The International Spread of Ethnic Conflict

The International Spread of Ethnic Conflict

FEAR, DIFFUSION, AND ESCALATION

DAVID A. LAKE AND DONALD ROTHCHILD, EDITORS

PRINCETON UNIVERSITY PRESS

PRINCETON, NEW JERSEY

Library of Congress Cataloging-in-Publication Data

The international spread of ethnic conflict: fear, diffusion, and
escalation / David A. Lake and Donald S. Rothchild, editors.
p. cm.
Includes bibliographical references and index.
ISBN 0-691-01691-7 (cloth : alk. paper).—ISBN 0-691-01690-9
(pbk. : alk. paper)
1. Ethnic relations. 2. International relations. 3. Conflict
management. 4. World politics—1989– I. Lake, David A., 1956– .
II. Rothchild, Donald S.
GN496.I595 1998   97-15031   305.8—dc21   CIP

The publisher would like to acknowledge IGCC for providing the
camera-ready copy from which this book was printed

This book has been composed in Berkeley

Princeton University Press books are printed on acid-free paper and meet the guidelines for
permanence and durability of the Committee on Production Guidelines for Book
Longevity of the Council on Library Resources

http://pup.princeton.edu

Printed in the United States of America

2   3   4   5   6   7   8   9   10

CONTENTS

FIGURES AND TABLES

A. Colin Cameron is associate professor of economics at the University of California, Davis. Professor Cameron's published research focuses on nonlinear regression, especially count data models, and applications in microeconomics, especially health economics. He is co-author (with Pravin Trivedi) of *The Analysis of Count Data*.

David R. Davis is associate professor of political science at Emory University. His research interests include the influence of domestic politics on international relations, political violence, and defense economics. He has recently published articles in *International Studies Quarterly*, *The Journal of Conflict Resolution*, and *The Journal of Peace Research*.

James D. Fearon is associate professor of political science at the University of Chicago. His current research focuses primarily on the explanation of interstate war and of interethnic conflict. Recent publications include "Signaling Foreign Policy Interests: Tying Hands versus Sinking Costs," *Journal of Conflict Resolution;* (with David Laitin) "Explaining Inter-ethnic Cooperation," *American Political Science Review;* and "Rationalist Explanations for War," *International Organization*.

Dan Froats is a Ph.D. candidate in political science, a MacArthur Fellow at the Center for International Security and Arms Control, and editor of the MacArthur Consortium Working Papers series at Stanford University. His dissertation research examines the European experience of international treaty guarantees for the rights of minorities.

Paula Garb is adjunct assistant professor of cultural anthropology and associate director of Global Peace and Conflict Studies at the University of California, Irvine. Her extensive field work in former Soviet republics since 1979 has focused on cultures of the Caucasus, ethnic relations, the role of culture in conflict, and conflict resolution. Her most recent chapters and articles include "Mediation in the Caucasus," *Anthropological Contributions to Conflict Resolution;* and "The Return of Refugees Viewed through the Prism of Blood Revenge," *The Anthropology of East Europe Review*.

Sandra Halperin is assistant professor of political science at the University of Pittsburgh. Her research focuses on conflict and social change, the development of the state, comparative political development, and Middle East politics. Professor Halperin has published articles on nationalism and state autonomy in modern Europe, and the politics of appeasement. She is author of *In the Mirror of the Third World: Capitalist Development in Modern Europe* and is completing a second volume on war and social change in modern Europe.

Stuart Hill is associate professor of political science at the University of California, Davis. He has published on policy analysis and information processing in the fields of American and comparative politics. His most recent book is *Democratic Values and Technological Choices*.

Bruce W. Jentleson is professor of political science at the University of California, Davis; director of the UC Davis Washington Center; and former special assistant to the director of the United States Department of State policy planning staff. Professor Jentleson has published widely on American foreign policy, international security, and international political economy. He is the co-senior editor of the four-volume *Encyclopedia of U.S. Foreign Relations*, editor of *Opportunities Missed, Opportunities Seized: Preventive Diplomacy in the Post-Cold War World*, and author of *New Era, New Century: American Foreign Policy After the Cold War.*

Cynthia S. Kaplan is associate professor of political science at the University of California, Santa Barbara, and director of the UC Program on Education Abroad Russian Study Center. She has published in the fields of Russian, Estonian, and ethnic politics; political participation; and political culture. Her most recent works appear in *Political Culture and Civil Society in Russia and the New States of Eurasia* (edited by Vladimir Tismaneanu); (with Henry E. Brady) *Referendums Around the World* (edited by David Butler and Austin Ranney) and *The Legacy of the Soviet Bloc* (edited by Jane Zacek and Ilpyong Kim); and *International Negotiation*.

Edmond J. Keller is professor of political science and director of the Center for African Studies at the University of California, Los Angeles. He has edited numerous collections, among them (with Louis A. Picard) *South Africa in Southern Africa: Domestic Change and International Conflict* and (with Donald Rothchild) *Africa in the New International Order: Rethinking State Sovereignty and Regional Security.*

David A. Lake is professor of political science at the University of California, San Diego and former research director for international relations at the University of California's Institute on Global Conflict and Cooperation. Professor Lake has published widely in international relations theory, international political economy, and American foreign policy. His most recent books include (co-edited with Patrick M. Morgan) *Regional Orders: Building Security in a New World*, (co-edited with Robert Powell) *Strategic Choice and International Relations*, and *Entangling Relations: American Foreign Policy in Its Century*.

Stephen D. Krasner is Graham H. Stuart Professor of International Relations at Stanford University. He has published widely on questions of international political economy and is working on a study of sovereignty.

Timur Kuran is professor of economics and Faisal Professor of Islamic Thought and Culture at the University of Southern California. His recent publications address various interdisciplinary themes, all involving social values and institutions. They include works on the dynamics of revolutions, the effects of public discourse on knowledge structures, the evolution of moral systems, the logic of Islamic economic thought, and linkages between Islam and economic development. He is the author of *Private Truths, Public Lies: The Social Consequences of Preference Falsification*.

Will H. Moore is associate professor of political science at Florida State University. His research focuses on violent political conflict behavior and can be found (with Ted Robert Gurr) in *American Journal of Political Science*, (with David R. Davis) *International Studies Quarterly*, and *Journal of Conflict Resolution*, among others.

Donald Rothchild is professor of political science at the University of California, Davis and an editor of the journal, *Nationalism and Ethnic Politics*. Among his books are *Racial Bargaining in Independent Kenya*; (co-editor) *State versus Ethnic Claims*; (co-editor) *The Precarious Balance*; (co-author) *Sovereignty as Responsibility: Conflict Management in Africa*; and, most recently, *Managing Ethnic Conflict in Africa: Pressures and Incentives for Cooperation*.

Stephen M. Saideman is assistant professor of political science at Texas Tech University. He has published articles on the domestic and international politics of ethnic conflicts. He is currently working on a book manuscript, *The Ties that Divide: Ethnic Politics, Foreign Policy, and International Conflict*.

I. William Zartman is Jacob Blaustein Professor of International Organizations and Conflict Resolution and director of the International and Conflict Management Program at the Paul H. Nitze School of Advanced International Studies of Johns Hopkins University. His books include *Elusive Peace: Negotiating an End to Civil Wars*; *Ripe for Resolution: Conflict and Intervention in Africa*; *Positive Sum: Improving North–South Negotiations*; *International Multilateral Negotiation: Approaches to the Management of Complexity*; *The Practical Negotiator*; and *The 50% Solution*.

ACKNOWLEDGMENTS

THIS VOLUME is the product of a multi-year research project sponsored by the University of California's Institute on Global Conflict and Cooperation and funded by the Pew Charitable Trusts. We are grateful to IGCC's Director, Susan Shirk, for her support. We are also indebted to the Pew Charitable Trusts, and especially Stephen Del Rosso, for their generous assistance. Without IGCC and the Pew Charitable Trusts this project could not have been undertaken.

All of the chapters in this volume were discussed at one or more meetings of the IGCC Working Group on the International Spread and Management of Ethnic Conflict, composed of approximately sixty-five west-coast academics who attended six meetings over eighteen months. We are grateful to the many participants for their insightful comments and probing questions. We would also like to thank the many guests from Washington, Moscow, several East European capitals, the United Nations, and elsewhere for helping bring scholars closer to the real world. The collaboration involved in these meetings extends far beyond the group of authors published in this volume and is reflected in the quality of the essays.

The first drafts of our chapters were discussed at the sixth and final meeting of the working group. We would like to thank Miles Kahler, Charles Kupchan, William Maynes, and Barnett Rubin for formal comments, and other participants for a lively and helpful discussion. Our chapters were also presented at the Pacific Council on International Affairs in Los Angeles, the World Affairs Council of San Francisco, an IGCC Policy Briefing in Washington, D.C, and an IGCC Teaching Seminar at the University of California, Davis. We thank the participants in these meetings, as well as Arnold Kanter, Timothy D. Sisk, Stephen John Stedman, and John Steinbruner, for their helpful comments.

An earlier and abridged version of Chapters One and Nine appeared as "Containing Fear: The Origins and Management of Ethnic Conflict," *International Security* 21, no. 2 (Fall 1996): 41–75. The expanded chapters are published here with permission of the President and Fellows of Harvard College and the Massachusetts Institute of Technology.

We are deeply grateful to IGCC's staff and acknowledge here our great debt to them for countless tasks large and small. Barbara Butterton organized six conferences from start to finish with great skill, kept track of what seemed an endless series of papers, and kept us within budget. Barbara was the "workhorse" of the project and deserves much of the credit for its successful conclusion. Fred Wehling, IGCC's academic coordinator for policy research, organized and chaired the policy panel at each meeting of the workshop; he was a vital link in the project. Kathleen Hancock served as an essential (and able) raportuer. Ron Bee managed the grant and the policy briefings. Bettina Halvorsen, from IGCC, and Martha Rehrman, from the Institute on Governmental Affairs at UC Davis, organized the teaching seminar. Jennifer Pournelle, IGCC's senior editor, oversaw the preparation of the manuscript and its transformation into printed pages by Stacy Moser-Simpson and Lynne Bush from The Page Group, who prepared the working typescript; Matt Baum and Richard Seroter who were tireless reference chasers and fact-checkers; and Lynn Edwards and Randy Stevens of Bookmark Media, who saw the proofs to press. Without the assistance of all, this project might have been started but it could never have been completed.

Don Rothchild also acknowledges the generous assistance of the Department of Political Science at the University of California, Davis, and the United States Institute of Peace during the period he worked on this project.

We are deeply grateful to Malcolm Litchfield at Princeton University Press, who recognized the unique nature and potential value of this book and and gave us wise counsel on difficult issues. We are indebted to him and his staff for all their assistance in producing this volume.

Finally, we are grateful to our families for their encouragement and understanding while we tried to unravel the mysteries of the international spread and management of ethnic conflict.

A B B R E V I A T I O N S

ANC   African National Congress
CGO   chief governmental officer
CNN   Cable News Network
COPDAB   Conflict and Peace Database
CPC   Confederation of Peoples of the Caucasus
CSCE/OSCE   Conference on/Organization for Security and Cooperation in
             Europe
ECOMOG   ECOWAS Cease-fire Monitoring Group
ECOWAS   Economic Community of West African States
IGCC   Institute on Global Conflict and Cooperation
JNA   Yugoslav National Army
NGO   nongovernmental organization
NPFL   National Patriotic Front of Liberia
OAU   Organization of African Unity
PM   political mobilization
PRIE   Politically Relevant International Environment
RC   rational choice
RFE/RL   Radio Free Europe/Radio Liberty
RMO   regional multilateral organization
RPF   Rwanda Patriotic Front
TPC   Tatar Public Center
UNAMIR   United Nations Assistance Mission in Rwanda
UNHCR   United Nations High Commission for Refugees
UNOSOM   United Nations Operation in Somalia
UNPROFOR   United Nations Protection Force
UNTAC   United Nations

PART ONE

Introduction

CHAPTER ONE

Spreading Fear: The Genesis of Transnational Ethnic Conflict

DAVID A. LAKE AND DONALD ROTHCHILD

BOSNIA. CHECHNYA. RWANDA. The early 1990s have witnessed a wave of ethnic conflict sweep across parts of Eastern Europe, the former Soviet Union, and Africa. Localities, states, and sometimes whole regions have been engulfed in convulsive fits of ethnic insecurity and violence. The early optimism that the end of the Cold War might usher in a new world order has been quickly shattered. Even before fears of nuclear Armageddon could fully fade, new fears of state meltdown and ethnic cleansing have rippled across the international community.

In this "new world disorder," many worry that ethnic conflict is contagious, that conflict in one locale can stimulate conflict elsewhere, and that initial outbreaks in the Balkans, the former Soviet Union, and Africa, if not quarantined, could set off an epidemic of catastrophic proportions. Analysts also fear that internal conflicts will escalate by drawing in neighbors and outside opportunists. Reflecting these concerns, James B. Steinberg wrote in 1993, "The war in the former Yugoslavia continues, and there remains a risk that it will spread, not only to other parts of Yugoslavia, but to its neighbors, as well" (27). In attempting to persuade the American people to support the deployment of U.S. troops to Bosnia under NATO command, President Clinton echoed this point. "Without us," he stated, "the hard-won peace would be lost, the war would resume, the slaughter of innocents would begin again, and *the conflict that already has claimed so many people could spread like poison throughout the entire region*" (Kempster and Pine 1995, A16, emphasis added). Almost daily reports of ethnic violence from around the world lend credence to these fears.

In this volume, we ask two central questions. First, how, why, and when do ethnic conflicts spread across national borders? Second, how can such transnational ethnic conflicts be best managed? In this and the following chapters, we sketch preliminary answers to these pressing questions.

The authors of the various chapters in this volume do not reach uniform conclusions about the causes of ethnic conflict, the propensity for ethnic conflicts to spread, or the management of conflict. As this is one of the first attempts to address the question of the international spread of ethnic conflict, we regard this diversity of views as a strength; it would not be helpful or appropriate to reach premature closure on this important topic. The essays in Part Two tend to draw relatively pessimistic assessments: the authors conclude that ethnic conflicts can and do spread across borders. The chapters in Part Three offer more optimistic judgments; without disputing that conflict can spread, they argue that ethnic conflict today is primarily a local phenomenon that is breaking out in many places simultaneously for similar but largely independent reasons. The essays in Part Four focus on the management of transnational ethnic conflicts.

In this chapter, we provide an intellectual foundation upon which the remainder of the volume builds. The other authors do not necessarily agree with all of our analysis, and their individual chapters do not necessarily depend upon all parts of it, but it serves, we believe, as a unifying framework for the study of transnational ethnic conflict.

We begin with a brief review of the concepts of ethnicity and ethnic groups. We take a middle ground in the relevant debates and emphasize, as many scholars now do, the socially constructed but persistent nature of ethnic identity groups. Their origins may be mythical, but they can nevertheless attract powerful loyalties and commitments as political elites mobilize ethnic kin for action.

We next examine the causes of ethnic conflict. We argue that ethnic conflict is not caused directly by intergroup differences, "ancient hatreds" and centuries-old feuds, or the stresses of modern life within a global economy. Nor were ethnic passions, long bottled up by repressive communist regimes, simply uncorked by the end of the Cold War. Instead, we maintain that ethnic conflict is most commonly caused by collective fears of the future. As groups begin to fear for their physical safety, a series of dangerous and difficult-to-resolve strategic dilemmas arise that contain within them the potential for tremendous violence. As information failures, problems of credible commitment, and the security dilemma take hold, the state is weakened, groups become fearful, and conflict becomes likely. Ethnic activists and political entrepreneurs, operating within groups, reinforce these fears of physical insecurity and cultural domination and polarize society. Political memories, myths, and emotions also magnify these fears, driving groups further apart. Together, these between-group and within-group strategic interactions produce a toxic brew of distrust and suspicion that can explode into murderous violence, even the systematic slaughter of one people by another.

Finally, we turn to the question of the international spread of ethnic conflict. In the last section of this chapter, we distinguish between diffusion, which occurs when conflict in one area alters the likelihood of conflict elsewhere, and escalation, which occurs when additional, foreign participants enter an otherwise "internal" conflict. Building upon the strategic dilemmas in the previous section, we then examine the principal causal routes by which ethnic conflicts can diffuse or escalate. Diffusion occurs largely through information flows that condition the beliefs of ethnic groups in other societies. Escalation is driven by alliances between transnational kin groups as well as by intentional or unintentional spillovers, irredentist demands, attempts to divert attention from domestic problems, or by predatory states that seek to take advantage of the internal weaknesses of others. In outlining the various causal paths, we identify differences between several of the chapters in Parts Two and Three. Our concluding chapter below draws more general analytic and policy lessons.

ETHNICITY AND ETHNIC CONFLICT

There are three broad approaches to the study of ethnicity and ethnic conflict. Although we have not tried to impose a single approach upon the chapters in this volume, and the authors do disagree among themselves, a perspective on the three approaches is necessary not only to provide a groundwork for some of the later issues we address but also to probe the limits of our ability to generalize the findings of this study to other types of conflicts—especially those that are less self-evidently ethnic in nature or do not possess an ethnic component at all. The three approaches are presented here as ideal types. We recognize that individual analysts may not fit well into any single category.

The *primordialist* approach takes ethnicity as a fixed characteristic of individuals and communities (Issacs 1975; Smith 1986; Kaplan 1993; and Connor 1994). Whether rooted in inherited biological traits (van den Berghe 1981) or centuries of past practice now beyond the ability of individuals or groups to alter, one is invariably and always perceived as a Serb, a Zulu, or a Chechen. In this view, ethnic divisions and tensions are "natural." Although recognizing that ethnic warfare is not a constant state of affairs, primordialists see conflict as flowing from ethnic differences and, therefore, not necessarily in need of explanation. Although analysts might probe the catalysts in any given outbreak of violence, conflict is understood to be ultimately rooted in ethnicity itself. As Anthony D. Smith writes, ethnic conflict follows inevitably from ethnicity: "Wherever ethnic nationalism has taken hold of populations, there one may expect to find powerful assertions of national self-determination that, if long opposed, will embroil whole regions in bitter and protracted ethnic conflict. Whether the peace and stability of such regions will be better served in the short term by measures of containment, federation, mediation, or even partition, in the long run there can be little escape from the many conflagrations that the unsatisfied yearnings of ethnic nationalism are likely to kindle" (1993, 40).

Analyses of conflict from within the primordialist approach stress the uniqueness and overriding importance of ethnic identity. Few other attributes of individuals or communities are fixed in the same way as ethnicity or are as necessarily conflictual. When viewed through this lens, ethnic conflict is sui generis; what one learns about ethnic conflict is typically not relevant to other social, political, or economic conflicts.

The most frequent criticism of the primordialist approach is its assumption of fixed identities and its failure to account for variations in the level of conflict over time and place. In short, the approach founders on its inability to explain the emergence of new and transformed identities or account for the long periods in which either ethnicity is not a salient political characteristic or relations between different ethnic groups are comparatively peaceful.

The *instrumentalist* approach, on the other hand, understands ethnicity as a tool used by individuals, groups, or elites to obtain some larger, typically material end (Glazer and Moynihan 1975; Steinberg 1981; Brass 1985; and Rothchild 1986b). In this view, ethnicity has little independent standing outside the political process in which collective ends are sought. Whether used defensively to thwart the ambitions of others or offensively to achieve an end of one's own, ethnicity is primarily a label or set of symbolic ties that is used for political advantage—much like interest-group membership or political-party affiliation. Given the existing structure of states, and the geographic concentration of individuals with common social or economic backgrounds within these entities, ethnicity may be a powerful and frequently used political tool, but according to instrumentalists this does not distinguish ethnicity fundamentally from other political affiliations.

It follows from the instrumentalist approach that the lessons drawn from ethnic conflicts can often—perhaps always—be applied to other sorts of conflicts. If politicized ethnicity is not inherently different from other forms of political association, ethnic conflict should not necessarily be different from other conflicts based on interest or ideology. In this view, ethnic conflict, however prevalent, is part of the larger conflict process.

Critics of instrumentalism counter that ethnicity is not something that can be decided upon by individuals at will, like other political affiliations, but is embedded within and controlled by the larger society. They point to the inherently social nature of all ethnic identities and argue, in contrast, that ethnicity can only be understood within a "relational framework" (Esman 1994, 13).

Finally, bridging the other perspectives and representing an emerging scholarly consensus, *constructivists* emphasize the social origins and nature of ethnicity (Anderson 1983; Dominguez 1989; Young 1993; and Brubaker 1995). Arguing that ethnicity is neither immutable nor completely open, this approach posits that ethnicity is constructed from dense webs of social interactions. In the constructivist view, ethnicity is not an individual attribute but a social phenomenon. A person's identity remains beyond the choice or control of that individual. As social interactions change, conceptions of ethnicity evolve as well. As but one example, until the late 1980s, the cosmopolitanism of urban areas and rewards offered by the federal state prompted many individuals in Serbia, Croatia, Bosnia, and the other constituent republics to evolve slowly toward a Yugoslav identity. As the state disintegrated, these same individuals, whether they wanted to or not, were quickly pressed by events to return to their more particularistic ethnic roots (see Brubaker 1995 and Kuran, Chapter Two in this volume).

As with instrumentalists, constructivists do not see ethnicity as inherently conflictual. Although ethnicity is robust, the turn toward violence still needs to be explained. For instrumentalists, as noted, conflict is largely stimulated by elites who mobilize ethnicity in pursuit of their own narrow interests. For constructivists, on the other hand, conflict is caused by certain types of what might be called pathological social systems, which individuals do not control. In this view, it is the social system that breeds violent conflict, not individuals, and it is the socially constructed nature of ethnicity that can cause conflicts, once begun, to spin rapidly out of control. "One of the great cruelties of ethnic conflict," John Chipman notes, "is that everyone is automatically labeled a combatant—by the identity they possess—even if they are not. Thus, ethnic conflicts in their extreme can become total conflicts" (1993a, 240).

Constructivist accounts of ethnic conflict are generalizable, but only to other conflicts that are also based largely on socially constructed groups and cleavages. This includes clan, religious, regionalist, or nationalist groupings but excludes class and other material interest-based conflicts more likely founded on individual attributes. Along with ethnic conflict, other "social" conflicts also appear to have increased in number and intensity over the last decade. Because of the generalizability of our principal findings, and the often amorphous but always permeable borders between ethnic, clan, religious, regionalist, and nationalist groups, we have not tried to draw sharp lines among these various types of conflicts. We believe ethnic conflict is part of a broader set of social relationships and that nearly all of our conclusions pertain equally well to other conflicts in this category.

On a final, methodological note, it is important to emphasize that there is no necessary contradiction between socially-constructed identities and rational, purposive choice by individuals and groups. As Hudson Meadwell (1989), Robert Bates and Barry Weingast (1995), and Russell Hardin (1995) argue—and as many of the papers in this volume demonstrate—the two processes and theoretical approaches are mutually reinforcing. Individuals may rationally choose an identity within the limited range that is socially available to them. Given some identity, individuals or groups can also rationally choose strategies that are the best means to their ends. These best responses can sometimes collectively produce conflicts with appalling levels of violence, but this does not necessarily indicate that the choices were ill-informed or irrational. Identifying those social systems or conditions most prone to violence is one of the theoretical and research frontiers.

THE CAUSES OF ETHNIC CONFLICT

By itself, ethnicity is not a cause of violent conflict. Most ethnic groups, most of the time, pursue their interests peacefully through established political channels. But when ethnicity is linked with acute social uncertainty, a history of conflict and, indeed, fear of what the future might bring, it emerges as one of the major fault lines along which societies fracture (Newland 1993, 161). Vesna Pesic, a professor at the University of Belgrade, a peace activist in the former Yugoslavia, and now a leader in the political opposition to Serbian President Slobodan Milosevic, says it well: ethnic conflict is caused by the "fear of the future, lived through the past."[1]

Fear of the future can take many forms. In the contemporary world, two broad types of fear seem particularly salient to ethnic groups. Some ethnic groups fear

---

[1] Remarks to the IGCC Working Group on the International Spread and Management of Ethnic Conflict, University of California, San Diego, October 1, 1994.

assimilation into a dominant culture and hegemonic state. This fear drives the politics of multiculturalism today—and underlies much of the ethnic politics found in developed countries. The struggle over the future of Quebec is one of the most pressing examples. Because of the power of the dominant culture and state, however, assimilationist conflicts are unlikely to become violent, as the fearful minority is weak in relation to the majority almost by definition.

Ethnic groups also fear for their physical safety and survival—especially when the groups are more or less evenly matched and neither can absorb the other politically, economically, or culturally. When such fears of physical insecurity emerge, especially when coupled with assimilationist pressures, violence can and often does erupt. Although fears of assimilation, if left festering, can eventually weaken states and evolve into fears of physical insecurity, our concern in the post-Cold War world and in this volume is primarily with violent conflicts driven by current concerns of safety and survival.

Collective fears of the future arise when states lose their ability to arbitrate between groups or provide credible guarantees of protection for groups. Under this condition, which Barry Posen has referred to as "emerging anarchy," security becomes of paramount concern (Posen 1993a, 103; Snyder 1993). When central authority declines, groups become fearful for their survival. They invest in and prepare for violence, and thereby make actual violence possible. Whether arising incrementally out of competition between groups or from extremist factions actively seeking to destroy ethnic peace, state weakness is a necessary precondition for violent ethnic conflict to erupt.

State weakness may not be obvious to the ethnic groups themselves or to observers—making the task of forecasting or anticipating ethnic conflicts especially difficult. States that use force to repress groups, for instance, may appear strong, but their reliance on manifest coercion rather than legitimate authority more accurately implies weakness. More important, groups look beyond the present political equipoise to alternative futures when calculating their strategies. If plausible futures are sufficiently threatening, groups may begin acting today as if the state were in fact weak, setting off processes, discussed below, that bring about the disintegration of the state. Thus, concerns that the state may not remain strong tomorrow may be sufficient to ignite fears of physical insecurity and a cycle of ethnic violence.

Situations of emerging anarchy and violence arise out of the strategic interactions between and within groups. Between groups, three different strategic dilemmas can cause violence to erupt: information failures, problems of credible commitment, and incentives to use force preemptively (also known as the security dilemma). These dilemmas are the fundamental causes of ethnic conflict. Within groups, ethnic activists and political entrepreneurs may make blatant ethnic appeals and attempt to outbid moderate politicians, thereby mobilizing members, polarizing society, and magnifying the intergroup dilemmas. "Nonrational" factors such as emotions, historical memories, and myths can exacerbate the violent implications of these within-group interactions.

Many readers will immediately recognize that the distinction between inter-group and intragroup strategic interactions parallels the traditional levels of analysis problem in international relations (Rothchild 1973, 3–4). In international relations, the distinction between interstate or systemic causes and intrastate or unit-level causes has been a useful organizing device, and it has helped us here in understanding the various origins of ethnic conflict. Nonetheless, the distinction is increasingly challenged, for good reasons, in international relations.[2] We do not accept the implication, drawn by many analysts, that the levels of analysis define separate and autonomous causal factors. Rather, we see between-group and within-group interactions (and, for that matter, inter- and intrastate interactions as well) as being inherently linked in a larger strategic calculus. In formulating political strategies, ethnic leaders anticipate the consequences of their within-group choices for relations with other groups and, in turn, incorporate the effects of their between-group choices into plans for dealing with their ethnic kin. These intergroup and intragroup interactions are intimately and necessarily integrated. Together, the choices made in these two arenas can combine to create a vicious cycle that threatens to pull multiethnic societies into violence.

Strategic Interactions between Groups

Competition for resources typically lies at the heart of ethnic conflict. Property rights, jobs, scholarships, educational admissions, language rights, government contracts, and development allocations all confer benefits on individuals and groups. Whether finite in supply or not, all such resources are scarce and thus objects of competition and occasionally struggle between individuals and, when organized, groups. As Hardin notes in describing relations between the pastoralist Tutsis and agrarian Hutus in Rwanda and Burundi, "the two groups do have an economic conflict—but it is merely a conflict for alternative uses of limited resources. They are like the warring kings of France and Spain, who, the French king said, were in complete agreement: They both wanted the same thing" (1995, 170).

Politics matter because the state controls access to scarce resources and the future income streams that flow from them. Individuals and groups that possess political power can often gain privileged access to these resources, and thus increase their welfare (Hardin 1995, 34–37; Esman 1994, 216). Because the state sets the terms of competition between groups, it becomes an object of group struggle. Accordingly, the pursuit of particularistic objectives often becomes embodied in competing visions of just, legitimate, or appropriate political orders.

In multiethnic societies, scarce resources and the struggle to control state policy produce competing communal interests. Groups claiming resources have two options. First, they can seek national policies that increase aggregate social

---

[2] For an elaboration of this critique and a "strategic" alternative, see Lake and Powell (h.d.).

wealth. Each group then gets a share of a growing resource "pie." Second, they can call for group-specific benefits or "rents" that typically distort the economy. "Rent seeking" reduces national wealth in the long run but may increase the well-being of groups in the short run. In brief, groups can seek a fixed share of a larger pie or a larger share of a fixed and perhaps shrinking pie. According to the logic of collective action, large, majority groups tend to have an interest in the first strategy of increasing aggregate wealth—of which they are the greatest beneficiaries—while smaller, minority groups prefer the second strategy of augmenting their own group wealth (Olson 1965 and 1982). As a result, the majority and the minority possess opposing policy preferences. These strategies may be reversed in cases where the commanding heights of the economy—and thus the highest returns to economic activity—are controlled by a minority ethnic group, as in South Africa, but the underlying policy disagreements remain. Countries with multiple minorities and no majority are likely to fall prey to redistributive conflicts, with no group supporting growth and all seeking particularistic benefits. Other issues, such as integration into the international economy, may also produce opposing policy preferences if those issues fall along existing ethnic fault lines.[3] Thus, in nearly all ethnically divided polities, groups possess competing policy preferences.

In Nigeria, for example, each ethno-regional group looks to the state to favor it when distributing public resources, producing, as the late Claude Ake (1985, 1,213) observed, an "over-politicization" of social life that gravely weakens the state itself. In Yugoslavia, Slovenians and Croatians resented the system of federal redistribution to the poorer regions of the country; their publics backed their leaders' expressions of indignation, ultimately fueling the demand for greater political autonomy (Woodward 1995a, 69–70). When groups conclude that they can improve their welfare only at the expense of others, they become locked into competition for scarce resources and state power.

Periods of declining growth, like those experienced by most of the communist societies immediately before and since the fall, can exacerbate and heighten intergroup tensions. Politics under conditions of extreme economic scarcity contribute to a win/lose mentality in which ethnic representatives seek favorable inclusion in the state—even domination—in order to avoid the risks of marginalization. Likewise, Jack Snyder (1993) argues that state incapacity frustrates the aspirations of individuals and groups, and can produce a nationalist backlash that fractures states as people seek to create political units more capable of meeting their needs. Diminishing resources increase competition between groups as they struggle to attain their goals.

Analytically, however, the existence of competing policy preferences is—by itself—not sufficient for violence to arise. Observers too often fail to recognize this important theoretical point and misattribute violence to competition over scarce resources. Violence, after all, is costly for all communal actors; people are

---

[3] For a discussion of the distributional implications of international economic integration, see Frieden and Rogowski (1996).

killed; factories, farms, and whole cities are destroyed; resources that might have been invested in new economic growth are diverted instead to destructive ends. As violence, and preparing for violence, is always costly, there must exist in principle some potential bargain short of violence that leaves both sides in a dispute better off than settling their disagreements through the use of force (Fearon 1993 and 1995); at the very least, the same ex post agreement could be reached without the use of force, and the resources that would have been expended in violence somehow divided between the parties ex ante. This holds irrespective of the breadth of the group demands or the extent of the antagonisms. The farther apart the policy preferences of the groups are, the greater the violence necessary for one group to assert its will over the other, and the greater the resources that can be saved by averting the resort to force.

Despite appearances, then, competing policy preferences by themselves cannot explain the resort to violence. All groups differ in their policy preferences, but most of the time these differences are successfully negotiated and compromised. The divorce between the two halves of Czechoslovakia is a sterling example of two ethnic groups, in conflict over the distribution of resources within their federal state but anxious to avoid the costs of war, developing a mutually agreeable separation to avoid a potentially violent confrontation.

A mutually preferred bargain must exist even if the resources available to groups are declining, because violence only further reduces the resource pool relative to possible agreements. Valerie Percival and Thomas Homer-Dixon (1995; also Adelman and Suhrke 1996) demonstrate this point empirically in their careful analysis of environmental scarcity and ethnic conflict in Rwanda; although widespread resource scarcity was an important factor in stimulating ethnic grievances, it was the fears of an elite faced with the prospect of losing power as the result of newly negotiated international accords that was the primary catalyst for one of the twentieth century's worst ethnic slaughters. For negotiations to fail to bridge the demands of opposing groups, at least one of three strategic dilemmas must exist. Each dilemma alone is sufficient to produce violent conflict. Nonetheless, they typically occur together as a dangerous syndrome of strategic problems.

INFORMATION FAILURES

Because violence is costly, groups can be expected to invest in acquiring knowledge about the preferences and capabilities of the opposing side and bargain hard, but eventually reach an agreement short of open conflict.[4] Groups might even be expected to reveal information about themselves to prevent violence from erupting. When individuals and groups possess private information and incentives to misrepresent that information, however, competing group interests can cause deep suspicion and produce actual conflict. We refer to this as an information failure. When information failures occur, groups cannot acquire or share the

---

[4] This subsection and the next draw heavily upon recent essays by James Fearon (1993 and 1995), two of the best theoretical works on conflict between organized groups.

information necessary to bridge the bargaining gap between themselves, making violence possible despite its devastating effects.

Private information is anything known by one group but not the other, including how intense their preferences are about specific policy objectives, how cohesive the group would be if challenged, or how military leaders would use their forces should fighting break out. Incentives to misrepresent private information exist in at least three common circumstances. In each, revealing true information undercuts the ability of the group to attain its interests. First, incentives to misrepresent occur when groups are bargaining over a set of issues and believe they can gain by bluffing. By exaggerating their strengths, minimizing their weaknesses, and misstating their preferences, groups seek to achieve more favorable divisions of resources. Through such bluffs, however, they increase the risk that negotiations will fail and violence arise.[5]

Second, groups may be truly aggressive but do not want to be branded as such. They may seek to minimize internal opposition, or to insulate themselves from repercussions in the broader international community. Although typically only minimal sanctions are imposed by other states, most groups attempt to avoid the label of an aggressor or violator of international norms and the political isolation that such a classification can carry.

Finally, in conflicts in which the groups are simultaneously negotiating and preparing for ethnic war, any attempt to facilitate compromise by having each side explain how it plans to win on the battlefield will seriously compromise the likelihood that it will win should war occur. Thus, groups cannot reveal their strategies or derive accurate predictions of their likely success. Paradoxically, each party is bound by its own self-interest to withhold the information crucial to bringing about an agreement. Concerned that private information they provide on how they intend to protect themselves or attack others will redound to their disadvantage, groups may refrain from revealing the information necessary to forge a mutually satisfactory compromise (Fearon 1995, 400).

Information failures are possible whenever two or more ethnic groups compete within the political arena. Groups always possess private information and, as these three circumstances suggest, often possess incentives to misrepresent that information. Information failures are thus ubiquitous in ethnic relations. In multiethnic societies, states can often communicate and negotiate successfully between groups, and thereby help preclude and resolve information failures. Indeed, communication and negotiation can be understood as two of the primary functions of the state. When effective, states create incentives and a sense of security that allow groups to express their desires and articulate their political aspirations and strategies. Not only do ethnic leaders respond to side-payments offered by state elites, but—in trying to curry favor—such leaders are sometimes more

---

[5] In game-theoretic terms, actors will choose to bluff depending upon first, the beliefs each actor holds about the other's "type" (i.e., the actor is more likely to bluff if it believes the other is "weak" and the second actor believes the first is "strong"), and second, the relative benefits (payoff) and costs (signal) of successful bluffing, unsuccessful bluffing, and not bluffing (that is, the higher the payoff from success and the smaller the cost of the signal, the more likely the actor is to bluff).

prepared to provide private information to a third party than to an ethnic adversary. As the state weakens, however, information failures become more acute and violence more likely. If one group believes that the other is withholding information, it too may begin to hold back crucial data or anticipate the failure of negotiations. Groups become suspicious of the intentions of others, and may begin to fear the worst. In this way, information failures and even the anticipation of such failures may drive groups to actions that undermine the ability of the state to maintain social peace. When this occurs, even previously effective states will begin to unravel. State capabilities, then, are at least partly affected by the magnitude of the information failures and the beliefs and behavior of the groups themselves.

Information failures cut two ways. On the one hand, all policy differences can be bridged—at least in theory—if the alternative is a costly conflict. Even cultural symbols and practices central to a people's conception of itself as a distinct ethnic entity may be negotiable if the known alternative is the outright destruction of the group. On the other hand, strategic incentives to misrepresent private information are a primary impediment to peaceful compromise, and these incentives may be present in a wide range of circumstances. Thus, skillful mediation by third parties who can probe the true preferences of groups and communicate them to relevant others is important for creating and maintaining cooperative ethnic relations. States able to arbitrate between groups are normally the preferred instrument to this end, but sometimes they too fall victim to the information failures they are designed, in part, to prevent. When this occurs, mediation by outside parties may be required (see Chapter Nine).

PROBLEMS OF CREDIBLE COMMITMENT

Ethnic conflicts also arise because groups cannot credibly commit themselves to uphold mutually beneficial agreements they might reach (Fearon 1993 and 1995; also Hardin 1995, 143; Weingast 1997). In other words, at least one group cannot effectively reassure the other that it will not renege on an agreement and exploit it at some future date. As exploitation can be very costly—up to and including the organized killing of one group by another—groups may prefer to absorb even high costs of war today to avoid being exploited tomorrow.

Stable ethnic relations can be understood as based upon a "contract" between groups.[6] Ethnic contracts specify, among other things, the rights and responsibilities, political privileges, and access to resources of each group. These contracts may be formal constitutional agreements or simply informal understandings between elites. Whatever their form, ethnic contracts specify the relationship between the groups and normally channel politics in peaceful directions.

Most importantly, ethnic contracts contain "safeguards" designed to render the agreement self-enforcing. They contain provisions or mechanisms to ensure that

[6] The term *ethnic contract* was, we believe, coined by Leonard Binder at the first meeting of the IGCC Working Group on the International Spread and Management of Ethnic Conflict, University of California, San Diego, May 13–14, 1994. On relational contracting more generally, see Williamson (1985); for an application to interstate relations, see Lake (1996).

each side lives up to its commitments and feels secure that the other will do so as well. As we elaborate in Chapter Nine, typical safeguards include: first, political power-sharing arrangements, electoral rules, or group vetoes that prevent one ethnic group from setting government policy unilaterally (Lijphart 1967; Horowitz 1985; Sisk 1995; and Weingast 1997); second, minority control over critical economic assets, as with the whites in South Africa or Chinese in Malaysia (Adam and Moodley 1993); and third, as was found in Croatia before the breakup of Yugoslavia, maintenance of ethnic balance within the military or police forces to guarantee that one group will not be able to use overwhelming organized violence against the other (Glenny 1992a; Hardin 1995, 58 and 159). These political checks and balances serve to stabilize group relations and ensure that no group can be exploited by any other.[7] In Barry Weingast's words, "reciprocal trust can be induced by institutions" (1997, 15).

The terms of the ethnic contract reflect the balance of political power between the groups and their beliefs about the intentions and likely behavior of one another. Safeguards are crafted to respond to the specific circumstances of each set of groups. However, ethnic contracts can be undermined and problems of credible commitment created by changes in either the ethnic balance of power or the beliefs of groups about others. These changes and their implications are captured in two separate but related models, one by Fearon (1993 and Chapter Five) that focuses on the balance of political power between groups and one by Weingast (1997) that emphasizes beliefs.

The political power of groups is determined by demography, the resources available to each group, and their capacity to organize effectively (Hardin 1995, 56). The first two determinants are "raw" capabilities, the third reflects the ability of groups to mobilize themselves for political action and depends, at least in the early stages of the conflict, upon the existence of other social institutions that bring together members of the ethnic communities. More powerful groups have a larger say in setting the terms of the contract. However, for the less powerful group to agree voluntarily to enter into and abide by the contract, its interests must also be addressed, including its concern that the more powerful group will try to exploit it and alter the terms of the contract at some future date. Indeed, it is the minority, fearful of future exploitation and violence, that ultimately determines the viability of any existing ethnic contract. When the balance of ethnic power remains stable—and is expected to remain stable—well-crafted contracts enable ethnic groups to avoid violence despite their differing policy preferences.

---

[7] Aleksa Djilas (1995, 99) argues that the Communist party served as the primary safeguard in Yugoslavia, largely through coercion and repression, and that the defeat of the party in the 1990 elections left a political vacuum. He faults the party for not developing "stable institutions that could have regulated relations among the republics' national groups and protected their political, cultural, and territorial rights. . . . Since Bosnia's Parliament, courts, press, and police, had no authority as impartial institutions, affiliation with one's national group emerged as the only source of protection, whether of one's human rights or physical security." Weingast (1997, 16 n.17 and 17), on the other hand, credits Marshall Tito for constructing a set of veto mechanisms institutionalizing trust among the groups.

However, the ethnic balance of power is almost always in flux, rendering safeguards transitory and creating insecurities between groups. As in Lebanon, disparities in population growth rates will eventually alter the balance between groups. Differing rates of modernization and access to resources may increase prosperity for some groups and poverty for others, also shifting the ethnic balance. When multiethnic polities fragment, as in Yugoslavia and the former Soviet Union, the relevant political space alters rapidly and the various ethnic groups that once counted their numbers on a national scale must now calculate their kin in terms of the new, smaller political units, and may find themselves in a stronger or weaker position. It is apprehension over the consequences of any dissolution, for instance, that motivates Protestants in Northern Ireland to hold tenaciously onto union with the largely Protestant United Kingdom, rather than merge with the predominantly Catholic state of Ireland. When such changes in the ethnic balance of power have not been anticipated, or if the safeguards are overly rigid and cannot be renegotiated easily, the ethnic contract will be at risk of collapse.

Problems of credible commitment arise whenever the balance of ethnic power shifts (Fearon 1993). As the influence of one side declines, previously enforceable ethnic contracts become unenforceable. The checks and balances that safeguard the agreement today become insufficient tomorrow. Even if the group that is growing stronger promises not to exploit the weaker group in the future, there is nothing to prevent it from breaking its promise when it actually is stronger. Recognizing this, the group that is growing weaker has no incentive to believe the promises made by the stronger. Fearon shows that the larger the differences in the policy preferences of the two groups, and the lower the costs of fighting (or, equivalently, the higher the weaker group's probability of winning in any resort to arms), the more likely the declining side is to choose to fight today rather than accede to an ethnic contract that will become increasingly unenforceable as time progresses. As John Chipman (1993a, 239) concludes, "All ethnic conflict is testimony to some prior failure of political arrangements that somehow once acted as a prophylactic to the organization of competition around ethnic claims."

It is important to note that conflict arises in this model from a combination of different policy preferences and commitments that lack credibility, not necessarily from a lack of information—thus distinguishing this dilemma from the information failures above and the model below. Both their differing policy preferences and changing power positions are well known to all parties to the conflict, but they choose to fight anyway. A focus on the ethnic balance of power demonstrates that even when fully rational and informed, groups may nonetheless decide it is better to fight now than risk exploitation later. In this instance, ethnic conflict is rooted in the competing policy preferences and changing power positions of the groups—characteristics of situations in which any ethnic contract becomes unenforceable and, therefore, not credible to the groups themselves.

Weingast (1997) and Bates and Weingast (1995) demonstrate that uncertainty by one group over the nature and intentions of another can also generate problems of credible commitment that are independent of changes in the ethnic balance of power. Specifically, they show that if information is incomplete and there are costs to becoming a victim in the future, changes in the beliefs of one group about the intentions of another can play a large role in setting the parties on the road to violence.[8] If a group believes that there is even a very small chance that it may become a target of a genocidal attack, it may choose conflict over compromise and the risk of future destruction. To provoke conflict, one group need not believe that the other really is aggressive, only fear that it might be. With incomplete information, even small changes in beliefs about the intentions of the other group can generate massive violence. Uncertainty over the intentions of others, as a result, can undermine ethnic contracts, create problems of credible commitment, and provoke intergroup conflict.

Information is costly to acquire and, as a result, there is always some uncertainty about the intentions of other groups. Although conflict and war may be costly, thus creating incentives to invest in acquiring more and better information, groups (and individuals) will still economize on this activity. As each additional piece of information is less useful than the last and increasingly costly to acquire, groups will stop short of obtaining full information about their political environment. Groups compensate for their informational limitations by acting on the basis of prior beliefs about the likely preferences of others (as well as the costs of resorting to violence and other variables). These beliefs are formed through historical experience—the "past" in Pesic's words—and represent each group's best guess about the other's intentions. Groups then update these beliefs as new information becomes available to them. Nonetheless, information is always incomplete and groups are forever uncertain about each other's purposes. Intense conflict, then, always remains possible in ethnic interactions.

As the ethnic balance of power is constantly in flux and some uncertainty over the intentions of others is ever present, problems of credible commitment in ethnic relations are universal.[9] Concerned that the balance of power may tip against them or that the other may have hostile intentions, groups worry that agreements made today will not be honored tomorrow. Effective states can help to mitigate these problems of credible commitment by enforcing existing ethnic contracts. When the future risk of exploitation is high, however, current relations and the state itself can quickly unravel. Fearful of the future, weaker groups may resort to preemptive violence today to secure their position in times to come. When this happens, outside peacekeepers or peace enforcers with sufficient military capabilities and political will may be the only means of ensuring ethnic peace.

---

[8] Beliefs are used here in their game-theoretic sense to refer to the conditional probably of an actor holding one set of preferences (intentions, in the text; payoffs from a game, more formally) rather than another. Beliefs are formed subjectively by actors, largely on the basis of past interactions.

[9] It is now commonplace to assert that recent demographic, social, economic, military, ideological or political changes—especially but not limited to the ending of the Cold War—have engendered the current wave of ethnic conflict (Esman 1994, 261). Yet, the broad types of changes frequently mentioned do not cause violence directly. Rather, such changes are mediated by both the balance of local political power between competing ethnic groups and their historically formed beliefs about each other's intentions. The changes associated with the end of the Cold War have had different effects in different areas, depending upon these local conditions.

Where information failures point to the importance of outside mediators in helping to manage and possibly prevent ethnic conflicts, problems of credible commitment point to a potential role for outside peace keepers or peace enforcers as guarantors of new ethnic contracts. Indeed, when the future risk of exploitation is high, but the declining group is still strong enough to possess some chance of victory, outside enforcers buttressed with sufficient military capabilities and political will may be the only way to ensure ethnic peace (Stedman 1996; Walter 1997). We return to the potential for conflict management through outside intervention in Chapter Nine.

THE SECURITY DILEMMA

Barry Posen has extended the concept of the security dilemma, first developed in international relations, to the study of ethnic conflict.[10] In the broadest sense of the concept, the security dilemma is understood to follow axiomatically from anarchy. Under anarchy, states are dependent upon self-help for their security and must therefore maintain and perhaps expand their military capabilities. This can threaten others, who react by maintaining and expanding their capabilities, creating a spiraling arms race and hostility. The dilemma follows from the inability of the two sides to observe each other's intentions directly; if each party knew that the other was arming strictly for defensive purposes, the potential spiral would be cut short. But because states cannot know the intentions of others with certainty, in Posen's words, "What one does to enhance one's own security causes reactions that, in the end, can make one less secure" (1993a, 104).

Understood in this broad way, however, the security dilemma more accurately rests on the information failures and problems of credible commitment just discussed. If preparing for war and actually using force is costly, groups will have substantial incentives to acquire information about the motivations and strategies of others and to construct safeguards to support negotiated solutions. By doing so, groups can lessen the severity of the dilemma and open up a larger bargaining space between the parties; as a result, if groups face a severe dilemma, it is in part because they cannot agree to solve it (Wagner 1993). It is not anarchy per se that precludes states from sharing information about their intentions or undertaking agreements not to engage in arms spirals but, rather, information failures and the inability to commit credibly to pacific strategies.

The unique analytic core of the security dilemma lies in situations in which one or more disputing parties have incentives to resort to preemptive uses of force. We use the term here to refer to these specific incentives. As Robert Jervis (1978) observes, incentives to preempt arise when offensive military technologies and strategies dominate more defensive postures, and thus the side that attacks first reaps a military advantage. The offense is likely to dominate when there are significant military benefits from surprise and mobility. Geography will also matter, because some kinds of terrain (such as mountainous areas) and settlement

---

[10] The security dilemma has a long pedigree in international relations. Jervis (1978) gave the concept its modern form. Posen (1993a) was the first to apply it to ethnic relations.

patterns (such as exclusive ethnic zones) are easier to defend than others (Posen 1993a, 105–9). When the offense dominates, even groups (and states) that favor the status quo, it follows, may be tempted to launch preemptive strikes to avoid a possibly worse fate.

When incentives to use force preemptively are strong, the security dilemma takes hold and works its pernicious effects. Fearful that the other might preempt, a group has an incentive to strike first and negotiate later. In ethnic relations, as in international relations, a cycle of violence can seize previously peaceful groups even as they seek nothing more than their own safety. By the same logic, previously satisfied groups can be driven to become aggressors, destroying ethnic harmony in the search for group security.

Where information failures can be mitigated by external mediators, and problems of credible commitment can be offset, in part, by external guarantees of ethnic contracts, the ability of third parties to moderate the security dilemma is very limited. External actors can seek to raise the costs of using force, in general, and preemptive uses of force, in particular, by themselves punishing groups that strike first. Through early intervention and mediation, external actors may also be able to shape military doctrines and force structures in groups beginning to prepare for self-defense. Nevertheless, once incentives to preempt are in place, there is little outsiders can do to mitigate the security dilemma.

Strategic Interactions within Groups

Strategic interactions between groups create the unstable social foundations from which ethnic conflict arises. Information failures, problems of credible commitment, and the security dilemma demonstrate that even when groups mean well and calculate the costs and benefits of alternatives realistically, conflict can still erupt. Even in "the best of all possible worlds," these strategic dilemmas can produce violence. Strategic interactions within groups, however, can also polarize societies and, by doing so, exacerbate the strategic dilemmas and potential for conflict.

Under conditions of actual or potential state weakness or lack of legitimacy, and as the strategic dilemmas described above begin to take hold, two catalysts—ethnic activists and political entrepreneurs—can produce rapid and profound polarization within multiethnic societies. Social polarization, in turn, magnifies the potential for violence described above. As we explain in this section, political memories, myths, and emotions also magnify the polarizing effects of activists and entrepreneurs, further accelerating the vicious cycle of ethnic fear and violence.

There are strong centripetal forces that unify each ethnic group. As Russell Hardin writes, "Individuals identify with such groups because it is in their interests to do so. Individuals may find identification with their group beneficial because those who identify strongly may gain access to positions under the control of the group and because the group provides a relatively secure and comfortable environment. Individuals create their own identification with the group through the information and capacities they gain from life in the group. A group gains power from coordination of its members, power that may enable it to take action against other groups. Hence, the group may genuinely be instrumentally good for its members" (Hardin 1995, 70).

Robert Bates, in turn, explains the persistence of ethnic groups in Africa by "their capacity to extract goods and services from the modern sector and thereby satisfy the demands of their members" (1983, 161). With resources such as land, state allocations, and high governmental positions in scarce supply and highly valued by all communal interests, ethnic membership is viewed as a means of maximizing the ability of individuals and groups to compete. Social interactions reinforce ethnic identities, carrying them beyond the purely material realm and giving them meaning in a wider range of relations. In particular, ethnic groups tend to possess strong norms of exclusion that override more diffuse universalistic norms, thus reinforcing group solidarity and promoting extremism (Hardin 1995, 101 and 140–41). As individuals interact with others in their social environment, ethnic groups thus have a strong tendency to form and become politically salient.

The centripetal forces that unite the group, however, do not necessarily lead to the polarization of the larger society. Ethnic identities and even vibrant ethnic organizations can coexist with a wide range of other, potentially cross-cutting identities and organizations. Two catalysts—ethnic activists and political entrepreneurs—are necessary to produce polarization.

All individuals desire to belong to groups, but the strength of this desire differs (Horowitz 1985). In a model of "ethnic dissimilation," Timur Kuran demonstrates in Chapter Two that ethnic activists—individuals with especially strong needs to identify with ethnic kin—can manipulate such desires to produce a process of social polarization that is rapid, apparently spontaneous, and essentially unpredictable. By persuading others to increase their public ethnic activity in order to maintain standing within the group, Kuran argues, ethnic activists can drive individuals to represent falsely their true preferences. Although they might prefer, for instance, not to associate exclusively with members of their own group, individuals are pressed by activists and the social pressures they spawn to alter their behavior in a more "ethnic" direction. In this way, Kuran concludes, ethnic activists can cause previously integrated communities to separate along ethnic lines.

Political entrepreneurs—individuals who may not share the beliefs of extremists but who seek political office and power—may reflect the polarization of societies and, through their actions, propel this process further. As Stephen Saideman notes in Chapter Six, ethnicity often provides a key marker for self-aggrandizing politicians striving to build constituencies for attaining or maintaining political power. As an identifiable (if not "fixed") characteristic, ethnicity allows for selective benefits to be targeted to specific communities—and for politicians representing those communities to claim credit for delivering the goods; at the same time, ethnic cleavages allow political entrepreneurs to mobilize grievances against distributions of benefits that are perceived to be unfavorable to the group. Thus, although ethnicity is certainly not the only political marker, it is a highly visible and easily used vehicle for political mobilization.

Politicians in the middle of the political spectrum or those who court ethnically heterogeneous constituencies are vulnerable, in turn, to political extremists seeking to draw electoral support only from a more ethnically homogenous and possibly more militant constituency, a phenomenon often referred to as ethnic outbidding (Rothschild 1981; Horowitz 1985). When faced with the threat of such challenges, even centrist politicians can be driven to embrace a more "ethnic" position and defend communal interests more vigorously. The smaller the constituency willing to support a universalistic program, the more likely politicians will be drawn toward the extremes.

Political entrepreneurs seeking power based on ethnic appeals also reinforce processes of social polarization. Like activists, they can highlight and legitimate ethnic associations and affinities and raise the political saliency of ethnic-based organizations. In framing issues for the public, moreover, political entrepreneurs can exaggerate the hostility of others and magnify the likelihood of conflict— thereby distorting public debate and images of other groups and driving co-ethnics toward them for power and support. President Milosevic's control over the media in Serbia, for instance, allowed him to present a one-sided view of Croat violence toward Croatian Serbs (Weingast 1997, 20). In short, political entrepreneurs both reflect and stimulate ethnic fears for their own aggrandizement.

Many analysts mistakenly focus on social polarization and the role of ethnic activists and political entrepreneurs in fomenting violence as the primary if not sole cause of ethnic conflict. Empirically, it is important to note that social polarization by itself does not necessarily lead to violence; Belgium provides a conspicuous example of a polarized society that manages to conduct politics on a peaceful if not necessarily always harmonious basis, partly because the state remains robust enough to prevent significant information failures, problems of credible commitment, and security dilemmas from arising. Ethnic extremists, in turn, are nearly always present, and they can be expected to become prominent whenever at least one of the strategic dilemmas above is initiated. Analytically, ethnic activists and political entrepreneurs are as much a product as a producer of ethnic fears, and are dependent for their "success" upon the underlying strategic dilemmas. Nonetheless, ethnic activists and political entrepreneurs do play an important role in exacerbating ethnic tensions and propelling societies along the road to violence.

The polarization of society is also magnified by such "nonrational" factors as political memories and myths, on the one hand, and emotions, on the other. Political memories and myths can lead groups to form distorted images of others and see others as more hostile and aggressive than they really are. Such memories and myths are often rooted in actual events, and probably could not be long sustained absent an historical basis. Yet, historical events can, over time, evolve into legends that justify the superiority of one group over another, stimulate desires for retribution, or sustain group hatreds.

Following decolonization in Africa, for instance, political memories of past conflict directly contributed to violent encounters, even instances of "selective genocide" (Lemarchand and Martin 1974). Imperial repression created communications gaps between rulers and ruled; it also allowed imperial officials great latitude in allocating fiscal resources and recruiting imperial adjuncts among the local population. Over time, however, these intentional and unintentional acts of ethnic preference spawned hurts and angers toward minority groups perceived as having close working relationships with the colonizers. With independence, the resulting perceptions of comparative disadvantage contributed to a spiral of fear and aggressive behavior, which grew precipitously whenever the stereotypic images of other groups were supported by actual events. Thus, substantive competition over land and other resources combined with symbolic hurts from past humiliations and denials of group status (for example, among the Hutu in Rwanda) to contribute to highly destructive outcomes. With the rough hand of the imperial buffer removed, centralized bureaucratic and military state power no longer kept ethnic adversaries at bay, and violent encounters ensued.

In Eastern Europe, political memories and myths have both defined the groups themselves and stimulated acute fears of mutual exploitation. The Croats and Serbs, for instance, formerly citizens within the same state and now enemies, have both used history and religion to support a view of the other as a tight ethnic bloc determined on a destructive course and therefore deserving of pitiless retaliation (Glenny 1992a, 85). In thus cultivating the enemy's image, leaders in the former Yugoslavia and elsewhere not only stereotype and express their hostility toward their opponents but they also force the appearance of conformity among their own group members. Such an insulation of an organized body of people from complex reality can be a harbinger of impending chaos and contention.

Emotions may also cause individuals and groups to act in exaggerated or potentially "irrational" ways that magnify the chances of intense conflict. We are suspicious of emotions as explanations of conflict, at least at a first stage. Many analysts leap prematurely to the conclusion that ethnic conflict—because it appears so counterproductive and so vicious—must be irrational by nature (see Connor 1994). In our view, many aspects of ethnic conflict can be understood as the perhaps unfortunate but nonetheless rational outcomes of group interactions. However, we would be remiss if we ignored such emotions as hostility and alienation as possible sources and catalysts of ethnic conflict.

Many analysts point to a deep psychological—perhaps even physiological—need for humans to belong to a group (Horowitz 1985). Part of this is a need to distinguish between "us" and "them" as individuals searching for belonging and security. This need underlies Kuran's model of ethnic dissimilation. In the process of drawing distinctions, however, individuals often overstate the goodness of their own group while simultaneously vilifying others. Where such emotional biases exist, groups are likely to interpret the demands of the other as outrageous, while seeing their own as moderate and reasonable; to view the other as inherently untrustworthy and likely to defect from any ethnic contract, while believing themselves to be reliable; to insist upon adequate safeguards against the possible defection of the other, but interpreting the efforts of the other to impose similar restrictions on them as a sign of "bad faith"; to believe that the other is withholding information or being purposively deceptive, while they are being open and honest; and so on. Emotions magnify both group solidarity and inter-group tensions (Van Evera 1994).

Under conditions of extreme scarcity, political competition and conflict can act as magnifiers of a people's uncertainty about its future. Individuals understand-ably fear the consequences of modernization and the application of programs of structural adjustment, anticipating the loss of jobs and status, and the need for massive readjustments in terms of new values, outlooks, and orientations (Rothchild and Groth 1995, 74–75). Under such circumstances, ethnic identities are more likely to become suffused with belligerent stereotypes, as hostility toward ethnic adversaries, fanned by the mass media, provide an outlet for exag-gerated fears and suspicions.[11]

The emotional power of ethnic attachments is typically increased by the unify-ing effects of what are perceived to be external threats. People who have little in common with others may unite when they feel threatened by external enemies. Thus, the shared identity of the Hutu in Burundi emerged only recently with the Tutsi repressions of 1972. An external threat of aggression led the organization-ally distinct Hutu of the north-center to join forces with those in the south-Imbo, something that Warren Weinstein has described as "enforced ethnicity" (Weinstein 1972, 27). Similarly, in Chechnya, when very disparate interests felt threatened by Russian power, they overcame their difference and made common cause in the face of Russian intervention.[12] This emotional pull may be cultivated by elites. After examining elementary school textbooks in former Yugoslavia, one analyst concludes that "Not a single act of heroism, or personal valor and death is mentioned for the sake of achieving freedom within the community. Only har-mony is required within so as to facilitate defending the community from the enemy" (Pesic 1994, 77). Much like the "rally round the flag" effect that takes place within states threatened by external aggression, ethnic leaders can mobilize their members against threats posed by other ethnic groups. Such mobilization creates cohesion against internal group "traitors," national minorities (such as Russians living in the Ukraine), and external state and ethnic enemies, and results in greatly strengthened collective capacities for good or evil (Brubaker 1995).

Whereas strategic interactions between groups call for external actors to medi-ate and provide information to the groups and, possibly, create credible guaran-tees of new ethnic contracts, strategic interactions within groups require chang-ing the incentives of the groups themselves and, especially, of the ethnic activists and political entrepreneurs who lead them. As discussed in Chapter Nine, tar-geted interventions are necessary to decrease the social and political salience of

---

[11] In both Serbia and Rwanda, the radio proved a powerful weapon for broadcasting elite messages of hostility. Thus, Serbia's president, Slobodan Milosevic, used the state radio to mobilize his sup-porters for war, while in Rwanda, Hutu ideologues employed the privately owned *Radio Mille Collines* to arouse their followers.

[12] As Paula Garb demonstrates in Chapter Eight, however, this common cause did not extend to ethnic allies in the broader region.

ethnicity and prevent the polarization of society. Such interventions are best taken early. Once the society has become polarized, there is little—at least in the short term—that outsiders can do to reintegrate the polity.

Because conflict can escalate dangerously when leaders and constituents become entrapped in a situation where political memories, myths, and emotions create menacing intergroup perceptions, it is also important that third parties take initiatives to clear up misperceptions and correct (or at least offset) emotionally generated fears and biases. Preferably, this should also occur at an early stage. At times, as in the 1971–1972 negotiations in the Sudan (Rothchild 1997), external intermediaries can be instrumental in encouraging rival parties to understand and empathize with each other's feelings and predicaments. They can help influence groups to see themselves as others see them, and to view others as they would want to be viewed. Provided such third-party actors are perceived as fair-minded and detached providers of information, they can often assist groups to recognize the distortions in the information they receive and correct for these distortions in evaluating the attitudes and emotions of other groups.

Together, strategic interactions between and within groups can produce environments of fear in which ethnic tensions and conflicts can grow. As Pesic recognizes, it is the future that threatens, but it is often interpreted through the past. Although each strategic dilemma alone is sufficient to produce and explain the outbreak of ethnic conflict, they almost always occur simultaneously. Ethnic activists and political entrepreneurs can polarize societies, exacerbating these strategic dilemmas. The tendency toward polarization, in turn, is magnified by political memories, myths, and emotions. Combined, these forces create a devastating brew of ethnic rivalry and violence.

THE INTERNATIONAL SPREAD OF ETHNIC CONFLICT

The fear that disputes may spread across state borders accounts for much of the increase in scholarly and policy interest in ethnic conflict today. Our discussion so far has focused on the origins of ethnic conflict within states. These origins, in turn, provide essential building blocks for understanding the international spread of ethnic conflict. Unfortunately, the magnitude of the problem and the processes through which ethnic conflict spreads remain poorly understood. Our analysis here is more tentative than that above, but provides an approach to conceptualizing and studying the problem. The chapters below provide more concrete analyses of this complex phenomenon.

Ethnic conflict spreads across state borders in two ways. *Diffusion* occurs when ethnic violence in one state increases the probability of conflict in a second. In other words, if conflict in Rwanda incites similar violence directly or indirectly in Burundi, the conflict will have diffused. *Escalation* occurs when a conflict in one country brings in new, foreign belligerents—whether neighbors or great powers with global reach. If Greece or Turkey were to become embroiled in the current

Balkan wars, for example, the conflict will have escalated.[13] Although analytically distinct, both processes can occur simultaneously in practice. The conflict in Rwanda, for instance, diffused to neighboring Zaire when Tutsi-related groups there emerged to challenge the state; the conflict also escalated when Tutsi-led Rwandan government forces intervened on an informal basis in support of their ethnic brethren and in an effort to check the extremist Hutus harbored in the refugee camps along its border.

Our focus on the international spread of ethnic conflict is not meant to imply that every such episode has an international dimension. Both scholars and policy makers need to recognize and respect the autonomy of particular ethnic conflicts from international pressures (Smith 1993, 28). It is also important to recognize that ethnic conflict is inherently self-limiting. Ethnic conflicts differ from ideological and, possibly, religious conflicts in that ethnic groups are by definition limited, whereas the latter principles are more nearly universalistic. Ethnic conflicts may still spread beyond the original kin groups, but they are not likely to produce global conflagrations unless they become linked with other issues (see Halperin, Chapter Seven). Nonetheless, the international spread of ethnic conflict—even within limited, regional contexts—is a legitimate and growing source of concern.

Like ethnic conflict in general, both diffusion and escalation are products of strategic interactions. The strategic dilemmas discussed above must be present for conflicts to spread beyond the initial belligerents. For conflict in one locale to alter the probability of conflict in a second, it must generate or worsen information failures, problems of credible commitment, or security dilemmas in the latter. Likewise, for third parties to join in as belligerents in an internal conflict, the same dilemmas must arise between the third party and at least one of the internal groups or, as before, between the groups themselves; in the absence of these dilemmas, the actors would benefit from a negotiated solution that stopped short of actual violence. Thus, the causes of ethnic conflict within a state are closely related to the causes of transnational ethnic conflict.

The strategic nature of transnational ethnic conflict has two important implications. First, ethnic conflict is most likely to spread to states that already face a risk of ethnic violence. Conflict abroad can exacerbate tensions within states, but it is unlikely to spread to societies that have worked out effective solutions to their strategic dilemmas. In states already at risk, however, conflict abroad can send dangerous signals to fearful groups.

---

[13] Spread, diffusion, escalation, and even contagion are often used as synonyms. We restrict the terms *diffusion* and *escalation* to the particular processes defined here and use the term *spread* for the more general tendency. Some analysts distinguish between positive diffusion, where an event increases the probability of a similar event occurring elsewhere, and negative diffusion, which reduces the probability. Similarly, some analysts differentiate between horizontal escalation, which increases the number of actors involved in the conflict, and vertical escalation, which increases the intensity or level of violence in the conflict. We are concerned here only with horizontal escalation, and use the term to refer to an increase in the number of actors. Our analysis suggests little about the level of violence in the conflict.

Second, as a strategic process, we need not observe conflict actually spreading to conclude that it is, indeed, a potential problem. To the extent that the ethnic groups themselves or third parties act to forestall the international spread of violence, any alteration in the current strategies of these actors may lead to greater diffusion or escalation in the future. To assess this potential requires a model of ethnic conflict that captures the strategic interactions of potentially warring groups.

Diffusion

The papers in this project reach different conclusions on the extent to which ethnic conflicts diffuse between states. Focusing on the aggregate level, Kuran (Chapter Two) and Stuart Hill, Donald Rothchild, and Colin Cameron (Chapter Three) develop models and provide evidence of how politicized ethnicity and the tactics of mass conflict spread to group members and their leaders in other countries who face similar political conditions. In studying specific cases, on the other hand, Fearon (Chapter Five) and Saideman (Chapter Six) locate the sources of contemporary ethnic conflicts primarily within states and question whether conflicts abroad play a significant role in precipitating violence. Sandra Halperin (Chapter Seven) argues that prior to 1945, social, economic, and political conditions in Europe, at least, did diffuse ethnic conflicts to other states, but that local circumstances today do not encourage such trends. This disparity in views underlines not a contradiction but an important insight. The seeds of ethnic conflict, while possibly blown in from abroad, germinate and take root only in fertile soil. Unless the local conditions are right—or, perhaps more appropriately, wrong—diffusion is unlikely; but when circumstances are receptive, ethnic conflict can take root and become devastating.

Building upon the causes of ethnic conflict discussed above, diffusion can occur in four ways. These four processes are not necessarily exclusive and all may occur simultaneously. First, events abroad may change directly the ethnic balance of power at home, disrupting the existing ethnic contract and precipitating violence. Through this first route, ethnic conflict may actually be contagious in the full sense of this overused term. For instance, refugee flows from a neighboring state may substantially alter the state's own ethnic composition (Newland 1993). Armed insurgents from one state may seek refuge in a second and stir up local conflicts in their wake, as in the recent violence in Zaire, where the presence of large numbers of Hutu refugees have prompted, in part, local Tutsi-related insurgents to declare war on their own government. As Edmond Keller notes in Chapter Twelve, these are constant concerns for many African states. Similar changes in the ethnic balance of power can occur in the breakup of federal states, even without the actual migration of peoples across recognized international borders. Once central political authority in Yugoslavia began to unravel, the relevant ethnic balance of power shifted from the federal level to the now independent republics. As this shift occurred, minority groups—previously protected by their kin in other regions—were left exposed and vulnerable. This emboldened the new majority and threatened the new minority in each state, undermining the ethnic contract and leading the groups into a spiral of violence (see Fearon 1993; Hardin 1995, 156–63; and Djilas 1995). In this way, Slovenia's relatively minor conflict with Serbia diffused to the other republics, and became more virulent with each additional occurrence.[14]

Second, ethnic conflict in one country may prompt groups in another to make more extreme demands. Groups in one state, witnessing ethnic mobilization or, more importantly, political success by ethnic groups in another, may increase their own political agitation and demand a significantly greater share of the resource pie—increasing the probability of conflict. Kuran (Chapter Two) develops a strong argument on the importance of this "demonstration effect" in stimulating ethnic dissimilation abroad. Similarly, ethnic conflict elsewhere may cause groups to update their beliefs about the likely demands of other groups in their own country. Even in the absence of any change in the underlying political power of groups or in the claims made, if the groups believe others are now more likely to challenge the existing ethnic contract and issue greater demands, their best response may be to strike preemptively before the others have actually increased their levels of mobilization. Thus, changes in beliefs about the likely behavior of others can precipitate conflict even in the absence of any manifest demands or actions. As groups update their beliefs about one another by observing events elsewhere, ethnic conflict can literally materialize out of thin air. Islamic fundamentalism appears to have stimulated greater concerns in France about its large Algerian minority and, especially, has raised fears that the latter is likely to make appeals for greater autonomy and a more favorable distribution of resources; although such concerns have stimulated sporadic violence by French rightists, the conflict has not to date reached the level of widespread violence.

Third, and in ways similar to those just discussed, ethnic conflict abroad may lead groups to update their beliefs about the efficacy of the political safeguards contained in their existing ethnic contracts. For example, if events abroad suggest that the economic leverage wielded by wealthy minority groups is less effective than previously believed, the poorer majority may become emboldened and the minority threatened—once again precipitating conflict without any manifest changes in the underlying conditions at home. In this context, Serbia's suppression of agitation for elevation to republic status in Kosovo in 1981 provided an important signal to other groups in Yugoslavia about the efficacy of existing federal safeguards. Hardin (1995, 157) dates the unraveling of Yugoslavia to this event.

Finally, ethnic conflict abroad may lead groups to update their beliefs about the costs of protest or, ultimately, violence and their probability of success. Effective protest or violence abroad may lead groups at home to believe that they too may be able to obtain valued ends through coercion. Hill, Rothchild, and Cameron

---

[14] Both Fearon (Chapter Five) and Saideman (Chapter Six) consider this domestic rather than international contagion. Admittedly, where one should draw the line between domestic and international is ambiguous. Refugee flows have also been important in the former Yugoslavia (Steinberg 1993, 53).

(Chapter Three) provide strong evidence for the diffusion of political tactics from one country to another. Slovenia's relatively easy break from Yugoslavia, precipitating a ten-day war between the Yugoslav National Army (JNA) and separatist forces that produced fewer than seventy casualties, gave "the impression that the dissolution of a country was not so difficult after all" (Woodward 1995a, 146). Similarly, if groups believe that violence will provoke the international community to insist on the punishment of ethnic aggressors, but events suggest that the international community is unlikely to impose such punishments, groups will then lower their estimated costs of using violence and become more likely to use force. For instance, Haiti's military leaders inferred from America's precipitant disengagement from Somalia, as well as its earlier pullout from Lebanon, that the United States lacked the will to absorb significant costs in a small, Third World country in an internal conflict and could be forced to back down—an inference that was confirmed when a diminutive group of demonstrators on the docks prompted the first American landing party to withdraw. American threats to intervene, in turn, only became credible once Haitian military leaders confirmed that the planes were in the air on their way to the island state. The various ethnic groups in Bosnia drew similar inferences, and reasonably doubted early attempts by the United States and NATO to intervene in the conflict; this may have led to the eventual deployment in Bosnia of a larger than otherwise necessary force to demonstrate the commitment of the United States.

In these four ways, then, ethnic conflict in one country may precipitate similar conflict in another. In all the paths, the beliefs of groups and ideas and information are crucial. Information and ideas, in turn, can jump borders easily and diffuse widely. Both Kuran (Chapter Two) and Hill, Rothchild, and Cameron (Chapter Three) highlight the possibility of global bandwagons of ethnic conflicts. Whether events have this effect, however, depends upon local conditions, the initial beliefs of groups on the scene, and the lessons drawn by these groups. For instance, adversaries may believe that resorting to violence is so costly that even substantial changes in these beliefs will still not produce manifest conflict. Conversely, the distribution of ethnic power or the beliefs of the groups about this distribution may be such that violence is inevitable; if so, events abroad may appear to cause the outbreak of conflict—and may in fact be a contributing factor—but conditions at home are the real driving forces. Identifying how conflicts diffuse requires a model of ethnic relations (such as the one posed in the previous section), estimates of the variables in this model, and close attention to how events abroad change these estimates and, especially, the beliefs of the groups.

It is important to note that all of the processes discussed above can both increase and decrease the likelihood of conflict. Successful conflict management abroad can reduce direct spillovers and lead groups to temper their own demands, reduce their expectations of the likely demands of others, have greater confidence in the safeguards in their existing ethnic contracts, and recognize the high costs of violence. For example, South African whites drew positive lessons from the earlier experiences of the minority communities in Kenya, Namibia, and Zimbabwe after the transfer of power to African-led majority regimes, thereby facilitating the recent transition to one person, one vote elections and a modified form of majority rule in that country. Even in the conflict-prone 1990s, the lessons drawn need not be one-sided. The peaceful transition in South Africa, the emerging but still fragile peace between Israel and its neighbors in the Middle East, and the peaceful divorce between the Czech Republic and Slovakia are shining examples of progress toward stable ethnic relations that may offset, in part, the harsh events that have occurred in Bosnia, Rwanda, and other recent tragedies. At the very least, some of the warning signs from the 1990s are more ambiguous than a focus on the overt conflicts alone might suggest.

There is, however, reason to expect that conflict may diffuse more readily than peace. The beliefs of groups are central to the outbreak of ethnic conflict within countries and the diffusion of ethnic conflict across countries. Information shapes these beliefs, and today flows mostly to groups from the international media. The media, in turn, contain an important selection bias. Conflict occurs in those countries in which the underlying conditions are most ripe—the balance of ethnic power is precarious, the demands made by each side are large, and the costs of conflict are small. It is a truism that we observe conflict where it is most likely. International news reports, which provide the raw material for the conclusions drawn by ethnic groups everywhere, are heavily biased toward conflict. The evening news does not feature balanced reports of deadly conflicts, on the one hand, and conflicts that did not happen or that were successfully nipped in the bud, on the other. This selection bias thus distorts the information received by individuals and groups and may cause them to see other groups at home as more threatening or prone to violence than they really are. The media sends one-sided messages and receivers may draw one-sided conclusions. This selection bias is likely to be even more extreme in the "partisan" press that is associated with one or the other side in a particular conflict.[15] Although diffusion can, in theory, work both ways—as a damper and spur to ethnic conflict—in practice the selection bias of the media will tend to heighten ethnic fears and provoke ethnic conflict abroad.

Coupled with this biased information flow are the emotions discussed above that often produce deep insecurities in individuals—especially when placed in environments they believe are becoming more threatening. An individual's desire to belong to and identify with an ethnic group can prove an emotionally satisfying experience when peace and regularized rules of intergroup relations prevail. However, when ethnic leaders exaggerate trends from abroad to stimulate fear and mobilize their supporters for competition and conflict, the result may be to entrap groups in deadly encounters from which there is no escape. Efforts to promote the security of one group then leave all groups with a heightened sense of

---

[15] Rational individuals will, of course, recognize the possibility of selection bias in the media. In turn, they will discount information on conflict when they update their prior beliefs. Correctly discerning the degree of bias, however, can be extremely hard, particularly for poorly informed individuals in a highly partisan environment. The likelihood of drawing the correct conclusion from the information most readily available is very low. If individuals are not fully rational, biased information flows may have much more extreme effects.

insecurity. Inter-group linkages become gravely weakened, leading to societal incoherence and, at times, to state collapse. As the actors retreat to their safe, ethnic containers, fewer and fewer of them are willing to risk contacts and cooperative initiatives with members of other communities, leaving them increasingly isolated and enmeshed in a Hobbesian world of group against group. Where polarization becomes complete and the state is dominated by a single ethnic group, it is only a short step to the communal killings of colonial Algeria, Bosnia-Herzegovina, Burundi, Rwanda, Sri Lanka, and Nagorno Karabakh.

Escalation

Ethnic conflicts also escalate to include additional, foreign belligerents.[16] Whereas diffusion occurs in part through information flows that condition the beliefs of ethnic actors elsewhere, escalation occurs through the more "traditional" routes of other interstate conflicts—alliances, spillovers, irredentism, diversions, and internal weakness. Nonetheless, all routes are contingent on the presence of information failures, problems of credible commitment, and security dilemmas.

Ethnic ties and antagonisms frequently motivate countries to become involved in ethnic conflicts elsewhere. In this form of "ethnopolitik," co-ethnics in one state are propelled by feelings of solidarity with their ethnic kin in a second. This typically occurs between neighbors where ethnic groups span national borders. India's intervention in Sri Lanka (Cooper and Berdal 1993, 186) and Hungary's attention to the treatment of its ethnic brethren elsewhere in Eastern Europe (Woodward 1995a, 219) are prime examples.

In their study of the escalation of international conflicts, Randolph Siverson and Harvey Starr (1991) find that states join ongoing wars when they possess opportunity, defined by shared borders, and willingness, represented by a preexisting alliance. Most states lack the ability to project force over long distances, and thus contiguity conditions the ability of states to become involved in a conflict. Alliances reflect a self-defined interest in the security of another belligerent. In a similar vein, in Chapter Four, Will Moore and David Davis reason that ethnic alliances—cases in which a majority group in one state is a minority group in a second—should have similar effects. Examining the behavior of all international dyads that are either contiguous or contain at least one great power (presumably possessing global reach), Moore and Davis find that ethnic alliances are an important source of interstate conflict. This effect is particularly prominent when the

---

[16] Countries also become involved in foreign ethnic conflicts, occasionally but not necessarily through international organizations, as peacekeepers or peace enforcers. As discussed in more detail in Chapter Nine, the distinction between belligerents and peacekeepers in one form or another is often hard to sustain in practice (Ruggie 1994, 99). Peacekeepers do not always remain impartial and can easily be perceived as belligerents. For every Cyprus, where the United Nations forces have remained neutral, there are the Somalias and Liberias, where UNOSOM II and ECOWAS, respectively, stepped over the border into belligerency. Nonetheless, the initial intent of the countries, at least, and the processes of involvement differ between these two primary routes. The escalation of ethnic conflicts to include additional belligerents is discussed here. Peacekeeping and peace enforcement are discussed in Chapter Nine.

minority kin group is politically mobilized, indicating a higher level of ethnic conflict within that state. Although there are obvious exceptions that have not resulted in heightened interstate conflict, such as the alliance between Catholics in Ireland and Northern Ireland and the ties between the Basques in Spain and France, the strength of the overall pattern is noteworthy.

Taking a longer-term and more explicitly constructivist view, however, Paula Garb (Chapter Eight) argues that the plasticity of ethnic identities renders such alliances problematic. In the Caucasus, she argues, distinct peoples nonetheless share strong ethnic bonds, embodied in the widespread "Caucasian idea." Seventy years of "divide and conquer" policies under Soviet rule, the state-building enterprises of the newly independent or more autonomous republican leaders, and the devastating force and brutality of the Russian invasion of Chechnya, she concludes, prevented ethnic alliances from escalating the local conflict into a regional conflict. In short, ethnic ties are a primary source of escalation, but they are flexible and contingent in their effects.

Ethnic alliances are likely to escalate conflicts whenever at least one party to the dispute, including the third party, suffers from one or more of the strategic dilemmas above. In turn, ethnic alliances may also cause conflict by exacerbating the strategic dilemmas between groups. When groups overestimate the support they may receive from their ethnic kin abroad, they may become intransigent and possibly hold out for a "better deal" than the other group is willing to accept. Likewise, if groups underestimate the support their opponents may receive (or believe they may receive), they may make "too few" concessions to avert violence. Thus, the possible presence of ethnic alliances complicates the strategic setting that faces groups, increases the likelihood that one or more strategic dilemmas will arise, and increases the probability of violence. Drawing on Garb's analysis again, the Chechens may have overestimated the likelihood that their ethnic allies would come to their aid while at the same time underestimating the brutality of the Russian response, perhaps expecting the international community or Russia's desire to curry favor with this community to restrain its reaction. Either or both of these incorrect estimates would have been sufficient to push the Chechens toward conflict rather than compromise.

Ethnic conflict within a state can act as a trigger for interstate conflict in four other ways. First, in processes similar to the first and most direct path of diffusion above, ethnic warfare may spill over into neighboring territories and draw states into violence. Ethnic combatants in one state may use the territory of a second for staging areas, retreats, and so forth—with or without the latter's consent. This spillover can lead to recriminations between the two affected states and, in cases of "hot pursuit," direct border clashes that may spiral out of control. As Keller (Chapter Twelve) again notes, such spillovers have been a frequent worry in Africa. In March 1991, in but one possible example, Charles Taylor's forces in Liberia joined with Sierra Leonean dissidents and invaded Sierra Leone (Wippman 1993, 170). There have also been problems in the former Yugoslavia, with minor incidents occurring at the Austrian border, Serbian/JNA overflights of Hungary and the bombing of a border village, and JNA forces withdrawing through Italian territory (Steinberg 1993, 52). Although potentially dangerous, and often used as an excuse for involvement by neighbors looking for a greater role, such spillovers can normally be resolved amicably. However, as borders become more fluid in areas of ethnic instability, and if the strategic dilemmas become acute, violent encounters may ensue.

Second, ethnic mobilization often contains within it an irredentist dimension, as ethnic leaders demand the reunification of an often mythical but nonetheless politically salient ethnic homeland—typically defined as the largest area of territory ever controlled or believed to have been controlled by the group (Carment 1994; Carment and James 1995). Examples include Somalia's invasion of the Ogaden region of Ethiopia, Nazi Germany's incorporation of the Sudetenland, and Pakistan and India's continuing conflict over Kashmir. In Chapter Five, Fearon concludes that irredentist conflicts are particularly prone to problems of credible commitment.

Third, ethnicity provides a strong basis for "diversionary wars" stimulated by political leaders beset by opposition at home and seeking to rally support for their continued rule by inciting conflict abroad.[17] Ethnicity and its emotional appeal to an "us versus them" outlook provides a particularly salient principle of organization and support. This was precisely the strategy used by Serbian President Milosevic; faced with growing opposition to his presidency and a majority that favored far-reaching economic reforms, which he opposed, the embattled president "played the ethnic card" and precipitated the collapse of Yugoslavia (Bates and Weingast 1995; Djilas 1995, 85 and 105).

Fourth, predatory states within the region may consider states with significant internal conflicts to be easy targets. With the other weakened by internal dissent, aggressor states may calculate that their prospects for an easy, cheap victory are now greater than before; challenging the target is thus more attractive. Ethiopia's internal weakness, for example, appears to have contributed to Somalia's 1977 challenge in the Ogaden (Carment and James 1995, 94). Such strategies may also backfire, however, as predatory states often appear to miscalculate the rally effect that their aggression provokes. This may have been the case in the Ogaden war, when Siad Barre sought to take advantage of the revolution in Ethiopia to settle outstanding territorial issues to his advantage; contrary to his expectations, Barre actually mobilized support for the new regime in Ethiopia and locked his country into a costly war.

Although still poorly understood, diffusion and escalation are real and, correctly, important concerns to policy makers worldwide. The chapters below shed light on these complex processes, but our understanding remains at a rudimentary level. For scholars and analysts interested in the international spread of ethnic conflict, no question is more important than how and why groups learn from conflicts abroad. Even at this stage, however, it is clear that both diffusion and escalation can result in devastating ethnic conflicts not only for the groups

---

[17] Diversionary wars are also called "conflict transformations"; Carment (1994) and Carment and James (1995).

involved but potentially for other states as well. Not only must such conflicts be managed to end the violence but they must also be controlled to inhibit their spread.

PLAN OF THE BOOK

The chapters below are organized into three sections. The first two examine the processes of diffusion and escalation, but arrive at different conclusions on the extent to which ethnic conflict is likely to spread within the modern world. The three chapters in Part Two suggest that ethnic conflict can and does spread across national borders. As discussed above, Kuran argues that ethnic dissimilation in one country can produce similar results elsewhere; Hill, Rothchild, and Cameron find that political tactics originating in one country diffuse widely to others; and Moore and Davis present evidence that transnational ethnic alliances produce higher levels of interstate conflict. The four chapters in Part Three, on the other hand, emphasize the local origins of ethnic conflicts and, while recognizing that conflict can spread across borders, they highlight the self-limiting nature of diffusion and escalation in today's world. As also discussed above, Fearon focuses on problems of credible commitment, Saideman highlights the domestic incentives of politicians, Halperin emphasizes internal socio-economic and political structures, and Garb examines the socially constructed nature of ethnic identity.

Part Four turns to the management of transnational ethnic conflicts. We begin with an overview of the problem of management and its relationship to the three strategic dilemmas. In Chapter Ten, Daniel Froats and Stephen Krasner examine the long history of international intervention on behalf of minorities within states and conclude that international efforts succeed best when they strengthen the position of domestic actors committed to the same goal. Cynthia Kaplan explores the complex interaction of domestic and international negotiations in two cases of potential conflict that—to date—have been handled successfully. Keller reviews important cases of transnational ethnic conflict in contemporary Africa and examines the potential and problems of regional peacekeeping and peace-making efforts. In Chapter Thirteen, Bruce Jentleson broadens the discussion to the more general problem of preventive diplomacy, arguing that it is possible, difficult, and necessary. I. William Zartman focuses on the equally difficult problem of finding stable solutions for ongoing violent conflicts; he concludes that success is dependent upon finding an appropriate formula made of identities and institutions for handling ethnic relations in the future. We conclude with a final essay that summarizes the analytic and policy lessons of the volume.

PART TWO

The International Spread of Ethnic Conflict

Ethnic Dissimilation and Its International Diffusion

TIMUR KURAN

MOST OF THE ALMOST two hundred members of the United Nations are ethnically heterogeneous, and in many of them, including ones developed and underdeveloped, democratic and authoritarian, federative and unitary, the social significance of ethnicity is rising. In particular, multitudes are asserting their ethnic distinctiveness and making it felt that their ethnic bonds are stronger than their national loyalties. Subnational groups that had appeared to be assimilating into geographically defined populations are now demanding ethnically based economic rights, political power, and social respect. Moreover, elections, development strategies, coups, and international treaties increasingly involve ethnic dimensions.[1] The process whereby the social significance of ethnicity becomes accentuated and ethnic particularities gain salience may be called, for lack of an established term, *ethnification*. To observe that a state is undergoing ethnification, that it is becoming *ethnified*, is to note that its members are treating ethnicity as increasingly relevant to their personal and collective choices.

The ethnic distinctions that individuals highlight in the course of an ethnification process need not be their own. Consider a population divided into two ethnic groups, g_1 and g_2. Members of g_1, who form a huge majority, start emphasizing their ethnicity and distancing themselves from members of g_2. Alarmed by the costs of exclusion from the majority, members of g_2 start behaving like individuals from g_1, hoping thereby to avoid rejection. In this illustration, ethnification is accompanied by *ethnic assimilation*: judged by observed behavior, the members of g_2 become increasingly indistinguishable from those of g_1.

In practice, however, ethnification often makes groups become less similar in behavior. Its outcome is ethnic dissimilation, our focus here.[2] Suppose, for an

Note: Drafts of this paper were presented at the March 1995 conference of the Institute on Global Conflict and Cooperation, held at the University of California at Davis, and the August 1995 conference of the American Political Science Association, held in Chicago. I received many helpful comments, especially from Paul Goble, Bernard Grofman, Sandra Halperin, David Lake, David Rapoport, Donald Rothchild, Etel Solingen, and two anonymous reviewers. Murat Somer provided exemplary research assistance.

[1] Gurr (1994) finds that ethnic conflict has become more common since around 1960. For impressionistic accounts supportive of this finding, see Pfaff (1993) and Moynihan (1993).

[2] The concept is distinct from ethnic fission, which occurs when a population considered to share a common ancestry splits into subpopulations thought to have different ancestries. Ethnic dissimilation commonly occurs without ethnic fission. Yinger (1981) distinguishes among the biological, cultural, psychological, and structural dimensions of the process.

illustration, that g_1 and g_2 are roughly equal in size. Members of g_1 start drawing together and publicizing their commonalities. Feeling excluded, members of g_2 tighten their intracommunal bonds through acts that make their own ethnicity more salient. In this second illustration, then, ethnification produces dissimilation, in that the behaviors of the two groups move apart. Ethnic dissimilation is not necessarily a source of intercommunal mistrust or violence, just as its converse, ethnic assimilation, need not foster social peace. Frequently, however, dissimilation heightens ethnic antagonisms and facilitates ethnic collective action. In its extreme forms, moreover, it causes states to become unglued, even to fall prey to ethnic warfare.[3]

When many countries undergo ethnic dissimilation simultaneously, the reason could be that factors common to all have heightened the significance of ethnicity through mutually independent mechanisms.[4] Without denying the significance of factors operating independently on each of many states, this paper presents a mechanism that captures the interdependencies among ethnic dissimilation processes. These interdependencies build on interpersonal behavioral linkages within the individual countries. In the overall argument, therefore, interdependencies exist at two levels: among individual choices and among national patterns.

The argument unfolds in stages. Concentrating first on a single ethnically heterogeneous state, I demonstrate how individuals who had appeared indifferent toward ethnicity may, through reactions and counter-reactions, bring about ethnic dissimilation. The crux of the reasoning is that people's ethnically meaningful behaviors shape the perceptions and incentives that drive the choices of others. Specifically, such behaviors pressure others into making frequent displays of their ethnicity, and they also raise the perceived advantages of ethnic solidarity. The consequent interdependencies may create multiple social equilibria, in other words, more than one self-sustaining pattern of ethnic activity. As we shall see, these equilibria may involve radically different amounts of *aggregate ethnic activity*, defined as the sum of the ethnically meaningful behaviors generated by the country as a whole.

The second segment of the argument recognizes that motives to perform ethnically meaningful behaviors are determined partly by the ethnic activities of other states. Ethnic strife within one state sensitizes people elsewhere to their own ethnic particularities, possibly raising their expectations of ethnic conflict at home. We shall see that international interdependencies can give certain countries disproportionate global significance. Under the right circumstances, in fact, a *bandwagon* that produces ethnic dissimilation within one country might

---

[3] Hechter, Friedman, and Appelbaum (1982, 425) observe that when ethnic groups become socially and economically segregated, their members become predisposed to mistrust other groups and readier to join ethnically based collective efforts. See also Hechter (1987) and Hardin (1995).

[4] The impetus could be technological progress that fosters greater awareness of group distinctions (Connor 1972, 343–44); the rising importance of government as a source of rent (Glazer and Moynihan 1975, 8–18); the collapse of legal structures that protect weak groups (Weingast 1997; Fearon, this volume, Chapter Five), among other possibilities.

touch off a *superbandwagon* that heightens the role of ethnicity in successive others. The argument accommodates the existence of conditions that accord ethnic relations within a particular country some immunity to ethnic dissimilation elsewhere; it is consistent with a persistent state of low ethnic activity. Moreover, states may influence one another asymmetrically. Because of the enormous influence of American culture, policies aimed at helping American ethnic minorities are likely to have an especially great impact on ethnic relations elsewhere.

In the presence of multiple social equilibria, small shocks to a country, whether internal or external, may spur huge changes. And if the interdependencies among individual behaviors are not readily observable, the changes will exhibit another characteristic: imperfect predictability. A key aspect of the model outlined below is that the interdependencies among individual behaviors are poorly observable. The source of unobservability is *ethnic preference falsification*, the act of misrepresenting one's ethnic needs under real or imagined social pressures.[5] In the presence of such preference falsification, ethnic dissimilation need not involve changes in ethnic dispositions or prejudices. It can occur without a prior buildup of ethnic mistrust or a prior escalation in the perceived need for ethnic solidarity. Moreover, the contributors to dissimilation may include individuals who would rather not alter their behaviors. In any case, whatever the attitudinal transformations that precede a dissimilation process, the consequent changes in the social importance of ethnicity may be disproportionately large. The possibility of disproportionality between causes and effects, coupled with the imperfect observability of the possible causes, lessens the predictability of ethnic dissimilation processes. At the same time, the very factors that make it difficult to forecast the course of ethnic relations facilitate retrospective explanation.

The implications of the model are consistent with certain often-noted patterns. In the 1960s, celebrated scholars failed to recognize the early manifestations of today's ongoing ethnic dissimilation processes. Nor did they anticipate the escalation of separatism among such groups as the Flemings of Belgium, the Basques of Spain, and the Kurds of Turkey (Connor 1987, esp. 196–200). In the 1970s and early 1980s, Yugoslavia was often portrayed as an example of successful ethnic integration and nation building; although everyone understood that memories of past conflicts had not disappeared, their potency seemed to be weakening. Equally important, almost no one was prepared for the rapidity and savagery of the subsequent disintegration (Glenny 1993, esp. ch. 1; Malcolm 1994, preface, chs. 14–15). Despite such predictive failures, there is no shortage of explanations for recent dissimilation processes. The following sections will show that these disjunctions between prediction and explanation are not aberrations. Rather, they are among the unavoidable consequences of behavioral interdependencies rooted in poorly observable motives.

---

[5] For a fuller definition and general analysis of preference falsification, see Kuran (1995).

PRIVATE ETHNIC PREFERENCES, PUBLIC ETHNIC BEHAVIORS

In the early twentieth century, Woodrow Wilson and other Western statesmen promoted the doctrine of national "self-determination." In its simplest form, this doctrine holds that "any self-differentiating people, simply because it *is* a people, has the right, should it so desire, to rule itself."[6] The promoters of self-determination maintained that some of the nations within the multinational empires defeated in World War I were unhappy with the prevailing political arrangements. Insofar as these nations appeared content, the reason was that they were reluctant to challenge the status quo publicly. Such oppressed nations had to be allowed to express their true loyalties freely and to develop political structures they considered their own. To these ends, the international community would organize plebiscites conducted by secret ballot. The promoters of self-determination thus recognized that publicly expressed political loyalties might depart from privately felt attachments. The secret ballot was to unveil private political aspirations under conditions free of pressures to engage in preference falsification.

Incentives to falsify group loyalties did not disappear, however, as multinational empires gave way to scores of new states. Rather, they began afflicting choices made within more finely subdivided communities. Because the new states carved out of the old empires were ethnically heterogeneous, the primary loyalties of their members could be toward subnations that we now classify as ethnic groups. The individual citizen of a state could feel a special attachment to his own ethnic group, and this attachment could make him discriminate against members of other groups. Sensing the vitality of subnational loyalties, the country's leaders could then seek to weaken these by discouraging their overt expression. Insofar as the strategy was successful, the individual would find it prudent to downplay, if not to conceal, his ethnic loyalties, acting as though he attached little significance to ethnicity. If the strategy was unsuccessful, social pressures would continue to favor ethnic solidarity over national solidarity, making it prudent for individuals to exaggerate, rather than hide, their ethnic loyalties, sentiments, and needs.

By definition, ethnic preference falsification entails an incongruity between *private ethnic preferences* and the preferences conveyed by *public ethnic behaviors*. It occurs when, for example, a Croatian-Yugoslav turns against her neighbors of Serbian extraction in order to appear supportive of Croat separatism, even though privately she remains committed to the ideal of Yugoslav unity. Private ethnic preferences are not directly observable, so the privately felt demand for ethnically meaningful behavior cannot be measured, except perhaps through controlled experiments. By contrast, public ethnic behaviors are observable.[7] In terms of these concepts, ethnic dissimilation raises aggregate ethnic activity as individuals undertake more and more actions that emphasize, celebrate, or deepen ethnic

---

[6] Connor (1972, 38, emphasis in original). See also Moynihan (1993, ch. 2).

[7] An individual may also engage in private ethnic behaviors, like paying special attention to news about his co-ethnics and humming ethnic tunes in the privacy of his home. Our concern here is with widely observable behaviors.

divisions. Because of the possibility of preference falsification, a rise in aggregate ethnic activity can occur even without changes in private ethnic preferences, although such changes can be a contributing factor. Individuals engage in ethnic preference falsification when they come under real or imagined social pressures to undertake, or to avoid, particular ethnic behaviors. A Malay living in a neighborhood served by two stores, one Malay-owned and the other Chinese-owned, may shop at the former for fear that his fellow Malays will frown on him if he does otherwise. Studies show that the citizens of Malaysia are aware that such pressures create tradeoffs between, on the one hand, social acceptance and, on the other, material benefits like lower prices and better quality.[8] Social pressures can also make people wear ethnic clothes, read ethnic newspapers, display ethnic symbols, attend ethnic rallies, and listen to ethnic speeches, all to gain acceptance and avoid sanctions.[9]

The point is not that ethnically meaningful behaviors are driven solely by social pressures. Even in their absence people would create ethnic boundaries through behaviors that draw attention to real or imagined differences. The reason lies in the common need to feel that one is not alone and that one is cared for. This need for belonging probably got hard-wired into the human brain when the survival probabilities of our hunter-gatherer ancestors depended on intraclan cooperation. Although we are just beginning to understand how the mind evolved,[10] we know that in units ranging from global empires to minute organizations people subdivide the groups to which they belong. Donald Horowitz (1975, 137) sees at work here a form of Parkinson's Law: "group identity tends to expand or contract to fill the political space available for its expression." He explains: "As the importance of a given political unit increases, so does the importance of the highest level of identification immediately *beneath* the level of that unit." Thus, soon after the partition of India in 1948, former Indians who had struggled as Muslims to secede from "Hindu" India began quarreling with each other as Bengalis, Sindhis, Muhajirs, or some other distinction more refined than "Muslim." Social forces obviously play a role in the emergence and deepening of such subdivisions. But the fact that no society escapes subdivisions suggests that genetic factors, too, must play a major, even a more basic, role. Within an ethnically heterogeneous

---

[8] See Banton and Mansor (1992). Experiments show that, left to themselves, Malaysian citizens would tend to ignore ethnic affiliations in certain contexts where, in practice, social pressures give practical significance to such affiliations. Sowell (1994, chs. 2, 4) provides additional evidence on the tradeoffs created by opportunities for cross-ethnic transactions.

[9] More extreme forms of ethnic preference falsification involve the projection of an ethnic identity that is not just exaggerated or downplayed but fundamentally contrived. Imagine a Yugoslav of mixed ancestry who considers himself a Yugoslav of Albanian extraction. If he conceals his Albanian identity by participating in Serbian nationalist rallies, he is undertaking a form of preference falsification that, in addition to raising aggregate ethnic activity, alters its character. Possibilities for this form of preference falsification were more limited when people's backgrounds were well known to most of the people with whom they came in contact. With urbanization and increasing mobility, they have grown. The model of this paper abstracts from the manipulation of one's identity; treating ethnic identity as preestablished, it focuses on the manipulation of associated needs.

[10] For recent insights, see Barkow, Cosmides, and Tooby (1992). An earlier attempt to explain ethnic identity in evolutionary terms was made by van den Berghe (1981).

state, awareness of the heterogeneity may be sufficient for the subdivisions to form along ethnic lines.

Additional support for the claim that ethnic bonds rest partly on genetic factors comes from social psychology. Certain psychological experiments show that individuals tend to evaluate and treat members of their own groups more favorably than those of other groups. Indeed, an "ingroup bias" shows up even in experiments in which the groups are created through random assignment (Turner 1982; Mullen, Brown, and Smith 1992). Apparently, *any* social division can have behavioral consequences. Specifically, the very perception that a country contains groups with different ancestries can induce behaviors that embrace group particularities rather than commonalities.

Human traits that evolved over thousands of generations are not necessarily uniform within a given generation. Just as artistic talent differs within cohorts, so ingroup bias and the desire for belonging may each vary across individuals. In fact, in the ingroup bias experiments the magnitude of the bias always differs among participants. Consistently with these experiments, people of a given ethnic background commonly differ in the strength of their ethnic identifications and the nature of their ethnic needs. Some individuals derive little of their self-esteem from their ancestry. Their happiness depends minimally on their ethnic associations. Barely conscious of their own ethnic backgrounds, they show little interest in those of others. At the other extreme are people who pay close attention to the ethnic markers that distinguish them from others and want the markers preserved. Such people take great pride in the achievements of their co-ethnics and get offended by criticisms of those achievements. Although they might cherish an ethnic custom for its practical advantages, they do so also, if not instead, for its contribution to preserving their group's cultural uniqueness.[11] Variations in *private ethnic preferences* may stem from genetics, socialization, or a combination of the two.

Whatever the variations, however, they imply that the members of any given society will differ in the tradeoffs they make between behaviors with and without ethnic meaning. For simplicity, suppose that behaviors fall into two categories: a *generic* category, which contains behaviors without ethnic significance, and an *ethnic* category. Behaviors that usually fall in the generic category include buying toothpaste and listening to the weather report; and ethnic behaviors include attending an ethnically exclusive picnic and donating funds to an ethnic party. In principle, any behavior can acquire ethnic significance. In southeastern Turkey the act of replacing stop signs by traffic lights has taken on ethnic meaning: red, yellow, and green are the colors of Kurdish separatists, whereas red and white, the colors of a stop sign, are those of the Turkish flag.

In terms of the distinction between generic and ethnic behaviors, ethnic dissimilation entails a rise in the share of resources that a society devotes to the latter. Such a rise can occur as individuals shift time, money, and other resources

---

[11] Diverse reasons for valuing ethnically based customs are identified by Sowell (1994, chs. 1–2) and Hardin (1995, chs. 6–7).

into ethnic behaviors; it can also occur as their generic behaviors assume ethnic significance. The cause of the consequent increase in aggregate ethnic activity may be changes in private ethnic preferences, or social pressures, or a combination of these elements. For example, a Mexican-American may take to reading Mexican-American literature because he develops a taste for Mexican-American authors, or because he expects thereby to earn praise and avoid censure, or a bit of both. What factors might generate a taste for ethnic literature? And who would create the social pressures? These questions go to the heart of the issue raised at the outset: what factors might propel ethnic dissimilation in many parts of the world at once? The possibilities include the technological, economic, and structural factors that analysts often invoke; such factors may transform people's private preferences and perhaps, therefore, their public behaviors. Another possibility lies in the efforts of *ethnic activists*, who are individuals self-motivated to promote public ethnic behaviors on the part of their co-ethnics. Ethnic activists pursue their objectives through two means: persuasion efforts aimed at transforming private preferences and social pressures directed at generating preference falsification. In practice, many of them expect to reap material benefits or achieve political power through their efforts. But their ranks also include individuals without such hopes. An uneducated and inarticulate person might become an ethnic activist simply because he is burning with anger toward people he considers outsiders.[12]

Ethnic activists are distinguished by their private preferences from the generally more numerous nonactivists, whom I shall call *ordinary individuals*. Having exceptionally great desires for belonging, the activists are internally driven to make their co-ethnics recognize ethnic differences, gain awareness of the ethnic motives behind social patterns, mistrust outsiders, and participate in ethnic activities. By contrast, ordinary individuals participate in efforts at social regulation only in response to social pressures. Insofar as they have genetically or socially created ethnic needs, they undertake public ethnic behaviors even in the absence of relevant pressures; however, these behaviors exclude efforts aimed at regulating the choices of others. Apart from ethnic activists and ordinary individuals, a society normally contains some *nationalist activists*, who are individuals self-motivated to resist ethnic divisions, and it may also contain *universalist activists*, who wish to obliterate even the divisions among countries. These activists with rival agendas compete over the behaviors of the masses.

Such competition occurs because as a rule activists cannot achieve their objectives without public support from the masses. In Titoist Yugoslavia the nationalists had the upper hand because vast numbers of Yugoslavs endorsed the Yugoslav melting pot through words and deeds, and because millions helped make life difficult for individuals fostering ethnic animosities.[13] As the social pressures

---

[12] Ethnic activists thus overlap with, yet are distinct from, ethnic "leaders," "elites," "vigilantes," and "agitators." The distinction differentiates the present theory from various theories, like those of Horowitz (1985, esp. ch. 6), Gagnon (1994–1995), and Laitin (1995b), in which the burden of deepening ethnic divisions falls on individuals with a stake in the character of ethnic relations.

[13] The acceptable behaviors varied across localities. See Malcolm (1994, ch. 14).

changed character after Tito's death, it became increasingly safe, and then increasingly prudent, to assert and promote ethnic particularities; in the process, ethnic activists gained influence at the expense of nationalists.

It bears emphasis that the individuals categorized here as "ordinary" base their behaviors on more than social pressures. Their private preferences play an important role, as do the satisfactions they derive from expressing themselves truthfully. As in other decision domains, the relative importance of expressive considerations can vary across individuals. Insofar as they are significant, ordinary individuals will exhibit some resistance to social pressures, simply to avoid the anger and resentment experienced by compromisers. Provided the pressures are sufficiently light, individuals will remain true to their private preferences, even at the risk of losing social standing.

Just as a dam that has held back a river might break as the water level rises, a person who has resisted social pressures might become responsive to them when they reach a critical level. If the magnitude of the pressures rises with aggregate ethnic activity, the level of such activity at which an individual becomes sensitive to social pressures defines what may be called his *threshold of responsiveness to ethnic activity,* or simply his *threshold.* When aggregate ethnic activity reaches a person's threshold, that person will start falsifying his ethnic preferences. Moreover, given that he had been unresponsive to ethnic dissimilation, his behavior will change discontinuously. In particular, he will shift resources from generic to ethnic activities in a discrete, and thus noticeable, manner.[14] By analogy, when a dam breaks, a huge volume of water rushes forward, even if the prior swelling had been continuous.

The water that inundates the plain beyond the dam will subsequently rise further if the river continues to surge. Likewise, an individual who makes behavioral adjustments to accommodate social pressures will make additional adjustments as ethnic dissimilation progresses. Consider a person who, at the start of a dissimilation process, meets his ethnic needs by keeping a few ethnic foods in his diet and attending one ethnic gathering a month. Faced with mounting social pressures to participate in the process, at first he resists altering his lifestyle. At some point, however, he gives in: he begins wearing clothes indicative of his ethnicity and subscribes to an ethnic newspaper. Still later, as pressures continue to mount, he also attends an ethnic rally and begins confining his social interactions to his own ethnic group.

THE PROCESS OF ETHNIC DISSIMILATION

Why should aggregate ethnic activity influence the level of social pressures? Insofar as the behaviors that account for it involve efforts to reward or punish others for their behaviors, the connection is obvious: the greater the rewards for

---

[14] For a formal demonstration, see Kuran (1998), where the model here receives a fuller treatment.

making public displays of one's ethnicity and the larger the punishments for failing to do so, the stronger are the incentives to substitute ethnic behaviors for generic ones. As we have seen, however, ethnic behaviors need not be aimed at influencing others; one can wear ethnic clothes without any intention of altering the criteria on which others base their own actions. Might such ethnic behaviors, too, become a source of social pressure?

When members of one ethnic group step up their ethnic activity, attention is drawn to society's ethnic divisions. Members of other groups are thus reminded of their outsider status vis-à-vis the group that initiated the ethnification. Motivated to ensure that *some* group accepts them, they feel pressured to develop a visible ethnic identity. Meanwhile, the members of the group that initiated ethnification notice that the standard of behavior within their group has shifted. They sense that to retain their group's acceptance, and thus to remain eligible for assistance and protection in the event of ethnic strife, they had better be more overt about their ethnicity. The upshot is that all ethnic behavior, provided it is public, magnifies the social pressures that make it prudent to shift resources from generic to ethnic activities.

If the ethnic identity that individuals cultivate is always their own, this ethnification process will result in ethnic dissimilation: with members of different groups adopting different sets of ethnic behaviors, the ethnic components of the state will appear increasingly different in terms of their observed behaviors. As already noted, some individuals, especially ones belonging to tiny ethnic minorities, may find it advantageous to change their public identity. In particular, they may attempt to assimilate into a larger ethnic group. For most people, however, such a strategy is generally not a viable option, especially over short time periods. A Yugoslav known to be of Croat descent cannot make his community believe, from one day to the next, that he is a Serb.

In the early years of the Sikh presence in Britain, Sikh men tended not to wear turbans. Members of the minuscule Sikh community sought to assimilate into British society. But with the arrival of more Sikhs and the establishment of Sikh communal organizations, Sikhs came under pressure to dissimilate by displaying their identity prominently. As some Sikh men sought to accommodate the pressures by putting on turbans, it became increasingly difficult for others to continue resisting without losing their standing among Sikhs. The Sikh community in Britain remained, of course, a small minority within the British population. At least initially, therefore, only some non-Sikhs were alarmed by the sight of more turbans.[15] By contrast, in Punjab, the Sikh heartland, efforts to make "good Sikhs" out of ones "who profess Sikhism but do not behave as Sikhs" have fed, and been fed by, campaigns to enforce orthopraxy within other ethnic (or ethnoreligious) groups. Thus, ethnification on the part of Sikhs has stimulated, and been stimulated by, ethnification on the part of non-Sikhs, thus generating ethnic dissimilation. It is significant that the methods used to make "fallen Sikhs" display the

---

[15] Banton (1985, 54–60). A poll indicated that one in five Britons wanted turbans banned, usually on the grounds that wearing one showed an unwillingness to integrate into the cultural mainstream. Four in five opposed such a ban.

conventional marks of Sikh identity (turban, beard, sword, shorts) included ridicule and the threat of violence.[16]

These methods also included persuasion, evidence that private ethnic preferences are malleable. Accounts of Sikh communities demonstrate, in fact, that Sikh conformism has been driven partly by changes in private preferences. Just as private ethnic preferences can change prior to an ethnic dissimilation process, they can be modified by the process itself. To retain analytical clarity, however, I shall rule out the latter possibility for the time being. Once we have explored the dynamics of aggregate ethnic activity under fixed private preferences, we can consider the question of when the variability of these preferences might make a difference. Suppose, then, that the members of a society somehow perceive that aggregate ethnic activity is rising. The perception pressures them to step up their own ethnic behaviors. Whether they make behavioral adjustments is determined, of course, by their thresholds. Depending on how thresholds of the nation's members are distributed, many outcomes are possible.

Figure 2.1 depicts a case in which perceptions of aggregate ethnic activity can change without any lasting effects. The horizontal axis of the figure registers the expected aggregate activity, and the vertical axis records the actual level. Aggregate activity is in equilibrium when the expected and actual levels are identical, so the possible equilibria lie on the diagonal. The curve identified as the *diffusion curve* captures the relationship between the expected and actual levels of aggregate ethnic activity. Its horizontal portion on the left indicates that at sufficiently low expectations small increases have no behavioral consequences. The diffusion curve has such a segment because people exhibit some resistance to social pressures.

The diffusion curve in Figure 2.1 eventually turns upward, an indication that personal resistance to social pressures is bounded. Two factors account for the positive slope: as expected ethnic activity rises, it crosses individual thresholds, and it makes people whose thresholds had already been crossed step up their ethnic activity. Where the diffusion curve lies below the diagonal, the realization falls short of the expectation, so the latter is subsequently revised downward; and where the curve lies above, the realization exceeds the expectation, producing an upward adjustment. The arrows on the curve indicate the direction of revision. They lead to a single point on the diagonal, which means that the equilibrium is unique. If the expectation rises even substantially above a, the subsequent adjustments will restore the original equilibrium; sustained ethnic dissimilation is impossible. By the same token, aggregate ethnic activity cannot disappear; it must stay positive because individuals genuinely want to engage in some public ethnic behavior.

Turn now to Figure 2.2, which features a diffusion curve that crosses the diagonal at three points. The curve's shape indicates that, in relation to the nation

---

[16] See Madan (1991, quotes, 600, 601). As Oberoi (1993) also documents, Sikh culture has never been monolithic—a fact that Sikh activists ignore. Like other communities, Sikhs have been divided by social hierarchy, ritual practices, and individual aspirations. One might add, with Cohn (1996, ch. 5), that Sikh culture has been anything but fixed. The turban itself was introduced to India by the British army.

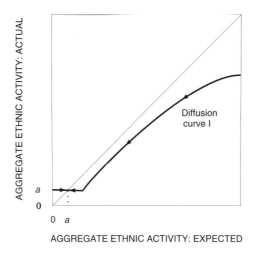

FIGURE 2.1
A single equilibrium: sustained ethnic dissimilation is impossible

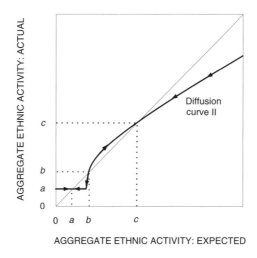

FIGURE 2.2
Three equilibria: sustained ethnic dissimilation is possible but unlikely

depicted in the previous figure, this one is more responsive to expected ethnic activity: at intermediate levels of aggregate ethnic activity, the curve lies above the diagonal. The arrows on the curve lead toward the lowermost and uppermost crossings of the diagonal, and away from the middle one. So equilibria *a* and *c* are stable, whereas *b* is unstable. The positions of the equilibria indicate that sustained ethnic dissimilation is possible but unlikely. It is possible because the perception of a large jump in aggregate ethnic activity, one from *a* to above *b*, would generate reactions and counter-reactions that carry the aggregate all the way to c. And it is unlikely because any smaller jump would carry the aggregate back to a. By itself, therefore, the existence of multiple equilibria does not imply sustained behavioral changes. It implies only that a sufficiently sharp rise in the expectation would induce multitudes to make lasting behavioral adjustments.

In an equilibrium, aggregate ethnic activity is self-confirming and thus self-perpetuating. If it is to move, therefore, something beyond the elements of Figure 2.2 must come into play. Activists destined to succeed will understand this. In particular, they will recognize that if aggregate ethnic activity is to rise above a permanently, one of two things must happen: the expectation must make a big jump or the incumbent equilibrium must be destroyed through an appropriate shift of the diffusion curve. One or both of these outcomes may be achieved through vivid public acts—in other words, widely noticed behaviors that arouse emotions, provoke images, seem personally relevant, and are committed to memory. For example, acts of civil disobedience, especially ones that are violent, can create the perception of an ethnic dissimilation process in progress, even if the acts have limited statistical significance. Cognitive psychologists find that vivid but scientifically inconsequential messages often persuade where scientifically compelling but pallid data leave perceptions uninfluenced (Nisbett and Ross 1980, ch. 3).

David Laitin (1995b) observes that the existence of groups willing to engage in violence on behalf of an ethnic cause may be decisive as to whether the cause gains widespread public support. I would add that the initial effect of ethnic violence is often to raise the perceived social pressures to undertake ethnic behaviors. And the violence may simultaneously alter people's intrinsic payoffs from ethnic behavior. Ethnic violence, along with the ensuing reactions, repression, and counter-violence, creates ethnic grievances, and it revives memories of past sufferings. Often, therefore, it makes people of all ethnic groups turn inward as a precaution against further violence.

It is one thing to dislike an equilibrium, another to pull off its destruction. Ethnic activists may want to alter expectations or private preferences, but they face resistance from their nationalist and universalist counterparts, actors with a stake in the status quo. Modeling the game played among these groups of players is beyond this chapter's scope. Let us simply assume, therefore, that conditions favorable to ethnic dissimilation have raised the levels of ethnic behavior that people privately desire. Through the changes, the diffusion curve shifts upward, as in Figure 2.3. The horizontal portion of the new curve, labeled III, lies above that of II. With a no longer in equilibrium, some dissimilation would occur even in the absence of preference falsification. In the presence of preference falsification, however, the dissimilation can be enormous. According to the figure, the behavioral adjustments initiated by changes in private preferences feed on themselves through preference falsification. We see that the new diffusion curve yields a unique equilibrium, d. The movement from a to d entails massive ethnification and, hence, dissimilation.

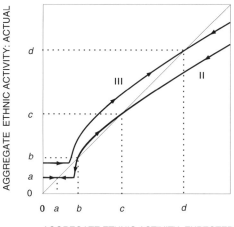

FIGURE 2.3
Massive ethnic dissimilation that is initiated by a shift in private preferences and compounded by widespread preference falsification

The diffusion curves in Figure 2.3 are not substantially different. Yet one promotes stability whereas the other yields large-scale dissimilation. The figure thus demonstrates that aggregate ethnic activity can be highly sensitive to individual characteristics. Indeed, under the right conditions a rise in a single person's need for belonging, or in his susceptibility to ethnically based social pressures, will cause a noticeable jump in aggregate ethnic activity. At the same time, there exist conditions under which substantial changes in the needs of huge numbers would leave aggregate ethnic activity unchanged. A society with low ethnic activity will tend to generate social forces that sustain the prevailing pattern; but once those forces have been overcome, massive ethnic dissimilation can occur through a bandwagon process. The speed at which the process runs its course will depend on how quickly individuals respond to changing social pressures.

A process that is highly sensitive to poorly observable individual and social characteristics is bound to generate many surprises. Even if the process itself is well understood, neither outside observers nor the players themselves will be able to forecast its outcomes infallibly. After all, the thresholds that govern behavioral switches are not public knowledge, so the shape of the diffusion curve cannot be determined with any certainty. For all practical purposes, the diffusion curve of Figure 2.1 is indistinguishable from that of Figure 2.2. The model thus illuminates why regional specialists often fail to recognize the potential for ethnic dissimilation stored within the social patterns they study. Of course, such specialists can identify ethnic activists as well as subgroups that are especially prone to ethnic preference falsification. Knowledge about the sizes and resources of such clusters may help identify latent tendencies toward ethnic dissimilation. But it can never overcome the obstacles to prediction.

Dissimilation processes that have come as a surprise may easily be explained in retrospect. Foresight and hindsight differ because the very process of ethnic dissimilation generates social patterns that make what has happened seem an obvious result of deep-seated ethnic suspicions and animosities. A dissimilation process can obviously be unleashed by preexisting ethnic mistrust that nationalist social pressures had kept unexpressed. However, dissimilation may just as well be a *source* of the apparent mistrust. Increases in aggregate ethnic activity create social pressures that make large numbers conform to the divisive plans of ethnic activists.

Figure 2.3 demonstrated that dissimilation can be unleashed by a shift in private preferences. If private preferences change further in the course of the dissimilation, the consequent behavioral adaptations may be reinforced. In particular, if individuals become more aware of ethnic particularities, more inclined to seek ethnic solidarity, and more suspicious of other ethnic groups, they may become readier to expand their ethnic activity, and their thresholds may fall. Under certain conditions, the changes in private preferences will critically affect the outcome. Turn to Figure 2.4, which depicts three successive diffusion curves. With the curve initially in position *I*, society is in equilibrium at *a*. Some time later, structural changes strengthen the ethnic activists, and private ethnic needs increase somewhat, driving the diffusion curve to position *IV*. The old equilibrium eliminated, aggregate ethnic activity moves toward *e*. If private preferences were fixed, the movement would stop there. But it continues, because a pro-ethnic shift in private preferences pushes the diffusion curve to position *V*, and aggregate ethnic activity jumps to *f*.

A major implication thus far is that the extent of ethnic dissimilation can be disproportionate to the factors that instigated it. Under certain conditions, small changes in the factors that govern ethnic behavior will generate massive dissimilation; and under other conditions, not much different, large changes will produce minimal dissimilation, if any at all. Herein lies a key reason why the technological, economic, and structural factors that influence private ethnic preferences are poor predictors of ethnic dissimilation processes. Although such factors are hardly irrelevant to ethnic behavior, their effects are both nonlinear and poorly observable.

THE INTERNATIONAL CATALYSTS OF ETHNIC DISSIMILATION

The foregoing analysis has treated the catalysts of ethnic dissimilation as internal to the nation in question. Removing this simplification, we now turn to the external factors that shape choices between generic and ethnic activities. Events and trends outside a country can have intended as well as unintended consequences for its own ethnic relations.

The intended international effects are analogous to those created by the efforts of local ethnic activists. Foreign ethnic activists can heighten a nation's awareness

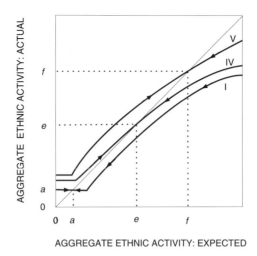

FIGURE 2.4
Ethnic dissimilation reinforced by changes in private preferences

of its divisions, and they can reward expressions of ethnicity. In the waning days of the Ottoman and Austro-Hungarian empires, various states and organizations assisted campaigns to accentuate the particularities and revive the rivalries of peoples within these empires. During the Cold War, both the United States and the Soviet Union fomented ethnic divisions within client states of the other. For yet another example, many world leaders have encouraged African ethnification by endorsing campaigns against economically successful ethnic minorities. In 1953, Indian Prime Minister Jawaharlal Nehru told a delegation of Africans of Indian descent that they were "guests" of the Africans. "If they do not want you," he continued, "out you will have to go, bag and baggage" (Sowell 1994, 139).

In acquiescing to discrimination against native-born Africans of Indian ancestry, and even to their imminent expulsion, Nehru was motivated by a desire to make India a leader of the nonaligned countries. Likewise, geopolitical considerations guided the efforts to achieve ethnic dissimilation in the Ottoman and Austro-Hungarian empires and, later, in the client states of the Cold War superpowers. Other motives that make people pursue dissimilation beyond their own state borders include the ethnic pride they derive from the distinctions of their kin. Even before the Balkan wars of the 1990s, expatriate Croats, including ones well assimilated into their adopted societies, were pouring money into the Croat separatist movement within Yugoslavia (Glenny 1993, 63). International campaigns are bound to remain ineffective, of course, unless the targeted country already shows ethnic divisions and strains. The Croat diaspora could not have forced their kin in Yugoslavia to renounce the ideal of a pan-Slavic nation. Under the right conditions, however, an international campaign can provide the push that activates a dissimilation process. Remember that where individual actions are interdependent small changes in personal or social variables can have momentous consequences.

The external push that activates a dissimilation process need not be intended. Self-reinforcing increases in ethnic activity may come about as unintended by-products of ideological currents, political shifts, cultural patterns, or social strains elsewhere. Under certain conditions, moreover, dissimilation in one country will instigate dissimilation in a second, which will then induce additional dissimilation processes. In other words, a bandwagon in one nation will activate bandwagons in others. A two-country illustration is in Figure 2.5. Ethnic dissimilation in country A, depicted in the top panel as a movement from a to a´, heightens ethnic consciousness in B. The diffusion curve of B thus shifts upward, carrying its aggregate ethnic activity from b to b´. The international process whereby one nation's dissimilation spawns additional dissimilations constitutes a *domino effect*.[17] This effect entails an international bandwagon. Moreover, insofar as the changes within the countries involve national bandwagons, the entire process forms a *superbandwagon*. Being a global bandwagon of local bandwagons, a super-bandwagon unites the numerical and spatial diffusions of ethnic activity.

Changing patterns within one country can create a domino effect through three distinct mechanisms. The first, the *demonstration effect*, operates through changes in private preferences. When ethnic discrimination becomes a dominant theme in the political discourse of country A, the citizens of B gain more exposure to the idea of such discrimination than they would otherwise. Becoming more sensitized to it, they start blaming their own disappointments on other ethnic groups. Moreover, they become increasingly inclined to think in ethnic categories, and they discover new advantages to ethnic solidarity. If the Québequois of Canada, the Bumiputra of Malaysia, and the Maoris of New Zealand all appear to be benefiting from separate identities, perhaps they, too, should start emphasizing their ethnic distinctions. Yet another form of the demonstration effect operates through the cynicism generated by attention to ethnic frictions. Individuals bombarded with tales of ethnic injustice start seeing themselves as victims of ethnic tyranny. They then react through discriminatory measures of their own, for both self-protection and the disbursement of justice.[18] Even consumption decisions that are free of discriminatory intent, like the act of collecting ethnic art, can fuel ethnic dissimilation a world away. By making ethnicity seem an essential component of personal identity, they may make people all over the world cultivate ethnic symbols.

The second mechanism, the *expectation effect*, operates through perceptions of the international diffusion of ethnic dissimilation. Indications of rising ethnic activity in one country, including news about self-determination movements, ethnic affirmative action policies, and racial repression, alert people everywhere to the possibility of dissimilation in their own societies. Individuals reason that if

---

[17] The domino effect has been studied in other contexts by Starr (1991), Kaempfer and Lowenberg (1992), and Schweller (1994).

[18] Wilson (1993, esp. chs. 1, 3) offers evidence that negative images of humanity promote socially destructive and divisive behaviors.

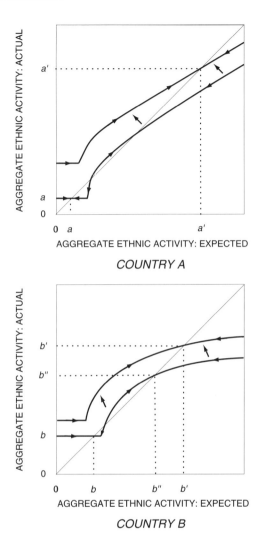

Figure 2.5
Ethnic dissimilation in country *A* triggers ethnic dissimilation in country *B*. In country *A*, ethnic activity jumps from *a* to *a'*. In response, ethnic activity in country *B* jumps from *b* to *b'*.

other states are becoming disunited, so might theirs. Under certain conditions, the consequent transformation in expectations will become self-correcting. For an illustration, turn back to Figure 2.5, and suppose that in country *B* the prevailing diffusion curve is the lower of the ones shown. Country *A* undergoes ethnic dissimilation, and the news reaches *B*. As long as *B*'s diffusion curve stays fixed, and expectations of ethnic activity change minimally, any effects will be transitory. But a sufficiently large jump in the expectations will produce an upward bandwagon to b". In any case, there is no guarantee that *B*'s diffusion curve will remain unaffected. If the expectation effect is accompanied by a demonstration effect that moves *B*'s diffusion curve upward, dissimilation will easily spread from *A* to *B*.

Remember that when one ethnic group starts emphasizing its particularities, groups with whom it interacts take countermeasures. Groups with whom it does not interact may take countermeasures of their own because of effects on their expectations. Their members will reason that, just as they themselves expect their country to undergo ethnification, so must the members of other ethnic groups. Geographically distant and historically unconnected groups may thus respond to each other's ethnification processes through preventive or preemptive ethnic activities of their own. Once in progress, therefore, ethnic dissimilation processes may feed not only on themselves but also on each other.

The third mechanism by which factors beyond a state can contribute to its ethnic dissimilation, the *reputation effect*, works through the rewards and punishments that its members derive from outsiders. Insofar as the individuals have international contacts, it may make a difference whether global public opinion treats the assertion of ethnic particularities as essential to self-realization or as a dangerous throwback to archaic tribalism. Likewise, it may make a difference whether global public opinion favors or opposes the breakdown of group distinctions. The rewards and punishments associated with the reactions of outsiders can transform existing equilibria and create new ones. So the ethnic dissimilation processes shown earlier in Figures 2.3 and 2.4 can just as well be triggered by a global public opinion sympathetic to dissimilation. Holding all else fixed, global public opinion is more likely to support a given nation's dissimilation if a wide variety of societies present salient ethnic divisions than if such divisions are generally indiscernible. Moreover, individuals are more likely to look favorably on dissimilation elsewhere insofar as they themselves are wrapped up in ethnic concerns. A Canadian will find it easier to understand why the former Yugoslavs are focused on their ethnic differences insofar as ethnic particularities carry social significance in Canada.

Ordinarily, the three international effects operate together, and they interact with factors internal to the state being acted upon. Consequently, the bandwagons that produce dissimilation are fueled by a complex mix of factors. The dissimilation of the Yugoslav nation was propelled by moves and countermoves on the part of various players, the resurfacing of ancient grievances, and not least, the support and encouragement that certain European governments gave to ethnically divisive acts. And these developments occurred against the backdrop of a global climate of opinion that has become receptive to two conflicting ideas. One is that cultural diversity, especially when reflective of ethnic divisions, is a valuable resource; the other, that ethnic groups tend to mistreat each other.

The international determinants of ethnic dissimilation are undoubtedly gaining importance. Societies now have great exposure to information originating from one another. They are getting linked ever more tightly by transportation and communication networks. And billions now receive news gathered and disseminated by global syndicates. Because of such trends, global influences are coming to play an increasingly significant role in the formation of perceptions, beliefs, and theories about social matters. At the same time, rising mobility is making people seek and receive more approval and encouragement from abroad.[19] These observations apply even to participants in movements that promote anti-modernism, xenophobia, or nativism. And they apply especially to movements committed to democracy, respect for minority rights, and individualism.

Before the emergence of modern technology, mountains, oceans, and sheer distance kept geographically separated countries essentially isolated from one another. Under the circumstances, norms and beliefs, however unusual, could survive indefinitely without facing outside challenges. Today, by contrast, global information flows can easily undermine local patterns. Ideas that do not occur to the members of a group, or that they are reluctant to articulate, may be drummed into their consciousness and inserted into their public discourses by travelers, publications, broadcasts, and other vehicles of international communication. This is not to suggest that expanding international contacts necessarily advance dissimilation. To the extent that global public opinion encourages the universality of civilized behavior, treats cultures as similar, and considers ethnic distinctions superficial, it will hinder ethnic dissimilation. But if it stresses cultural relativism,[20] glorifies ethnic solidarity, and labels ethnic particularities as immutable, it will stimulate dissimilation.

For the sake of argument, suppose that global public opinion becomes favorable to ethnic dissimilation. Does it follow that cascading dissimilation processes will occur throughout the world? Will the triggered processes provoke additional ones, which then produce further reactions in a widening array of countries? The extent of a chain of dominoes need not be indefinite. For the same reason that a given dissimilation process may stop before the point where ethnic activity absorbs all resources of the relevant population, a sequence of international effects and counter-effects will normally cease well before its logical limit. Similarly, for the same reason that a given nation's dissimilation may leave some of its members unaffected, dissimilation may spread across certain borders but not others. The logic of threshold-governed behavior allows collectivities, like their individual members, to exhibit varying degrees of resistance to alterations in the criteria governing their choices. The behavioral effects across states need not, then, be symmetric. Just because ethnic relations in country *A* have influenced those of *B* does not mean that *B* must have a reciprocal influence on *A*. Major behavioral changes can afflict *B* without producing any behavioral changes in *A*, even if some changes occur in the private preferences of *A*'s members.

ASYMMETRIES, REVERSALS, AND VARIATIONS IN DIFFUSION

There are more basic reasons why international influences are typically asymmetric. Economically and militarily backward peoples are generally more eager to emulate outsiders than are advanced ones. Populations also differ in their contributions to the production, interpretation, and dissemination of information. In particular, the economically developed peoples more or less determine global

---

[19] For complementary insights, see Rosenau (1984).

[20] The idea that all cultures are equally functional and valuable.

information flows. Finally, variations in geopolitical position and military potential make some populations command more attention than do others.

The Rwandan genocide of 1994 received attention from the international media, but until then few people outside Rwanda knew its ethnic composition or the history of discord between Hutus and Tutsis. And after the killings subsided, Rwanda's ethnic problems quickly receded from the headlines, until hostilities in neighboring Burundi refocused attention on Hutu-Tutsi troubles. By contrast, ethnic disputes involving few deaths, even none at all, sustain prolonged attention when they occur in nuclear-armed Russia or the strategically critical Middle East. And ethnically charged events in the United States routinely make the world's headlines. The beating that Rodney King, a black motorist stopped for speeding, suffered at the hands of white police officers was watched repeatedly by television viewers throughout the world.

We live in an age when Euro-American civilization in general, and American culture in particular, contributes heavily to global understandings, myths, sensitivities, and attitudes. People everywhere watch American movies and receive news from American press services. And throughout the world large numbers want to rebuild their countries in the image of the United States. The global impact of American culture is akin to the influence that Roman-Hellenic culture once enjoyed in the Mediterranean basin. The relevant consequence here is that ethnic relations in the United States set salient examples from which people in other countries draw lessons, authority, and inspiration. Although the United States does not shape global expectations unilaterally, the influences that it exerts are highly disproportionate to its global share of population, even perhaps to its global share of income.

The United States used to be committed to the ideal of the American melting pot. The ideal was never pursued fully or consistently, the most significant departure being the separate status forced on black Americans. Yet, for a long time, expanding segments of the American nation favored lowering ethnic barriers, and the American government did not try to nourish the cultures of new immigrants. In spite of occasional setbacks, the trend to about 1970 was toward limiting racial segregation and discrimination.

Since then, however, the United States has abandoned the goal of obliterating the social significance of ethnicity. Affirmative action policies require Americans to pay close attention to ethnicity; perversely, they expose the users of color-blind selection procedures to charges of racism. The multiculturalism movement that has captivated the media, schools, and the government keep Americans focused on ethnic particularities, obscuring their shared interests as citizens. Americans are now taught that their ethnic components are enmeshed in an evil system of oppression and subordination. Where the founders of the United States recognized that a multiethnic state requires what Ernest Renan ([1882] 1939) would later characterize as "collective forgetting,"[21] huge efforts are now under way to

---

[21] Related ideas are developed by Shriver (1995), who stresses the importance of forgiveness in enabling peaceful social interactions.

keep Americans focused on the sufferings some of their ancestors inflicted on some of their other ancestors. Unlike earlier generations who learned to distance themselves from their ancestral histories, present generations are thus becoming habituated to treat ethnic guilt as heritable. Various application forms, including official ones, encourage applicants to declare their ethnic origins; they generally relegate the designation "American" to the category of "other." Voting regulations adopted in 1990 institutionalized ethnic gerrymandering—the drawing of voting districts to concentrate the electoral power of designated minorities. These examples, to which more could be added (see Schlessinger 1991), demonstrate how the United States is undergoing ethnic dissimilation. This interpretation is consistent with surveys that find interest in ethnicity to be greater among young Americans than among their elders (Alba 1990, 105–16, 307).

There have been countertrends. For example, the consumption patterns of all major ethnic groups have accommodated the steady flow of new consumer goods. And they have been equally quick to adopt new production technologies. Such trends undoubtedly influence global perceptions concerning the social significance of ethnicity in the United States. But they do not offset the influence of policies and statements that celebrate ethnic rights and differences. As in other domains, it is the perception of reality that guides individual responses, not reality itself; and the perception is shaped largely by trends that receive attention. If American public discourse emphasizes the negative dimensions of American ethnic relations, other countries will be exposed to indications of ethnic dissimilation in the United States, possibly missing signs of the continuing vitality of the American melting pot. An important reason why American public discourse has been sympathetic to ethnic dissimilation is that individual Americans have tended to avoid expressing reservations about policies that promote dissimilation, lest they be accused of racism or ethnocentrism. For a quarter-century, polls have consistently shown that most Americans privately reject ethnic quotas, guidelines, and timetables.[22] But it is their public actions and statements that outsiders observe, not their private reservations.

An illustration of the global influence of American ethnic policies lies in an episode that occurred during Tansu Çiller's 1993 visit to the United States, her first as Turkey's premier. During a joint news conference with President Clinton, she was asked how she would deal with Kurdish unrest in Eastern Anatolia. Attempting to explain her position in terms familiar to Americans, she replied that the Turkish state would remain an ethnic melting pot. The Turkish press treated this response as a gaffe, and commentators cited it as proof of her inexperience and simplemindedness. Moreover, her embarrassed advisors took pains to make her aware that in advanced countries the ideal of the melting pot has given way to that of the "salad bowl."[23] What might have happened had an American president stated in Ankara, where the Turkish melting pot remains a

---

[22] For recent evidence, see Sniderman and Piazza (1993). Typically even majorities of the intended beneficiaries of affirmative action stand opposed, although such findings are sensitive to how questions are worded. For interpretations, see Steele (1990) and Kuran (1995a, ch. 9).

[23] *Cumhuriyet*, October 22, 1993, 1, 15.

popular ideal, that the United States should remain a salad bowl? The American press would probably not have considered the statement a blunder, if it took notice at all. Where most Turks want to adapt to international political norms, Americans generally believe that others should look to *them* for political guidance. The international demonstration and reputation effects of American ethnic relations thus swamp the corresponding effects of ethnic relations within Turkey.

In suggesting that the dominant international norms are fueling ethnic dissimilation, I am not proposing that global public opinion has become supportive of everything done in the name of ethnic rights. Extreme acts of violence, like Kurdish terrorism on European soil (which Europeans find menacing) and ethnic cleansing in the Balkans (which horrifies people everywhere) draw adverse responses. Yet less vivid acts of violence often go unnoticed, and where noticed, global public opinion tolerates them. The European press has been sympathetic to Kurdish separatism: leading publications glorify it, and they generally turn a blind eye to atrocities committed in the name of Kurdish rights. The global media are particularly sympathetic to campaigns aimed at preserving ethnic distinctions. And they are receptive to assertions that past conflicts create insurmountable barriers to ethnic harmony in the present. With respect to the former Yugoslavia, the press has commonly treated as axiomatic that the country's principal ethnic groups hate each other so intensely that they can never live together harmoniously, except under compulsion.[24]

Many world leaders have contributed to this perception. Albert Gore has characterized the Yugoslav conflict as "a tragedy that has been unfolding for a long time, some would say for 500 years."[25] And John Major has argued that "the biggest single element behind what has happened in Bosnia is the collapse of the Soviet Union and of the discipline that that exerted over the ancient hatreds in the old Yugoslavia."[26] Major's claim overlooks that the discipline exerted by the Soviet Union ended in 1948 when Yugoslavia broke away from the Soviet Bloc. Equally serious, his statement, like that of Gore, ignores the long periods in Balkan history when various ethnic groups got along remarkably well even as they preserved certain cultural distinctions. Nevertheless, statements in this vein have had the effect of legitimizing the fragmentation of the Balkans.

The charter of the United Nations proclaims "the principle of equal rights and self-determination of peoples." In providing safeguards for persecuted minorities, this principle also provides a legal crutch to ethnic activists bent on dividing their nations. It allows self-proclaimed spokespersons for groups that appear to be underperforming others to launch campaigns for special privileges. Moreover, it makes such activists believe that if they succeed in triggering massive ethnic dissimilation global public opinion will endorse their demands for ethnic autonomy, even for secession. Oddly, as Daniel Patrick Moynihan (1990, ch. 7) observes, the United Nations and other international organizations have continued to encourage ethnic activism even as events demonstrate their inability to prevent the

[24] For an influential version of this argument, see Kaplan (1993).
[25] "Larry King Live," Cable News Network, June 5, 1995.
[26] As quoted by Malcolm (1994, xx)

human tragedies that such activism produces. Their impotence in the face of the genocides in Bosnia and Rwanda illustrates the point.

There are signs that Americans troubled by their government's domestic ethnic policies will not remain as quiescent as they became after around 1970. The Supreme Court has declared unconstitutional the most egregious forms of ethnic gerrymandering. The voters of California have repealed their state's affirmative action laws. The University of California, the country's largest state university system, has sent shock waves through the higher education establishment by repealing its affirmative action guidelines. FInally, numerous politicians have signaled their preparedness to restrict, if not to scrap, the federal government's affirmative action mandates. Such developments are unveiling reservations that many have long harbored about the role that ethnicity plays in American life. One cannot know whether they will fuel a bandwagon that ends up reducing the emphasis on ethnic rights. But if a major shift does occur, there may be repercussions in other countries. Just as the twentieth century saw ethnic movements grow and spread, the twenty-first might see them lose strength.

After World War II, in certain regions of the world, including Europe, ethnic assimilation gained legitimacy partly because crimes carried out in the name of German, Italian, and Japanese nationalism made ethnic movements suspect. This reaction was also fueled by the fact that influential branches of scholarship interpreted the observed dip in ethnic activity as evidence that modernization was reducing the significance of ethnicity.[27] The unfolding public backlash to affirmative action in the United States may well help activate another global decline in ethnic dissimilation. Combined with the horrors generated by the recent ethnic cleansings in Africa, the Balkans, and elsewhere, the turns in American public discourse and official policies could jolt nations into recognizing the dangers of ethnic divisiveness. Accordingly, they may serve as watershed events that make people everywhere reconsider incumbent policies.

The ultimate consequences of events that make people reconsider prevailing structures are not perfectly predictable, however. Because the individual decisions that determine aggregate ethnic activity in any given country, and also the outcomes of countries, are interdependent, slight differences in individual responses can produce huge differences in global trends. Likewise, intrinsically minor differences in such factors as the global spread of information, the interpretation of trends, and the organizational capacities of activists can make an appreciable difference. The effects of the relevant factors are thus both nonlinear and nonmonotonic in ways that do not lend themselves to exact identification.

One possible scenario hinges on the responses of nationalist activists. Recall that such activists are self-motivated to resist ethnic divisions. As such, many are committed to the preservation of existing states. In the course of an ethnic dissimilation process, their efforts are eclipsed by those of ethnic activists. Alarmed by the extreme consequences of dissimilation, like ethnic riots and ethnic cleansing, the nationalist activists redouble their efforts to focus attention on national

[27] Connor (1979) critiques the logic of this interpretation.

commonalities, trying to make ethnic divisiveness disreputable. Insofar as they succeed, individual thresholds of responsiveness to ethnic activity climb, thus making the pressures of ethnic activists less effective. In any given society, then, the diffusion curve shifts downward, possibly destroying the incumbent equilibrium that features high ethnic activity. Turn back to Figure 2.3, and suppose that aggregate ethnic activity is d. Through the efforts of nationalist activists, the diffusion curve shifts to position II, lowering ethnic activity to c. There is no guarantee, of course, that the nationalist activists will be successful, for the ethnic activists will counter their assimilationist efforts. Also, small differences in opposing efforts can dramatically influence observed behavioral patterns.

An ethnic dissimilation or assimilation process within a given country need not affect other countries uniformly. Dissimilation in A may trigger massive dissimilation in B without any visible effects in C. An obvious reason could be that the preexisting equilibrium of B was more vulnerable to a perturbation than that of C. Another might involve differences in cultural affinity with A. The demonstration, expectation, and reputation effects of ethnic dissimilation within a Latin American country are likely to be greater on other Latin American countries than on Middle Eastern ones. Still another source of variation could involve similarity in ethnic mix. When the social significance of ethnicity rises in a country with a large Kurdish minority, the change will be felt most strongly where there exist significant Kurdish populations. Multistate ethnic groups, including Russians, Serbs, Arabs, Tamils, and Chinese, may thus play a critical role in the international diffusion of ethnic dissimilation.

CONCLUSIONS AND POLICY IMPLICATIONS

In a world of declining communication and transportation costs, one society's social patterns are increasingly likely to influence those of others. Yet political actors and observers routinely overlook the linkages among domestic and foreign matters. For example, domestic pressure groups promote policies without any attention to international consequences. And although students of international relations recognize that domestic concerns help shape foreign policies, those of domestic politics rarely pay attention to the external repercussions of developments within states. The foregoing sections have shown that neglecting the linkages between domestic and international trends can produce serious errors of interpretation. It can make policy makers and analysts ascribe ethnic dissimilation processes to shifts in domestic technology, government, or laws, overlooking international stimuli.

By no means are all ethnic processes driven by external factors. Ethnic consciousness can deepen and ethnic particularities gain salience even in the absence of international influences. The Albanians of Kosovo have not needed a global intellectual climate conducive to ethnic divisions to make them realize that the government in Belgrade desires their elimination. Nor have they needed any international encouragement to realize that the Serbian threat makes it prudent to cultivate Albanian solidarity. Yet, individuals are more likely to consider themselves victims of ethnic discrimination and oppression insofar as global public discourse condemns cultural integration and ethnic assimilation. Likewise, they are more likely to seek ethnically based solutions to their problems when international public opinion predisposes them to exaggerate the ethnic dimensions of social patterns.

International linkages among ethnic patterns are observable only imperfectly, because private dispositions, openness to information flows, and sensitivities to social pressure do not lend themselves to exact measurement. So predictions of how a country's policies will affect ethnic relations elsewhere always stand a chance of being dead wrong. Not even a powerful government that controls a vast intelligence agency can micromanage global ethnic relations. Under the right conditions, a policy with a limited objective, like moral support to an organization working to preserve some ethnic art, might trigger a massive dissimilation process. Also, a given policy might produce very different effects in countries that appear similar from a distance.

Another implication relates to interpreting the impact of past events and trends. The fact that a certain ethnic policy or process has had no obvious international effects does not establish its irrelevance. The developments may well have raised the possibility of dissimilation in various parts of the world through their effects on private preferences, thresholds, and expectations. Though appearing to have had no international impact, they could be paving the way for a string of dissimilation processes. Just as social developments may make an individual increasingly prepared to extend his ethnic activities without actually changing his observable behavior, so the same developments may make entire societies increasingly ready for ethnic dissimilation without actually triggering the process. Because public ethnic behaviors are interdependent and because they may differ from the underlying private preferences, observed ethnic patterns of ethnic activity can hide possibilities for change.

What policy proposals flow from these observations? Nothing in the above argument implies that political actors should work to abolish ethnic affiliations or to prevent ethnically meaningful behavior. Efforts to hinder ethnic activity risk making individuals refrain from meeting socially harmless needs rooted entirely in their own personalities. What the observations do imply is that policy makers should avoid glorifying, promoting, or subsidizing ethnic activity. A step in this direction would be to bar governments from pursuing policies that discriminate on the basis of ethnicity or even take account of ethnic particularities. The proposed restriction would be akin to rules that make governments keep religion out of the affairs of state. In various countries, the secularization of government has provided safety both *for* and *from* religion. While preventing individuals from forcing their own religions on others, it has also enabled them to practice religion as they see fit. Regulations to keep the world "safe for and from ethnicity" will yield similar benefits.[28] In contrast to measures that alleviate specific ethnic tensions, they will help solve a recurrent set of problems. The prevailing asymmetries in cross-country influences impose a special responsibility on culturally

---

[28] The phrase belongs to Moynihan (1993b, 173).

commanding political entities, like the United States and the European Community. They must be particularly careful to prevent their power holders from encouraging ethnic activity.

Recent decades have seen a tendency for major international players to treat group rights, including the rights of ethnic groups, as an integral component of human rights. Whatever the benefits that ethnic rights provide to certain individuals, they also invigorate ethnic distinctions and bolster pressures to engage in ethnic preference falsification. Properly interpreted, human rights encompass both the right to nurture ethnic particularities and the right to disregard them. Ethnic rights enshrined in state constitutions and international charters promote the former right and neglect the latter. They also create pressures that jettison individual needs to develop an ethnically composite identity. Such needs were captured by a poster that the journalist Christopher Hitchens (1992, 236) noticed in Sarajevo as the city was being pounded by Serbian gunfire. The poster featured "a combined logo featuring the Star of David, the Islamic star and crescent, the Roman Catholic cross and the more elaborate cruciform of the Orthodox Church. *Gens Una Summus* read the superscription, 'We Are One People.'"

The millions committed to the Yugoslav ideal ought to have been able to continue living as Yugoslavs. And once Yugoslavia's ethnic troubles escalated, global public opinion should have recognized and supported the Yugoslavs who wanted their nation preserved. Rather than harping at every opportunity on "ancient hatreds," world leaders should have signaled an understanding of the social forces making Yugoslavs pull themselves apart. If other countries are to avoid Yugoslavia's fate, we must find ways of protecting the individual right to refrain from ethnic behaviors. The task will require an appreciation for two types of interdependencies: those among individual ethnic behaviors and those among the levels of ethnic activity within separate states.

CHAPTER THREE

Tactical Information and the Diffusion of Peaceful Protests

STUART HILL, DONALD ROTHCHILD, AND COLIN CAMERON

The goal of the demonstrations in Selma, as elsewhere, is to dramatize the existence of injustice and to bring about the presence of justice by methods of nonviolence. Long years of experience indicate to us that Negroes can achieve this goal when four things occur:

1. Nonviolent demonstrators go into the streets to exercise their constitutional rights.

2. Racists resist by unleashing violence against them.

3. Americans of conscience in the name of decency demand federal intervention and legislation.

4. The Administration, under mass pressure, initiates measures of immediate intervention and remedial legislation.

—*Martin Luther King*, Saturday Review, *April 3, 1965*

In the spring of 1968 there was much rethinking within the CRA (Civil Rights Association) leadership; the tactics of Martin Luther King in America had been absorbed inasmuch that it was felt by some that only public marches could draw wide attention to what we were trying to achieve by normal democratic means.

—*Ann Hope, member of the executive committee, Northern Ireland Civil Rights Association, interview in 1976.*

CURRENT EXPLANATIONS of mass conflict tend to focus attention on the impact of changing political opportunities rather than on grievances as causes of political protest. Shared feelings of injustice may be a necessary condition for moving citizens into the streets but, taken alone, they are seen as insufficient for causing mass discord. Instead, it is seen that the disaffected begin mobilizing when at least one person from their ranks reaches the conclusion that the time is ripe and devises a strategy for shaping political outcomes. If other group members come to similar conclusions, there is a broad range of factors identified by the literature that influence political opportunity, such as a group's resources, its internal organization, its access to selective incentives for encouraging participation, and growing disagreements among its opponents (see, for example, Tilly 1978; McAdam 1982; Chong 1991; Lichbach 1995; and Tarrow 1995).

Assuming that opportunity plays such a critical role, a key and relatively unanalyzed step in explaining the expansion of conflict is understanding how large numbers of group members reach common conclusions about what are often complex judgments (Hill 1992). Political events may, on rare occasions, unambiguously cause all members of a particular group to conclude that the timing is right and specific tactics are appropriate for them to take action to improve their welfare. But the dynamic political processes, such as shifting coalitions, of open, pluralistic societies often shroud political opportunity in ambiguity. In such situations, even highly educated and well-informed individuals often reach different conclusions regarding the chance of success that unconventional tactics might have at a specific point in time. As a consequence, credible knowledge about political opportunity will probably be scarcer, which suggests that common conclusions about political opportunity will not spontaneously appear among group members but will *diffuse* from skilled tacticians to individuals with less expertise. The rate and extent that any particular group can expand mass conflict will be constrained by how fast and how far credible knowledge of new political opportunities spreads among its members.

In the opening quote above, a principal architect of the American civil rights movement, Reverend Martin Luther King, illustrates the importance of political expertise and of using common tactics to change the political status of African Americans. King's plan revealed a sophisticated understanding of the limited options available to African Americans in the early 1960s. Although African Americans had made gains in federal courts, Congress was the only institution that could truly transform their second-class status. At that time blacks had few means of directly influencing Congressional representatives, for they were largely disenfranchised in the South, where their numbers were the greatest. The U.S. electoral system, moreover, required that successful candidates win a plurality of votes in single-member districts, a daunting hurdle for a group that numbered little more than 12 percent of the total population in the United States. Hence King proposed that African Americans make a dramatic and convincing appeal to the informed public in the country as a whole (Weisbrot 1990).

This strategy was complex and it required, as most strategies of mass action do, that demonstrators follow the same plan of action. King contended that a direct challenge to Southern officials by means of nonviolent protests could be expected to provoke violent responses. He anticipated that repeated viewing of televised images of that violence would significantly undermine the legitimacy of existing racial policies among whites. This shift in public attitudes would pressure members of Congress to support key legislative initiatives for reform.

However, if protesters broke ranks and even a few responded violently, expectations of success would probably disappear. In the event that protester discipline

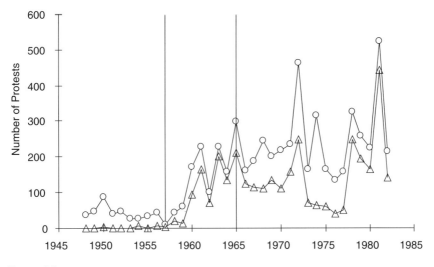

FIGURE 3.1.
Incidence of protests in Western Europe, Canada, and the United States.
○ total protests in Western Europe, Canada, and the United States
△ protests in the United States

collapsed, Southern officials could argue that violence by the police was neces-sary to maintain law and order in the face of illegal behavior (Chong 1991). A positive impact on outside public opinion would then be lost and past gains might even be endangered. In such a situation, how does a new strategy requir-ing that demonstrators conform to a challenging script diffuse rapidly and widely, convincing large numbers of people to work in concert?

The spread of tactical knowledge among group members can be facilitated through technological developments that broaden access to political information. A strategist can reach many group members, either by making a case for acting in a particular manner or by training from example, mounting mass action that serves as a model for emulation. Improved means for disseminating information also spreads new ideas about mass conflict to other groups. The development and widespread adoption of television in Western democracies after World War II, for example, created an enormous audience around the time when mass resistance movements began in earnest with the confrontation over racial policies in the United States. The upper series plotted in Figure 3.1 indicates that the incidence of protests in Western Europe, Canada, and the United States grew rapidly dur-ing and after the period 1957 to 1965, just as the American civil rights movement mobilized. Television now provided a national and international stage for playing out the drama of mass discord.

Consider the impact of the example of the demonstrations in Selma, Alabama, that King mentions above. The month before King penned these words, he met with President Lyndon Johnson and was told that a bill would soon be introduced in Congress guaranteeing federal intervention to protect the voting rights of

African Americans. Johnson left King with the difficult task of mobilizing public opinion, especially white public opinion, in support of this new legislation. King organized a march from Selma to Montgomery, Alabama, as a means of symbolically petitioning Alabama's governor, George Wallace, to protect African Americans who tried to register to vote. Predictably Wallace refused to provide the guarantees that King sought and banned the march. About six hundred protesters set off for Montgomery on March 7, 1965. The demonstrators were met by police at the Edmund Pettus Bridge outside of Selma. Given two minutes to disperse, they refused and bowed their heads in prayer. Police charged on foot and horseback, beating men and women with billy clubs, some encased in barbed wire. This dramatic spectacle was made available through television that same day to almost 90 percent of Americans and a smaller but substantial portion of citizens in Western Europe. All three domestic networks interrupted their broadcasts with the Selma story and showed compressed, edited scenes of violence repeatedly during the next week. King finished the march to Montgomery, keeping the story a major focus on the nightly news and holding Congressional attention for more than a month. In the end, the Voting Rights Act introduced during the confrontation in Alabama passed both houses of Congress within four months by almost four-to-one majorities (Weisbrot 1990).

The apparent effectiveness of this tactic held great appeal to other groups in the United States and in Western Europe who faced similar circumstances. For example, Ann Hope's remark quoted above reveals that Catholics in Northern Ireland drew inspiration from what they saw in Selma (Purdie 1990). They believed that their treatment bore similarities to that of African Americans in the United States, and they directly modeled their actions on the methods employed by the American civil rights movement (Rose 1971). The same process has been reported by other ethnic minorities, as well as by those who demonstrate for causes as diverse as opposition to foreign wars and protection of the environment (McAdam 1988). This process of diffusion across groups raises the possibility that some portion of the growth in protest activity following the success of the U.S. civil rights movement may result from external diffusion, for the tactics employed in Dr. King's struggle were adapted to promote other political objectives.

Widening access to political information, however, does not mean that most or all of the recipients will reach common conclusions about how to proceed. For dissension within a group to expand beyond the core group, an additional number of citizens must perceive the hypothesized stimulus, evaluate it in a common manner, choose to participate in unconventional collective action at the same time and, in doing so, exhibit some semblance of a similar strategy and tactics. The literature on public opinion for the last forty years indicates that most members of the mass public are ill-equipped for this task. The vast majority of citizens have a minimal awareness of and knowledge about politics, and they exhibit an incomplete and rudimentary understanding of political issues and the procedures for making political decisions (see Neuman 1986). They also pay little or no attention to the vagaries of policy-specific debates (Zaller 1992). The very groups that activists seek to organize in demonstrations, moreover, are typically less edu-cated about and attentive to politics than the average citizen (Smith 1989).

The causal path for linking emerging political opportunity to the mobilization of group members to attain a common strategy can be quite long. Lowering the costs on information about political opportunity through technological change only increases the *potential* audience. Mobilization could still stall in the face of inattention, or alternative indicators of opportunity might be followed. If their background and political education differ from one another, protesters who have recently joined a struggle may draw divergent conclusions about the tactics of mass action, and unity of action may suffer.

The current literature readily admits that there are strong incentives for infor-mation about political opportunity to diffuse within and across group boundaries. What is missing is an explanation of how this process of internal and external dif-fusion operates at the level of individual cognition. If we wish to understand how far and wide mass conflict will spread, we must explain how information about mass conflict is attended to and interpreted by individuals who are bound by common goals but who vary considerably in their background and level of polit-ical knowledge. In the remainder of this chapter, we will address this question.

THEORIES OF POLITICAL OPPORTUNITY

Theories of political mobilization and rational choice explain mass conflict by focusing on the impact of changing political opportunity. The term "political mobilization" represents a broad range of theoretical approaches—resource mobilization, political process, and political opportunity—that view mass discord as purposively driven to fulfill collective interests.[1] From this perspective, mobi-lizing large numbers requires an organizational network for the diffusion of polit-ical knowledge from elite tacticians to rank-and-file group members. As new members are brought into the "movement," they learn about particular tactics (such as boycotts, strikes, and protests) or "repertoires," and the importance of coordinated action (Tilly 1978, 1983). Direction about when and where to act flows from a "core group" in the center to those at the periphery who recently joined. Knowledge about timing and tactics also flows externally across group boundaries. The senders and recipients of that expertise are group leaders who have the requisite backgrounds for assessing new developments and shaping them to their advantage (McCarthy and Zald 1973, 1977; Tarrow 1995). Changes in access to political information facilitates the spread of news about changing opportunity, primarily from the leadership of one group to the elites who lead others (McAdam and Rucht 1993). "Cycles of protest" periodically emerge as elites from one or more groups learn more fully about the weakness of current

---

[1]James Rule (1988) identified the common characteristics of this type of theoretical approach but he did not employ the label *political mobilization*.

authorities and the best means for pressuring them (Buerklin 1987). As government elites counter the rising threat or as groups fail to sustain or increase collective discord, mass action declines (Tilly 1975; Tarrow 1989).

Political mobilization (PM) theory identifies where information flows among groups and to which individuals, being primarily those who occupy key roles within these groups. Variation among group members is not of great interest, because PM theorists assume that these individuals share common interests and political grievances. Failing to specify how different individuals become convinced to follow a single approach leaves open the question of how far protest behavior will spread within or across group boundaries (Lichbach 1995). The scope of this problem is narrowed if we understand the important role played by organizational networks. They may well provide the only story that potential participants hear when political information is inaccessible or costly to acquire. Some provocative PM investigations have analyzed periods of mass discord at a time, over two hundred years ago, when such conditions were common (Tilly 1986). However, knowledge about access to information does not tell us how individuals with relatively little background in politics come to the same conclusion that particular political conditions or tactics will make success likely. Overcoming this theoretical omission becomes particularly important in periods when access is widely available and political novices are exposed to a diverse array of cues about the incidence and tactics of mass conflict.

Rational choice (RC) explanations fill in a piece of this puzzle because they examine whether value differences among group members affect their willingness to engage in mass demonstrations. Theorists assume that all individuals carefully allocate their resources to the preferences that maximize their satisfaction. Intense feelings of grievance alone do not provoke mass discord; only the prospect of success in addressing them leads large numbers to commit the time for and take the risks of mass action. (Mason 1984; DeNardo 1985; Muller and Opp 1986; Muller, Dietz, and Finkel 1991). Consequently, acquiring credible knowledge about the factors that determine success are critically important. Learning that another group has achieved an important victory by applying mass pressure against a particular government, for example, can provoke similar behavior. Other groups now believe that this government and states in similar circumstances are more vulnerable than analysts previously believed. Mass conflict also has its own "production function" or technology of how to proceed (Lichbach 1995). Innovations in the means of mass discord are particularly attractive. They spread quickly within and across state boundaries because they increase the efficiency of collective action by lowering the costs of applying collective pressure, raising the expected benefits, or accomplishing both simultaneously (Hirschleifer 1983, 1987).

Let us assume for the moment that information about a group's political opportunities and the specifics of timing and tactics for influencing politics are unambiguous and available to all group members. Under this condition, rational choice theory explains how variation in individuals' preferences can have a significant impact on the initiation and spread of collective discord. Choosing to act first requires a potential participant to identify a compelling reason why he or she should commit scarce time and resources when the contribution any single individual makes is unlikely to influence the final outcome. At the time this obstacle was originally identified, the attraction of "free riding" could only be circumvented by coercing participation or offering selective rewards to those who supported a particular cause (Olson 1965; Tullock 1971).

These solutions are now seen as playing a minor role in explaining voluntary participation in mass discord (Mason 1984). Theorists recognize that other incentives and case-specific conditions are likely to be more important in promoting mobilization, such as obtaining social rewards (Chong 1991), fearing social penalties (Hardin 1995), conforming to internalized norms of political action (Muller, Dietz, and Finkel 1991), and self-consciously cooperating to promote collective rationality (Hardin 1982; see Lichbach 1995 for a more comprehensive list of "solutions"). In addition, the assessments that individuals make regarding the worth of the "public good" that their group wants to provide influences when they participate and how much they are willing to risk. For example, a few "extremists" in a particular organization may value a proposed change in public policy more intensely than other group members, and choose to "test the waters" by protesting at the first sign of a positive shift in political opportunity, even though the anticipated costs of their actions are expected to be quite high. Moderates for whom the proposal is less salient will wait until the chances of success have risen and the personal costs appeared to have declined (DeNardo 1985; Lohmann 1994).

This type of analysis can be logically extended by examining how utility-maximizing individuals interact under dynamic conditions. Many studies begin by identifying how the interaction of individuals within a group influences their relations with other groups. For example, social pressures to exhibit public support for one's ethnic identity (such as wearing distinctive clothing or choosing an "ethnic" diet) can persuade individuals who share that identity to conform. Observing this group's newly found solidarity provokes other groups to respond in kind, heightening intergroup tensions and raising the risk of a future confrontation (see Kuran, Chapter Two). Using the analytic framework of game theory, the number of participants in a demonstration or riot can be modeled as an "assurance game" in which the marginal joiner looks to gain social and normative benefits from mass action only if he or she can be confident that others of like mind will appear (Chong 1991). Rational choice analysts also examine the structure of conflicting incentives between competing group elites or between a group elite and a state elite to learn how it yields predictable patterns over time. Two groups with a past history of violence, for example, can live in peace when their security is assured by the state or an external power. If that security guarantee disappears, civil war and secessionist movements become more likely as a means to resolve this internal threat (see Fearon, Chapter Five and Saideman, Chapter Six).

Understanding the role of individual wants and their variations across group members adds specificity to predictions about the diffusion of information on timing and tactics, and about the impact of that information in stimulating additional mass discord. The RC conclusion is contingent: information on political opportunity will spread and promote further conflict within and across groups only when it offers the individuals who receive it a reasonable prospect of further net gains.

This view of the diffusion process, however, rests on the premise that individuals who have common goals and who have access to the same information will make the same choices about participation. Doubts about a political movement's chances of success do not alter this expectation. When faced with uncertainty, rational choice theory tells us that satisfaction-maximizing individuals weigh the quality of the available information and gather more if they believe that the expected benefit will outweigh the cost in producing a better decision. Again, identical preferences and access to information produce similar choices.[2] But if individuals who share identical wants and availability to information choose *not* to draw on the same facts about political opportunity, then the logical implication is that they may follow divergent courses of action.

Consider how this might occur. Serious efforts at producing major social change for a particular group are not only uncertain, they also occur rarely, involve multiple institutions and political actors, and take considerable time to unfold. It seems reasonable that the large and pervasive differences in the political backgrounds of group members will systematically shape their ability to assess these political events. For the vast majority of any group's members, the analytic frame they bring to this task will include a small portion of the major political actors and institutions in their country. With limited knowledge, they will not use the same indicators of political success or failure that one finds among the well-informed. Consequently, individuals who want to achieve indistinguishable political goals could, when faced with the choice of whether to participate in an emerging political movement, draw on different facts from the same pool of information and reach dissimilar interpretations about its significance.[3] Rational choice does not tell us how variation in background or prior information shapes the diffusion of information about the timing and tactics of mass conflict.[4] If political opportunity is going to play its critical role in causing discord, we need to fill

[2]Some theorists use rough rules of thumb to claim that after one or two apparent victories individuals will believe that a strategy is sound, without telling us what process of reasoning would consistently produce that assessment for different citizens (see Chong 1991). Game-theoretic analyses suffer from the same problem. The payoffs for any game subsume a host of tactical judgments on which reasonable people could disagree. Yet, theorists believe that the structure of the game typically yields self-evident estimates of the payoffs. Rarely do analysts check to see if their theoretical inferences have any empirical support (Selten 1990). James DeNardo (1995) recently found that he could not replicate the payoffs that theory predicts for games of nuclear deterrence among novices or experts.

[3]One reason similar individuals could reach divergent interpretations is that they did not share the same access in the past to resources for higher education. Yet even citizens who reach similar levels of educational accomplishment may encounter and learn dissimilar theories of political change simply because they happen to attend different universities and learn different accounts.

[4]Signaling expert judgments from elites to followers does not solve this problem because followers must still identify and judge the quality of the source for this type of decision. Their ability to assess will be constrained by the limits of their past experience.

in this explanatory gap by examining cognitive rather than evaluative processes.

Before we consider how cognitive processing might offer the analytic means for addressing this problem, it is important to take note of a factor that may have been prematurely discarded. As noted earlier, recent work on mass conflict plays down the role of changes in political grievances as a conspicuous cause in producing mass discord. This logic appears to be soundly based. Few concrete examples exist in which groups mobilize without improvements taking place in political opportunity. Yet this conclusion does not eliminate the possibility that group members' heightened feelings of grievance might also speed the rate of mobilization *during* periods when their political advantage changes for the better. Indeed, if there is considerable disparity in the knowledge that long-term activists and new recruits bring to a dispute, new participants may experience growing feelings of injustice as they learn more about their group's systemic mistreatment. With this possibility in mind, it is now time to examine how information is processed.

COGNITIVE EXPECTATIONS

Current explanations of information processing suggest that differing levels of political experience and background should play a large role in shaping the diffusion of information about political opportunity. Cognitive psychologists start from the premise that individuals employ a common mechanism for processing information (Newell, Rosenbloom, and Laird 1989). Explaining how this mechanism operates at any particular moment in a given domain requires examining how current information processing has been structured by past experience.

Individuals access and manipulate information in short-term or working memory. Working memory is highly constrained in the number of distinct, unrelated bits of information that can be simultaneously processed (Baddeley 1986). As a result, individuals are serial processors and attend to only a few bits of data at one moment. Yet, the capacity to store information in long-term memory is prodigious (Bahrick and Hall 1991). Individuals expand the processing ability of working memory by encoding and storing patterns of multiple bits of information or "chunks." When faced with similar patterns in the future, long-term memory enables individuals to recognize and manipulate each multi-bit chunk as one distinct piece of information. With more experience in encoding commonplace patterns we increase our ability to recognize and process more data in the future (Miller 1956).

As experience accumulates in specific domains, individuals distill from specific examples prototypical views of particular people, objects, or activities they commonly encounter. These knowledge structures or "schemas" are defined as "organized prior knowledge, abstracted from experience with specific instances" (Fiske and Linville 1980, 543). Schemas explain how the attributes and characteristics of the world are typically related to one another in particular contexts. Thus an event schema or "script" tells us what to expect when we take part in activities as diverse as a birthday party or a budget hearing (Schank and Abelson 1977).

Because individuals continually face far more stimuli than they can perceive or understand at a given moment, they employ schemas to structure what they see and how they interpret it. Schemas direct where we look for relevant material in a given situation or what information we retrieve from memory to address a particular problem. When important "facts" are not provided, this type of knowledge structure can fill in "default values" (Rumelhart and Ortony 1977). With greater experience, a more general knowledge structure is constructed within which additional specific cases or attributes are categorized and understood (Taylor and Crocker 1981). The more developed a schema becomes, the more instructive it is in the future, as it allows a person to take in and interpret more detail in a wider variety of contexts.

Because schemas set our expectations of how events will unfold or individuals will act in particular circumstances, they frequently trigger evaluative or judgmental reactions based on how closely these expectations are met (Fiske 1982). Individuals can develop strong affective feelings about the prototypical activities and people (such as mothers or politicians) that schemas explain, and the degree of "fit" or match that an individual perceives in a specific instance can determine the extent to which those feelings are engaged. Identifying additional examples for an evaluative knowledge structure can widen the range of one's assessment by applying the same judgment to more cases (Fiske and Taylor 1984; Fiske and Pavelchak 1986). A general evaluative schema is likely to be triggered more often than one that is narrowly defined. Thus changes in knowledge can shape the scope of evaluation and the frequency with which an assessment is brought to mind and the judgment is felt.

The diverse range of schemas any single person constructs is linked within long-term memory by the degree to which they are associated together in daily activities. These connections can be made when distinct phenomena appear in close proximity, as they frequently do. Individuals' goals also structure how they organize the content of their thoughts, linking schemas that are integral for performing common physical or mental tasks. As individuals navigate their daily lives, different objects and activities will continuously cause a "spread of activation" in long-term memory among the specific knowledge structures that are most instructive to the task at hand. When a particular schema is stimulated or "primed" it will highlight connections to related schemas if further reflection is required (on how to deal with problems, for example, or identify a novel case, and so forth). Just as any single knowledge structure becomes more developed with increased experience and thought, the linkages between schemas become more tightly interconnected as one observes and studies relationships at a higher level of analysis among multiple, discrete phenomena. By encoding common patterns of attributes *across* different prototypes, such as identifying familiar "stories" from complex chains of events, individuals begin to construct expectations about dynamic relationships in a variety of contexts (Anderson 1990).

This analysis argues that differences in the level of background and reflection in a specific domain have important implications for understanding *current* information processing. Individuals who have a wealth of past experience can identify the extended causal chain of events within which specific episodes are seen as one step in a larger process. Unusual attributes will be noticed and catalogued by veteran observers because of their similarity to more familiar patterns from their past. In developing this expansive view, individuals can gather many examples and generalize narrow knowledge and evaluation structures to a broad level. Confidence and scope of understanding grow with additional opportunities to apply this knowledge system to new objects and events. A robust framework accumulated from the past thus imposes order on the variable flow of external events in the present.

By contrast, individuals who lack extensive background in a particular domain will not see an extended causal chain in which immediate events are embedded. Their internal library will fail to notice and identify many key attributes, events, or people as commonplace patterns. To the extent that their restricted schemas carry an assessment, individuals will apply them to the restricted range of examples from which they were constructed. Lacking a highly ordered internal structure, individuals' perceptions and interpretations will be shaped or "framed" by the most prevalent pattern of external events in the present. They will focus on proximate indicators of activity, and their predictions about the future will be derived from the trends of these indicators at the moment.

The impact of past experience in structuring current processing reinforces the prevailing belief that group leaders and tacticians have strong incentives for speeding the diffusion of information about political opportunity. When background for attending to and interpreting news about political opportunity is limited, however, our analysis indicates that we need to reconsider current views of how diffusion unfolds.

Cognitive constraints bolster the claim that it is extremely difficult and time-consuming to develop an analytic frame of reference that is comprehensive enough to make reliable inferences about the timing and tactics of mass conflict. Devising a plan for a group that must employ *un*conventional tactics suggests that a group's status is low and their policies for reform are unpopular. Plotting to overcome these substantial obstacles compels the tactician to examine a wide political horizon that includes a number of possible pathways of influence. The high costs for devising this strategy de novo provides strong incentives for identifying how someone else solved similar problems under roughly comparable conditions. Understanding the constraints on individual cognition for addressing such demanding questions just adds another reason to the incentives the literature already identifies for tactics to diffuse from one group to another.

Rational choice analyses have always had a difficult time explaining why elites are willing to bear the substantial burden of organizing a mass movement. The expectation that knowledge structures can carry evaluative assessments offers one explanation. When prospective leaders begin to research how to overcome the political impediments for addressing their "problem"—discrimination, corrupt practices, wasteful use of resources, and so on—they will often discover a wider array of examples than they expected and conclude that the problem is more widespread than they originally believed. Generalizing their evaluative knowledge structure in this manner increases the number of objects or events that trigger this assessment. Consequently, they "feel" their grievance more often, helping to redouble their commitment in the face of a long, difficult struggle.

The most distinctive contributions of this analysis are in explaining the reaction of those who bring comparatively little background to a dispute and in predicting how elite ideas will diffuse among them. From limited political experience the average group member will encode small, disaggregated (or to use Philip Converse's [1964] term, *morselized*) chunks of knowledge about particular topics such as personal mistreatment, their political identity, their group's partisan affiliation, and a vaguely defined sense of the current direction of general economic and political conditions. Even though they may be aware that recent political change—election of a new legislature or chief executive—raises the possibility of improving their group's political condition, they will not know how to act on that unlikely prospect in an efficacious manner.

Knowledge from elites diffuses to and mobilizes the group members to action through one of two distinct conduits. An elite representative can fill in the missing links in the members' fragmented understanding of political opportunity and broaden their sense of grievance. Group organizers can convey the idea that current conditions offer historic opportunities for pressuring key political actors with the carefully timed use of common tactics. Given the large numbers of participants that need to be mobilized and the limits of their formal education, organizers will find it counterproductive to provide recruits with general explanations of current political trends. Instead, they can offer low-level shorthand explanations of immediate political events and concentrate on the operational tactics for taking advantage of this emerging opportunity.

Recruits will be likely to judge their leaders, just as rational choice theorists maintain, in terms of whether the tactics "work" in achieving tangible success. Because new participants know little about what to expect, however, elites can shape their expectations of how quickly they will achieve specific goals. They can also help stiffen participants' resolve by revealing that the problem that brought them together is far more pervasive than most realize. Doling out additional examples can have the effect of progressively widening their sense of grievance, and the very experience of mass action can provide new evidence to explain why further action is required. Furthermore, the manner in which elites define their group's grievance can be used to justify and strengthen support for specific tactics. (For example, Martin Luther King invoked scripture to justify the cause of civil rights and the tactics of nonviolence.) Limited backgrounds thus need not be a liability. With sufficient time and contact, elites can turn that deficit into a strength. They can shape a common understanding of how to proceed and what participants should expect.

Organizational contact from group representatives is not the only conduit by which information about timing and tactics diffuses from elites to group members. Exposure to the act of mass conflict is another means by which individuals can learn that political pressure is being applied on their behalf. Before information became widely available through the mass media, group members were exposed to episodes of mass action if they lived in large cities and directly observed these activities or learned of them by word of mouth. As the scope of mass conflict grew, it could attract additional participants even though they had no direct contact with a group's representatives.

The advent of the electronic media, particularly television, has greatly expanded the potential impact of exposure of this kind. More than 90 percent of citizens in the United States and Western Europe now have access to television. Even as early as the mid 1960s, when mass discord exploded, television was available to almost 80 percent of Americans and 50 percent of citizens in Western Europe (Noam 1991). Television is especially influential in disseminating political information because using it does not require reading skills, and most individuals think that information from television is less biased than other sources of political news, such as newspapers and radio. The visual nature of the medium substantially increases its credibility because most citizens maintain that "seeing is believing" (Roper 1991).

Nearly universal access to political events will not provoke political novices to change their habits substantially or pay close attention to measures of political opportunity and signs of the emergence of mass conflict. Without the benefit of direct contact with a group attempting to organize them, their view of political events—to the extent that they pay any attention at all—will be present-oriented, framed by the few stories (the economy, war, crime) that are most prevalent on the news at any given moment. Actually "seeing" people like themselves take to the streets in one of these stories, however, should rivet their attention because it immediately brings to mind their personal feelings of grievance (Hill and Rothchild 1986). The more times they observe these political acts, the more often they will think about and feel that emotion, and more tightly identify that feeling with the political causes and solutions discussed in the mass media. Because of their limited backgrounds, they will know little about the specific history of past conflicts or how these demonstrations are supposed to produce political change. Without that background they will focus on the present struggle and gather information about changing political opportunity during the brief time—typically little more than weeks or months—after this dispute captures their attention. Their best indicator of opportunity and the focus of the news stories will be the number and size of protests during this period of conflict. After a rapid upsurge in these events, they will infer that opportunity is improving because members of their group are applying pressure in greater numbers. With larger audiences exposed to periodic spikes of activity, more group members should be motivated to join.

Unlike instruction from an organizational contact, the scope and specificity of information from news stories is extremely limited. Observers will not be told why they need to follow common tactics or apply pressure at particular points in time that group leaders believe are politically efficacious (Iyengar 1991). To predict the dynamics of their response we need to understand how mass attention and inferences are shaped within a highly truncated view of politics. The marginal participant focuses attention on the immediate context within which events occur. This means that an upsurge in activity will attract more notice and new recruits if there has not been protest activity in the recent past. The media is more likely to give each episode of a new, "breaking" story of this type more coverage than a similar number of events that are part of a long-term campaign. For some-one who perceives politics in terms of what is most prevalent at the moment, a wave of activity that suddenly emerges within a short time signals that this devel-opment is significant. Indeed, there is some truth to this perception. An abrupt, large change will attract considerable attention, stimulate widespread discussion, and even place the issues of the demonstrators on the national agenda, if only for a brief period (Jones 1994).

By the same logic, large increases in mass conflict in the surrounding region can provoke a similar reaction. Events in neighboring states typically receive less coverage than domestic news, and the average citizens' knowledge about foreign affairs is even lower than their limited awareness of national affairs. But demon-strations that engulf a region can capture a nation's attention. Suddenly learning that mass discord is pervasive would increase the frequency with which the mar-ginal joiners reflect on their groups' grievances and also lead them to infer that the growing prevalence of this activity suggests that it is an efficacious time to act. Assuming that at least one group leader is willing to take advantage of this activ-ity, we should see an increase in domestic conflict in response to particularly high levels of external discord.

Protesters who respond to exposure to ongoing mass conflict offer organizers a new means of influencing political outcomes. Yet the volatility of their reactions to domestic and foreign discord suggests that they cannot easily be directed or managed. From the perspective of group leaders, perhaps the most troubling effect of mass exposure is that new recruits do not have the benefit of direct con-tact with their organizations' representatives. Consequently, they do not know how they are supposed to act or see the importance of following common tactics. Marginal joiners may show up for no other reason than that they have recently seen people like themselves pressuring their opponents to change. When they arrive, exhortations by organizers to behave in a disciplined manner can have lit-tle impact on them if they have no understanding of how the means of conflict produces particular results. Because of their limited background, their feelings of injustice will be narrowly defined, increasing the probability they will express a message defined by their personal experience rather than by the political objec-tives of the leadership.

Increasing the level of exposure to mass conflict should thus increase the num-ber of protesters and protests, but this additional strength is an unwieldy tool for influencing politics. Participants who respond to exposure to conflict will vary dramatically in number and purpose as the dynamics of mass action and televi-sion coverage change.

Estimating Effects of Political Background on Mass Conflict

The post-World War II period in the United States and Western Europe is an excellent time in which to test these propositions. As noted earlier, protest activity increased rapidly, so that by the mid-1970s scholars identified the entire era as one of a few distinctive "cycles of protest." Because this period began with the emergence of the civil rights movement in the United States and the use of innovative tactics, we can test whether current expectations that tactics diffuse across groups have empirical support. The postwar period also offers an almost unique opportunity to examine a burst of mass action at the same time that access to political information rapidly expanded to include most citizens in this region. The proportion of citizens with access to television was essentially zero after World War II and grew to roughly 90 percent by the late 1970s. Although the literature concurs in the belief that knowledge about timing and tactics diffuses from elites to rank-and-file members of a group's organization, it leaves unspecified how and with what effect that information spreads by exposure through the mass media to individuals with little political knowledge. The hypotheses just deduced from principles of information processing can be tested to fill out this important lacuna in our current understanding.

The data for this investigation have been obtained from *The Third World Handbook of Political and Social Indicators* compiled by Charles Taylor (see Jodice and Taylor 1981). The *Handbook* measures the incidence of indicators of mass conflicts such as the number of peaceful protests and riots for varying periods of time (days, quarters, years) and the various aggregate factors that might influence the timing and scope of this activity (such as GDP, availability of newspapers and televisions, and so on.). The time frame of these data from 1950 to 1982 perfectly brackets the period of theoretical interest.[5]

Our dependent variable is the monthly incidence of peaceful protests in seventeen Western industrialized nations. We selected those countries that maintained democratic institutions throughout the entire thirty-five-year period. Given our theoretical interests, we wanted to concentrate on states where the dissemination of information was not under direct political control. We chose to explain the incidence of peaceful protests because this is the specific type of mass action that characterized the initial stages of this "cycle" of conflict and that we hypothesized would spread within and across groups. We selected the monthly incidence of protests because it reflects the hypothesized time frame of the marginal joiner and allows us to examine the dynamics of signaling and response. Thus the dataset is structured as a cross-sectional monthly time series of seventeen countries for thirty-five years, with 6,698 observations.

We compiled thirty-eight independent variables to explain the incidence of protests. The model is a fixed-effects model, so dummy variables were con-

---

[5]The available data on protests begins in 1948, but we have good comparable measures on gross domestic product per capita only since 1950. As a result, the statistical analysis begins in 1950.

structed for sixteen out of the seventeen states. In addition, we included measures for contextual factors such as a state's population ($\ln[pop_1]$), gross domestic product per capita ($GDP/capita_1$), and in early runs its inflation and unemployment rates. Because we did not want to attribute incorrectly effects that might be purely internal to a dispute, we controlled for the past history of conflict with lagged versions of the dependent variable, or the incidence of peaceful protests, for up to three months ($\ln[prot_{1-3}]+0.5$).[6]

The first hypothesis, which we share with rational choice and political mobilization analyses, is that knowledge about political opportunity diffuses within and across groups. In the postwar context, we believe that the success of the tactics of nonviolence that African Americans employed in the United States spread to groups in states who faced similar political circumstances. We identified those political conditions on four interactive dimensions. The first and second conditions are states with ethnic diversity and high thresholds for winning legislative representation.[7] States with both conditions should have a higher incidence of protest behavior because ethnic groups would be constrained in their ability to pursue conventional forms of political change, and would have strong incentives to look for unconventional tactics that could be used to change their status. This variable is constructed as an interaction term, reflecting a contingent relationship. Each component of this variable considered separately does not capture the hypothesized effect. By combining ethnolinguistic fractionalization ($ethnofrac_1$), or the degree of ethnic and linguistic divisions, and the minimum proportion of the vote required to win legislative representation in a particular state ($legthres_1$), we measure the conflict between group divisions and limited electoral options. Interaction terms are frequently used in this analysis because most of the propositions about diffusion refer to contingent causes.

The third condition that facilitated the diffusion of nonviolence was access to television. As television becomes more readily available in states with ethnic groups and high thresholds, it offers the means of revealing how nonviolent demonstrators are treated (tv_1 is coded from 1–5, with 1 equal to 0 to 20 percent of the population having access, 2 equals 21 to 39 percent, and so on). King benefited from the advent of television because scenes of violence against civil rights protesters were sent directly into the homes of most Americans. Television also facilitated the mobilization of African Americans as they observed the civil rights movement unfold over five years.

The fourth and final condition examines whether the incidence of protest behavior was greater under these conditions *after* 1960, when the tactics of the civil rights movement were put on public display (the final interaction term is $1960*ethnofrac_1*legthres_1*tv_1$). If peaceful protests emerged under these conditions before this date, they were obviously not due to the diffusion of tactics from the American civil rights movement.

[6]Ln denotes the natural logarithm. In addition, the constant .5 has been added to prot to avoid the prospect of taking the logarithm of 0.

[7]The measures for each state's legislative thresholds were drawn from Lijphart (1994).

The second hypothesis investigates the claim that wide exposure to a surge in mass conflict will increase the number of future protests. We measured a rapid increase in protests by constructing an interaction term that multiplied past protests lagged by one month times past protests lagged by two months $(\ln[\text{prot}]_1{}^*\ln[\text{prot}]_2)$. Our prediction is that when both increase, this represents an upsurge in protest activity. If most of a state's citizens are exposed to this behavior through access to television $(\ln[\text{prot}]_1{}^*\ln[\text{prot}]_2{}^*\text{tv}_1)$, we believe that there will be more protests than when similar outbursts of discord and the availability of television are low.

Our third hypothesis builds on the second. As the time between protests increases, the incidence of future peaceful protests should typically decline. Extended periods of quiet usually mean fewer people are organized. We predict that an upsurge in protests that occurs after a long period without protest activity should capture widespread attention and produce additional protests if that information is transmitted to large numbers of citizens via television (the interaction term is $\ln[\text{prot}]_1{}^*\ln[\text{prot}]_2{}^*\text{tv}_1{}^*\text{timeprot}_3$).[8]

Mass attention should also be responsive to periods of large-scale external discord. Our fourth hypothesis predicts that the most visible indicators of mass conflict in the region should be followed by higher protests within each state (region-prot$_1$). Because television coverage of foreign domestic affairs faces severe time constraints, only the most sensational events receive extended coverage. Past analysis of news coverage suggests that a large number of protesters in other states will attract more foreign news coverage than increased incidents of protest alone.

Our fifth and last hypothesis tests whether tactical unity declines as increased exposure attracts more marginal participants. By focusing on the tactics of nonviolence that dominated the early 1960s, we can infer how much consensus there was by examining the response to violence. If the commitment to nonviolence is strong, as we believe it was when elite organization and direction were particularly strong in the early years of the civil rights movement from 1958–1962, then we should have few protests in the immediate aftermath of mass violence or riots. Nonviolent protesters would want to dissociate themselves from those who use violence as just another tool of mass pressure. Thus the number of protests in the month following a riot (1958–1962*riot$_1$) should decline. As the time since an episode of rioting increases (1958–1962*timeriot$_2$), peaceful demonstrations should become more prevalent. When the civil rights movement and other protest movements rapidly expanded in the subsequent period, from 1963 to 1982, we should see signs of greater disunity in the use of peaceful demonstrations. A high rate of expansion should attract more marginal joiners who lack the background and training in tactics of their predecessors. The negative response to high levels of rioting that we hypothesize for the 1958–1963 period should weaken or disappear in our dependent variable from 1963–1982 (1963–1982*riot$_1$). Rioting will be for the marginal joiner another indication of disaffection, and we should

---

[8]Timeprot is lagged by three months because it measures the number of months without protests prior to a two-month upsurge of demonstrations. In hypothesis 5 we analytically divide riot$_1$ and timeriot$_2$ in the same fashion.

not see more protests as the amount of time since a period of violent mass action increases ($1963-1982*\text{timeriot}_1$).

Estimating these relationships should take into account how the data are distributed. Our dependent variable—the number of peaceful protests—is a classic example of "event count" data, where the count is a non-negative integer that has no effective upper limit. Ordinary least squares regression is inappropriate for this analysis because it can predict negative outcomes. More importantly, the distribution of the data does not fit the ordinary least squares assumptions of homoskedastic errors, and the relationships do not conform to its linear functional form. The difference between zero and one events, for example, is not the same as between fifteen and sixteen events (King 1988, 846). Poisson regression is often used for estimating relationships for count data, but a Poisson distribution assumes that events are independent within the time period in which they are tallied—in this case, the number of protests in each month. Clearly that is not our expectation. We believe that protests within each month will often be linked. When events within each time period are interdependent, the most appropriate technique is negative binomial regression with maximum likelihood estimation.

Count regression models have typically been applied to cross-section data. Here we estimate a dynamic model using panel data. The dynamics are handled by using the markov regression approach of Zeger and Qaqish (1988). In the simplest case of one lagged dependent variable the number of protests at time t, prot_t is negative binomial distributed with mean $\exp(x_t*b + a*\ln[\text{prot}_{t-1}+0.5])$, where x_t is a vector of regressors, b is a vector of parameters, and the constant term 0.5 is added to prevent the obvious problem that would otherwise arise when prot_{t-1} equals zero. This approach can then be directly applied to panel data (see for example Fahrmeier and Tutz 1994, 205). The only adaptation is the inclusion of country-specific fixed effects. Thus for country i at time t, $\text{prot}_{i,t}$ is negative a binomial distributed with mean $\exp(x_{i,t}*b + a*\ln[\text{prot}_{i,t-1}+0.5] + c_i)$. In the reported results, three lags of prot are similarly included. As in the case of linear dynamic panel data regression with fixed effects, consistency requires the number of time periods to go to infinity.

Before reviewing the results, it is important to point out that we are well aware of the limits of what aggregate data can tell us about individual behavior. Clearly we are not directly testing the cognitive or motivational states of the individuals who engaged in peaceful protests during this period. However, theory can identify specific patterns of collective behavior that are consistent with individual-level hypotheses. We believe that the strength of the test increases and becomes easier to disconfirm as the predicted pattern of collective behavior becomes more precisely and narrowly defined. With this in mind we predicted more peaceful protests when two, three, or even four conditions occurred simultaneously. Three propositions are consistent with the general belief held by theories of rational choice and political mobilization regarding the diffusion of mass conflict within and across group boundaries (hypotheses 1, 2, and, to some extent, 4). Testing these expectations is important because the claim that diffusion occurs, particularly at the intergroup level, remains controversial. The remaining two hypotheses, 3 and 5 (and to a lesser degree, 4), make predictions that distinguish our approach from the current literature; these claims indicate that competing claims at the individual level can yield divergent and meaningful collective-level hypotheses.

The results of the negative binomial regression can be found in Table 3.1. The chi-square statistic, 2,796, reveals that the model as a whole is statistically significant. The model also fits the data well, with a deviance R-squared measure (Cameron and Windmeijer 1996) of 0.484. Given the very different mean level of counts across countries, much of the explanatory power is due to inclusion of country dummies. But the remaining regressors are still statistically significant overall, with a chi-square test statistic of 670 when tested against a country-dummy-only model. Overall the most important explanatory variables a priori are statistically significant and have the predicted sign.[9] It is important to note at this point that interpreting the coefficients is complicated because they measure the proportionate—not linear—changes in the dependent variable that result from unit changes in the independent variables. Thus the column labeled Impact in Table 3.1 measures the percentage change in one standard deviation in the dependent variable of an increase of one standard deviation in each explanatory variable. We can see that a standard deviation increase in $\ln(\text{pop}_1)$ has a comparatively large and predictably positive effect on the number of peaceful protests (+552%), just as a standard deviation increase in GDP/capita$_1$ lowers the expected level of discord by a proportionately much smaller amount (–58 percent). (See Appendix Table A3.1 for the means and standard deviations for the complete dataset.)

Although these results reveal something about the relative importance of the explanatory variables, combining variables in interaction terms makes it difficult to identify the separate impacts of each variable. We cannot isolate the independent effect of tv, for example, because an increase in this variable will simultaneously change the value of the three interaction terms of which it is a part. Because the theory and hypotheses focus on the combined impact of two or more explanatory variables at high values, however, this need not be an intractable problem. The difficulty arises when more than one interaction term is involved in testing a particular hypothesis. Although the final and most theoretically important term may be significant with the appropriate sign, in several cases the lower-order interactions move in opposite directions, raising the question of whether the total impact conforms to our expectations.

We address this problem by constructing illustrative scenarios for each hypothesis, using the five states with the most protests: United States, United Kingdom, France, Germany, and Italy. In each case we first establish a baseline that measures the predicted level of protests using the state's mean levels during a period of time that is theoretically relevant to the hypothesis in question. We then generate a scenario by increasing the value of each of the variables that contribute to a particular hypothesis's final interaction term by one standard deviation. The value for all variables that interact with these terms are also changed by this amount, while all

---

[9]Because twelve out of the seventeen states in the analysis have relatively low levels of protest, we should point out when we drop the states with low numbers of demonstrations from the analysis all of the theoretically relevant variables retain their predicted sign and remain statistically significant.

TABLE 3.1

Negative Binomial Regression on the Number of Peaceful Protests in Seventeen States, 1950–1982

Variables	Estimates (std. errors)	Impact
GDP/capita$_1$	−.000254 (.0000648)[a]	−58%
ln(pop$_1$)	3.165 (1.341)[c]	552
ln(prot$_1$)	.330 (.047)[a]	26
ln(prot$_2$)	.300 (.047)[a]	24
ln(prot$_3$)	.062 (.043)	5
legthres$_1$	−.215 (.117)	−27
ethnofrac$_1$*legthres$_1$	.793 (.452)	578
ethnofrac$_1$*legthres$_1$*tv$_1$	−.001 (.117)	−31
1960*ethnofrac$_1$*legthres$_1$*tv$_1$	.013 (.003)[a]	42
tv$_1$	.157 (.058)[b]	27
ln(prot$_1$)*ln(prot$_2$)	−.337 (.135)[c]	−41
ln(prot$_1$)*ln(prot$_2$)*tv$_1$	.057 (.028)[c]	34
timeprot$_3$	−.011 (.004)[b]	−57
ln(prot$_1$)*ln(prot$_2$)*timeprot$_3$	−.047 (.012)[a]	−121
ln(prot$_1$)*ln(prot$_2$)*tv$_1$* timeprot$_3$	.018 (.003)[a]	118
regionprot$_1$	.00000059 (.0000002)[b]	8
riot$_1$	.024 (.043)	5
1958–1962*riot$_1$	−.127 (.062)[c]	−7
1963–1982*riot$_1$	−.022 (.045)	−4
timeriot$_2$	−.022 (.007)[b]	−197
1958–1962*timeriot$_2$	.026 (.007)[a]	82
1963–1982*timeriot$_2$	.019 (.007)[b]	168
Canada	−2.386 (4.704)	
United Kingdom	8.204 (3.410)[c]	
Ireland	21.460 (8.125)[b]	
Netherlands	13.334 (5.594)[c]	
Belgium	13.382 (5.364)[c]	
Luxembourg	23.316 (9.894)[c]	
France	10.615 (4.418)[c]	
Switzerland	14.435 (5.744)[c]	
Germany	10.943 (4.873)[c]	
Austria	15.421 (6.324)[c]	
Italy	10.027 (4.584)[c]	
Finland	14.749 (6.743)[c]	
Sweden	15.234 (6.332)[c]	
Norway	18.710 (7.463)[c]	
Denmark	16.816 (6.706)[c]	
Iceland	26.656 (10.567)[c]	
constant (United States)	−43.551 (16.751)[b]	
Number of cases	6,698	
log likelihood	−4375	
X^2	2,796	
Prob > chi^2	.000	
deviance R^2	.484	

[a] p < .001   [b] p < .01   [c] p < .05

other variables in the model are held at their mean values. In this manner we can determine the net effect of a system of explanatory variables and their interactions.

Hypothesis 1

This hypothesis tests whether peaceful protests are higher in ethnically divided states that were exposed to the innovative tactics of the American civil rights movement. These tactics should diffuse to groups in other states who faced political conditions similar to those African Americans confronted in the late 1950s. Specifically, when a state had substantial ethnic divisions (ethnofrac$_1$), high thresholds for winning legislative representation through "conventional" politics (legthres$_1$), widely available access to television (tv$_1$), and the people had seen nonviolent tactics used effectively in the United States after 1960, then we should expect greater numbers of peaceful protests.

The final interaction term that measures this effect, 1960* ethnofrac$_1$*legthres$_1$*tv$_1$, found in Table 3.1, is positive and statistically significant at the .001 level. Yet a single explanatory variable (legthres$_1$) and a lower-order interaction term (ethnofrac$_1$*legthres$_1$ *tv$_1$) are negative. Table 3.2 shows the total impact of the four variables and their interactions that contribute to this hypothesis for specific states. This scenario uses the mean values of the large protest states for 1950–1970, evenly bracketing the period in which tactics changed in the United States during the late 1950s to early 1960s. The baseline at state-level estimates for each country lists the model's predictions when 1960* ethnofrac$_1$*legthres$_1$*tv$_1$ = 0 and all other explanatory variables are held at their mean values. In scenario 1, 1960* ethnofrac$_1$*legthres$_1$*tv$_1$ is then set to its mean value for the 1960–1970 period.

It is not surprising, based on the historical record, that the United States shows a substantial impact from this change—an average increase of 1.144 protests per month from a base of 1.323 per month or close to a net gain of 100 percent. The effect on states with more limited ethnic divisions and access to television during the 1960s, such as the United Kingdom and France, are proportionately more moderate (+.225 and +.172 from bases of .539 and .693, respectively), whereas homogeneous states with low legislative thresholds such as Germany and Italy show virtually no increase (.003 and .001, respectively). Although this analysis

TABLE 3.2
Hypothesis 1, Using 1950–1970 Means

State	Ethnofrac/ legthres/mean tv	Baseline	Scenario 1
United States	.505/35%/4.2	1.323	+1.144
United Kingdom	.325/35%/3.1	.539	+.225
France	.261/35%/1.8	.693	+.172
Germany	.026/ 5%/2.0	.717	+.003
Italy	.038/ 2%/1.5	.551	+.001

cannot establish a causal relationship between events in the United States and the increased incidence of peaceful protests in states such as the United Kingdom and France, the pattern and level that emerges is consistent with the claim that tactics diffuse across group and state boundaries to those in similar political circumstances.

Hypothesis 2

This hypothesis examines whether an upsurge in protests (interpreted as two consecutive months of high protests) prompts more demonstrations when televised stories of the protests reach most citizens, compared with situations in which televisions are available to only a minority of the electorate. The final interaction term—$\ln(\text{prot}_1)^*$ $\ln(\text{prot}_1)^*\text{tv}_1$ is positive and significant at the .05 level, supporting the claim that wider access to visual information on protest activity contributes to a sharp increase in protest activity. The fact that the interaction of past protests lagged one and two months ($\ln[\text{prot}_1]$ $^*\ln[\text{prot}_2]$) taken alone achieves statistical significance and is *negative* suggests that the increased availability of television may have a substantial impact in prolonging further demonstrations.

To investigate that possibility, Table 3.3 constructs a baseline that sets $\ln(\text{prot}_1)$ and $\ln(\text{prot}_2)$ at their mean levels for the 1963–1982 period and tv_1 at 3, where television is available to between 40 and 59 percent of the state's population. This time frame was selected because it represents a period in which the number of protests was at times high and variable—certainly high enough to attract the attention of marginal joiners—and access to television continued to grow for every country except the United States.[10] Thus we could investigate scenarios in which both the past level of protests and access to television varied in a range that was theoretically interesting.[11] Scenario 1 increases television to level 4, where television is available to between 60 and 79 percent of households, and past protests, lagged one and two months, to one standard deviation above the mean for each country. In scenario 2, television is set to level 5, where television is available to between 80 and 100 percent of the population, and protests for the past two months are boosted by two standard deviations above their means. Again, the corresponding changes are made in the appropriate interaction terms.

The results for the first scenario reveal that the level of protests increase by at least 100 percent when compared with the baseline. For example, the number of protests in France under baseline conditions is .979 and increases by +1.103 protests in scenario 1. (Note that the values in scenarios 1 and 2 are always measured against the baseline.) The most noticeable effect, however, occurs in sce-

[10]The United States adopted television at an exceptionally fast rate, reaching level 3 by 1956 and level 5, or 80–100 percent of the population, by 1958. As a result, the baseline in Table 3.3 for the United States is artificially low because it forces tv = 3 with corresponding changes made in the appropriate interaction terms.

[11]Using this time frame also has the advantage of consistently using the dummy variables concerning riots and timeriot that apply after 1963. Thus 1958–1962*riot and 1958–1962*timeriot are set to 0 for this analysis.

TABLE 3.3
Hypothesis 2, Using 1963–1982 Means

State	Mean prot/std. dv. prot/mean t	Baseline	Scenario 1	Scenario 2
United States	12.6/20.9/5	4.122	+4.321	+27.181
United Kingdom	3.0/ 8.7/4.8	1.566	+2.382	+8.954
France	1.1/ 2.1/4	.979	+1.049	+4.196
Germany	1.1/ 3.6/4.3	.707	+.745	+4.200
Italy	1.1/ 3.3/3.8	.683	+.785	+2.964

nario 2. The smallest expansion in protest activity from the baseline is 375 percent for Italy (a baseline value of .683 and an increase of +2.964 demonstrations) and the largest escalation in mass action is over 600 percent for the United States (a baseline of 4.122 that grows by +27.181 protests). The effects from scenario 2 are large, but so is the shock being considered. These outcomes are predicted to occur *only* under the special circumstances when there is a high level of protests—two standard deviations above the mean—for two consecutive months and the impact typically endures for one month.[12] The particularly large, nonlinear increase in protest activity under scenario 2, moreover, nicely fits our theoretical expectations. Only at the higher levels of protest activity and access to political information would we expect an issue to be placed on the national agenda and begin to attract the attention of large numbers of marginal joiners. Smaller spikes in mass action will entice disproportionately fewer observers because the story will fail to reach a level sufficient to prompt sustained coverage from the national or even regional media.

Hypothesis 3

The context in which an upsurge of protest activity takes place also determines how much attention an episode of mass action attracts and ultimately produces additional demonstrations. The marginal joiner who knows little about what is required to change the direction of public policy is more likely to pay attention and conclude that political opportunity is rapidly improving when a dramatic episode of mass action takes place after a period of no protest activity. Therefore, hypothesis 3 adds another condition to hypothesis 2: the longer the time since the last period of protest activity the greater the impact of a rapid escalation in peaceful demonstrations and widespread access to that information through television coverage.

Hypotheses 1 and 2 represent new empirical tests of how mass action spreads, but those predictions, particularly hypothesis 1, are consistent with explanations of mass conflict based on rational choice and political mobilization. Hypothesis 3 moves into new territory. Indeed, if there is a prediction from the existing litera-

---

[12]This analysis examines only short-term dynamics. It does not tell us what the long-run impacts of increasing the level of protests would be.

ture about the amount of time prior to an eruption of demonstrations, it would be that increasing the time without protest activity before an outbreak of protests will lower rather than increase the subsequent number of demonstrations. Protest episodes that are packed closely together, from this perspective, are a better indicator of improving political fortunes. The problem with this prediction is that it presupposes an average level of attentiveness to current politics and background knowledge about political change that we believe most citizens lack.

In Table 3.4, we examine the same baseline and scenarios as those employed in Table 3.3. The only change is that we increase timeprot$_3$ by one standard deviation from its mean in scenario 1 and by two standard deviations in scenario 2. Thus in scenario 1 we have an outbreak of protests that erupts after the following conditions are met: there is an increase of one standard deviation above the mean time between protests for that country, the outbreak remains one standard deviation above the mean level of past protests for two months, and is broadcast to a minimum of 60 percent of the population. Scenario 2 boosts past protests and timeprot$_3$ to two standard deviations above their mean and increases access to television to a minimum of 80 percent of a state's citizens. Corresponding changes are also made in the variables with which timeprot$_3$ interacts for both scenarios. By comparing the scenarios in Tables 3.3 and 3.4 we can identify the added impact of increasing the time between protests.

Because the United States has a short time between protests for this entire period (a mean of 1.004 months and a standard deviation of .064), the results indicate very little additional growth in the number of peaceful demonstrations beyond the level predicted for each scenario in Table 3.3. (The model estimates that there would be an additional 4.432 protests in scenario 1 and 27.181 in scenario 2 in Table 3.3 and an increase of 4.432 and 29.909 protests for scenarios 1 and 2, respectively, in Table 3.4.) Except for the United Kingdom, no other country shows a noteworthy response to scenario 1. Dramatic effects, however, emerge again in the second scenario. For countries other than the United States, with its low mean time between protests, increasing the amount of time between protests expands the number of protests by a minimum of 250 percent. For example, the predicted number of demonstrations for Italy in Table 3.3 under scenario 2 is +2.964 above the baseline. By increasing the time between protests by two standard deviations this grows to 7.443 above the baseline (see Table 3.4). The other states show even more impressive gains. Germany—the state with the largest and most variable mean times between protests among the high-protest states—leads the way, growing by +64.081 additional demonstrations above its baseline of 4.2 demonstrations. This unusual confluence of events—an outbreak of high protest activity broadcast to virtually the entire country after an extraordinarily long period of quiet—appears to evoke a correspondingly large reaction.

Hypothesis 4

Compared with the complexity of the other predictions, this hypothesis is straightforward. Large demonstrations in the surrounding region attract mass attention, increase the perception that opportunity for political gain is improving,

TABLE 3.4
Hypothesis 3, Using 1963–1982 Means

State	Mean timeprot (std. dv.)	Baseline	Scenario 1	Scenario 2
United States	1.004 (.064)	4.122	+4.432	+29.909
United Kingdom	1.7 (1.372)	1.566	+8.954	+22.096
France	3.013 (3.667)	.979	+1.103	+10.684
Germany	6.117 (12.492)	.707	+.850	+64.081
Italy	3.346 (3.799)	.683	+.699	+7.443

and lead to a higher incidence of demonstrations the following month. The measure of impact, 8 percent, for this variable found in Table 3.1, suggests that the effect of large variation in the number of regional protesters is modest. Table 3.5 confirms that expectation. The baseline sets all variables at their mean values for the 1963–1982 period; scenario 1 increases $regionprot_1$ by one standard deviation above its mean value, while scenario 2 bumps $regionprot_1$ by two standard deviations.

The overall impact of exposure to a two-standard-deviation spike in regional protest activity yields a maximum increase in the United States of +.875 protests, or fewer than one additional protest in the month following this upsurge in discord. Measured in proportionate terms this is only a 7.4 percent increase above the baseline for this country. For smaller states such as the United Kingdom and France, the absolute impact of regional protests is smaller, +.463 and +.244, respectively, but when compared with their baseline values, are proportionately larger than for the United States: 20 percent for both the United Kingdom and France. This result is intuitively reassuring because it suggests that the largest protest states "export" proportionately more mass discord than they "import."

Hypothesis 5

Our final proposition predicts that tactical unity declines as wider exposure to protest events attracts increasing numbers of marginal joiners. Mass commitment to employing nonviolent tactics could be expected to emerge in the early years of the American civil rights movement, 1958–1962, as newly trained, peaceful protesters actively disassociated themselves from those who use violence to exert

TABLE 3.5
Hypothesis 4, Using 1963–1982 Means

State	Mean regionprot (std.dv.)	Baseline	Scenario 1	Scenario 2
United States	31,568 (59,272)	11.755	+.421	+.857
United Kingdom	68,066 (155,391)	2.280	+.221	+.463
France	73,041 (153,988)	1.121	+.117	+.244
Germany	74,380 (155,045)	.855	+.082	+.172
Italy	74,093 (156,344)	.780	+.076	+.214

political pressure. Thus as the number of riots in any given month grew during this period, fewer peaceful demonstrations in the following month could be anticipated. Nonviolent protests are also predicted to increase with each additional month after an episode of mass violence. As the ranks of peaceful protesters rapidly expands with more marginal joiners after 1962, we expect that this response to collective violence will weaken, if not disappear.

In Table 3.1, we find support for a negative reaction to rioting during the 1958–1962 period. The explanatory variable, $1958–1962*riot_1$, is statistically significant with a negative sign. Our measure of the response of peaceful demonstrators to rioting after this period, $1963–1982*riot_1$, shows the predicted change: the coefficient is still negative, but it is smaller and no longer statistically significant.

The results in Table 3.6a provide further confirmation. Using the mean values for the 1950–1970 period—a time that encompasses the hypothesized change—we estimated a baseline in which all of the dummy variables concerning $riot_1$ and $timeriot_2$ were set to equal 0. In scenario 1, we estimate the impact of rioting at the mean level and a two-standard-deviation increase above the mean for each country for the 1958–1962 period (this impact appears in the parentheses under scenario 1). The average number of riots produces a substantial reduction in peaceful protests in the United States of −.855 or about 30 percent of the baseline of 2.697 protests, and a more moderate response elsewhere. Germany, for example, is typical, declining by 7 percent or −.04 protests from a base of .581. A much higher level of rioting, at two standard deviations above the mean, lowers the incidence of peaceful demonstrations by 30 percent or more in Western Europe and evokes a dramatic reduction in protest activity in the United States of close to 100 percent (a decline of −2.443 protests from a base of 2.697). By comparison, the reaction to the *same* level of rioting during 1963–1982 yields a considerably weaker response. In scenario 2, a month of rioting two standard deviations above the mean in the United States lowers peaceful demonstrations by −.864, or essentially the same response as the *mean* level of rioting produced in 1958–1962 of −.855, a comparison that holds for all other states listed in Table 3.6a.

The level of peaceful protests should also increase with each additional month since the last episode of collective violence, particularly during the time in which we believe tactical unity to be high. We see in Table 3.1 that there are positive and statistically significant coefficients for the explanatory variables measuring the response to timeriot for both periods, 1958 to 1962 and 1963 to 1982. To determine which interval produces a stronger reaction, Table 3.6b lays out scenarios that are similar to those in Table 3.6a. They measure the impact of the mean value and two standard deviations above the mean for the time since the last riot for each period. Scenario 1 reveals that for 1958–1962 the response is stronger than the outcomes displayed in scenario 2 for 1963–1982. Thus the mean time since a riot for the United States produces +.192 protests in 1958–1962 but falls to +.138 protests after 1963, a reduced impact of +.054 demonstrations, or a little more than 25 percent. Other states such as France drop as much as 48 percent in their responsiveness to the mean value of timeriot, from +.305 protests in 1958–1962 to +.158 protests after 1963.

TABLE 3.6A
Hypothesis 5a, Using 1950–1970 Means

State	Mean (std. dv.) riot	Baseline	Scenario 1	Scenario 2
United States	3.008 (7.820)	2.697	−.855 (−2.443)	−.163 (−.864)
United Kingdom	.614 (1.549)	.755	−.057 (−.284)	−.006 (−.056)
France	.514 (1.490)	.686	−.043 (−.245)	−.007 (−.048)
Germany	.490 (1.108)	.581	−.040 (−.194)	−.007 (−.036)
Italy	.988 (2.460)	.450	−.053 (−.237)	−.009 (−.052)

TABLE 3.6B
Hypothesis 5, Using 1950–1970 Means

State	Mean (std. dv.) timeriot	Baseline	Scenario 1	Scenario 2
United States	2.684 (3.266)	2.697	+.192 (+.690)	+.138 (+.484)
United Kingdom	9.824 (13.850)	.755	+.216 (+1.223)	+.151 (+.762)
France	11.10 (14.612)	.686	+.305 (+1.248)	+.158 (+.768)
Germany	5.392 (5.701)	.669	+.100 (+.361)	+.073 (+.246)
Italy	3.460 (3.172)	.450	+.042 (+.129)	+.030 (+.090)

CONCLUSION

Explanations of mass conflict increasingly identify variations in political opportunity as an important determinant of mass conflict. Findings from public opinion research suggest that there are large differences in the ability of leaders and followers to judge when and how a group should employ unconventional methods of political pressure. We have argued that current accounts offer an incomplete explanation of how credible information about timing and tactics diffuses from a group's strategist to the people who join a mass movement in its period of rapid expansion. Understanding the *cognitive process* by which that information spreads—or not—is significant because the spread of information can shape the rate of diffusion and the degree of tactical unity that emerges across different political actors, and can directly influence success or failure.

Using concepts from cognitive psychology, we have argued that marginal joiners who have little background knowledge about politics focus on the immediate history of their group's protest activity—a period of a few weeks or months—to evaluate the dynamics of political opportunity. In the early stages of a protest movement, we share the expectations of theories of rational choice and political mobilization that innovative new tactics spread to groups that face conditions for which these new techniques have proven efficacious. Lowering the costs of acquiring timely information on protest events should also widen the audience and extend periods of intense protest activity. As support for a particular mass action builds, however, our theoretical approach identifies predictions that diverge from the conventional wisdom. More time between outbreaks of mass conflict, rather than less, attracts greater attention and response to new episodes of mass action from marginal joiners. As there is a rapid expansion, with new recruits who have little political expertise, tactical unity inevitably declines and the pace of protest varies, in part, with the protest activities of citizens in neighboring states. Using data from Western Europe, Canada, and the United States from 1950–1982, we found support for the hypotheses whereby we agree with theories of rational choice and political mobilization about the diffusion of mass conflict. Our investigation also provides empirical evidence for our claims concerning how the cognitive process of diffusion diverge from the expectations of these theoretical approaches.

APPENDIX

TABLE A3.1
Means and Standard Deviations for Model Variables for Seventeen States, 1950–1982

Variable	Mean	Standard Deviation
prot	.861	5.135
GDP/capita$_1$	6307	2263
ln(pop$_1$)	9.105	1.744
ln(prot$_1$)	−.370	.788
ln(prot$_2$)	−.370	.788
ln(prot$_3$)	−.370	.787
legthres$_1$	12.604	12.499
ethnofrac$_1$*legthres$_1$	4.412	7.292
ethnofrac$_1$*legthres$_1$*tv$_1$	12.675	32.220
1960*ethnofrac$_1$*legthres$_1$*tv$_1$	14.072	31.297
tv$_1$	3.033	1.714
ln(prot$_1$)*ln(prot$_2$)	.538	1.212
ln(prot$_1$)*ln(prot$_2$)*tv$_1$	1.946	6.018
timeprot$_3$	35.090	52.579
ln(prot$_1$)*ln(prot$_2$)*timeprot$_3$	15.695	25.731
ln(prot$_1$)*ln(prot$_2$)*tv$_1$*timeprot$_3$	34.472	66.888
regionprot$_1$	59591	147316
riot$_1$	.316	1.955
1958–1962*riot$_1$	.051	.577
1963–1982*riot$_1$	.206	1.799
timeriot$_2$	67.021	88.181
1958–1962*timeriot$_2$	9.078	31.709
1963–1982*timeriot$_2$	50.086	90.4

Transnational Ethnic Ties and Foreign Policy

WILL H. MOORE AND DAVID R. DAVIS

CONSIDER the following stylized account of events in northern Zaire in the fall of 1996.[1] Zairean rebels of Tutsi heritage launched military attacks with the avowed goal of toppling Mobutu Sese Seko's regime. This rebellion followed a shift from Hutu to Tutsi control of the Rwandan state, which borders Zaire to the north. One consequence of the Tutsi rebellion in northern Zaire was strained relations between Rwanda and Zaire: conflict short of war. These events provide an example of what we refer to in this study as an "ethnic alliance," and provide a concrete example of the phenomenon explored here: the extent to which shared ethnic ties between a group that controls a state and kin who are disadvantaged in a neighboring state lead to international tension between the two states.

The Zairean case is but one example of ethnic conflict behavior in the 1990s, and these events have produced an upsurge in interest among international relations scholars, policy makers, and pundits. Concern over ethnic conflict might be driven by a number of motivations: first, a partisan interest in the winners and losers; second, a humanitarian interest in stopping the suffering and killing; and/or third, a security-driven interest in global peace. The first motivation is generally held by politicians and pundits with axes to grind whereas scholars typically hold either the second or third motivation, or a mix of both. Like the others in this volume, this chapter is motivated by the third interest.

Several scholars have sought to contribute to our understanding of conflict resolution, peacekeeping, and policy prescriptions for third parties who seek to intervene (Halpern 1964; Modelski 1964; Luard 1972; Suhrke and Noble 1977;

Note: Earlier versions of this paper have been presented at the International Spread and Management of Ethnic Conflict Workshop and the 1995 annual meetings of the International Studies Association and American Political Science Association. The authors would like to thank David Carment, Ted Robert Gurr, Keith Jaggers, Pat James, David Lake, Brett Ashley Leeds, Doug Lemke, and Suzanne Werner for comments and suggestions on this project. This project was supported in part by a grant from the National Science Foundation (SBR-9423762). Moore's contribution was also supported in part by the Institute on Global Conflict and Cooperation and the Academic Senate of the University of California, Riverside. Davis's contribution to this effort was supported in part by the University Research Committee, Emory University. The order of the authors' names was determined by a coin toss.

[1] We would like to thank David Pion-Berlin for suggesting that these events illustrate our argument.

Touval and Zartman 1989; Ryan 1990; Stedman 1991; Licklider 1993; McGarry and O'Leary 1993b; Carment and James 1997). Yet, as Lake and Rothchild note in the introductory chapter, it is difficult to find work that theoretically specifies the linkage between ethnic conflict and global peace. Further, although it is possible to find assertions that such a linkage exists, there is little systematic, empirical work that demonstrates the existence of such a linkage. This paper addresses those shortcomings.

What is the conventional wisdom regarding the escalation of ethnic conflict (that is, the relationship between domestic ethnic conflict and international conflict behavior)? Until recently, little has been said beyond "ethnicity matters." Let us examine the state of the literature. Maynes (1993) criticizes the Clinton administration's efforts to employ a collective security solution to contain ethnic conflict. His argument is motivated by the contention that ethnic conflict must be contained because "animosity among ethnic groups is beginning to rival the spread of nuclear weapons as the most serious threat to peace that the world faces" (5). This assertion rests on the claim that an ethnic conflict between Russia and the Baltic states would dim "many of the hopes for a new, more cooperative world" (5). Beyond that, Maynes does not explain this assertion. Perhaps he, like Moynihan (1993), is drawing "lessons" from the past. Moynihan approvingly cites Halévy (1930) and Schmitt (1958), who contend that World War I was the outcome of conflict between minorities and states over the right to self-determination. He then asserts: "The ethnic perspective can lay claim to some predictive power. Only some. But enough to warrant more respect than it has perhaps received" (Moynihan 1993, 32). Moynihan is not speaking solely about international relations, but it is clear that he believes that ethnicity ought to be considered as an important variable when discussing international relations and global order and peace. Yet he, like Maynes, fails to specify for us precisely what linkage exists between ethnic conflict and foreign policy behavior. Surely, there is more that we can say than "1914!"

In fact, Midlarsky (1992, 173) sketches for us "an influence of communal violence on the probability of systemic war" (that is, war that leads to the breakdown of the international system). He embeds his analysis in his (1988) model of systemic war in which resource inequality triggers alliance formation, and memory of past conflicts can then generate an overlap in conflict domains or structures. He contends that this is typically followed by an actual or perceived change in the balance of power, which leads to systemic war. What is the impact of communal conflict on this sequence? Midlarsky contends that the most likely entry points are the distribution of resources—triggering resource inequality—or the balance of power. Presumably, some sort of balance or power image undergirds the arguments made by Maynes and Moynihan. Hence, Midlarsky sketches a theoretical argument that enables one to identify a linkage between ethnic conflict and international conflict: it directly or indirectly upsets the balance of power and can lead to systemic war. That said, we must note that Midlarsky (1988) identifies only eight systemic wars between 500 B.C. and the present. Thus, although these linkages clearly can have an enormous impact, they apparently do not do so frequently. It is worth asking whether these linkages exist not only in the case of systemic wars or crises but also in run-of-the-mill foreign policy behavior.

Carment and James (1995, 1997) and Brecher and Wilkenfeld (1995, 1997) have also studied the impact of ethnicity on international crises. Carment and James (1995) begin by rejecting the distinction that is frequently made between affective and utilitarian models of ethnic conflict in favor of a rational choice synthesis of the two. They then propose a series of hypotheses suggesting that crises with an irredentist dimension will be more violent and drawn out. They use the International Crisis Behavior (ICB) data to demonstrate that crises with an irredentist dimension display higher levels of perceived threat, more conflictual crisis management techniques, and greater violence. In a different study, Carment and James (1997) develop a two-level game theory argument about the linkages between ethnic national mobilization and international crisis behavior. They hypothesize that states that are ethnically homogeneous and have low constraints are most likely to be involved in interstate conflict, and those that are ethnically heterogeneous and highly constrained will be the least likely to be involved in interstate conflict, with the others filling out the continuum. They further hypothesize that the same rankings will be observed across the types of states with respect to the extent to which the conflicts become protracted, and the opposite rank order will be observed with respect to the effects of ethnic affinities and cleavages on the severity of the violence that results from the crisis. They perform a data analysis using the ICB data, and find support for the second and third hypotheses, but not the first.

Following work by Carment (1993; Carment and James 1995), Brecher and Wilkenfeld (1995, 1997) engage in more ad hoc hypothesis-generating exercises. They simply propose that crises that have ethnic dimensions are likely to be distinct from those that do not. More specifically, ethnic crises are more likely to: have more violent triggers; involve higher perceived threats to basic values; induce a resort to violence and to higher levels of violence; involve the use of violence as the primary means; induce political rather than military activity by major powers; attract greater participation by global organizations; have a higher incidence of stalemate/compromise outcomes; and to be terminated by less formal agreements. Although the data analysis—also using the International Crisis Behavior data—does not provide unequivocal and strong support for each of their hypotheses, most receive some support, and the general pattern that emerges is that interstate crises with an ethnic dimension do differ from those without one.

Marshall (1993) argues that an unnecessary and counterproductive dichotomy between interstate and intrastate conflict has been constructed, a situation that needs rectification. He develops a macrosociological theory of social conflict that seeks to explain communal conflict and systemic war as driven by a single process. Preliminary statistical analyses (1997) offer support for the hypotheses derived from his theory. Without either presenting or critiquing his work, we wish to make note of another point he makes during his critique of extant construction of conflict typologies: wars are rare events. Further, so are crises. However, states interact with one another with high frequency. Whereas studies like those by Midlarsky, Carment and James, and Brecher and Wilkenfeld limit their analyses to events like systemic wars or crises, we wish to explore whether ethnicity influences conflict and cooperation more generally. That is, we suspect that if ethnicity matters at all—and it appears to—it ought to matter all the time across the entire range of foreign policy behavior, not only during crises and war.

In fact, Davis, Jaggers, and Moore (1997) specify a statistical model that purports to account for variance in conflictual behavior short of war as well as war itself. In that study the dependent variable includes the entire range of cooperative and conflictual foreign policy behavior as measured by the Conflict and Peace Databank (COPDAB) (Azar 1980). However, rather than develop a theoretical argument, that paper presents some ad hoc hypotheses that are developed by assuming that a linkage exists, and asks what it might look like. The only theoretical contention advanced in the study is that the results undermine the realist project. The current project addresses that shortcoming by developing an argument that produces a hypothesis that a linkage exists and then tests it (along with some secondary hypotheses) using an expanded spatial domain, controlling for democracy.

Preliminary studies of international conflict behavior suggest that ethnicity matters: we find support for Moynihan's contention that ethnicity has some explanatory utility. In this paper we seek to develop an argument, albeit a very simple one, to explain why it does. We contend that ethnicity is important because ethnic ties among peoples across state borders in the international system act as unstated alliances among those people. The term *alliance,* in this case, refers to "a similarity or relationship in character, structure, etc.; affinity"[2] rather than the more traditional meaning of the term in international relations. Transnational ethnic ties may represent an opportunity for elites in many societies to mobilize political support by using ethnic appeals to vilify a rival state for its treatment of ethnic brethren (Horowitz 1985, 291). Further, the elites of the ethnic minority in the second state have an interest in forging a relationship with the first state, particularly if geography makes an irredentist option feasible. In this manner, we contend that similar ethnic groups distributed across different states will be likely to form what are, in effect, alliances. These ethnic alliances should behave much as alliances between states have been hypothesized to behave in international relations. These hypotheses are developed more fully below.

ARGUMENT AND HYPOTHESES

In our earlier study (Davis, Jaggers, and Moore 1997) we found support for the argument that there is a connection between the dyadic conflict level between two neighboring states and the presence of a disadvantaged ethnic minority in one state when members of that same minority group are in power in the other. How can we explain that linkage? Some would contend that ethnic affinity or a

[2] *Webster's New Universal Unabridged Dictionary,*

similar "affective" explanation would suffice. We pursue an alternative possibility. As noted above, we contend that it is useful to conceptualize ethnic linkages among people across state boundaries as functionally equivalent to alliances between two states. Siverson and Starr (1991) identify alliances as a major factor in the diffusion of war. They contend that "alliances can be seen as important components of the incentive structures available for states" (24). From there they argue that "borders and alliances create the salience and/or the ease of interaction that significantly increases the probability that states will join ongoing wars" (93). That is, even though doing so involves putting one's soldiers in battle, states often honor their commitments to allies and join wars: war diffuses through the international system as a consequence of alliances.

We are not interested in the diffusion of international conflict per se; rather we are interested in the escalation of ethnic conflict to international conflict. If alliances affect decision making, interactions, and the size of international wars, what does conceptualizing ethnicity as an alliance purchase? Siverson and Starr develop their argument in a geopolitical context that takes into consideration similar policy preferences, and suggest that states form alliances because they share similar geopolitical goals. We contend that different members of the same minority group will—rightly or wrongly—assume that their kin share similar policy preferences. We are not simply arguing that some kind of ethnic "affinity" leads to alliance-like bonds between ethnically homogeneous elites. Rather, we are contending that they expect to share policy preferences, and that they therefore expect to share similar geopolitical preferences. Hence we do not measure the presence or absence of such shared preferences in our sample. Instead, we assume that it exists and tease out the implications of that assumption for dyadic conflict behavior in the international system. Further, we note parenthetically that a threat to kin across a border can aid state building by providing a state with an issue around which to mobilize popular ethnic support for the regime. These arguments lead us to suggest the following stylized set of interactions:

> t: An ethnic group experiences increasing persecution from State B (where it does not have access to power), or mobilizes and challenges State B's authority/sovereignty, which leads State B to countermobilize against the ethnic group.
>
> t+1: If members of the ethnic group share power or are dominant in State A and State B falls within the Politically Relevant International Environment (PRIE; Maoz 1997) of State A, then State A will take an interest in the relations between State B and the ethnic group, and will respond to the situation by increasing its hostility toward State B.

In other words, conflict between a state and an ethnic group will escalate to the international level when other elite members of that same ethnic group play a role in policy making in another state and that state finds the first state to be politically relevant, given its resource constraints.

This stylized scenario leads us to posit the following hypotheses, which we divide into three categories: attributes, discrimination/grievances, and mobilization.

Attributes

Dyads (that is, a pair of states) with a transnational ethnic tie, in which members of the ethnic group are disenfranchised in one of the states, will produce higher levels of conflict behavior than other dyads. That is, we expect the following attribute to have a statistically significant impact on dyadic conflict behavior: when both states contain group members from the same ethnic group, but the group is incorporated into the power structure in only one of the two states.

H1: The level of conflict between two states will be higher if both states contain group members from the same ethnic group, and one of the co-ethnics is politically privileged in its society, but its brethren in the other state are not.

Discrimination/Grievances

Because they provide ethnic kin in a rival state a stronger case upon which to mobilize ethnic supporters, and because mobilization contributes to the state building project when the kin without access to state power are victims of discrimination, the conflict escalation effect of transnational ethnic ties will be intensified.

H2: High levels of discrimination against the ethnic kin in state B or the perception by State A that such grievances exist will lead to higher levels of dyadic conflict.

Mobilization

High levels of ethnic mobilization in State B provide allied elites in state A with better opportunities to realize the goal of similar policies across the two states. We further contend that state A's expectation that state B (that is, the state with the disenfranchised group) will engage in scapegoating behavior in an effort to mobilize its supporters against both the dyadic partner and the ethnic group will be likely to contribute to conflict behavior (i.e., state B will blame state A for meddling in state B's internal affairs and stirring up trouble).

H3: High levels of ethnic mobilization in state B will be associated with high levels of dyadic conflict.

RESEARCH APPROACH, MODEL DEVELOPMENT, AND OPERATIONALIZATION

In an attempt to understand the impact of ethnicity on international relations, we examine the influence of ethnic ties on the behavior of each state in the international system in 1977–1978 in dyadic interactions with each member of the state's PRIE (Maoz 1997). Through the use of the COPDAB (Azar 1980) events dataset, we employ a broad conceptualization of our dependent variable *international interactions* and include measures of the complete range of state interactions. We examine three components of international interactions. *Conflict* includes events ranging from minor verbal displays of discord to threats, to the imposition of political and economic sanctions, and full scale militarized hostilities. *Cooperation* includes events ranging from meetings of officials and verbal statements of support, to military and economic agreements, establishing joint military commands, and jointly fighting a war. Cooperation is neither the absence nor the opposite of conflict but a separate indicator that measures a different type of state behavior. Both of these components are also incorporated in the broader measure of *net interactions*, which represents the overall flow of relations from a state to its dyadic partner.

In the COPDAB dataset, events are coded on a fifteen-point scale with categories one through seven measuring cooperation and nine through fifteen measuring conflict. In order to create indices of cooperation, we assign weights to cooperative events according to their intensity and then sum the weighted values across a temporal unit — in this case the year — to create aggregate scores (see Azar and Sloan 1975 for a discussion of the intensity weights). This aggregate score is then divided by the number of events to create a measure of the average level of cooperation sent by an actor to its dyadic partner in a given year. Indices of conflict are created in the same manner for events in COPDAB categories nine through fifteen. Net interactions is a measure of the difference between the average level of cooperation and the average level of conflict. Positive values indicate that the relationship is generally cooperative; negative values indicate a conflictual relationship.

Our primary independent variables measure three facets of ethnicity: *ethnic alliance, minority mobilization,* and *minority discrimination/grievances.* An ethnic alliance is said to exist in cases where an advantaged minority lives in one state and members of the same minority group are at risk in the other state; an advantaged minority is a group that has access to the existing power structure. Minority mobilization is a measure of the extent of political organization and activity by the minority in the target state. Minority discrimination/grievances is a measure of the extent of discrimination of the minority group in the target state. Data measuring each of these variables was taken from Phase I of Gurr's (1993) *Minorities at Risk* dataset. The unit of analysis in the Gurr dataset is the minority group. The authors created the measure of ethnic alliance by "translating" Gurr's measures of the existence and status of the minority group into the PRIE dyads. To aggregate the data from the group level to the dyadic level for grievances and discrimination, we aggregated both measures at the level of the state by taking the highest group score on each variable. The amount of violent and nonviolent protest of the minority group during the 1975–1979 time period was summed into a measure of total protest mobilization.

Our study examines the interactions of each state in the international system with all other states within its PRIE in 1977–1978. Unfortunately, 1977–1978 is the last time period that COPDAB covers. PRIE was developed by Maoz and "represents the set of political units whose structure, behavior and policies have a direct impact on the focal state's political and strategic calculus" (1997). A state's PRIE contains all other states with which it is geographically contiguous and all major and regional powers that are capable of interacting militarily with the focal state. Our unit of analysis is state behavior toward a PRIE dyadic partner in

1977–1978. Employing the PRIE method of case selection allows us to avoid inflating our sample with implausible pairs. However, we have also coded contiguity for each state because of the salience of transnational movements of people across borders.

Davis, Jaggers, and Moore (1997) show that the ethnic composition of states has an impact on dyadic conflict behavior, but their analysis fails to control for potentially relevant variables, and their findings may thus be spurious. To address that shortcoming, we construct a mutlivariate statistical model that enables us to control for the influence of potentially confounding factors, and we include a number of important control variables that influence international interactions. In particular, we find substantial evidence in the scholarly literature which suggests that strategies of reciprocity, joint democracy (that is, a dyad composed of two democratic states), the level of state development, economic growth, and power capabilities have a strong impact on dyadic foreign policy behavior. As a result, we include measures of these factors in our model.

Recent work on international cooperation and conflict—particularly among rival states — has focused on reciprocity (Ward 1982; Dixon 1986; Goldstein and Freeman 1990; Rajmaira and Ward 1990; Goldstein 1991; Goldstein and Freeman 1991; Ward and Rajmaira 1992. Results indicate that states tend to respond to the actions of others in kind. We expect that the behavior received by an actor from its dyadic partner will influence the state's behavior toward its counterpart; for all types of activities a strong positive relationship should exist between behavior received and behavior sent. Consequently we include a measure of the behavior of the target state toward the actor as an explanatory variable in each equation.

We adopt the same operationalization of regime type employed by Maoz and Russett (1993) for the measure of democracy. Maoz and Russett (1993) develop their indicator of regime type from the Polity II dataset (Gurr, Jaggers, and Moore 1989) by subtracting a state's autocracy score from its democracy score and multiplying this quantity by the state's power concentration score. From this continuous measure, we create a dummy variable representing joint democracy for all dyads in which both states have regime type scores greater than thirty.

It has been argued that more developed states behave differently toward other actors in the international system. Cooperation, for instance, may be heavily influenced by the wealth of a state actor. Wealthy states are generally more extensively integrated into the international system. They have numerous transnational ties and involvements. They also tend to be more satisfied with the system (see for instance Organski and Kugler 1980; Lemke 1995). We generally expect more developed actors to exhibit more cooperative international behavior. A second, related argument posits that economic well-being has an important influence on the foreign policy behavior of states. Russett (1990) posits that states experiencing economic decline are far more likely to engage in foreign policy belligerence. Therefore, we include measures of the level of development and economic growth in our model. Data measuring the level of development were collected from the United States Arms Control and Disarmament Agency (various years). For each state we calculate national income per capita as a percentage of the U.S. per capita national income for each year. States with per capita incomes of at least 30 per cent of the U.S. per capita income in the given year are coded as developed. Data measuring the growth rate of GNP were collected from the International Monetary Fund's *International financial statistics* (various years).

Another potentially influential factor in determining the character of certain dyadic interactions are the relative capabilities of the states involved. We, like Bremer (1993), control for the difference between the capabilities of the actor and the capabilities of the target. Many hypothesize that particular power distributions are violence prone (for a detailed discussion of the debate see Sullivan 1990; Waltz 1979; and Organski and Kugler 1980). The value of the capabilities score for each state was constructed in accordance with Bremer (1993) and reflects the percentage of the total systemic capabilities controlled by each state in the given year.

Because we want to be able to determine whether the hypothesized relationships hold for aggregate foreign policy behavior, conflictual foreign policy behavior, and cooperative foreign policy behavior, or only for a subset of the three, we estimated the parameters for each of the following three equations:

$$NS = a + b_1{}^*NR + b_2{}^*EA + b_3{}^*MG + b_4{}^*MM + b_5{}^*DD + b_6{}^*EG + b_7{}^*LD + b_8{}^*C + b_9{}^*PD + e \quad [1]$$
$$CNS = a + b_1{}^*CNR + b_2{}^*EA + b_3{}^*MG + b_4{}^*MM + b_5{}^*DD + b_6{}^*EG + b_7{}^*LD + b_8{}^*C + b_9{}^*PD + e \quad [2]$$
$$CPS = a + b_1{}^*CPR + b_2{}^*EA + b_3{}^*MG + b_4{}^*MM + b_5{}^*DD + b_6{}^*EG + b_7{}^*LD + b_8{}^*C + b_9{}^*PD + e \quad [3]$$

Where:
NS = Net behavior sent by the actor to the other member of the dyad
NR = Net behavior received by the actor from the other member of the dyad
CNS = Conflict sent by the actor to the other member of the dyad
CNR = Conflict received by the actor from the other member of the dyad
CPS = Cooperation sent by the actor to the other member of the dyad
CPR = Cooperation received by the actor from the other member of the dyad
EA = Ethnic alliance
MG = Minority grievances
MM = Minority mobilization
DD = Joint democracy dummy
EG = Economic growth
C   = Contiguity
LD = Level of development
PD = Power differential between actor and target

Below we present the results of the estimation of equations 1 through 3 in Tables 4.1 through 4.3, respectively. The same set of independent variables are included in each equation. All three equations were estimated using an ordinary least squares technique. We tested for collinearity, heteroskedasticity, and autocorrelation to ensure that the assumptions of the ordinary least squares model were met. Because of the volume of output from the auxiliary R^2 tests for collinearity and Goldfeld-Quandt tests for heteroskedasticity, we merely report that no auxiliary R^2 value exceeded .35, and the Goldfeld-Quandt F-statistics for each independent variable were insignificant, indicating variances were homoskedastic. The Durbin-Watson statistics for autocorrelation are reported in each table. All test statistics indicate that the OLS estimator is appropriate.

Results

The results from the regression analyses are presented in Tables 4.1 through 4.3. Regression analysis enables one to determine the impact of each variable on the dyadic foreign policy of what might be described as a typical dyad. The major objectives of our regression analyses are first to determine whether the given variable has a statistically significant impact on dyadic foreign policy behavior (that is, whether we can reject the hypothesis that the variable does not affect dyadic foreign policy behavior), and second, when the variable is found to have a statistically significant impact, to determine the direction of the impact (that is, whether positive changes in the variables increase or decrease the amount of dyadic foreign policy behavior). To reiterate our hypotheses about the impact of ethnic alliances and the status of minorities on international interactions, we expect that the existence of an ethnic alliance will be positively related to the occurrence of conflict and negatively related to net interactions and cooperation. We also expect that if the minority group is mobilized or discriminated against, the parameters measuring these two facets of the status of the minority group will also be positively related to conflict and negatively related to net interactions and cooperation.

The results in Table 4.1 support the contention that dyads with shared ethnic groups experience less cooperative overall relationships: the parameter for ethnic alliances is statistically significant at the .01 level and exhibits the expected negative sign. However, the parameters for mobilization and discrimination of the minority group are not statistically significant, indicating that the treatment of the minority group has little impact on overall relations. Two control variables are significant—net interactions received from the target state and joint democracy— indicating that relationships are reciprocal and that democratic dyads exhibit significantly more cooperative relations than other dyads. The overall fit of the equation is reasonable, with R^2 equal to .36.

When we separate foreign policy behavior and examine only cooperation (see Table 4.2), the ethnic alliance parameter is in the expected direction, but is not statistically significant. Hence, although ethnic alliances affect overall relations, they do not have a perceptible impact on cooperation. Neither of the minority status variables is significant either, indicating that the manner in which the minority group is treated has little impact on the levels of cooperation within the dyad. Two control variables are significant—cooperation received and contiguity, indicating that bordering states cooperate more and that reciprocity is a strong norm. Thus, although we find support for our three hypotheses when we examined net foreign policy behavior, when we disaggregate foreign policy behavior and exam-

TABLE 4.1
Ethnic Alliances and Net Interactions

Dependent Variable	Independent Variable	Estimated Parameter	Standard Error
Net interactions sent	Net interactions received	0.570[a]	0.022
	Ethnic alliance	−3.607[a]	1.089
	Minority grievances	0.032	0.049
	Minority mobilization	−0.208	0.119
	Democratic dyad	2.004[b]	0.081
	Economic growth	0.088	0.050
	Level of development	0.704	0.735
	Contiguity	1.014	0.570
	Power differential	0.005	0.004
	(constant)	1.117	0.583

[a] $p < .01$; [b] $p < .05$; Adj. $R^2 = .36$; N = 1,328

ine only cooperative activity, we fail to find support for the hypotheses. The implication is that although the ethnic composition of the states that compose a dyad influences their overall foreign policy behavior, it has no impact on cooperative foreign policy behavior.

Table 4.3 presents the results of the estimation of equation 3. These results provide additional support for the contention that the ethnic attributes of dyads influence patterns of conflict. The parameter for ethnic alliance is significant at the .01 level and indicates that states with shared ethnic groups exhibit considerably more conflict than other states (that is, the sign is positive, as expected). Further, the parameter for minority mobilization is also significant and positive, indicating that if the minority group is mobilized in pursuit of political ends, the relationship between the two states is considerably more conflictual. Three control variables are significant. The positive parameter for conflict received once again indicates support for the arguments about the reciprocal nature of interna-

TABLE 4.2
Ethnic Alliances and Cooperation

Dependent Variable	Independent Variable	Estimated Parameter	Standard Error
Cooperation sent	Cooperation received	0.685[a]	0.001
	Ethnic alliance	−0.047	0.719
	Minority grievances	−0.023	0.032
	Minority mobilization	−0.509	0.708
	Democratic dyad	0.956	0.534
	Economic growth	0.001	0.001
	Level of development	0.557	0.487
	Contiguity	1.309[a]	0.384
	Power differential	0.005	0.004
	(constant)	1.768[a]	0.396

[a] $p < .01$; Adj. $R^2 = .52$; N = 1,328

TABLE 4.3
Ethnic Alliances and Conflict

Dependent Variable	Independent Variable	Estimated Parameter	Standard Error
Cooperation sent	Cooperation received	0.475 [a]	0.002
	Ethnic alliance	2.993[a]	1.852
	Minority grievances	−0.053	0.039
	Minority mobilization	0.296 [a]	0.094
	Democratic dyad	−0.819	0.630
	Economic growth	−0.962 [b]	0.039
	Level of development	0.147	0.575
	Contiguity	0.949[b]	0.447
	Power differential	−0.002	0.003
	(constant)	1.438[a]	0.453

[a] $p < .01$; [b] $p < .05$; Adj. $R^2 = .25$; N = 1,328

tional relations. The parameter measuring the impact of economic growth is also significant. The sign of this parameter indicates that states experiencing low or negative levels of economic growth are more likely to be involved in conflictual relationships. This finding supports the contention of Russett (1990). Finally, contiguity has a significant impact on conflict, supporting the findings of Bremer (1993) among others.

Taken as a group, what do these results indicate? First, we find support for two of the three hypotheses. Ethnic alliances lead to greater dyadic hostility, especially when the disadvantaged group is politically mobilized. On the other hand, we fail to find support for our second hypothesis, which suggests that the extent to which the disadvantaged group experiences relative deprivation increases dyadic tensions. Second, we demonstrate that although cooperative activity is not affected by ethnic alliances, conflictual behavior is higher in dyads with ethnic alliances. Finally, and most importantly, we demonstrate that these relationships hold when theoretically important control variables are included in the analyses: the impact of ethnic alliances is not spurious.

CONCLUSIONS

By way of conclusion we wish to consider the implications for the major theoretical approaches in international relations of our findings that the ethnic composition of states has an impact upon foreign policy behavior. Much of the theorizing to date in international relations has concentrated, for good reason, on the causes of war. In addition, the literature has devoted considerable attention to the behavior of the so-called "great powers" and the occurrence of war among them. Although the argument made by scholars that war among the major powers has determined the structure of the international system may be valid (for a discussion of the importance of this issue see Rasler and Thompson 1994; Gilpin 1981; Kennedy 1988; or Organski 1968), this has had the unintended consequence of leaving international relations theory with a relatively limited conceptual framework for addressing the relationship between ethnicity and international behavior. Although the two schools of thought, realism and liberalism, that have emerged as the dominant theories for explaining international relations do not explicitly address the influence of ethnicity on international conflict, it is possible to consider implicit linkages from within their respective frameworks.

Realism

The traditional realist paradigm (see Morgenthau 1948) and its more systematic neorealist version (as developed by Waltz 1959, 1979) argues that behavior (specifically making war) in the international environment is primarily driven by the structure of the system. Unitary states are the principal actors, and they exist in an international system characterized by anarchy. There is little difference between states: they are all driven by the same goal—self-preservation—the maintenance of which is accomplished by developing a preponderance of power over others or, at a minimum, preventing other states from gaining a preponderance of power. There are two primary means for achieving this goal—military buildups and alliance formation. However, an individual state's attempts at increasing its security through arms buildups or the forging of new alliances are likely to be perceived as threatening by its neighbors. As a result, all states face security dilemmas: if they increase their capabilities in order to improve their security situation, other states are likely to feel threatened and do the same.

Because security concerns dominate the hierarchy of interests of all states, other types of interactions among states, including economic, social, environmental, and cultural ties, are far less important. Further, cooperation is simply a tool states use to pursue lesser interests or to support self-preservation via the maintenance of economic competitiveness. Within this perspective, sub-systemic factors are deemed to be far less important than systemic constraints in the drive for national security. Particular characteristics or attributes of states, such as ethnic divisions, should have little impact on the behavior of states unless they influence self-preservation.

Although realist scholars are generally silent on the issue of ethnicity, the following linkage between ethnicity and international conflict patterns is implied by the realist perspective: since one tool for improving a state's security situation is to increase its relative capabilities, ethnic divisions within other states could provide states with opportunities to weaken potential rivals by exploiting their ethnic vulnerabilities. One could further argue that an ethnic minority that is mobilized and actively pursuing greater autonomy or separatist goals in a rival state represents a vulnerability, but an ethnic group that is assimilated into the society or incorporated into the political and/or economic structure of the state does not. Naturally, efforts to "destabilize" a rival state could take the form of covert or overt support of the ethnic minority. However, it might also take the form of increased foreign policy belligerence (with or without the direct support of the ethnic group).

Liberalism

Liberal arguments about the international system differ from those of the realists on four major counts (for a comprehensive overview see Haas 1964; Keohane and Nye 1977; Krasner 1978; and Keohane 1984). First, within the liberal perspective, states are not the only important actors in the international system. International organizations, multinational corporations, ethnic and religious groups, and other transnational movements of people can directly and indirectly influence international relations (Krasner 1978; Keohane and Nye 1977). In particular, international institutions can constrain and condition state behavior, often by helping to overcome the insecurity associated with the anarchic nature of the international system. Second, liberals contend that states are more usefully conceptualized as being composed of a variety of actors, who often have competing interests, and all of whom attempt to influence the formation of policies (e.g., Allison 1971; Jervis 1976). States can have a difficult time determining exactly what is in the national interest as different intergovernmental and interest groups attempt to manipulate information and influence policy to further their particular goals or the goals of their constituencies. Third, because of the difficulty of clearly defining goals, state decisions are often determined through bargaining, coalition building, and clashes among the various components of government. Individually rational behavior may result in collectively irrational decisions as groups pursue their individual interests at the expense of national interests. Finally, other issues beside national security concerns are often pursued by the state. Social, economic, political, cultural, and ecological agendas are often the focus of state behavior.

Building on this set of assumptions, liberal theorists have argued that the international system has the potential to move beyond the cycles of warfare that have characterized international relations since the Peace of Westphalia. In particular, increasing economic interdependence, the spread of democratic governments, and the growth of institutions have all contributed to the evolution of the international system. Economic interdependence is said to constrain states from employing violence in the international system because of the threat warfare poses to the increasing gains from trade (Rosecrance 1986; Nye 1988). In addition, the discovery of a lack of hostilities between democratic states leads liberal scholars to argue that the democratization of the international system has important implications for the occurrence of war (Doyle 1986; Chan 1984; Maoz and Russett 1993). Some scholars have gone so far as to argue that a system made up of only democratic states would be free of war (Rummel 1979). Finally, as international institutions increase in number and grow in importance, liberal theorists have pointed to their influence in conflict management and the manner in which they constrain state behavior (Keohane 1990).

What, then, does the liberal approach imply about linkages between the ethnic composition of states and dyadic foreign policy conflict? We submit that liberalism identifies one set of factors that could conceivably increase the likelihood of ethnic conflict affecting international relations, and another set of factors that might diminish the likelihood of an international dimension to ethnic conflict. To address the first set, the fact that the state is not conceptualized as a unitary actor leads one to expect that the interests of particular groups are more likely to become the focus of state behavior. Thus, it is reasonable to expect that certain states might pay attention to the demands of domestic ethnic groups or other interest groups to act on behalf of ethnic brethren in other states. A second factor identified by liberalism is international norms. Hence, concern about the treatment of ethnic groups could lead states to become belligerent toward a rival. In the same vein, states may be willing to participate in efforts by international institutions and/or nongovernmental organizations aimed at overcoming ethnic discrimination or oppression.

On the other hand, liberalism also points to factors that would limit the influence of ethnicity on dyadic foreign policy behavior. In particular, international institutions are likely to constrain the willingness of states to take direct action, in favor of allowing the institution to attempt to manage or resolve the situation, especially if a state contains an ethnic minority of its own. Second, the growth of democratic regimes, which tend to be more inclusive of groups within their societies, may limit the appeal of ethno-nationalist aspirations and separatist movements. Finally, liberalism suggests that increasing economic interdependence should constrain states from risky foreign policies.

With respect to the major theoretical frameworks in international relations, our findings have a number of important implications. Most significantly, our results indicate that the ethnic characteristics of states have an influence on foreign policy behavior. This finding presents difficulties for realist theories that neglect state-level characteristics, and adds further impetus for expanding the scope of liberal theories that focus on the characteristics of states. In many ways, these findings point to the importance of further critical thinking and reconceptualizing. Having discovered empirical evidence to support the contention that ethnicity matters, we find ourselves in a situation not unlike that characterizing international relations during the last ten years, in which scholars have found themselves attempting post hoc to develop theories to explain the newly realized democratic peace. Developing better theories for understanding the dynamics and processes through which ethnicity influences international interactions is important.

PART THREE

The Limits to Spread

CHAPTER FIVE

Commitment Problems and the Spread of Ethnic Conflict

JAMES D. FEARON

IF INTERNATIONAL POLITICS among the major powers turn hideously ugly in the next twenty years it will be a simple matter to use hindsight to show how this was "inevitable." Frightening analogies to the 1920s and 1930s can be spun out. A protracted, costly war has ended with the collapse of one of the combatants, its economy ruined and chaotic, its people resentful and ripe for mobilization by authoritarian demagogues who can easily argue for restoring national pride by means of expansion—Weimar Russia, as some have termed it. The largely pathetic response of the Western states through NATO and the UN to Serbian aggression in Croatia and Bosnia has already recalled the impotence and incoherence of the League of Nations. And for a time the major powers' reactions to "the Third Balkan war" produced divisions reminiscent of older alignments that might conceivably foreshadow a return to insecurity in Western Europe. Russia, France, and Britain have tended to favor Serbia while Germany and the United States have leaned toward Croatia.[1]

Continuing the analogy, the principle of national self-determination remains as powerful and problematic today as it was in the 1920s and 1930s. No one seriously questions the principle,[2] but in the former Soviet Union and Eastern Europe after communism, "self-determination" strongly pursued would seem to imply an endless succession of irredentist and secessionist wars, state repression of minorities, ethnic cleansing, enormous numbers of refugees and attendant problems, and perhaps fertile grounds for escalation to major-power conflict. In the 1930s, according to some, Chamberlain and company's acceptance of the principle of self-determination deeply influenced their initial response to Hitler's expansionist program (Taylor 1961, 189). In responding to diverse ethnic conflicts and nationalisms to the East, the Western powers have been similarly torn between the desire for peace and stable borders on the one hand, and acceptance

---

Note: For helpful comments on an earlier version I wish to thank participants at an IGCC conference held in March 1995 at the University of California, Davis and especially David Laitin, David Lake, Timur Kuran, Donald Rothchild, and Steve Saideman.

[1] Thomas L. Friedman, "Boris, Bill, and Voltaire," *New York Times*, February 26, 1995, sec. 4, p. 15.

[2] Etzioni (1992–1993) is a recent exception.

of the principle of self-determination on the other.[3] Could this confusion foster ethnic wars and allow them to spread across borders in such a way as to ignite serious major power conflict?

In this paper I develop two related arguments. First, the analogy sketched above is probably not warranted. It is unlikely that the upsurge of ethnic conflict observed in Eastern Europe and the former Soviet Union since the end of the Cold War will repolarize the major powers and reintroduce severe security conflicts among them. I argue that under present conditions ethnic wars and conflict in Eastern Europe and the former Soviet Union are likely to be self-limiting. They will rarely spread far, and if they do this will tend to occur gradually rather than in major, simultaneous conflagrations. Although the Western states' failures in the former Yugoslavia are disgraceful on humanitarian grounds, they are not comparable to the League's failures regarding Italy, Japan, and Germany in the 1920s and 1930s because the conflict in the Balkans is much less likely to spread so as to engage fundamental security interests of either the Western powers or Russia.

Nonetheless, the Western powers have a range of other good reasons to try to understand, prevent, and contain these conflicts. These reasons include humanitarian objectives (the value of preventing slaughter), economic objectives (the value of trade with prosperous states in the region), and to some extent ideological objectives, in that the success of exclusivist ethnic programs in Eastern Europe may contribute to undermining the legitimacy of liberal democratic "civic" notions of citizenship in the West. The second main argument of the paper concerns the causes of the so-called resurgence of ethnic violence in the former Communist countries. Understanding the causes of these conflicts is a precondition for understanding the circumstances under which they might spread and the likelihood that different policy instruments can succeed in containing them.

Though increasingly criticized, a standard view in the U.S. media is that "ancient hatreds" explain the increase in ethnic violence in the former Communist countries. A typical story line is: "These people, the Xs and Ys, have hated and warred against each other for centuries; this is their natural condition. While strong, Communist domination kept them from killing each other, but ultimately the 'pot' boiled over (or it boiled over when the lid was removed)."

Although I agree that the end of Communist domination was a critical factor, I argue for a different mechanism connecting it to the onset of large-scale ethnic violence. In brief, I argue that the collapse of Communist central governments has in several places created a *commitment problem* that arises when two groups find themselves without a third party that can credibly guarantee agreements between them. The problem is that in post-Soviet Eastern Europe, ethnic majorities are unable to commit themselves not to exploit ethnic minorities in a new state. Ethnic minorities, such as the Serbs in Croatia, Armenians in Azerbaijan, and possibly Ossetians in Georgia, anticipate that regardless of what the ethnic major-

---

[3] The Western reaction to Chechnya—opposed to the brutal suppression of a movement for self-determination, but reluctant to condemn Yeltsin's regime for acting against the further dissolution of the state—provides a dramatic illustration.

ity's leaders agree to now, there is no solid guarantee that the leaders will not renege in the future, due to the play of majority politics in the new state to come. Given this anticipation, fighting now in hopes of winning secession from a weak, barely formed state may appear the superior alternative. However, the ethnic war that ensues may leave both majority and minority worse off than if the majority could make a credible commitment not to abuse the minority in the new state.[4]

This commitment problem is definitely not the only source of ethnic violence in the former Communist countries. For example, the internal dynamics of nationalist movements within groups also seem quite important (Gagnon 1994–1995; Laitin 1995b). I will argue, however, that even when other factors matter they frequently interact with and are shaped by this underlying commitment problem. Moreover, by specifying this mechanism fairly sharply, I am able to identify several conditions under which it will or will not work to produce violence, suggesting hypotheses that might explain why ethnic violence has occurred in some places rather than others. Finally, understanding how this commitment problem can operate to produce ethnic conflict has implications for understanding factors that will promote or discourage its spread across borders.

The paper has three sections. The first argues that in present circumstances ethnic conflicts in Eastern Europe and the former Soviet Union will tend to be self-limiting. In the second section I present a simple model of the commitment problem as a cause of ethnic conflict and briefly discuss its application to the case of the war in Croatia in 1991–1992. The final section concludes, drawing out implications of the commitment problem model for thinking about the spread of ethnic conflict.

CONSTRAINTS ON THE SPREAD OF ETHNIC CONFLICTS

Journalists and academics frequently use fire metaphors when discussing ethnic conflicts. Mixes of ethnic groups in a territory are compared to "kindling" or "tinder" that could easily be "ignited" by extremists who then start a "wildfire." Similarly, ethnically mixed areas are explosives that will go off with the slightest "spark." "Kosovo could blow at any time" says *The Economist*.[5] These metaphors suggest that ethnic conflicts have an inherent potential to spread rapidly and catastrophically. Since its start in 1992, Western observers of the war in Yugoslavia have repeatedly prophesied its spread throughout and possibly beyond the Balkans—to Kosovo, then Albania, Macedonia, Greece, Turkey, . . . Russia? NATO?[6]

Although the fire image may correctly represent some of the dynamics of increasing ethnic conflict "on the ground" in a particular area, the suggestion that

---

[4] In an important article, Barry Posen (1993b) has also argued that ethnic wars in Eastern Europe and the former Soviet Union may stem from the effects of anarchy. I discuss differences between our approaches below.

[5] "Minorities: That Other Europe," *The Economist*, December 25, 1993–January 7, 1994, p. 17.

[6] See especially George Kenny, "From Bosnian Crisis to All-out War," *New York Times*, June 20, 1993, sec. 4, p. 17.

such conflicts are prone to spread like wildfire from one state or region to another needs to be questioned. Indeed, the opposite might be the more reasonable explanation. I argue in this section that ethnic conflicts have properties that should tend to make them self-limiting in geographic extent. Further, if and when they do spread in Eastern Europe, they are unlikely to engage basic security interests of the Western powers.[7]

In the first place, ethnic conflicts that turn violent are typically "about" irredenta or attempts to secede to found an independent nation state. This means that the claims that give rise to ethnic conflicts will typically extend only as far as there are "brethren" to bring into Greater Ruritania, or brethren for Ruritania to intervene to protect. Moreover, the progress of a Greater Ruritania only directly threatens neighboring states with non-negligible Ruritanian populations, or states that are unlucky enough to possess territory that was at some point in the past allegedly controlled by Ruritanians. In the cases of, say, Serbia, Croatia, Albania, Macedonia, Hungary, Romania, and Slovakia, the bulk of any such irredentist project involves only some borders with only some immediate neighbors. And although border conflicts among minor powers can be notoriously long-lived and difficult to settle, they tend to "simmer" rather than explode, and they have not in the past made for general wars or caused tremendous grief among the major powers.[8]

Even if and when irredentist projects in Eastern Europe cause significant tensions or war, the major powers are not likely to be seriously threatened by them, for two major reasons. First, whereas before 1945 major powers often had to worry a lot about who would fight with whom in the event of a war, a number of developments since 1945 have made this central concern of old-school balance-of-power politics almost a non-issue. If the first line of defense against these worries is the "pluralistic security community" of Western Europe and a general European zeitgeist that views war as unthinkable, the final and sturdiest line of defense is the nuclear revolution. This has had the crucial effect of making major powers far less dependent on allies than they ever were before. The nuclear revolution means that the progress of a Greater Serbia or even a Greater Hungary would not create a state large enough to tip any relevant "balance" of concern to the major powers—the alliance preferences of minor powers simply do not matter as much as they did in the non-nuclear past. For example, in the eighteenth and nineteenth centuries competition between Prussia, Austria, Russia, and the Ottoman Empire over the control of Eastern Europe was motivated in part by concerns about how alliances and influence in the region would affect the overall balance of power, and World War I grew in part from Austria-Hungary's fear of expanding Russian influence in the Balkans. More recently, Stalin wanted

[7] I should make it clear that I am using "self-limiting" to refer to the spread of ethnic conflict from one group or place to the next, on and on across borders. Within a particular region, ethnic conflict may in some circumstances be "self-catalyzing" rather than self-limiting. Indeed, the commitment problem model of ethnic conflict developed below has this flavor.

[8] The First and Second Balkan wars were handled reasonably well by the major powers—it was a conflict between a minor power and major power that started the Great War.

imperial control of Eastern Europe both because it meant that the first line of defense could be stationed far from the homeland and that he would not need to worry about multipolar alliance politics in which Eastern European states might enter a hostile coalition against the Soviets. The nuclear revolution has undercut or at least greatly diminished the motive for such balancing and "spheres of influence" behavior.[9]

The second main reason why the spread of ethnic conflict in Eastern Europe need not engage the major powers' security interests is that for the most part ethnic conflicts are particularist rather than universalist.[10] Anyone can ascribe to the principles of Marx and Lenin or classical liberals, but not anyone can be a Serb, Hungarian, or Russian. For regimes founded on universalist ideological principles, the expansion and relative success of regimes founded on alternative universalist principles poses an indirect threat by calling domestic legitimacy into question—if *their* regime principles are doing so well and attracting new adherents, what is wrong with *our* principles? The Cold War was not simply about geopolitics but was also a struggle for "hearts and minds" in this sense. Except at the margins or perhaps in the long term, ethnic conflicts cannot be a struggle for hearts and minds since ethnic identity is presumed to be ascriptive. Greater Serbia does not envision converting Hungarians en masse into Serbs.[11] Thus the progress of irredentist projects does not have nearly as direct implications for the domestic politics of the major powers as the ideological struggle in the Cold War did. More generally, this is another feature of ethnic conflicts that should tend to make them self-limiting rather than highly liable to spread from state to state.[12]

One could object to or counter the above arguments on several grounds. First, although it may be true that irredentist projects in Eastern Europe can only extend so far, what about the possibility of diffusion through *chain reactions?* Ethnic conflicts typically produce large numbers of refugees, whose arrival in a new place may cause new tensions and problems. For example, the government

[9] Russian leaders vigorously object to a NATO that excludes them and extends up to present Russian borders, but they would be much more inclined to take drastic actions to stop the expansion if it were not for nuclear weapons. And it seems unlikely that Gorbachev could have "let Eastern Europe go" in the first place without facing much stiffer opposition from the military had it not been for nuclear weapons.

[10] Both Huntington (1993) and S. Kaufmann (1996) make this distinction and develop other implications.

[11] This is not to claim that ethnic identities are unalterably fixed by objective characteristics, but rather that the social understanding of ethnicity holds that it is not a matter of choice, as is a universalist ideology.

[12] Nazi Germany illustrates the possibility of an irredentist/expansionist program that envisions not converting but murdering other ethnic types in order to take their land and eliminate "inferior" groups. This could happen again, but it is important to note that the social Darwinist premises of this approach are not seriously advocated by state leaders anywhere (as far as I know). Lebensraum is "out," replaced by the more democratic premise that all countries are created equally and have an equal right to control territory and to sell characteristically national tourist items. Universalist religions (Islam, Orthodox Christianity) could conceivably mobilize large numbers of converts across political boundaries in Eastern Europe and the former Soviet Union, although this seems unlikely, and even if it occurred it might not threaten the legitimacy of the (secular) Western republics.

in Belgrade has tried to resettle Serbs fleeing Croatia and Bosnia in Kosovo, where their presence adds to tensions with the ethnic Albanians who make up the vast (and oppressed) majority.[13] Likewise, refugees from Rwanda may recently have heightened ethnic tensions in Burundi,[14] as they have on numerous occasions in the past.[15] There is no doubt that the presence of Hutu refugees and militia in eastern Zaire following the 1994 violence in Rwanda figured directly in the uprising of Zairian Tutsi and other groups against the refugees and the Zairian government. In the worst case, then, one can imagine a chain reaction in which ethnic war causes refugees, who de-stabilize a new place, causing more war, causing more refugees, and so on.

A closely related argument concerns possible *demonstration effects* of ethnic conflict. Even without flows of refugees or some other material transborder impact, it could be that if people in state B simply observe increased ethnic conflict in state A this will increase the risk of similar violence in state B.[16] Seeing pictures and hearing stories of killing due to ethnic antagonisms in state A could make people in state B more fearful and worried about the dangers posed by ethnic others in state B—"if it can happen there, why couldn't it happen here?" Heightened fears and suspicions could then play into the hands of ethnic political entrepreneurs seeking to mobilize an ethnically based political coalition, and so increase the ethnification of politics in state B. Lemarchand (1994a, 60) argues that exactly such a demonstration effect exacerbated ethnic tensions in Burundi in the 1960s and subsequently: "no other event did more to sharpen the edges of ethnic hatred in Burundi than the Hutu revolution in neighboring Rwanda [1959–1962]. . . . By identifying their political aims and aspirations with their Rwanda kinsmen, [some Hutus] imputed to the Tutsi of Burundi hegemonic motives that the Tutsi did not at first possess but to which they eventually gave a substance of truth. Conversely, many Tutsi saw in the Rwanda upheaval an ominous prefiguration of their own destinies. A kind of self-fulfilling prophecy was thus set into motion."

Demonstration effects might also work through learning by political elites. For example, observing how Milosevic successfully used the ethnic card in Serbia to cement his hold on power might encourage other politicians in trouble to try similar tactics.[17]

Although chain reactions and demonstration effects are without doubt possible mechanisms for the cross-border spread of ethnic conflict, these arguments tend to neglect the countervailing incentives that potentially affected publics and gov-

---

[13] See Schmidt (1994) and "Serbia's Apartheid Victims," *New York Times*, December 12, 1996, A12.

[14] Donatella Lorch, "Specter of Hate Stalks Burundi, Too," *New York Times*, April 26, 1994, A9.

[15] For example, Lemarchand (1994a, 61) notes that Tutsi refugees from the Rwandan revolution (1959–1962) had an interest in supporting a Tutsi-dominated government in Burundi to obtain aid for retaking power in Rwanda.

[16] Kuran (Chapter Two) develops a theoretical rationale for this based on the idea of a tipping game. For an empirical study suggesting that demonstration effects of this sort may take place, see Hill and Rothchild (1992).

[17] On Milosevic's maneuvering, see Gagnon (1994–1995) and Woodward (1995a).

ernments often have to slow, contain, or arrest such processes. Concerning demonstration effects, for instance, ethnic conflict in state A need not inevitably lead people in state B to become more hostile to ethnic others in their own country. Instead, they might respond that "such things must not be allowed to happen here." And regardless of public reactions, governments can surely have strong incentives to counter possible demonstration effects or chain reactions. Empirical evidence suggests that governments worry about the impact of refugee flows and other means of transmission, and may respond preemptively. For example, as they observed the severity of the Bosnian war, Albanian leaders in Tirana dramatically moderated their calls for active pursuit of autonomy and secession of Kosovo province, in large part from fear of war with Serbia or a major refugee crisis.[18] With the encouragement of the leadership in Tirana, the Kosovan Albanians constructed a shadow government and a private, underground educational system as part of a strategy that seeks autonomy while avoiding bloodshed.[19] Finally, the war in Yugoslavia has served as a powerful object lesson in what can happen if political leaders foment, and mass publics support, interethnic hostility. Rather than increasing the legitimacy and power of ethnic appeals in Eastern Europe, the war may have the opposite effect, in part through the action of international organizations interested in acting more aggressively to prevent similar conflicts from developing.[20] This is not to argue that countervailing forces will always undermine demonstration effects and chain reactions—the Rwanda-Burundi-Zaire case suggests otherwise—but that it is wrong to suppose that they will always or even usually produce rapid cross-border transmission of ethnic violence.[21]

A third, much stronger objection to the "self-limiting" argument concerns Russia, the major power most likely to be directly affected by or implicated in the spread of ethnic conflict in the region. The assertion that particularist ethnic conflicts have minimal implications for the domestic legitimacy of major power governments has less weight regarding Russia, since Moscow faces numerous possible secessionist struggles within its current territory. Russian leaders might fear that successful irredentist or secessionist wars to their east will encourage more secession attempts within their already diminished borders. And the millions of ethnic Russians living in the "near abroad" of course create the possibility of the largest irredentist project ever, one that could conceivably make for a major-power war (though I would argue that this is still very unlikely).

---

[18] That is, if Milosevic decided to "cleanse" Kosovo violently the Tirana leadership would feel compelled to support Kosovo's Albanians and would certainly face a refugee crisis. See Schmidt (1993) and Zanga (1992). Western pressure seems also to have been significant.

[19] The possibility of an intifada-like struggle in Kosovo is growing, although this would hardly count as a case of rapid, trans-border spread of ethnic conflict. See references in note 13.

[20] Experts on the former Soviet Union have noted a strong trend away from popular support for would-be "romantic nationalist" leaders in the successor states. Although there are surely many factors behind this trend, one may be a popular concern that such leaders can bring on the sort of trouble and destruction observed in Yugoslavia and Chechnya. See, for an example, Garb (Chapter Eight).

[21] It should also be noted that the ethnically matched and bipolar case of Rwanda and Burundi is highly unusual, even in Africa.

There are two possible dangers here that concern the cross-border spread of ethnic conflict. Regarding the first, it seems something of a leap to argue that the demonstration effect of ethnic conflict in Eastern Europe would be decisive for would-be secessionists in Russia—they are much more likely to pay close attention to how the Russian government responds to demands for increased autonomy within the federation (as in Tatarstan) and for independence (Chechnya). The second danger—that increasing Russian irredentism will have the effect of fomenting and spreading ethnic conflict in the former Soviet republics—seems much graver and more probable. There is a variety of mechanisms by which a more openly irredentist leadership in Moscow might directly or indirectly bring about ethnic violence in the former republics, from military reconquest to offering support for Russian-speaking separatists and extremists. Countervailing incentives may work to dampen the effects of some of these mechanisms; for example, the danger of Russian irredentism gives the leaders of majority ethnic groups in Ukraine, the Baltic states, some Central Asian states, and Moldova strong incentives not to foment ethnic discord or encourage its spread.[22] Nonetheless, the fact that countervailing incentives or forces exist does not mean that they will be enough (of course, in the case of direct military intervention by Moscow, countervailing forces are almost entirely irrelevant). As I argue below, the mere presence of an overtly irredentist government in one state can exacerbate a commitment problem that can lead to increased ethnic conflict in neighboring states, despite the existence of countervailing incentives for the neighboring state governments to prevent such escalation.

ETHNIC WAR AND THE PROBLEM OF POLITICAL COMMITMENTS BY THE RULING GROUP

Although there are reasons to doubt the "wildfire" metaphor as it concerns the likelihood that ethnic conflicts will spread rapidly from state to state, it may be more compelling as a description of the dynamics of ethnic conflict *within* particular communities.

Yugoslavia provides some striking examples here. Full-scale war between Serbs and Croats erupted in the Krajina region of Croatia in late June 1991, more or less immediately following the Croatian parliament's declaration of independence on June 25. Although interventions by the Serb-dominated Yugoslav National Army (JNA) made for some of the worst fighting, it is significant that the conflict was characterized by very local-level, house-to-house warfare—Serbs and Croats in the mixed communities of Krajina and Slavonia were almost completely polarized at the time of the declaration and took up arms against the other group. Indeed, ethnic polarization and conflict in this case has the look of "wildfire," in that the two communities were not nearly so divided only months earlier. Journalists traveling in the region in 1990 reported that most people seemed to have had no use for or interest in the exclusivist arguments pushed by the minority of extremists.

---

[22] On the moderation shown by Ukrainian leaders since independence, see Laitin (1995b).

Misha Glenny (1993, 19) writes that "before May 1991, Croats and Serbs lived together in relative contentment throughout the regions which have now been so dreadfully ravaged." He reports on "a network of Serbs in Knin [home of the highest concentration of 'gun-toting' Serb extremists] who believed that Babic [an extremist Serb leader in Krajina] was driving them towards a senseless war" (20). Commenting on a town in Banija district where the first large-scale fighting of the war occurred, Glenny states that "Babic had been sending emissaries from Knin in an attempt to undermine the social democratic forces in Glina in favor of the militant Serb nationalist line. The Serbs in Glina resisted Babic's bloody entreaties until June [1991] but by then they felt that they no longer had a choice—it was Croats or Serbs, and they were Serbs" (93). On the Croatian side, Glenny discusses the case of a well-respected local leader in Slavonia who, in the first months of 1991, "was determined to stop distrust between Serbs and Croats from sliding into open hostility. For weeks before his [assassination], he traveled tirelessly from village to village striking local deals to prevent the extremists in both [Serb and Croat] communities from assuming a dominant influence" (106). At a higher political level, a group of Croatian intellectuals and politicians evidently tried to persuade the Croatian leader Franjo Tudjman in the summer of 1990 to change his policy on Krajina in order to avoid a war (14).

A reporter for the *Frankfurter allgemeine Zeitung,* Michael Schmitz (1992) confirms these impressions. He found that in 1990, Serbs in Krajina "were reluctant to follow the strategy of confrontation" favored by the extremists: "When I talked to people in the streets, in shops, and bars I found few people who asserted they felt a threat. On the contrary, Croats and Serbs were peacefully working and living together. In interviews they talked convincingly about friendship, inter-marriage, and tolerance among the different religions (Christian Orthodox and Roman Catholic). At that time the militants appeared at first sight as an exaggeratedly nervous splinter group. 'That's just politics,' commented common people." (25).

These reports, along with many similar observations by other reporters and scholars, argue against the view that the war was made inevitable by deep and wide nationalist passions crossed with conflicting territorial claims.[23] It appears that most Serbs and Croats in Croatia were not from the outset intent on having separate, ethnically pure nations. On the contrary, with the exception of a relatively small number of extremists led by Milan Babic, Serbs and Croats in the mixed population areas recognized that war would be costly and viewed it as unnecessary—until the spring of 1991. These months, according to Glenny, saw a rapid and nearly total "homogenization" of opinion.[24] Serbs and Croats who had resisted the extremists' appeals finally opted for division and war.

The rapid polarization of Serbs and Croats in Croatia represents a puzzle. It is inconsistent with an "ancient hatreds" explanation, according to which we would expect to find seething and widespread hostility waiting to erupt at any time. This is very definitely not what we find in 1990 and even early 1991, except in the

[23] For example, see John F. Burns, cited in Fearon 1993, and Gagnon (1994–1995, 132n10).
[24] See, for example, Glenny (1992a, 85).

case of some extremists. It is also a puzzle for more "top-down" arguments that argue that elites, primarily in Belgrade, directly created ethnic polarization. In this account, extremists like Milan Babic were simply pawns of Slobodan Milosevic operating in Belgrade (which is probably true), and they were able to force polarization by means of terrorism, intimidation, and assassinations.[25] Although there is something to this, it should be noted that these activities were going on from early 1990 (following multiparty elections in Croatia in May), but rapid and thorough polarization appears not to have occurred until shortly before the declaration of independence in June 1991.

I argue that the rapid polarization of ethnic opinion and the subsequent conflict in Croatia is explained by a commitment problem operating between the majority Croats and the minority Serbs in Croatia. With the declaration of independence, Serbs in Croatia, whether extremist or utterly indifferent to such things, faced the prospect of entering the new state of Croatia with no credible guarantees on their political status, or economic and even physical security. And although the Croatian majority government could have done much more to try to assure the Serb minority, there was nothing credible they could do to commit themselves not to pursue policies detrimental to Serb welfare and security in the future, after the Croatian state had grown stronger. Faced with this prospect, it could make sense for even nonextremist Serbs to try to fight now rather than later, despite the costs of civil war and the existence of bargains that majorities on both sides might have preferred.

To make this argument more precise, it is helpful to use a simple game model of the problem faced by a majority and minority ethnic group after the disintegration of an "imperial" authority previously over both of them. I sketch and analyze this model next.[26] It is a stylization intended to make clear a particular political dynamic that I argue is empirically important, even if the way the dynamic operates in particular cases is invariably more complicated and qualified than in the stylized model. In particular, whereas in the model I treat the majority and minority groups as unitary actors, the discussion of the Krajina case (below) indicates that in reality intragroup politics matter significantly. To understand exactly *how* it matters, however, I argue that one needs a prior understanding of the core commitment problem clarified by the simple model.

A Model of the Commitment Problem

Consider a majority group *M* and minority group *m*. Suppose that living together in one state affords the groups total "benefits" worth *B*, which will be divided between the two according to the political rules of the game in the new state. We can think of *B* either as solely economic or including political and other benefits as well. In Croatia, Serbs and Croats cared not only about access to state patronage and consideration for jobs in the public and private sectors but also about

---

[25] This is the flavor of Gagnon's (1994–1995) account.

[26] The model presented here is a simpler version of that presented in Fearon 1994. See that paper for a fuller treatment.

the curricula taught in schools, the alphabet used on street signs, symbols of the new state, and a range of things connected to views of relative status. We can think of each group's share of B as representing its value for a given resolution of all such issues.

In the first period of the game, the minority group will decide whether to fight for secession or to acquiesce and enter the new state. If they fight, a war occurs that is won by the majority with probability p_1, and which costs $c_M > 0$ for the majority and $c_m > 0$ for the minority. Victory for the minority means successful secession, in which case it receives benefits b_m, the value of independence for the group. The majority, on the other hand, receives b_M, the benefits of living in the smaller state it is left with. If the majority wins a military conflict, it will take all the benefits B, leaving nothing for the minority, which is forced to remain in the majority's state.[27] It follows that the expected payoffs for civil war in the first period are $pB + (1 - p_1)b_M - c_M$ for the majority, and $p0 + (1 - p_1)b_m - c_m = (1 - p_1)b_m - c_m$ for the minority. I assume that $b_m + b_M < B$, so that the total benefits of living together in the new state exceed the sum of the groups' values for separation. If this is not the case, then there is no reason for the groups not to separate happily and peacefully as soon as they can.[28]

If the minority decides to enter the new state instead of opting for secession, then I assume that "majority rule" means that the majority group decides on a division of the total benefits between the two groups. Let α be the proportion of B that the majority proposes to keep for itself in the new state. After the majority makes its demand (which might in practice represent the specification and implementation of a constitution), the minority will decide a second time whether to try a war of secession. Payoffs are the same as for civil war in the first period, except that now we assume that the probability that the majority defeats the minority *increases* to $p_2 > p_1$. The idea here is that it will be more difficult for the minority to secede after the majority has consolidated its control of the new state and begun to build up the police, army, and security apparatus.[29]

The appropriate solution concept for the model specified above is subgame perfect Nash equilibrium. In a subgame perfect equilibrium, players cannot rely on threats or promises that they would not want to carry out if they actually had to make the choice. This is natural for the strategic situation considered here, where it is obvious that what the minority wants to do in the first period depends on its expectations about how the majority would divide up the benefits B in the

[27] This can be justified more thoroughly as follows: If the minority loses, it has revealed that it cannot secede successfully by force, so in the future its probability of winning secession by war drops close to zero. Since fighting is costly this means the minority will accept an offer of zero rather than fight.

[28] In the case of $b_m + b_M > B$, a transfer from the minority might be necessary if the majority's value for peaceful separation (b_M) is less than its expected value for forcibly trying to prevent secession; it is conceivable that problems with bargaining or commitment might engender conflict in this particular case.

[29] It may also be more difficult for the minority to obtain help from ethnic brethren in nearby states or from the international community after it has already agreed once to enter the new state.

new state. Likewise, the division proposed by the majority will depend on its expectations about what the minority would be willing to accept.

Working backward, in the second period the minority does best to accept any offer of benefits worth more than its second-period value for fighting to secede. Thus any division α such that $(1 - \alpha)B \geq (1 - p_2)b_m - c_m$ will be accepted in preference to war. Given this fact, the majority does best to push the minority just up to its willingness to fight in the second period, choosing a division α^* such that $(1 - \alpha^*)B = (1 - p_2)b_m - c_m$ if $(1 - p_2)b_m - c_m \geq 0$, and $\alpha^* = 1$ if $(1 - p_2)b_m - c_m < 0$. Thus if the minority were to acquiesce rather than fight in the first period, peace would prevail and payoffs would be α^*B for the majority and $(1 - \alpha^*)B$ for the minority in the second period.

But here is the dilemma. As long as the minority group would prefer fighting in the first period to receiving none of the benefits in the new state (i.e., $[1 - p_1]b_m - c_m > 0$), then it will strictly prefer to fight for secession in the first period. Acquiescing yields a peaceful settlement worth $(1 - \alpha^*)B = (1 - p_2)b_m - c_m$, whereas fighting in the first period yields $(1 - p_1)b_m - c_m$. Because the minority is more likely to succeed at war in the first period than in the second $(1 - p_1 > 1 - p_2)$, secessionist war in the first period is strictly better than being "pushed to the wall" short of war in the new state. That is, it is better to fight for secession now than be forced to live with a worse situation in the new state, albeit peacefully.

The outcome of immediate civil war, however, makes both majority and minority worse off than they ideally could be. It is easy to show that since war is costly, there will always be peaceful settlements in the new state that both groups prefer to a violent conflict in either period. For example, the majority would ideally like to commit itself in advance to offer a division $\alpha' < \alpha^*$ such that the minority would prefer to receive this in the new state rather than fight to secede in the first period (i.e., α' such that $[1 - \alpha']B$ is just greater than $[1 - p_1]b_m - c_m$). If the minority could be guaranteed that the majority *would* in fact implement this division in the new state, the minority would then prefer not to fight. *But the majority cannot credibly commit itself to make such moderate demands in the new state,* because at that point its bargaining power will have increased due to the consolidation of police and army capabilities. Costly ethnic war is thus explained as the result of the majority's inability to make a credible commitment to the minority.[30]

This commitment problem may help explain the rapid polarization of ethnic groups in Croatia following the declaration of Croatian independence in June 1991. For Serbs, the Croatian declaration of independence meant that they were

[30] It is important to note that cultural differences, disagreements, and misinterpretations between ethnic groups (which are almost always present) are not enough to explain why violent conflict sometimes occurs between them. Even if there are disagreements and resentments, fighting is costly—in the case of ethnic war obviously so—so that groups should have strong incentives to settle their differences without war. Of the literally hundreds of geographically contiguous or interspersed ethnic groups in Eastern Europe and the former Soviet Union, only a tiny fraction has engaged in widespread, serious violence since 1991 (Fearon and Laitin 1996). Arguments such as the commitment problem story given here are required to explain such costly violence, at least on the presumption of roughly rational actors. For a more general version of this argument applied to interstate war, see Fearon (1995).

entering a new state in which they lacked any serious indication that the government would and could credibly guarantee Serb rights. And even if the government did seek verbally to reassure the Serbs that their rights would be respected, the Serbs could not be sure that such policies would be faithfully implemented in the future, given diverse majority pressures for jobs for Croats and possibly for efforts at cultural homogenization or exclusion. According to Glenny (1992a, 31), "when Croatian independence was declared on June 25 . . . , Glina's Serbs, fearing the worst, sided with the thuggish forces of the Marticevci [Chetnik irregulars]," whom they had previously resisted.

If the commitment problem model does capture something of what was going on in Croatia, then we might expect to find evidence of Croatian leaders trying to work out guarantees with Serb leaders. In fact, in addition to offering verbal assurances of equal treatment on numerous occasions, the Croatian President Tudjman met with the leader of the Serbs in Croatia, Jovan Raskovic, several times in the summer and fall of 1990 to discuss precisely the issue of commitment to guarantees on the Serbs' status and "cultural autonomy."[31] The talks failed. Raskovic stated that he believed Tudjman wanted to offer stronger and more credible guarantees, but was prevented from doing so by extremists within his party, the Christian Democratic Union (HDZ).[32]

That the model captures an important aspect of what was happening in Croatia prior to the outbreak of war is indicated by the centrality of the question of guarantees and commitment in both Serb-Croat and intragroup political debate in 1990 and early 1991. The case also shows, however, that the model sketched above is too simple in that it leaves out important dynamics that bear on whether groups will be able to resolve the problem. In the Croatian case, it is significant that while Tudjman did offer verbal reassurances to the Serbs and negotiated on guarantees with their political leadership, he also took actions that had the opposite effect of frightening the Serbs. For example, symbols of the wartime Ustashe regime hated by Serbs were adapted for use by the new Croatian government, and in 1990 Tudjman's party pushed through constitutional reforms that removed supramajority rules for votes on (among other things) ethnically sensitive issues. Such actions would tend to exacerbate the majority's commitment problem, and so are inconsistent with the model.[33]

Two factors are left out of the model that seem to bear directly on Tudjman's motivation to try to construct a credible set of guarantees for the Serb minority. First, in the model I assume that the two ethnic groups can be represented as "unitary actors," when in fact what "the group" decides to do is the product of complicated internal political dynamics. In the Croatian case, Tudjman had been

---

[31] According to Glenny (1993, 19), Raskovic never demanded outright secession.

[32] See sources cited in Fearon 1994.

[33] At least, they are inconsistent with a simple and straightforward interpretation of the model. One could, however, argue as follows: if the problem really is unresolvable (there is no way that the majority can credibly commit itself), then any negotiations and discussions will just be for show, and the leaderships of the two groups will have no reason not to take provocative actions if this helps them gain support within their own group.

elected in May 1990 on a platform whose central elements were increased autonomy for Croatia within the federation and "decommunization," which was understood to imply a reduction of Serb representation in Croatian public-sector jobs
(Woodward 1995a, 118–19). Thus, to appear to make concessions on this matter was to appear to cede ground to the (largely Croatian) opposition parties that
had argued against him and which constituted a significant share of the legislature. Further, Tudjman's election campaign had done surprisingly well (though it
still did not win a majority of votes cast) in a large part because he had been mas-
sively funded by wealthy émigrés with (typically) extremist views about kicking
out the Serbs—émigrés do not bear the costs of civil war that Croatians living in
Krajina recognized they would. Thus intragroup political dynamics can militate
against efforts to construct credible guarantees for the minority.[34]

The second key factor affecting Tudjman's interest in constructing a credible
commitment concerns the role of Serbia. For good reasons, Tudjman and other
Croats strongly suspected that Milosevic and some important military leaders in
Belgrade were actively trying to create a Greater Serbia that would include
Krajina—that is, that Milosevic was an irredentist. This increased the risk of
committing to the Serbs in Croatia, since to do so credibly might entail actions
(such as letting them keep their arms or control police stations in some towns)
that could hurt Croatia in the event of war with Serbia.

Although the case is more complicated than the model (as is always true), the
complexities are harder to order and make sense of without a clear statement of
the underlying problem of commitment by the majority to the minority. Though
I lack the space to do so here, the basic commitment problem described here
appears to operate in a number of other cases as well. The war over Nagorno
Karabakh is probably the best example: The disintegration of Soviet authority led
Armenians in Nagorno Karabakh to try to fight for secession right away rather
than face an uncertain future as a minority in the new state of Azerbaijan. By
February 1993, with the costs of supporting the war effort crippling Armenia, the
Armenian president was reported to see the only way to end the conflict as
"through international guarantees for the security of Armenians living in Nagorno
Karabakh, which Azerbaijan has been unable to provide."[35]

The commitment problem model also implies a number of hypotheses on the
question of why ethnic violence occurs (or is more likely) in some cases rather
than others. I will sketch these in the next section, after some observations on
how the argument given here differs from Barry Posen's analysis of the "security
dilemma" as a source of ethnic war, which also stresses anarchy as a causal factor.[36] Whereas my argument identifies and examines a specific commitment prob-

---

[34] Intragroup dynamics, chiefly in the form of intimidation by the extremists supported by
Belgrade, also affected the Serbs' disposition to compromise with the Croats.

[35] Celestine Bohlen, "Amid War for Enclave, Armenia Sees Little Hope," *New York Times*, February
12, 1993, A3.

[36] See Posen (1993b). The commitment problem and security dilemma arguments are sometimes
said to be similar (e.g., Cederman 1996).

lem that may occur between a majority and minority group and may cause ethnic war, Posen argues that first, interspersed settlement patterns create offensive advantages, which (following Jervis 1978) exacerbate the security dilemma, and second, "the complexity of these situations makes it possible for many competing groups [simultaneously] to believe that their prospects in a war would be better earlier rather than later" (34); thus preventive wars become likely. The specific commitment problem I have described does give rise to a sort of preventive war undertaken by the minority, although it is motivated by the majority's inability to commit to certain political bargains in the future rather than by mutual miscalculations of the course of relative power. In addition, the security dilemma is typically assumed to explain how the structural condition of anarchy can make for escalating hostility or even violent conflict between actors that are interested *only* in their own security and have no fundamentally aggressive or revisionist desires. By contrast, for the commitment problem I describe to operate, there must be some set of substantive issues over which the minority and majority have conflicting preferences, either in the present or in the future. Otherwise, the minority has nothing to fear concerning what policies the majority will implement in the new state, and the fact of anarchy is then inconsequential. In the security dilemma argument, hostility is said to grow not from a specific mechanism that requires conflicting preferences, shifting relative power, and anarchy, but rather from mutual uncertainty about the other side's intentions. It is not made clear, however, why signaling between states or groups cannot be used to reduce this uncertainty, if in fact the parties are interested only in security.[37] Finally, the commitment problem account gives an explicit answer to the question of why the groups in conflict cannot bargain to a settlement both prefer to a costly war, whereas the security dilemma account does not (Fearon 1995, 384–85).

Factors Affecting the Severity of the Commitment Problem

The model allows the identification of several factors that should influence the question of whether the commitment problem will produce ethnic war or peace. These are: one, the military strength and cultural preferences of the minority; two, the pattern of settlement of minority and majority groups; three, the presence of external guarantors or ethnic brethren in a neighboring state who are both willing and able to threaten credibly to intervene on behalf of the minority if they are abused in the new state but not otherwise; four, the extent of the minority's expected decline in ability to secede in the future; and five, the value of the "exit" option for individuals in the minority group, and the social and political organization of the minority.

---

[37] See Kydd (1997) for a strategic analysis of the security dilemma problem that takes signaling into account, and finds that security seekers will often be able to communicate their intentions by means of costly signals. Note also that uncertainty about group intentions plays no necessary role in the commitment problem argument (although minority uncertainty about the majority's future policy preferences could easily be incorporated).

RELATIVE MILITARY STRENGTH AND CULTURAL PREFERENCES OF THE MINORITY

In the model, the commitment problem operates only if the condition $(1 - p_1)b_m - c_m > 0$ holds, which in words means that the minority would prefer to fight in the first period rather than accept zero benefits in the new state. ("Zero benefits" should be interpreted as the policies the majority would follow if the minority had no military bargaining power at all.) The commitment problem does not operate if fighting now is worse for the minority than the worst situation they would face under the new regime (i.e., $[1 - p_1]b_m - c_m < 0$). Thus, if either the minority is very weak relative to the majority ($p_1 \cong 1$), or if its costs for fighting are very large relative to its (cultural) value for secession, the minority will prefer simply to acquiesce and there will be no war. Conversely, if the minority is militarily strong relative to the majority (as with Serbs in Krajina and Bosnia), then the commitment problem is more likely to operate.[38]

Many small ethnic groups in Eastern Europe and the Soviet Republics may fit this case. For example, in 1988 Milosevic pushed through constitutional changes that rescinded Kosovo's status as an "autonomous province," a move widely and correctly interpreted by the vast Albanian majority to presage greater oppression (Woodward 1995a, 94–95). Although some violence occurred, Kosovars did not fight en masse to secede, mainly because they lacked any serious prospect of success at a reasonable cost—it was better to accept greater oppression (and probably a lower ability to fight for secession in the near future) than to fight for secession in the present.

SETTLEMENT PATTERNS

In the game analyzed above, if the minority wishes to secede it must "fight its way out." This formulation implicitly assumes that the minority and majority groups are interspersed in the area in question. In cases where the groups are not intermixed—that is, if minority-held territory within the new state is relatively compact—then nothing stops the minority from simply declaring their own autonomous region or state. This puts the burden of violent escalation on the majority group, and if the majority prefers fighting later ($p_2 > p_1$), then the majority will want to wait. On the other hand, if the minority and majority groups are highly intermixed, then the minority cannot simply declare political autonomy or sovereignty and have the declaration be effective. To control the territory they need to eject (or subjugate) members of the majority group. Thus, when populations are highly intermixed, to "secede" means to fight, and we should expect war by the logic of the model (assuming other conditions are fulfilled).[39]

[38] It is worth stressing that the commitment model makes no a priori assumption about the relative military as opposed to political strength of the majority and minority groups (formally, the minority's probability of winning at war in the first period could be greater than 1/2). It is entirely possible for a numerical majority group to be relatively weak militarily, as in the case of Hutus in Burundi prior to 1993, or Muslims in Bosnia.

[39] In Posen's (1993b) account, by contrast, interspersed populations are more prone to violence because of greater offensive advantages.

In Czechoslovakia, for example, Czechs and Slovaks were not highly inter-spersed, so that a declaration of independence by Slovakia would not raise diffi-cult questions about the control of territory populated by members of both groups. This was not the case for Croatia and the Krajina region in 1991, so that to declare any meaningful independence Krajina Serbs had to fight to secure their grip on the territory. In line with the above argument, once the war largely emp-tied Krajina of Croats, the onus of escalation then fell to Tudjman, who waited for an auspicious moment (maximum $p_2 > p_1$) to try to regain control. Likewise, to control Nagorno Karabakh, Armenians there had to eject an Azeri minority.

For cases of little mixing in settlement patterns, it is possible that even the knowledge that the minority does not have to fight to secede may make the com-mitment problem easier to resolve in the first place. Russians live almost entirely within one part of Estonia, so if they ever anticipate worsening oppression, they can simply declare independence and put the onus of violent escalation on the Estonian government. Further, anticipation of this fact may give the Estonian government incentives not to push the Russians too far. The logic of constitu-tional secession clauses is captured here—if everyone knows they can be unilat-erally implemented, an officially sanctioned exit option might smooth relations by reducing the majority's ex post incentives to exploit the minority.[40]

EXTERNAL GUARANTORS AND THE ROLE OF THE MINORITY GROUP'S "HOMELAND"

Of course, the commitment problem can be eliminated if there is some powerful third party willing and able to commit to intervene if the majority does not respect political commitments to the minority.[41] Due to the costs and character of ethnic wars, international organizations will rarely be able to make such commit-ments credible.[42] On the other hand, it is possible that if the minority in the new state has nearby brethren in a powerful state of their own—Serbs in Serbia, Hungarians in Hungary, Russians in Russia, etc.—then the anticipation of a reac-tion from this state may allow the majority in the new state to commit credibly.

The case of Serbia illustrates that not every "homeland" will be willing or suit-ably positioned to play this role. In fact, Milosevic's initial desire for a Greater Serbia implied that his interest was in *fomenting* abuse of Krajina Serbs by Croats rather than reducing it, thus aggravating the commitment problem. Likewise, if a

---

[40] On the downside, however, a secession clause could conceivably aggravate relations by giving the minority group the option of "holding up" legislation or other decisions by threatening to exit if not given a better deal (Quebec may illustrate this problem).

[41] The game can be modified to allow a third party to choose whether to intervene with force con-ditional on the division α chosen by the majority in the new state. If the third-party threat is credi-ble, then the effect on the game is the same as if the minority's prospects for war in the second period do not fall. See Van Houten 1995 for a careful analysis and discussion, which is the first to explore this possibility formally. Considering the problem of resolving civil wars, Barbara Walter (1997) has argued that a commitment problem similar to that considered here can be ameliorated by effective external (third-party) guarantees.

[42] See Walter (1997), however, for an argument that for civil wars in progress, external guarantees can provide crucial help in forging negotiated peace settlements.

government comes to power in Russia with irredentist leanings, the commitment problem will be likely to "kick in" in a number of the former republics, exacerbated as in Yugoslavia by Moscow-supported Russian groups of local extremists. Irredentists in Moscow would have the effect of increasing the value of a struggle for secession for minority Russian groups, thus making it more likely that the commitment problem could come into play. Further, if irredentists in Moscow help instigate incidents of ethnic violence in the former republics, the local Russians' fears of majority intentions might increase so as to make them worried about future reneging on the existing "ethnic contract" by the majority-controlled government. Increasing irredentism in Russia probably poses the greatest and most likely danger for a rapid, cross-border spread of ethnic conflict through the region.

EXTENT OF THE ANTICIPATED DROP IN ABILITY TO SECEDE

The more the minority expects that its prospects for seceding will fall if they enter the new state, the more likely it is that the conditions for the commitment problem to produce violence will hold.[43] This is significant for applying the model to cases in which a minority is already living in an established or consolidated state run by a distinct ethnic majority, such as, for example, the case of African Americans or other minorities in the United States. Here, we should expect large-scale violence or secession attempts only when something happens to make the minority fear a sudden and irreversible drop in bargaining power, meaning the minority's ability to fight for secession or autonomy.[44] For instance, once the Kosovan Albanians had accepted the drop in bargaining power following Milosevic's rescinding Kosovan autonomy in 1989, they faced no commitment problem until the next time something happened to shift relative military prospects further away from the Kosovars.

VALUE OF THE "EXIT" OPTION FOR MEMBERS OF THE MINORITY
AND THEIR SOCIAL AND POLITICAL ORGANIZATION

For simplicity, the model treated both majority and minority groups as unitary actors. In fact, *individuals* in both groups face a very difficult decision, and not all will choose the same way due to variation in individual circumstances. For example, faced with a future risk of oppression by the majority, a member of the minority might well choose simply to exit (emigrate) rather than take up arms and fight. Massive numbers of Serb refugees testify to the relative appeal of this option—fighting is very costly and very dangerous. We should expect, then, that the better the exit option, the lower the chance an individual will stay and fight.

In general, we would predict that urban dwellers with professional or other modern-sector skills would do better by exiting than would rural farmers (who lose their means of livelihood, land).[45] And by the same logic noted above, the

---

[43] For the formal argument, see Fearon 1994.

[44] Other conditions noted above need also to be met for the commitment problem to operate.

[45] Also, some research suggests that social networks among urban people are badly suited for mobilizing the kind of groups of young men needed for a guerrilla struggle, so that the value of the "fight" option would be higher for rural people as well. See Petersen (1992).

better one's expected exit option in the future, the lower the majority's incentive to oppress you in the future, so that the commitment problem might operate much more strongly for rural people than for urbanites. Largely consistently with these expectations, urban Serbs in Zagreb either took the exit option and became refugees in the early phase of the conflict, or have remained in Croatia, while the fight was prosecuted almost entirely by rural Serbs (aided by the JNA).

Implications for the Spread of Ethnic Conflict

The commitment problem argument is consistent with the view of the first half of this chapter, that ethnic violence in Eastern Europe is likely to be self-limiting for the most part. The principal causes of conflict in this account are particular to relations between two groups concerned with a certain patch of territory, rather than something likely to spread "like wildfire" across borders.

Nonetheless, the commitment problem argument does suggest two interesting points about the most likely paths for the international spread of ethnic conflict, should this occur. I briefly discuss these by way of a conclusion.

First, the commitment-problem logic is most likely to foster the rapid and catastrophic spread of ethnic conflict in the case of what might be called *nested minorities*. Diverse histories of nationalism and the construction of ethnicity have left, in several places around the world, the following sort of arrangement. Members of group A are a minority within an administrative unit dominated by members of group B, but group B can at the same time be viewed as a minority within some larger administrative, state, or regional unit in which group A constitutes a majority.[46] Some examples: 1. Serbs were a minority within Croatia, whereas Croats would have been a minority within a Serb-dominated Yugoslavia without Slovenia. 2. There was an Azeri minority within the Nagorno Karabakh Autonomous Oblast, whereas the Armenian majority within Nagorno Karabakh was a distinct minority within the Soviet Socialist Republic of Azerbaijan. 3. Irish Catholics have been a minority within Protestant Northern Ireland, whereas Protestants would be a minority within a unified Irish Republic; furthermore, Catholic Ireland may be viewed as a "minority" of sorts in the shadow of the United Kingdom. 4. Tamils are a minority within Sri Lanka, although in the larger region, including Tamils in nearby India, the Sinhalese are the minority.[47] In these examples, minority-majority relations are nested or linked together at successive administrative, state, and regional levels.

When there are nested minorities, a change of power relations or state collapse at one level can ramify via the commitment problem through the other levels. In the case of Yugoslavia, Tito's construction had solved the nested commitment problems by relying implicitly on a balance of power—Slovenia and Croatia bal-

---

[46] Donald Horowitz (1990, 454) discusses essentially this phenomenon, referring to ethnic minorities with an "external affinity." See also Kaufman (1996, 114).

[47] Tambiah (1986, 110) notes that the Sinhalese fear of being "engulfed" by south India inspires actions against the Tamils that risk making this true in a "self-fulfilling prophecy."

anced Serbia. Slovenia's decision to exit the federation implied that if Croatia remained in the federation, it would be a minority beneath the Serbs, and there was no question of the Croat leadership accepting any verbal or paper commitments from a Milosevic-led Serbia. In turn, however, the decision of Croatia to exit the federation implied a commitment problem for the minority of Serbs in Croatia, as argued above. Similarly, greater autonomy for Azerbaijan in the late 1980s increased the fears of the Armenians in Nagorno Karabakh, whose desires for their own autonomy then ramified into conflict with the local Azeri minority.

Fortunately, Yugoslavia appears to have contained the only major instance of such a nested-minorities problem in Eastern Europe (possibly Moldova-Transdnestr would count as well), so that the further spread of ethnic conflict due to their "unraveling" will not occur. Probably more significantly, the second (and related) way that the majority-minority commitment problem can play into the spread of ethnic conflict concerns the cross-border effects of irredentist politics. As noted above, increasing irredentism in one state, even at the level of declaratory rather than implemented foreign policy, can exacerbate the commitment problem in neighboring states with significant numbers of the minority perceived as co-ethnics of the irredentists. The biggest danger here obviously concerns Russia.[48] To date, Yeltsin's government has sent mixed signals concerning the "near abroad," speaking frequently of the rights of the Russian speaking minorities while being ambiguous and sometimes contradictory as to Russia's role in "protecting" them.[49] A more actively and openly irredentist policy might raise the value of the military or secessionist option for Russian-speakers in the "beached diaspora,"[50] thus raising the risk that the commitment problem between majority and minority could subsequently be activated. Alternatively, as the fear of Russian "fifth columns" grows in ex-republic majority governments, existing implicit bargains between majority and minority groups may be undermined. It may be that the Western powers and relevant international organizations can do little to prevent this from happening, but it surely makes sense to consider the possibility and what might be done about it—country by country—in advance.

[48] Increasing irredentism in Hungary, which is possible though less likely, would also exacerbate commitment problems in Romania and Slovakia.

[49] See the perceptive analysis by Van Houten (1995).

[50] The phrase is from Laitin (1995a).

Is Pandora's Box Half Empty or Half Full? The Limited Virulence of Secessionism and the Domestic Sources of Disintegration

STEPHEN M. SAIDEMAN

DOES SECESSION spread? If so, can it be contained? These two questions must be addressed to understand the challenges posed by ethnic divisions within and between states today, as secessionist conflicts have perhaps been the most controversial and internationalized form of ethnic conflict.[1] The coincidence of the disintegrations of the Soviet, Yugoslav, and Czechoslovak federations suggests that secession spreads with potentially nasty consequences. Further, there seems to be more secessionism today than ever before. Consequently, we need to comprehend the processes through which separatism within a particular state may or may not spread, causing conflicts within and between states. The heart of the argument here will be that secessionism is less likely to spread between states than previously thought, though it may spread quite rapidly within a state, as the events and institutions within states' boundaries greatly shape the incentives of politicians and the fears of ethnic groups. Separatist crises may generate dynamics that encourage separatism elsewhere, but to understand where it will (or will not) spread, we must study the conditions that foster separatism.

An alternative approach to this question is presented here, focusing on two interacting domestic processes that further separatism: the use of ethnic identities by politicians to gain and maintain power, and the ethnically defined security dilemmas faced by politicians' constituents. Although this interaction between ethnic politics and ethnic security dilemmas can be applied to ethnic conflict in general,[2] the focus here is on ethnic secessionist movements for three reasons: first, this article is responding to the conventional wisdom concerning contagion which, in turn, focuses on the threat of ethnically driven secessionism; second, the disintegration of the three states in question was the result of ethnic seces-

---

Note: Marijke Breuning, Miles Kahler, Stuart Kaufman, Lisa Martin, James Fearon, and two anonymous reviewers have provided insightful criticisms and suggestions. The latter half of this chapter was published as "The Dual Dynamics of Disintegration: Ethnic Politics and Security Dilemmas in Eastern Europe," *Nationalism and Ethnic Politics* 2, no. 1 (Spring 1996): 18–43. Any remaining difficulties are the author's responsibility.

[1] Not all secessionist movements are ethnic in nature, nor do all ethnic disputes become secessionist conflicts.

[2] For a similar approach focusing directly on ethnic conflict, see Kaufman 1996.

sionist movements, not just ethnic conflict in general; and third, focusing on a single form of ethnic conflict, secession, may help to isolate key dynamics that can then be applied to other forms of ethnic conflict.

This chapter isolates and compares some of the crucial events and dynamics driving the Yugoslav, Soviet, and Czechoslovak disintegrations.[3] This study indicates that the contagion at work was not secessionism but the processes spawned by the end of the Cold War—democratization and economic transition—and their impact upon the interests of politicians and the fears of their constituents.

Do Ethnic Dominoes Fall?

Conflict centered on ethnic identities (racial, linguistic, kinship, and/or religious identities) is not a new problem, nor are fears of contagious separatism. Secession and fears of it have haunted Africa since before most states gained their independence. Due to the weakness of the new African states and because of the perceived artificiality of their boundaries, a belief developed that any change in existing boundaries to reflect more accurately the distribution and demands of ethnic groups would challenge the legitimacy of all African boundaries. This fear has many names, including Pandora's box, balkanization, and the ethnic domino theory; and it has two key aspects: secessionism was thought to be contagious (diffusion); and fears of such contagion inhibited states from supporting secessionists or boundary alterations in Africa (escalation). This chapter takes issue with the former aspect of the ethnic domino theory: does separatism cause itself to spread?[4]

This chapter asserts that *positive reinforcing* dynamics developed within Czechoslovakia, the Soviet Union, and Yugoslavia, but that spatial diffusion was more limited than is often argued.[5] In other words, secessionism within each state increased the probability of more secessionism within each, but that the consequences of secessionism within one state for separatism in other states were not, and are not, so clear. There are two ways to consider how a political phenomenon diffuses: through processes generated by its occurrence (contagion), and through the lessons drawn by others from observing the occurrence (demonstration effects). To argue that secessionism is contagious would require showing that there is some process inherent within secessionist crises that causes it to spread

---

[3] One reviewer was concerned about the applicability of this argument beyond Eastern Europe, but this should not be a problem since the argument was derived mostly from the comparative politics literature on ethnic conflicts in Africa and South Asia and cases in these regions.

[4] This article solely deals with diffusion and not escalation, as defined by Lake and Rothchild (Introduction to this volume). The model developed in this article was originally intended to explain escalation—under what conditions states are likely to take sides in secessionist crises (Saideman, 1997).

[5] To clarify, the occurrence of a particular event may increase or decrease the likelihood of subsequent occurrences (Midlarsky 1970, 75). Diffusion may occur over time or space: a phenomenon may spread within a state or repeat itself over time (reinforcement), or it may spread beyond the boundaries of a state (spatial diffusion) (Siverson and Starr 1991, 12).

beyond a state's boundary. One kind of contagion may be inherent in secessionism: the departure of one ethnic group and its territory from a state may upset the political balance and cause other groups to secede. The discussion of the Soviet and Yugoslav cases below will illustrate this.

Another means by which a phenomenon spreads is through the lessons learned by policy makers, activists, and ethnic groups elsewhere—demonstration effects. As others in this volume develop the demonstration effects argument, I will focus here on a key problem with this approach. Any event provides a great deal of data to observers, who can then absorb a variety of lessons from the event. Arguments concerning demonstration effects often assume that politicians and followers will learn only one kind of lesson—one that encourages further political action, leading to repeated occurrences of the first event, that is, positive spatial diffusion. Reality is not so simple, as different individuals can consider the same event and draw completely different conclusions.[6] Was the legacy of Vietnam that the United States should not intervene abroad or that it should if it followed a different strategy? Are observers of Yugoslavia's disintegration encouraged by Slovenia's escape or discouraged by Bosnia's plight?[7] The lessons people learn may depend on their preferences before the observed event.[8] Although Hill and Rothchild argue that demonstration effects shape outcomes, they assert that "the propensity to engage in protest is structured by past conflict and cued by current protest events" (1992, 195–96). This opens up the question about whether the process at work is reinforcement or spatial: is the past conflict causing present conflict, or are external events? The impact of an external event will vary as the relevant actors differ in their inclinations to learn particular lessons.

Do political entrepreneurs and their followers learn from a secessionist movement's success that they can achieve similar success? Given the relatively simultaneous breakup of Yugoslavia, the Soviet Union, and Czechoslovakia, it would not be unreasonable to argue that successful secessionist movements encourage other separatists to act more aggressively as their goal seems more realistic, and as states seem to be less antagonistic to separatism and less supportive of the international norms of territorial integrity (Young 1992). The timing of the three federations' breakup would suggest that either one helped to cause the others (diffusion), or that their causes are related.

A successful secession may demonstrate by providing multiple lessons, causing elites leading ethnic groups elsewhere to change their beliefs. For a successful secession to encourage (rather than discourage) secessionist efforts by others, it must indicate that: the gains of seceding are greater than previously believed or

[6] For similar arguments, see Legro (1995, 101, 223); and Mercer (1996).

[7] There is evidence to suggest that elites within Eastern Europe are perhaps being discouraged because of Bosnia. Prominent Hungarian and Bulgarian elites have toned down their nationalist appeals and have worked toward agreements that pledge respect for minority rights (New York Times, March 25, 1995, H4).

[8] Hill, Rothchild, and Cameron (Chapter Three in this volume) attempt to explain how a single lesson can be generated by experts who are organizing collective action. However, their use of schema theory tends to undermine their argument since schema theory can explain how different people learn different lessons from the same event due to their predispositions (Jervis 1976).

that the costs of seceding are less than expected; success is more likely than previously believed; or some, many, or key states are less hostile to secessionism, so that one's efforts will probably face less international opposition than previously supposed.

The relatively low costs of the disintegration of the Soviet Union may have encouraged others. Though the Baltic republics did not gain independence quickly or without cost, relatively few lives were lost and relatively little damage was done, compared to the secessionist efforts of the Bengalis, the Croats, or the Bosnians. The Baltics' relatively low costs may have encouraged Slovakia to secede from Czechoslovakia, and it certainly encouraged other states within the Soviet Union to seek more autonomy. However, the severe costs incurred by Croatia and Bosnia as they seceded from the Yugoslav federation provide an important counter-demonstration, indicating that secession can be tremendously costly. It is not clear why outside observers would choose to learn from those that seceded cheaply, rather than learning from those that bore high costs for their efforts.[9]

Potential separatists may be encouraged to secede if their perceived likelihood of success is changed by a successful secession. The mere fact that a state could successfully secede probably has a huge impact on potential secessionists because success was so rare between World War II and 1991: only Singapore and Bangladesh were able to make the break. The breakups of Yugoslavia and the Soviet Union, along with the secession of Eritrea, indicated what could now be achieved. Like the wall falling in Berlin, the success of others encourages one's efforts as the estimated probability of attaining independence increases. Not all recent secessionist movements, of course, have been successful in attaining independence. The new peace accord may reduce violence within Bosnia, but Bosnia's government will not control almost half of its territory. Georgia's plight indicates that recognition may not mean independence, as it has been coerced and dominated by Russia (Hill and Jewett 1994). The Republic of Somaliland provides another discouraging example, as it has gained de facto independence from Somalia, but no state has recognized it. These counterexamples do not demonstrate that secession has been less successful recently than in the past. Instead, they indicate that potential secessionists have conflicting data as they reevaluate chances for success. Moreover, although few separatist movements succeeded before 1990, the failures of many attempts did not discourage others from trying.

Perhaps the biggest perceived sea-change in the international politics of secession, and the most encouraging one for potential secessionists, is that states are less opposed to secessionism than in the past. During the Cold War, few secessionist movements received significant support and they were rarely given diplomatic recognition. Since 1991, all the constituent republics of the Soviet Union have been recognized, Eritrea is now considered a state by the international community, and four former Yugoslav republics have received recognition and vary-

---

[9] See Fearon (Chapter Five) for a discussion of the tendency of demonstration effects arguments to omit countervailing forces.

ing levels of material support. Potential separatists may now believe that they will receive assistance or, at least, face less opposition from other states. Thus, the less hostile international environment may encourage ethnic groups to secede.

However, the record of opposition to secessionism before 1990 has been greatly exaggerated (Saideman, 1997). Although secessionist movements did not receive much assistance from most states during the Cold War, several groups did obtain significant support. Katanga's attempt to secede from the Congo was assisted by arms, finances, and mercenaries provided by Belgium, France, the Federation of Rhodesia and Nyasaland, and South Africa. Biafra received arms from France and the People's Republic of China through Gabon, the Ivory Coast, and Tanzania, as well as recognition from the latter three states plus Zambia. Bangladesh's secession was made possible by India's assistance and intervention. These cases are not meant to suggest that the international community encouraged secessionist movements, but that recent changes are less drastic than commonly thought. Though potential secessionists of the 1990s may believe they will face less opposition than before, the difference is one of degree and not of kind.

Recent secessionist conflicts do present many lessons for elites and ethnic groups considering secessionist strategies, but these lessons are ambiguous. Recent events suggest that both positive and negative spatial diffusion dynamics may be at work. Whether they cancel each other out is not clear. Although some ethnic groups were able to succeed while incurring relatively few costs, Croatia, Bosnia, and even Eritrea may serve as cautionary tales, possibly discouraging as much as the other cases encourage. The number of recent successful secessions is startling, and may encourage some dissatisfied ethnic groups to secede, but many other secessionist movements continue to make little or no progress toward their goals, including the Tamils in Sri Lanka, the Québecois, and several movements in India and Pakistan, to name just a few. The most encouraging development for potential separatists has been the increased apathy of the international community toward secessionism. This is tempered, however, by the international community's failure to stop the inheritors of the disintegrating state's institutions and resources from preying on other states that seceded from the broken state: for example, Serbia's conquest of portions of Croatia and Bosnia and Russia's coercive diplomacy in its "near abroad." Though the many counterexamples do not prove that secessionism will not spread, again they do show that recent events may discourage secessionism as much as encourage it.

Although demonstration effects may be positive or negative (or both), arguments based on the influence of demonstration effects upon separatism have a critical flaw: they ignore or gloss over the causal processes within states that drive some groups to secede, whereas others do not try or do not achieve success. Not all ethnic groups seriously consider secession; a change in the perceived probabilities and costs of secession (the demonstration effect) cannot be the only causal force at work. Why, then, do ethnic groups seek to secede? Focusing on the incentives of elites and the threats perceived by ethnic groups may provide a causal model that can begin to address these questions and explain whether secessionism spreads.

The Individual Pursuit of Power and the Collective Search for Security

Because the preceding analysis questions whether secessionism diffuses, we need to consider what caused three federations to disintegrate. Two distinct dynamics often interact, to varying degrees, intensifying ethnic conflict: politicians use ethnic identities to mobilize support to maintain and improve their positions; and ethnic groups fear for their security, a dynamic also known as the ethnic security dilemma. Studies of the former dynamic focus on competition within an ethnic group for political support, and analyses of the latter deal with competition between ethnic groups. These two kinds of competition will interact, increasing the intensity of both. The transition from communism and authoritarianism to market capitalism and democracy caused competitive processes to intensify by creating opportunities for political entrepreneurs to use ethnic identities for political gain and by increasing the level of threat that ethnic groups sensed. Here, I sketch out the two distinct dynamics—ethnic politics and ethnic security dilemmas, show how they interact, and then suggest how these interacting processes may cause or prevent secessionism.

Ethnic Politics

Ethnic identity often presents political entrepreneurs who seek to enhance or maintain their positions with tantalizing opportunities and/or tight constraints. The existence of ethnic diversity means that policies can be aimed at helping certain groups and gaining their support at the expense of others. The ethnic composition of a politician's pool of potential supporters shapes the likely ethnopolitical strategies that can be followed.[10] By specifying a few assumptions, the core dynamics of ethnic politics can be delineated. First, before maximizing any other interest, politicians must care about gaining and maintaining power, as this is the prerequisite for almost all other goals attainable through politics (Mayhew 1974; Ames 1987). The second assumption is that all politicians require supporters to attain and maintain their positions—the supporters forming the politicians' constituency. Leaders cannot rule without some support. How the constituency supports an elite varies, depending on the regime and on existing political institutions. In a democracy, the constituency's support comes through voting for individuals and parties. In an authoritarian regime, the constituency of the leaders consists of those who control the means of repression.

Once in positions of power, democratic and authoritarian elites care about preventing these supporters from leaving their coalition, that is, exiting (Hirschman 1970). When politicians' supporters exit from their coalitions and support a competing politician, the former may become less able to maintain their political positions. Thus, the supporters' potential for exiting is a crucial constraint for incumbent politicians and a vital opportunity for challengers. The degree to which

---

[10] Indeed, the specific design of federalism within Yugoslavia, the Soviet Union, and Czechoslovakia may help to explain their disintegrations, as the boundaries shaped the politicians' pool of potential supporters.

exiting is a threat to a politician's position depends upon how the constituents support the politician. If constituents support politicians with votes, then the question becomes: how much do the votes matter? Votes matter the most, and the political system is the most competitive, when the gain or loss of relatively few votes greatly changes the balance of political power. Likewise, if the constituency of a politician is the army, then the military's preferences are very constraining, particularly when there is someone else or some policy option around which the military can rally.

Responses to exiting depend upon who is exiting and who might exit. Policies aimed at attracting exiters or avoiding potential exiters' alienation require identifying these individuals or groups and their interests. Ethnic identity serves as one way politicians distinguish between actual, potential, and wavering supporters and their preferences. People care about policies affecting the group to which they belong.[11] Politicians, therefore, try to develop policies that favor groups to which their constituents belong, and avoid policies that hurt their constituents' groups. Consequently, the ethnicity of the politician's constituents is a key determinant of *who* might exit, *why* they should wish to exit, and *what kinds of policies* politicians may seek to avoid or embrace to prevent them from exiting.

Political entrepreneurs thus take positions and follow policies that emphasize a particular ethnic identity if it binds their supporters together. A politician needing the support of a religiously homogenous military will probably stress that religion to keep the key constituency together. Ethnic cleavages can also serve as a constraint upon politicians, making some policies politically difficult to advocate. Politicians try to avoid positions that might offend some ethnic groups in their constituencies, even if such positions are favored by other constituents. For instance, politicians needing the votes of both blacks and whites will try to avoid the issue of affirmative action.

However, how strongly politicians care about their constituents' ethnic identities depends upon the degree of competition politicians encounter for constituents' allegiance. A leader who does not have to worry about supporters exiting does not have to worry as much about alienating them. On the other hand, if the exit of supporters crucially weakens the politician and strengthens the competing politician, then each politician will be compelled to take increasingly strong stands in favor of policies that match the constituency's preferences, a process known as ethnic outbidding (Rothschild 1981; Horowitz 1985). Ethnic outbidding is a situation in which competing elites try to position themselves as the best supporters of a group's interests, each accusing the others of being too weak on ethnic nationalist issues. When conditions foster ethnic outbidding, the exit of ethnically defined supporters can change the balance of power domestically; most, if not all, politicians are compelled to take extreme stands favoring the ethnic group's interests.

This discussion of ethnic politics reveals some conditions that cause secessionist sentiment to develop. Political competition for the support of specific ethnic

---

[11] See Hardin (1995) for a rational choice explanation of why ethnic identities and ties matter.

groups often causes ethnic conflict to increase, because the competition forces politicians to support policies that hurt the economic opportunities, and sometimes physical security, of other ethnic groups in the polity. Sri Lanka exemplifies this dynamic, as competition among Sinhalese politicians for Sinhalese voters produced policies that increasingly marginalized and disenfranchised the minority Tamils, leading to a very violent secessionist movement. Where ethnic outbidding develops among politicians representing an ethnic group that is out of power and is the subject of discrimination, the outbidding process frequently leads to demands for secession. One of the big assumptions of ethnic politics models in general, and of this chapter specifically, is that individuals determine their interests through their ethnic identities and ties. This may be a huge assumption, but it is less heroic in contexts of ethnic insecurity.

Ethnic Security Dilemmas

"The proximate source [of extreme ethnic nationalism] is fear. It is fear for one's property and family, for one's ancestral graves and one's history, that leads people to 'cleanse or be cleansed.'" (Bookman 1994, 33).[12] This fear or insecurity is not supposed to exist at the level of domestic politics and society, but it is usually considered normal for international politics. When this insecurity exists, domestic politics can be similar to international relations.

The difference between international politics and domestic politics is the existence of a government in the latter that can adjudicate disputes and assure security for all citizens. International politics is a system of self-help, but domestic politics is supposed to be different. However, this theoretical distinction may be drawn so starkly that it obscures similarities between the two realms. The conflicts between states on the one hand and between ethnic groups on the other do share some characteristics so that theories developed to understand the former can be applied to the latter. Barry Posen (1993b) has taken the security dilemma and applied it to the relations between ethnic groups in collapsing empires. The approach taken here also applies the security dilemma to domestic ethnic politics, but differs from Posen (and Lake and Rothchild) by focusing on the continued existence of varying levels of authority and hierarchy, rather than on the translation of traditional military-strategic variables.

The security dilemma in international politics refers to the situation in which states, having no higher authority to protect them, have to take measures to ensure their security. These measures are seen as threatening by neighboring states, forcing them to respond, causing all states to be less secure (Jervis 1976). Posen argues that similar dynamics develop when empires collapse, as neighboring ethnic groups view each other as potential threats; the more a group coheres and mobilizes, the greater the threat it poses to others. He then applies several variables central to international security analysis to the politics of imperial decline. Although

---

[12] The following discussion is largely an extension of Horowitz's (1985) understanding of ethnicity and insecurity, though his discussion of secessionism differs from mine.

his discussion of these variables does present interesting insights, Posen's approach may be less useful for understanding the ethnic security dilemmas that exist in empires before they completely collapse and within existing states because he omits the state and existing authority from his discussion.

To understand ethnic security dilemmas, we must consider the role of the state in mediating or influencing the competition by ethnic groups for security. In an ideal state, there is no such competition because the state monopolizes the means of violence, and all ethnic groups are guaranteed security and fair adjudication of disputes. Where no state exists, as Posen portrays, ethnic groups compete with each other as if they were states, and act according to their military advantages. In between these extremes, states exist and shape the course of ethnic politics. In many political systems, the state may be biased toward or against particular ethnicities, so competition is waged among different ethnic groups for control of the state. If my group does not capture the state, someone else's will, and then we will be at the mercy of the state. Because of the state's resources, it can be an ethnic group's greatest ally or adversary. This is the heart of the ethnic security dilemma within existing states, and distinguishes it from the security dilemma in international relations. If the state cannot protect the interests of all ethnic groups, then each group will seek to control the state or secede so that they can control their own state, decreasing other groups' security and decreasing the state's ability to provide security for any group. Consequently, some of the dynamics present in international politics emerge domestically (Fearon, Chapter Five). For instance, each group will consider their interests and actions to be limited and benign whereas those of other groups are seen as irreconcilably hostile (Jervis 1976, ch. 3).

It is important to consider what is meant by security and insecurity in this context. Members of ethnic groups may be insecure about many things, but here security will refer to economic, physical, and political security. Economic security refers to a variety of issues shaping one's life-chances, including income, inflation, employment, and investment in one's region. Where ethnic differences already exist, economic competition can be perceived as a competition between ethnic groups for economic opportunities and resources, and "when economic conditions deteriorate, competition becomes more ferocious and fuels nationalist ideology" (Bookman 1994, 6). Ethnic groups that do better than average feel that they are being pulled down by the other groups. Ethnic groups that do worse than average are insecure, as they feel exploited. Any economic improvement by one ethnic group is frequently perceived as an example of favoritism by the center: the ethnic security dilemma has an economic component, as all sorts of motives and fears are read into any change in the economic status of each ethnic group. The economic insecurities will be most intense, of course, when a group has little control over the government, and when it fears that its economic well-being depends on the will of others.

Like economic security, physical security ultimately depends on whether an ethnic group has some control over the state. Physical security refers to the more basic aspects of life-chances: is my life at risk? Will my ethnic group survive

(Horowitz 1985, 175–81)? Fears about physical security are most concerned with first, other ethnic groups' perceived intentions and capabilities, and second, the state's ability and resolve to restrain the other ethnic groups and to protect one's group. Ethnic insecurity will increase: if leaders of ethnic groups threaten to expel members of other groups; if ethnic groups arm and form militias; if the state is perceived as being unable to stop violence perceived to be ethnically motivated; or if the state takes sides, abetting the efforts of one ethnic group and deliberately not protecting others. Although an ethnic group will become insecure if the outbidding politicians of other groups advocate threatening policies, this insecurity will greatly intensify if the group also has no control over the state. If it can block efforts by the state to abet other groups, then ethnic security exists. If an ethnic group has no such capability, it will seek it by trying to take control of the state or by trying to secede. Thus, like economic security, the question of physical security rests upon whether groups have political security: can they shape the decisions of the state?

Ethnic groups will feel most secure if they have control, or share control, over policies that affect them—political security. Political insecurity will be most extreme when a particular ethnic group captures the state, or an ethnic group is denied access to the state, or when the state is not yet captured but can be seen as susceptible to domination by one group.[13] When a single ethnic group controls all of the state apparatus, all other ethnic groups will be threatened, as they can no longer rely upon an impartial adjudicator of disputes or an unbiased protector. Instead, the resources of the state may be used against ethnic groups out of power in favor of those in power. Again, two responses are likely—attempts to gain control over the state or to opt out of it.

A similarly insecure situation exists when a single ethnic group is excluded from power, even if the regime itself is multiethnic. Pakistan before 1971 exemplifies the insecurity of excluded ethnic groups, as the Bengalis had no voice in the government nor any high-level officers in the military. After the 1970 election, which would have given the Bengalis a dominant role in the government, was contested by the military and the West Pakistanis, the only remaining solution for the Bengalis was to secede. Secession is one solution to exclusion: it is very difficult to be excluded from your own government.

The third situation, in which the state may be captured, is as prevalent today as it was during the period of decolonization. During transitions, it is not necessarily clear which groups will rule, which ones will be excluded, whether old guarantees will endure, and whether institutions designed to resolve or mediate conflict will operate successfully.[14] The cases discussed below fit into each of these categories, but particularly into the last one, as the economic and political transitions of the Soviet Union, Yugoslavia, and Czechoslovakia tended to increase the insecurity felt by all ethnic groups, including those that were advan-

---

[13] Political security will be affected by political institutions, which may give minority ethnic groups some insurance in the forms of federalism, minority vetoes, and other electoral laws that help minority parties (Lijphart 1977).

[14] See Fearon (Chapter Five) for the difficulties of making credible commitments in these contexts.

Ethnic Security

Threat of Supporters Exiting from Politician's Constituency	Relatively Insecure	Relatively Secure
High	[1] **Secessionism**	[2] Politicians are ignored, or increase insecurity
Low	[3] Strategies change, or security may develop	[4] **No secessionism**

FIGURE 6.1
Ethnic Politics, Ethnic Insecurity, and Secessionism

taged. In such situations, it makes sense for each group to try to gain control over the state or, if a group cannot, then to secede.

Interaction between Ethnic Politics and Ethnic Insecurity

Ethnic politics and ethnic insecurity interact, each reinforcing the other as the preferences of potential constituents, and thus the preferences and strategies of politicians, are shaped by their perceived security. Moreover, a state's ethnic security depends crucially on what politicians are doing: if politicians take radical stands favoring some ethnic groups at the expense of others, the security climate deteriorates. On the other hand, if politicians downplay ethnic identities, building multiethnic constituencies and developing civic or other nonethnic ideologies, then ethnic groups feel more secure. Using a two-by-two matrix (Figure 6.1), we can focus on four possible outcomes produced by the interaction of these two processes.

The two processes produce two relatively "stable" outcomes, and two outcomes in which either groups' security or the political entrepreneurs' strategies are likely to change.[15] In cell 1, politicians, fearing the exit of their supporters, emphasize ethnicity, reinforcing the existing context of ethnic insecurity. Politicians will opt for ethnically oriented policies, as their supporters' preferences will be quite intense due to their perceived insecurity. These policies will then favor some groups at the expense of others, causing the losing groups to seek more political power to ensure their security by means that may include secession, and causing the winning groups to be more dependent upon the state and upon their politicians for protection. As a result, conflict between ethnic groups will probably escalate, resulting in separatism by groups that cannot influence the state. This is a "stable" situation because politicians face little incentive to change their strategies and because the security of ethnic groups will not improve.

In cell 4, the two dynamics produce a more appealing stable outcome: relatively little conflict. Again, the two dynamics reinforce each other. Politicians will

[15] The word *stability* may seem strange here, as a situation characterized by extreme ethnic insecurity and ethnic outbidding may not seem stable, but it can be considered stable in the sense that politicians and their supporters will repeat their behavior over time.

be less interested in emphasizing ethnic identities and ethnically oriented policies if their constituents are relatively less interested in such issues, which they will be if their ethnic groups are secure. Politicians avoiding ethnic identity will support policies that favor all or most ethnic groups, building a more ethnically secure environment, with little support for separatism.

In cell 2, politicians try to use ethnic identities to mobilize support even though ethnic security exists. This is not a stable outcome, because either the politicians will not be successful in their efforts, as potential constituents do not care that much about ethnic identities, or the politicians' efforts will alter the context of the society, making ethnic identity an issue and ethnic groups increasingly insecure.

Cell 3 is not a stable situation, either: this is the case in which politicians avoid ethnic identity despite existing ethnic insecurity. This circumstance is unlikely to last long. Politicians will be tempted and even compelled to engage in ethnic politics when their potential supporters face extreme insecurity because of their ethnic identities. The supporters will demand that their politicians protect them, or find ones that will. Or politicians avoiding ethnic identities will create policies that alleviate the perceptions of ethnic insecurity, changing the state's political climate for the better.

Of course, neither cell 1 nor cell 4 is so stable that states would never go from no conflict to high conflict or the reverse, but such change will be more likely and easier in situations that are represented by cells 2 and 3. Recent events in Eastern Europe and the former Soviet Union show how these dynamics play out and interact, causing ethnic conflict to break out in several states virtually simultaneously without ethnic conflict diffusing across international boundaries, though these dynamics do cause ethnic conflict to diffuse over time—that is, through positive reinforcement.

Is Separatism Contagious in Eastern Europe?

Did any of the breakups of Yugoslavia, the Soviet Union, or Czechoslovakia cause the breakup of either of the others? The answer seems to be no—secession did not spread from the first to the second to the third state. Because the same initial conditions were present in each state, political and economic liberalization sparked similar processes in each state—ethnic politics and ethnic insecurity—spreading from one part of each state to the entire political system without causing other states to disintegrate.

Applying the distinctions and arguments drawn earlier will illuminate the key causal processes. What kinds of diffusion dynamics were at work in Eastern Europe in the late 1980s and early 1990s? As will be seen below, the dynamics of ethnic political competition within ethnic groups (ethnic outbidding) and between ethnic groups (ethnic security dilemmas) did have diffusing effects over time, in the form of positive reinforcement. The outbidding of politicians created and sustained the fears of ethnic groups, and the insecurities of ethnic groups resulted in support for outbidding politicians who then gained power and followed through on their promises, including the promise to seek independence. Reinforcement occurred in another way, as the attempted secession of one group from a state changed the interests of other groups within that state, because the balance of power within the state and the security of all remaining ethnic groups were altered.

Positive spatial diffusion of secessionism is hard to disprove, but was probably not a significant force in the three disintegrating federations. Did elites and ethnic groups reconsider their chances for success and the benefits of secession as they evaluated what was going on elsewhere? Such an argument might address Czechoslovakia's disintegration, since the processes that drove the Czechs and Slovaks apart largely began after the breakup of Yugoslavia and the Soviet Union were well underway. However, the positive spatial diffusion approach is less credible when applied to Yugoslavia and the Soviet Union, as the disintegration of each was the product of a long series of policies, crises, and events combined with the effects of similarly designed political institutions. The disintegration of both Yugoslavia and the Soviet Union was driven by elites and followers whose attention and interests were focused on dynamics internal to their state. The boundaries between states mattered for two reasons: first, each ethnic group's greatest threats were internal to their respective states—other ethnic groups and frequently the state itself; and second, politicians and movements were interested in gaining and maintaining power, which generally meant focusing on domestic institutions and constituencies: voters and other potential constituents largely resided within existing boundaries.

The disintegrations of Yugoslavia, the Soviet Union, and Czechoslovakia indicate that the contagious processes that did extend across the boundaries of Eastern Europe and the Soviet Union were democratization and economic liberalization. These changes spread from the Soviet Union throughout Eastern Europe and back, undermining the old order, causing politicians to consider different strategies for maintaining their positions, and intensifying the fears of ethnic groups. The end of communism meant that elites needed new ways to mobilize support. Elections compelled elites to compete with each other for the support of particular groups, leading to political campaigns that promised to use the state to benefit certain groups economically and politically at the expense of others, which, in turn, intensified the security dilemmas facing ethnic groups. Economic liberalization threatened great harm to groups that had been favored by the old system and posed new opportunities to previously disadvantaged ethnic groups, increasing the value of controlling the state or of creating new states to govern one's territory. The cases below will show how ethnic politics and ethnic security dilemmas combined to cause secessionism to spread within states from republic to republic, but not between states.

The Worst Case Scenario: Yugoslavia

Previously considered the ideal of ethnic accommodation with high rates of intermarriage and power-sharing institutions, Yugoslavia's carnage has alarmed Europe and the world. The original dispute between Serbia and its autonomous republic, Kosovo, increased tension between Serbia and Yugoslavia's other constituent republics, leading Slovenia to secede after a short battle with the Yugoslav army and catalyzing a war between Croatia and Serbia that spread to Bosnia. Despite the NATO-enforced peace agreement, there is still concern whether conflict will spread to Macedonia or Kosovo, potentially drawing in neighboring states. Yugoslavia's destruction shows how the incentives of politicians and the insecurities of ethnic groups can interact in ways that hurt nearly everyone's interests.

Although the combatants in the Yugoslav conflict can trace their disputes back to World War II and before, the pivotal period was the mid-1980s. The circumstances were ripe for politicians to engage in ethnic politics. Economically, two factors essentially invited politicians to engage in ethnic politics: the extreme decline of Yugoslavia's economy in the 1980s and the uneven development of Yugoslavia that corresponded with republic boundaries (Woodward 1995b). Indeed, the distribution of wealth, jobs, technology, and future economic growth was more uneven in Yugoslavia than in any other socialist country, with Slovenia, Croatia, and Vojvodina being much better off (Bookman 1992, 58). This inequality created resentment among the favored, who felt that they were subsidizing the others, and among those who were doing poorly, with the result that all groups developed strong but conflicting preferences about the direction and pace of economic reform. Fears of physical security were especially easily manipulated because of the memories of atrocities during World War II. Politically, incentives existed for elites to take advantage of ethnic identity. Because power was regionally focused, each republic having its own party system, resources, and political institutions, it made sense to play to a limited audience: the key supporters within the existing republic boundaries. This particular federal structure meant that politicians could gain and maintain their positions if they attracted support from only one ethnic group: Serbs in Serbia, Croats in Croatia, and Slovenes in Slovenia.

Specifically, the stage was set for the rise of Serbian nationalism, which resulted from Slobodan Milosevic's efforts to gain power in Serbia. In 1987, the League of Communists of Serbia was divided, facing the difficult problem of maintaining legitimacy in the face of economic disaster. Milosevic found a successful formula for providing the party with a mission and for his leadership of the party: defending Kosovo's Serbs against the Albanian majority. The approaching six hundredth anniversary of the Battle of Kosovo gave Milosevic the opportunity to take a stand on the Kosovo issue, creating a supporting coalition of nationalists and conservatives. Because Kosovo has a critical role in Serbian history and nationalism, Milosevic was able to purge the party of those who opposed his nationalist strategy, thereby gaining control of the Serbian Communist party (Gagnon 1991, 21).

Milosevic's successful use of the Kosovo issue to build a nationalist coalition had two important effects on the politics of Yugoslavia. First, it increased the insecurity of non-Serbs in Yugoslavia, particularly as Milosevic's statements and actions threatened to alter the existing institutions that gave other ethnic groups some control over Yugoslav decision making. Reasserting Serb control over

Kosovo threatened to alter the balance of power within federal institutions, as Serbia could add Kosovo's vote to Montenegro's and its own (and later, Vojvodina's), giving Serbia the ability to block decisions at the federal level. Indeed, the final act that broke the Yugoslav federation was Serbia's obstruction of the presidency's normal rotation to a Croatian politician in May 1991, triggering the secession of Slovenia and Croatia a month later. The policies taken toward Kosovo were perceived to be part of a larger effort to recentralize the Yugoslav political system, which would lessen the ability of the various ethnic groups to control their destinies. The growing insecurity in each republic was revealed by the success of politicians who promised extreme policies to support their particular ethnic groups.

The second effect of Milosevic's Kosovo strategy was to demonstrate how successful a nationalist strategy could be in Yugoslavia, so that Milosevic continued to pursue nationalist policies, and politicians in Yugoslavia's other constituent republics began to emphasize ethnic nationalism as well. In the election campaigns following Milosevic's rise, competing politicians promised to follow chauvinist policies to defend their ethnic group against the others in Yugoslavia. "The results of the first free elections in Yugoslavia since World War II, held in 1990, set the stage for the civil war that broke out in summer and fall 1991. In those elections, strongly nationalist parties or coalitions won in each of the republics" (Hayden 1992, 654). Each of the winning parties or coalitions then kept their promises. Once in power, Croatia's Franjo Tudjman began using Croatian nationalist symbols, including those from the fascist Ustashe regime, and ceased to recognize the existence of minorities within Croatia, particularly the Serbs. This, in turn, reinforced the threat perceived by Serbs living outside Serbia.

Politicians engaged in competition to be the best nationalists, leading to policies and promises that threatened the livelihood, rights, and security of minorities within each republic. The increased insecurities of ethnic groups led to greater support for politicians who promised protection of certain groups, including secession as means of assuring security (Woodward 1995a). Ethnic politics and ethnic insecurity reinforced each other, causing the conflict to escalate. Remaining within the federation was no longer possible for Croatian and Slovenian politicians because they had based their political ambitions on promising secession and because their supporters were increasingly alarmed by the rise of Serbian nationalism. Over the course of six months in 1990, support for secession within Slovenia went from 28 percent of the population to a clear majority (Bookman 1992, 96).

Ethnic conflict spread swiftly within Yugoslavia because changes in the federal structure influenced the security of all ethnic groups. Slovenia and Croatia were threatened by any increase of Serbia's influence at the federal level, and they also wanted to protect their economies from the downward-spiraling Yugoslav economy (Bookman 1992, 95–96). Bosnia and Herzegovina and Macedonia felt insecure in a Yugoslavia without Croatia and Slovenia, compelling them to also secede despite their initial reluctance. However, ethnic conflict has not been as virulent as often feared. Perhaps the most remarkable aspect of this crisis is that it has not yet spread beyond the boundaries of what was Yugoslavia. Although refugee flows into neighboring states and sanctions have hurt these neighboring states, armed conflict has still respected Yugoslavia's boundaries. This case indicates that secessionism does tend to spread within the body politic, but not necessarily beyond it. Positive reinforcement occurred within Yugoslavia as the efforts of each group to improve their security decreased the security of the others, intensifying the ethnic security dilemma for all ethnic groups, and causing a cascade of seceding territories.

Sudden Disintegration: The Soviet Union

The breakup of the Soviet Union is such a large and complex event that this chapter cannot do it justice. This section will focus instead on how the central questions of this chapter apply to the Soviet Union's disintegration: were the dynamics of ethnic politics and ethnic insecurity important? How did secessionism spread within the Soviet Union? Though the specific events and processes were not identical among the fifteen constituent republics, the politics and conflicts of all were shaped by changing political opportunities, economic fortunes, and security caused by Gorbachev's three key reforms: *glasnost*, *perestroika*, and democratization. These reforms gave politicians greater incentives to use ethnic identities to mobilize support, increased the economic stakes involved, and exacerbated the threats felt by many ethnic groups. In this section, some of major events and processes of the Soviet Union's disintegration will be discussed, with an emphasis on the Baltic republics as they led the independence efforts.

As the Baltic republics of Estonia, Latvia, and Lithuania were the last to be incorporated into the Soviet Union, it makes sense that they were the first to try to leave it. Indeed, the process by which they "joined" the USSR eventually catalyzed the process that ended in their independence. Glasnost in the Soviet Union resulted, among many other things, in the release of information about the Molotov-Ribbentrop pact that divided Poland between Nazi Germany and Stalin's Soviet Union and gave Stalin the Baltics. The inclusion of the Baltics in the Soviet Union required forceful exportations and executions that also became public knowledge with *glasnost* (Lieven 1993, 222). Shortly thereafter, popular movements arose and people began to organize protests on anniversaries of the pact and of other salient events. Initially, the demands of Baltic popular fronts, and those in other republics, focused on economic and environmental issues. Chernobyl was a catalyst, causing each republic to seek greater control over its environment and economic development. Glasnost mattered because it gave individuals more information about the past and about ongoing events within the Soviet Union and within Eastern Europe, and it allowed individuals to organize and voice their protests (Gellner 1992, 249). The success of some individuals and groups within the Baltics to voice their demands without repression demonstrated to potential activists elsewhere in the Soviet Union that the government was not going to repress dissent as much or as forcefully as it had in the past.

Similarly, perestroika increased the interest each ethnic group had in gaining more autonomy. Perestroika was the effort to reform the economy, which would have distributive consequences, hurting some groups more than others. For instance, because of the peculiar division of labor, a new project in Estonia might require immigrants from other republics, especially Russians. Such projects stimulated opposition because of the increasingly perceived threat that the titular nationalities of the Baltics—Lithuanians, Latvians, and Estonians (especially the latter two) —were being overwhelmed demographically by other ethnic groups, especially Russians. This was both an economic and a political threat, because changes in the demographic balance might prevent the "native" ethnic groups from winning elections in a more democratic system if such changes were allowed to continue. Perestroika increased the tensions between the Baltics and Moscow as inflation accelerated and shortages of various goods developed. The Baltic countries demanded their own currencies to buffer themselves from Soviet inflationary pressures, and pushed for a faster pace of reform so that the center's control over trade, which was blamed for shortages, would be removed (Bookman 1992, 99–100). These economic demands reinforced the Baltics' desire for more political control.

The third key reform was democratization, whereby the constituency of politicians changed from the party apparatus to each republic's citizens. Rather than appealing to those higher up in the party, politicians increasingly had to appeal to masses of citizens participating in the political process (Roeder 1994). Although the competitiveness of elections varied among the republics, the results of elections mattered within the Baltic republics, causing incumbents to lose and nationalists to gain seats in legislatures. Because of past events and ongoing economic problems, those politicians who took nationalist stands tended to do well. Sajudis, the Lithuanian Reconstruction Movement formed in 1988, called for sovereignty in February 1989. It won thirty-six of Lithuania's forty-two seats in the Soviet Union's Congress of People's Deputies and dominated the 1990 elections by winning 80 percent of the seats in Lithuania's Supreme Soviet (Krickus 1993).

Elections in the Baltics and elsewhere not only meant that politicians had to gain popular support in terms of votes, but they also had to compete with others for such support. Elections caused each nationalist front to take increasingly extreme positions, eventually leading to declarations of independence. "The leaders [of the Popular Front for Latvia], however, were generally more moderate than the membership at large. Their room for maneuver was constrained, not only by their program and radicalized membership, but also by the more militant groupings on their political flanks who were quick to cry 'Betrayal!' at the first sign of compromise by the Front" (Muiznieks 1993, 199). The Estonian Popular Front [EPF] also faced ethnic outbidding, as a competing institution developed—the Congress of Estonia (Furtado and Hecter 1992, 196). Because its supporters were exiting to back a competitor, the EPF tried to outbid the competition, pushing for independence. Even the local Communist parties tried to take stands on nationalist issues to regain legitimacy and support (Lieven 1993, 220).

Ethnic outbidding and political and economic insecurity thus produced independence movements that won elections and gained power in the Baltics. The tremendous popular support for these efforts and the unsuccessful efforts to repress these movements led most observers, as well as participants in Russia's political system, to acknowledge that the Baltics could and would become independent. Their secession did not mean that the Soviet Union was no longer viable, but did spur a set of processes that resulted in fifteen independent states standing in the wreckage of the Soviet Union. The Baltics' separatist efforts encouraged activists' efforts in other Soviet republics and forced Soviet officials to consider a new Union treaty, which, in turn, set the stage for the August coup of 1991.

Many of the events and reforms pushing the Baltics toward independence also influenced the politics of other Soviet republics. The combination of glasnost and Chernobyl energized opposition to the Communist party and to the Soviet Union in the Ukraine and elsewhere. The ability of Baltic movements to organize and protest demonstrated to Ukrainian activists what was possible in Gorbachev's Soviet Union (Krawchenko 1993, 75). Unlike other reputed "demonstration effects," there was a clear, positive lesson to be learned, and it influenced activists' actions because the same federal government that allowed the Baltics to speak more freely also ruled the Ukraine. Indeed, some compromises made by the Soviet government with the Baltics were then generalized to the rest of the republics, including greater economic freedom (Hazard 1993, 120). Nagorno Karabakh became a crucial issue within Armenia because glasnost, perestroika, and democratization allowed information about the plight of Armenians there to be known and to be used by opportunistic politicians (Dudwick 1993). The path chosen by Georgian elites to political success and independence was not particularly democratic, but was still influenced by the same forces that shaped the other separatist movements (Jones 1993, 294). As a result, Georgian political movements competed with each other in their efforts to exclude the other minorities in the republic, including the Abkhazians and the South Ossetians, which would have severe consequences for the newly independent Georgia.

To deal with the republics, Gorbachev negotiated a treaty to determine the powers and rights of the republics and the new Union of Soviet Sovereign States, which did not include the Baltic republics, Georgia, or Moldova. This treaty was to be signed on August 20, 1991. However, on the day before, forces within the Soviet Union seeking to maintain its integrity launched a coup to prevent the signing of the Union treaty. Their failure delegitimated key federal institutions, the last remaining ties holding the Soviet Union together, and increased each republic's insecurities. Although many did not like the pace or content of Soviet reforms, the possibility of finding themselves in a Soviet Union ruled by conservatives and nationalists was too much, and intensified the ethnic security dilemma. The first act of the State Council, a body including the presidents of the republics and the president of the USSR, was to recognize the independence of the Baltics (Hazard 1993, 130). After the coup, attempts to develop a new Union treaty were blocked by the republics as each made new demands. Once the Ukraine held its elections on December 1, 1991, resulting in majorities favoring independence, even in the predominantly ethnic Russian Crimea, the Soviet Union's end was near (Krawchenko 1993, 92).

Although physical insecurity varied among the republics, ethnic outbidding was consistently present once politicians had to appeal to voters and had to compete with others for those votes. Increased political competition by itself was not the cause of the Soviet Union's disintegration, but the strategies used by politicians and the preferences articulated by the masses did help cause the collapse, because they largely focused on ethnic groups' rights and interests. The first parties to organize were devoted to protecting various national groups' interests, as the "Western" model of parties competing on a left-right spectrum made little sense in a "classless" society.

Ethnic insecurity also developed in several republics as the independence movements progressed. Minorities within these republics had relied upon the Soviet government to guarantee their security. With the decline of the center and the rise of politicians who made their careers by promising to favor the titular nationalities, Russians outside Russia, Abkhazians and South Ossetians in Georgia, and the Chechens in Russia, to name just a few, had much more to fear. Although they might not have been happy under the old Soviet Union, these minorities did not have to worry as much then about the state being used by an ethnic group to deprive them of their land, their jobs, or their political rights. Now the old guarantees are gone, the states that have replaced the Soviet Union are not seen as impartial adjudicators of potential disputes, and so the ethnic security dilemmas have become acute, leading to separatism within the successor states.

The Velvet Breakup: Czechoslovakia

Czechoslovakia's disintegration is remarkable for its nonviolent nature. Not only was force not used to maintain the integrity of the state but the seceding ethnic group, the Slovaks, did not perceive a physical threat. However, they certainly did perceive an economic threat, which helped to motivate both voters and politicians. Since Czechoslovakia was the last of the three Eastern European federations to break up, it is plausible that actors within this state were influenced by the examples set by separatist movements in Yugoslavia and the Soviet Union. However, the political consequences of economic reform were the primary force at work.

Czechoslovakia faced problems in reforming their polity and economy similar to those of Yugoslavia and the Soviet Union. Reforming the economy had very clear distributional consequences as the Slovaks were certainly going to bear the brunt of the pain because their region contained most of the obsolete factories and industries. Reforms exacerbated existing resentment over policies perceived to favor the Czech lands at the expense of Slovakia. Investment by

Czechoslovakia in Slovakia focused on two areas, raw materials and the defense sector, while final production and high tech industries were concentrated in the Czech lands, appearing to limit Slovakia's industrial development (Bookman 1992, 97–98). The combination of a poorly developed economy and economic reform that would hurt Slovakia caused economic insecurity as Slovaks feared for their jobs.

Economic insecurity caused Slovak voters to support parties promising to slow the reform process and protect the interests of Slovaks. In the Czech lands, popular sentiment favored a relatively faster pace for reform efforts to create links with Western Europe. The election of 1992 produced results that could not be reconciled to create a stable government. Vladimir Meciar led the Movement for a Democratic Slovakia, promising to increase Slovakia's autonomy and to slow the pace of economic reform. Vaclav Klaus led the conservative, promarket reform Civic Democratic party in the Czech Republic. These two parties won pluralities of seats in their respective republics, and had little room to form a coalition due to their differences on market reform and on the desired degree of the constitution's centralization. Meciar sought a confederation with an essentially sovereign Slovakia, whereas Klaus favored either a federal state or two independent states. After a series of meetings, the two leaders agreed on June 20, 1992, to divide Czechoslovakia into two independent states. They also agreed *not* to hold referendums on this issue. Once the issue of secession was decided, they were able to negotiate the split fairly easily and with no violence at all (Pehe 1993).

The one lesson that actors within Czechoslovakia may have learned from external events was that nationalism was a useful tool for gaining political office. Meciar's campaign was not unlike those of politicians in Soviet republics or Yugoslav republics, as he emphasized the rights and insecurities of Slovaks, seeking to gain the votes of that one ethnic group. Consequently, he alienated the Czechs, who were more influential in the federal system, and offended the Hungarian minority in Slovakia. Though the Slovaks did not fear the Czechs as much as the Croats feared the Serbs, the ethnic outbidding by Meciar and Klaus, along with the perceived bias of economic reforms, did poison the political atmosphere, making compromise impossible and disintegration more likely. Again, politicians' promises and policies created insecurities, increasing their incentives to use ethnic politics: the dynamics reinforced each other, causing ethnic conflict to intensify, leading to demands for autonomy and secession.

Comparative Disintegration

Because the breakup of the Yugoslav, Soviet and Czechoslovak federations occurred within the span of a single year, it is plausible that the first secessionist efforts encouraged favorable conditions for later separatist movements. Although this is clearly the case within each country, it is not the case that separatism and ethnic conflict within one state greatly encouraged or exacerbated similar processes within other states. The rise of nationalism within Serbia did foster nationalism and secessionism in Slovenia and Croatia, which, in turn, caused Macedonia and Bosnia and Herzegovina to secede, as well. The separatist efforts of the Baltics did encourage each other and help to foster similar movements in other Soviet republics. However, the disintegration of Yugoslavia did not cause or catalyze the breakdown of the Soviet Union or vice versa. The federal government of each state did not disappear overnight as it became clear that federations in Eastern Europe were becoming an endangered species. Instead, each state broke apart after a series of events and rising nationalism dating back to the mid-1980s, which were produced by ethnic politics and ethnic insecurity. The parallels between these states, particularly between Yugoslavia and the Soviet Union, are the result of the fact that these states faced similar political problems in similar circumstances: specifically, the problem of how to recreate polities, economies, and societies after the collapse of communism, and how to maintain power.

Perhaps the key reason why Czechoslovakia, Yugoslavia, and the Soviet Union fell apart almost simultaneously was the timing of the first relatively competitive elections. Yugoslavia's first fairly free elections were in 1990; the various Soviet republics held elections between 1989 and 1991; and Czechoslovakia's first federal elections in June of 1992 were its last. "In the more democratic environment, nationality leaders, armed with the structural resources control of the union republics provides, have greater incentives to actively mobilize their ethnic constituencies, and in turn face new pressures from them" (Young 1992, 92). Elections meant new opportunities for new politicians and movements, increased competition for political support, and decreased security as perceived by ethnic groups, who now had to worry about who would govern them, but who might be able to do something about it. In each country, incumbent politicians and nationalist upstarts faced similar political dilemmas and resolved them with comparable strategies. Moderation tended to be punished as those who weakly supported nationalist causes faced serious competition that promised to defend the nationality's interests better.

Politicians outbidding incumbents and competitors on ethnic issues were successful because changing political institutions and the perils of economic reform caused most ethnic groups to perceive threats to their economic, political, and physical well-being. Once they acted to protect themselves, other ethnic groups within their political systems felt threatened, setting off a spiral of insecurity. Policies favoring Serbs caused Croats and Slovenes to feel less secure, as well as making other minorities within Serbia more fearful. Policies, including secession, promised and enacted by Croatian and Slovenian elites to favor the titular nationalities made the Serb diaspora feel insecure, causing them to rely upon Serbia's protection, which exacerbated the insecurity of all Yugoslavia's ethnic groups. Likewise, the efforts of the Baltic titular nationalities to gain control over their governments increased the insecurity of minorities in the region, including Russians. This has become an issue that nationalists within Russia have used to criticize Yeltsin. These criticisms have occasionally pushed Yeltsin to make statements about protecting the rights of Russians in the near abroad.

The politicians' strategies worked because the masses of voters, who could now reasonably threaten to exit to competitors, perceived themselves to be insecure. The promises kept by winning politicians to seek autonomy and/or develop discriminatory economic and other policies reinforced existing fears. Each of these three states faced similar political and economic problems left in communism's and authoritarianism's wake, providing incentives for politicians to emphasize ethnic identities and creating insecurities in the minds of ethnically defined voters.

States' boundaries largely contained these processes because elites and ethnic groups were responding to threats and opportunities within these boundaries. Although elites could learn lessons from the experiences of other states, their incentives were shaped by existing international and republican boundaries. With the onset of democracy (or at least semi-democratic processes), politicians had to focus on new constituents, either voters or the remnants of the state, who largely lived within preexisting boundaries. Thus, they paid more attention to cues from within the state than from outside it.

Ethnic threats are also largely, though not entirely, confined to within state boundaries. The worst thing that can happen to an ethnic group is for the state within which it resides to be captured by an adversarial ethnic group. Hungarians in Slovakia are much more concerned with the behavior of the Slovakian majority and the state they dominate than with Serb actions in Vojvodina because Slovakia's state apparatus can be directly used against them.

Finally, the nature of secession implies that the focus of movements will be on the state's behavior itself and not on external actors. Secession is an attempt to separate an ethnic group and its territory from an existing state. Thus, the first question one must ask of any secessionist movement is why those people would want to leave that state, and the answer will invariably focus on the previous abuses and the potential policies of the state where they reside. These threats are influenced by the interaction of ethnic politics and the ethnic security dilemma. Secession will not occur simply because a politician or a group realizes that it is more possible or less costly now than it was before. Although elites and ethnic groups in the Soviet Union, Yugoslavia, and Czechoslovakia certainly were aware of events in other Eastern European countries, and may have consciously adopted strategies that were similar to the more successful movements, their desires to secede were largely determined by events, opportunities, and threats within their respective states.

CONCLUSION: GOOD NEWS AND BAD NEWS

Secessionism is probably not as contagious as it is often portrayed, and the mechanisms by which it is thought to spread need to be seriously reconsidered. Diffusion, in the form of demonstration effects, does not have the clear consequences analysts often argue. The lessons to be learned from the Yugoslav crisis may or may not encourage potential separatists, depending on whether potential separatists consider themselves to be more like Slovenia or Bosnia, which in turn partly depends on their predispositions. Instead, ethnic conflict and secessionism tend to be generated and reinforced by the internal interacting dynamics of ethnic politics and ethnic security dilemmas. This offers both good news and bad.

Because demonstration effects are clearly not as influential as often perceived, secessionism is not as likely to spread as is commonly thought. Ethnic strife can be managed by states if they ameliorate the insecurities perceived by existing ethnic groups and give politicians relatively few incentives to play the ethnic card. Such states will not break apart merely because they contain ethnic groups, who might observe such events occurring elsewhere.

The bad news is that ethnic conflict and separatism spread quickly within states and are hard to cure. Because ethnic conflict reinforces existing insecurities and provides politicians with additional incentives to gain support through mobilizing ethnically defined supporters, it tends to spread within the state as it causes ethnic groups to seek control of the state or opt out of it. Unless it is treated quickly, such ethnic conflict can spread within the body politic so that it soon becomes unmanageable.

Further, contagions can be quarantined, but the causes of ethnic conflict and secession are more complex and harder to eliminate. If the processes by which ethnic conflict develops are ethnic politics and ethnic insecurity, there are some possible institutional solutions that might be recommended. The approach taken here stresses the imperatives of political competition between and among ethnic groups. Although the obvious answer would be to advise repression, that may merely delay the onset of conflict, as the Eastern European experience testifies.

Instead, there are two very different methods to deal with ethnic politics in democracies: compel politicians to rely on multiple ethnic groups for support (through vote-pooling) or create a single party for each ethnic group (consociationalism). Vote-pooling works by causing politicians to appeal to more than one ethnic group, forcing them to moderate their positions and creating disincentives for ethnic outbidding (Horowitz 1985). Consociationalism works by limiting the ability of supporters to exit and by giving each ethnic group a share of power. If the only other parties are those representing other ethnic groups, there is little interest in exiting, and if each ethnically defined party controls some of the reins of the state, each group feels more secure (Lijphart 1990).

Because the key dynamics are related to politicians' interests and ethnic groups' insecurities, international efforts must focus on these dynamics. The United States, its allies, and international organizations must offer incentives to politicians to moderate their policies and give assurances to ethnic groups that they need not fear for their security. Recent efforts to tie membership in NATO's Partnership for Peace program and preferential access to the European Union to treatment of minorities may help to finesse the ethnic security dilemmas in Eastern Europe and the former Soviet Union. The success of NATO's peacekeeping mission in Bosnia will depend on whether every group feels secure. If not, politicians will gain by playing on fears of insecurity.

More work needs to be done on these issues. This chapter's purpose has been to question existing understandings of how separatism spreads and to develop an alternative understanding that places the key sources of ethnic conflict and secessionism within the confines of each state. External events matter less than the strategies of opportunistic politicians and the insecurities of ethnic groups.

CHAPTER SEVEN

The Spread of Ethnic Conflict in Europe: Some Comparative-Historical Reflections

SANDRA HALPERIN

EUROPE during its supposed "one hundred years of peace" (1815–1914) was the scene of recurring ethnic conflict (see Appendix, Table A7.1). Ethnic conflict was endemic throughout the region and had, as well, a high propensity to spread. After World War II, there was a sharp decrease in the number of ethnic conflicts in Europe, and where they occurred, they did not spread.

This chapter is concerned with structures and processes that contributed to the generation and spread of ethnic conflict in nineteenth- and early twentieth-century Europe. It argues that the generation and spread of ethnic conflict during that period was associated with certain features of European society that were destroyed in the course of the world wars and that, as a result, ethnic conflicts occur far less frequently in Europe today and, where they occur, they no longer have a propensity to spread.

Other contributors to this volume predict that ethnic conflict in Europe today will not spread. James Fearon, in this volume, argues that "Ethnic conflicts have properties that should tend to make them self-limiting in geographic extent," because the principal cause of ethnic conflicts—a "commitment problem" involving lack of guarantees of minority rights—"are particular to relations between two groups concerned with a patch of territory" rather than something "likely to spread 'like wildfire' across borders." But at times ethnic conflicts have "spread like wildfire." They did in Europe before 1945, as is shown in Table 7.1.

Clearly, at certain times and places, ethnic conflict is not self-limiting.

To explain why, it it necessary to analyze socio-economic and political structures that facilitate the spread of ethnic conflict, rather than individual groups, or their strategic interactions. Arguments that focus on dynamics that operate within or among individuals and groups tend to emphasize factors that are always and everywhere present. As David Lake and Donald Rothchild observe, "the ethnic balance is constantly in flux and some uncertainty over the intentions of others is ever present," thus "*problems of credible commitment in ethnic relations are universal*" (Chapter One in this volume, emphasis added). Combining the analysis of such factors with models of diffusion processes can show how alterations in the environment may move a society from intercommunal coexistence to conflict; however, neither models of strategic interaction nor models of diffusion, nor their

TABLE 7.1
The Spread of Ethnic Conflict in Europe Before World War II

Date	Event
1830s	
1830–1831	Polish insurrection
1830–1833	Belgian revolution
1830–1831	Bosnian revolt
1831	Uprising in Rome, Parma, Modena, Bologna
1831	Rebellion in Albania
1831	Uprising in Hungary
1831	Uprising in Bulgaria
1831	Uprising in the Danubian principalities
1832	Sonderbund rising in Switzerland
1832–1842	Rebellion in Montenegro
1832–1835	Rebellion in Albania
1833	Insurrection in Serbia
1833	Insurrection in Albania
1833–1840	Basque uprising
1834	Rebellion in Bosnia-Herzegovina
1835	Uprising in Turnovo, Bulgaria
1837	Catholic riots in Rhineland, Westphalia, Posen
1840s	
1846	Uprising in Galicia
1847	Civil War in Switzerland
1/1848	Milan uprising
1/1848	Uprising in Sicily
1/1848	Uprising in Palermo
2/1848	Uprising in Naples
3/1848	Sardinian conflict
3/1848	Berlin uprising
3/1848	Milan uprising
3/1848	Piedmont-Austrian war
3/1848	Uprising in Vienna
3/1848	Uprising in Pesth
3/1848	Uprising in Posen
3/1848	Uprising in Venice

combined insights, can predict when and where an initial wave of ethnic conflicts will begin, or which countries will follow the example of the first.

This chapter explains when and why ethnic conflict is not self-limiting by linking the generation and spread of ethnic conflict to socio-economic and political structures that were prevalent throughout Europe in the nineteenth and twentieth centuries but that were eliminated in the course of the world wars. The first

TABLE 7.1 (continued)
The Spread of Ethnic Conflict in Europe Before World War II

Date	Event
3/1848	Insurrections in German states
4/1848	Insurrection in Baden
5/1848	Uprising in Vienna
5/1848	Riots in Milan
5/1848	Serbo-Hungarian civil war
6/1848	Uprising in Wallachia
7/1848	Insurrection in Ireland
8/1848	Uprising in Livorno
9/1848	Insurrection in the Ionian Islands
1848–1849	Hungarian insurrection
1848–1849	Piedmont-Austrian war
3/1849	Insurrection in Naples
1900–1921	
1900	Revolt in Albania
1901	Polish riots in Posen
1903	Uprising in Macedonia
1903	Uprising in Bulgaria
1903	Rebellions in Albania
1905	Pogrom in Russia
1905	Rebellion in Kroya and Argirocastro, Albania
1906–1907	Insurrection in Elbasan, Albania
1908	Revolt in Macedonia
1909	Armenian massacres
1910–1912	Insurrection in Albania
1911	Uprising in Galicia
11/1913	Anti-Prussian riots in Zabern and Alsace
1914	Rebellion in Albania
1915–1923	Armenian massacres
1916	Conflict in Turkestan
1916	Irish rebellion
1917	Flemish Separatist movement in Belgium
1917–1921	Russian nationalities

section specifies the process by which ethnic conflict spreads across national borders. The second section discusses conditions in Europe during the nineteenth and twentieth centuries that facilitated the spread of ethnic conflict. The third section shows how the world wars, by changing the ethnic map of Europe, destroying the traditional social structure of the region, and placing the economies of Europe on a wholly different footing, eliminated the conditions that had fostered the generation and spread of ethnic conflict in Europe during the nineteenth and early twentieth centuries. Applying the discussion of previous sections to the recent conflict in Bosnia, the fourth section shows how the presence of the structures characteristic of Europe before the world wars gave conflict in Bosnia a propensity to spread in 1914, and how their absence today has inhibited the spread of the recent Bosnian conflict, either through diffusion or escalation. However, in a postscript, the prospect of a reemergence in Europe of both the structures and the conflicts of the pre-World War II era is considered.

How, Why, When, and Where Ethnic Conflicts Spread

"Ethnic Conflict" is conflict about "political, economic, social, cultural, or territorial issues between two or more ethnic communities" (Brown 1993, 5).[1] Ethnic conflict in one state can spread to other states in either of two ways: by igniting similar conflicts in other countries (diffusion), or by drawing other states into the fighting (escalation).

Ethnic conflict spreads by diffusion when the "reference group" of the belligerents extends beyond the boundaries of the state. In these cases, the outcome of a conflict in one state will bear on the relations of power between members of the same groups living in other states. Two conditions increase the likelihood that this situation will arise. The first is where the ethnic map of a region is sharply incongruent with its political map, as was the case in Europe throughout the nineteenth and early twentieth centuries. During this time, national integration remained incomplete and highly problematic in the states of Western Europe, and Eastern Europe was a virtual mosaic of "nested" ethnic communities. The second condition is the presence of social revolutionary conflict. At these times, ethnic conflict may fuse with the more general or larger social conflict. As Anthony Smith points out, "national aspirations tend to combine with other non-national economic, social, or political issues, and the power of the movement often derives from this combination . . . neglected, oppressed, or marginalized ethnic communities or categories fuse their national grievances and aspirations with other non-national aspirations and grievances" (1991, 145). During the 1830s, the 1840s, and the beginning decades of the twentieth century, ethnic conflicts in Europe fused with transnational labor and enfranchisement conflicts and, as they swept through Europe in waves of revolutionary violence, ethnic conflict spread, as well.

Ethnic conflict also spreads by drawing in other states (escalation). States will intervene in an ethnic conflict in another state for two reasons. First, states will intervene when an ethnic conflict in a neighboring state fuses with social revolution. In Europe in the nineteenth and twentieth centuries, revolutionary uprisings

---

[1] An "ethnic community" is "a named human population with a myth of common ancestry, shared memories, and cultural elements; a link with a historic territory or homeland; and a measure of solidarity" (Smith 1993, 28–29).

in one country (such as in France, Naples, and Russia) tended to trigger similar uprisings elsewhere in Europe. As a result, other states viewed social revolution anywhere in Europe as a threat to the dominant system throughout the region and operated in concert to suppress revolution wherever it occurred (see Appendix, Table A7.3b).

During the nineteenth and twentieth centuries, states everywhere in Europe were continually beset with domestic conflicts growing out of efforts either to challenge or to defend existing structures: for or against extension of the suffrage, redistribution of the national product, changes in property relations, higher wages, shorter working days (see Appendix, Table A7.2).

Because the upper classes of Europe held identical positions and had the same privileges, social revolution anywhere in the region threatened not only the dominant class at home but also the dominant European social class system. Thus, the balance of power among contending forces within one state was of critical concern to all other states in the region.

Historically, elites have allied with elites in other states to put down class challenges to the existing order. In the nineteenth and early twentieth centuries, European elites joined together to suppress local uprisings and revolutions that threatened to undermine their power and privileges. British, French, and Spanish forces in Spain (1820, 1821, 1826–1833), Austrians and Piedmontese nobles in Naples (1820, 1848), British and Portuguese in Portugal (1833–1840), French and Italians in Rome (1849) and in Sicily (1860), Austrians and Russians in Hungary (1849), German and Finnish forces in Finland (1918), and Romanians and Hungarians in Hungary (1919) joined together, fighting side by side with "foreign" class allies, to suppress dissident and revolutionary elements from among their own countrymen. The military intervention by Great Powers in European domestic affairs helped to preserve the essential contours of local class structures in Europe until 1945.

That periods during which ethnic conflicts in Europe spread by diffusion (see Table 7.1, above) coincided with waves of social revolutionary violence throughout the region can been seen in Figure 7.1.[2]

States also intervene for essentially imperialistic motives. Ethnic conflicts in the Balkans during the 1800s, 1820s, and 1870s spread by means of escalation because they provided opportunities for Balkan groups and European states to pursue imperialist goals in the area (Table 7.2).

Although it may be true, in general, that ethnic conflict is inherently self-limiting, it is not self-limiting when it fuses with labor or enfranchisement struggles, or when surrounding states are seeking opportunities for imperialist expansion (Table 7.3).

---

[2] Data for this chart are listed in the appendix. Class conflict includes violent demonstrations for the extension of the suffrage; and strikes, riots, and demonstrations by wage workers and the unemployed that are severe enough to provoke state action, such as police or military operations, and/or the imposition of a state of siege or of martial law.

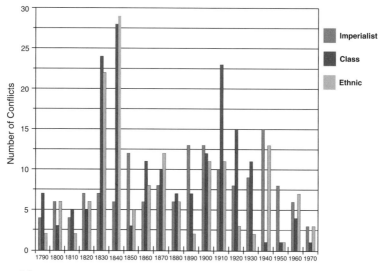

FIGURE 7.1
European conflicts, 1790–1970

CONDITIONS LEADING TO THE GENERATION AND SPREAD OF ETHNIC CONFLICT
IN EUROPE[3] IN THE NINETEENTH AND EARLY TWENTIETH CENTURIES

A period of conflict and change began in Europe with the industrial revolution at
the end of the eighteenth century, and culminated in the world wars at the beginning of the twentieth century.

Following the French Revolution of 1789 there were twenty-five years of
almost uninterrupted warfare in Europe (1792–1815), "warfare on a scale
unprecedented since the barbarian invasions" (Blainey 1973, 75). These wars
were a symptom of revolutionary change. During that quarter of a century of
warfare, the framework of European society was shaken to its foundations. The
end of that world war (1815) and the beginning of the next (1914) marks a
period of social conflict. The conflicts that occurred in Europe during that time—

---

[3] European Russia is treated here as part of "Europe." During the nineteenth and early twentieth
centuries, Russia officially recognized the crest of the Urals and of the Caucasus as its European limits, though the boundaries of the Russian administrative divisions bore no relation to these. These
areas were considered by other states to be part of Europe and were claimed and fought over by
Romania, Czechoslovakia, Germany, Poland, and Finland. On the other hand, areas of Asian Russia
in contention among European powers were considered as part of Asia and thus as potential colonial
acquisitions rather than as a division of European territory.

The provinces of the Ottoman Empire that lie on the continent of Europe are also treated as part
of Europe. These provinces were part of Europe prior to the fourteenth century, and the populations
of those areas considered themselves and were considered by Europeans to be European. In the nineteenth and early twentieth centuries, they were clearly bound up with European movements and
events. Balkan nationalist movements were among the first to emerge on the continent following the
French Revolution, and the revolutions of 1830 and 1848 reverberated throughout the Ottoman
Empire's European provinces (although not in the Asian portion of the empire.)

TABLE 7.2
The Spread of Ethnic Conflict in the Balkans

Date	Event
1800–1810	
1804–1813	Uprising in Serbia
1807	"Rebellion of Tican" in Srem, Austria
1807	"Rebellion of Djak" in the Banat
1807	Insurrection in Bosnia
1809	Rebellion of Jancic in Bosnia
1809	Uprising in Tyrol
1820s	
1820	Uprising in Piedmont
1820	Massacre of Turks at Petras, Greece
1820–1821	Revolt in Naples and Sicily
1821	Piedmont revolt
1821	Insurrection in the Danubian principalities
1821–1830	Greek revolt
1870s	
1871	Croat rebellion in Rekovica
1875–1876	Uprising in Bosnia-Herzegovina
9/1875	Insurrection in Bulgaria
1876	Serbia, Montenegro versus Turkey
1876	Bulgarian uprising
1876	Bulgarian massacre
5/1876	Rebellion in Macedonia
1876–1878	Insurrection in Crete
1877–1878	Insurrection in Thessaly

primarily, but not exclusively, ethnic, class, and imperialist—were generated by the vast restrictive system that allowed landowners and wealthy industrialists to monopolize land as well as the entire field of industry and trade. Restrictions on ethnic minorities and on labor provided the conditions for the fusion of ethnic and class tensions. They also prevented the expansion and integration of domestic markets, and so made states dependent on the acquisition of foreign markets and investment opportunities. Eager to protect their monopoly position at home and reluctant to mobilize a mass base, elites promoted imperialist expansion abroad in order to avoid the development of the home market. In the two-phased world war at the beginning of the twentieth century (1914–1918 and 1939–1945), the old social and political world in Europe was swept away. The enormous material changes that took place in Europe in the course of the wars reduced the incidence and spread of conflict in Europe by radically altering its ethnic map, eliminating sharp political and economic inequalities, and restructuring economies in ways that eliminated the need for imperialist expansion as an engine of growth.

TABLE 7.3
Summary: How, Why, Where, and When Ethnic Conflict Spreads

	Ethnic conflict spreads	
By means of	Because	Where and when
diffusion	the reference group of the belligerents extends beyond the boundaries of the state	the ethnic map of a region is not congruent with its political map
	ethnic conflict fuses with transnational class conflict	political and economic rights throughout a region are denied to ethnic minorities or lower classes
escalation	other states fear the spread of revolutionism and attempt to contain it	the structure of rights throughout a region advantages and disadvantages the same groups
	other states seek to exploit opportunities for imperialistic expansion	unwilling to extend rights to the mass of the population, state elites seek abroad for markets and opportunities rather than develop domestic ones

The Ethnic Map of Europe

European states, like those in the Third World, were deliberately constructed entities, as numerous scholars have pointed out (e.g., Duby 1980; Poggi 1978; Anderson 1974; Strayer 1970; Mattingly 1955). They came into existence and defined their boundaries by the use, or the threatened use, of force. Nation states in Europe did not evolve gradually from preexisting communities: they were not based on cultural uniformity, and they did not correspond to historic or ethnic divisions. The older states of Western Europe were formed through the conquest and assimilation by a dominant "core" of culturally distinct "peripheries" (e.g., Great Britain, France, Spain). Political entities were formed elsewhere in Europe with total disregard for the ethnicity of the subject populations. Thus, conflicts involving ethnic minorities were a constant threat to peace in Europe: in the 1820s in southern Europe and the Balkans, after 1830 in Western Europe, and in 1848 and following World War I throughout Europe.

After the Napoleonic Wars, Poland was divided up among Russia, Prussia, and Austria; Norway became a subordinate unit of Sweden; Finland was made a subordinate territory within the Russian Empire. The Czech people lived under the domination of a foreign ruling class. Belgians were dominated by the Dutch until 1830 (and by the Germans between 1914 and 1918). Ireland, which had been subjugated by force to English rule, continued to be dominated by a favored minority of ex-conquerors throughout the nineteenth century. During the nineteenth century, not a single decade went by without some crisis over the Irish

Question.[4] In Germany, the territorial duchies (e.g., Bavaria, Saxony, Swabia, Franconia) remained the focus of patriotic sentiment throughout the century. During the 1920s, there were separatist movements in the Rhineland and in the Bavarian Palatinate.[5] Germany also contained significant ethno-linguistic minorities, most prominently French and Polish. Catholics rioted in Germany in 1836, in 1864 and 1866, and in 1874–1875. There were anti-Semitic riots in eastern Prussia in 1881 and in Hamburg, Frankfurt am Main, Würzburg, Karlsruhe, and smaller places in 1919.

From 1903–1905, a tide of pogroms against Jews swept Russia in Belostok, Odessa, Nikolaev, Kiev, and some sixty-six other towns and villages, leaving hundreds of Jews dead and thousands destitute (Urusov 1908, chs. 4 and 5). One of the principal factors contributing to the Revolution of 1917 in Russia was the disaffection of the major non-Russian nationalities. All the revolutionary parties of Russia counted among their leaders members of the educated classes of many nationalities (Aspaturian 1968, 143). In 1896, Kurds and regular Turkish troops slaughtered between five and eight thousand Armenians in Constantinople. A Turkish and Kurdish massacre of one million Armenians began in April 1915 (Bryce 1972; Arlen 1975; Pearson 1983). In the Balkans, there were uprisings of Albanians throughout the nineteenth and early twentieth centuries. There was recurring discontent and armed insurrection in Bosnia-Herzegovina between 1878 and 1914. The war in Europe in 1914 was instigated by the attempt by traditionalists and conservatives in the Hapsburg Empire to end the drive of the Slavic peoples in the empire for national autonomy.

The spread and management of ethnic conflict was an issue of increasing international concern in Europe throughout the nineteenth and early twentieth centuries, and was a direct cause of World War I. The minority system set up by the League of Nations after the war was an expression of this concern.[6] However, neither the League's Minority Treaties, nor the revision of frontiers and the reshuffling of populations following World War I, resolved the problem of ethnic minorities in Europe. Although some minorities were eliminated by the transfer

[4] Robert Goldstein records a continual stream of agrarian uprisings and riots in Ireland throughout the century, as well as the crises these events engendered in London (1983, 229–30, 252, 257, 258–62).

[5] In September 1923, separatists seized Düsseldorf, and a month later, the "Rhineland Republic" was proclaimed at Aachen (October 21) and at Coblenz (October 25). Bonn, Wiesbaden, Treves, and Mainz were also occupied by separatist forces. The "Autonomous Government of the Palatinate" was proclaimed at Speyer on November 11 and was officially recognized by the French high commissioner (Mowat 1927, 254–57; Benns 1930, 394–402).

[6] The basic documents relating to the League minority system include the following: Protection of Linguistic, Racial and Religious Minorities by the League of Nations (1927.I.B.2); Official Journal, Special Supplement no. 73, Documents Relating to the Protection of Minorities by the League of Nations (1929); Protection of Linguistic, Racial or Religious Minorities by the League of Nations (C.8.M.5.1931.I). C. A. Macartney (1934) combines general analysis of the problem with an evaluation of the minority work of the League of Nations. Useful, too, are de Azcárate (1972), and Stone (1932).

and reshuffling of populations, others, including Jews, the Poles of German Upper Silesia, and the Macedonians, continued to hold minority status in states dominated by other nationalities. Still other masses of people, among them large numbers of Germans, Hungarians, Albanians, and Bulgarians, were converted by the settlement into new national minorities. In the new state of Lithuania, approximately 2 million, or 16 percent, were minorities: Jews, 8 percent; Poles, 3 percent; Russians, 2.5 percent; and others, 2.5 percent (League of Nations 1926, 106). In the new state of Latvia, of the population of 1.6 million in 1920, 1.35 million were Lettish-speaking Latvians; the remaining .25 million consisted of Russians, Lithuanians, Germans, and Jews (104–5). The Treaty of Neuilly assigned some 3 million Magyars to Czechoslovakia, Romania, and Yugoslavia. The seven hundred thousand Magyars of Slovakia, the eastern province of Czechoslovakia, resisted assimilation into the ruling Slovak majority, and complained of political and economic exploitation (Janics 1975). Local reforms, in particular national discrimination in land reforms undertaken during the interwar years in parts of Central and Eastern Europe, exacerbated interethnic tensions.[7] Ethnic tensions were also exacerbated by border disputes after the war. Vilna and Galicia were annexed by force. Germans and Poles disagreed over Silesia; Russians and Poles disagreed over boundaries; so did Czechs and Magyars, Serbians and Bulgarians, Russians and Romanians, Romanians and Magyars, and Greeks and Turks. Throughout the interwar period, statesmen grounded demands for frontier changes on the argument that it was their national duty to rescue co-national minorities from oppression by "alien" masters. This became a key element in the propagandistic scheme used by Hitler to justify his expansionist policy.

Class Conflict in Europe in the Nineteenth and Early Twentieth Centuries

During the nineteenth and early twentieth centuries, the struggle of ethnic minorities in Europe to secure equal rights merged with the more general struggle of lower classes for extension of the franchise and workers for better living conditions.

"Class conflict" is conflict between classes over rights and privileges, including the right to vote, secure bread at an affordable price, organize, raise wages, shorten hours of employment, and work in safe conditions.[8] Class conflict, thus, includes enfranchisement conflicts, food riots, and labor unrest.

[7] For instance, in Transylvania, Slovakia, Backa, and Banat, where landless Hungarian peasant laborers lived side by side with Romanian and Serbian peasants, Hungarian peasants were considered to be part of an "enemy nation" and received a less than equitable share of the lands of their former Hungarian masters (Seton-Watson 1945, 79, 297).

[8] Classes represent locations, places in the social structure, defined in terms of structural relations of inequality with regard to some fundamental or central distributive value, i.e., power, wealth, status, or some combination of these. Classes are sets of individuals that can be defined by certain common interests, by the fulfillment of certain functions, and the holding of certain positions.

During the nineteenth and early twentieth centuries, powerful landowning classes and wealthy elements of the industrial bourgeoisie sought to maintain legal, social, and land institutions that effectively excluded ethnic minorities and lower classes from political life and from opportunities for economic advancement. As industrialization proceeded within this system of restrictions, states were continually beset with domestic class conflicts growing out of efforts either to challenge or to defend this system.

In the course of the nineteenth century, the monopolization of land, industry, and trade in Europe led to increasing inequalities of income and to the growing impoverishment of the mass of the population. In 1900, the gulf between rich and poor was greater than in any previous or subsequent period of European history (Romein 1978, ch. 13). On the eve of World War I, England consisted of "small islands of luxury and ostentation surrounded by a sea of mass poverty and misery" (Joad 1951, 558). Widespread poverty, squalor, and poor health were characteristic features everywhere in Europe. As organized labor replaced the peasant masses, and the strike replaced the food riot, conflicts between rich and poor reached unprecedented levels.

In nearly all states in Europe, the franchise remained highly restricted until well into the twentieth century. European "democracy" before 1945 was a severely limited form of representative government. Universal, equal, direct, and secret suffrage became the norm throughout Western Europe only after World War II. On the eve of World War I, Norway was the only country in Europe with universal and equal suffrage. Before World War II, except for Norway, democracy was everywhere constructed on the basis of a highly restrictive, means-tested suffrage, which excluded the majority of the population from participation in the political process. Like democracy in the ancient world, it was really an "egalitarian oligarchy," in which "a ruling class of citizens shared the rights and spoils of political control" (MacIver 1932, 352). Universal adult suffrage would have enfranchised 40 to 50 percent of each country's population. In 1910, only some 14 to 22 percent of the population was enfranchised in Sweden, Switzerland, Great Britain, Belgium, Denmark, the Netherlands, and Germany (Table 7.4). Where the suffrage did include members of the poorer classes, three-class and other weighted and plural voting systems, as well as open balloting and restrictions on and biases against working-class organizations and parties, made it futile for poor people to vote. Thus, the figures listed in Table 7.4 do not reflect the actual number of people who were permitted to vote under the systems existing at the time.

In every decade of the nineteenth century, violent conflict erupted over efforts to expand or preserve the existing structure of rights within European societies. The landed upper class was eventually willing to extend democratic rights to the upper reaches of commercial and industrial wealth; but after 1848, both wings of the propertied class closed ranks to oppose further extensions of the franchise to minorities and the lower classes. Because the Great Powers of Europe operated in concert to suppress civil wars and put down revolutionary forces throughout the region, these conflicts frequently escalated.

TABLE 7.4
Percent of European Population Enfranchised, 1910 (by Country)

Finland	45	Austria	21
Norway	33	Sweden	19
France	29	United Kingdom	18
Spain	24	Denmark	17
Bulgaria	23	Portugal	12
Greece	23	Romania	16
Serbia	23	Russia	15
Germany	22	Netherlands	14
Belgium	22	Italy	8
Switzerland	22	Hungary	6

Source: Goldstein 1983, 241.

Throughout the nineteenth and early twentieth centuries,[9] ethnic minorities and working classes tended to be similarly situated with respect to economic opportunities, political participation, and rights of citizenship. As a result enfranchisement conflicts and conflicts involving ethnic minorities and labor were thoroughly intertwined.

Ethnicity and class, in fact, were often overlapping social-class categories. In the nineteenth and early twentieth centuries, different ethnic or national groups often represented particular economic classes within societies. In some areas of Central and Eastern Europe, there was a threefold national and social distinction: the upper classes, the urban classes, and the serfs, and they belong to three different nationalities. In certain parts of Hungary, for instance, the landed gentry were Magyars, the urban middle class German-speaking, the peasants Croat or Slovak natives. Successive waves of conquest had originally left two distinct classes: one formed by the conquerors—Magyars, Germans, Swedes, Turks, Poles—and the other by the conquered—Czechs, Slovaks, Serbs, Slovenes, Vlachs, Ruthenes, and White Russians, the Finnish and Lithuanian nations of the Baltic, and the non-Turkish races of the Balkans.[10] Later, colonization left a threefold national and social class structure: the privileged conquering races; the conquered serfs; and midway between the two in legal status, the German, Polish, or

[9] It is difficult to distinguish clearly between labor struggles and enfranchisement struggles. Most strikers simply wanted to improve their wages, hours, and working conditions. The overwhelming majority of strikes after 1850 arose from wage disputes, especially between 1910–1911 when inflation threatened to erode working-class living standards (Geary 1981, 122–25). But strikes were a bargaining tactic for other issues, including the right to vote. In Belgium in 1902 workers went out on strike in an attempt to force an extension of the franchise. In 1906, the Free Trade Unions and Social Democrats adopted the same weapon to combat a proposed restriction of the suffrage in Hamburg (Evans 1979).

[10] Why did successive waves of conquest leave two classes and not more? The upper classes of the conquered population tend to assimilate culturally to the conquerors. For instance, when the Poles became the ruling class north of the Carpathians, the nobles of Ruthene origin became Polonized. As a result, there were Polish serfs, but there were no Ruthene nobles.

Jewish colonists.[11] The social division coincided with the racial, the conquerors occupying the position of landowners and administrators; the colonists supplying the urban and artisan classes, and in some cases the military's, while the conquered tilled the land (Macartney 1934, 82–83). Thus, class and minority issues were thoroughly intertwined in the 1848 revolutions or when, for instance, Slovak or Ruthenian serfs rose up against their Magyar or Polish lords, as in Austria-Hungary and in Poland in 1831, 1846, and 1910. When a revolt against the Austrian Landwehr law in Boka Kotorska in June 1881 spread to Krivosije, the proclamation of martial law there provoked an insurrection that spread to the regions along the frontier with Montenegro and toward southern Bosnia, and lingered on in eastern Herzegovina until November 1882. These were both ethnic and class conflicts, precipitated by a combination of denationalization policies and agrarian conditions. Although ethnic and class conflicts were often fused in Europe during the nineteenth and early twentieth centuries, they are not fused of necessity: conflicts involving ethnic minorities are "ethnic conflicts" when they are largely concerned with nationalism, issues of nationality, or national rights may appropriately be called "ethnic conflicts"; "labor conflicts" are those in which labor issues are clearly at the center of concern.

Like conflicts involving ethnic minorities, labor conflicts were seen by the League of Nations as a potential threat to international peace. After World War I, the League set up an International Labor Office (ILO) and imposed upon all its members the obligations of becoming members of the organization and of performing the duties involved by such membership. The constitution of the ILO begins by recognizing that: "the League of Nations has as its object the establishment of universal peace, and such a peace can be established only if it is based on social justice; . . . conditions of labor exist involving such injustice, hardship, and privation to large numbers of people as to produce unrest so great that the peace and harmony of the world are imperiled."

However, labor conflicts after World War I grew in strength and number. After World War I, Western states confronted both newly organized labor movements at home and a Bolshevik revolution abroad. During the interwar period, with revolutionary turmoil throughout Europe, traditional and conservative elites organized against domestic labor movements through a variety of corporatist arrangements, and internationally, supported Germany's rise as a bulwark against communism. The Second World War was the result of these policies.

Imperialism in Nineteenth- and Early Twentieth-Century Europe

Imperialism—the attempt by a state to seize the land or territory of another state, or to establish direct or indirect forms of control over territories outside its own borders—was endemic in Europe throughout the nineteenth and early twentieth

---

[11] The colonists were, in most cases, invited into the area by the landowners. Or, as in the case of the Saxons in Transylvania, the colonists filled an existing economic and social need and did not displace or come in conflict with the earlier conquerors.

centuries (see Appendix, Tables A7.3a and A7.3b). Monopoly[12] placed limits on growth and generated pressures for expansion. Expansionist policies designed to establish protected "spheres of influence," secure cheap sources of raw materials and labor, and redress the balance of forces (class or ethnic) within states, gave rise to more or less continual imperialist rivalries in Europe. Concerned to maintain political and economic restrictions on other classes and on minorities, landed and industrial elites proposed and advocated imperialism abroad as an alternative to the development of the home market, and as a means of alleviating land hunger and pacifying peasants.[13] In fact, industrial capitalist development in Europe was fed by expansion. Throughout the nineteenth and early twentieth centuries, European states annexed other territories and engaged in imperialist rivalries and wars, both in Europe and outside the region.

Economic development in Europe before World War II proceeded principally by means of lateral gains, through the acquisition of spheres of interest, rather

[12] Monopoly is generally understood to mean a position in law or in fact enabling the monopolist to produce or sell particular goods to the exclusion of all competitors. A number of writers maintain that all monopoly gives rise to a tendency to decay and stagnation. Lenin argues, for instance, that "as monopoly prices become fixed, even temporarily, so the stimulus to technical and consequently, all progress, disappears to a certain extent" (1948, 120–21). However, other writers view monopoly as a condition of economic progress and of growth. The strongest defense of monopoly is the Schumpeterian argument which holds that innovation—and thus expansion—will not come about unless there is an expectation that a monopoly position and the profits that go with it can be obtained. Monopoly means security, and without security there would be no steady investment, no constant expansion of the market, no research into new techniques. Therefore the existence of monopoly is a condition of progress, and monopoly profits are the mainspring of growth (Schumpeter 1947, 87–91).

But typically the pursuit of monopoly has been a speculative gamble, rather than a search for security. Its aim is to achieve domination, not innovation or the general good. As Braudel points out, at the top of the English East India Company, the Hudson's Bay Company, and all such enterprises were "small ruling groups, obstinately attached to their privileges, thoroughly conservative and in no sense looking for change or innovation" (1979, 2: 446). The aim of agricultural protection was not to develop agriculture, or to advance the public good by making the state more self-sufficient, but to keep prices high in a noncompetitive sector.

[13] The notion that the acquisition of new territory, accompanied by a subsequent increase in state wealth, is a means of mediating internal conflict, is an old one. Francis Bacon, counselor to James I, argued that the colonization of Ireland would relieve English overpopulation, reduce the risk of internal rebellion due to food shortages, and simultaneously strengthen the authority of the crown (in Maxwell 1923, 270). In *Federalist Paper No. 7*, James Madison advocated American expansion on the western frontier as a solution to the growing conflict between different sectoral interests in the economy. In the nineteenth and twentieth centuries both socialists and capitalists suggested that imperialist expansion might enable the metropolitan industrial proletariat to escape immiseration through an absolute increase in wages and standard of living. In their attempt to prove the material advantage of colonialism, imperialists "stressed the value of the colonies chiefly as a market for British emigration" (Burt 1956, 446). Cecil Rhodes has been quoted as having remarked in 1895: "I was in the East End of London yesterday and attended a meeting of the unemployed. I listened to the wild speeches, which were just a cry for bread, and on my way home I pondered over the scene and became more than ever convinced of the importance of imperialism....My cherished idea is a solution for the social problem, i.e., in order to save the forty million inhabitants of the United Kingdom from a bloody civil war, we colonial statesmen must acquire new lands to settle the surplus population, to provide new markets for the goods produced by them in factories and mines....If you want to avoid civil war you must become imperialists" (in Lenin 1948, 79).

than by intensive gains, through improved organization or productivity. Imperialism was, above all, a form of protection for dominant groups seeking to avoid the further development of the home market, and thus to preserve their monopoly position at home. Before 1945, foreign investment was pursued in many European countries at the expense of domestic investment and to the detriment of domestic growth. In Britain and France, the two largest foreign investors during the nineteenth century, domestic industry clearly suffered because investors failed to exploit opportunities at home (Trebilcock 1981; Lewis 1972, 27–58; Cameron 1961, 123, 152; Cairncross 1953, 225; Lévy 1951–1952, 228; Sée 1942, 360). Inasmuch as it led to the neglect of domestic investment and the development of domestic markets, imperialism and colonialism helped to create the conditions that eventually led to social polarization and economic stagnation in the colonizing countries.

Europe itself was an arena of imperialist rivalry and expansion from Napoleon's Continental System at the beginning of the nineteenth century to the fascist crusade to recreate a Roman empire at the beginning of the twentieth. Europe was riven by imperialist rivalries throughout the nineteenth and early twentieth centuries. During this period, there emerged a Great Germany crusade, a Russian Pan-Slav movement, and movements for a Greater Serbia, a Greater Bulgaria, a Great Slav state, a Greater Greece, a Greater Romania, a Greater Macedonia, and a Greater Croatia. Polish nationalists sought the resurrection of the Polish Commonwealth; Lithuanians sought the resurrection of the Kingdom of Lithuania.

Each of the five Great Powers to emerge from the Napoleonic Wars (Russia, Prussia, Great Britain, Austria-Hungary, and France) endeavored to exploit ethnic divisions in the Balkans and in other Ottoman territories. As a result, the expected (or hoped for) breakup of the Ottoman Empire (the so-called "Eastern Question") was a permanent cause of crisis in Europe throughout the nineteenth century (starting with the Greek uprising in the 1820s, which was considered a threat to the whole European system). Britain and France exploited ethnic distinctions in the Ottoman Empire in their quest to control the sea and land routes to India. Russian imperialist ambitions with respect to Moldavia and Wallachia led to war with the Ottoman Empire in 1806–1812, 1828, 1853 (the Crimean War), and 1878. Serbian and Bulgarian ambitions with regard to Bosnia and East Rumelia, respectively, led to war between those countries and the Ottoman Empire in 1876, 1878, and 1885. Austrian imperialist ambitions in Bosnia-Herzegovina generated a series of conflicts from 1878 until the start of World War I.

In the 1850s and 1860s, uprisings and wars in Italy became a Europe-wide issue as Austria endeavored to maintain her hold on the peninsula. After 1866, Austrian interest turned more and more to the Balkan area, the only region in Europe where there was still a possibility of expansion. Austria sought to acquire both commercial and political control of the Balkan states. Its desire to acquire ports on the Aegean led to conflict with both Russia and Serbia. Because of its imperial rivalry with Britain, France, and Russia, Germany sought to foster links with the Ottomans through arms sales and military aid, and by economic and diplomatic activity in the empire. By the eve of World War I, Germans had begun to reorganize the Ottoman army, and the two states were planning the coordination of their railway systems. In 1914, imperialist rivalries in the Balkans helped to transform a local conflict between Austria and Serbia into a Europe-wide conflagration.

THE WORLD WARS AND AFTER: WHAT CHANGED AND WHY

The ethnic, class, and imperialist conflicts that recurred in Europe throughout the nineteenth and twentieth centuries culminated and came to end in the course of the world wars. The wars radically altered the ethnic map of Europe, as well as its traditional social structures and patterns of development. As a result, ethnic conflict has been relatively rare in Europe since World War II; where it has occurred, it has not spread.

The world wars altered Europe's propensity for ethnic conflict for a number of reasons. Genocide, expulsion, flight, and border shifts between 1912 and 1948 brought the ethnic map of Europe into much closer agreement with its political divisions. Massive population transfers in Europe—the largest since those associated with the breakup of the Roman Empire—began during the Balkan wars of 1912–1913, and continued throughout the 1940s. During the Balkan wars about 100,000 Turks fled before the advancing Balkan armies; 15,000 Bulgars fled before the Greek army; 10,000 Greeks left Serbian and Bulgarian Macedonia; 70,000 Greeks left Bulgarian Western Thrace; 48,750 Muslims left West Thrace; and 46,764 Bulgars, East Thrace. In 1914, 265,000 Greeks were expelled from Turkey, and 85,000 deported to the interior; 115,000 Muslims left Greece; and 134,000 left the other Balkan states for Turkey. During World War I, the Bulgars deported 36,000 Greeks from West Thrace. From 1915 onward about 1,600,000 Armenians were massacred or expelled from Turkey. After the Armistice, about 240,000 Greeks returned to East and West Thrace and Asia Minor, but nearly all of these had to flee again in 1922, together with the balance of the Armenians (Pallis 1925; Ladas 1932). These movements had the effect of profoundly modifying the racial geography of Macedonia, Thrace, and Anatolia.

Forced population transfers initiated by the Nazis during World War II, and accelerated by the liberated peoples in 1945–1946, resulted in a consolidation of the various national groups (Kulischer 1948, ch. 10). After the war, a massive migration removed all but a tiny minority of Germans from Central and Eastern Europe. Between 10 and 12 million Germans—4 million from Poland, 3 million from Czechoslovakia, 2 million from the Baltic states, and smaller numbers from Hungary, Yugoslavia, Rumania, and Russia—were forced into Austria, East Germany, and West Germany (Wiskemann 1956, 118). Some 10 million Soviet citizens displaced eastward by the war moved from central and eastern Russia toward the west and northwest. Five million Poles left western Russia and eastern Poland to resettle within the new Polish boundaries. Nearly two hundred thousand Czechs and Slovaks moved from eastern to western Czechoslovakia,

TABLE 7.5
Minorities in Europe, 1910–1930 (as percent of total population)

	1910	1930	1950
Austria	67	3	1
Hungary	52	8	5
Germany[a]	7	1	—
GDR	—	—	0.1
Poland	—	31	3
Bulgaria	26	12	12
Romania	7	25	13
Albania	—	9	4
Greece	—	12	8
United Kingdom	12	6	6
Finland	—	11	10

Source: Krejci and Velimsky (1981, 66).

[a] In German Upper Silesia, 42 percent of the population was made up of minorities (Macartney 1934, 517).

one hundred sixty thousand Turks were expelled from Bulgaria, and four hundred thousand persons moved from southern to northern Yugoslavia (Wiskemann 1956, 213) where they replaced some three hundred thousand Italians and an equal number of Germans. This simplification of ethnic boundaries "solved" some of Europe's most intractable problems (Table 7.5). The world wars leveled domestic economies, destroyed the industrial structure of the region, and changed the balance of class power throughout Europe.

After the end of World War II, the class structures of the states of both Western and Eastern Europe were radically changed. These changes in class structures made possible the establishment of a new economic and political order in the region on the basis of interest groups, parties, unions, and other organizations linked to sectors of the economy that had formerly been excluded from power. Workers became a powerful organized force. Parties representing labor became legitimate participants in the political process in most countries of Western Europe, and the dominant power in Eastern Europe. Although parties representing labor had participated in government in several countries before 1945, their presence in government had been strenuously and sometimes violently resisted by the Right. It was only after 1945 that socialist and labor party participation in European governments was treated as fully legitimate. New trade unions were organized and unions, which before the war had been hindered by police repression, acquired significant numbers of new members and were reorganized. In Western Europe the average level of real earnings of industrial or manual workers in 1948 was almost a fifth higher than in 1938 (Milward 1984, 486). In the German Democratic Republic (GDR) real wages more than tripled in this period; in Bulgaria, Yugoslavia, and Romania they rose by over 150 percent (Aldcroft 1978, 212–15). Workers also benefited from the lowering of housing rents and the greater security of employment than before the war.

The restructuring of social and political elites made possible the expansion of the powers and responsibilities of central governments. Throughout Europe, most governments were committed not just to rebuilding economies but to changing its method of functioning. In contrast to prewar economic policies, postwar policies were designed to expand domestic markets through increased production, rather than to divide up and exploit national markets through restrictive practices; to encourage competition rather than cartels; to raise the level of earnings and of welfare of the working classes, and to increase and regulate domestic investment. Very large wage increases were conceded by many governments as one of their first acts following the war. In addition, raising the level of employment was treated as a high priority in the formulation of development strategies and plans, and in the laying down of investment criteria.[14] After 1945, policies were designed to produce sustained growth characterized by a more equitable distribution of income as well as rising income per head.

The social transformation effected in the course of the world wars eliminated the conditions that had generated recurring conflict throughout the nineteenth and early twentieth centuries in Europe. After World War II, a radical change in the number and status of minorities brought the ethnic map of Europe into closer agreement with the political map. The collapse of the region's traditional social structure enabled states in Europe to gain greater autonomy and thus to pursue policies of redistribution that put economies on a fundamentally different footing. After 1945, growth centered on the home market. Europe experienced unprecedented growth after World War II and this growth was the result not of the exogenously driven processes that had generated capitalist expansion previously, but of a far-reaching process of internal restructuring made possible by a new balance of class power throughout Europe.

After 1945, Europe also enjoyed relative stability. Most of the wars involving European states after 1945 resulted from the attempts on the part of some West European states to hold on to colonial possessions: Britain in Malaya (1947–1952), Palestine (1948), Kenya (1953), Cyprus (1955–1959), Suez (1956), and the Falkland Islands (1982); France in Madagascar (1947), Indochina (1947–1954), Tunisia (1952–1954 and 1961), and Algeria (1954–1962); Portugal in Angola (1962–1963), Goa (1961), and Mozambique (1965); Belgium in the Congo (1960–1964); and the Netherlands in Indonesia (1947–1949). In addition to these colonial wars, Britain became involved in civil wars in Lebanon (1958) and in North Yemen (1962–1967); Greece fought in Cyprus (1963–1964, 1974), Yugoslavia, Albania, and Bulgaria were involved in the Greek Civil War (1946–1948). The Soviet Union put down a revolution in Hungary (1956) and fought a war in Afghanistan (1979–1988). In 1968, the armies of five Warsaw Pact countries invaded Czechoslovakia in order to halt a reform process initiated by a wing of the Communist party.

---

[14] On the investment criteria debate of the 1950s, see Sen, 1960; Dobb, 1960; Galenson and Leibenstein, 1955.

There was a sharp drop in the number of ethnic and class conflicts in Europe after 1945. Ethnic conflict continued in Belgium, Spain, and in Northern Ireland: tensions emerged between the Flemish and the Walloons in Belgium in 1966 and in 1968; the Basque Euskadi Ta Ezkatasum separatists assassinated numerous high-ranking Spanish officials, including Spain's prime minister in 1973; Northern Ireland was a continual battleground. There was other domestic violence, as well: insurrectionary strikes throughout France, and frequent rioting and conflicts with police during 1947–1948; riots in Poland and street battles in Budapest in 1956, touched off by hopes for reform; strikes in Belgium in 1960, and in Spain in 1962; bombings and political murders in Italy in the 1960s and 1970s. After street battles between students and riot police in Paris in May 1968, a general strike involving 10 million workers closed down most businesses in the country; that month, demonstrations at the universities of Milan and Trento spread and eventually paralyzed the Italian university system, and street battles took place in Prague between students and Soviet troops sent in to crush reforms. In 1970, Italian troops fought with left- and right-wing guerrillas, and demonstrations in Poland were held to protest increases in the prices of basic food items. In 1973, government troops killed thirty-four students in street battles in Athens; in 1980, Polish workers in Gdansk began large-scale protests demanding the right to form independent trade unions. Demonstrations and strikes took place throughout the final years of the 1980s in the Soviet Union. In 1989, a wave of demonstrations swept through Eastern Europe—in Poland, Czechoslovakia, the GDR, Romania, Bulgaria, Albania, and Yugoslavia. These were the prelude to relatively peaceful "revolutions" which, that year, brought about a change of government in Poland, Czechoslovakia, the GDR, Romania, and Bulgaria.

A reappearance of flux, uncertainty, and more intense conflict in political life in Europe became apparent during the 1960s, in both the east and the west. At the same time, in both parts of Europe, it was possible to discern the formation of a new class structure, with features reminiscent of nineteenth-century European society and, as a result, a resurgence of nationalism and class conflict.

In the post-World War II period, refugees from rural Eastern Europe and East Germany furnished labor for the expanding industry of West Germany. In subsequent years, millions of people from the rural underdeveloped south of Europe—Portugal, Spain, southern Italy, Yugoslavia, and Greece—and from Turkey to Algeria have moved into the factories of industrial Europe—France, Germany, northern Italy, Switzerland, and other countries. Pakistanis and West Indians have migrated to Britain (Castles 1984, 146–48). In Switzerland immigrant workers comprise about one-third of the total labor force, and almost the whole of the manual working class. The proportion of immigrant workers is also considerable in France and Germany.

By the 1960s, this massive import of foreign workers had begun a process of new class formation in West European societies. Today, these workers represent a new "subproletariat." For the most part, they work at the least attractive and worst-paid manual jobs. Their rates of unemployment are higher than those of indigenous workers and, in periods of recession, their unemployment rises faster (Castles 1984, 149). Unrepresented in the government and unorganized, they are unable to bring effective pressure on either employers or government for higher wages, shorter hours, or better working conditions. Foreign workers played a leading role in the events of May 1968 in Paris and elsewhere (ibid., ch. 1). Other waves of strikes in Western Europe since then have been led by these workers (for example, a wave of militant strikes in West Germany in the summer of 1973 that involved mainly foreign workers). The immigrant groups are often content with or resigned to less space and comfort than older workers. This is particularly true of the immigrants from poorer lands. The result, as David Landes observes, is a situation reminiscent, in the small, of the industrial slums of the early nineteenth century (1969, 501).

New ethnic minorities are being formed as immigrants and their descendants form groups characterized by nationality, language, culture, and lifestyle. As many of the immigrants have become settlers and more and more are sending for their dependents, racism is on the upsurge in all the countries of immigration, expressed in media campaigns against immigrants, racist attacks, the growth of neo-Nazi organizations, and the emphasis on racial problems in the policies of major political parties (Castles 1984, ch. 1).

After the 1960s, there were also changes in Eastern Europe and in the Soviet Union reminiscent of pre-1945 Europe. In Eastern Europe, the relative decline in the material and social standing of the proletariat and the corresponding advancement of the new white-collar professions has resulted in a class stratification system which is now in many ways similar to that of Western capitalism (Parkin 1969).

Starting in the 1960s, reforms were introduced in nearly all Eastern European countries aimed at instituting greater market freedom. The immediate consequence of these reforms was the widening of income differentials (Parkin 1969, 261–64). Yugoslavia, which instituted market reforms earlier and far more radically than the other socialist countries (Landy 1961), became also the most politically volatile and the scene of the greatest communal violence.

At the end of the 1970s, the economies of Eastern Europe began to slow dramatically. The East had overinvested in heavy industrial sectors while not introducing technological advances rapidly enough. East European governments sought therefore to increase the efficiency of their economies in the 1970s by importing advanced technology from the West. Because of the high prices of this technology and the low quality of East European manufactured goods, these countries began to borrow from Western banks, governments, and international agencies. The slower growth and decline of the world economy in the late 1970s and 1980s made it difficult for the Eastern European countries to repay their loans, and the burden of debt contributed to severe economic crises in Poland, Romania, and Yugoslavia, and to increasingly difficult conditions throughout the East (Tipton and Aldritch 1987, 248–52).

The revolutions of 1989 were aimed at accelerating the shift to a market economy begun in the 1960s. They were initiated by those elements within the increasingly de-proletarianized Communist parties (see, for example, Taborsky 1961, 32–37; and von Lazar 1966) best able to take advantage of markets and capitalist forms of ownership. The revolutionaries were members of the old nomenklatura seeking a future in new "market" fiefdoms (see, for example, Tismaneanu 1989, 31; and Lipski 1989–1990, 19–21). It was this element of the ruling elite in East Europe that sought to accelerate the conversion of East European economies to market systems. It was also this element that was in the best position to take advantage of this conversion. A marked increase in class conflict in Eastern Europe has followed in the wake of the revolutions. As a result of the revolutions, societies have become much more visibly stratified. There has been a further decline in living standards. For the first time in the post-World War II order within East Europe, armies of the unemployed have emerged, alongside the new entrepreneurial classes. The reemergence of inequality in Eastern European societies is already much in evidence, as are class tensions and, perhaps, the early beginnings of a process of class struggle.

In multiethnic states, the tensions that emerged in Europe after the mid-1960s exacerbated ethnic, as well as class, conflict. In these states, "nationalist" elites, struggling to exclude other groups from new sources of wealth and to institutionalize new privileges, promoted nationalist ideologies and movements. However, wherever ethnic conflicts occurred, they did not spread.

Previous sections of this chapter have argued that in Europe political and socioeconomic structures before World War II gave conflicts there a high propensity to spread, and that these structures were destroyed in the course of the two world wars. We should expect, therefore, that in the absence of these structures, ethnic conflicts occurring in Europe today will not trigger similar conflicts in neighboring countries or encourage other states to intervene. That this is, in fact, the case, can be demonstrated by contrasting the conflict in Bosnia in 1914 with the more recent conflict there.

CONFLICT IN BOSNIA, YESTERDAY AND TODAY

In 1914, a conflict involving Austria and the Bosnian Serbs widened to engulf all of Europe. The spark that set off the war was the assassination of the Archduke Franz Ferdinand, heir to the Austro-Hungarian throne, in Bosnia-Herzegovina. Despite the absence of any evidence of Serbian government complicity in this event, the assassination of Franz Ferdinand led to war between Austria and Serbia because of Austria's unwillingness to extend democratic rights to minorities living within the empire.

The Serbian quest to establish a Yugoslav state had acted as a magnet on Serb and other Slav minorities living within the Austro-Hungarian Empire. In consequence, Austrian leaders feared that Serbian success in establishing a Yugoslav state would mean the ultimate dismemberment of the empire. Together, the Slav nationalities in the Austro-Hungarian Empire constituted half the population. Between 1905 and 1914, and with Franz Ferdinand's active encouragement, improved representation had been extended to non-German minorities within the empire.[15] The assassination of Franz Ferdinand cleared the way for a conservative backlash against the liberalization that had taken place under his direction.

In an international setting dominated by imperialist rivalries and ambitions, the conflict between Austria and Serbia quickly widened to engulf all of Europe. In 1914, when war broke out in the Balkans, France was plotting to reacquire Alsace-Lorraine and Germany was obsessed with keeping control of it; Russia was seeking to gain control of the Dardanelles for access to the Mediterranean; Britain was involved in a naval building race with Germany and feared that Germany would gain control over the channel ports.

World War I unleashed an imperialist frenzy among European states. According to treaties concluded among the Allies, at the end of the war the members of the Allied camp were to receive the following territories: Great Britain—southern Mesopotamia and Bagdad, Haifa and Acre in Syria, and a part of the German colonies; France—Syria, territory in Asia minor, Alsace-Lorraine, the Saar Valley, territories on the left bank of the Rhine, and a part of the German colonies; Russia—Constantinople, Turkish provinces in Europe, the Bosphorus and Dardanelles, the Sea of Marmora, full liberty in northern Persia, further territory in Asia Minor, and those parts of Poland that were in 1914 under Prussia and Austria; Japan—parts of Shantung and the Pacific Islands; Romania—Transylvania, the Banat, and Bukovina; Serbia—the southern Dalmatian coast and parts of Albania; Italy—the Trentino, southern Tyrol, Trieste, Istria, the Istrian Islands, the Dalmatian Islands, islands of the Aegean, territory in Asia Minor, and an extension of its colonies in Africa. The Central Powers were also seeking territorial gains: Austria-Hungary—part of Russian Poland, part of Serbia, Montenegro, control over Albania, and Venice; Bulgaria—Macedonia; Germany—substantial acquisitions in Eastern Europe, retention of some form of effective control of Belgium, and annexation of French coal regions.

The recent conflict in Bosnia has taken place in a radically altered international environment. Thus, at no time since 1992, when violent conflict erupted in Bosnia between Muslims and Serbs and between Croats and Muslims, has the conflict threatened to spread either by diffusion or escalation. Today, there are no Serb or Croat communities in neighboring states. There is a Muslim community in Bulgaria, but because rights of citizenship are an issue for Bosnian or Bulgarian Muslims, transnational Muslim ties have not become a factor in the conflict.[16] In fact, the alteration of class structures that took place following World War II makes it unlikely that class relations in Europe will provide either a motive for uprisings or a vehicle for spreading the current conflict beyond the borders of the

---

[15] By the Moravian Compromise of 1905, the Bukovina Compromise of 1910, and the Polish-Ruthenian Compromise of early 1914.

[16] The Arab Muslims fighting in Bosnia—Egyptians and Algerians, probably armed and funded by Iran/Sudan, and viewed by their own governments as radical dissidents—and the arms and training provided to Bosnians by Iran have not lead to a spread of the conflict, either by triggering a similar conflict in neighboring states with Muslim populations (such as Albania, Bulgaria, or, a bit further afield, Turkey) or by drawing in other states (such as Egypt, Algeria, or Iran).

former Yugoslavia. Nor is the conflict likely to spread through escalation. The international environment of Europe today is not one in which the acquisition of territory is the primary motor of development. In the absence of a system of restrictions on minorities and the lower classes, such as existed before World War II, development in Europe is generally based on the expansion of the home market rather than on processes of territorial expansion and the transfer of surplus from imperial or colonial holdings.

CONCLUSIONS

Ethnic and class conflicts were endemic in Europe during the nineteenth and early twentieth centuries. They were related to the dominant social structure and pattern of development in the region before World War II. These were the products of attempts by a pan-European landed and industrial elite to monopolize gains from economic development, and to exclude other classes and ethnic groups from political and economic life. Elites blocked land reform and, through the creation of cartels and syndicates, monopolized trade and industry. Other policies restricted the mobility of foreigners and minorities and placed restrictions on the suffrage and on labor organization.

After World War II, and in both East and West, a new economic and political order was established throughout the region. In both East and West, in different ways and by different means, workers became a powerful organized force and labor and minorities became fully legitimate participants in the political process. The integration of minorities and labor into the political process and changes in their status and level of welfare ended the labor conflicts that had recurred more or less continually throughout the nineteenth and early twentieth centuries. Reinforced by regional organizations, states eliminated protection and monopoly; this, plus increased domestic investment and the rising real wages of the work force, altered the structure of demand for domestic goods and services. The resulting expansion of domestic markets put an end to the pursuit of profit through colonialism and imperialism.

Thus, after World War II, both the ethnic and political avenues for spreading ethnic conflict were no longer relevant in Europe. The ethnic avenue was closed because the status, as well as the number of minorities within European states radically changed in the course of the two world wars and their immediate aftermath. The political avenue closed because changes in domestic socio-economic structures brought the Great Game of imperialist competition to an end. Though political institutions were fundamentally different in East and West, it was the elimination of sharp inequalities and the expansion and integration of domestic markets that closed the political avenue in both parts of Europe. In recent years, however, tensions within Western and Eastern European societies have reemerged. In both parts of Europe, the transition toward a system of class stratification has, because of its greater inequality, generated ethnic and class divisions and tensions reminiscent of pre-World War II Europe.

TABLE A7.1
European Conflicts, 1790–1945

Date	Event
1794–1795	Civil War in Zurich
1798	Irish uprising
1804–1813	Uprising in Serbia
1807	"Rebellion of Tican" in Srem, Austria
1807	"Rebellion of Djak" in the Banat
1807	Insurrection in Bosnia
1809	Rebellion of Jancic in Bosnia
1809	Uprising in Tyrol
1819	Anti-Prussian riots in German states
1815	Uprising in Serbia
1820	Uprising in Piedmont
1820	Massacre of Turkish population at Petras, Greece
1821	Piedmont revolt
1821	Insurrection in the Danubian principalities
1821–1830	Greek revolt
1823	Separatist riots in the Rhineland
1830	Uprising in the Netherlands (Belgian Revolution)
1830–1831	Bosnian revolt
1830–1831	Uprising in Poland
1831	Uprising of Slavs against Magyars in Hapsburg lands
1831	Rebellion in Albania
1831	Uprising in Hungary
1831	Uprising in Bulgaria
1831	Uprising in the Danubian principalities
1831	Uprising in Rome, Parma, Modena, Bologna
1832	Sonderbund rising in Switzerland
1832	Nationalist uprising in the Palatinate, Germany
1832–1835	Rebellion in Albania
1832–1842	Rebellion in Montenegro
1833	Rebellion in Serbia
1833–1840	Basque uprising
1834	Rebellion in Bosnia-Herzegovina
1835	Uprising in Turnovo, Bulgaria
1836	Catholic riots in Rhineland, Westphalia, Posen
1841	Insurrection in Crete
1841	Insurrection on the Ionian Islands
1841	Insurrection in Nis, Serbia
1844	Insurrection in Italy
1845	Rimini revolt in Romagna, Italy
1846	Uprising in Galicia
1846	Uprising in Denmark
1847	Civil war in Switzerland
1847	Riots in Milan, Palermo
9/1847	Riots in Messina

TABLE A7.1 *(continued)*
European Conflicts, 1790–1945

Date	Event
1/1848	"Smoking riots" in Milan
1/1848	Uprising in Palermo
2/1848	Uprising in Naples
3/1848	Milan uprising
3/1848	Piedmont-Austrian war
3/1848	Uprising in Vienna
3/1848	Uprising in Pesth
3/1848	Uprising in Posen and Silesia
3/1848	Uprising in Venice
5/1848	Uprising in Vienna
5/1848	Riots in Milan
5/1848	Serbo-Hungarian civil war
6/1848	Uprising in Wallachia
7/1848	Insurrection in Tipperary
8/1848	Uprising in Livorno
9/1848	Insurrection in the Ionian Islands
1848–1849	Hungarian insurrection
1849	Insurrection in the Ionian Islands
3/1849	Insurrection in Naples
1850	Insurrection in Bulgaria
1852–1853	Revolt in Herzegovina
1853	Turco-Montenegrin War
1857–1858	Uprising in Herzegovina
1858	Uprisings in Bosnia
1861–1862	Insurrection in Herzegovina
1862	Serbian uprising
1862	Uprising in Bulgaria
1862	Montenegrin uprising
1863–1865	Polish uprising
1864	Catholic riots in Germany
1866	Catholic riots in Germany
1866	Revolt in Epirus
1866–1867	Crete insurrection
1868	Uprising in Albania
1872–1876	Uprising of minorities in Spain
1872	Catholic riots in Germany
1874–1875	Catholic riots in Germany
1875–1876	Uprisings in Bosnia-Herzegovina
9/1875	Insurrection in Bulgaria
1876	Bulgarian massacre
1876	Serbia and Montenegro versus Turkey
5/1876	Rebellion in Macedonia
1876–1878	Insurrection in Crete
1877–1878	Insurrection in Thessaly

TABLE A7.1 *(continued)*
European Conflicts, 1790–1945

Date	Event
1878	Uprising in Bosnia-Herzegovina
1878–1879	Rebellion in Macedonia
10/1880	Rebellion in Macedonia
1/1881	Rebellion in Albania
1881	Dalmatian revolt
1881	Anti-Semitic riots in Pomerania, Germany
1882	Uprising in Herzegovina
1885	Rumelian struggle
1894–1896	Armenian massacres in Turkey
1896–1897	Insurrection in Crete
1900	Revolt in Albania
1900	Riots in Bulgaria
1901	Polish riots in Posen, Germany
1903	Uprising in Macedonia
1903	Uprising in Bulgaria
1903	Rebellions in Albania
1903–1905	Pogroms in Russia
1905	Rebellion in Kroya and Argirocastro, Albania
1906–1907	Insurrection in Elbasan, Albania
1908	Revolt in Macedonia
1909	Armenian massacres in Turkey
1910–1912	Insurrection in Albania
1911	Uprising in Galicia
11/1913	Anti-Prussian riots in Zabern, Alsace, Germany
1915–1923	Armenian massacres
1916	Rebellion in Ireland
1916	Conflict in Turkestan
1917	Rebellion of Russian nationalities
1917	Flemish separatist movement in Belgium
1917	Russian nationalities
1919	Uprising in East Galicia
1919–1922	Rebellion in Ireland
1920	Revolt in Albania
1924	Revolution in Albania
1928–1934	International Macedonian Revolutionary Organization in Bulgaria
1933	Uprising in Catalonia
1938	Revolt in Crete
1938–1939	Czechs versus Sudeten-German Czechs
1940s	Jews expelled and massacred throughout Europe; ethnic conflict in Yugoslavia

TABLE A7.2
Class Conflicts in Europe, 1790–1945

1790	Peasant uprising in Bohemia
1790	Peasant uprising in Saxony
1791	Priestly riots in Birmingham
1793–1795	Peasant uprising in Silesia
1795	Bread and wage riots in Britain
1798–1799	Peasant uprising in Silesia
1799–1801	Bread riots in Britain
1800	Lancashire riots
1808	Lancashire riots
1809–1810	Bread and wage riots in Britain
1811–1813	Food riots in England
1812–1813	Food and wage riots throughout Britain
1816	East Anglia (Ely and Littleport) riots in England
1819	Peterloo massacre in England
1819	Riots in Hamburg, Frankfurt am Main, Würzburg, Karlsruhe
1820	Army revolt in Russia
1822	East Anglian riots
1825	Decembrist revolt in Russia
1826	Peasant uprisings and rebellions in Russia
1830	"Swing" riots in England
1830	"Tithe War" in Ireland
1830	Wage riots in Wales
1830	Insurrections in Germany
1830	Paris revolt
1830–1832	Rebellion in Bosnia (nobles against economic reform)
1831	Insurrection in Russia
1831	Peasant uprising at Novgorod, Russia
1831	Colliers' riots in Derbyshire, England
1831	Wage riots in Glamorgan, Ireland
1831	Uprising in Lyons, elsewhere in France
1831	Uprising in Rome, Parma, Modena, Bologna
1831	Riots in Saxony, Hessen, and Hannover
1831	Insurrection in Göttingen, Germany
1831	Peasant uprising at Novgorod, Russia
1832	Huge demonstrations in the Palatinate, Germany
1832	Uprisings in Paris, elsewhere in France
1834	Uprising of silk workers in Lyons, France
1834	Insurrection in Paris
1835	Poor Law riots in England
1835	"Fireworks Revolt" of Berlin journeymen
1839–1844	"Rebecca riots" (peasant uprising) in Wales
1839	Insurrection of the Seasons in France
1839	Chartist demonstrations in England
1840	Strikes in Paris
1841	Tax rebellions in the southwest of France
1842	Peasant insurrection, Kazan province, Russia

TABLE A7.2 (*continued*)
Class Conflicts in Europe, 1790–1945

1844	Uprising of Silesian weavers
1844	Uprising of textile, railway workers in Prague
1845	Strike of woolen workers in Lodève, France
1845	Rimini revolt in Romagna, Italy
1846	Frankfort riots in Germany
1846–1847	Food riots outside Paris
1847	Food riots, the "potato war," in Berlin
1847	Peasant uprising in Bulgaria
1847	Revolt of serfs in Russia
2/1848	Uprising of workers in Paris
3/1848	Uprising in Vienna
3/1848	Uprising in Pesth
3/1848	Uprising in Posen and Silesia
3/1848	Uprising of workers in Berlin
3/1848	Insurrections in German states
4/1848	Insurrection in Baden
5/1848	Uprising in Vienna
5/1848	Riots in Milan
6/1848	Paris uprising
6/1848	Uprising in Wallachia
11/1848	Uprising of workers in Paris
6/1849	Insurrections in Baden, Rhineland, Dresden, Bavaria
6/1849	Insurrection in Paris
6/1849	Insurrection in Lyons
1850	Riots in Prussia
1851	Paris insurrection
1854	Insurrection in Madrid
1860	Uprising, attacks on landlords in Sicily
1861	Peasant uprisings in Italy
1862	Riots, demonstrations in Sicily
1865	Riots in Palermo
1866	"Seven and a Half Revolt" in Palermo
1866	Riots in Germany
1868	Macinato revolt in Italy
1868	Revolution in Spain
1868–1869	Demonstrations, riots throughout Italy
1869	Labor violence throughout Germany
1869 1870	Violent strikes in St. Etienne and Aubin, France
1870	Insurrection in Pavia, Piacenza, Bologna, Genoa
1871	Paris Commune
1871–1872	Violent agricultural strikes, Lombardy
1873	Violent textile strike in Pisa
1873	Riots in Frankfurt am Main
1874	Bread riots in Tuscany, Emilia-Romagna
1874	Insurrection in Bologna-Taranto
1876	Peasant uprising in Bulgaria

TABLE A7.2 *(continued)*
Class Conflicts in Europe, 1790–1945

1877	Insurrection in Benevento-San Lupo, Italy
1878	Insurrection in Mote Labro (Tuscany)
1882	Strikes, demonstrations in Cremona, Parma
1883	Strikes, demonstrations in Verona region of Italy
1884	Strikes, demonstrations in Polezine, Italy
1885	"La Boje" revolt in Mantovano, Italy
1886	Trafalgar Square riots in England
1889	Violent miners' strikes, Ruhr, Silesia
1889	Violent strikes in Lombardy
1889	London Dock strike
1890	Violent strike in Ravenna area of Italy
1890	Clash between socialists and police in Berlin
1893	General strike in Belgium
1893	Revolt in Sicily
1896	Demonstrations in Milan, Italy
4/1898	Violent demonstrations in Milan, Florence
1900–1901	Insurrectionary strikes at Belfort and Marseilles
1902	Strikes at Louvain, Belgium
1903	Uprising in Bulgaria
1903	Strikes in the Netherlands
1905	Peasant/worker uprisings in Russia
1906	Strikes of tobacco workers in Bosnia
1906	Strikes of railwaymen in Bulgaria
1907	Strikes in Belgrade, Serbia
1907	Romanian peasant uprising
1908	Strikes at Nantes, France
1909	General strike in Spain
1909	Strikes at Salonika, Macedonia
1910	Violent strikes in Berlin
1911	Liverpool riots in Great Britain
1911	Uprising in Galicia
1912	Violent strikes in the Ruhr
1913	General Strike in Belgium
1917	Bread riots in Bavaria, Silesia, Stettin, Düsseldorf
1917	Russian Revolution
1917	General strike, insurrection in Italy
1918	Finnish civil war
1918	Socialist uprising in the Netherlands
1918–1919	Strikes in Andalusia suppressed by troops
1918–1920	Russian upper classes versus Bolshevik Revolution
9/1918	Peasant uprising in Bulgaria
11/1918	Revolution (Kiel); socialist revolution (Munich); right-wing military putsch attempt (Berlin)
1/1919	"Spartacus Revolt" in Berlin
3/1919	Communist coup d'etat in Hungary
3/1919	Communist revolution in Bavaria

TABLE A7.2 (*continued*)
Class Conflicts in Europe, 1790–1945

1919–1920	Violent strikes in Italy
1919	General strike in Switzerland
1919	Uprising in East Galicia
1919	Royalist uprising in Portugal
1919	Strikes in Bulgaria
1919–1920	Strikes and demonstrations in Romania
1920	Violent strikes in Italy
1920	Strikes in Bulgaria
1920	Strikes in Slovenia, Bosnia, Croatia, Yugoslavia
1920	Spartacist outbreak, coup, Kapp Putsch in Germany
1921	Strikes in Russia
1921	Kronstadt massacre in Russia
1921	Strikes, communist revolts in Germany
1921	207 killed, 819 wounded in fascist attacks in Italy
1922	Riots, demonstrations in Germany
1923	Nazi Beer Hall putsch
1923	Bulgarian repression
1926	General strike in Great Britain
1927	Leftist uprising in Portugal
1929	May Day riots in Berlin
1930	Violent strikes, Mansfeld mining area, Germany
1930–1934	Massacre of Kulaks, USSR
1932	Riots in France
1/1933	Leftist revolt in Spain
12/1933	Revolt in Aragon, Spain
2/1934	Civil war in Austria
2/1934	Rioting in Paris
3/1934	Uprising in Andalusia, Spain
3/1934	Four-week general strike in Sargossa
6/1934	Uprising in Asturias, Spain
1936	Strikes in France
1936–1939	Spanish Civil War

TABLE Λ7.3A
Imperialist Conflicts in Europe

		Imperialist Objective
1805–1815	Napoleonic Wars	France, to acquire German and Italian lands
1806–1812	Russia versus Turkey	Russia for Moldavia and Wallachia
1808	Russia versus Sweden	Russia to annex Finland
1815	Austria versus Naples	Former King Murat of Naples backed by Austria for Naples
1820	Uprising in Naples	Austria, to maintain control of Naples
1821	Uprising in Piedmont	Austria, to maintain control of Piedmont
1828	Russia versus Turkey	Russia for Moldavia and Wallachia
1848	Revolt in Milan	Austria, to maintain control
1848–1849	Piedmont–Austria	Austria, to maintain control
1848–1850	Prussia–Denmark	Prussia, for Schleswig-Holstein
1853–1856	Crimean War	Russia, for Moldavia and Wallachia
1852–1853	Turco–Montenegran War	Montenegro, for expanded boundaries
1858–1859	Turco–Montenegran War	Montenegro, for expanded boundaries
1859	Italy–Austria	Italy and Austria, for Italy
1860–1861	Italy–Sicily	Piedmont, for Italy
1864	Prussia–Denmark	Prussia, for Schleswig–Holstein
1866	Italy–Austria	Italy and Austria, for Venetia
1866	Austro–Prussian War	Prussia, for South German States
1870	Franco–Prussian War	Prussia, to acquire South German States
1876	Serbia, Montenegro versus Turkey	Serbia, to acquire Bosnia
1878	Russo–Turk War	Russia, to reacquire Bessarabia; Serbia and Bulgaria, for expansion
1878	Austria versus Bosnia–Herzegovina	Austria, to occupy Bosnia–Herzegovina
1885	Bulgaria versus Turkey	Bulgaria, for acquisition of East Rumelia
1885	Serbia versus Bulgaria	Serbia, for territorial compensation; Piedmont for territory
1896–1897	Greco–Turk War	Greece, to acquire territory
1911	Italy versus Turkey	Italy, for Dodocanese and Tripolitania
1912	First Balkan War	Bulgaria and Serbia versus Turkey, for territory
1913	Second Balkan War	Serbia versus Bulgaria, for division of territorial spoils
1916	Turkestan	Russia, for colonization
1918	Russo–Polish War	Poles, for expansion
1919	Hungaro–Romanian War	Romania, for territory
1919–1922	Greco–Turk War	Greeks, for expansion
1920	Vilna	Poles, for expansion

TABLE A7.3A *(continued)*
Imperialist Conflicts in Europe

		Imperialist Objective
1920	War in Anatolia (1920)	Russia, for Constantinople
1938	Germany annexes Austria	
1939	Germany annexes Czechoslovakia	
1939	Italy conquers Albania	
1939	Germany occupies Poland	
1939	Russia occupies E. Poland	
1939	Russia versus Finland	Russia, for territory near Leningrad
1940	Germany invades Norway, Denmark, Romania, and Luxembourg	
1940	Russia occupies Lithuania, Latvia, Estonia, Bessarabia	
1940	Bulgaria annexes part of Dobruja (Romania)	
1940	Hungary annexes part of Transylvania (Romania)	
1941	Germany occupies Bulgaria, Hungary	

TABLE A7.3B
Extra-Regional Imperialist Conflicts Involving European Powers

		Imperialist Objectives
1807–1837	Central Sumatra	Dutch, for trade and dominion
1810–1824	Spanish-American War	Spain, for commercial exploitation
1811–1814	Anglo-American War	Britain, to blockade U.S. ports, ban U.S. trade with France
1823–1826	Burmese War	Britain, to acquire Arkan and Tenas Serim, control over Assam
1825–1828	Persia	Russia, Armenians for Georgia
1825–1830	Tasmania	Britain, to secure control
1833–1936	Zambesi and Delagoa Bay	Portugal, to gain control
1836–1852	War in La Plata	France and Britain, to control Argentina
1838–1842	British-Afghan War	Britain, to prevent Russian influence in Afghanistan
1839–1842	First Opium War	Britain to open Shanghai, Canton, Amoy, Foochow, and Ningpo to trade
1839	Khivan	Russia, for expansion
1839–1847	Conquest of Algeria	France, for expansion
1843	Gwalior, India	Britain, for dominance, order
1843	Conquest of Sind	Britain, to annex Sind to British India
1845–1846	British-Sikh War	Britain, to acquire land
1846–1849	Bali	Dutch, to secure control
1848–1849	British-Sikh War	Britain, to annex the Punjab
1850–1852	South-East Africa	Britain, to secure property
1853	Burma	Britain, to annex Pegu
1856–1857	Anglo-Persian War	Britain, fearing Russian influence
1856–1860	"Opium War"	Britain and France, for trade
1857	Senegal	France, to control Senegambia
1857–1859	Britain in India	Britain, to transfer authority from East India Company to British Crown
1859–1863	South Borneo	Dutch, for control of coal mines
1859–1860	Spain versus Morocco	Spaniards to extend the boundaries of Spanish settlements
1859–1860	South Celebes	Dutch, to secure control
1859–1864	Circassia	Russia, for expansion
1861–1867	Mexican Expedition	French, Spaniards, British for control
1865–1868	Bokhara	Russia, for Samarkand and the Oxus
1867–1868	British–Abyssinian War	Britain, to secure control
1871–1872	Algeria	France, to maintain control
1873–1874	Ashanti	Britain, for free trade
1873–1908	War in Achin	Dutch, for direct rule over the Achinese sultanate
1878–1880	British–Afghan War	Britain, against Russian influence and to advance frontier at Pishin
1878–1881	Sieges of Geok Tepe	Russia, for expansion

TABLE A7.3B *(continued)*
Extra-Regional Imperialist Conflicts Involving European Powers

		Imperialist Objectives
1879	Zulu War	Britain, about a disputed boundary
1881	Tunisia	France, to govern Tunisia
1881–1885	Revolt of the Mahdi	Britain, for control
1882	Egypt	Britain, for control
1882–1885	Tongking War	France, for trade route to China
1885–1886	Britain versus Burma	Britain, to complete annexation
1885–1895	Sudanese Independence	Britain, for reconquest
1891–1894	Malay Archipelago	Dutch, to extend direct rule
1892–1894	Eastern Congo War	Belgium, for ownership
1894–1896	Italo–Abyssinian War	Italy, for control
1894–1901	Conquest of Madagascar	France, to annex
1896–1900	Sudan Campaigns	Britain for establishment of an "Anglo–Egyptian Sudan"
1897–1898	Northwest Frontier of India	Britain, to maintain control
1897–1901	Uganda	Britain, to maintain control
1898	Sierra Leone	Britain, to affirm, extend control
1898	Spanish–American War	Spain, to control Cuba
1899–1900	Chinese Boxer Rising	Russia, Britain, France, Germany, Italy, Austria for commercial privileges
1899–1902	South African War	Britain, to annex Transvaal and the Orange Free State
1903–1908	Southwest Africa	Germany, for colonization
1904–1905	Russo–Japanese War	Russia, concerning rival interests
1906	Zulu Revolt	Britain, to maintain control
1911–1917	War in Libya	Italy, for expansion
1912	Morocco	France, to maintain control
1916–1917	Morocco	France, to maintain control
1920	Syria	France, for control of its Mandate
1920–1921	Iraq	Britain, for control of its Mandate
1920–1927	Northern Morocco	France, for control
1920–1932	War in Libya	Italy, for expansion
1925–1926	Syria	France, for control of its Mandate
1929–1933	Morocco	France, to extend control
1930–1931	Indochina	France, to maintain control
1935–1937	Ethiopian War	Italy, to annex
1940–1947	Britain in Palestine	Britian, for control
1941	Vichy French versus British	Both, for control in Syria
1945	Algeria	France, to reestablish control
1945	France in Lebanon	France, for control

Ethnicity, Alliance Building, and the Limited Spread of Ethnic Conflict in the Caucasus

PAULA GARB

THE PAST two centuries of history in the Caucasus offer dramatic examples of attempts to build alliances among linguistically and/or culturally related ethnic groups for the purpose of combating military invasions. These alliances have been based on promoting the idea of a shared cultural identity and there have been temporary successes—for instance, during periods of wars in the Caucasus against Russian conquests in the latter eighteenth and nineteenth centuries (Henze 1992). Overall, however, the alliances have been short-lived and not pivotal.

In this study I examine the most recent, failed attempts at alliance building in the context of the war in Chechnya. This case shows that despite the strong factors that could cause the spread of conflict across borders where ethnic groups are related, and even when concerted efforts are made toward this end, the factors that limited the spread were more potent.

This was not what we would have expected. Chechnya's declaration of independence from Russia and Russia's military response prompted predictions from astute, close observers and regional experts that there was considerable potential for the fighting to spread. Not long after the Chechen republic declared its independence from Russia, Marie Bennigsen Broxup (1992, x) pointed out that "The present crisis in Chechnya is a logical consequence of two centuries of Russian onslaught on the North Caucasus, and may similarly discredit the Russian democratic leadership. The situation is strongly reminiscent of the 1917–1920 Civil War period during which the North Caucasian peoples made a desperate bid for freedom. Ultimately, Moscow's heavy-handedness may well promote the long-held aspiration for a Pan-Caucasian confederation. . . . The divided Muslim peoples of the North Caucasus have shown that they are quite willing to unite to fight for a common goal when faced with the real danger of a Russian military intervention, and quite capable of such action."

Yuri Kalmykov (1993, 4), Russia's former minister of justice, who resigned this post to protest his government's intervention in Chechnya, also predicted that the whole Caucasus would rise up over a war in Chechnya: "it is impossible to frighten the Chechen Republic with military preparations. If any actions are undertaken against this republic the whole North Caucasus will revolt. Nobody will politely ask permission from the leaders of the republics for such actions."

When Russia finally launched a military assault on Chechnya, Fiona Hill (1995, 4) also maintained that the armed conflict had potential to escalate to involve other republics in Russia as well as other countries: "The North Caucasus is a tinderbox where a conflict in one republic has the potential to spark a regional conflagration that will spread beyond its borders into the rest of the Russian Federation, and will invite the involvement of Georgia, Azerbaijan, Turkey, and Iran, and their North Caucasian diasporas. As the war in Chechnya demonstrates, conflict in the region is not easily contained. Chechen fighters cut their teeth in the war between Georgia and Abkhazia,[1] the Chechen and North Caucasian diaspora in Turkey is heavily involved in fund-raising and procuring weapons, and the fighting has spilled into republics and territories adjacent to Chechnya."

Other experts maintained that the conditions did not exist for the spread of conflict. Pavel Felgengauer (1994) predicted in the early weeks of the war in Chechnya that it would not spark a repetition of the wars in the Caucasus because "other mountain peoples would hardly help Dudayev[2] and his supporters. Neighbors are not liked in the Caucasus, and many would, most likely, only rejoice if misfortune were to befall the Vainakh tribes."[3] In March 1995, at a workshop for this research project, similar analyses were provided by Emil Pain and Andranik Migranyan, advisors at that time to Yeltsin on ethnic relations.

It is difficult to draw firm conclusions while conflicts are in progress. When I began writing this paper during the first weeks of the war in Chechnya, it seemed that other Caucasians were poised to join the fight if certain cultural "buttons" were pushed. Within a few months, when I returned to the area for more interviewing, informants were resigned to the war and clearly had no intentions of joining the Chechens in the battlefield. During a third rewriting of this chapter (late February 1996), leaders of Chechnya's closest neighbors—Daghestan and Ingushetia—were warning that Russia's military operations on their territories could ignite a North Caucasian wildfire. These neighbors showed restraint in the face of provocation both by Chechen militants and Russian forces operating in their republics. This could have changed, depending on developments in Russia's policies in Chechnya and the North Caucasian republics. We know how fluid ethnicity can be and how dramatically it can be reconstructed in response to contextual changes in the situation.

In their broader study of ethnicity, ethnic alliances, and international relations, Moore and Davis (Chapter Four in this volume) tell us that ethnic alliances have a significant impact on conflict and that ethnic ties across inter-state boundaries help elites pursue more conflictual relations with a neighboring state. This may be statistically true when examining fixed cases or cases in the short term. This has not been proven so far in closely examining the North Caucasus case over time.

---

[1] Abkhazia is a disputed territory within Georgia, one of the fifteen former republics of the Soviet Union that is now an independent state. The North Caucasian entities remained inside Russia when the Soviet Union collapsed, and constitute seven of Russia's twenty-one ethnically based republics.

[2] Dzhokhar Dudayev was the Chechen leader until the Russians claimed they had killed him in an air attack in April 1996.

[3] Vainakh is the indigenous term the Chechens and Ingush use to call their people.

Looking at attempts to build a North Caucasus alliance that includes Abkhazia (the North Caucasus is in Russia, whereas Abkhazia is not) shows that identity is malleable and evolves over time; it can be invented and reinvented, and it can reinforce or weaken ethnic alliances, depending on the circumstances of its development. This case study shows the importance of a longitudinal and in-depth view of such fluid phenomena as ethnic identity and ethnic alliances. It also shows that third parties, in this case Russia, are crucial factors to be considered. Incorporating the findings of such case studies in the quantitative methodologies can serve to strengthen such research.

In order to understand this case better and why the conflict in Chechnya did not spread beyond its borders, we will look at the factors that have promoted and discouraged the development of such alliances. In this study I examine the potentially powerful symbolic and affective factors (Adam 1990; Connor 1993; Douglass 1988, and Monroe 1996) that can shape a Pan-Caucasian identity and alliance, how they have been utilized by political activists, and why they did not mobilize a significant Pan-Caucasian solidarity movement. By stressing local and indigenous ideas about personhood, self, the group, and their relationship to conflict and the issues of power (Avruch and Black 1991; Wolf 1990; Starr and Collier 1989), I attempt to show how the actors in this drama have perceived and influenced the situation.

I argue that this alliance movement, not unlike other "Pan" ideologies, could not supersede the powerful forces of state-building in the newly constituted republics, and the attendant reinforced ethnic identities and particularism (Fearon, Chapter Five in this volume). No one has yet made a comprehensive comparative study of Pan ideologies, in part because these ideologies have grown in different environments, and therefore their ideologies, aims, forms, and methods are diverse. However, some similarities, relevant to this study, have been identified (Landau 1995): 1. Pan ideologies generally arise in response to a perceived threat from another nationalism, or another Pan ideology; 2. people are mobilized into these movements around beliefs in common cultural and linguistic roots; 3. Pan movements have zig-zag destinies; 4. these movements are most visible during wars and at other times when there is opportunity for redrawing borders; 5. they are successful when they gain international support, or the support of states where these movements arise; 6. when they do not have such support, or face obstacles at the state level, the beliefs in common roots are not enough to sustain the movements. Competing particularist identities triumph. As Landau (1995, 191) concludes, "Nationalism has a better chance of success than Pan movements in the political arena—as history has often demonstrated—thanks to its ability to generate stronger sentiments and deeper loyalties."

I show how the factors that have led to the demise of other Pan movements have been at work in the case of the Caucasus. These factors have prevented the peoples of the republics neighboring Chechnya from crossing over their state boundaries to become involved in the fight against the Russians. There were also other factors specific to the Chechnya case. The wars in Chechnya and in Abkhazia depleted these people's ability to unite, and reinforced the specific identities of the Chechens and Abkhazians, who had been the prominent leaders of the Pan-Caucasian movement. Furthermore, neighbors watched developments in Chechnya with horror as the Russian armed forces turned cities into heaps of rubble and killed tens of thousands of civilians. Russia's demonstration of military power of monstrous proportions was a factor in discouraging the military involvement of any other group that might have shown solidarity with the Chechens.

The study is based on anthropological fieldwork in Abkhazia, the North Caucasus, and Moscow, beginning in 1979. Over the years I developed close friendships with some of my informants. I have lived in their homes, shared in the births, deaths, joys, and sorrows of our respective families. In the past few years I have mourned the loss of cherished friends and acquaintances who died at war. I have agonized at the sight of scorched buildings and shattered lives on a land where so many of my own values and those of my children (whom I dragged into the field) were shaped. This, I believe, has enabled me to experience the power of the symbolic and affective aspects of Caucasian culture that I strive to convey. The opportunity of having worked with people in the region for so long, together with recent frequent trips, provides insights into the changes in this dynamic situation.

I began interviewing leaders of the region's alliance movement, the Confederation of Peoples of the Caucasus (CPC), at the outset of the organization in 1989, and periodically since then. My most recent interviews were in September 1996. Other informants for this study are Abkhazians and North Caucasians who live in Abkhazia and the North Caucasus, and in the Moscow diaspora. Some have been involved either as combatants or as medics in the wars in Abkhazia and Chechnya. Most are intellectuals, mainly academics in the social sciences or humanities, journalists, and teachers, the men and women in their cultures who construct their people's identity, who publish the articles, make the speeches and teach the young, those who influence (and are influenced by) the thinking of their fellow citizens. Whenever possible I present their ideas in their own voices. I do not identify informants due to my promise of confidentiality. Another source of information is from books as well as interviews with Caucasians published in Russian newspapers.

First, I explain the "Caucasian idea," the philosophical foundation of alliance building in the Caucasus and its contemporary manifestations. This will include a presentation of how North Caucasians and Abkhazians regard their common roots, shared history of Russian domination, and cultural values. Second, I will describe the results of this effort of alliance building and examine reasons for the failures.

THE CAUCASIAN IDEA

The CPC, the Association of Peoples of the Caucasus, various groups uniting Circassians, and the Association of the Commonwealth of Nations were the leading organizations born of efforts to build a sense of common ethnicity among the diverse peoples of the Caucasus. The philosophical foundation of these organizations and of what might be considered an embryonic Pan-Caucasian movement is referred to as the Caucasian idea.

The most central question facing Caucasianists is whether there is a Caucasian identity. Cases for and against are constantly argued (Huttenbach 1995). According to Yuri Anchabadze (1995), the first record of the concept of a Pan-Caucasian identity can be traced to Leonti Mroveli, a Georgian historian of the eleventh century who claimed in his history of the Kartvelian (Georgian) czars that all peoples of the Caucasus originated from one ethnarch. Until relatively recently linguists maintained that the indigenous Caucasian languages originated from the same roots and were classified under the Iberian-Caucasian family, which is further divided into four groups—Kartvelian, Abkhaz-Adyghe, Nakh, and Dagestani (Arutiunov 1994). This linguistic theory also contributed to the belief of common origins.

The idea was at its peak during the Caucasian wars of the nineteenth century, and then again in the early twentieth century with the rise of the North Caucasus Confederation, when efforts were made in 1917–1920 to create a united state of these peoples. The idea continued to thrive among émigré Caucasians in Turkey and the Middle East who have participated in efforts to revive it in the homelands of their ancestors. Not all the Caucasian peoples were involved, either at all or to the same degree, in the resistance to Russian expansion in the nineteenth century, nor in the North Caucasus Confederation. When I have asked informants from the North Caucasus or Abkhazia to list all the peoples they consider to be related and therefore potential allies, I have made almost as many different lists as the number of people I have questioned. Yet each person gives me a rather long list, showing acceptance of the "Caucasian idea" in one or another form.

Anchabadze, who studies manifestations of the "Caucasian idea" in today's conflict situations, particularly its influence on peacemaking efforts in the region, maintains that all proponents of this idea, no matter what their political or ideological motivations, agree that the Caucasian peoples share ethnic and cultural similarities, have a common historical destiny, uphold independence and sovereignty as important values for regional ethnic-political and intellectual development, believe in the ideas of peace and accord, and have an aversion to coercive solutions to controversial issues (1995, 6).

To understand how the Caucasian idea is used to shape the notion of a common identity we will examine its components.

Common Roots

Generally North Caucasians (Chechens, Ingush, Daghestanis, Kabardians, Ossetians, Cherkess, Adyghey) and Abkhazians tend to see themselves as related to each other, in terms of culture and/or language. There does not seem to be disagreement over whether North Caucasians and Abkhazians have similar roots and cultural histories. We know this is perhaps the most powerful defining factor in the politics of ethnicity (Williams 1994; Vayrynen 1994). At the core of ethnopsychology is a conviction that members of the nation are all ancestrally related. Kinship phraseology that uses the images of blood, family, brothers, sisters, mothers, ancestors, home is a powerful tool in appealing to ethno-national sentiments (Connor 1993). This is a typical statement made by North Caucasians and Abkhazians about what they have in common: "Look at our dances, listen to the music, read the tales of the Narts, our legendary heroes. You can see by the similarities that we have had the same culture since ancient times."

Another common argument I have heard from North Caucasians and Abkhazians about their pre-Russian history in the Caucasus is that there were no real borders between them, as though they lived in one country: "We rode our horses from one area to another, not knowing any boundaries. Under Soviet government artificial borders were drawn to separate us from each other. We almost forgot that we were related."

Anthropologists and historians of the Caucasus also know about the widely practiced customs of fosterage, adoption, and intermarriage across language groups, customs that were practiced in order to forge strong bonds and alliances among the diverse groups. The idea that the Caucasian peoples were genetically and culturally similar was not denied in the Soviet Union. The Caucasus was designated as a separate historical-cultural region, thus promoting the concept (Anchabadze 1995, 6). Even today the idea is being promoted, no doubt unintentionally, by the newly invented bureaucratic term *litsa kavkazskoi natsional'nosti* (literally, people of Caucasian nationality). It is a term used by the Russian militia and mass media as part of the campaign to drive Caucasians out of Russian cities. This term refers not only to North Caucasians but also to Georgians, Azerbaijanis, and Armenians, who have not been involved in the alliance building of the North Caucasians and Abkhazians. Officials in the militia and other organizations have profited from the bribes of those who resist eviction. Caucasians who live in Moscow and have been victims of frequent passport checks in public places, among other indignities, have said that this phenomenon and the new term are bound to make Caucasians feel related, if only in their victimization.

There does not seem to be any ambiguity among Circassians (Abkhazians, Abazins, Adygheys, Kabardians, Cherkess) about their common roots. Gueorgui Otyrba (1994, 283) confirms the potency of this belief about a common identity: "After the Russian conquest the Abkhazians and the North Caucasian peoples had no means of continuing active anti-colonial resistance, and so they resorted to passive resistance. Their historical connections may have weakened, but the Abkhazians, Adygheys, Circassians [also known as Cherkess], and Kabardians never forgot that they were members of one ethnic group who were artificially separated by tsarist Russia and then by Soviet nationality policy. Whenever an opportunity presented itself to take their destiny into their own hands, such as at the time of the Bolshevik Revolution, they revolted. In between, passive resistance persisted."

Recent manifestations of Circassian identity and its mobilizing power are alive and well within the framework of the Caucasian idea. Igor Chernov (1995) predicted that if the war in Chechnya were compounded by a resumption of armed hostilities in Abkhazia it would "certainly stir up the whole of the Caucasus and then a second Caucasus war will probably be a reality."

Bagrat Shinkuba, a prominent Abkhazian writer, told me that in the 1970s he was first made aware of the extent to which some Circassians had maintained this sense of common identity. When he was visiting a Kabardian village, one of the local elders told Shinkuba that in all likelihood the elder was an Abkhazian and Shinkuba was a Kabardian. The elder then proceeded to tell the confused writer a story of how long ago a vendetta was about to be carried out between a Kabardian and Abkhazian family, and that it had the potential to turn into warfare between the two peoples. In a successful effort to prevent such developments the elders of both communities agreed that one hundred Abkhazian and one hundred Kabardian mothers would exchange their infants, thus making the peoples relatives and therefore exempt from the rules of blood revenge. That is how in the mind of the Kabardian elder it was entirely possible that Shinkuba was really a Kabardian and vice versa.

An Abkhazian friend in her late thirties told me that her grandfather, a prominent academic, continually reminded her from her childhood that Abkhazians had ethnic relatives in the North Caucasus. "My grandfather would often tell me, pointing to the veins on his arms, 'Don't ever forget that we all have the same blood running through our veins.'" But not all Abkhazians had grandfathers who taught their young this unauthorized ethnic history. An Abkhazian woman in her late twenties who spent the whole Abkhazian war as a field medic said that she grew up having no idea that Abkhazians were related to these other peoples in the North Caucasus. She remembers becoming aware of North Caucasians and their relationship only after 1990, when the CPC organized cultural festivals among related ethnic groups. During the war she and many of her Abkhazian friends associated for the first time with other Circassians, Chechens, etc., who formed volunteer combat units. So, for broad sections of the population, the notion of common ancestry is relatively new.

A Common History of Oppression

The Caucasian wars provide a powerful historical symbol to the peoples of the North Caucasus. It is the most common justification offered for the need for a Pan-Caucasian movement. However, there is not always clarity on details about the composition of the alliances that fought the Russians, the actions of these recalcitrant peoples, or the reasons for defeat.

One reason is that this history was totally neglected in the Soviet Union, and many important issues have not been treated in Western historiography. Sociologists in Adyghey have concluded from analyzing public opinion surveys that the falsification of history is contributing to tensions in the area: "The true history of the Caucasian Wars has still not been written. Such processes [falsifying history] . . . can generate conflicts, since the thirst for historical truth gives rise to surrogates, to all sorts of ethnosocial myths that increase interethnic tensions" (Khanakhu and Tsvetkov 1995, 10).

What North Caucasians and Abkhazians seem to be clear about is that there was a lack of coordinated action by their ancestors, and that they were overrun unjustly by Russia. This is a relevant theme in reasoning about the need for an alliance like the CPC and why the Abkhazians should be included: "As history has taught the peoples of the North Caucasus, unity among them is the only hope they have to withstand the inevitable attempts to suppress their desire for national and cultural self-realization. . . . The history and destiny of Abkhazia are closely connected with those of all the peoples of the North Caucasus. Today they share a common history of suffering and oppression, of deportations and cultural destruction, and of fighting powerful enemies. They also share a determination to protect themselves against a repetition of history" (Otyrba 1994, 289, 292).

Finally, there is a strong belief among these peoples that they are invincible, no matter what the odds against them. Ruslan Aushev, president of Ingushetia (Chechnya's closest neighbor and home of co-ethnics) and a veteran of the Afghan war, said it best: "The people can be stifled. But they cannot be beaten. Nobody has yet managed to crush the mountain people" (1995).

Shared Cultural Values

To understand why the North Caucasians and Abkhazians speak with such confidence about their ultimate invincibility, it is helpful to focus on some of their shared core values that promote an ethos which I believe can be summed up in three interrelated words—freedom, respect, and honor. They are words used repeatedly in my most recent conversations with North Caucasians and Abkhazians about the conflicts in the region. Not everyone I talk to agrees about the extent to which each of these peoples has maintained what they consider to be ancient traditions of customary law, nor has customary law been practiced in exactly the same way among all the peoples. However, these concepts of freedom, respect, and honor come up often enough among all my diverse informants that I think they are important to understanding some factors influencing individual and group behavior today.

Ruslan Khasbulatov (1995), chairman of the former Russian parliament, has pointed out this freedom-loving aspect of the Caucasian ethos: "All the Caucasus peoples, including the Chechens, have an extremely strong sense of freedom. I knew that they would resist if Russian tanks and the army entered the Chechen Republic." Ismail Munayev (1994), a Chechen linguist, explained: "An everyday Chechen greeting to another Chechen is "may you be free." This is our most important value, and all the other values follow from it. Not to be free means to have nothing. Personal wealth means nothing compared to freedom."

As Ian Chesnov (1994) and Georgi Derluguian (1995) have pointed out, freedom has long traditions in Chechnya and to varying degrees among all the related peoples, who never gave their leaders much power over their lives, except in time of war. It is freedom that was traditionally based on ownership of land (a critically important demand today) and possession of weapons in every home.

The Process of Alliance Building and the Role of Ethnicity

The CPC unites community organizations of most peoples of the North Caucasus. In the late 1980s and early 1990s, before the wars in Abkhazia and Chechnya, it attempted to build a regional administrative structure: all-Caucasian ministries parallel to those in the republics, a council of ministries, and a parliament. CPC leaders tried to pattern the organization after the European community. They encouraged the governments and presidential structures of the North Caucasus to coordinate cultural, economic, educational endeavors, even to form a council of presidents.

The founding of the CPC occurred after riots in Abkhazia in July of 1989. When fighting erupted between Georgians and Abkhazians, several dozen young North Caucasians spontaneously went to support their ethnic relatives. They say they came with the blessings of their elders, who told them it was the right thing to do. This sparked the idea of building a confederation of peoples that would come to each other's aid in such situations. Abkhazians were among the most active organizers because of their escalating conflict with Georgians. Chechens were also heavily involved in the leadership because of their independence drive. Both Abkhazians and Chechens were motivated to mobilize their related Caucasian neighbors, because, among other things, they sought to tip the balance of power in their favor by multiplying their numbers with the help of this solidarity movement. Some members cherished the goal of establishing a North Caucasus confederation that would include Abkhazia and southern Russia, including the Russian Cossacks (Krasnodar, Stavropol, and Rostov regions) as a confederation of states (Otyrba 1994).

In the early stages of the CPC, Abkhazian participants told me that their people were the intellectual and spiritual center of the alliance, but tried to keep a low profile. Most of the administrative work was done by the Chechens, and the chair was a Kabardian.

It was not easy to build unity. In addition to representatives of related linguistic groups, the North Caucasus is home to distinctly different ones, most notably Iranian and Turkic, with their own histories and cultures, setting them somewhat apart from the more ancient indigenous Caucasians. Tensions between some of the ethnic groups have had long histories. The conflict between the Ossetians (Iranian speaking, Christian heritage) and Ingush (Vainakh speaking, Muslim heritage) over disputed territory was a primary impediment to unity. In addition, the leaders of the CPC had their own interpersonal conflicts, which they tried to mediate.

The strongest arguments used by mediators in the Caucasus to encourage compromise and reconciliation are appeals to ethnicity, common values, and public opinion. In the case of the Abkhazians the use of culture-specific values is closely linked with the people's acute awareness of their small numbers and endangered culture. In building the alliance of North Caucasian peoples, the appeal to ethnicity in a broadened sense was used and referred to as Caucasian ethnicity. The purpose of the CPC was to promote the idea that all parties were ethnically and culturally related. The Abkhazian members of the CPC told me how they helped to reinforce this belief in a shared "Caucasian ethnicity" by using the ancient Vainakh (Chechen-Ingush) tradition of slaughtering a bull to make a whole village related once they all consumed the bull's blood. I was told about one such effort when a whole Chechen village carried out this ritual with its Abkhazian visitors. This committed the village to fight by the side of Abkhazians, and vice versa.

Intermarriage has also been encouraged and even facilitated by the organization. A leader in the CPC gave this explanation after citing several examples of Abkhazian men or women marrying representatives of the groups: "When people have contact with each other, marriages are inevitable. For years we really had no contact with them. When we had our CPC meeting in Nalchik (Kabardino-Balkaria), one Abkhazian student fell in love with a Kabardian woman. It just works out that way. Emotionally people are prepared for this because they read articles about our contacts, our good relations, how the different people support us. It's an interesting phenomenon, because none of these peoples ordinarily wants their daughters to marry outside the group, but they will now allow marriage with Abkhazians."

LIMITS OF THE ALLIANCE

Despite the power of the "Caucasian idea" in building an alliance, by the winter of 1994, when the the war in Chechnya began, the CPC, the only Pan-Caucasian effort that had remained on the political scene for any length of time, and the only one with some experience as a military alliance, was clearly not a force in the North Caucasus to be reckoned with by Moscow. The reasons are complex and interrelated. These are what I see to be the most important:

First, the CPC ultimately could not resolve conflicts between member groups, most notably between the Ingush and Ossetians. It did not succeed in building a viable alliance with non-Caucasians, especially the Cossacks. These are extremely difficult conflicts to manage, of course, especially because Moscow has a hand in them. Ultimately, the CPC's ineffectual mediation seriously undermined the organization's prestige in the region.

Second, the CPC could not overcome the parochial concerns of the nomenklatura and political parties in the republics. This is the result of the solidly pro-Moscow orientation of the North Caucasian republics that are controlled by the former elites whom Kalmykov (1993) calls the "modern mafiosi." As he says, "They have acquired possibilities neither the sovereign princes nor the secretaries of party committees ever dreamt of enjoying." Moscow gives them these possibilities, so it is not in their interests to join forces with other Caucasian leaders against Moscow. Kalmykov laments: "The princes were at least respectful of their freedom-loving nations. . . . [The present leaders] are much more anxious about their own destinies and private affairs than about those of their state. They sing praises and 'hallelujah' to the Center and vow everlasting fidelity to Russia." Under Soviet government there was no history of regional integration, so people in the republics had no experience with the process of integration (Hill 1995). Apparently they had no real interest in it either, since their goal was to get the most out of privatization and increase their own status (Arutiunov 1995; Shnirelman 1996). All the ethnic areas were upgraded to republics. These were essentially new states with the former party bosses promoted to presidents.

Third, the leaders of the Pan-Caucasian movement were not experienced in politics, let alone the politics of integration (Hill 1995). Most were intellectuals—historians, poets, writers. No one leader could be accepted by all ethnic groups. No leader has appeared in the North Caucasus who can unite the peoples as did Shamil, the Daghestani leader of the resistance against the Russian conquest of the North Caucasus. Shamil was able to unite people on the basis of the idea of an Islamic holy war. Today, however, Pan-Islamic ideas do not seem to play that kind of role.

Fourth, the integrative efforts begun by the CPC were exhausted by war, first in Abkhazia and later in Chechnya. Whatever creative spirit this idea had and was capable of materializing was diverted into organizing for war. Such a weakened CPC was unable to help Chechnya when its turn came.

Fifth, the enormous firepower that Russia was willing to use against Chechnya discouraged anyone besides the Chechens from thinking of counteracting Moscow's military might. Those Caucasians who might have been motivated to help the Chechens knew that it was a futile cause. They would be destroyed in the effort, especially since they could not count on international support. They knew that to unite as they did in the Caucasian wars, they needed similar outside help. In the last century their allies against Russia were Turkey, Britain, France, and Germany. No such foreign allies exist today. One informant described the situation this way: "The international community sees Russia as a big bear that they are all afraid of, because it's so huge, clumsy, and unpredictable. The United States and other countries will do anything to appease the bear with sugar. 'Here', they say to the bear, as they offer a cube of sugar while keeping their distance, 'take Chechnya, have Abkhazia.'"

War has another consequence—it magnifies nationalistic sentiments. This is key to my discussion of the role of ethnicity in alliance building and its limits. After Georgian forces were driven out of Abkhazian territory, an Abkhazian war veteran described a shift in thinking away from the Pan-Caucasian identity that had been cultivated before the war: "If anything the war reinforced Abkhazian identity, showed us we were capable by ourselves of doing more than even we thought possible." Undoubtedly, the Chechen war victories also increased Chechen nationalism and particularism, and subverted notions of a broader Caucasian identity.

THE POWER OF ETHNICITY AND THE POVERTY OF ALLIANCE

Caucasians conceptualize the differences between themselves in various ways, and the idea of similar ethnic heritage and cultural traits has not translated into a clear Pan Caucasian identity, let alone a strong alliance. People tend to blame their differences and tensions on the old Soviet structure of the state which was a patchwork quilt of nationalities, especially in the North Caucasus. They point to the Soviet policies of divide and rule that have left an indelible mark, and the large proportion of non-Caucasians who live among them. This is a common remark I heard among informants, no matter where they live in the North Caucasus: "The Caucasus will never unite because we've been divided beyond repair, so much that we cannot trust one another. . . . Besides, we can never fully unite because not only Caucasians live here, but also large Russian communities. And the Cossack movement is being revived."

Caucasians also look inside themselves and at their own traditions of clan and religious rivalry to understand what went wrong. The following statement was made by a prominent Ingush physician about Chechen and Ingush culture: "We have clans that represent contradictory political and economic interests, and different religious trends within Islam. Islam is not the unifying force it was in the nineteenth century. My cousin and I are of these two different groups. KGB agents among us use this small religious difference. They say to him, 'you're more pure than your cousin,' and they say the same to me. This makes us want to fight each other. In the Caucasus we can be like roosters or cocks that are ready to attack one another over the slightest provocation. I would like to be able to resist this provocation. But we have our interests to protect."

Informants also criticized themselves for not being "Caucasian" enough, for allowing traditions to degenerate. This argument is used to explain why there was not a more significant number of North Caucasian volunteer soldiers signing up to fight with the Chechens against Russian forces. An Adyghey graduate student made this complaint: "Caucasians will never fight the Russians en masse because they have degenerated. They no longer follow their ancient traditions to the extent necessary for men to take up arms on a scale that would be meaningful. Our men say they are ready to fight for their ethnic brothers and cousins, but few really are. I suppose this makes their mothers happy, but to me it is a sad state of affairs."

As has been mentioned, Abkhazians and North Caucasians did not have much contact before the Gorbachev era. When they became reacquainted in the course of building the CPC and then fighting in the battlefields of Abkhazia they came to know each other better. Closer contact did not necessarily improve the relationship. This is how some Abkhazians explained their combat experiences with North Caucasians: "In the battlefield we got closer to our brothers from the North Caucasus and our diaspora, and realized how very different we were. It's like marriage. When you get close you find out about a person's shortcomings." The sanctions against Abkhazia, its closed borders with Russia, Georgia, and Turkey, and lack of contact make it especially difficult for the Abkhazians to continue working on these relationships.

Among the diverse peoples of the North Caucasus there was much more interaction and contact than with the Abkhazians. Living in close contact can also be a source of tensions. Great mistrust was generated by the Ingush-Ossetian conflict over disputed territory, which erupted in armed conflict in 1992. Practically the same conversation takes place when talking to Ingush about Ossetians and to Ossetians about Ingush. The blame and stereotypes hurled in either direction sound very much alike. This is a typical statement that I heard on both sides of the Ingush-Ossetian border: "They aren't like us. They are tricky and thieves. They reaped all the benefits of the republic, lived much better than us, and then they turned on us."

The Kabardians did not rush to the aid of the Chechens, although they constituted a sizeable contingent of North Caucasian volunteers who fought in Abkhazia. One common explanation I heard was that they fear living in a North Caucasus independent from Russia because the Chechens historically seized part of Kabarda, and therefore might take even more, if it were not for Russia's protection. Also, the Kabardians have their own headaches trying to keep under control their internal ethnic tensions with the Turkic Balkars, the republic's other titular nationality.

When Russian troops were first introduced in Chechnya, and in January and February 1996, after the hostage crisis in Daghestan and Russian shellings of Ingush villages, these two closest neighbors of the Chechens were considered the most likely territories in which fighting could spread. The powder keg consisted of large numbers of refugees in these republics, the numerous communities of Chechens on the Chechen-Daghestani border, and the ethnic affinity of the Ingush and Chechens. In the summer of 1995 the hostage incident in Budyonnovsk, southern Russia, was on the verge of sparking armed conflict in Russia when the Russian prime minister negotiated a peaceful solution.

These types of incidents had the potential to escalate the fighting. Daghestan and Ingushetia demonstrated restraint in the face of Russian or Chechen intervention on their territories. Ingushetia had several good excuses to declare war against Russia for shelling its border villages, but limited itself to sending diplomatic notes of protest. The Ingush president, Ruslan Aushev warned that his people might start fighting Russian troops if operations on Ingush territory continued. "Who can stop people whose brothers, fathers, mothers, and relatives are being destroyed?" he asked. An Ingush villager told a Reuters' reporter, "If they start killing innocent people then we'll get weapons and fight the Russians. It's either fight or die" (Reuters Information Service, February 25, 1996).

During the January 1996 hostage crisis in Daghestan, police and government efforts focused on preventing Daghestanis from attacking the Chechen militants holding Daghestani hostages. Later, their efforts were turned to quelling anti-Russian sentiments after Russian forces, in their mismanaged rescue operation, killed innocent Daghestani hostages who had been taken by Chechen militants. In this context, the chair of the Daghestani parliament, Mukhu Aliyev, expressed concern that public discontent over Moscow's Chechnya policy could have caused an outburst of separatist sentiments in the region (*Monitor*, [Washington, DC, Publication of the Jamestown Foundation], Vol. 2, No. 40; February 27, 1996).

Russia's inadvertant or, perhaps, deliberate attempts to provoke Chechnya's neighbors into armed conflict could have counted on the long-standing animosities and grievances of Chechnya's closest neighbors, especially in Daghestan. At the outset of the war in Chechnya in the winter of 1995, Daghestanis told me that the Chechens were bad neighbors before the war and therefore did not deserve any assistance from the Daghestanis. Even at the height of the brutal bombings of Grozny, Muslim anti-Russian demonstrators in Daghestan's capital city never numbered more than two thousand.

When Chechen militants first took hostages in Daghestan in January 1996, Daghestani officials made colossal efforts to suppress anti-Chechen outrage, to prevent the crisis from being compounded. The Daghestanis could not afford to let any ethnic conflict on their territory turn violent: the republic comprises at least thirty different ethnic groups, some of which have long-standing animosities. Any small upset in the delicate ethnic balance of Daghestan would have enormous repercussions for the whole region.

The Ingush carry their own resentments against Chechens because of the way they were treated when Chechnya drew the border after it declared its independence from Russia in 1991, and counted Ingushetia out. Because no border agreement was ever made between Chechnya and Ingushetia, there are disputed territories that both republics claim to be their own. While supporting the Chechen cause, several Ingush also expressed to me their concerns about how they can expect negative treatment from Chechnya should it win complete independence from Russia. So there is also potential for hostilities to be provoked in Ingushetia against Chechens.

None of the Chechens that I have spoken to have criticized their North Caucasian neighbors for not helping them fight the Russians. Abkhazia, potentially the most likely military ally, could not afford to help Chechnya and alienate Russia while it was trying to maintain Russia's support in its bid for independence from Georgia, especially since Georgia supported Russia's effort to keep Chechnya. Abkhazia's precarious position vis a vis Russia and Georgia made it politically dangerous to provide aid to the Chechens, and it was logistically impossible because of Abkhazia's sealed borders controlled by Russia and Georgia.

Some Chechens say they never expected help from anybody, least of all the Abkhazians. They understood that it would be politically suicidal for the Abkhazians to come to their aid. However, I have heard some Chechens express disappointment with the general absence of volunteers from neighboring republics. The resentment does not seem to run very deep. A Chechen representative of Dudaev in the United States told me: "At first we were surprised there were so few volunteers. But we have accepted that. We're sure that we will win our independence eventually, and then the others, seeing our success, will be willing to unite and leave Russia too."

CONCLUSION

I have outlined the factors that could promote or discourage the development of a Pan-Caucasian identity as they apply to a discussion of ethnicity and alliance building and the spread or escalation of ethnic conflict in the context of the war in Chechnya. I have examined the symbolic and affective factors that can shape a Pan-Caucasian ethnicity. I have presented Caucasians' views of their specific and common identities, what it means to them to be Chechens, Abkhazians, etc., as well as what it means to them to be Caucasians.

The Caucasian wars represent a clear and poignant symbol that has been used in efforts to unite these groups. These peoples are not always in agreement about the details of the alliances and actions of their ancestors in those events of the last century. They share, however, a general sense that there was a lack of coordinated action that weakened them, and believe that history can repeat itself for the same reasons. Alliance building in the spirit of the Caucasian idea has been aimed at preventing such disunity.

So far, a Pan-Caucasian ethnic identity is barely embryonic. The Soviet and pre-Soviet forces of division are still deeply ingrained. The boundaries that lie between these peoples are largely the same as they were under Soviet government. Many of the key decision makers are also the same. The elites of the republics feel that Russia still provides them with more stability than they would have if they broke away from Moscow. Furthermore, even if this dependence were to decline and there were economic and political incentives for secession, Russia's demonstration of military might and of how far it was willing to go to quell the Chechen independence movement discouraged any North Caucasian group, alone or aligned with others, from launching a military operation against Russia.

The absence of a strong Pan-Caucasian identity and movement is further reinforced by the process of state building and privatization, and the attendant prominence of individual ethnic identity over a common Caucasian ethnicity. This process could not help but limit efforts to forge a Pan-Caucasian alliance. The internal interests of each group were primary and were dominant in motivating the alliance. Just as Otyrba (1994) said: "As history has taught the peoples of the North Caucasus, unity among them is the only hope they have to withstand the inevitable attempts to suppress their desire for national and cultural self-realization." This self-interested motivation was enough to doom the alliance effort to failure. Ostensibly the alliance was an integrative enterprise, but in fact the particularistic interests of the groups were the driving force and therefore impeded its success. The wars in Abkhazia and in Chechnya dealt the final blow, further reinforcing ethnic nationalism among the diverse peoples. This has doomed to failure the most recent resurgence of the Pan-Caucasian movement.

PART FOUR

The Management of Transnational Ethnic

Conflict

Containing Fear: The Management of Transnational Ethnic Conflict

DONALD ROTHCHILD AND DAVID A. LAKE

EFFECTIVE MANAGEMENT of ethnic conflicts by local elites and governments and by external states and organizations is a complex and ongoing process. To foster stability and constructive ethnic relations, the rights and positions of minority groups must be secured. Only if minorities are confident of their physical and cultural security can stable and peaceful ethnic relations prevail.

Confidence-building measures undertaken by local elites and governments are the most potent instruments to secure minority rights. In light of group fears and individual ambitions, however, international intervention may be necessary and appropriate, either to support local leaders in their confidence-building efforts or to enforce new, externally imposed ethnic contracts. Even so, confidence-building measures and international interventions are imperfect. Unlike other, more optimistic observers, we see no permanent resolutions, only temporary "fixes." In the end, ethnic groups are left without reliable safety nets. There is no form of insurance sufficient to protect against the dilemmas that produce collective fears and violence. We can only hope to contain ethnic fears, not permanently eliminate them.

In this chapter, we examine the problem of managing ethnic conflicts. We feel that ethnic conflicts, even when they spread from abroad, are most effectively managed by the state and its institutions. After a brief introduction, we therefore turn first to the main measures for building confidence among minorities about their future within the state: respect, power sharing, elections, and regional autonomy and federalism. We then address the motivations behind and efficacy of external interventions in bringing about a return to peaceful relations. This and the following chapters concentrate on general measures for coping with the spread of conflict. In Chapter Fifteen we focus on some specific measures for controlling the international spread of ethnic conflict.

COPING WITH FEAR

The variety of ethnic experiences makes the development of generic guidelines for conflict management extremely difficult. Where ethnic groups possess effective safeguards, share pacific expectations, and feel secure in their relationship with the state and each other, intergroup competition tends to be constructive. Ethnic leaders are not fearful for their group's future and can operate within existing political institutions to maximize group interests. These elites abide by the rules of the game because they perceive the possibility of achieving beneficial outcomes for themselves and their ethnic constituents. The result over time is a growing sense of confidence on all sides about the intentions of ethnic rivals. As rivals demonstrate their commitment to deliver on bargains, confidence evolves and elites develop pragmatic, even positive, perceptions of each other. The possibilities for such constructive interethnic relations should not be underestimated. Ethnic groups have lived side by side in amity for centuries in many areas of the world. To focus exclusively on the destructive side of ethnic relationships perpetuates dangerous political myths.

But where safeguards, shared norms, and pragmatic perceptions are absent, the prevailing incentive structure may encourage ethnic leaders to adopt damaging courses of action. Destructive relations are not the norm, but they can surface when the strategic dilemmas outlined in Chapter One make violence seem expeditious. Facing information failures, problems of credible commitment, or security dilemmas, political leaders may choose to play the ethnic card in a calculated effort to benefit themselves and their constituents, even though the costs are high in terms of the common good. Threatening language and action can lead to societal polarization, precipitating a situation of grave suspicion and uncertainty for all. As David Rieff notes, "the Bosnian Serbs won because they knew how to take old fears and old complaints, repackage them, and cause otherwise decent Serbs, people from a national community with no more of an innate predilection for murder than any other national community, to commit genocide. . . . What began as a tactic of pure massacre and terror in villages," he continues, "had evolved within six months into a sophisticated *system* for the destruction of a people" (Rieff 1995, 112, emphasis added). In light of such menacing possibilities, and especially its planned, genocidal variant, can ethnic brutality be constrained? Can confidence-building mechanisms within the state and international pressures and guarantees reassure uncertain peoples as to their future and make cooperation possible?

As shown in Chapter One, it is difficult to transcend the dilemmas that produce collective fears. As a consequence, we have little alternative but to recognize that there is no form of insurance sufficient to protect against dilemmas of this sort, only the possibility of limiting their impact. There are no reliable safety nets in our anarchic world able to secure the cultural or physical survival of beleaguered ethnic peoples. Nonetheless, we believe confidence-building measures and international interventions can promote cooperative interethnic relations (Stein 1990, 111).

We turn first to the negotiation of confidence-building measures that hold out some promise of promoting interethnic cooperation. The acceptance and implementation of these measures can enhance prospects for interdependence through iterated encounters, possibly culminating in a growth of confidence in each other's goodwill.

However, because some conflicts cannot be expected to end by this process, the situation may require external intervention to enforce stability and encourage the building of a consensus among the contending state and ethnic actors. In the post-Cold War world, interventions in intrastate ethnic conflicts are likely to encounter strong public resistance in the advanced industrial states—even though "the greatest need for U.S. forces is peacekeeping and peace enforcement" in precisely such confrontations (Maynes 1995, 109). The very process of mobilizing ethnic constituencies for the bitter intrastate wars that can follow inhibits Western democracies from becoming involved militarily in what promise to be protracted engagements. Croatia's ruthless treatment of its Serbian population in the early 1990s went virtually unrecognized in the Western press. In Bosnia, international appeals by the contact group and the United Nations had little influence on Serbian treatment of the Muslim population. The fall in eastern Bosnia of such safe-areas as Srebrenica and Gorazde, and the ruthless ethnic cleansing and presumed murders that followed, are stark reminders of the limited influence of the international community. Only the NATO bombings of September 1995 appear to have penetrated the cycle of conflict in Bosnia, but it is still too soon to tell whether this intervention, the Dayton Peace Agreement that followed, and now the deployment of the NATO-led Implementation Force will produce a long-term peace. The aborted restoration of hope in Somalia provides a second telling reminder of the limited ability of the international community to mitigate collective fears. In the end, the safety nets for ethnic minorities remain fragile.

CONFIDENCE-BUILDING MEASURES

Confidence-building measures seek to reassure ethnic peoples about their future. As Saadia Touval puts it, "actors may resort to insurance and other forms of risk management in order to reduce risks" (Touval 1982, 19). Through packages of coercive and noncoercive incentives, the state attempts to assure ethnic minorities about their place in society. By means of these concessions, it seeks to get recalcitrant elites to rethink their belligerent practices and cooperate in joint problem-solving initiatives.

To overcome minority fears, confidence-building measures must be appropriate to the needs of those who feel vulnerable to the majority-backed state. The challenge, as I. William Zartman observes in Chapter Fourteen, "is to keep the minority/ies from losing." Such safeguards, if handled sensitively over the years, may be able to cope with the central questions of sharing private information and making credible commitments. Although there is a wide variety of possible trust-building mechanisms for reassuring minorities and thereby reducing strategic dilemmas, we concentrate here on four major mechanisms that we feel have the greatest practical potential for providing incentives for interethnic cooperation. We recognize that other mechanisms—such as constitutional guarantees, mutual vetoes, reserved seats in the legislature, gerrymandering, corrective equity in appointments and revenue allocations, quotas, controls on land sales, bills of rights, ombudsmen, judicial interpretation and review, and others—can also prove important. Nevertheless, we regard the four approaches or measures highlighted here as critical to the difficult but necessary task of redesigning political institutions to ease ethnic minority feelings of insecurity.

Demonstrations of Respect

The security of ethnic peoples is in no small way based on a reciprocity of goodwill and respect. Unless each side views its opponent as having legitimate interests, relations are likely to be marred by a history of intended or unintended affronts that widen social distance between groups and exacerbate fears among ethnic minorities that their children will be relegated indefinitely to second-class status.

Relations in Bosnia, worsened by polarization and increasingly hostile perceptions, have been further aggravated by the contempt Serbs have shown their Muslim adversaries. Describing themselves as the only people in former Yugoslavia "who have the talent, energy, experience, and tradition to form a state," they characterize their adversaries as representing "all that is base, undesirable, and naturally subordinate" (Cigar 1995, 74–75). In the Sudan, southerners, with strong memories of slavery and perceptions of low status, bridle at any new evidence of disrespect. Thus, they viewed the Sudanese government's decision to apply Islamic (shari'a) law to them as well as to the Muslims living in the country's north as a confirmation of their second-class status (Amnesty International 1995, 57). Their resentment boiled over in 1994, when the minister of state in the president's office, at the mediation talks in Nairobi held by the Inter-Governmental Authority on Drought and Development (IGADD), allegedly treated both southerners and the IGADD mediators with contempt when rejecting the southerners' call for self-determination and a secular state (*Sudan Democratic Gazette* 1994, 3).

The fears of ethnic minorities may often be overstated. Minorities in Eastern Europe are described as having "an exaggerated fear of the loss of identity," a legacy of distrust of majority authorities that causes them to make broad demands for legal guarantees. The majorities, fearful that this will start them down the slippery slope toward the breakup of their states, refuse to consent to these demands (Watts 1995, 92–93). But to build confidence it is imperative that dominant state elites take minority ethnic resentments and anxieties into account. Unless old psychological hurts are taken seriously, regimes will be unable to avoid the problem of "wounded tigers" in years ahead. Those involved in the management of ethnic disputes can learn much from C. E. Osgood's Graduated and Reciprocated Initiatives in Tension Reduction (GRIT) strategy for easing conflict between the superpowers during the Cold War (Osgood 1962). His suggested approach of repeated overtures (in this case by a dominant majority controlling the state) without expectations of an immediate tit-for-tat response could stimulate full negotiations between equals. Unless past wrongs are redressed and the sting of disparagement is removed from current ethnic interactions, internal negotiations will remain clouded by an overhang of bitterness and suspicion; minority uncertainty regarding adversary intentions will contribute to serious problems of credible commitment and security dilemmas.

Power Sharing

Conflict management requires an effort by the state to build representative ruling coalitions. In conceding to ethnic minority members a proportionate share of cabinet, civil service, military, and high party positions, the state voluntarily reaches out to include minority representatives in public affairs, thereby offering the group as a whole an important incentive for cooperation. In South Africa, for example, President Nelson Mandela agreed to include power-sharing provisions in the interim constitution in an effort to reconcile the economically dominant local white community as well as to build confidence among mostly white investors abroad. Significantly, this concession was withdrawn in 1996 with the enactment of a new majority rule constitution. National Party leader F. W. de Klerk was quick to describe the ending of broad multiparty participation in cabinet decision making as a "mistake" that would cause a loss of confidence in the country (*ANC Daily News Briefing*, May 9, 1996).

Power sharing can be informal (e.g., Kenya in the 1960s) or formal (e.g., Nigeria in 1979), and can take place in settings that are authoritarian (e.g., Zambia in the 1980s) or democratic (e.g., South Africa in the mid-1990s). In both Eastern Europe and Africa, there has been a mixed pattern of "hegemonic exchange" regimes: centrally controlled one- or no-party regimes that allow a limited amount of bargaining to take place between state, ethnic, and other elites. Under the authoritarian administrations of Josip Broz Tito in Yugoslavia or Félix Houphouët-Boigny in Côte d'Ivoire, nationality or ethnic representatives met with the president in cabinet sessions, where strong differences were sometimes aired by group spokespersons behind closed doors. The resulting power-sharing systems are quite diverse, yet they have in common a form of coordination in which a somewhat autonomous state and a number of less autonomous ethnic-based and other interests engage in a process of mutual accommodation in accordance with commonly accepted procedural norms, rules, or understandings (Rothchild 1986a, 72). These elite power-sharing arrangements are inevitably fragile and temporary because the ethnic pillars upon which they rest remain firmly in place and resist the integrative pulls that would lead to countrywide loyalties. Even so, while these arrangements last they can provide some security for political and ethnic minorities.

Pacted democracy, with its rough reflection of the configurations of elite power, can prove relatively easy to organize in an interim constitutional situation. Such pacts are a form of "mutual security agreements" among ethnic and other elites (possibly including militia leaders) who accept limitations on their autonomy to gain a measure of security for themselves and their supporters (Sisk 1996, 81). Elite pacts can provide a relatively stable form of governance during a transitional period, but if they remain unresponsive to public demands for change over too long a time, then the pactmakers risk becoming isolated from their supporters, allowing new uncertainties to surface (Karl 1986, 217–18). In principle, there is no logical reason why such structural arrangements cannot lead to a more open system of sharing—even full democracy, as happened in South Africa.

Because of the fragility and temporary nature of these state-inspired inclusive coalitions, such mechanisms are likely to provide only minimal assurances to ethnic minorities. With ethnic balances of power constantly evolving and information limited, these arrangements are necessarily transitional ones. If poorly negotiated and implemented, the incomplete ethnic contracts may be rejected eventually by the groups they are designed to protect. The number of people appointed to the cabinet or civil service, for example, is not in and of itself a guarantee of proportional group influence (Mattes 1993, 76). Minority representatives can, as in the Sudan at various times, be assigned insignificant portfolios and therefore wield only minor influence. Majority and minority parties may also pull back from power-sharing arrangements, regarding these arrangements as coopting them into a system they view as still potentially threatening. In Sri Lanka, hard-line elements within the minority Tamil community rejected President Chandrika Kumaratunga's 1995 proposal giving them control over a semiautonomous region in the north, a proposal also opposed by some of the more nationalist Sinhalese in her own cabinet; at the same time, the insurgent Liberation Tigers of Tamil Eelam reportedly charged that the government's tactic of peace negotiations was in fact a pretext to cover its planned military offensive. Similarly, hard-liners among the majority Hutu in Rwanda, resentful of the power-sharing provisions of the 1993 Arusha accords, launched a preemptive strike that included a genocidal assault against both the Tutsis and some Hutu moderates.

When not applied with great care, power-sharing arrangements can backfire. In Rwanda, extremist Hutus feared the consequences of the power-sharing provisions of the 1993 Arusha accords their government had been pressured into accepting. These provisions gave the Tutsi-led Rwandese Patriotic Front responsibility for five of the twenty ministries (including the Ministry of the Interior) as well as 40 percent of the enlisted ranks and 50 percent of the officer positions in the new army. In the case of Rwanda, then, the power-sharing agreement itself "contributed to [a] polarization of political tensions," because the Hutu hard-liners viewed it as jeopardizing their position of political influence in the country (Newbury 1995, 15). Fearing for their future under this agreement, the extremists launched a highly destructive preemptive strike.

As Chaim Kaufmann (1996, 156) observes, the core problem with power-sharing arrangements is their essentially "voluntaristic" natures. Ethnic elites must be prepared to interact continuously with other elite representatives they find personally repugnant, something difficult to do under normal circumstances but especially so where the norms of collaborative politics are not firmly in place. In order to achieve inclusiveness, should those crafting power-sharing structures bring ethnic extremists into decision-making bodies to build greater confidence? Again, local circumstances are critically important in assessing the appropriate course to follow. For instance, in situations in which a majority African government has perceived its local white community to be useful in achieving its developmental objectives as well as in reassuring others abroad about the safety of their investments in the country—as in Kenya, Zimbabwe, or South Africa—government authorities have restrained their anger over the humiliations of colonial times and have included white representatives in important cabinet positions. However, in situations in which Africa's ethnic groups regard each other's ambitions for control of the state and its hold on publicly controlled resources suspiciously, as in Burundi and Rwanda, their essentialist perceptions of their rival's intentions frequently lead to an inflexible stance in favor of appointing their group members or conciliatory outsiders to high government positions. It may be possible to justify an exclusion of radical adversaries in such circumstances: including Hutu extremists in a post-Arusha government in Rwanda, for example, is not likely to have led to an easing of interethnic tensions.

Where the majority-dominated states remain unprepared to respond to legitimate minority demands for full participation in decision-making activities, power-sharing schemes are likely to unravel and become themselves a source of grave insecurity. Power sharing by itself is not a solution to ethnic fears. Although it does offer some incentives for cooperation, it cannot prevent extremist elites and their supporters from polarizing society and pulling on the social fabric. Certainly, as Kaufmann (1996, 156) points out, power sharing cannot be expected to thwart ethnic violence once group leaders have mobilized for intense conflict and war.

Elections

Although elections represent only a brief episode in a larger political process, they can have enormous influence on intergroup collaboration and conflict. Where favorable circumstances prevail (that is, an agreement on the rules of the political game, broad participation in the voting process, and a promising economic environment), elections can promote stability. In democratic regimes, where institutionalized uncertainty provides many players with an incentive to participate, the election process can legitimate the outcome (Przeworski 1991, 26). All groups have a reason to organize and, through coalitions with other parties, they are given an opportunity to gain power in the future. This prospect of competing in accordance with the procedural norms of the system can be reassuring to minority interests; not only do they have a chance to advance their individual and collective interests but they are encouraged by the majority's commitment to the electoral contract. The effect is to preempt conflict, probably the best form of minority reassurance available.

The implications of elections, however, can also be troubling at times in multiethnic settings. Even where minority groups are represented in the legislature, there is a real possibility that they will remain shut out of the decision-making process. Hence, unless election mechanisms can be linked with other types of political institutions such as multiparty coalitions, regional autonomy, or federalism, they may not be able to provide security against ethnic discrimination.

Moreover, with opportunities limited and competition for positions and resources intense, some leaders can choose to further their individual and collective interests, even at a high cost in terms of the society's overall well-being. When ethnic entrepreneurs seek to outbid their centrist rivals through militant appeals to their ethnic kinsmen, elections can increase strife and undermine the frail, cross-cutting linkages that buttress democratic regimes. Ethnic outbidding heightens minority insecurity. Groups make greater demands on the state and on one another. They strain against their own commitments to the existing ethnic contract and worry about the promises of the other. Values of restraint and civility are weakened, and suppressed emotions of dominance come to the fore in majority circles. In some circumstances leaders can repackage and play upon latent grievances in such a way as to foster a collective response highly damaging to their stereotypic enemies. As a result, elections in certain circumstances can prove very destabilizing, threatening minorities with the possibility of discrimination, exclusion, and even victimization.

Electoral systems have been organized in two ways to promote inclusive coalitions. First, electoral rules can be set so that candidates are forced to appeal to more than one ethnic group. In an effort to give presidential candidates an incentive to attract support from a broad cross section of communal groups, for example, both the 1979 and 1995 (draft) constitutions in Nigeria provided that if there are two candidates for election, a candidate would be deemed to be elected when that person secured a simple majority of the total number of votes cast as well as one-quarter of the votes cast in at least two-thirds of the states. In securing a majority of votes in this multiethnic society, moderate appeals, with their overarching themes, were expected to win out over parochial ones. Nigerian constitutional experts anticipated that the adoption of such an electoral system would build a measure of confidence among ethnic minorities regarding their future political status.

Second, electoral rules can also be crafted to ensure some minimal representation of all ethnic groups in the society. Those seeking to encourage minority representation in party lists and in ruling coalitions have looked favorably on various systems of proportional representation (PR). For example, in structuring the elections for the Russian State Duma (the lower chamber of parliament) in 1993, legal drafters provided for a chamber of 450 members, half on the basis of single-member constituencies and half on the basis of PR. Constituencies vary enormously in population size, ranging from as few as 13,800 to over 700,000. Such a system ensures the representation of smaller ethnic peoples in the State Duma. In South Africa, the African National Congress agreed, somewhat reluctantly, to use PR to give racial and ethnic minorities a sense of security at a difficult time of transition (Sisk 1993, 87). Although the PR system seemed cumbersome and failed to generate close links between a member of parliament and his or her constituents, ANC leaders nonetheless agreed to continue use of this mechanism for electing members to the National Assembly under the 1996 Constitution.

The way that state elites structure electoral arrangements, then, is likely to prove critical in building confidence in minority circles. A broad-based electoral formula, like that of Nigeria, and proportional representation are two possible ways of encouraging minority ethnic participation and inclusion; yet they are likely to endure only as long as they retain support among key groups and state elites. If the majority shifts its concern away from the values of representativeness, a change in electoral rules can take place. Unless this change is handled fairly and with extreme sensitivity, it can be perceived by minority elements as inimical to their interests. As a consequence, considerable experience is required before minorities come to see electoral laws as reliable foundations for their security.

Regional Autonomy and Federalism

Political and administrative decentralization can also play an important role in managing political conflict. By enabling local and regional authorities to wield a degree of autonomous power, elites at the political center can promote confidence among local leaders. Measures on decentralization, regional autonomy, and federalism featured in peace negotiations in Bosnia, Sri Lanka, Cyprus, Sudan, Angola, Mozambique, and South Africa. In each, they provided insurgent militias with an important incentive for responding positively to proposals by the government or a third-party mediator for settling the conflict. The U.S.-brokered peace initiative in Bosnia achieved a key breakthrough in the September 1995 negotiations, for example, when the Bosnian government agreed to recognize an autonomous Bosnian Serb entity, called Republika Srpska. In exchange, Serbia and Croatia accepted the legal existence of Bosnia and Herzegovina with its present borders and endorsed the division of the country, 51 percent of the territory to the Bosnian government and Bosnian Croats, and 49 percent to the Bosnian Serbs. All three parties perceived control of Bosnia's space to be critically important for their survival once peace came into effect.

In attempting to create a new balance between state and society, groups turn to decentralization as a means of placing institutional limitations on unbridled central authority. Politically marginalized groups have vivid memories of excessive state penetration and a continuing fear of majority domination. Decentralization and the authority these schemes allow local elites can, therefore, become confidence-building mechanisms that safeguard the place of minorities in the larger society. In Ethiopia, for example, President Meles Zenawi looks to a scheme of ethnic federalism as a means of reversing the repressive, hegemonic practices of previous governments that have led to internal wars (McWhirter and Melamede 1992, 33). The 1994 constitution gives the nations making up Ethiopia wide powers, including an unconditional right of self-determination and secession. Appearance, however, must not be confused with reality. Although he accepts that the new Ethiopian constitution grants the states increased autonomy, Edmond Keller (Chapter Twelve) emphasizes the practical limitations that are placed on the maneuverability of state politicians. The ruling Ethiopian People's Revolutionary Democratic Front, which created the various ethnic parties in the first place, remains in a strong position to control the activities of these local political leaders by manipulating the fiscal resources made available to them.

Nevertheless, experiments with decentralized systems in India, Pakistan, Cyprus, Sri Lanka, Kenya, Uganda, South Africa, Sudan, and Ethiopia reveal serious practical difficulties in securing majority-backed state acceptance for these attempts to insulate minority interests from central authority. Determined to prevent the fragmentation of the state, public officials have taken firm action to avert a weakening of control. In extreme cases, they have revoked previous concessions. Thus, as Yugoslavia began to disintegrate in 1989, President Slobodan Milosevic rescinded the autonomous provincial status within Serbia that Tito had given to largely Albanian-populated Kosovo. Sudan's President Gaafar el-Nimeiry, who had been the main advocate of political accommodation with the Southern Sudan Liberation Movement insurgents in 1972, backtracked on his commitments formalized in the Addis Ababa accords, and in the late 1970s began to dismantle the quasi-federal compromise; to placate hard-line Muslim elements within his government, Nimeiry intervened in southern regional elections, changed regional boundaries, redivided the southern region, applied shari'a law to non-Muslims, and ultimately, abrogated the agreement itself. In these and other cases, the voiding of concessions on autonomy heightened tensions and led to new or renewed violence.

Although regional autonomy and federalism have been used as safeguards, they have had, in some instances, unintended consequences that have actually increased conflict. Despite efforts to decentralize power in South Africa and Ethiopia, the fiscal dominance of the political center has tended to undercut the significance of regional authorities. Moreover, efforts to delineate boundaries have increased conflict between ethno-regional identity groups. In contemporary Russia, the arbitrary way in which internal boundaries divide ethnic peoples has been a major source of tension (Lapidus and de Nevers 1995, 3). In Ethiopia, the regional boundaries set up by the government appear to favor Tigray and the Afars, at the expense of the formerly dominant Amhara and the Somali Isaks in the Awash Valley. Unless carefully crafted, decentralization schemes may worsen rather than improve interethnic relations.

Confidence-Building Measures Evaluated

Confidence-building measures are potentially creative instruments by which states can reassure ethnic minorities. They indicate a sympathetic concern on the part of those in power toward the fears and uncertainties of minorities. By acknowledging and showing respect for difference and by agreeing to share resources, state positions, and political power with exposed and vulnerable groups, these measures reduce the perceived risks of association and provide incentives for cooperation with other groups. They can also become the basis over time for an iterated process that can culminate in a shared sense of common fate among diverse communities. States seeking ethnic accommodations have used confidence-building measures effectively in the past, and they will continue to do so in the future. The international community should encourage states at risk of significant ethnic conflict to make use of confidence-building measures.

However, such confidence-building measures represent conflict management, not conflict resolution. They can reduce some of the factors giving rise to ethnic fears, but they do not alter the basic dilemmas that cause these fears to emerge in the first place. The risks in ethnic encounters remain in place, even if papered over by concessions. Because there is always the possibility that groups will repeal their accommodating measures and adopt more threatening forms of interaction, these confidence-building measures never eliminate the information failures, problems of credible commitment, and security dilemmas that are embedded in ethnic encounters. As Adam Przeworski astutely observes, "if sovereignty resides with the people, the people can decide to undermine all the guarantees reached by politicians around a negotiating table. Even the most institutionalized guarantees give at best a high degree of assurance, never certainty" (Przeworski 1991, 79).

EXTERNAL INTERVENTION

If states fail to restrain the incentives for violence rooted in the strategic interactions of groups, it is necessary to turn to the international environment and ask whether external intervention can safeguard minorities against their worst fears. For many observers, sovereignty is linked to responsibility: state elites are expected to guarantee minority rights and provide the means for establishing and maintaining regularized patterns of state-society and interethnic relations. The state, with its monopoly of force, is often in a position, as one South African mediator described it in 1995, to "enforce stability" between local warring parties (in this case, in the East Rand townships in his country). But who will intercede if the state is unable or unwilling to secure the safety of its minority peoples? What forms will this intervention take? Which kind of intervention, if any, is likely to have a significant impact on intrastate conflicts?

At the outset, it is important to note that some states in Eastern Europe, the former Soviet Union, and Africa are notably "soft" and unable to enforce regulations throughout their territory. As pointed out in Chapter One, the decline of the state contributes to an environment in which inter-group violence can take place. Other states, lacking effective control and unwilling to live with the uncertainties of ongoing negotiations, opt for heavy-handed repression in an effort to compensate for their weaknesses (Lapidus and de Nevers 1995, 35). In such abusive contexts, such as Siad Barre's Somalia, the state itself can become the source of intense conflicts with ethno-regional opponents. In these situations, external intervention may not only be warranted but required to promote peaceful interethnic relations.

The principle of sovereignty has never been articulated or respected in the clear-cut manner often assumed by scholars of international relations. When international action is sanctioned, external actors, concluding that sovereignty is not being exercised in a responsible manner, can decide to intervene in intrastate conflicts to protect minority interests and to insulate the international community against spreading violence. As Daniel T. Froats and Stephen D. Krasner demonstrate in Chapter Ten, states have a long history of intervention in the ethnic (and religious) affairs of other countries, using various international pressures, unilateral pledges, and treaties to protect the rights of minorities (also see Krasner

1993). Many of the treaties settling European affairs in the aftermath of World War I contained provisions obligating states to protect the political and religious rights of their minorities as a condition for admission to the League of Nations. Because the new governments viewed these treaty provisions as externally imposed, however, and because they often lacked domestic support and major-power commitment, they frequently proved difficult to implement. More recently, the United Nations Charter affirmed an international commitment to basic human rights and fundamental freedoms. Former U.N. Secretary General Boutros Boutros-Ghali has said that "the time of absolute and exclusive sovereignty . . . has passed" (Boutros-Ghali 1992, 9). The Conference on Security and Cooperation in Europe (now the Organization on Security and Cooperation in Europe) has always sought to promote human rights within states, with a meeting of national experts on minority problems stating in early 1991 that "issues concerning national minorities, as well as compliance with international obligations and commitments concerning the rights of persons belonging to them, are matters of legitimate international concern and consequently do not constitute exclusively an internal affair of the respective state" (quoted in Kampelman 1993, ix). Lori Fisler Damrosch, in turn, observes that "large segments of the international community have been willing to endorse strong collective action in a wide range of situations," including genocide, interference with the delivery of humanitarian relief, violation of cease-fire agreements, collapse of civil order, and irregular interruption of democratic governance (1993, 12).

Nonetheless, since 1945 there has been a strong insistence by many countries on the protection of national autonomy afforded by the juridical principle of sovereignty. This emphasis on internal autonomy has often been strongest where states themselves were weakest (Jackson and Rosberg 1982). Yet today, ethnic conflicts and their possible spread have thrust issues of "humanitarian" intervention onto the policy agendas of the United States and many other countries. As Edmond Keller indicates in Chapter Twelve, even in Africa, where the norm of juridical sovereignty is strong, there is a new willingness on the part of state leaders to entertain limitations on the notion of sovereignty. This reflects their shock over the extreme brutality of ethnic wars and the inability of states with limited legitimacy and low capabilities to surmount these challenges (Obasanjo 1996). Despite this change in attitude, it remains an open question whether these leaders will be prepared to sanction international interventions directed against their own countries.

External intervention takes three broad forms: noncoercive intervention, coercive intervention, and third-party mediation during both the negotiation and implementation stages. We look briefly at each of these forms, drawing conclusions in each case about their anticipated effects on intrastate conflicts.

Noncoercive Intervention

In our shrinking global environment, international actors are increasingly distressed over the violation of minority rights taking place in other countries. They are also concerned with the possibility of diffusion—with demands for self-determination spreading and civil wars spilling over into neighboring territories—as seen in Liberia, Rwanda, and Bosnia. This sense of alarm has, intermittently, prompted outside states and multilateral organizations to protest infractions or exert pressure on the transgressors. Western governments, encouraged by their domestic publics to denounce breaches of human rights in Bosnia, Chechnya, Rwanda, Burundi, and Sudan, have criticized these abuses through quiet, behind-the-scenes diplomacy and at public forums.

Assertions of international norms are important in raising the costs of unacceptable behavior, especially when their advocates offer an alternative set of interests around which defectors can mobilize and challenge the ensconced ethnic leaders (Gagnon 1994–1995, 139). States are also in a strong position to use inclusion in or exclusion from the international community to reward or punish regimes and ethnic leaders who deviate from internationally accepted norms. The promises of inclusion or the pains of exclusion can at times create strong incentives to behave in a more responsible fashion. Thus Milosevic's desire to be accepted by Europeans and North Americans enabled Western diplomats to influence his behavior at the bargaining table, even causing him to make concessions on the emotionally charged issue of Bosnian government control over a unified Sarajevo. This concession brought him into contention with the Bosnian Serb representatives at Dayton, and with some hard-liners in the capital city, exposing deep within-group differences to the world community. Similarly, conditions on membership in international organizations appear to be mitigating ethnic conflicts in Hungary and Romania, while Turkey's desire for acceptance in Europe may be limiting its actions against its Kurdish minority.

In South Africa, external protests and sanctions raised the costs of doing business, access to technology and raw materials, and travel. Sanctions physically punished the regime, something that became painfully evident in South Africa's loss of dominance in the air war over Angola, brought on in part by the air force's inability to secure modern weaponry and spare parts. The symbolic impact of sanctions was also important because it represented a clear statement of sympathy for black hardship and moral disapproval of apartheid policies by the international community (Strack 1978, 12). Above all, international condemnation challenged state and governmental legitimacy. Although the costs of sanctions were discomforting and burdensome, they did not hurt the main body of the white constituency sufficiently to alter priorities—until President F. W. de Klerk's remarkable change of heart on negotiating with the anti-apartheid opposition in the early 1990s (Sisk 1995).

Given the emotionalism over security issues that brings aggressive ethnic leaders to the fore in the first place, we are skeptical that external appeals, exhortations, and pressures will in and of themselves dissuade determined elites from their abusive courses. Bosnian Serb leader Radovan Karadzic, Bosnian Serb military commander Ratko Mladic, and their ilk remain sufficiently insulated from world pressures that what transpires at diplomatic meetings or in the global press will probably have little immediate impact on them or their militant followers.

Pointing to the crimes of "ethnic cleansing" or to the violation of safe areas in Bosnia, for instance, did little to deter Karadzic, Mladic, or their supporters. In fact, the crimes that were committed actually eliminated dissenters and waverers within the Bosnian Serb community and bound members together more tightly than before.

Frustrated by this ability to ignore external censure, international actors have sought to influence local parties through the use of various pressures, including refusals of diplomatic and economic support, mandatory sanctions, the denial or threatened denial of recognition, and the provision of intelligence information. In Chapter Eleven, Cynthia Kaplan concludes that the pressure of third parties was decisive in gaining a Russian-Estonian agreement on troop withdrawals during the 1993–1994 negotiations. To be sure, the actions of Estonia's president in conceding the right of retired Russian military officers to reside permanently in his country represented a face-saving compromise for President Yeltsin in his relations with Russians at home and abroad. Nevertheless, it was the European and American reaction to Yeltsin's demand to link the issue of troop withdrawal with the issue of human rights that proved critical. Western leaders threatened that unless the Russians agreed to withdraw their troops from Estonia, it might lead to delays in the next Russian/U.S. summit; moreover, efforts by the United States Senate to tie economic assistance to a Russian agreement were also telling. External pressures facilitated the negotiations, leaving the Russian president with a limited freedom to maneuver. The West has also been actively involved in easing Eastern European insecurities by engaging majority governments in a discussion of their ethnic problems, facilitating communications between majorities and minorities, and pushing the parties toward accommodation wherever possible. The effect, notes Larry Watts (1995, 95), has been to ease the siege mentality and the sense of vulnerability of local actors; nevertheless, it remains unrealistic to hope that these pressures alone will compel regional governments to change their basic policies.

Noncoercive interventions, as well as other forms of intervention discussed below, place the initiating party or parties in a dilemma. On the one hand, seeking to overcome the dilemmas of between-group strategic interactions, initiating countries need to engage in confidence-building in order to establish trust and to reassure majority and minority groups. On the other hand, targeting within-group interactions, the efforts of third parties to alter the incentives of leaders and punish particular groups (the Hutu in Rwanda or the Serbs in Bosnia) complicate the process of building trust across groups. In dealing with this dilemma, the initiating states can benefit from precise information on such subjects as within-group points of tension and capabilities and from the adoption of a mix of policies gauged to promote conciliatory behavior on the part of target groups.

In brief, noncoercive interventions can be helpful in raising the costs of purely ethnic appeals and in structuring the incentives of group leaders prepared to accept international norms for the purposes of recognition, acceptance, and inclusion in the international community. Where conflicts are intense, however, exhortations and international warnings may not deter or end violence. The most that noncoercive intervention can do in such situations is to create a climate in which ethnic appeals and violence are perceived by all as illegitimate and, therefore, marginally less likely to be used.

Coercive Intervention

Third parties intervene militarily in intrastate conflicts in a peacekeeping or peacemaking role for a variety of reasons: to ensure food deliveries to the starving (e.g., Somalia, Bosnia), protect designated safe areas (e.g., Iraq, Bosnia), defend threatened peoples (e.g., Liberia, Rwanda), and establish a new regime (e.g., Uganda). States may be motivated by hegemonic ambitions, concerns for regional stability, sympathy for oppressed groups, a sense of international responsibility, or simple humanitarianism (Cooper and Berdal 1993, 197). They may also intervene to maintain their own moral values, deter the possible use of weapons of mass destruction, or forestall further diffusion (Brown 1993, 16–20). Whatever the motive of states, the rise in ethnic conflict today creates new demands and opportunities for coercive intervention by outside states and international organizations.

External interventions have two primary effects. First, intervention can alter the internal balance of ethnic power and may lead groups to moderate their demands. Except perhaps where the sides have reached a "hurting stalemate" (Zartman 1985) and the purpose of the intervention is exclusively to separate the forces and keep the peace, interventions always have political implications (Betts 1994; Carr 1993). Even in Somalia, where negotiations on establishing a transitional national council led to hopes for a settlement in 1993, the initial humanitarian mission eventually favored one claimant to power (Ali Mahdi Mohamed) over the other (Mohamed Farah Aideed), ultimately causing the politicization of the mission (Hirsch and Oakley 1995).

Typically favoring, by design or default, the weaker side in any internal conflict, external powers reduce the stronger side's chances for success. This, in turn, restrains the stronger party's demands. To the extent that such restraint takes hold, intervention can improve the prospects for agreement. However, the weaker side is likely to increase its demands and ask for more at the bargaining table as its prospects of failure decline and its chances of success improve (Wittman 1979). For instance, once the NATO countries intervened decisively in September 1995 on behalf of the Bosnian government, and against the Bosnian Serb forces, the latter—pressured by Milosevic—quickly moderated their demands and moved toward accepting the territorial partition they had earlier rejected.[1] At the same time, however, the Croats saw new opportunities on the battlefield and at the negotiating table, and the United States and its allies had to exert pressure on the Bosnian government and Croatia not to exploit their

---

[1] Milosevic's role in the October 1995 negotiations was important, because it carried with it an implied threat: if the Bosnian Serbs refused to be more accommodating at the bargaining table, their Serb kinsmen across the border could further reduce their military support.

increased leverage. With both effects occurring simultaneously, the "bargaining gap" between the parties remained as wide as ever.

As the Bosnian case demonstrates, unless pressure is exerted on both sides to moderate their demands, intervention by itself will not necessarily enhance the prospects for agreement. In this case, however, the United States did place pressure on all the combatants and brought the parties to an agreement in Dayton. The partisan effects of interventions must be recognized and incorporated into any plan for bringing the disputants to a successful agreement. Even so, intervention, by itself, does not solve the information failures that may have thwarted agreement in the first place. On this score, intervention is an instrument of limited effectiveness.

The second primary effect of intervention is to provide guarantees for new ethnic contracts between the warring parties, at least during an interim period. As discussed in Chapter One, problems of credible commitment hinder the efforts of groups to resolve their differences peacefully. The primary attraction of external intervention is that an outside state can enforce an agreement, thereby providing the necessary credibility that is otherwise lacking. Indeed, when the future risk of exploitation is high, but the declining group is still strong enough to possess some chance of victory, outside enforcers may be the only way to ensure ethnic peace (Stedman 1991; Walter 1997). Thus, in Namibia in 1989, the third-party enforcer was in a position to raise the costs of breaking agreements by monitoring the implementation process, highlighting violations of the peace agreement, and focusing an international spotlight on any breaches that occurred (Fortna 1995). The lack of any equally effective third-party enforcer in neighboring Angola following the signing of the Bicesse accords and UNITA President Jonas Savimbi's poor showing in the first round of the 1992 elections increased incentives to defect from the agreement and resume the civil war.

The promise of the post-Cold War world is that the great powers, freed from the shackles of superpower competition, can now intervene to mitigate ethnic conflicts by providing external guarantees of social order. If the warring parties themselves cannot make credible commitments to uphold their pacts, external powers can lead the groups to peaceful solutions by enforcing any agreement they might reach. The paradox of the post-Cold War world, however, is that in the absence of the bipolar competition that drove them into the far reaches of the globe, the United States and other powers now lack the political will necessary to make a sustained commitment to the role of external guarantor. This lack of resolve partly reflects the vagaries of public opinion. For example, during the 1994 Rwanda crisis only 28 percent of the American public surveyed in June 1994 favored sending U.S. troops to stop the killing (quoted from CBS News, June 20, 1994); two months later, however, when the policy objective shifted to humanitarian aid, 69 percent of respondents favored such a strategy (quoted from Yankelovich Partners Inc., August 4, 1994). As these data indicate, intervention is a weak reed upon which to rest hopes for the successful management of transnational ethnic conflict. Certainly, the outcomes of these initiatives are less than inspiring. For every successful military intervention, as in the Congo or Persian Gulf crisis, there are the failed efforts in Sri Lanka, Somalia, and Lebanon.

The key issue in determining the success of any external guarantee is the commitment of the international community. In a way not sufficiently appreciated by current policy makers in Washington and elsewhere, external guarantees work only when the local parties to the conflict believe that the outside powers are committed to enforce the ethnic contract in a fair manner into the indefinite future. The behavior of the external powers today is not the crucial factor. Rather, a more fundamental question is whether the warring parties or potential combatants believe the external powers will be there to protect them tomorrow, and in the days and years after that. In the absence of a belief in the fair-mindedness and stamina of the external powers, intervention in any form will fail to mitigate the conflict.

Unfortunately, even countries with strong interests in intervening often find themselves unable to offer credible external guarantees. Countries vitally affected by the fighting or the outcome either tend to be partisan or are perceived by the combatants as partisan, as was the case with France's intervention in Rwanda in 1994. One or both sides to the conflict, therefore, will doubt the willingness or ability of the outside power to enforce the new ethnic contract in an evenhanded manner, and they will be less likely to reach an effective and enforceable agreement. Likewise, having essentially taken sides in the Bosnian conflict, the United States and its NATO allies may have forfeited their status as credible guarantors; although many in the West worry about Russian involvement in peacekeeping operations in Bosnia, in part because the Russians are viewed as favoring the Serbs, this may be the only way of checking the bias or feared bias of NATO and ensuring that the warring parties accept external oversight. The more partial the external guarantor, the less likely the sides will be to reach an effective and enforceable agreement. However, when outside powers have an interest in a stable outcome, rather than in the victory or loss of either side, they may be perceived by all as fair-minded facilitators. Britain's role in Zimbabwe in the 1970s is a positive example of an interested party able to work with a coalition of external mediators to push negotiations ahead to a successful outcome.

Countries with weak interests in the conflict, on the other hand, will tend to lack or will be perceived as lacking the political stamina to enforce any new ethnic contract into the future. The East African countries making up the Inter-Governmental Authority on Drought and Development have launched mediatory initiatives in recent years in the Sudan, but they lack the economic and military capabilities to enforce an agreement between the combatants at this juncture. Likewise, the United States was unwilling to bear any substantial cost in human lives to guarantee the peace in Somalia, although some casualties are probably inevitable in all peacemaking operations. When the interest of the outside power in the conflict is weak, each of the warring parties is more likely to believe that the external guarantor will default on its commitment, and the adversaries will therefore continue fighting. An external guarantee that the parties fear will soon evaporate is no guarantee at all.

There are many reasons why states might possess only weak interests in guaranteeing a new ethnic contract. First, political instability abroad is typically broad but shallow in its effects; conflicts that may diffuse across borders or instability that threatens to breed centers of international terrorism and crime affect all countries, but none intensely. It is a collective bad, if you will, subject to the usual tendency to free ride on the efforts of other states (Olson 1965). Although the international community might benefit significantly from ending the conflict, it is in no country's interests to pay unilaterally the substantial costs of resolving the dispute by acting as the world's policeman. This is one plausible interpretation of the hesitancy of the United States in taking a leadership role in Bosnia. In this view, presidents George Bush and Bill Clinton held back, hoping that the Europeans would step forward and carry the financial and military burden; only when the Europeans proved unprepared to assume the costs did the United States take the lead.

Second, false understandings of the nature of ethnic conflict can also increase the reluctance of states to become involved. Analysis or political rhetoric that portrays ethnic conflicts as primordial contests of centuries-long duration subtly raises the expected costs of any possible intervention and reduces the expected benefits; natural or inevitable conflicts appear to be harder to resolve than other, more "man-made" conflicts. In this case, the widespread acceptance of the view that the present Balkan conflict is based upon ancient hatreds is both an impediment to action and an excuse for inaction.

Weak interests, however, need not preclude states from becoming involved in ethnic conflicts. Especially after the Cold War, states are freer to respond to international events according to their own internal, domestic political whims and fancies. Humanitarian intervention is driven by many of the same information flows that drive the process of diffusion (see Chapter One). As John Chipman writes, "The flow of information and the effect of television mean, especially for the great powers who retain power projection capabilities, that public opinion might support the deployment of force for preventive diplomacy, humanitarian aid, peacekeeping, or pacification, even without the national interests of the 'expeditionary state' being remotely engaged. This impels states to become involved in the parochial quarrels of others. Leaders may know that their citizens will not support heavy casualties where no great strategic interest is at stake, but often the demand 'to do something' cannot be refuted by reasoned argument" (1993a, 239). Public exposure to information about human tragedies may thus induce an emotional response sufficient to draw an outside power into a conflict. These same emotions, however, are likely to prove insufficient to sustain interest once the full costs of the mission become apparent.

Weak commitments produce ambiguous policies that may, in the end, exacerbate rather than resolve conflicts. Public commitments encourage the weaker party to believe that the external power supports it, thereby prompting the party to fight on and hold out for a better deal than its position on the battlefield warrants (Djilas 1995, 102). Ambiguity and vacillation, however, may simultaneously persuade the stronger party that the external power does not possess sufficient stamina, and that it too may improve its position by continuing to fight. Indeed, the strong party may even target the external power in an attempt to raise the latter's costs of intervention and force its withdrawal from the conflict. This ambivalent commitment is the true tragedy of the current United States policy in the Balkans. One of the most important lessons from this analysis is that if external powers are going to intervene in ethnic conflicts, either alone or in concert with others, they must do so in a way that is credible to the groups involved.

Although easier to organize, external intervention by a single actor represents an intermittent and somewhat unreliable means of responding to ethnic violence in the contemporary period. Even though the French did enter Rwanda in the later stages of the 1994 crisis, this was a belated and atypical initiative. More common is the case of the Sudan, where a decade of brutal encounters has engendered diplomatic maneuvers by third parties but no decisive military intercession between the warring sides. As noted above, with the end of the Cold War, elites in the developed, Western countries are looking inward, reluctant to take on the challenge of risky humanitarian interventions and peace enforcement in distant countries.

Intervention by multilateral regional or global organizations can help mitigate problems of political legitimacy and burden sharing that might otherwise thwart effective international commitments. The problems of coalition building, financing, and domestic public opinion remain, but the collective nature of the intervention tends to blunt opposition at home and abroad. To some extent, the Economic Community of West African States (ECOWAS) intervention in Liberia in 1990, where it prevented the National Patriotic Front of Liberia from taking over Monrovia (and with that city's fall, a possible threat to the Krahn and Mandingo peoples living there), represents a pioneering effort to protect vulnerable ethnic groups.

The difficulties of funding the ECOWAS effort and building up a larger force to ensure a sustained commitment, however, point up some of the larger problems associated with multilateral peace enforcement. International organizations, after all, are state-based institutions that rely upon their members to support their activities. They cannot cope with the burgeoning problems of intrastate conflict unless their members pay their dues promptly and provide the necessary military equipment, logistical support, and trained manpower (Boutros-Ghali 1995, 11). Smaller states such as Ghana have expressed their uneasiness about continuing what seems an indefinite commitment of scarce resources in Liberia (*West Africa*, December 26, 1994 to January 8 1995, 2208); large and wealthy states, such as the United States, are slow to meet their financial responsibilities and appear intent on reducing their contributions to United Nations peacekeeping and peace-enforcing activities in the years ahead. To achieve "acceptable costs," international organizations will, without doubt, have to make some difficult choices on which humanitarian interventions to undertake (Haass 1994, 27). Only in special cases, then, can multilateral interventions be expected to demonstrate the kind of long-term commitment necessary to restore peace and stability.

In sum, external interventions are not likely to solve the underlying problems associated with ethnic insecurity and violence or to change the local balance of power between the parties. Interveners can attempt to reinforce international norms and enforce agreements, but in the final analysis, conflict management requires an effort by the local parties to work out acceptable rules of interaction. This is not to say that containing conflict is not an important achievement, only that containment by itself is not a permanent solution. External intervention does not solve the strategic dilemmas discussed above or create a desire among the parties to restore normal relations.

Third-Party Mediation

Given the limitations of confidence-building measures and external interventions, there are few alternatives to negotiations if both sides are to be brought into the solution. At times, however, external mediators have succeeded in encouraging adversaries to reconsider their alternatives and opt for peaceful, negotiated solutions to their differences. For a mutually satisfactory peace to take place, a two-step negotiating process is essential: first, among the key elements within each group, and then between the groups themselves. Operating rules must be hammered out in these talks regarding inclusive coalitions, proportionality in recruitment and allocations, citizenship, autonomy, provisions on electoral competition, and so forth. The ensuing negotiations are likely to be protracted and difficult, largely because the various factions and groups lack a clear chain of command (making commitments difficult to produce) and because they understand fully that the terms they accept will cast a long shadow over their future. But if each of the parties concludes that its alternatives are limited, its present course unduly costly, and its stake in its rival's willingness to cooperate with an agreement significant, they may then begin to negotiate in good faith.

External mediators can play an important role in facilitating negotiations by encouraging adversaries to open up channels of communication, to reconsider their alternatives, and to opt for peaceful, negotiated solutions. A mediator's ability to influence the strategies of the adversaries must not be overstated; nevertheless, the ability of a third party to make effective use of pressures and incentives can prove decisive, especially if the parties to the conflict have nowhere else to go.

In intense ethnic disputes, mediators can use a variety of noncoercive and coercive incentives to increase the information available to the adversaries, facilitate a change in their strategies, or find a way to save face. Noncoercive incentives extend benefits or rewards for compliance, whereas coercive incentives punish or threaten to punish a targeted actor to bring it into line with preferred types of political behavior. Provided that the demands of the two sides are negotiable and neither party can anticipate a military victory, mediators can make use of a package of carrots and sticks in the hopes that the targeted party (or parties) will accept a compromise and thus allow some degree of mutual cooperation to materialize (Rothchild, 1997c).

Normally, noncoercive incentives will be preferred by third parties because of their low cost and expected impact. Thus, mediators frequently make use of side-payments to enlarge the pie and alter the payoff structure, thereby enhancing the benefits of making concessions (as occurred most dramatically in the Egyptian-

Israeli negotiations at Camp David in 1978). Third parties can also influence the choices of ethnic minorities by guaranteeing them against possible future abuses at the hands of the majority after an agreement has been reached.

However, when ethnic conflicts grow in intensity and can no longer be resolved by means of rewards, it sometimes becomes necessary for the third party to force movement toward cooperation by means of threats or punishments. These coercive incentives become increasingly punitive as they move from diplomatic pressure to economic sanctions to military intervention, as occurred at different stages in the Bosnian confrontation. In the contemporary period, only a coalition of mediators seems likely to have the political capacity to create the mix of noncoercive and coercive incentives necessary to overcome a stalemate and move the parties toward a negotiated settlement.

The scope for third-party initiative at both the negotiation and implementation stages is, thus, highly circumscribed. Internal wars are particularly difficult to negotiate, largely because ethnic enmities tend to be so deep and the stakes so high. Data on negotiations indicate that settlements are difficult to achieve and at least as difficult to maintain, even where a third party is prepared to step between the adversaries. Roy Licklider, largely reconfirming earlier studies by Stephen Stedman and Paul Pillar, finds that only fourteen out of fifty-seven civil wars between 1945 and 1993 were settled through negotiations (Licklider 1995, 684; Stedman 1991, 5–7; Pillar 1993, 25). This relatively low percentage reflects the strength of state and ethnic identifications and the difficulty that intrastate groups have in compromising with their adversaries. As Charles William Maynes (1995, 111) contends: "There is . . . a desperate quality to civil wars that makes them particularly hard to control once they start." Despite its emphasis on opening channels of communication and facilitating the flow of information, third-party mediation cannot wholly eliminate potential information failures. The conflicting groups are bound by the same incentives not to reveal all of their private information, even to third parties. Moreover, problems of credible commitment loom large. Barbara Walter (1997) suggests that interstate wars are actually easier to bring to a negotiated conclusion than civil wars; in the former, the two parties remain on opposite sides of their border, but in the latter the disputants must again merge themselves into a single unit and face larger problems of credible commitment as a result. Particularly in cases where insurgencies have an ethnic or nationality dimension, a mediated agreement may be difficult to arrange because highly sensitive issues of legitimacy are involved (Frei 1976, 70).

The difficulties normally associated with mediation are compounded by the obstacles to implementation. Several laboriously negotiated agreements have been signed only to fall apart at the implementation stage—for example, in Ethiopia and Eritrea (1962), Sudan (1982), Uganda (1985), Angola (1975, 1992), and Rwanda (1994). Unlike the ending of wars by means of military victory or capitulation, where the power of identity groups to resist central authority is largely eliminated, negotiated settlements leave ethnic entities with sufficient space to frustrate the ambitions of state elites (Licklider 1995, 685). The concessions necessary to bring about agreement often result in a complex and indeterminate process at the consolidation stage. Because deep distrust of an opponent remains in place at the time an agreement is set in motion, commitments made at the bargaining table may not be credible. Within-group rivalry may come into full view after the agreement, the provisions of the agreement may be vague and cause new tensions, and the world community may not be prepared to give sustained support to peacekeeping and peacemaking. The presence of such dilemmas continues to threaten the renewal of violence.

Accordingly, it was prudent for chief American negotiator Richard Holbrooke to state at the 1995 talks on Bosnia that, with several of the main issues still unresolved, there could be no guarantee that any settlement would hold (Sciolino 1995). Even now, after an agreement has been laboriously worked out, the Dayton peace accord may still unravel. After all, armies remain separate and mobilized, and ethnic leaders continue to fear a preemptive strike. The Bosnian Serbs rejected a power-sharing arrangement in 1992 and, during the current implementation phase, may fail the commitment test again. Although the human costs of partition are high, the separation of the adversaries territorially may be the only way of coping with the various strategic dilemmas we have identified (C. Kaufmann 1996).

The failure of agreements, however, is also partly attributable to the unwillingness of the international community to provide mediators with the economic, logistical, police, and military support needed to oversee the processes of disarmament, integration of the armed forces, repatriation of refugees, and holding of general elections. In addition, the guarantees made to one or more rivals by foreign governments and multilateral organizations may come to lack credibility in the eyes of local actors if domestic publics lose interest in far-off conflicts and retreat from commitments made at the high point of the struggle.

As wars reach a mutually hurting stalemate and leaders on both sides perceive an "intolerable situation" with little expectation of military victory, there is a chance that the exhausted parties will come to the table and bargain in earnest (Zartman 1985, 232). Despite the emotionalism and organizational imperatives surrounding ethnic-related struggles and civil wars, a number of them—including Cambodia, Nicaragua, Zimbabwe, Angola, Namibia, Mozambique, and possibly now Chechnya, Bosnia, Palestine, and Israel—have been or are close to being settled by means of negotiations. One must not anticipate too much from mediatory efforts, but a grim outlook is also not appropriate and could be self-fulfilling.

The Limits of Intervention

International interventions may prove necessary but not sufficient to ensure long-term commitments to peaceful relations. Where confidence-building measures fail to overcome ethnic fears, the state can fragment and the international community become by default the guarantor of last resort for desperate peoples caught up in intense civil wars. Yet even here, the safety net is frail, dependent on the goodwill of local adversaries and the sustained concern of foreign governments and publics.

External interventions, whether they are noncoercive, coercive, mediatory, or—as is common—a combination of the three, are not likely to solve the underlying strategic dilemmas that produce ethnic fear and violence. Information failures remain possible, despite the efforts of outside actors to facilitate communication and protect the parties from the potentially disastrous consequences of revealing private information. Enforcing ethnic contracts depends upon the credibility of the external parties, who often have far less at stake in the conflict than the warring groups themselves. External actors can seek to raise the costs of using force, in general, and preemptive uses of force, in particular, by punishing groups that strike first; such initiatives or the threat of such initiatives may have a moderating effect on the security dilemma. Through early action, they may also be able to determine military doctrines and shape force structures in groups beginning to prepare for self-defense. Nevertheless, once incentives to use force preemptively are in place, outsiders can do little to restrain the security dilemma. In the final analysis, conflict management requires an effort by the local parties to engage in efforts to work out acceptable rules of interaction. External intervention does not by itself create a desire among the parties to restore normal relations. This is not to say that international efforts to contain conflict are not important, only that containment is not by itself a solution.

Preventive diplomacy appears to be the most appropriate form of action available to domestic and international leaders. International intervention is far more effective if it occurs before the frenzied ethnic killings begin and before such confrontations create vested interests in prolonging the crisis. Fearing another downward spiral into widespread violence in Burundi, the Clinton administration and the international community have taken a series of preventive measures to bolster moderate forces and to "deter extremists from fomenting violence or overturning the current fragile power-sharing arrangement," including the facilitation of local dialogues, the deployment of military observers, radio appeals, the strengthening of the judicial system, high-level visits to reassure moderate politicians that the world community remains concerned, and the provision of developmental assistance (Friedman 1995). To date, this preventive action has helped stabilize a very risky situation.

For Bruce Jentleson (Chapter Thirteen), it is hard to deter conflicts from escalating into crises because, in practice, preventive measures are difficult to formulate and implement. Thus Jentleson and others conclude that preventive diplomacy involves complicated political and military decisions regarding the domestic jurisdiction of states, the timing of interventions, and problems of political will and capacity on the part of intervening states and organizations (Stedman 1996; Lund 1995, 161–63). The difficulties in the way of preventive action are illustrated by the crisis in Rwanda, where the international community was not prepared to develop effective strategies for dealing with rising ethnic tensions in advance of the widespread killings. However, as Jentleson stresses, even though effective preventive diplomacy may be complicated, it nonetheless remains necessary and possible. The risks that ethnic conflict will diffuse to the surrounding region or escalate are substantial, but these risks can at times be reduced, as the case of Macedonia indicates.

CONCLUSION

Most of the time, most ethnic groups live side by side in amity with each other. Even in cases where ethnic minorities might otherwise be at risk, some states have been determined to promote stable ethnic relations on their own, and have made concessions on minority group inclusion, participation, autonomy, and access to resources. These adjustments to the grievances and insecurities of smaller or less powerful ethnic groups, for the most part, ease intergroup tensions. However, an awareness that regimes can always change their preferences and retract these concessions leaves minorities fearful of the future. Information failures, problems of credible commitment, the security dilemma, and the risk that ethnic activists and political entrepreneurs will polarize society lurk in the background of all ethnically divided polities. Violence always remains a possibility.

In their fear, ethnic minorities, recognizing the state's limited capacity to maintain order and its potential to act repressively in some cases, look outward to the international community for protection. They hope the international community will restore a balance of power and hence make systematic, state-sanctioned ethnic killing too costly for the hard-line majority leadership to condone. The international response, however, has all too often been feeble and unconvincing. Western countries condemned ethnic cleansing in Bosnia and Sudan and appealed for negotiated settlements; they have also mediated peace agreements between the adversaries with some success in recent years. However, as these situations continue to degenerate, these same external powers are inhibited by calculations of prudence and fail to intervene more forcefully. The effect is to leave the aggressive nationalists with an incentive to stay their murderous course. In a world community in which domestic publics oppose external interventions and many states are inclined to free ride on the efforts of others, only fragile safety nets are held out for the vulnerable.

Minority Rights and the Westphalian Model

STEPHEN D. KRASNER AND DANIEL T. FROATS

IN AN IDEAL Westphalian order, political relations between rulers and ruled are territorially bounded and not subject to any external authority. Actors within the territorial boundaries of a state can structure their relationships independently of outside forces. They may enshrine civil liberties or ignore them; they may treat men and women in the same or in different ways; they may recognize and preserve minority cultures or suppress them. Rulers may wield absolute power or very little. It is the absence of any external authority, rather than the internal organization of the polity or the degree of actual power wielded by the government, that is the defining characteristic of Westphalian sovereignty.

Many see international concerns for human rights and minority rights as a revolutionary development, since the principle that individuals or groups are endowed with inherent rights implies that public authorities are not free to structure relations between rulers and ruled in any way that they see fit. One scholar avers that "the international law of human rights is revolutionary because it contradicts the notion of national sovereignty, that is, that a state can do as it pleases in its own jurisdiction" (Forsythe 1983, 4). Another observes that international human-rights law has "broken through the armour of sovereignty" (Hailbronner 1992, 117). Rulers are said to face unprecedented political, economic, and in some cases military pressure if they violate human rights standards held to be universal.

The view that recent developments signal a fundamental change in how international relations are ordered in fact—rather than in theory—is myopic both empirically and analytically. Empirically, the view that international concerns for minority rights represent a substantially new development ignores the long history of external involvement in the treatment of minorities within states. Relations between rulers and ruled have been an enduring international concern. The principles of nonintervention and territoriality, which define the Westphalian model, have persistently been challenged by alternative principles such as universal human rights, toleration, and ethnic self-determination. Every major peace settlement of the modern period has addressed the fate of minorities, defined in

Note: An earlier version of this essay appeared as a working paper of the Institut für Interkulturelle und Internationale Studien, Universität Bremen. For helpful comments and criticisms, the authors wish to thank David Holloway and Stephen Stedman. Responsibility for errors remains with the authors.

terms of religious affiliation and later ethnic identity. With the end of the Cold War, minority rights have again become a focus of international concern.

Conceptually, the Westphalian model of states, which emphasizes the centrality of exclusive authority within a given territory, has never provided an adequate explanation for the behavior of rulers. The Westphalian order is only weakly institutionalized. It has never been so taken for granted that rulers could not imagine other ways of doing things. Indeed, they have frequently chosen to violate the domestic autonomy of their own or other states. The international system is anarchic; rulers always have the option of compromising their own autonomy or intervening in the internal affairs of other states. There has been no authority that could prevent rulers from signing, by choice or duress, agreements that alter their relationship with their own subjects, nor any enduring consensus on how to balance minority-rights concerns against demands for sovereign autonomy. A variety of often mutually inconsistent principles have been used to legitimate policy.

Rather than being an accurate description of what has happened in the international environment, the Westphalian model is best understood as a default. If no other choices are made, then state authority structures do have exclusive control over relations between rulers and ruled within their own territory. But other choices have, in fact, frequently been made.

Where significant internal support exists for minority rights, international guarantees can help to prevent violent oppression and assimilation of communal groups by making liberal policies more credible and more difficult to reverse. Where this support is insufficient, minority protection has relied on external rewards and threats. Historically, coercive threats have been the most common but least reliable path to minority protection. Whether voluntary or coercive, international efforts to protect minorities succeed primarily by strengthening the position of domestic actors who are themselves committed, for reasons of interest or principle, to safeguarding the future of minorities.

PROTECTING MINORITIES IN A WESTPHALIAN DEFAULT SYSTEM

Where are international minority-rights guarantees likely to emerge? Can they change the behavior of rulers toward vulnerable groups within the domain of the state? To be consequential, international minority-rights commitments must lead rulers to respect minority rights where they would not or could not otherwise, due to competing domestic pressures.

Minority-rights guarantees involve specific commitments by rulers or governments concerning the treatment of minorities, as individuals and/or groups. Minorities have been constituted in different ways historically: the salience of religious affiliation has declined in comparison with ethnicity, defined as a shared identity based on language, physical characteristics, history, kinship, region, or culture.

Minority-rights guarantees have arisen through two distinct paths. First, where there is significant domestic support for minority rights, international guarantees can strengthen the capacity of rulers to implement liberal policies, sometimes by empowering liberal forces within civil society. Second, where domestic support has been limited, minority rights guarantees have been the result of incentives or threats given by more powerful states.

By voluntarily accepting external standards and implementation mechanisms, rulers can signal a credible commitment to respect minority rights, obtain political cover for unpopular policies, and obligate successors to implement liberal policies. These "self-binding" commitments insulate policies against the competing interests of other domestic political agents. They may empower domestic authorities or constituencies with a stake in enforcing constraints. Or rulers may give international institutions the capacity to monitor implementation and punish defection. External enforcement alters the domestic political calculus of current and future stakeholders. External constraints lend credibility to commitments made by state leaders. Commitments can not always be reversed without cost by future leaders, even those who have different views. Historically, self-binding commitments have occurred primarily through international human-rights conventions, which legitimate and reinforce certain conceptions of rights without reference to the behavior of other states.

In practice, these commitments have worked best for democratic states whose rulers have sought to be bound. In more authoritarian political systems pledges can be too easily reversed without engendering domestic political resistance. The rule of law in most of Western Europe after 1945 has enabled enforcement of regional human-rights standards even where these were unpopular with incumbent governments.

Since rulers in most states have historically not sought to protect minority populations, minority-rights guarantees have had to operate through the prospect of external sanctions and rewards. In what we term "contracting," rulers commit themselves to certain domestic policies subject to external rewards or concessions. Contracting is strategic in that the way each party acts is conditional on the behavior of other parties. In cases of symmetrical minorities, where the majority or ruling group in one state forms a minority in another state and vice versa, rulers may respect minority rights with the expectation of concessions by their counterparts. Rulers might prefer to assimilate minorities domestically while preserving co-ethnics or co-religionists within the borders of other states, but fear of reprisals limits incentives to defect from a mutual guarantee. All sides are then presumably better off than they would be in a situation in which both parties defect, threatening a spiral of oppression and dislocation.

Since contracts are strategic and often depend on linkages across issue-areas, they may be thwarted by breakdowns in the overall relationship among states and are unlikely to persist among potentially warring states. During the European religious wars of the sixteenth and seventeenth centuries and during the recasting of the Ottoman Empire in the nineteenth and early twentieth centuries, most rulers sought to eliminate minorities in their midst. Only exhaustion from war and (in the Balkans) outside imposition of territorial settlements made possible tentative mutual guarantees of respect for religious and linguistic minorities.

External actors can also seek to compel changes in policy toward minorities through the threat of sanctions (coercion) or physical force (imposition). Coercive threats make the target worse off: the target cannot refuse while maintaining its status quo ante. For instance, the imposition of sanctions against South Africa's apartheid governments meant that they could not maintain racist policies and still have free access to international organizations and markets. Imposition denotes cases in which the target has no choice: powerful actors can implement their preferences through military force, or can threaten to eliminate the rulers or would-be rulers as actors.

Coercive threats and direct imposition have been the most common means for altering state-society relations within target units. Major-power decisions to recognize or withhold recognition from would-be states have had a profound influence on state-minority conflicts by shaping the ethno-demographic composition of states. The major state-creating settlements of the past century—the Versailles settlement, the dismemberment of European overseas empires, and the breakdown of the Soviet Union—can be viewed broadly as international efforts to promote stability in the successor states of defeated and untenable multiethnic polities. Sadly, in all three periods, the dismembering of foreign domination has often fueled rather than quelled exclusionary policies on the part of newly ascendant regimes.

Since they require the continuous application of threats by outside actors, external attempts to coerce toleration on the part of recalcitrant states have frequently failed to overcome domestic resistance. Outside states must be willing to impose sanctions that punish failure to adopt and comply with external standards. If threats to impose sanctions or to destroy the target state lose their credibility over time, the rulers of the target state will abandon minority-rights commitments. Even when major powers have imposed these standards on very weak states, typically in the aftermath of armed conflict, they have not been willing and able to police their implementation against the resistance of targets.

CHRISTIAN MINORITIES IN THE ISLAMIC WORLD

Concerns by political rulers in one political entity about the treatment of some defined group in another realm have been an enduring characteristic of international politics. This was true not only before notions of autonomy and nonintervention became widely understood (if not necessarily practiced) in the West, but afterward as well. For Western Christendom, such efforts were first directed at the Islamic world following the crusades. The rulers of the major European powers always regarded the treatment of Christians within the Ottoman (Osmanli) Empire as a matter of concern. European rulers asserted that Christians within the Ottoman Empire had special rights and pledged to intervene on their behalf if necessary. Initially, when Europe was weak and the Ottoman Empire strong, they could offer little more than rhetorical pledges to protect coreligionists. Later, they signed conventions that affirmed principles of autonomy under Ottoman law. As the Porte weakened, however, the European powers engaged in coercion, securing treaties that affirmed their right to intervene on behalf of Christians.

European rulers made unilateral commitments to protect Christians in the Muslim-dominated Levant as early as the thirteenth century (these pledges were later reaffirmed, for instance, by Louis XIV in the seventeenth century). However, little came of this saber rattling, given that the Ottoman Porte was at the height of its power. European rulers also sought agreements to affirm autonomy for religious minorities and to secure better treatment for their nationals abroad. The Capitulations treaty of 1536 provided that French nationals and other merchants and travelers were to be judged by French law in consular courts, were not subject to Ottoman taxation, and would face limited customs duties on foreign goods (these treaties lay the early basis for French domination of the Levant). These treaties were consistent with the organization of political life within the Ottoman Empire, where the *millet* system gave religious communities considerable control over their own affairs.

As the Porte weakened, however, the major European powers used coercion to secure expanded rights for resident Christians. The Western powers sought to dominate commerce within the Ottoman Empire and to promote the interests of Armenian and Greek Orthodox merchant communities. In 1673, France secured concessions for the Jesuits and Capuchins. The Treaty of Karlowitz of 1699 gave the Polish ambassador the power to raise issues concerning the treatment of Catholics with the sultan, and gave Austria the right to intervene on behalf of Catholics, a right that was renewed in 1718, 1739, and 1791. The Treaty of Kutchuk-Kainardju (1774) gave the Russian ambassador standing to represent all Christians. European monarchs used these powers cynically, protecting coreligionists only when it served other political purposes. The pretense for intervention which these treaties gave the European powers contributed to the decline of the Ottoman Empire (Macartney 1934, 161–63; Laponce 1960, 25; Blaisdell 1929, 24; Mansfield 1991, 80).

RELIGIOUS TOLERATION IN EARLY MODERN EUROPE

Virtually every major peace settlement in Europe from the 1555 Peace of Augsburg to the 1815 Congress of Vienna contained provisions for the treatment of religious minorities. These quid-pro-quo settlements among the major powers were contracts, compromises intended to prevent religious warfare. Toleration was not initially viewed as a desirable policy: the persecution of religious minorities or heretics was a central feature of medieval Christendom, and increased in the initial decades of the Reformation and Counter-Reformation.[1] Rather, toleration was accepted in specific areas as a matter of political necessity.

The Protestant Reformation fueled over a century of religious wars, both domestic and international. France was wracked by religious wars starting in 1562. Religious conflict in England twice destroyed Stuart monarchs. Later Germany was devastated by the Thirty Years War, which resulted in the death of 40 percent of the population in some areas (Beller 1970, 345–46, 357; Jordan 1932, 19–25, 38). It became increasingly evident, that heretical beliefs could not easily be suppressed by the sword but nevertheless, intolerance remained the norm.

Limited toleration emerged as a result of domestic and international settlements reached only after protracted wars.[2] The Peace of Augsburg of 1555 recognized both the Catholic and Lutheran faiths (Calvinist rulers were recognized later). At the same time, it endorsed the principle that the prince could set the religion of his territory (cuius regio, eius religio), an explicit break with the medieval world, which presumed a unified Christendom but hardly an endorsement of toleration for religious minorities. Augsburg reflected the view that domestic religious unity was necessary for the state but that state religions might differ. Cuius regio eius religio was entirely consistent with the Westphalian model.

Even the Augsburg settlement, however, made some provision for religious toleration. Rulers did not have unlimited rights over religious practices: at a minimum dissenters were not to be executed but rather were to be allowed to emigrate. Although the state could regulate public worship, it generally could not intervene in private practices. In eight imperial cities of the Holy Roman Empire inhabited by both Lutherans and Catholics, people of the two faiths were given the right to coexist. The rulers of ecclesiastical states could not change the religion of their domains. The Habsburg ruler Ferdinand I also promised, in a secret agreement not formally part of the Peace, that Lutheran nobles and townspeople living in ecclesiastical territories could continue to practice their faith. Augsburg,

---

[1] The persecution of non-Christians and heretics characterized Christianity from its adoption by Constantine as the Roman state religion through the early modern period. Theodosius imposed the death penalty on a heretic in the fourth century. Saint Augustine endorsed persecution designed to open the minds of those who had embraced error, though he rejected the death penalty. Catholic intolerance included the persecution of Jews, heretics, and (later) accused witches. Lutheran and Calvinist state churches became persecutory as well: both Calvin and Luther persecuted and banished those who did not subscribe to their beliefs (Bainton 1951, 26, 38–53; Jordan 1932, 31).

[2] The toleration clauses of early modern Europe built on old and new ideas about the illegitimacy of coerced beliefs. It had long been an accepted tenet of Christian thought that true belief could not be coerced, although what constituted coercion (including what level of torture) was contested. Even before the outbreak of the religious wars in France, many educated French had concluded that religious toleration was a moral good, and not simply a political necessity. At the beginning of the sixteenth century, Postel had argued that all the major religions of the world were based on a common universal truth. Bodin later endorsed religious toleration in his 1576 Six Books of the Commonwealth. Locke stated in his 1689 Letter Concerning Toleration that "neither Pagan nor Mahometan, nor Jew, ought to be excluded from the civil rights of the commonwealth because of his religion" (Jordan 1932, 42; Skinner 1978, 244–54; Lewis 1992, 49).

however, failed to secure religious peace and political stability in Europe (Scribner 1990, 195–97; Gagliardo 1991, 16–21; Jordan 1932, 36–37; Little 1993, 324–25).

The toleration provisions of the 1648 Peace of Westphalia (consisting of the treaties of Münster and Osnabruck) are of particular interest, given the common perception that Westphalia played a critical role in creating the modern state system. In its extensive provisions for religious minorities, and in other ways, the Peace of Westphalia itself violated what later came to be understood as the Westphalian model. Although *cuius religio eius religio* was rhetorically embraced, many specific articles provided for religious toleration in Germany. Catholic orders were to stay Catholic; Lutheran orders were to stay Lutheran (Treaty of Osnabruck 1648, Article v: 11–23). Catholics who lived in Lutheran states and Lutherans who lived in Catholic states were to be given the right to practice their religions in the privacy of their homes, to educate their children at home, or to send them to foreign schools. Subjects were not to be excluded from the "Community of Merchants, Artizans or Companies, nor depriv'd of Successions, Legacies, Hospitals, Lazar-Houses, or Alms-Houses, and other Privileges or Rights" because of their religion. Subjects were not to be denied the right of burial nor were they to be charged an amount for burial different from that levied on those of the state religion (Article v: 28). Dissenters (Catholic or Lutheran) who did not have any rights of religious practice in 1624 and who sought or were ordered to move were granted the freedom to emigrate and had five years to sell their goods (Articles v: 29–30).

Catholics and Lutherans in specific mixed cities (Augsburg, Dunckelspiel, Biberach, Ravensburg, Kauffbeur) were to have freedom of religious practices; in the first four of these cities, offices were to be divided equally between Catholics and Lutherans (Treaty of Osnabruck 1648. Article v: 7). Members of the Silesian nobility who were Lutherans were granted by the Emperor the right to continue to practice their religion provided that they "do not disturb the publick Peace and Tranquillity"; they were also given the right to build three churches (Article v: 31). Magistrates of either religion were admonished to forbid any person from criticizing or impugning the religious settlement contained in the agreement and in the earlier Treaty of Passau (Article v: 41).

Catholics and Lutherans were to be equally represented in imperial assemblies, and religious issues were to be decided by consensus (Article v: 42). Representatives to the imperial courts were to be divided by religion. If the judges of the two religions voted uniformly against each other in a case, the case could be appealed to the Diet. If there were cross-cutting cleavages with respect to religion, then a case could not be appealed (Article v: 45). Rights given to Lutherans and Catholics were extended to Calvinists (Article vii: 7).

Where the religion of a ruler changed from one Protestant sect to another (for example, from Lutheran to Calvinist), the ruler was to have the right of worship of his own religion, but was prohibited from attempting to change the religion of his subjects or churches, hospitals, schools, and revenues. The new ruler was enjoined from giving "any trouble or molestation to the Religion of others directly or indirectly." The community was given the right to name ministers, and the prince was to confirm them "without denial" (Article vii).

The terms of toleration were shaped by the interests of the rulers of the major powers, the Habsburgs, the King of France, and the King of Sweden. The Holy Roman Emperor, Ferdinand III, endorsed religious toleration within Germany to settle a devastating war, but refused to accept it in other Habsburg lands. Austria, ruled by the Habsburgs but not part of the Empire, was not included. Toleration was limited to Lutherans, Calvinists, and Catholics (Treaty of Osnabruck 1648, Article vii: 240). The rulers of France refused to accept provisions for religious toleration.

The Peace of Westphalia was a major step in ending religious strife but there were conflicts over implementation and unilateral attempts to defect. The Westphalia clauses were put into effect beginning in the winter of 1648–1649 (Gagliardo 1991, 83–85), but there was tension over their implementation, particularly in the free cities.[3] Those states that could sidestep the terms of Westphalia did so. The Habsburgs expelled Protestants from Styria and Upper Austria while tolerating them in such outlying areas as Silesia and resettling many in Transylvania "for state economic reasons" (Gagliardo 1991, 178). The Habsburgs refused to abide by some provisions for the repatriation and restitution of Protestants and the expulsion of dissidents whose situation was not explicitly protected (Holborn 1959, 370). The archbishop of Salzburg expelled Protestants in 1731. Such actions were typically followed by reprisals against Catholics in the Protestant northern German territories. Calvinists and Lutherans also clashed, particularly in Saxony and Brandenburg-Prussia.

The ecclesiastical boundaries set by the treaty remained surprisingly intact in Germany until as late as 1945. After 1648, there was a slow but general abatement of religious conflict. Yet this may have been due primarily to the fact that states were more homogenous in 1648 than in earlier years and to the relatively few religious conversions of princes after Westphalia (Holborn 1959, 370–71; Gagliardo 1991, 177–188; Hughes 1992, 134–36). Only slowly did the principle of toleration implied in the Peace of Westphalia come to prevail in Western Europe.

After 1648, it became common for a sovereign taking over a territory to pledge respect for existing religious practices within that territory. The treaties of Oliva (1650), Nijmegen (1678), Breslau (1742), Dresden (1745), Hubertusburg (1763), and Warsaw (1772) all had such provisions. The Treaty of Utrecht of 1731, in which France ceded Hudson Bay and Arcadia to Britain, provided that the Roman Catholic subjects of these areas were entitled to practice their faith

---

[3] The Westphalian simultaneum system, which gave corporate status to two or all three recognized faiths in specific divided areas, was continually challenged and maintained only by a tense balance of threats. For instance, the 1697 Treaty of Ryswick allowed Catholics in the Palatinate to retain the privileges accorded to them by the occupying French, a threat to simultaneum. Intense conflict among the three religions ensued, until in 1718 the Elector of the Palatinate tore down the wall separating the Calvinist section of the Church of the Holy Spirit in Heidelberg and claimed the church as his own. The Protestant and Catholic German states (and their allies) would have gone to war but for the intervention of the emperor (story in Hughes 1992, 134–36).

"insofar as the laws of England permit it" (quoted in Laponce 1960, 24). A similar provision was included in the Treaty of Paris of 1763, in which the British monarchy again agreed that Catholic subjects in Canada would be entitled to the same rights as those in Britain (Laponce 1960, 23–24; Macartney 1934, 158–59).

In the settlement of the Napoleonic Wars, provisions were made to protect religious minorities in parts of Belgium assigned to Holland and in areas of Savoy ceded to Geneva. Belgian Catholics were to have liberty of conscience, equal access to administrative positions, and representation in political bodies. These provisions were to be written into the Dutch constitution and could not be changed. Detailed measures for religious coexistence were also made for parts of Catholic Savoy ceded by the King of Sardinia to Calvinist Geneva.[4]

The 1815 settlement also included, for the first time, provisions for an ethnonational minority. In the Congress of Vienna Final Act, Austria, Prussia, and Russia were committed to provide Poles "a Representation and National Institutions . . . that each of the Governments to which they belong shall judge expedient and proper to grant them" (Article I). This provision reflected in part Castlereagh's (accurate) view that Polish national sentiment could not fully be suppressed, even though Poland had disappeared as an independent country in 1795. These efforts to assuage Polish nationalism and defend Polish identity failed, and the Poles rebelled several times in the nineteenth century.[5]

In sum, limited toleration for religious diversity and for absorbed populations emerged hand in hand with the state system in early modern Europe. Stipulations regarding religious minorities were part of larger contractual agreements to end wars and were a condition of the transfer of territory among rulers. These conditions violated the very Westphalian model of sovereignty that these same treaties

[4] Article 3 of the protocol of May 29, 1815, ceded parts of Savoy, which had been ruled by Sardinia, to Geneva. The protocol stipulated that Catholics in the ceded territory would be able to continue their existing practices. In areas where the Catholic population exceeded the Protestant, schoolmasters would always be Catholic, and no Protestant "temple" would ever be established except in the town of Carrouge, where only one could be built (quoted in Laponce 1960, 26). The mayor and vice-mayor would always be Catholic. If the Protestant population grew and exceeded the Catholic one, then there would be rotation in office and a Catholic school would always exist even if a Protestant one were built. The new government would continue to provide, at the existing level, support for the clergy and religion. In these areas Protestants could worship privately and hire private Protestant schoolmasters. Catholics were to have equal civil and political rights. Catholic children were to be admitted to public education although religious instruction would be conducted separately. The King of Sardinia could bring complaints to the Diet of the Helvetic federation (Laponce 1960, 26–27, 39; Macartney 1934, 158–59).

[5] Russia did establish distinct institutions for "Congress Poland" after 1815, including a separate constitution and parliament, but the 1830 revolt of Polish army cadets caused Nicholas I to abolish local autonomy. The French government protested, but the British, anxious to avoid enmity with Russia, refused to take any significant action (Fouques-Duparc 1922, 115, 122–26; Claude 1955, 7; Laponce 1960, 28–29). Austria strictly forbade manifestations of political nationalism among the Poles (Macartney 1934, 112). The 1863 Warsaw Uprising precipitated more repression and more intense assimilative measures by Alexander II (Pearson 1983, 72–74). Prussia engaged in Germanization campaigns after 1830 and 1848, and after 1867 excluded the Polish language altogether and expelled Russian Poles (Pearson 1983, 128–29; Janowsky 1945, 25–27). See also Breuilly (1994, 115–20).

are said to have created. An uneasy religious détente emerged in Europe, which was only later reinforced by principled ideas about the virtues of toleration and religious freedom.

THE BALKANS IN THE NINETEENTH CENTURY

As the Ottoman Empire unraveled in the nineteenth and early twentieth centuries, all of the successor states (Greece, Romania, Serbia, Montenegro, Bulgaria, and Albania) as well as the weakened Ottoman regime accepted external constraints on their treatment of religious and later ethno-national minorities. Unlike religious toleration in Western Europe, minority protection in the Balkans was the result of external coercion by the European "great powers," which wielded great leverage over Balkan states at the point of their independence. The rulers and would-be rulers of new states preferred complete autonomy with respect to the treatment of groups within their own borders. The rulers of the major powers, however, compelled them to commit themselves to nondiscrimination. Policymakers in Britain, France, Germany, Russia, and Austria-Hungary were motivated primarily by concerns about international stability: religious and ethnic strife could destabilize Balkan polities and draw outside states into conflicts that they would have preferred to avoid. World War I proved these anxieties all too prescient. Public outrage, notably in Britain, over massacres that were well publicized (even without CNN), and later concerns over the unwanted emigration generated by discriminatory policies strengthened major-power resolve to "manage" conflict in the region.

These efforts to protect minorities were not successful. Recognition was a major source of leverage available to the great powers but, once extended, could not easily be withdrawn, in part because the major powers needed Balkan interlocutors to pursue their interests. After independence, the rulers of the Balkan states enhanced their national power bases, and it became more costly for the major powers to threaten sanctions or forceful intervention. The mechanisms for monitoring were rudimentary.

Greece was the first Balkan polity to become independent from the Ottoman Empire, a status secured only through the intervention of Britain, France, and Russia.[6] By 1830, these states were committed to creating a formally independent Greek entity, but it was hardly to be a Westphalian state. The British wanted to avoid granting Russia naval access to the eastern Mediterranean, Russian leaders did not have the military power to impose their own settlement. Greece was established as a monarchy, even though most of the Greek revolutionaries would have preferred a republic. Otto, the underage second son of the King of Bavaria, was chosen as monarch because he did not have close ties with the ruling houses

---

[6] The Greek revolt began in 1821. By 1827, the Ottomans, with the help of a fleet provided by Mehmet Ali (the quasi-independent ruler of Egypt), were on the verge of suppressing the rebellion. A joint British, French, and Russian force destroyed Mehmet Ali's fleet at the Battle of Navarino and the Ottoman army was then defeated. Greek independence was recognized in 1832.

of any of the major powers. Greek public finance was constrained by the terms of a loan from the major powers (Schwartzberg 1988, 139, 301, 303; Temperley 1966, 406–8; Anderson 1966, 74–75; Dakin 1973, 289–90, 310–12; Jelavich and Jelavich 1977, 50–52).

The Western powers insisted that religious toleration be included in Greek law. An 1830 protocol stipulated that in order to preserve Greece from "the calamities which the rivalries of the religions therein professed might excite . . . the subjects of the new State, whatever their religion may be, shall be admissible to all public employments, functions and honours, and be treated on a footing of perfect equality, without regard to difference of creed, in their relations, religious, civil or political" (quoted in Macartney 1934, 164–65).

Toleration clauses were expanded in subsequent Balkan settlements. In the 1856 Treaty of Paris, which granted independence under Ottoman suzerainty to Wallachia and Moldavia (the two Ottoman provinces that were to become Romania) and a subsequent agreement in 1858, the Western powers sought to guarantee equal treatment for all, including Jews. During the late 1860s, leaders in both Britain and France vainly protested against the treatment of Jews in Romania. In Britain, Lord Stanley argued that the treatment of Jews in Romania was an affair that touched Christians as well as Jews, because, "if the suffering falls on the Jews, the shame falls on the Christians" (translated from Fouques-Duparc 1922, 102). The British claimed the right to enforce Article 46 of the 1858 Paris treaty providing for political and economic equality for Jews under great-power guarantee (98–106). Yet the Romanian constitution of 1866 gave only Christians the right to apply for Romanian nationality. Romanian authorities ignored the vaguely worded treaty provisions and subsequent protests.

Western powers sought in more limited terms to prod the Ottoman regime toward religious and political toleration. After the Crimean war, they pressured the Sultan to issue the firman (edict) of Hatti-Humayoun committing the Porte to administrative reform and to religious privileges for Christians (Blaisdell 1929, 25). Despite external pressure, however, Ottoman rulers would not or could not fully accommodate (or suppress) religious and ethnic divisions in their realm.

The efforts of the major powers to establish religious toleration in the Balkans reached their apogee at the Congress of Berlin in 1878, organized to settle the armed conflicts that began with a Christian revolt in Bosnia.[7] The Congress recognized Serbia, Montenegro, and Romania as independent states and Bulgaria as

---

[7] In 1875 Christians in Bosnia and Herzegovina rebelled against Ottoman authorities. The Austrian Foreign Minister, Count Andrassy, proposed that the Porte grant religious liberty to the two provinces and abolish tax farming. The Porte agreed, but was too weak to implement this accord and unrest continued. A revolt the following year in Bulgaria was suppressed. Serb forces unsuccessfully attacked with Russian assistance; in 1877, Russia intervened directly with the hope of creating a Bulgarian state with access to the Mediterranean that would be beholden to Russia, an outcome that was threatening to Britain. With the aid of Russia, the various Slavic groups in the Balkans defeated the Ottomans, and Russian and Bulgarian gains were secured in the March 1878 Treaty of San Stefano. The Western major powers organized the Congress of Berlin later in 1878 to roll back Russian and Bulgarian gains and to prevent further Balkan wars. See Langer 1964, 138; Jelavich and Jelavich 1977, 143–53; Anderson 1966, 182.

a tributary state of the Ottoman Empire. Austria-Hungary, with British support, secured the right to occupy and administer Bosnia-Herzegovina and the Sanjak of Novi Bazar, although these areas remained formally part of the Ottoman Empire.

As a condition of recognition, the major powers insisted that the new states grant political equality to all faiths. The Treaty of Berlin provided that in Bulgaria, Montenegro, Serbia, and Romania,"the difference of religious creeds and confessions shall not be alleged against any person as a ground for exclusion or incapacity in matters relating to the enjoyment of civil and political rights, admission to public employments, functions, and honours, or the exercise of the various professions and industries in any locality whatsoever. The freedom and outward exercise of all forms of worship shall be assured to all persons . . . as well as to foreigners, and no hindrance shall be offered either to the hierarchical organization of the different communions, or to their relations with their spiritual chiefs" (Articles 5, 27, 35, and 44, respectively). The Ottoman Porte endorsed similar language as a "spontaneous declaration," with additional provisions for the political organization of minority communities and the rights of foreigners: "The freedom and outward exercise of all forms of worship are assured to all, and no hindrance shall be offered either to the hierarchical organization of the various communions or to their relations with their spiritual chiefs. Ecclesiastics, pilgrims, and monks of all nationalities traveling in Turkey in Europe, or in Turkey in Asia, shall enjoy the same rights, advantages, and privileges. . . . The rights possessed by France are expressly reserved, and it is well understood that no alterations can be made in the status quo in the Holy Places" (Article 62).

The Treaty of Berlin also included guarantees for a specific ethnic minority, Armenians. The Porte agreed to implement local reforms in Armenian territories and to guarantee Armenian security against the Circassians and Kurds. It made this pledge in order to secure the withdrawal of Russian forces. The Porte was to inform the Powers of the steps it had taken and the Powers would "superintend their application" (Article 61; Mansfield 1991, 75, 81; Macartney 1934, 167).

The minority provisions of the Berlin settlement were the result of imposition and coercion. The targets were not involved in drafting the settlement. The would-be rulers of Romania, Bulgaria, Montenegro, and Serbia were not interested in religious toleration per se. They accepted conditions as the only way to secure greater external recognition and gain land. The Ottoman leadership agreed to protect Armenians only to secure the withdrawal of foreign troops, an unambiguous example of compulsion.

The major powers as a group sought religious toleration primarily to stabilize the volatile Balkans. Orthodox religious concerns had provided a pretext for Russian intervention in the Balkans and Anatolia, which threatened British interests in the eastern Mediterranean. The Habsburgs were apprehensive about ethnic nationalism that might spill over into the Dual Monarchy. This fear had prompted the occupation and later annexation of Bosnia and Herzegovina, hardly a first best solution for the empire, since it brought more Slavs under Habsburg rule. Bismarck was anxious to maintain Germany's alliance with both Austria-Hungary and Russia, an alliance continually strained by conflict in the Balkans.

Humanitarian concerns and interest-group pressure were also influential. British public opinion was agitated by reports of Turkish atrocities against Bulgarians in 1875–1876; William Gladstone's exploitation of this issue was one of the factors that led to his return as prime minister in 1880. Jewish groups in the United States and Great Britain pressured their governments to protest Romanian treatment of Jews. Later in the century, American officials pressed Romania for reforms with the hope of limiting the flow of new Jewish emigrants (Macartney 1934, 169, 281; Fouques-Duparc 1922, 112; Pearson 1983, 98).

The treatment of Jews in Romania epitomizes the failure of intermittent major-power attempts to secure minority rights in the Balkans. Romania was not recognized by the major powers until February 1880, when Romanian officials publicly declared that a Jew could become a citizen, but, in practice, policy hardly changed. Although non-Christians could nominally obtain citizenship, it required an act of parliament for each individual Jew. Of the 269,000 Jews in Romania, only 200 attained citizenship. Noncitizens had to pay for primary school, were excluded from professional schools in 1893, and from secondary and higher education in 1898. Jews were prohibited from living in rural areas. By the 1900s, almost 90 percent of Romanian émigrés to the United States were Jewish (Fouques-Duparc 1922, 98–112; Jelavich and Jelavich 1977, 178; Pearson 1983, 98).

Nor did European states prevent the killing of very large numbers of Armenians in the Ottoman Empire. There was a series of semi-organized massacres starting in 1894. Despite formal protests from the Western powers, including the dispatch of two British warships in 1909, massacres continued and culminated in 1915, when perhaps one million Armenians perished (Macartney 1934, 167, 170).

Unlike the development of religious liberty in Western Europe, the effort to secure minority rights in the Balkans was founded neither in domestic political support nor in a stable balance of capabilities in the region that would allow reciprocal concessions toward minorities. The stable (if not liberal) millet system of religious and cultural pluralism could not be sustained, given the declining power of the Ottoman Empire. The rulers of Balkan states sought domination by the titular group and cultural homogenization. Only the decisive application of outside pressure could have brought peace and toleration to the region. Although the major powers did protest massive humanitarian violations, they were unwilling to apply direct economic or military pressure except where it suited their narrow strategic interests.

MINORITY PROTECTION IN THE VERSAILLES SETTLEMENT

International efforts to secure minority rights culminated in the Versailles settlement of the First World War. All of the new polities as well as several established states whose boundaries were changed signed minority-rights treaties or made unilateral pledges regarding minority rights. The prospective rulers of some states (especially Hungary and Czechoslovakia) favored the minority-rights treaties, but leaders of other states, especially those with large internal minorities (including Poland, Romania, and Yugoslavia) saw the treaties as a product of external coercion or imposition (Bartsch 1995, 84–85). Unlike earlier settlements, the Versailles arrangements provided for monitoring and enforcement through the League of Nations and the International Court of Justice. In the end the Versailles settlement failed, and not just because of the triumph of Nazism in Germany.

Minority rights were established in treaties concluded by the Allied powers in 1919 with Poland, Austria, Czechoslovakia, Yugoslavia, Bulgaria, and Romania, in 1920 with Hungary, Turkey, and Greece, and again in 1923 with Turkey; in declarations made as a condition for admission to the League by Albania in 1921, Lithuania in 1922, Latvia and Estonia in 1923, and Iraq in 1932; and through League guarantees for the treatment of minorities in bilateral conventions concerning the Free City of Danzig and Upper Silesia (Poland/Germany, 1920 and 1922), the Aaland Islands (Sweden/Finland, 1921) and the Memel Convention (Lithuania/Germany, 1924) (Lerner 1993, 83; Claude 1955, 16; Jones 1991, 45).

The protections were detailed and elaborate. In the Polish minority treaty, the model (verbatim in most cases) for League minorities obligations, the Polish government undertook "to assure full and complete protection of life and liberty to all inhabitants of Poland without distinction of birth, nationality, language, race or religion. . . . Differences of religion, creed or confession shall not prejudice any Polish national in matters relating to the enjoyment of civil or political rights, as for instance admission to public employments, functions and honours, or the exercise of professions and industries" (Articles 1 and 7). It granted citizenship rights to all individuals habitually resident or born within its territory of habitually resident parents even if the latter were not currently in Poland, a provision that reflected concern about the exclusion of Jews in earlier decades. (The Romanian government was forced to signed similar provisions). Minority-language schooling would be provided in areas with a considerable number of non-Polish speakers, although the teaching of Polish could be obligatory (Article 8). Additionally, Jews could decline official duties that would violate the Sabbath, and Polish leaders were committed "to refrain from ordering or permitting elections, whether general or local, to be held on a Saturday." (Article 11, reprinted in Macartney 1934, 502–6; see also Sharp 1979, 174; Fouques-Duparc 1922, 112).

For the dominant figure at Versailles, Woodrow Wilson, the international protection of minority rights represented a key pillar of a peaceful postwar order in Europe. This order was to be based on collective security, the principle that peace-loving states would join together to resist depredations by any aggressor. Only liberal democratic states would make such commitments. Liberal democracy, in turn, was founded on self-determination, yet ethno-national populations were inextricably mingled in much of Europe. The treaties sought to resolve this problem by making minorities loyal citizens of the states in which they happened to reside. If minorities were ill-treated, they could cause disorder within their countries of residence and threaten international peace if a patron state came to their assistance (Macartney 1934, 275, 278, 297). In Wilson's words at the Paris Peace Conference, "Nothing, I venture to say, is more likely to disturb the peace of the world than the treatment which might in certain circumstances be meted out to minorities. And therefore, if the major powers are to guarantee the peace of the world in any sense, is it unjust that they should be satisfied that the proper and necessary guarantees have been given?" (quoted in Sharp 1979, 175). The Wilsonian vision of collective security trumped the Westphalian norm of nonintervention.

From the outset, rulers in Romania, Poland, and Yugoslavia protested the minority treaties. These leaders all confronted large minority populations within the borders of their state, while only a small percentage of their co-ethnics lived in other countries. Bratianu, the Romanian leader, argued at the peace conference that the minority treaty violated Romania's sovereignty as well as the principle of sovereign equality, and that the possibility of external intervention undermined internal stability. Disaffected rulers also pointed out that the regime was unfair. The victors, especially the United States and Britain, accepted no standards for the treatment of the Welsh, Irish, African- and Asian-Americans, and other minorities within their own societies. Italy refused to accept a treaty governing the German-speaking minority south of the Brenner Pass. The United States, along with New Zealand, Canada, and Australia, blocked efforts by Japan to introduce a clause endorsing racial equality into the League Covenant (Macartney 1934, 252; Sharp 1979, 181–83; Sharp 1991, 61; Janowsky 1945, 126–29; Claude 1955, 17, 32–33; Trachtenberg 1993, 27; Bilder 1992, 65–66; Bartsch 1995, 75–76).

The major powers justified minority-rights guarantees in terms of established norms and diplomatic precedent. The defining justification of the League minorities system, the 1919 letter from French leader Georges Clemenceau accompanying the Polish minorities treaty, illustrates that the Westphalian norm of nonintervention was explicitly contradicted by other norms endorsed by the ascendant powers: "This Treaty does not constitute any fresh departure. It has for long been the established procedure of the public law of Europe that when a State is created, or even when large accessions of territory are made to an established State, the joint and formal recognition of the Major powers should be accompanied by the requirement that such States should, in the form of a binding international Convention, undertake to comply with certain principles of Government . . . it is to the endeavours and sacrifices of the Powers in whose name I am addressing you that the Polish nation owes the recovery of its independence. . . . There, rests, therefore, upon these Powers an obligation, which they cannot evade, to secure in the most permanent and solemn form guarantees for certain essential rights which will afford to the inhabitants the necessary protection, whatever changes may take place in the internal constitution of the Polish State" (quoted in Macartney 1934, 238).

Unlike earlier toleration clauses, the Versailles minority-rights guarantees had extensive provisions for monitoring and enforcement. In treaties with Poland,

Austria, Bulgaria, and Czechoslovakia, minority protections were made basic constitutional law as well as international obligations. The treaties provided that the laws related to the treatment of minorities would not be changed without the approval of a majority of the League Council (Bilder 1992, 64; Laponce 1960, 40; Lerner 1993, 85).[8]

Individuals as well as states could petition the League Secretariat. Petitions were considered by an ad hoc Minorities Committee composed of the president of the Council and two appointed members. If the Committee could not resolve a complaint informally, it was placed on the Council's agenda and a Committee of Jurists could determine if the state had violated its international obligations. The Committee could ask the Permanent Court of International Justice for an advisory opinion (Veatch 1983). Between 1921 and 1938 the League received 473 petitions. Poland was the most frequent target of complaints (203 petitions), followed by Romania with 78 (Janowsky 1945, 117–21; Claude 1955, 20–28; Bartsch 1995, 103–4).

The rights of minorities were protected in some countries during much of the interwar period. The Baltic states, Hungary, and Czechoslovakia did conserve most of their minority populations and integrate them into civil society. Hungarian leaders were sympathetic to the minority rights regime because there were large Hungarian minorities outside of Hungary, and minorities constituted only a tenth of the Hungarian population. A multiethnic alliance from the start, Czechoslovak leaders embraced and in many respects implemented minority treaty provisions, hoping that they would make pan-German appeals less attractive for the large German minority. Public reaction was positive, at least initially. Yet even in Czechoslovakia, some minorities did not fare well: commitments for an autonomous Carpathian region and for Slovak autonomy were never fully implemented, and Ruthenian peasants in Carpathia received developmental assistance primarily to undermine Magyar domination of the area. And even the relative security of the German minority in Czechoslovakia did not prevent its representatives from complaining to the League, and eventually providing a pretext for the takeover of Czechoslovakia itself (Azcárate 1972, 40–42; Pearson 1983, 155; Bartsch 1995, 81–83; Macartney 1934, 413–15; Robinson et al. 1943, 169).

The enforcement procedures were not implemented vigorously against states that aggressively opposed minority-rights guarantees. Some specific victories were pyrrhic. For instance, in one of the few cases to go through the entire procedure, the League was petitioned in 1921 concerning challenges to the property rights of Germans who had settled in what became Poland after the First World War. The three-member ad hoc Minorities Committee failed to secure an infor-

---

[8] The bilateral minority protections were also subject to enforcement by the League. The Geneva Convention of May 15, 1922, between Germany and Poland established an elaborate regime with regional enforcement machinery and appeal to the League. Minority- rights provisions applicable to Danzig were governed by a high commissioner who could refer cases to the League; the local parliament of the Aaland Islands could direct complaints to the League. See Veatch 1983; Macartney 1934, ch. 7.

mal settlement and the case was referred to the full League Council in 1922. The Poles rejected the Council's request for restraint as well as the findings of a committee of jurists, and expelled the Germans. The Council referred the issue to the Permanent Court of International Justice, which also ruled against Poland. The Poles refused to reverse the evictions but did finally agree to pay compensation of 2.7 million zlotys. In another case brought in 1928, Russian peasants complained that their land was being unjustly taken by Lithuania. No one in the League was anxious to press the issue. The Lithuanian government stalled and the case was dropped a year and a half after it had been initiated (Janowsky 1945, 121–22, 125n8).

Despite historical precedent, a clear rationale, and monitoring and enforcement procedures, minorities did not fare well in the disaffected states. The experience of minority populations in Poland, whose minority treaty was a model for all others, was mixed at best (Gutman 1989, 103-5; Pearson 1983, 188–89). The commitment not to schedule national elections on Saturday was honored (law of July 28, 1923); however, other provisions related to the observance of the Sabbath and Jewish schools were not implemented (Robinson et al. 1943, 237). Anti-Semitic pogroms and campaigns were at a minimum tolerated by public officials; complainants to the League were persecuted (176). The emigration rate of Jews was five times that of Poles. The Eastern Slavic minorities, seen as a security threat, were actively suppressed by the Polish state. Belarusians were Polonized after 1924 by means that included closures of schools, societies, and newspapers, and the establishment of a concentration camp at Beresa Kartuska, and Ruthenes (Ukrainians) were violently pacified by the Polish cavalry in 1930 (162–64).

The interwar experience demonstrates the difficulty of coercing and imposing minority-rights provisions upon states where these provisions have weak domestic support. For intervention to succeed where leadership within the target continues to oppose it, the initiator must monitor and credibly threaten to punish violations. Instead, the major powers went their separate ways: the United States withdrew from the League, and French leaders sought alliances with the new East European states against Germany. Eastern European states built coalitions in opposition to League intervention. The Western powers, especially France, did not want to hold relations with these states hostage to minorities issues.

One cannot ultimately say how much worse minorities might have fared in the interwar period without the League minority provisions; however, the roots of its ultimate collapse lay in the vigorous opposition of states in which minority rights did not have a strong base of domestic support, and in the failure of outside powers to back these commitments. The Polish government formally renounced its minority-rights commitments in September 1934. Nazi Germany also renounced its League obligations in 1934. Once the League could no longer guarantee the security of Eastern Europe against Germany, and had demonstrated that there would be no reprisals against Poland, the League minorities system became defunct.

MINORITY PROTECTION AFTER 1945

In the aftermath of the Second World War, the international protection of minorities was almost abandoned, a position made evident at Potsdam, when the four powers accepted the deportation of millions of Germanic residents in areas ceded to Poland and other parts of Eastern Europe. These policies reflected the preferences of the superpowers and general disillusionment with the interwar experience. Only a handful of specific agreements in Europe in the twenty years following World War II were concerned with minority rights. Instead, international human-rights concerns focused on the rights of individuals.

The architects of the postwar order rejected minority protection in principle because of the perceived failure of the League treaties and the discrediting of ethnic nationalism. The fascist interlude and the horrors of the Nazi Holocaust, which had decimated Jewish and Roma (Gypsys) minority populations across Europe, had shown the failure of international monitoring and enforcement. Group rights appeared to be a dangerous principle, since the Nazi regime had used German-speaking minorities as a pretext for expansion (Alcock 1979, 226–27). Thus the 1947 peace treaties with Bulgaria, Hungary, Italy, and Romania prohibited discrimination but gave no means for members of aggrieved groups to seek redress.[9]

The United States emerged from World War II as the dominant state in the international system, powerful enough to project its values on the postwar order. Though toleration is a validated norm, America's governing ideology emphasized the individual, not the group. Undersecretary of State Sumner Welles argued, "in the kind of world for which we fight, there must cease to exist any need for the use of that accursed term 'racial or religious minority'" (May 1943, quoted in Claude 1955, 74–75).

Soviet leaders eschewed international minority-rights guarantees for different reasons. Presiding over a realm of astonishing ethnic diversity with a history of resistance to centralization, Moscow had much at risk from granting international access to minority representatives. Soviet nationalities policy fused socialist internationalism, Leninist self-determination (in which cultural and national groups were granted formal autonomy), and the exigencies of Stalinist centralism. Soviet military hegemony and party rule suppressed ethno-national political movements.

Due in large part to the opposition of the United States and Latin American states, minorities were not mentioned in the UN Charter, and received only lim-

---

[9] The Austrian State Treaty of 1955 offered special protections for Slovenes and Croats in specific areas. Each was guaranteed elementary school instruction in its own language. Slovenian and Croatian would be accepted as official languages along with German. The two groups were to participate in the cultural, administrative, and judicial systems on equal terms with German speakers (Laponce 1960, 37). Each of the 1947 peace treaties stipulated equal rights for all citizens. Hungary and Romania, during whose fascist interludes the Holocaust had been particularly abominable, were instructed to compensate victims of racial persecution but only if claims were presented within six months of the treaty coming into force (Articles 27 and 25 respectively). The Eastern European peace treaties, eclipsed by Cold War politics, soon became dead letters.

ited mention in the International Covenant on Civil and Political Rights.[10] The chief proponent of the Universal Declaration of Human Rights, Eleanor Roosevelt, successfully excluded minority rights (Sigler 1983, 67, 77). Although minority issues gained some attention within specialized UN organs, most notably the Sub-Commission on Prevention of Discrimination and Protection of Minorities and UNESCO, their activity was inconsequential until the late 1980s.

Instead, democratic leaders in postwar Western Europe sought to institutionalize the rights of individuals in regional and international conventions, most notably through the European Convention for the Protection of Human Rights and Fundamental Freedoms (1950) and the European Court and Commission of Human Rights, which enforce it among Council of Europe member states.

Later, the 1975 Helsinki Final Act establishing the Conference on (now Organization for) Security and Cooperation in Europe (CSCE/OSCE) recognized the right of persons belonging to minorities to equality before the law and equal human rights (Principle 7). The Helsinki agreement was a contract between the Western and Soviet blocs in which the West recognized the borders of Eastern Europe, and the East additionally recognized human-rights standards. Helsinki commitments were not binding and there were no provisions for enforcing them.

Minority rights were the subject of agreements of a small number of bilateral accords. In 1946 the occupied Italian and Austrian governments reached a bilateral understanding on regional autonomy and minority rights for German speakers who were a majority in South Tyrol/Alto Adige (which had been ceded to Italy after World War I and whose population had been subject to repression under the fascist regime). Although autonomy and some language rights were granted in 1948, authority remained in the hands of Rome and the larger Trentino-Bolzano region in which German speakers were still a minority. Italian speakers remained overwhelmingly dominant in the economy and administration of areas whose residents were predominantly German speaking. Eventually, renewed pressure from Austrian leaders (Austria having regained formal sovereignty in 1955) and local resistance campaigns by minority extremists led Italian governments to renegotiate a package of commitments to autonomy, which were implemented starting in the late 1960s. Since then, the region has become a model of successful local autonomy and state-minority cooperation (Hailbronner 1992, 126–27; Woodward 1995a, 475n17).

The London Treaty of October 1954, which divided the Free Territory of Trieste between Italy and Yugoslavia, stipulated equality between Italians and Yugoslavs in the area. Special schools, which could not be closed without the approval of a mixed Italian-Yugoslav committee, were designated to teach in one of the two languages. In areas where the nonstate group constituted more than half the population, public documents were to be promulgated in both languages (Laponce 1960, 38). A second bilateral agreement concluded at Osimo in 1974

[10] The International Covenant on Civil and Political Rights solicits states not to discriminate against "persons belonging to minorities...in those states in which ethnic, religious, or linguistic minorities exist" (Article 27), but state authorities are free to determine how to implement the clause, and to deny the distinctive language, culture, or history of minorities (as many have done).

provided that all groups were to have equal political and economic rights; each was entitled to its own schools and to the use of its language in official communications (Hailbronner 1992, 127).

When Britain gave up control of Cyprus, the 1959 Treaty of Guarantee between Cyprus, Greece, Turkey, and the U.K. provided for the protection of the minority Turkish Cypriotes. Each ethnic group had its own chamber in the parliament. Turkish Cypriotes had to be represented at all levels of government and wielded veto power in many areas. Key constitutional provisions could not be amended, and amendments to some other provisions required the approval of Turkey. Unification with Greece (Enosis), the preferred outcome of the Greek majority on Cyprus, was in effect prohibited. If there were violations, the signatories were to consult, but if an accord was not reached each reserved the right to take action aimed at reestablishing the state of affairs specified by the treaty. When Greeks reasserted control in 1974, Turkey used the treaty to justify invasion and partition of the island (Bilder 1992, 69–70; Platias 1986, 153–57).

State-minority conflicts did not disappear from the international stage after the failure and rejection of the interwar experience, even though almost no collective action on the issue could be sustained across Europe's bipolar divide. Bilateral disputes continued to fuel discord; the resulting accords met with varying degrees of success. In Western Europe, the success of the Council of Europe in reinforcing basic human rights led to diminished fears of excesses against minority groups.

MINORITY PROTECTION AFTER THE COLD WAR

The end of the Cold War accompanied, and in some cases induced, a resurgence of interethnic strife. The new salience of state-minority conflicts—"the New Europe's old issue" (Cuthbertson and Leibowitz 1993)—led to renewed efforts to promote international stability by securing minority rights within existing states.

International minority-rights standards are now codified in the 1992 UN General Assembly Declaration on the Rights of Persons Belonging to National or Ethnic, Religious, and Linguistic Minorities, the first post-World War II convention explicitly focused on the rights of minorities. At a regional level, minority rights issues in Europe have received the most attention. The 1990 CSCE/OSCE Copenhagen Document specified extensive rights for national minorities, including the free use of the mother tongue in public and private, the incorporation of minority history and culture into the school curriculum, and the right of contact with co-ethnics in other countries (reprinted in Brownlie 1992, 424–48). Anti-Semitism and discrimination against Roma were condemned. There were modest provisions for monitoring: signatories agreed to provide within four weeks a written response to inquiries from another member state. The 1991 Charter of Paris for a New Europe further extended these minority-rights provisions. The office of the High Commissioner on National Minorities was established at the 1992 Helsinki summit to provide early warning and mediation in state-minority conflicts that could affect peace and stability (Bloed 1993, 95–96; Moravcsik 1994, 48–49). The OSCE has established on-site observer and mediation missions in several states experiencing severe instability, including Estonia, Moldova, the former Yugoslavia, and most recently Russian Chechnya.

Minority rights received prominent attention in European diplomacy in relation to the breakup of Yugoslavia. In December 1991, European Community foreign ministers made acceptance of the Carrington Plan the prerequisite for recognition of former Yugoslav republics.[11] The Carrington Plan stipulated guarantees for human rights and civil liberties regardless of sex, race, color, language, religion, or minority status (ch. 2). The republics were to protect the rights of national and ethnic minorities as elaborated in UN, CSCE/OSCE, and Council of Europe conventions, and to guarantee the cultural, political, and educational rights of minorities, establishing special regimes where they formed a local majority. A permanent Court of Human Rights would monitor these special areas and resolve disputes among the republics. Croatia, Slovenia, Macedonia, and Bosnia formally accepted the plan, but it was not implemented.

In January 1992, after the European Community had recognized Croatia and Slovenia, the EC Arbitration Commission (Badinter Commission) ruled that Slovenia and Macedonia had met the conditions specified in the Carrington Plan (Woodward 1995a, 190–91). The Croatian government, pressured by the EC, also complied: in May 1992, it passed the Constitutional Law of Human Rights and Freedoms and the Rights of National and Ethnic Communities or Minorities, many of whose provisions were drawn verbatim from the Carrington Report. The law endorses UN human rights accords, the Helsinki Final Act, the Paris Charter for a New Europe, and other CSCE/OSCE documents related to minority and human rights. Article 4 commits Croatia to assist national and ethnic minorities to establish relations with their parent country. Special districts were designated in which minorities were to be educated in their own language using a curriculum adequate to present their history, culture, and science if such a wish were a expressed (Article 49). Representatives of minorities totaling more than 8 percent of the population of the whole country were entitled to proportional representation in the Croatian parliament, government, and supreme judicial bodies. Those with less than 8 percent were entitled to elect five representatives to the House of Representatives of the Croatian parliament (Article 18). Issues regarding minority and human rights were to be decided by the Court of Human Rights that would be established by all the states created out of the territory of the former Yugoslavia.

---

[11] Under the Carrington Plan, republics were to guarantee the cultural rights of minorities, equal participation in public affairs, and the right of each individual to choose his or her ethnic identity. Ethnic minorities could participate in the "government of the Republics concerning their affairs" (ch. 2.4). In areas where members of a minority formed a local majority, they were to be given special status, including the right to show their national emblem, an educational system "which respects the values and needs of that group" (ch. 2.5.c), a legislative body, a regional police force, and a judiciary that reflects the composition of the population. Such special areas were to be permanently demilitarized unless they were on an international border. The rights established in the convention were to be assured through national legislation. The Carrington Plan's Court of Human Rights was to consist of magistrate nominated by each of the Yugoslav republics and an equal number plus one of nationals from European states who would be nominated by the member states of the European Community. No two members were to be from the same republic or European state. Court decisions were to be taken by majority vote (ch. 4).

Annex 6 of the Dayton Accords provided for human rights guarantees and the creation of an ombudsman and a Human Rights Chamber. For at least five years the ombudsman was to be appointed by the chair of the Organization for Security and Cooperation in Europe and eight of the fourteen members of the Chamber were to be appointed by the Committee of Ministers of the Council of Europe. Neither the ombudsman nor the eight members appointed by the Council of Europe were to be from the former Yugoslavia.

The elaborate minority-rights provisions for the former Yugoslav republics were adopted as a result of coercion. The prospective rulers of these new states would have preferred not to be encumbered by such international obligations. The commitments had limited domestic support. But their acceptance was a condition of recognition by the European Community. Recognition was an important resource for the rulers of these insecure protostates, because it facilitated contracts with other states and served as a signal of legitimacy to domestic populations.

However, the major powers continued to need interlocutors in the region. Although the Tudjman and Milosevic regimes had violated minority-rights commitments domestically and with regard to Bosnia-Herzegovina, both leaders were reaffirmed in the 1995 Dayton settlement, because outside states were unable to impose a solution without the consent of governments in Zagreb and Belgrade.

Finally, the end of the Cold War has also prompted a number bilateral contractual agreements. For example, Germany and Denmark have made parallel declarations regarding the treatment of ethnic groups within the other country, stating that each minority would be given the right to establish schools, would enjoy proportional representation in local government committees, and would be able to maintain religious, cultural, and professional ties with its home country (Hailbronner 1992, 128). Hungary has signed agreements with neighboring states with large Hungarian-speaking populations, as has Russia vis-à-vis successor republics of the former USSR with Russian-speaking populations.

In some instances, bilateral accords were the result of Western pressure by leading European Union states backed by the United States. In the negotiations leading to the 1995 European Stability Pact, European Union member states (led by French Premier Eduard Balladur) conditioned future consideration for EU membership on resolution of minority disputes among Eastern European states, especially those related to the situation of Hungarians and Russians in neighboring states. Since these states (Poland, the Czech and Slovak republics, Hungary, and Slovenia in particular) rely critically on economic and military relations with the West, they have little choice but to reach at least nominal bilateral agreements.

The end of the Cold War brought a renewal of international attempts to guarantee minority rights because ethnic conflict again threatened peace and stability and mobilized public concern worldwide.

Conclusion

The fate of minorities is an old item on the international agenda. The most enduring motivation to protect minority rights has been fear that internal strife would cause international instability, drawing rulers into unwanted and costly wars. Religious conflict in early modern Europe provoked an uneasy détente among the recognized faiths. Ethnic antagonisms in the Balkans in the nineteenth century inevitably engaged the major powers of Europe because each feared that potential rivals would secure influence in the region at its expense. The minority-rights conditions imposed after 1918 were motivated by a broader vision of international stability through democracy, self-determination, and the security of minority groups. The minority-rights provisions of the 1959 Cyprus independence agreements were designed to prevent armed conflict between Greece and Turkey, and when the agreement was violated by Cypriote efforts to unite with Greece, Turkish troops did intervene. In recent years, the political costs of hosting refugees have added to interests in quelling state-minority conflicts at their source.

Ideological and ethical commitments of rulers and their constituencies have also motivated efforts to secure minority rights by compromising the domestic autonomy of states. European concern about the fate of Christians in the Ottoman Empire reflected commitments to coreligionists in addition to commercial and strategic interests. Accusations of Turkish atrocities increased British concerns about ethnic conflict in the Balkans. The arrangements concluded at Versailles did not reflect immediate security threats to the major powers so much as beliefs about how the world could be more safely organized according to democratic principles. European Union involvement in the former Yugoslavia was motivated by desires to prevent renewed genocidal violence at acceptable cost.

Rulers have also entered into external commitments in order to bolster their capacity to recognize minority rights, and to constrain the behavior of successors. For centuries, Ottoman authorities saw fit to recognize the autonomy of Christian communities in agreements with outside powers. After World War I, democrats in Czechoslovakia sought League intercession to assure German minorities of their place in the country's political and economic system. Since 1945, Council of Europe human-rights commitments have made increasingly unlikely a liquidation of religious and ethnic minorities within member states. Yet where these commitments have not been built on a base of domestic support, they have done little to modify the harsh treatment of minorities.

Minority-rights agreements have had some success, most notably the development of religious toleration in northwestern Europe from the sixteenth to the nineteenth centuries. (The Holocaust painfully demonstrated the incomplete and contested nature of this toleration.) Toleration was often the result of developments within polities, but these domestic changes were reinforced by international agreements. These agreements were Pareto-improving and mutually contingent: rulers adhered (at least initially) in part because they feared that violations could precipitate retaliation against coreligionists in other countries and lead to war. Where rulers feared the disorder of communal strife more than they desired communal uniformity, international protections have provided an equilibrium to which all parties adhered because defection would leave each worse off.

Efforts to establish toleration through coercion and imposition have usually failed. In the Balkans in the nineteenth century, after the First World War, and in Yugoslavia after 1991, major powers made the acceptance of minority rights a condition of international recognition. In most of these cases, the rulers or would-be rulers of the target states objected to these constraints, but were too weak to refuse. Once recognition was accorded, however, the initiators lost their major source of leverage. Withdrawing recognition was problematic because recognized local rulers became interlocutors without which the powerful could not pursue their interests. As rulers gained resources, they were able to sidestep, ignore, or abrogate minority-rights commitments.

It is often held that the sovereign state system has excluded alternative princi-ples and political forms that could accommodate the legitimate interests of groups not possessed of a state—in short, different forms of self-determination. The prin-ciples of juridical sovereignty, including nonintervention in the internal affairs of other states, are widely affirmed. Now that juridical states monopolize the world's land mass, all communal groups are formally subject to state authority, and countless languages and cultures have perished in the process. Yet rulers have always been able to conceive of alternatives to the Westphalian model and have frequently limited their sovereign capacity with regard to minorities. Given that two-thirds of politically salient minorities worldwide have significant populations in more than one state (Gurr 1992, 16), neither minorities nor minority-rights guarantees are likely to disappear soon from the international stage.

The status of minorities, and relations between rulers and ruled more generally, are always subject to challenge by external actors motivated by alternative inter-ests and ideologies. Norms, rules, and practices are plural and contested in the anarchic international environment in which nothing prevents rulers from ceding their sovereign authority, or rulers in more powerful states from coercing or imposing their preferences on those in weaker ones. Very strong states such as the United States can resist such challenges. Rulers in weaker polities must engage in contracting or, as in the Balkans for most of the nineteenth and twentieth cen-turies, submit to coercive pressure.

International efforts to resolve state-minority conflicts and strengthen ethno-cultural pluralism are dependent on the domestic interests of target state rulers. Without a strong base of domestic support, these efforts hinge on external rewards and threats that are unlikely to persist except in situations of symmetri-cal and stable interdependence. Where rulers at least initially support minority protections, however, credible international commitments can help institutional-ize toleration.

The Westphalian model is not deeply embedded. The principle of autonomy has always been challenged by alternatives, including religious toleration, and human and minority rights. The outcomes of these challenges are a function of the power and interests of rulers who must respond both to domestic con-stituents and external pressures.

CHAPTER ELEVEN

Ethnicity and Sovereignty: Insights from Russian Negotiations with Estonia and Tatarstan

CYNTHIA S. KAPLAN

ETHNICITY and sovereignty appear at the core of interstate conflict as the twentieth century draws to a close. This combination is not accidental, as it reflects the absence of established legitimacy in the unconsolidated regimes of post-Soviet Eastern and Central Europe and the developing world. Although ethnicity in its primordial form may exist as a latent factor, it is its politicization in the context of rapid political, economic, and social change that makes it such a potent catalyst of interstate conflict. Unlike other issues connected with economic and territorial disputes, ethnicity once politicized makes compromise and the peaceful settlement of differences difficult. Ethnicity in its most radical forms assumes an indivisible quality of moral right and wrong in which there can only be winners and losers. In this context, extending the range of participants within the ethnic communities only intensifies nationalism, thus increasing the likelihood of violence. In this respect, ethnic disputes differ from nonethnic ones.

Yet violent conflict between states and armed intervention by third parties are not the only means to "settle" differences in the highly charged context of politicized ethnic differences. There have been cases when negotiations have succeeded in avoiding open conflict and its spread. This chapter examines two such instances when negotiations succeeded despite the politicization of ethnicity.

Russian negotiations with Estonia and Tatarstan occurred in the wake of the Soviet collapse at a time in which the meaning and basis of statehood were yet to be fully defined. Old and new political elites searched for new bases of legitimacy. Representative institutions began their existence in societies where established rules of the game promoting compromise and tolerance were absent, political organizations were weak, and respect for minority rights was not yet the norm. Under such conditions ethnicity offered an easy basis for political mobilization. Although two cases can only suggest hypotheses and not confirm them, it would appear that, given the absence of stable political institutions, practices, and shifting political groupings (which may be considered as necessary, but not sufficient conditions), the more threatened the position and legitimacy of the president by nationalist forces, the more likely it is that he will turn to external validation through negotiations or agreements. His objective is to defuse nationalism as a weapon against presidential authority. This is the case when the president has chosen not to politicize the national issue himself. Although a variety of mecha-

nisms may be chosen to defuse nationalism in the domestic arena, such as providing benefits to domestic participants, another option is to undermine the institutional basis and organizational strength of these opponents.

We do not examine instances in which presidents or "state" leaders themselves
politicize ethnicity, but hypothesize that interstate conflicts in such cases are more
likely to lead to violence, which ends only when a clear winner or loser emerges,
if there is no third-party intervention. This is the case of Chechnya.

The seeds for nationalist movements in the USSR were long present, but sub-
merged sentiments entered the public realm during the Soviet collapse.
Gorbachev's attempt to negotiate a new Union Treaty (spring 1991) and its
prospective signing served to legitimize ethnic discontents which may have actually precipitated the August 1991 coup attempt and the dismantling of the USSR.
In the aftermath of these historic events, the former Union Republics (including
Estonia) regained their independence and the Autonomous Republics (including
Tatarstan) sought to redefine their relations with Russia. In the cases of Estonia
and Tatarstan, the urge for independence and its accompanying political manifestations were quite similar during the Soviet endgame (Kaplan 1995b). Yet,
although conflict was avoided in both cases, the consequences—state status,
domestic political configurations, and institutions—were quite different. These
differences are at least in part due to the formal independence of Estonia as
opposed to Tatarstan, but they also reflect differences in the assumed conditions,
that is, the strength of institutions and respect for rules of a democratic political
game.

A focus on either international systemic or domestic determinants alone cannot account for the differences evident in the selected cases. Russia could have
chosen to use force against Tatarstan as it did in the case of Chechnya and to
ignore Estonia's demands for the removal of Russian forces. In fact, neither
Russia's, Estonia's, or Tatarstan's international status alone, nor the constellation
of domestic political forces within these states alone, can explain the settlements
reached. An approach that surmounts the level of analysis problem, the two-level
negotiations game, allows for international and domestic factors to be taken into
account simultaneously. It reveals how the presidents of Tatarstan and Estonia
were able to reach agreements with Russia over a new Sovereignty Treaty and
Russian troop withdrawals, respectively, despite strong domestic political opposition to these agreements. These cases focus our attention on the critical role that
the presidents of these countries played in connecting interstate and domestic
policy preferences. Yet without fully appreciating the constraints that shifting
domestic forces exerted, it would be impossible to understand how these presidents changed their own positions during the course of negotiations.

Besides elucidating cases of potential conflict that ended peacefully, two important theoretical insights arise from the exploration of these cases within a two-
level game paradigm. The importance of context—in this instance, state status
and the international aspirations of Estonia—created a critical role for third parties and alliance partners in overcoming recalcitrant domestic coalitions and the
negotiating partner's preferences. A second finding drawn from the Tatar case

reinforces the synergistic characteristics of two-level negotiations as a key to the evolution of regime type and the restructuring of domestic political groups in contexts where the basis of regime legitimacy and institutions are weak and few democratic rules of the game are observed.

Two-Level Negotiations

As scholars of international relations have argued, a systemic perspective in which domestic determinants are viewed as residual variables cannot explain real-world outcomes, nor can domestic determinants alone successfully reveal why agreements are reached (Putnam 1988; Moravcsik 1993; Katzenstein 1976; Gourevitch 1978; Schoppa 1993). The two-level game metaphor first presented by Robert Putnam provides a logic of interaction between negotiating parties which recognizes the linkages that may exist between negotiators, that is, governments that are reaching agreements (level I) and domestic constituents who must ratify such agreements (level II). In this context, "Central executives have a special role in mediating domestic and international pressures precisely because they are directly exposed to both spheres" (Putnam 1988, 432). The model also focuses our attention on transgovernmental, transnational, and cross-level relations as a means of understanding how win-sets are, or are not, achieved at both levels I and II (Knopf 1993, 600). Win-sets are either the range of positions supported by each of the negotiators (level I) —which overlap, thus making agreement possible—or those that exist among the domestic political forces (level II) of each of the states—which overlap with those negotiating on behalf of their state. The latter, level II win-sets, are also mediated by the existence of state institutions. Ultimately, the negotiators' win-sets must overlap in order to reach agreement, and to the degree that domestic political forces must ratify such agreements their win-sets must overlap with those of their negotiators.

The two-level negotiations model has found its strongest support in studies of economic issues, with fewer tests in the field of strategic studies. Peter Evans concluded in a volume focusing on the application of the two-level negotiations model that "Our cases show clearly that territorial conflicts between long-term military adversaries are least likely to evoke the complex domestic divisions that make synergistic issue-linkage possible. Issues of sovereignty and national security generate few transnational alliances. . . . If it is true, as seems plausible, that adversarial negotiations over territory and formal sovereignty represent a declining proportion of current negotiations, the tendency toward an increasing role for synergistic strategies follows" (P. Evans 1993, 424–25).

Although economic issues seem to conform to the model, we need only look at recent events in Central and Eastern Europe and the former Soviet Union to see that in this part of the world, issues of territory and formal sovereignty have not declined in importance but actually increased at an alarming rate. In some instances, peaceful agreements have led to the creation of new states, such as the Czech and Slovak republics, but in others, such as the former Yugoslavia and

Chechnya, armed conflicts ensued. Although these cases differ in a variety of ways, they all share a central issue—ethnicity. The centrality of ethnicity in defining sovereignty describes a set of cases that are poorly understood and for which the probability of successfully negotiated outcomes is difficult to determine. An inescapable characteristic of these cases is irredentism. Irredentism constitutes a quintessential basis for heterogeneity within the domestic constituencies (level II). "Lines of cleavage within the level II constituencies will cut across the level I division, and the level I negotiator may find silent allies at his opponent's domestic table" (Putnam 1988, 444). It also creates the possibility of transnational alliances between political groups that seek to represent their ethnic compatriots. For all these reasons, the two-level model should be tested in the context of ethnicity. The initial supposition that issues of sovereignty make synergistic issue linkage difficult may need to be qualified as being valid only when the negotiators are instrumental in politicizing ethnicity, and may not be true in all cases in which ethnicity and sovereignty are involved. Thus, our cases characterized by issues of both ethnicity and sovereignty pose most "difficult" cases for the two-level paradigm. If the logic of the model is found applicable to them, the mechanism through which peaceful settlements are reached and violence is avoided should be elucidated.

The Two-Level Game Model as a Prism

As suggested by Andrew Moravcsik (1993, 18) empirical evidence from case materials should be analyzed in terms of the "success or failure in reaching agreement" and "the distribution of gains and losses." To achieve this, he states that "It is essential to specify the preferences of and constraints on the major actors. Three essential theoretical building blocks are needed: specification of domestic politics (the nature of the 'win-sets'), of the international negotiating environment (the determinants of interstate bargaining outcomes), and the statesman's preferences" (23).

    As will be shown in analyzing domestic constraints—interest-group configurations, representative institutions, and uncertainty (Moravcsik 1993, 24)—some of the assumptions of the two-level model must be violated. For example, it is not at all clear that relative costs and benefits of negotiated alternatives remain constant through long negotiations. Indeed, in the case of Russia, changes in the strength of domestic constituents and a change in the salience of nationalism may affect both the domestic win-set and the strategy and preferences of the chief governmental officer (CGO). Most studies have stressed the patterns of mobilization on the domestic scene and "participation expansion" (Schoppa 1993, 370) as a means of shaping domestic coalitions and thereby, level II win-sets. The cases to be examined below suggest that the demobilization of particular groups and audiences may also play an important part in reaching agreements. This may be achieved, in part, through payoffs and a change in strategy, but not in goals.

    The above observations also speak to a statesman's preferences. The statesman's "acceptability-set" may also change in light of changes in the negotiating partner's position. CGOs may choose to capture an issue from domestic constituents through international negotiations. Through the application of "synergistic strategies" CGOs may not only restructure domestic coalitions, but through "alternative specification" (Schoppa 1993, 370) may entirely restructure the domestic political agenda. In doing so in unconsolidated polities, the nature of the institutions themselves may be changed. This is possible through the legitimization that successful negotiations themselves provide the CGO and through the strategic use of payoffs. Thus, a hypothesis suggested by the Tatarstan case is that the less institutionalized a political system is when the position of the CGO or president is threatened by domestic nationalist forces, the more likely that international negotiations will be linked to institutional reform. As will be seen in the case of Tatarstan, the president's ability to reshape entirely the configuration of domestic political forces and to reform the very institutions of government demonstrates the potency of CGO synergistic strategies.

A final observation concerns the nature of the cases to be examined. Some may object to examining cases in which one state, Estonia, is formally sovereign and independent, while the other, Tatarstan, remains within the Russian Federation. There is no doubt that this shaped the two sets of negotiations. The independent status of Estonia allowed its president to ignore the parliament and reach a behind-the-scene agreement with the president of Russia through the inclusion of third parties from the international arena. The European Union and the CSCE's High Commission for National Minorities made the agreement possible both domestically and internationally. Of course, this alone might not have been sufficient had public opinion not legitimized President Meri's activities. Had Estonia not had legal independence, third actors, such as the European Union and the Baltic Council, could not have made it possible for the CGO virtually to ignore the level II win-set, that is, the issue of ratification. As Jeffrey Knopf has noted, the impact of alliances "creates different contexts within which two-level interactions can occur" (Knopf 1993, 600). This suggests a way in which domestic preferences (level II win-sets) may be at least partially ignored and level I win-sets modified.

Estonia clearly fits within the realm of relevant cases, but what about Tatarstan? Without legal recognition of independence, the context of negotiations is not constrained by international factors in the same manner as found in the Estonian case. Russia can and does claim that relations with Tatarstan and other former Autonomous Republics, such as Chechnya, are solely a matter of domestic concern. To the extent that international concerns shape the context of negotiations, issues of human rights tend to exert the strongest influence.

Nonetheless, within Tatarstan, the necessary elements of the two-level model exist—domestic politics that are autonomous from those of Russia proper and a separate set of CGO preferences. The degree of interpenetration is much greater, and as a consequence Tatar sovereignty is much weaker than that found in an independent state. This alone, however, should not lead us to exclude this case. Tatarstan, like many other new states, has a sense of national interest, a concept of territory, and people. The complexities that define the Russian Federation provide a context in which many cross-level and transnational alliances are possible. Intergovernmental alliances were also possible during the initial period of negotiations. In light of these possibilities, Tatarstan would appear to be a particularly difficult case for a negotiated agreement—witness Chechnya—but an agreement was successfully negotiated and armed conflict avoided. Thus, the cases of Estonia and Tatarstan provide variation in terms of state status (international context).

What can we learn from the actual negotiations between Russia and Estonia and Tatarstan? What distinguishes these cases? We have suggested that they vary in terms of state status, but variation is also introduced by the differences in domestic political forces and institutions that serve to constrain CGO negotiations. The cases also provide evidence, albeit in different ways and for different reasons, of the ability of CGOs either to change the level II win-set or to ignore it successfully. In both cases the issue of nationalism had either to be captured or the forces of nationalism de-mobilized. In seeking greater sovereignty, two very different presidents for different reasons sought to depoliticize the issue of nationalism, or at least to reshape it. These are not isolated cases. One can think also of the situation in Ukraine and Kazakhstan. Perhaps successful negotiations over ethnic issues require the president's acceptability-set to be positioned toward the center on the issue of nationalism, not at the "radical" extremes.

A more formal hypothesis may be formulated from the above observations: the less extreme a president is on the issue of nationalism, the more likely he is to introduce nonethnic issues onto the domestic political agenda. These nonethnic issues, such as economic integration, may allow for "payoffs" necessary for the neutralization of disaffected domestic political groups. Thus due to either initial preferences or shifts in domestic constituencies, a president may seek a moderate position that fosters successful negotiations.

As alluded to above, domestic factors constraining the CGOs of Estonia and Tatarstan differed—that is, domestic institutions, political parties, and groups. Yet these countries share one very important characteristic, the presence of a large Russian ethnic community. In Estonia approximately 30 percent and in Tatarstan 43 percent of the residents are ethnic Russians. The history of these Russian populations is very different, as are settlement patterns. Whether the politics of the Russian ethnic communities produce transnational alliances will be explored. State policies affecting Russians—in particular, citizenship laws and state language laws—also clearly differ. These defining characteristics provide a background against which to explore the impact of domestic heterogeneity on level II "win-sets."

The most important factor uniting these cases is their negotiating partner, Russia. In the Estonian case we examine negotiations over Russian troop withdrawals, that were successfully concluded in July 1994 (ratified by Estonia in December 1995; unratified by Russia). Tatarstan negotiated its status within the Russian Federation through a Sovereignty Treaty with Russia that was signed in February 1994. From the collapse of the Soviet Union until the conclusions of these negotiations, the position of President Yeltsin and the nature of Russian domestic politics changed significantly. By selecting the Estonian and Tatar negotiations with Russia, we are able to examine these two states' ability to negotiate with the same partner whose own acceptability and level II win-set shifted dramatically. In analyzing these cases, we hope to learn not only about the applicability of the two-level negotiations model to issues of ethnicity, but how CGOs' preferences link their activities on the international level with their respective domestic contexts as they reach negotiated settlements.

CASE STUDIES

In order to maximize comparability, each case will examine domestic constraints understood as political groups, parties, coalitions, interest groups, the impact of institutions, and public opinion; the international negotiating environment; and statesmen's preferences. How "win-sets" at each level emerged will allow us to examine the role of transnational alliances, transgovernmental alliances, and cross-level ties. In this context, we will deduce the distribution of costs and benefits that might produce the relevant win-set. We will also attempt to provide a sense of how win-sets may have varied over time in order to provide a dynamic that is usually missing in the literature on two-level negotiations. We will examine statesmen's acceptability-sets and how they may have interacted with domestic preferences (level II win-sets). The dynamics of win-sets and how they affected the final negotiations will be presented in the context of the Tatar and Estonian case material. In this context we will explore the strategies employed by the presidents of these countries paying special attention to the use of synergistic approaches and the role of third parties from the international arena. Since case materials are by their nature detailed, we will provide background for the negotiations before providing more specific evidence. We begin with the collapse of the Soviet Union and the emergence of Russia under the leadership of President Boris Yeltsin.

The Russian Federation

THE END OF THE SOVIET UNION

The national referendum on the Union Treaty held on March 17, 1991, was meant to affirm the transformation of the Soviet Union, but instead demonstrated the weakness of the state (Brady and Kaplan 1994).[1] By the August 1991 coup attempt, referendums had already been used by Union Republics, such as Estonia, as a mechanism by which to acquire popular legitimacy for their proclamations of independence (March 3, 1991). Autonomous Republics, such as Tatarstan and Bashkortostan, raised the issue of Union Republic status and pro-

---

[1] Although approximately 56 percent of the population voted in favor of a new Union Treaty, six of the fifteen Union Republics refused to hold the referendum, and among the remaining Union Republics some chose to change the wording of the question.

claimed sovereign status. Tatarstan declared its state sovereignty on August 30, 1990, and held a referendum on it in March 1992 (Sheehy 1992, 2). The nature of the state was defining the Soviet political agenda.

For Russians within the Federation the issue of regime type was at the fore during the late spring and summer 1991. The dynamics of political authority and power will be seen to be consistent with shifts in Yeltsin's policy positions. Yeltsin, the first popularly elected president of Russia (June 1991), challenged an increasingly conservative Gorbachev. The issue of state boundaries perhaps weighed less heavily on Russia at this stage than the issue of who or which forces would control the state. In his contest with Gorbachev, Yeltsin appealed to the regions and republics to take as much authority as they wanted, thus using them against the Communist center. He stood for democracy, which included the liberal concept of self-determination. It was his use of the term *democracy* which defined him at this time. Russian nationalism was not yet an issue on the political scene. After the August 1991 coup attempt and the destruction of the USSR in December 1991, Boris Yeltsin was at the height of his popularity, riding a wave of democratic euphoria.

DOMESTIC COALITIONS

A brief review of shifts in domestic political groupings is necessary in order to analyze changes in Yeltsin's policy preferences. Initially, umbrella organizations such as the Democratic Union and Democratic Russia organized democratic forces against the ancien régime (1988 through 1990). The Communist Party of the Soviet Union, although outlawed immediately after August 1991, reemerged as a number of new parties, some of which espoused democratic socialist ideas, but others of which stood for old-fashioned orthodoxy. Communist strength increased during 1992–1993 as the incoherence of political life grew.

The center of the political spectrum is perhaps best understood as representing the democratic, liberal segment which also included a segment supporting state power. Although most democrats supported a strong presidency and Yeltsin, some grew disenchanted with him and moved into opposition. Among the factors promoting this switch was a rejection of their initial support for national rights within the USSR and growing adherence to the idea of a unified Russia with a strong central government. Thus the focus on a strong state among domestic political forces served to shape Yeltsin's alternatives as he confronted rising demands for sovereignty and independence. Toward the left of center were located a number of parties that represented private economic interests, stability, and a strong state. The more liberal democratic elements of this sector rejected the emphasis on state power and chose to oppose Yeltsin selectively.

Perhaps the most important factor shaping Yeltsin's options was the emergence of the right wing of the political spectrum. Although slower to develop than other political forces, it became quite strong by 1993. In Russia, a conservative in favor of state power may be categorized as on the left or the right. Indeed, several rather infamous meetings occurred between the so-called reds and blacks. The best-known representative of the extreme right is Vladimir Zhirinovsky's Liberal

Democratic Party, which promotes the reestablishment of a Russian empire. Nationalist parties are also found here. The growth of the far right calling for a new USSR based on the great-power status of Russia began to limit Yeltsin's room to maneuver.

The above schematic overview suggests the chaotic and often tumultuous nature of Russian political life and is evidence of the absence of established and legitimized political institutions. Presidential and parliamentary relations became increasingly strained. The Russian parliament at first granted Yeltsin extraordinary powers in order to address the issue of reform (November 1991). Individual leaders from both the left and right who wanted a strong leader supported Yeltsin, but for different reasons (Brady and Kaplan 1994). When the economic costs to society of reform began to accumulate and Yeltsin began to exercise power in an increasingly authoritarian manner, liberal democrats were dismayed, but had nowhere else to go.

Politicians who were more toward the extremes, right or left, went into opposition. Their groups' institutional strength resided in the Russian parliament, a leftover from the Soviet era. A stalemate between Yeltsin's reformist desires and the parliament's more cautious approach to economic change was evident by late fall 1992. Parliament refused to confirm Yeltsin's reformist Prime Minister Gaidar or to extend Yeltsin's extraordinary power to rule by edict. A struggle for power ensued in which the parliamentary leadership, representing the forces on the right, went into open opposition against Yeltsin. In this struggle, which was to dominate political life until the attack on the Russian White House, the parliament building, in October 1993, the overarching issue was the balance of power between the president and parliament and the nature of the new Russian state. During this crisis, Yeltsin turned increasingly to the heads of the republics and the executives (governors) of the provincial governments for support. This institutional crisis created an opening for demands for both regional and ethnic autonomy and sovereignty. Russia still lacked a new constitution that defined the rights of the provinces (*oblasts*), and republics.

What began as an institutional crisis assumed an increasingly ethnic character when the governors began to worry that the provinces did not have the same rights as the republics (*RFE/RL* January 11, 1993). The representatives from the republics who formed the "Sovereignty and Equality" faction were concerned that the referendum through which Yeltsin wished to demonstrate his power vis-à-vis the parliament would "increase inter-ethnic tensions" (*RFE/RL* February 5, 1993). The heads of local administrations came out against the referendum because they feared that some republics and regions might add questions on sovereignty. The Council of the Heads of Republics stated that the "referendum would inevitably lead to the politicization of society and distract people from economic problems" (*RFE/RL* February 2, 1993). The referendum, which was initially to include a vote on a new constitution, turned instead into a contest between the president and parliament.

The increasing importance of ethnic issues in the context of institutional stalemate led parliament to hold hearings on the integrity of Russia (*RFE/RL* February

23, 1993). "The Chairman of the Council of Nationalities Ramazan Absulatipov noted two tendencies in regional policy. On the one hand there was super-centralization, and on the other the crumbling of the state through the transfer of many powers to the subjects of the federation" (*RFE/RL* February 23, 1993).[2]

Yeltsin, who had earlier encouraged the independence of the Union Republics and the transfer of power to the new republics of the federation, began to move toward the center. He won the referendum, but turnout was low and the referendum was not held in all the republics. By August, Yeltsin proposed a Federation Council "overseeing the process of constitutional reform, helping to realize a new Federal Treaty, and debating the most important policies in the country" (*RFE/RL* August 17, 1993). The stalemate with parliament dragged on until Yeltsin issued an ultimatum for the members to disband, which they refused to do. In October 1993 Yeltsin sent troops and tanks against the parliament.

Opposition to a new constitution continued. Yeltsin insisted that the "federal treaty be exclude[d] from the text of the constitution, that the words *sovereign* and *sovereign state* with regard to the republics be removed, and that the republics and other subjects of the federation should have equal rights" (*RFE/RL* November 4, 1993). During a meeting with the heads of Russian republics and regions, "The chief sticking point was the relative status of the republics and regions, with the republics still insisting on their superior status." A referendum on the new constitution that strengthened the presidency did eventually pass, approved by 54 percent of eligible voters. However, in nine republics the referendum on the constitution was either not held, the turnout too low to be valid, or the vote simply went against it (*RFE/RL* December 1993). Even after the dissolution of the parliament, the shift away from democratic forces continued, as testified to by the results of the December parliamentary election.[3] Thus, the weakening of Yeltsin's own position in light of increasing challenges from Russian nationalists appears strongly related to his own shift in preferences.

Yeltsin moved toward a more right-centrist position. Despite having encouraged republican autonomy when he was in opposition to the center, Yeltsin now found it difficult to deal with an increasingly autonomous periphery. Yet, he could not abandon the periphery from whom he continued to need support. Yeltsin also had to prevent the extreme right from capturing the nationalist issue. He sought to achieve these contradictory ends by standing for the integrity of Russia. Thus Yeltsin, who had been a strategic partner in the independence drives of the Union

[2] At these hearings, the deputy prime minister responsible for nationalities policy set out eleven theses of Russia's nationalities policy. Among the eleven theses, which the newspaper *Nezavisimaya gazeta* lists (February 23, 1993), are the equality of all peoples of the Russian Federation, federalism, territorial unity, and the integrity of the Russian Federation and its subjects, the depoliticization of nationalities policy, reliance on the legally elected bodies of power whether they are to the liking of the center or not, the absolute priority of political methods of solving conflicts, the principle of consistency in small matters, and the need to take into account the complexity of the religious composition of Russian society (*RFE/RL* February 24, 1993).

[3] Out of a total of 450 seats in the lower chamber, 96 went to pro-Yeltsin forces, whereas 70 went to supporters of the nationalist Zhirinovsky, and 65 to Communists. Anti-reformist elements held 182 seats, as compared to the 164 of the pro-reformist groups (*RFE/RL* December 27, 1993).

Republics and efforts toward republic sovereignty in the immediate aftermath of the USSR's collapse, now found himself in need of support or at least neutrality from the republics. If agreements with Estonia and Tatarstan were not reached, nationalist sentiments among Estonians, Tatars, and Russians might be inflamed. These sentiments could then be used by the rightist, nationalist wing of the political spectrum in Russia.

Public Opinion in Russia

The distribution of the new political forces reflects the electoral preferences of the Russian public. Based on a large-scale representative survey by the author on political participation in politics, it is apparent that two characteristics of public opinion played a defining role in the evolution of politics in regard to two-level negotiations.[4] The trend toward the right is understandable in terms of where the public was located on economic issues and regime preferences as compared to the elite and liberal intelligentsia. Based on an analysis of political attitudes toward regime type, economic reform, trust in institutions, and political leaders, the author and Henry Brady concluded that on the eve of the August coup attempt, the political parties and intelligentsia tended to favor more radical economic reform and either a mixed socialist-capitalist or Western-type political system, while the mass public supported much more conservative alternatives. In particular, "what is stunning is that the new parties and organizations (with the exception of the Socialist Party) are located near people who . . . want Westernization and those who want capitalism and socialism. There are virtually no new organizations located where 60 percent of the population place themselves" on these issues (Kaplan, Brady, Smirnov, and Andreenkov 1992, 26, fig. 6).[5]

The other rather striking finding from our survey was the extent of support for the independence of the union republics. Among all of our 15,309 respondents, 65.4 percent favored independence as did 66.3 percent of those who were members of the Communist party. Even among supporters of reactionary political groups, 55.6 percent supported independence. However, the strongest support

---

[4] Data used in this analysis are from a survey on Citizen Participation in Politics conducted from the end of May through the beginning of August 1991. A representative sample of 12,309 respondents from Russia were interviewed in person. The authors of the survey were Cynthia S. Kaplan, William V. Smirnov, Vladimir G. Andreenkov, and Henry E. Brady. The first stage survey from which the data are drawn was supported by the John D. and Catherine T. MacArthur Foundation and the Soviet Academy of Sciences, with initial assistance from the International Research and Exchanges Board and the American Council of Learned Societies. Field work was supervised by Vladimir Andreenkov, the Center for Comparative Social Research, Moscow, Russia. Additional assistance was provided by the Center for Political Studies, Institute of State and Law, Moscow, Russia.

[5] This particular analysis examined groups based on their answer to "What do you think is the best course of development for your country?" The question offered six closed responses: "revival of the pre-1917 monarchy; return to the system of 1930–1950; return to the system of 1960 to the early 1980s before *perestroika* began; build a society on the basis of humane, democratic socialism; and build a society based on a combination of capitalism and socialism at their best." We realize the imperfections of this question, but it does tap important issues as they were understood in Russia at that time.

for independence was found among those labeled Westernizers, an overwhelming 87.2 percent (Kaplan, Brady, Smirnov, and Andreenkov 1992, 20).

This strong support for the independence of the republics of the Soviet Union would suggest a quick agreement with Estonia over realizing the conditions of independence. However, as negotiations dragged on, there emerged new political organizations on the right that politicized ethnicity, changing the terms of the political debate in Russia. Whereas the new political movements of fall 1991 did not reflect public preferences on economic and political issues, those that emerged during 1992 and 1993 sought to do so. Thus it is not surprising, in the context of institutional stalemate, that when elections were called in 1993 new post-Soviet political organizations and parties would be able to capture the preferences of and take strength from the growing alienation of the Russian public. This helps to account for the shift toward a more conservative set of dominating coalitions on the Russian political scene.

Win-Sets at Level I and Level II in Russia

There was a clear shift in domestic coalitions during the period of negotiations, considerably narrowing the Russian win-sets at both levels. What might have been acceptable in the fall 1991 was not by 1993 and 1994. Yeltsin's loss of extraordinary powers in November 1991 and the instability and disaffection caused by economic reforms made him vulnerable to pressure by the newly emergent nationalist forces.

At first, the status of ethnic Russians abroad was not politicized since many Russians abroad had supported some change in status from the old Soviet Union without realizing what the implications might be for them. Russian democratic forces had been closely associated with forces in the Union Republics seeking independence. In this context, Yeltsin had urged the taking of as much sovereignty and power as republics wished. This comment, however, was directed against the center. At the time of the August 1991 coup attempt, Tatarstan, acting with this encouragement, was on the verge of becoming a Union Republic.[6]

By December 1992 the situation had changed. The issues of institutional power within Russia—decentralization, local autonomy, and sovereignty—were now linked. Over time, the issue of decentralization of power became politically charged as regions claimed the same rights as the new republics, which were already calling for sovereignty or even independence. In addition, the advent of Russian refugees from Central Asia and the Caucasus further contributed to politicizing the national issue. This allowed politicians on the right to use Russian communities now in a new diaspora for their own political advantage. The rightist parties, along with those on the far left in Russia, used the laws on citizenship in the Baltic states as evidence of the mistreatment of Russians and the need for Russia to play a special role in this so-called "near abroad" (Kaplan 1995a). By

---

[6] Private communication to the author by a prominent political activist in Tatarstan who was involved in these negotiations.

linking the issues of institutional authority and nationalism, a conservative coalition emerged, as witnessed by Yeltsin's call for the April 1993 referendum and the December 1993 electoral results.

Groups on the right in Russia sought to speak on behalf of as well as to organize ethnic Russians within the newly independent states. Rumors abound regarding not just political contacts (transnational alliances) that were public, but financial assistance and, in some instances, aid and strategic advice from institutions within the Russian state to groups abroad (cross-level alliances). This was true in both the Estonian and Tatar cases.

In agreeing to the treaty with Tatarstan and troop withdrawals from Estonia, Russian domestic political coalitions could claim that benefits were given to Russian retired military officers that they would not otherwise have received, and that Tatarstan was not given its independence but rather some type of vague autonomy. In the end, however, it was still support from the democrats and less radical groups that made these agreements possible. Nevertheless, the rightist groups attempted to use nationalism against Yeltsin and the democratic forces.

Yeltsin's win-set shifted consistently as the result of constraints posed by the emergent nationalist forces. As suggested previously, Yeltsin had initially encouraged independence and autonomy claims as a means of weakening the center. However, once he was in control of the government the exercise of these claims weakened the Russian state—clearly something undesirable. Yet declining support by conservative forces meant that Yeltsin could not afford simply to write off backing from the heads of the republican governments. Furthermore, although Yeltsin could assume support from democratic reformers, this somewhat limited the policies he might adopt. Thus, if initially Yeltsin might be viewed as a partner in a transgovernmental alliance encouraging autonomy and sovereignty claims, as the consequences of this alliance became clearer and domestic opposition emerged, he had to maintain the support or at least the neutrality of republic leaders at home while depoliticizing the nationality issue or coopting it so that it could not be used against him by conservative forces. This helps to explain what appear to be contradictory policies and demonstrates the potent influence of domestic constraints on CGO choices.

Consequently, Yeltsin appeared increasingly more conservative on nationality issues, as exemplified by claims of human rights violations in the Baltics, yet he also reacted to pressure from the OSCE, the United States, and Germany (*RFE/RL* May 27, 1994, and July 28, 1994). Yeltsin benefited from reaching an agreement with Estonia that extended rights to the Russian retired officers, but within a few months took a hard stand on border issues with Estonia. Clearly, he attempted to capture nationalist support while reacting to outside pressure.

In the case of Tatarstan, beyond the signed agreement that granted an ill-defined sovereignty, very little in the way of power was actually delegated. Yeltsin shared with President Shaimiev an interest in preventing a more radical Islamic movement from gaining power, thereby avoiding an open clash, as later happened in Chechnya. This logic is enticing, but how can Chechnya be explained? Although it is not the purpose of this paper to do so, it is worth noting that the role of Yeltsin's presidential advisors had increased by December 1994, which may be a critical part of the decision to use troops in Chechnya. Of equal importance is the fact that the leader of Chechnya had politicized ethnicity as a means of seeking independence from Russia.

In the two cases presented here, Yeltsin was able to use a more constrained level II win-set in making claims during negotiations. In the case of Estonia, third-party pressures were probably decisive, whereas in the case of Tatarstan, retaining political support by the heads of the republics probably allowed an agreement, but one that granted relatively little substantial change. The agreement had relatively low costs and allowed Yeltsin to claim to have defended Russian nationals abroad and the integrity of the Russian state.

The Cases of Tatarstan and Estonia

MOVEMENTS TOWARD INDEPENDENCE AND SOVEREIGNTY

At first glance it is surprising to find ethnic groups that represent two distinctive traditions evidencing such similar tendencies in their attempts to redefine their status during the Soviet period.[7] In the Estonian case, sovereignty was declared in November 1988 and a resolution "On the State Status of Estonia" on March 30, 1990, restored the interwar Republic of Estonia and announced a period of transition to independence (*Restoration* 1991, 3-4, 22–23). This was followed by the March 3, 1991, referendum in which 77.7 percent of the 83 percent of the population that voted favored independence. Irredentism can affect transnational contacts and the disposal of domestic forces. Although the Russian population in Estonia did not support independence, their position shifted from one of supporting the Union to sovereignty within a new Union (Saar 1990, 14; and *Molodezh' Estonii* March 5, 1991).

The Supreme Soviet of the Tatar SSR declared its sovereignty on August 30, 1990, but held a referendum on sovereignty only after the collapse of the Soviet Union in March 1992. Despite the strong opposition of the Yeltsin government, 61.4 percent of those voting in the Tatarstan referendum favored sovereignty. The yes vote was higher in rural areas, in which Tatars constituted most of the population (75.3 percent), while in Kazan, a city of Russian and Tatar inhabitants, 51.2 percent voted against sovereignty. Overall, 50.3 percent voted in favor of sovereignty (Khakimov 1993 and Sheehy 1992, 3).

Moscow's worry was that Tatarstan was pursuing a course of independence rather than sovereignty, especially in light of its refusal to sign the Federation Treaty and the claim for independence already made by the Chechens. It took until February 24, 1994, before a treaty was signed between Russia and Tatarstan (Teague 1994, citing *Rossiskaya gazeta* February 17, 1994).

As noted, the transition processes in Estonia and Tatarstan were in some ways surprisingly similar. These similarities allow us to isolate those factors which led

---

[7] Estonians are mostly Protestant and their capital, Tallinn, was a Hanseatic city, while Tatars are Muslim and played an important intermediary role between ethnic Russians and the Muslims of Central Asia before the Russian Revolution.

to successful negotiation from those constraints which help to distinguish the manner in which the CGOs reached settlements. In both cases there ensued a "war of laws" in which Estonia and Tatarstan proclaimed the primacy of their laws over those of the USSR and the RSFSR (Furtado and Chandler 1992, 103–6; Laas 1991; Khakimov 1993). Initial moves toward sovereignty were anchored in the need for economic reform (Kaplan 1992; Taagepera 1993, 127–214; Raviot 1994; Iskhakov 1992; and Drobizheva et al. 1994). A desire to preserve titular languages was central to both national movements. In both cases umbrella reformist organizations emerged: the Popular Front in Estonia, and the Tatar Public Center.

Among the most important distinguishing factors are differences in the nature of the nationalist movements and institutions. In Estonia, nationalist movements in favor of independence, such as the National Independence Party, managed to influence the Popular Front by playing on the latter's fear of losing mass popularity. This helped to move the Popular Front from seeking autonomy to seeking independence. By contrast, in Tatarstan the nationalists failed to pull more neutral groups toward independence.[8]

Critical to the outcome of the cases is the differing fates of the local Communist parties. In Estonia, the party suffered a fatal split in March 1990. A Russian-dominated Communist party maintained its allegiance to Moscow, whereas the Communist Party of Estonia (CPE), composed primarily of ethnic Estonians, was independent. The former sought to maintain the USSR, whereas the latter sought some kind of autonomy for Estonia within a new union. Given the strong association of the CPE with the center, the organization's position did not offer a viable alternative for the majority of ethnic Estonians. In Tatarstan the leading members of the Communist party, including President Shaimiev, had supported the putsch of August 1991. This left them without a base of legitimacy. Nonetheless, the Communist party in Tatarstan and its nomenklatura retained power and reorganized itself in December 1991.

An alternative representative institution in Estonia, the Congress of Estonia, eventually shared power with the Supreme Soviet, while in Tatarstan, the Milli Medzhilis functioned as a national assembly including Tatars from throughout the former Soviet Union, but never becoming an official state body. These differences may have affected the perceived legitimacy of representative units in their respective countries.

A number of puzzles emerge as Estonia regained independence and Tatarstan succeeded in signing a separate treaty with Russia. The first of these puzzles is how what appeared to be a viable independence movement in Tatarstan collapsed with the reemergence of a strong presidency after the August 1991 attempted coup. The answer to this question must be sought in the synergistic strategies of President Shaimiev, made possible through his use of negotiations with Russia. The second puzzle is how President Meri was able to ignore the Mart Laar gov-

---

[8] Radical national groups in Tatarstan, such as Ittifak, had only 2.5 percent of the popular support in August 1991 as opposed to the 27 percent still enjoyed by the Communist Party (Drobizheva et al. 1994, 110).

ernment's preferences and reach an agreement on Russian troop withdrawals. Eventually, President Meri was even able to have the agreement ratified by the parliament. The Estonian case highlights the importance of state status in the involvement of third parties in negotiations.

TATARSTAN

The political setting within Tatarstan was a critical component in understanding President Shaimiev's strategy. Three types of political movements arose during the denouement of the Soviet Union: nationalist, democratic, and cultural/societal (Drobizheva et al. 1994, 110). The democratic forces included political move-ments and parties, some of which were branches of Russian organizations. These movements developed somewhat more quickly than those native to Tatarstan, but appealed only to a small segment of the ethnic Russian population as well as some Tatars. More central to the disposition of domestic political coalitions were the democratic and cultural movements of Tatar origin. The central umbrella organi-zation was the Tatar Public Center (TPC). This organization initially based its appeal on cultural and linguistic issues; later, it became more political. The TPC enjoyed considerable popularity immediately after the collapse of the USSR, when the future of the president of Tatarstan and the nomenklatura were unclear.

Ittifak, the most radical organization demanding independence for Tatarstan, based its claims to statehood on Islam. However, its popularity as well as that enjoyed by all independence-oriented organizations dropped soon after the USSR's collapse. The TPC's popularity declined from a high of 20.6 percent in 1989–1990 to 6 percent after August 1991 (Drobizheva et al. 1994, 109), while Ittifak was supported by only 2.5 percent of the population and approximately 46 percent supported no political organization (109).

If the new political organizations in Tatarstan were weak, they still attracted popular support. The democratic movement claimed that it could get fifty thou-sand people out onto the streets of the capital, Kazan, and later, Ittifak did gather approximately twenty thousand supporters wearing Islamic headbands to sur-round the presidential buildings. This ability to mobilize the public declined as splits within and between the organizations developed. The TPC was in almost constant crisis, and a formal split occurred over the new constitution and whether Tatarstan should seek immediate independence or sovereignty within the Russian Federation (Iskhakov 1994, 12, 13). In fact, this was the divisive issue between radical movements such as Ittifak, which insisted upon independence, and the democratic movements, such as the Democratic Party of Russia, which empha-sized human rights, liberal economic reforms, and the integrity of Russia. By spring 1993, the nationalist movements stopped being a decisive force in politi-cal life (14). Thus, although nationalist organizations posed a potential threat to President Shaimiev's power and could call upon popular support against Russia, it can be argued that Shaimiev's strategy contributed to their collapse.

Initially, despite considerable Russian pressure, Tatarstan adopted its own con-stitution in March 1992. A referendum affirmed the constitution by a vote of 66 percent (Iskhakov 1994, 10). However, the momentum for national independence had begun to dissipate due to socio-economic problems within Tatarstan. Here the strategy of President Shaimiev came to the fore. The old *nomenklatura* represented by the president claimed that the economic problems of Tatarstan could only be solved within the context of the Russian Federation (25). A new coordinating council in Tatarstan that united nationalist and democratic forces opposed Yeltsin's April 1993 referendum and the December 1993 Russian Federation elections, but supported negotiations with Russia and the election of March 1993 (17). This council ultimately supported the agreement between Tatarstan and Russia as necessary, but still expressed doubts as to whether it fully recognized that two equal entities were involved. Many of the leaders of the TPC were disillusioned by the agreement (19). The more radical groups continued to reject negotiations with Russia and demanded the resignation of the president and vice president (17). Ultimately, the defining issue for the domestic coalition was whether to cooperate with the nomenklatura. Ittifak viewed itself as leading the opposition and was only willing to cooperate with democratic forces, and did so even when those forces were supported by ethnic Russians (27–28). President Shaimiev transformed the central political issue from solely one of independence to whether the government and president should be supported in negotiations with Russia.

How did President Shaimiev manage to promote a compromise between the more centralist forces within the TPC and the nomenklatura? The key to Shaimiev's success was to use economic claims against Russia—the issues of privatization and taxation. As Jean-Robert Raviot noted, "it would not have been possible to create the outward image of a reformist Tatarstan without a skillful internal policy concentrated on removing the national movements from the decision-making process so as to ensure the lawful authority a monopoly on the endogenous definition of the Republic of Tatarstan" (Raviot 1994, 74). This was possible through Shaimiev's synergistic approach, which linked economic issues with those of national sovereignty. Shaimiev used progressive members of the Communist party who were members of the Tatar Supreme Soviet to implement this policy. He transformed the party apparatus into the state apparatus by presidential appointment, granting it executive authority based in local administrative districts without need to resort to representative institutions (76).

What factors arising from the domestic scene may have encouraged President Shaimiev to adopt a policy that was clearly at odds with his support of the August 1991 putsch? The Islamic demonstration in October 1991, which led to an open conflict (Raviot 1994, 77), may have encouraged Shaimiev to become more sympathetic to the position of the TPC. Thus, a compromise approach to negotiations with Russia allowed the president to derive support from those supporting independence, while distancing himself from more radical movements, thereby not alienating ethnic Russians who preferred that Tatarstan remain in the Russian Federation. Of course, the Russian democratic movements still opposed these maneuvers, but they lacked widespread public support. The compromise approach was adopted first in the Tatar Constitution (November 1992) in which Tatarstan was described as "a sovereign state, a subject of international law, asso-

ciated with the Russian Federation on the basis of a treaty of the mutual delega-
tion of powers" (Teague 1994, 19 cites *Sovetskaya Tatariya*, December 13, 1992).
The actual bilateral treaty signed in February 1994 "makes no mention of
Tatarstan as a sovereign state," nor as "associated with Russia," but as a "state
united with Russia, on the basis of the constitutions of the two states and the
Treaty on the Delimitation of Spheres of Authority and the Mutual Delegation of
Powers" (Teague 1994, 26). Although this was disliked by many groups in
Tatarstan, it was nonetheless accepted.

WIN-SETS

Tatarstan represents the extreme case of a chief executive with little legitimacy
(August 1991) confronted by a growing nationalist movement under conditions
of economic and institutional instability. As noted initially, the president of
Tatarstan was presented with a puzzle after the August coup attempt on how to
reestablish legitimacy and maintain his base of support within the old nomenklatura. An orthodox Communist, he had not supported nationalist claims before
the Soviet collapse. Aware of the dangers of radical Islamic movements, however,
he moved toward the more moderate wing of the TPC, while providing economic
benefits for those who might be less enthusiastic about this ideological transformation. In this process, he transferred the center of political authority to his
administrative cadres. Indeed, after the signing of the treaty, a new electoral and
representative system was created in time for the March 1995 elections in which
the upper house consisted of the "elected" heads of regional administrations and
the lower house lacked formal representation by political parties.[9] Thus,
President Shaimiev was able to undermine and transform domestic political
forces and institutions.

   Due to political splits and an economic crisis, President Shaimiev was able to
transform the Communist nomenklatura into a state nomenklatura that would
supplant many of the functions of the Supreme Soviet and could engineer a constellation of political forces more favorable to the president. In a sense, the compromise approach to state status supported by Shaimiev coopted the issue of
nationalism, while arguing that remaining in the Russian Federation had side
benefits, especially economic payoffs. This also provided a basis for appealing to
the ethnic Russian population which was interested in the integrity of the Russian
Federation, but probably less so in the democratic ideas of the Russian political
parties transplanted to Tatarstan.

   The two-level negotiations model allows us to connect logically the considerable number of transnational, transgovernmental, and even cross-level alliances
that occurred within this ethnically heterogeneous setting. At the transgovernmental level Shaimiev and Yeltsin had initially shared interests in republican
autonomy. When this started to unravel for Yeltsin, Russia tried to exert pressure
on Tatarstan, using such threats as to cut off the Tatar oil pipeline (Teague 1994,

   [9] Interview by the author with the head of the Presidential Election Commission, March 1995,
Kazan, Tatarstan.

20). However, Russia had an interest in maintaining Tatarstan within the federation for economic as well as political reasons. Although Shaimiev could use the potential of Ittifak as a means to stress constraints on his ability to negotiate and as a potential threat, Yeltsin and Shaimiev both appreciated the threat that Russian nationalists, such as Zhirinovsky, posed to both of them.

During the process of negotiations, members of the Russian parliament and Constitutional Commission visited Tatarstan, trying to influence the adoption of the Tatar Constitution. They wanted to take part in a caucus of the Accord pro-Russian opposition faction, but were told by the chairman of the All-Tatar Public Center, Marat Mulyukov, that "the guests [should] not interfere in the sovereign republic's internal affairs" (*Current Digest* 1992b; *Nezavisimaya gazeta* October 20, 1992). Another typical situation recognized in two-level negotiations occurred-when members of both negotiating teams recognized compatriots across the table. For example, "Citizens of the Russian Federation, a public political movement in Tatarstan, [is] preparing a statement on disavowing the (ethnic) Russian members of Tatarstan's delegation at the talks with Russia. According to the movements chairman, Aleksandr Salagayev, they are not defending the interests of Tatarstan's Russian population" (*Current Digest* 1992a cites *Nezavisimaya gazeta,* September 11, 1992). These contacts were in addition to those that occurred between members of Russian political movements in Tatarstan which were branches of organizations established in Moscow and also in addition to the broad outreach to Tatars living in the diaspora made by members of Tatar political organizations. Indeed, the alternative parliament, Milli Medzhilis, and the series of Congresses of the Tatar People clearly sought to bring pressure to bear on Russia. These transnational alliances probably provided information on the situation, but were unlikely to have been decisive. Government-to-government envoys, including parliamentary delegations, probably raised the pressure for some sort of agreement. According to a number of political leaders interviewed in Kazan during March/April 1995, tensions between Russians and Tatars had increased until the signing of the bilateral agreement.

Ultimately, the final agreement left the meaning of sovereignty vague, but allowed Shaimiev to claim a special status for Tatarstan as compared to those republics that had signed the Federation Treaty in April 1992. It also provided him with a means of increasing his own authority and as part of a synergistic strategy shifted authority from representative institutions to those of the state administration. Although domestic political forces (the level II win-set) may have constrained Shaimiev initially, they also permitted him to restructure his approach to the negotiations (acceptability-set), establish a basis for his own legitimacy, capture the issue of sovereignty, and demobilize some of the more radical proponents of independence. Had there been no negotiations with Russia, the linkage of economic policies and political sovereignty would not have been possible. Instead, the initial trend supporting political independence might have been strengthened, with the increasing interethnic tension contributing to conflict both within Tatarstan and between Tatarstan and Russia. Witness the tragic situation of Chechnya and Russia. Thus, the puzzle of how the president of

Tatarstan, who left without political support and legitimacy in August 1991, reemerged as a popularly supported and authoritative leader who could transform the political institutions of Tatarstan and reach agreement with Russia, can only be fully understood in the context of two-level negotiations. Without President Shaimiev's strategy, the TPC might have matured into a full-blown independence movement. For Yeltsin, the peaceful conclusion of a model agreement with Tatarstan was of benefit in the political debates over the integrity of Russia, and helped him to contain the issue of nationalism. Both leaders sought to coopt nationalism and to use it against domestic political opponents.

ESTONIA

The Estonian case highlights the importance of the international community. International involvement may permit CGOs a wider array of options than would otherwise exist in light of domestic constraints. International pressure on CGOs may affect level I win-sets. We will assume the distribution of political strength within the Estonian parliament without providing a detailed political history of its evolution, since it remained relatively stable during the period under consideration (Kaplan 1995b; Kaplan and Brady 1995; Raun 1991; Taagepera 1993). As suggested by our examination of Russian domestic political coalitions and President Yeltsin's initial position, relations with Estonia were at first quite positive. Yeltsin's visit to Tallinn on January 12, 1991, after the events in Lithuania and Latvia was greatly appreciated. Formal recognition of Estonian independence on August 24, 1991, and the Protocols of Intergovernmental Relations between Estonia and the Russian Federation were signed in September 1991. Yet, relations began to sour by the beginning of 1992 (Vares 1993; and Zhuryari-Ossipova 1993). By October 1992, President Yeltsin stopped Russian troop withdrawals and "connected his order with the violation of the rights of the Russian-speaking population in the Baltic States" (Vares 1993, 17). When this occurred, Estonia sought third-party intervention by the Western states (Zhuryari-Ossipova 1993, 125). In November 1992, the United Nations General Assembly demanded an immediate agreement on the removal of Russian troops.

Negotiations over troop withdrawals seemed to cycle back and forth between accusations of human rights violations by the Russians and pressure applied by the Baltic countries, Western Europe, and the United States. Although Russia announced the withdrawal of its troops by August 31, 1994, statements by various spokesmen in the Russian Foreign Ministry, Foreign Minister Kozyrev, General Grachev, and Yeltsin himself linked the troop withdrawals with the treatment of Russian speakers living in Estonia. Additional threats were made, such as the introduction of additional troops into Estonia, the claim that Russia had special interests in the "near abroad" (Klatt 1994, 24), and the denial of economic benefits to Estonia. The Russians often tried to use international forums for these purposes. Ultimately, Yeltsin linked not only the rights of Russian speakers to the withdrawal of troops, but more specifically the rights of retired Russian military officers to receive permanent residency permits in Estonia with permission to privatize their housing.

The Estonians used international forums, such as the Council of Europe, to claim that Russia was attempting to interfere in the internal affairs of Estonia and that the laws that Russia objected to, such as the Citizenship Law, the Law on Aliens, and the Electoral Law, had been reviewed by the Conference on Security and Cooperation in Europe and were found to be in conformity with international standards (*RFE/RL* June 23, 1993). Public interchanges between Estonia and Russia were quite acrimonious.

The Pro Partia faction that led the Estonian government took a strong nationalist stand, often openly hostile to Russia. It was clearly not willing to compromise with the Russians, particularly in light of their accusations and threats. Indeed, one of its leaders even noted that threats such as those by Grachev (later withdrawn) made it easier for them to explain why no agreement had been reached (*Current Digest* 1994b).

It was President Meri who was at the forefront in bringing Western countries' influence to bear on Russia. He repeatedly met with members of the Baltic states, Nordic countries, Germany, and with the president and vice president of the United States. On such occasions, these third parties supported Estonia's demand for immediate Russian troop withdrawals without any linkage with other issues. Throughout 1993 and 1994 the United States used every opportunity to note that linkage was unacceptable (*RFE/RL* October 20, 1993; *RFE/RL* March 11, 1994). At times this became almost embarrassing, as when President Clinton after discussing the matter with President Yeltsin at the G-7 Meeting in July 1994 thought there was an agreement of sorts, but Yeltsin at a news conference when asked whether the troops would be out by August 31, 1994, said "no." Later he admitted that he had "promised Bill" to "try to solve this problem" (*Current Digest* 1994a). What did emerge from this meeting, however, was crucial. Yeltsin promised to meet with President Meri.

Before the presidential talks, the Russians used government figures outside of the formal negotiations to suggest possible consequences and alternative bases for agreements. These included the autonomy of the northeast area of Estonia, which has a large Russian-speaking population. These "suggestions" often entailed contacts and support for elements within the Russian-speaking community, such as the Russian Assembly within Estonia (cross-level alliance). Another suggestion was dual citizenship as a means of addressing human rights issues (*RFE/RL* April 28, 1994). When such "suggestions" crossed the boundaries of acceptable practice—like accusing Estonia of genocide and threatening troop invasions—they were withdrawn or disowned as private opinions. These accusations increased the pressure on Estonia. It is possible, of course, that some of the statements coming from members of parliament and the military *were* their own views. If so, then these may also fit into a pattern of constraints stemming from domestic forces on President Yeltsin.

The Estonians simply awaited the result of international pressure on Russia during the years of threats and increasing demands. As late as July 20, 1994, President Yeltsin said "We have no intention of withdrawing our troops as long as Estonia does not conform with international human rights law" (*RFE/RL* July 21,

1994). (International commissions had already found Estonia in compliance with human rights observances.) By this time, however, not only had Clinton clearly rejected linkage on the issue of troop withdrawals, but his secretary of state, Warren Christopher, reinforced this position at a meeting with Russian Foreign Minister Kozyrev during which he noted that the absence of an agreement on troop withdrawals from Estonia might delay the next Russian-U.S. summit. Even the U.S. Senate attempted to influence the situation by linking aid to Russian troop withdrawals (*RFE/RL* July 14, 1994). This pressure, along with continued support for Estonia from the Scandinavians, Germans, and British, pressured Yeltsin into meeting Meri.

WIN-SETS

The central issue in the Estonian case is how President Meri was able to ignore domestic constraints in seeking a compromise settlement. We assume everyone involved sanctioned the use of third parties in pressuring Moscow. Part of the answer to this question is the unraveling of the domestic coalition, beginning in the summer of 1994. The Pro Partia group split apart, undermining the Mart Laar government, which fell by early fall 1994. Public opinion also played a role. The population of Estonia had turned from the politics of negation with its focus on anti-Soviet and anti-Russian issues to a growing concern with economic issues. A decline in support for the strong nationalist stands espoused by Pro Partia was also evident (Kaplan 1995a) in the March 5, 1995, elections that rejected the Pro Partia group in favor of centrists and left centrists. Thus, the domestic coalition did not actually shift its position toward the agreement with Russia, but was weakened. Those who later replaced the coalition were much more predisposed toward positive relations with their Russian neighbor.

The large Russian-speaking community in Estonia provided an opportunity for Russian interference in the domestic arena. Some non-Estonian residents, such as retired military officers, ultimately opted for Russian citizenship. It is primarily those who chose Russian citizenship who were in contact with radical Russian politicians, such as Zhirinovsky. However, most ethnic Russians living in Estonia did not wish to leave. They recognized the legitimacy of the Estonian government, even if they did not always agree with its policies. A decline in tension with Russia served their interests. Among those with the most to gain were ethnic Russians in the burgeoning business community in Tallinn, the capital. Thus, although transnational alliances existed between the most radical of Russian nationalists in Estonia and nationalists in Russia, this was a fairly small group within the entire community. More moderate forces in Russia were later to make public contact with other segments of Russian society in Estonia. Members of these more moderate groups sought to become a legitimate opposition within the Estonian parliament. Thus irredentism, although a focus of Russian rhetoric, had relatively little influence on domestic forces within Estonia.

President Meri, although a strong supporter of national independence, was a pragmatist. He offered a compromise to Yeltsin that allowed retired Russian military officers to gain permanent residence in Estonia. Meri recognized that the terms of the agreement increased the actual number of retired military remaining in Estonia by only several thousand. Thus, while giving Yeltsin evidence that he had defended the rights of Russian speakers, Meri had achieved his ultimate aim—the removal of all Russian troops. Without continued pressure from third parties during the 1993 and 1994 negotiations, it is doubtful that an agreement would have been reached, given the domestic pressures on Yeltsin. The agreement on troop withdrawals did not mean that either the Russian government or Yeltsin stopped taking a strong nationalist stand. Witness Yeltsin's position on the unilateral declaration of the Russian-Estonian border. Nonetheless, pressure from third parties in the context of two-level negotiations made the agreement on troop withdrawals possible. The agreement allowed President Meri to ignore his domestic coalition win-set, knowing that it was weakened and that he enjoyed third-party legitimization for his agreement plus popular support. Indeed, the ratification of the agreement in Estonia required still additional pressure even on the new, more moderate parliament as well as tactical maneuvering by President Meri (*Postimees,* December 21, 1995).[10] This was possible because of Estonia's desire to conform to the standards set by its European partners so that it could join in formal alliances. President Yeltsin claimed that Estonia had compromised and that he had maintained a hard position on other issues, so as not to appear to have reached the agreement due to the pressure of Western powers.

Conclusions and Observations

Two-Level Negotiations

The logic of the domestic and international outcomes found in the two cases analyzed could not be easily understood without resort to the two-level negotiations approach. The critical role played by the presidents (CGOs) in linking the international and domestic arenas is key to understanding the negotiating process. Although it was originally suggested that the issue of sovereignty might not be particularly appropriate for this approach, the case of Tatarstan suggests the utility of its application. The two-level model in a somewhat modified form, as suggested by Knopf (1993), also captures the effect that third parties can have on both domestic and international win-sets. The existence of heterogeneous level II coalitions, which almost by definition exist in ethnically charged situations, supports the use of this approach.

What Do We Learn from the Two-Level Negotiation
Model about Negotiations over Ethnic Issues?

Here we are concerned not with the theoretical or generic, but with what the specific characteristics of the cases examined tell us about successful negotiations involving ethnicity and how conflict can be avoided or managed. First, these types

---

[10] Representatives were forced to vote up or down on the July agreement as a single package.

of cases often, but not always, include shifts in win-sets over time. Ethnicity is a charged issue subject to politicization that affects win-sets at levels I and II. In our successful cases of negotiations, we found that agreements were reached not by expanding participation or increasing mobilization, as has often been suggested in the literature on two-level negotiations, but rather through the cooptation of the issue and the demobilization of potentially radical nationalist groups. Thus, instead of politicizing ethnicity, the CGOs actually needed to alter the agenda somewhat, thereby coopting the issue and to some extent depoliticizing it.

The role of institutions was also important in our cases, although in a somewhat specialized manner. Rather than simply specifying rules affecting winning domestic coalitions, the strength of the state and its institutions helped to determine how important level II win-sets would be. Thus, through the use of synergistic policies both Yeltsin and Shaimiev attempted to shift the focus of power away from representative institutions. To the degree that nationalism can be used to support a strong presidency, representative institutions within unconsolidated regimes may suffer. Thus, it is not always the coalition or a shift in the coalition and its preferences that is important, but the way that the process of negotiation may actually be used to affect the role of institutions themselves.

Finally, the cases examined showed a shift in the preferences of CGOs in connection with changing domestic political coalitions. Perhaps the most interesting aspect of these shifts was the location of the presidents on the issue of nationalism. Unlike presidents of states involved in open ethnic hostilities, these presidents had not introduced or politicized the issue of ethnicity themselves. Instead, they reacted to its politicization so as to coopt the issue and to build their own legitimacy on the basis of it. This need to depoliticize the issue or at least take it away from potential domestic opposition allowed them, although not without difficulty, to reach compromises leading to successful negotiations. In the instance of Estonia, where level II win-sets within Estonia and Russia made an agreement particularly difficult, President Meri's strategy of using third parties neutralized his domestic coalition and changed what was acceptable to his negotiating partner, Boris Yeltsin.

Successful negotiations in the arena of ethnic politics appear to require leaders who are not themselves politicizing ethnicity but rather trying to coopt the issue in order to gain the political support of more moderate groups in society. They attempt to deny the issue to their opponents. In instances where radical forces dominate the domestic scene but all political forces express strong desires to be accepted within the international community, third parties can play a decisive role in creating conditions in which negotiations can be successfully concluded. The nature of leadership is critical in the avoidance of ethnic conflict, particularly within political systems that remain unconsolidated.

Transnational Ethnic Conflict in Africa

EDMOND J. KELLER

SINCE 1960, Africa has witnessed more than a score of civil wars, and in just the past decade between 2 and 4 million people have died in such wars. In 1993 alone, there were 5.2 million refugees and 13 million displaced persons in Africa. Domestic insecurity in Africa, then, has had an increasingly high propensity to spill over borders, resulting in new regional security dilemmas. For example, in a matter of weeks the 1994 civil war in Rwanda resulted in five hundred thousand deaths, and in more than 3 million refugees fleeing to Zaire and Tanzania. It is clear that what were once thought to be mere domestic conflicts are now increasingly seen as potential sources for regional insecurity. Domestic ethnic conflicts in places such as the former Yugoslavia, Iraq, and Rwanda have led to intense and bloody internal wars, massive refugee flows, and threats to the continuity of multiethnic nation-states.

Following the analytical framework spelled out by Lake and Rothchild in the Introduction, the purpose of this essay is fourfold: first, to identify the origins and transformation of ethnic conflicts in selected African states that have on occasion become transnationalized (Lake and Rothchild, Chapter One);[1] second, to identify the factors that contribute to the politicization of ethnicity and those that seem to explain why some incidents of politicized ethnicity spill over national borders and others do not; third, to identify the ways in which the most intense incidents of ethnically based conflict have been dealt with by regional and international institutions; and fourth, to assess the increasing challenges posed to external and regional actors who might consider some form of intervention for the purpose of assisting in the management of domestic conflicts that have or could become transnationalized.

The international community has always found it difficult to broker political solutions to the most severe incidents of ethnic conflict once they have become intense civil wars that have spread regionally (Rothchild 1995, 211). A classic example of this can be seen in the regional morass created when the Rwandan civil war in 1996 spread into eastern Zaire, as Hutu militia took refuge in camps in that region and launched attacks against the Tutsi-led government, prompting elements of the Rwandan army to penetrate into Zaire in hot pursuit. These devel-

---

[1] For the purpose of this essay, transnational conflicts are defined as those domestically based ethnic conflicts that spill or have a high potential to spill across borders or draw ethnic allies from across borders into an internal conflict. This spillover can be in the form of war, refugee flows, or ideas, and result from *diffusion* or *escalation*.

opments had devastating consequences for regional security. This and other incidents of transnationalized ethnic conflict are now challenging policymakers to come up with new and more effective approaches to conflict prevention and management.

The discussion is divided into three main sections. The first section attempts to sketch the broad dimensions of the problem in a selected number of African countries, tracing its origins to historical as well as more immediate causes. The second looks at the problem of managing transnational ethnic conflict from an intellectual as well as a policy perspective. The last section examines the policy challenge of transnational ethnic conflict in contemporary Africa.

The Origins of Transnational Ethnic Conflict in Africa

The end of the Cold War and the onset of what is being termed the "new world order" has coincided with and in some cases fueled the politicization of ethnically based nationalism, particularly in Eastern Europe and sub-Saharan Africa. The postwar international political environment had until recently been characterized by ideological competition and conflict between the United States on the one hand and the Soviet Union and Communist China on the other. Both ideological camps as a matter of policy discouraged the representation of groups based upon a distinctive ethnic identity (Ryan 1990, xix–xxi). Instead, there was an active attempt in policy circles to establish the viability of multiethnic states. This tendency in the realm of public policy was reinforced in social science scholarship, which generally ignored ethnic nationalism as a politically salient variable and focused on what was described as the process of national political integration (Young 1993, 21–23). To the extent that it existed and was relevant, scholars generally agreed that ethnic identity was different from nationalism in that it did not require separation from a given multiethnic state and the creation of an ethnically pure nation state. Today, however, in parts of Eastern Europe and Africa, the notion of the inviolability of artificially created nation states is being seriously called into question, as ethnic groups assert their right to self-determination up to and including separation from the multiethnic state. With the demise of Soviet communism, ethnically based republics that had been forcefully incorporated into the Soviet Empire took advantage of openings in the political opportunity structure, and acted upon their claim to self-determination by cutting their ties to Russia (Esman 1994, 10).[2] Crawford Young notes that in the first years of African independence secessionist movements emerged in eighteen out of fifty-two states, but were largely suppressed (except for the Eritrean struggle for national liberation between 1962 and 1991), until the end of the decade of the 1980s (Young 1993, 29).

---

[2] Esman argues that the political opportunity structure provides the context in which groups shape their strategies, tactics, and ideological goals. Openings in such structures might make it possible for even subjugated states to take action to break away from a hegemonic state.

In recent years domestic ethnic conflicts have been more common than inter-state conflict, and when these conflicts are diffused and escalate, they threaten regional security. Diffusion involves information flows from one state or ethnic community to another state or ethnic community that already contains a high potential for ethnic conflict. The new information, whether true or not, serves to inflame ethnic tensions. Escalation, on the other hand, involves ethnic groups forging alliances with transnational kin groups, with the results often being inten-tional or unintentional spillovers, irredentism, or border conflicts (Lake and Rothchild, Chapter One).

The central question addressed in this section is: how, why, and when do eth-nic conflicts in Africa become transnationalized? The roots of transnational eth-nic conflict can be traced to the perception of ethnic groups that their physical security is in jeopardy at the hands of some other ethnic group or groups (Lake and Rothchild, Chapter One). When such a situation obtains and the state is either unwilling or unable to mediate between groups or to provide them with assurances that they will be protected, groups that perceive a serious threat will at the very least prepare for violent conflict, and may even go so far as to engage in a preemptive strike. Myths and memories of exploitation, discrimination, and violence perpetrated on one group by another drive the groups further apart (Gurr 1993, 5–6).

Whether or not ethnic conflicts become transnationalized depends on certain historic and/or immediate circumstances. The historic factors can largely be traced to the invention of tribes, and with the removal of colonial social control mechanisms, the stage was set for the unleashing of *tribalism* in the post-inde-pendence period (Davidson 1992, 11–12). The more immediate causes can be categorized either as precipitant or facilitating factors. Precipitant causes might include economic or political crises with ethnic undertones, inflammatory rhetoric on the part of ethnic entrepreneurs, or real or imagined fears of an eth-nic group that incumbent elites are either unwilling or unable to make credible commitments to protect them against ethnic hostilities (Fearon, Chapter Five). Facilitating factors might include the total collapse of national government and/or the availability of massive amounts of weapons of war, as was the case in north-east Africa following the end of the Cold War. The removal of the stabilizing effects of superpower competition in the region made it much more likely that violent ethnic conflicts might occur.

Lake and Rothchild (1996a) note that under conditions of extreme insecurity and ethnic distrust, the situation is ripe for a diffusion and/or escalation of ethnic conflict across borders. Fears are diffused within states and sometimes between them. When there exist kin groups in neighboring states, ethnic conflict can either intentionally or unintentionally become transnationalized. Much depends on political opportunities as perceived by ethnic entrepreneurs. For example, Hutu militia driven out of Rwanda by the Tutsi-led Rwanda Patriotic Front in 1994, continued to wage war from across the border. By 1996 Tutsi soldiers were fighting the Hutu militia inside Zaire, and the Zairean army seemed powerless to do anything about it. In the process, the "softness" and weakness of the Zairean state was laid bare, giving rise to the emergence of internal rebel groups bent on bringing down the Mobutu regime.

The remainder of this section focuses on five cases that amply illustrate how ethnic conflict has become transnationalized in present-day Africa, particularly since the end of the Cold War. In each of these cases, over time, the primary impetus to transnationalization has shifted. In the case of Somalia in its conflict with Ethiopia over the Ogaden in 1977–1978, the near collapse of the Ethiopian nation state seemed to present an opportunity for the government of the Republic of Somalia to lend massive support to Somali irredentists in Ethiopia's Ogaden region in an effort to recapture what were claimed to be "lost" Somali lands. In other words, Ogadeni Somali irredentism, under conditions of state weakness in Ethiopia, provided the impetus for the escalation of ethnic conflict in Ethiopia as represented in the transnational alliance of Somalis against Ethiopian hegemony.

The conflict between the north and south in Sudan began as a simple quest for social justice on the part of the people of the south, but over the years it has grown into a struggle for self-determination. The diffusion of ethnic fears in the south of northern oppression largely inspired the first Sudanese civil war (1955–1972); and the failure of the Sudan national government to remain true to commitments to political and social equity in the south fueled the second, beginning in 1983.

The third and fourth of our cases, Rwanda and Burundi, represent nicely the recent social construction of distinct and hostile ethnic identities, and the diffusion and escalation of violent ethnic conflict to the extent that the scope and the intensity are widened and become transnationalized. The final case, that of the Liberian Civil War, has elements of diffusion and escalation, but is notable in the extent to which political elites, with their own personal agendas, manipulated the ethnic factor to secure the support of ethnic kinspeople, while at the same time their movements remained open to alliances with elites from other ethnic groups even as their personal political objectives remained the central focus.

Somali Irredentism

Somalia has traditionally been viewed as an ethnically homogenous state, and therefore, not very likely to be destroyed by ethnic conflict. In fact, outside observers have historically been more concerned with the territorial ambitions of a Somali state bent on reuniting what some Somali leaders argued was an historic Somali nation-state. However, what led to the collapse of the Somali state in 1991 was a combination of historical and contemporary factors.

The Somali people can trace their history as far back as 500 B.C. They claim to be the descendants of a single founding father, Samaale, and they are therefore assumed to be related by blood. On the basis of language and culture, the Somalis can be considered a nation, composed of six clan families organized along the lines of a lineage system. These are further broken down into clans, sub-clans, sub-sub-clans, and so on down to the nuclear family (Laitin and Samatar 1987).

Traditionally, the Somali people were seen to adhere to no central political authority. Yet the irredentist claims of the Ogaden Somali of Ethiopia is based upon the myth of a unified Somali state that was coterminous with the nation. This fiction became an invented memory, and inspired the Ogaden War of 1977–1978 (Adam 1995). When British and Commonwealth forces liberated Ethiopia as well as British and Italian Somaliland from the Italian fascists in 1941, some British politicians held out hope to the Somalis that life would be given to Greater Somalia once Italian East Africa was dismantled. Many Somalis came to feel that this gave legitimacy to their claim to self-determination as a coherent, pristine Somali state. However, this was not to be, as the Horn of Africa was returned to the status quo ante once the British retreated from the area.

In neighboring Ethiopia, following the demise of the imperial regime in 1974, the country descended into a state of virtual anarchy. In addition, the alliance of more than twenty years between the United States and Ethiopia was ended, and Ethiopia was vulnerable to enemies both inside and outside the country. It was in this context that the president of Somalia, Siad Barre, decided to commit massive military support to the irredentist claims of Somalis living in Ethiopia's Ogaden region. In the process Somali irredentism escalated to include kinspeople from the Republic of Somalia itself (Carment and James 1995).

In June 1977, Ethiopia was invaded by regular Somali military forces and destabilized internally by Ogadeni guerrillas. In other regions of the country the state was being challenged by other ethnic guerrilla movements. The Somali onslaught continued until early 1978, and in the process almost the entirety of the Ogaden fell briefly into Somali hands. However, Ethiopia quickly turned to the Soviet Union and its allies for assistance, and was able by the spring of 1978 to oust the Somali army and to send Ogadeni guerrillas into flight to isolated regions of the country or across the border into Somalia.

When the effort to liberate the Ogaden failed, politics reverted to its traditional intraethnic modality, at times involving whole clan families against other clan families, and at others being confined to sub-clan conflicts. Under normal circumstances this type of conflict might have remained local, but because of the massive amounts of arms in the region as a result of intensive superpower involvement in Cold War competition there, civil war became transnationalized, creating arms and refugee flows back and forth across borders. When civil war broke out in Somalia in the early 1980s, guerrillas from ethnic groups that opposed Siad Barre's clan-based pogrom took refuge in Ethiopia, and for almost a decade relied upon Ethiopia not only for safe haven but also for the military support needed to wage war against the Somali government. A 1988 peace accord between Somalia and Ethiopia forced Somali opposition groups to fight their way back into the country. The ultimate result was the complete collapse of the Somali state in early 1991.

Southern Sudan Separatism

The historic roots of the conflict in Sudan can be traced to two factors: first, Arab slave trade activities in what is presently southern Sudan, and second, the pattern of British colonial rule in Sudan. At roughly the time of the European scramble for Africa, the Sudanese state was consolidating itself under the leadership of the

Islamic spiritual and political personality known as the Mahdi. In the process, the animist and largely Nilotic south was incorporated with the Islamic and Arab north. The south was seen as nothing more than a reservoir of slave labor for sale in various parts of the Arab world. When the British assumed direct administration of Sudan in the late nineteenth century, its administration was relatively lax; in the 1920s, however, it decided to institute formal colonial rule, resulting in the administrative separation of the north from the south. The policy involved the expulsion of all northern Arab and Muslim influences from the south, and allowing the southerners to rule themselves in a traditional manner. In addition, Christian missionaries were allowed to proselytize and to erect schools in the region. At the time, the British tried to orient southern Sudan more toward its colonies south of the Sahara. The three southern provinces were declared closed districts, and Arabs and Muslims were not allowed to travel or trade there. However, as independence approached, it became clear that Britain was prepared to accede to political forces in the north that were pressing for the independence of a unified Sudan. Independence was granted on these terms in 1956 (Woodward 1990).

In the political competition that accompanied the period immediately after independence, the social, economic, and political backwardness of the south were laid bare. Many southerners came to feel that the benevolent, if neglectful, British colonial rule had been replaced by a tyrannical Arab and Muslim post-independence government, bent on Islamicizing the entire country (Viorst 1995). Despite the fact that Muslim politicians proclaimed their commitment to the equality of rights of all Sudanese, for many southerners this commitment was not credible. Some of them reverted to the historical memory of the slave trade to explain why they mistrusted the intention of the northerners. Such feelings were evident in the eruption of a mutiny among southern soldiers in August 1955. Fear and mistrust were diffused throughout the south. The mutiny marked the beginning of a seventeen-year-long civil war that only ended in 1972 following the mediatory efforts of Emperor Haile Selassie I of Ethiopia.

The uneasiness of what independence would mean for the southerners seemed to be justified by what occurred to them as soon as the independent government assumed power. Southerners became the victims of discrimination, intimidation, and disrespect in their dealings with northerners. It is important to note, however, that at this time no southern group claimed to be an historic nation with a right to self-determination. Also, although there was a diffusion of ethnic tensions in the south, conflict in the first civil war never became significantly transnationalized.

When the regime of General Gaafar Nimeri assumed power in 1969 as the result of a military coup d'état, one of its first priorities was the settlement of the civil war and the establishment of a sense of trust and cooperation in the south. Whereas successive northern-dominated governments had attempted to control the south in a hegemonic fashion, Nimeri tried to allay the fears of the south by providing the region with a measure of governmental autonomy (Lake and Rothchild 1996a, 34–35). Another manner in which southern trust was cultivated was by the government's abandonment of its efforts to create an Islamic state. For about a decade, the government sought to improve conditions in the south, while at the same time more effectively exploiting the region's natural resources.

In the end, Nimeiri's commitment to the semi-federal compromise with the south proved not to be genuine. Over the years he systematically undermined the south's autonomy, and drifted closer and closer to the Muslim Brotherhood. In 1983, he decreed a return to the shari'a (Qur'anic) laws. This prompted an immediate resumption of the civil war, and it has raged ever since. Federalism and other forms of decentralization can serve as effective confidence-building measures, but such experiments must be carefully crafted (Lake and Rothchild, Chapter Nine).

Importantly, continuing discrimination, rather than a long historical memory of ethnic chauvinism, along with an attempt to impose an assimilationist Islamic culture on the people of the south, prompted this reeruption of war (Salih 1991).

Whereas the first Sudanese civil war had been relatively contained, several factors contributed to the transnationalization of the current conflict. First, the rebels of the Sudanese People's Liberation Army were initially able to secure military assistance from Libya and Ethiopia, and later from Israel and Uganda. Second, Nimeiri was overthrown by a popular uprising in 1985. This led to a temporary restoration of secular democracy, but in 1989 Sudan witnessed a military coup by officers staunchly committed to the establishment of a unitary Islamic state. This led in turn to a dramatic expansion of refugee flows across Sudan's southern borders, and the expansion of the ranks of southern opposition forces. On the basis of their past experiences, many southerners felt that their physical security and group rights would not be respected by a government committed to shari'a law.

Third, the availability of massive quantities of arms introduced into the region as a result of superpower competition throughout the late 1970s and early 1980s has made the current conflict much more disruptive than the first civil war. Both sides have been guilty of horrendous atrocities against their adversaries. The Sudanese government has practiced a scorched-earth policy, and its forces have repeatedly engaged in indiscriminate aerial bombing in the south, forcing hundreds of thousands of southerners into refugee camps in Uganda, Ethiopia, Zaire, and Kenya (Human Rights Watch/Africa 1994). Cross-border incursions on the part of Sudanese forces led to the severing of diplomatic relations with Eritrea in 1994 and Uganda and Ethiopia in 1995, and a year later to UN-imposed sanctions against the Khartoum government.

The Invention of Tribalism in Rwanda and Burundi

The current ethnic tensions in Rwanda and Burundi are similar and yet different. In both cases the roots of conflict can be traced to the colonial era. On the one hand, the historical memory of the Hutus of Rwanda can be traced to recollection of Tutsi collaboration with Belgian colonialists, brutal administrative practices, and systematic discrimination throughout the colonial era (Newbury 1988). On the other hand, Belgian colonialism and Tutsi overlordship during the colonial era was not as violent in Burundi as in Rwanda. Instead, the Burundi tensions can be traced to the diffusion effect of Rwanda's troubles.

Ethnically, Rwanda and Burundi are virtual mirror images of one another. In each country the Hutu make up about 85 percent of the total population, and the Tutsi account for about 14 percent. The two groups speak the same language, Kirundi in Burundi and Kinyarwanda in Rwanda. They share the same customs, and historically lived relatively harmoniously for centuries before the colonial period. However, the overrule of the minority Tutsi was more rigidly institution-alized in Rwanda than in Burundi (Lemarchand 1994b).

In Rwanda, because of their ownership of cattle, the Tutsi historically estab-lished a patron-client relationship with the Hutus. When they took over the colo-nial rule of Rwanda from the Germans following the First World War, the Belgians, like the Germans before them, ruled through the existing political arrangements and showed preference toward the Tutsi in the assignment of administrative and military positions, as well as in educational opportunities. The overrule of the Tutsi became extremely harsh toward the Hutus. It was in this context that there emerged a sense of collective Hutu identity, and by the late 1950s, with the "winds of change" blowing all over the colonized world, includ-ing colonies neighboring on Rwanda, a Hutu national movement began to take shape (Newbury 1988, 114–16). Its ethnic character was reinforced in the polit-ical competition that accompanied the struggle for independence. In 1960, after several years of guerrilla warfare, Hutu insurgents succeeded in overthrowing the Tutsi political leadership. A year later the Tutsi monarchy was abolished, and independence came in 1962. Tutsi were purged from the government and the army, and systematically discriminated against. What was most important, how-ever, was that some Tutsi became refugees in countries surrounding Rwanda.

Those Tutsi who went into exile in Uganda initially were totally marginalized in that country, but eventually many young Tutsi who were descendants of Rwanda refugees joined the ranks of the National Resistance Movement of Yoweri Museveni in his fight to overthrow Idi Amin and subsequently the regimes of Milton Obote and General Tito Okello (de Waal 1994). Many Rwandans in Uganda had never forgotten either the manner in which they were deprived of their Rwanda birthright, or the periodic pogroms of the Hutu-dominated gov-ernment in Rwanda against Tutsi throughout the post-independence era.

The Tutsi have an ethnic affinity with the Hima people of Museveni, and some observers suggest that it was this connection that provided the Uganda govern-ment with the rationale for supporting the efforts of the Rwanda Patriotic Front (RPF) to return home and attempt to reclaim Tutsi citizenship rights. The ethnic tensions within Rwanda escalated when an RPF force of ten thousand armed combatants invaded northern Rwanda in October 1990, causing havoc through-out the country. Hutus, now intensely fearing for their physical safety, conjured up memories of alien Tutsi from "Ethiopia" returning to impose once again feu-dal rule over the numerically dominant Hutu (Misser 1995, 33). For many Hutu, this was an unacceptable prospect.

A cease-fire and political settlement were brokered by the Organization of African Unity (OAU) in Arusha, Tanzania, in 1992. Consequently, a formula was worked out for powersharing. However, because of differences of opinion within the Hutu leadership, the commitments of their negotiators at Arusha proved not to be credible. President Habyarimana was closely allied with Hutu militia hardliners, and he did nothing to control their excesses.

The moderate Hutu leadership that agreed to the accord came to be perceived by Hutu hard-liners as traitors, and ethnic tensions after this point intensified, culminating in the assassination at the hands of Hutu militia of President Habyarimana in April 1994. Thus was unleashed a frenzy of genocide against the Tutsi by hard-line Hutus and Hutu civilians who got caught up in the hysteria and succumbed to the spell of their leaders, who systematically called upon them to purge the society of Tutsi. Some eight hundred thousand Tutsi and moderate Hutus were murdered in a brief three-month period. The weapons used to commit genocide in most cases amounted to nothing more than farm implements and traditional weapons.

In an effort to halt the carnage, the RPF resumed full-scale war against the Hutu militia and the Rwanda army, routing them and forcing millions of civilian Hutus to flee across the borders into Zaire and Tanzania. The RPF now controls the country and is attempting to establish a government of national reconciliation, albeit under Tutsi hegemony. Yet for many Hutus in exile, this commitment is not credible not only because of past experiences but also because of the fear of vengeful retribution on the part of the Tutsis who would like to see those involved punished for their deeds.

In contrast to Rwanda, ethnic stratification in Burundi was less rigid, and Hutu-Tutsi ethnic conflict is more recent (Lemarchand 1994b). A mediating role was played in Burundian society by the institution of *ganwa*, the princely oligarchy. Princes could be from either ethnic group, but custom regarded them as ethnically distinct from either group. However, Belgian colonial rule, as in Rwanda, came to undermine the traditional system. The colonialists handed out ethnic identity cards and established a caste system very similar to that found in colonial Rwanda. The Tutsi came to be favored in all aspects of life.

There was a peaceful transition to independence under Tutsi leadership. Although some Hutu played a limited role in government just after independence, most were purged from power by subsequent regimes, both military and civilian. Some Hutus, inspired by the social revolution in Rwanda, attempted to push for their group's rights in Burundi. At the same time, the Tutsi leadership in that country was determined not to suffer the fate of the Tutsi overlords in Rwanda. They feared that a Hutu-dominated government would systematically violate their rights as citizens. Burundian Hutus attempted revolts in 1965, 1972, 1988, and 1991, but they were brutally repressed.

After 1990, at the encouragement of France and other external patrons, Burundi's Tutsi leadership began to open up the political system. In 1992, the first multiparty constitution was introduced. Subsequently in national elections in June 1993, the first Hutu president of Burundi, Melchior Ndadaye, was elected. However, the military continued to be dominated by the Tutsi, and hard-liners in

Tutsi society, including the armed forces, refused to compromise. At the same time, Hutu extremists pushed for a rapid purging of Tutsi from positions of power. Ndadaye chose a gradualist strategy, utilizing a generous formula for including Tutsi in his government and another for integrating Hutus into the military officers' corps.

Ethnic tensions continued to be diffused until Ndadaye was assassinated in October 1993, and the Tutsi-dominated military seized power once again. In the aftermath of the coup, an estimated one hundred thousand people on both sides lost their lives. Both Hutu and Tutsi used rumor and myth to incite the killings and to justify extreme acts of ethnic violence. In contrast to the recent events in Rwanda, however, this outbreak of violence seems to have been spontaneous. As many as seven hundred thousand Burundians fled to neighboring countries, and more than a million others were displaced inside the country. Through the mediation of outside actors such as the UN and the OAU, Burundi was able to restore a fragile democracy by April 1994, under Hutu leadership. The OAU engaged in preventive diplomacy in an effort to head off the escalation of ethnic conflict, but this effort failed as a Tutsi-led military coup toppled the civilian government less than two years later.

Disjointed Ethnic Conflict in Liberia

Lake and Rothchild (p. 19) have noted that, "ethnicity often provides a key marker for self-aggrandizing politicians striving to build constituencies for attaining or maintaining political power" (also Saideman, Chapter Six). In some cases the ambitions of political entrepreneurs is what drives them to encourage ethnically based conflict. This is clearly represented in the Liberian civil war.

Although the military coup staged by Sergeant Samuel K. Doe, an ethnic Krahn, in 1980 against Americo-Liberian President Tolbert had ethnic undertones, the resulting conflict remained contained inside the country. The depth of ethnic tensions in Liberia did not become manifest until after a failed coup in 1985 (Fleischman 1993, 56). Doe believed that the coup was instigated by members of the Gio ethnic group, and he systematically began to persecute that group and their kin, the Mano. On December 24, 1989, a well-organized opposition force, the National Patriotic Front of Liberia (NPFL), invaded Liberia from the Côte d'Ivoire. It was headed by a former cabinet member in Doe's government, Charles Taylor, an ethnic Gio. The NPFL targeted Krahn and Mandingo (their ethnic kin) supporters of Doe. The Liberian opposition splintered in the early 1990s, and currently is composed of at least six ethnically based armed movements, the most significant of which are the NPFL of Taylor and the United Liberian Movement for Democracy, the latter of which has a Mandingo as well as a Krahn faction. The Armed Forces of Liberia is the remnant of the forces loyal to Doe.

The level of ethnic violence reached astounding proportions, prompting the Economic Community of West African States (ECOWAS) to establish in 1990 a peacekeeping force ECOMOG, or the ECOWAS Cease-fire Monitoring Group (Vogt 1996; and Mortimer 1996). This five-nation force, led by Nigeria, was successful in at least containing the fighting by 1994, but because of the transnational nature of the situation and the lack of a unified opposition, peace has been difficult to achieve. The Côte d'Ivoire, Sierra Leone, and Guinea continue to support the NPFL; and the NPFL supports opposition forces in Sierra Leone. The support of various rebel forces by neighboring states has contributed greatly to the escalation and protraction of the conflict, despite the best efforts of external actors to make peace.

The conflict in Liberia has resulted in more than seven hundred fifty thousand Liberian refugees, and civil war and the destabilization activities of the NPFL have contributed to the creation of one hundred thousand refugees in neighboring Sierra Leone (Lyman 1991, 556). Until early 1996, the Liberian conflict had a diffusion effect on politics in Sierra Leone, where civil war also erupted.

The roots of the present conflict in Liberia, in contrast to those in Somalia, Sudan, Rwanda, and Burundi are recent, and can be attributed mostly to elite political entrepreneurship that came to be pegged to ethnic affinity. In this circumstance, historical memory is less important than an immediate sense of relative deprivation or a sense of vengeful retribution based on personal grievances that are tied by an ethnic entrepreneur to recent ethnically based excesses against one's own group.

Managing Transnational Ethnic Conflict in Africa

Although transnationalized ethnic conflict is relatively rare in Africa today, there is increasing concern in the international community with finding mechanisms for the management of domestic conflicts that have the potential to spill over borders. History has shown that permanent solutions to such conflicts are nearly impossible; therefore, success is most likely in the prevention and management of deep and potentially violent ethnic conflict. Individual countries might engage in various strategies for internally eliminating or managing ethnic differences.

Conflict Elimination

The most common options available for the *elimination* of ethnic differences range from genocide to total assimilation (McGarry and O'Leary 1993a). The incidents of ethnic cleansing that were attempted in Rwanda in 1994 clearly could be considered genocidal. This option is almost impossible to implement effectively today because of the outcry it ultimately raises in the international community. Genocidal adventures today normally are halted before they can run their course.

The assimilation option is also difficult if not impossible in situations where integration is tantamount to the establishment of hegemonic control according to the cultural preference of the ruling ethnic group. Successive Sudanese governments, including the present one, have attempted this project but have failed precisely because the objects of assimilation are not willing to abandon their own cultures completely. All of the governments of modern Ethiopia, except the present one, had tried and failed to assimilate disparate ethnic communities into a state with a common, if multiethnic, identity.

Another common option for eliminating ethnic differences that might become transnationalized would be partition or secession. This was attempted by the Ogaden Somali in 1977–1978; it is today a goal of some members of Ethiopia's Oromo ethnic group; and it is now also being seriously considered by both sides in the Sudan conflict (*Sudan Democratic Gazette* 1995, 1).

Conflict Management

Methods for *managing* ethnic differences, as opposed to eliminating them, within a country vary from the strategies of national leaders to the intervention of external actors (G. Evans 1993, 9). Domestically, leaders might engage in policies of hegemonic control or transparent state-society relations. The objective of the second alternative is to build trust. Lake and Rothchild (Chapter Nine) identify four main trust-building options for national leaders: one, demonstration of respect for all groups and their cultures; two, formal or informal power sharing; three, elections according to rules that ensure either power sharing or the minimal representation of all ethnic groups in national politics; and four, federalism or regional autonomy.

African leaders are increasingly realizing that hegemonic control is not a wise long-term ethnic conflict-management strategy. Wherever this has been tried, it has failed. This point is amply made by the Ethiopian and Sudanese examples mentioned above.

As difficult as they are to achieve, trust-building approaches to managing ethnic conflict in Africa seem to hold the most promise. In almost all cases where national leaders adopt such approaches they are likely initially to be viewed with suspicion by groups who have previously felt insecure. However, through actions and policies that demonstrate the commitment of government to respecting all groups and cultures, confidence and trust can be engendered.

Power sharing is becoming increasingly popular in Africa, with the most recent experiments being in Burundi, Djibouti, and South Africa (Shezi 1995, 199). In each of these cases a conscious attempt was made to assure ethnic groups that they had group representation at the level of national government and some measure of regional autonomy. Confidence-building measures such as these are best seen as new ethnic contracts.

Rather than genuine power sharing, however, it is more common for political leaders in Africa to demonstrate only tentative commitment to power sharing, and to present only the appearance of attempting to form governments that are characterized by broad ethnic representation at the leadership level, and that give the indication of being concerned with social equity and the equal worth of all individuals and groups. In Ethiopia, for example, the new government has introduced a number of policies intended to show its respect for all of the country's nationalities. The constitution calls for the creation of ethnically based states that possess considerable autonomy. At the same time, politics has been structured in

such a way that the Ethiopian People's Revolutionary Democratic Front dominates at all levels. So progress toward trust-building must be measured in small
degrees. Yet, it would appear that the regime recognizes its importance.

South Africa's first all-race, multiparty elections were held in 1994, according
to modified proportional representation rules. No one party was able to achieve
an absolute plurality, and a few nonviable parties were canceled out (Reynolds
1994). Subsequent negotiations resulted in the sharing of executive power by the
two strongest parties, the African National Congress and the National Party, and
the appointment of the leaders of other parties who did well in the elections to
significant cabinet posts. This seems to have been enough to engender wide confidence in South African society that the country's leaders were committed to protecting the rights of all citizens no matter what their race or ethnicity.
Consequently, negotiation over a new social contract as represented in a permanent constitution proceeded with a minimum of serious conflict or ethnic/racial
tensions.

Federalism or regional autonomy are other approaches that can be used to
build trust among groups that formally felt threatened. However, this approach is
likely to fail unless leaders are willing to make credible commitments and to
demonstrate consistently that they respect all citizens. Sudan unsuccessfully
attempted a regional autonomy strategy. It was undermined by what proved to be
a hegemonic project on the part of Islamic fundamentalists. Nigeria has been relatively more successful at making federalism work in the wake of the Biafran Civil
War. Presently, Nigeria has thirty-one states. Federalism was chosen as a strategy
in 1979, following the war, in an effort to avoid future severe ethno-regional conflict. Since then, there have been no further serious threats to the maintenance of
Nigeria's national boundaries.

No matter what strategy is chosen, success depends greatly upon the commitment of leadership. If leaders are not prone to compromise and to operate trans-
parently, ethnic tensions are bound to reemerge. And in some cases the resulting
tensions will turn into conflicts.

Increasingly some observers believe that *preventive diplomacy* should be
employed to address both interstate and intrastate sources of conflict. The objective of such a strategy would be to head off conflicts through diplomacy before
they erupt. This approach has two dimensions: early preventive diplomacy and
late preventive diplomacy. Early preventive diplomacy involves good offices and
skilled diplomacy as soon as tensions become apparent; and late preventive
diplomacy involves efforts to persuade adversarial groups to desist when conflict
appears to be imminent. A corollary to this approach would be the preventive
deployment of peacekeeping troops in order to serve as a deterrent to conflict (G.
Evans 1993, 39). To be most effective, such deployments should be robust,
involving a sizable contingent of appropriately armed peacekeepers with clearly
defined rules of engagement.

Once conflicts occur, preventive diplomacy and preventive deployment must
give way to *peace making*. In such cases, arbitration and mediation on the part of
third parties is called for. Such actors might be internal to the troubled country,

and represented by a person of high moral standing, or someone who appears to be neutral to the given conflict, or an individual with widespread charismatic appeal. However, with regard to the most intractable conflicts in Africa, the trend seems to be toward the intervention of external actors: individuals such as former President Jimmy Carter or Archbishop Desmond Tutu and President Nelson Mandela of South Africa; government officials representing one or another major power; representatives of the UN, the OAU, or sub-regional organizations such as ECOWAS and the Intergovernmental Agency for Drought and Development (IGADD). Under the auspices of the OAU, former Tanzanian president Julius Nyerere provided good offices between 1995 and 1997 to stem the spread of the ethnic conflicts in Rwanda and Burundi.

In the aftermath of the Cold War, the controls exercised by the superpowers over regional clients in Africa have been removed, and the possibility of growing numbers of incidents of transnationalized ethnic conflicts is increasing. The realities of this situation have encouraged African leaders seriously to reconsider the norms of external intervention for the purpose of settling domestic disputes (Keller 1997).

The UN, like the OAU, has historically supported the idea of the inviolability of the national boundaries of African states that existed at the time of independence. Consequently, it has been unwilling to become involved in adjudicating boundary disputes among neighboring states, and it has generally stayed out of mediating domestic conflicts. Until recently, the UN intervention in the Congo crisis in the early 1960s was the only incident in which the UN decided to commit troops in an effort to restore peace in Africa (Jackson 1982). At the time many observers seemed to believe that this action would serve notice that the UN would intervene anywhere in Africa where a communist threat was perceived. However, the Congo operation proved to be unique and was never repeated.

Despite its record in this area, in the 1990s the UN began to rethink the notion of state sovereignty and the norms of intervention in domestic disputes. This was prompted by Iraq's brutal repression of the Kurds in the aftermath of the Gulf War (Stremlau 1991). Also, civil war in Somalia catalyzed the UN into action first on humanitarian and then on political grounds. In the spring of 1992 the organization committed peacekeeping troops to Somalia in an operation called United Nations Operation in Somalia (UNOSOM) I. The primary motivation was humanitarian. The force was to clear the way for desperately needed food deliveries to an estimated 1.5 million Somalis threatened by war-induced famine. In late 1992 the Security Council authorized the deployment of a U.S.-led military force, UNOSOM II, to protect relief workers as they attempted to reach at-risk populations. Whereas the United States defined its role in strictly humanitarian terms, the UN envisioned a wider role for UN forces: to disarm the armies of local warlords and create an enabling environment for the restoration of a Somali national government. The latter objective proved to be a failure, as the UN was unable to make peace among warring leaders of ethnic factions or to build peace by creating an enabling environment for the return of civil government grounded in the trust of the general population.

The lessons of Somalia have forced the leaders of the international community to look more carefully at the possibility of regionally based approaches to the regulation of ethnic conflicts that either are or have a good possibility of spreading regionally. Following the UN's embarrassment in Somalia, its former negotiator in the conflict, Mohamed Sahnoun (1994, 54), asserted, "The UN headquarters must establish strong permanent and functional relationships with the regional organizations so that they can coordinate their response to specific needs in different regions of the world. The current system is not adapted to the post-Cold War international environment and routinely reacts to crisis through improvisation."

Apart from the failure of adversaries to make credible commitments in the course of third-party negotiations, much of the blame for failures in such efforts must be laid at the feet of the international community, which has always been reluctant to intervene either coercively or noncoercively in conflicts where they do not perceive their vital national interest to be at stake (Lake and Rothchild, Chapter Nine). Even when regional actors, despite lacking the resources to do so effectively, are willing to attempt to manage their own problems, the international community has historically been reluctant to provide support for regionally based interventions. This has particularly been so in the case of African disputes.

The OAU has from time to time been willing to try and engage in peacekeeping in domestic conflicts that have become regionalized, but it has not had the wherewithal to do so effectively. Such was the case in the first major OAU peacekeeping effort in Chad in 1981–1982. It was underfinanced, and plagued by logistical problems.

The most successful inter-African peacekeeping effort to date has been that mounted by ECOMOG in 1991, with the objective of restoring peace and order in Liberia. After five years of peacekeeping, the West African units of ECOMOG were augmented by troops from Uganda and Tanzania. By August 1995, some semblance of order had been restored, and a government of national reconciliation had been agreed to by warring parties (*Los Angeles Times,* August 1995, p. A10).

Although it was founded to manage conflict among member states and to represent their interests in international forums, the OAU has played more of a reactive role in addressing threats to national and regional security, working through informal channels rather than through established mediation and conciliation institutions.

POLICY CHALLENGES OF TRANSNATIONAL ETHNIC CONFLICT IN AFRICA

African leaders have increasingly come to feel that the security, stability, and development of every African country affects every other African country, and Africa cannot hope to make progress toward development or democracy without creating the conditions and institutions necessary for lasting solutions to problems of security and instability. In this spirit, at the 1992 OAU Summit in Dakar,

Senegal, a resolution was passed calling for the establishment of an OAU Mechanism for Conflict Prevention and Resolution (Organization of African Unity 1993). The Mechanism was formally approved the following year, even though it was unclear as to how much authority it would have to intervene in the affairs of member states. Early indications are that the member states of the OAU have not adopted an attitude conducive to the establishment of Wilsonian multilateral collective security management system. In other words, it is not clear whether the notions of state sovereignty and the norms of intervention will indeed be altered in the process of implementing the Mechanism.

The primary objective of the Mechanism is said to be the "anticipation and prevention of conflicts." In situations in which conflicts have occurred, the Mechanism is supposed to be responsible for undertaking peacemaking and peace-building activities. In cases of severe conflict, there is a provision for OAU cooperation with the UN. Such was the case in late 1996, when African troops were committed to the humanitarian force organized under UN auspices to ensure the delivery of food and other relief supplies to Rwandan refugees in the war-torn Great Lakes region of Central Africa.

The obstacles to the successful implementation of the Mechanism are formidable. Chief among these is cost. Bilateral aid donors and the UN have made contributions, but many more resources are needed (Washington Office on Africa 1995). At its 1995 Summit, the OAU made some tentative strides toward addressing some of its funding needs. First, the secretary general threatened to cut off speaking and voting rights for the leaders of countries behind in their dues, which resulted in the immediate infusion of some $20 million (*Pretoria News* 1995). Second, the leaders in attendance, demonstrating a firm commitment to the Mechanism, agreed to place their armed services on standby for possible intervention in increasingly unstable Burundi. These actions were preceded by the inauguration of the Cairo Center for African Crisis Solving, which hosted a one-month training course for twenty-eight military officers from fourteen African countries on conflict prevention and management. A similar center is planned for Harare, Zimbabwe. Eventually the OAU plans to create a continental "rapid deployment force." Troops would be drawn from standing national armies and trained and deployed from one of the two centers. The force would operate under the aegis of the UN (*Agence France Presse* 1995a).

At the root of the funding difficulties is the fact that, Africa is composed of fifty-three of the poorest countries in the world, many of which are characterized by unstable politics and food insecurity. Their militaries are small and they already spend too much on military purposes. How then will they afford over time to participate in the Mechanism? Who is to pay for the training and upkeep of the elite troops that a country must make available to the inter-Africa peacekeeping force?

Another pitfall has to do with state sovereignty and the norms of external intervention. Will the OAU in fact be able to assert its assigned authority when crises emerge? Will the Mechanism be obstructed by member states who have yet to buy into the new conceptualizations of state sovereignty and the norms of intervention? Although African leaders tend to agree that the Mechanism is needed, it is unclear what most would do if they were confronted with a situation in which the OAU Mechanism had been employed to resolve conflicts in their own country. Certainly such intervention would be more likely in smaller and weaker states (such as Burundi). But even then, the decision to intervene in any country will not be taken easily. For example, at its 1995 Summit in Addis Ababa, Ethiopia, the OAU secretary general received widespread support from member states in attendance to make some of their troops available for peacekeeping duties in Burundi (*Agence France Presse* 1995b); however, low-intensity ethnic warfare has continued in Burundi, and the OAU has only committed military and civilian monitors to the country. The OAU might also feel more impelled to intervene in places where the state has completely collapsed (such as Somalia and Liberia), but peacemaking would be very difficult if not impossible when armed conflict is intense and the mutual mistrust of the adversaries is high. The OAU is least likely to contemplate direct intervention in larger and stronger states or where a state is highly unstable but still coherent (such as Sudan and Nigeria).

In cases of the most severe conflicts, the OAU continues to support subregional initiatives such as the peacekeeping efforts of ECOMOG in Liberia and the mediation of IGADD in the case of Sudan and Somalia. Such regional capacities, however, are still in their incipient phases, and fraught with all the problems attributed above to the new OAU mechanism. For example, the ECOMOG operation is very expensive and it is unclear how long the participating nations can continue to maintain a presence in Liberia. In Sudan, IGADD in 1995 tried to impose some conditions for negotiation on the government of Sudan, the IGADD Declaration of Principles (Legum 1995, 32). The Principles call for the right to self-determination for all Sudanese people up to and including secession, and the commitment to a separation of religion and the state. These principles have resulted in a stalemate in the mediation process, and in the meantime Sudan's relations with its neighbors (except for Kenya) have badly deteriorated.

What has become abundantly clear by the mixed results of the intervention of regional and international actors in efforts to bring peace to the most severe cases of ethnically and culturally based conflicts in Africa such as Sudan, Somalia, Liberia, and Rwanda is that constructing peace is a multifaceted process. It works best when such an intervention preempts the eruption of ethnically or culturally based conflicts in deeply divided societies.

External intervention would be most effective if it were indirect and represented in the material and logistical support of UN or regional efforts. Rich countries such as the United States, Britain, and France could make significant contributions through behind-the-scenes mediation and financial and technical assistance to regional peace initiatives.

In cases where conflict has erupted and spread regionally, the activities of outside actors cannot be confined to peacekeeping—that is, the containment of actual military activity on the part of ethnic adversaries. The further challenge is to develop effective political strategies for peacemaking. Most often severe ethnic conflicts are inspired and promoted by leadership with their own personal agendas. Unless leaders declare that they are committed to peace, and are willing to demonstrate that they are serious, tensions will remain and may even escalate. Depending upon the character of a given state and the size and military capacity of the ethnic groups in question, a conflict may or may not be highly likely to become transnationalized. In the Lilliputian state of Djibouti, for example, the Front for the Restoration of Unity and Democracy (FRUD), representing the minority Afar people in a struggle with the Issa-dominated government of Hassan Gouled Aptidon, has been unable to separate Djibouti's northwest area from that country; nor has it been able to rely upon safe haven in Ethiopia from which to launch attacks against the government. FRUD now appears to be willing to settle for social justice within the context of the current state (*Humanitarian Monitor* 1995, 37). By contrast, in South Africa, Chief Mangosuthu Buthelesi, claiming to be the leader of a Zulu nation with historic roots, has recently encouraged his followers to resist the imposition of federalism on the Zulus by any means necessary. The South African state would appear to be sufficiently strong in military terms to stave off the secession of Zululand. However, unless preventive diplomacy or other peacemaking measures are taken early, the result could be an ethnic rebellion that spreads widely and causes severe problems of regional and national security. The Zulu are South Africa's largest African ethnic group, with ethnic kinspeople in several neighboring countries. Zulu identity, to be sure, is a relatively recent social construct that has been dramatically expanded throughout the twentieth century. Currently, in the context of the rapid political and social changes taking place in South Africa, the potential for severe ethnic conflict in the Zulu areas is real, and calls out for immediate domestic and international peace initiatives.

CONCLUSION

Severe ethnically based conflicts, as we have seen, are generally based on elements of a group's historical memory, fear of physical insecurity, and upon perceived or real discrimination, inequalities, or inequities. Any peace effort must find ways of addressing these problems through public policies and programs to build trust of one another among constituent ethnic groups; and to engender a sense that government is credibly committed to respecting and protecting the rights of all groups. The securing of the commitment of political leaders to social justice, establishing a government that is transparent and honest, and making sure that the political system operates according to the principles of democracy would go a long way toward effective conflict management and peace-building.

CHAPTER THIRTEEN

Preventive Diplomacy and Ethnic Conflict: Possible, Difficult, Necessary

BRUCE W. JENTLESON

THE BASIC LOGIC of preventive diplomacy is unassailable.[1] Act early to prevent disputes from escalating or problems from worsening. Reduce tensions that if intensified could lead to war. Deal with today's conflicts before they become tomorrow's crises. It is the same logic as preventive medicine: don't wait until the cancer has spread or the arteries are nearly fully clogged; or as the auto mechanic says in a familiar television commercial as he holds an oil filter in one hand and points to a seized-up car engine with the other, "Pay me now or pay me later."

Indeed, invocations of the need to expand and enhance the practice of preventive diplomacy have been heard from virtually all quarters of the post-Cold War world:

- from the outset of the Clinton administration, as in the emphasis by then-Secretary of State Warren Christopher in his 1993 confirmation hearings on the need for "a new diplomacy that can anticipate and prevent crises . . . rather that simply manage them"; the advocacy by then-National Security Advisor Anthony Lake for "greater emphasis on tools such as mediation and preventive diplomacy" so that "in addition to helping solve disputes, we also help prevent disputes"; and the assertion by AID Administrator J. Brian Atwood that whereas "containment of communism defined our national security policy for nearly half a century . . . the Clinton administration has made crisis prevention a central theme of its foreign policy" (Binder and Crossette 1993; Atwood 1994).

- from the United Nations, as in the January 1992 call by the UN Security Council, in its first-ever summit meeting at the level of heads of state and government, for "recommendations on ways of strengthening . . . the capacity of the United Nations for preventive diplomacy, for peacemaking and for peacekeeping," and the ensuing report by UN Secretary General Boutros Boutros-Ghali, *An Agenda for Peace,* which devoted a full chapter to preventive diplomacy (Boutros-Ghali 1992: 13–19);

Note: The author thanks Alexander George for his comments on an earlier draft. A version of this chapter appeared under the same title as University of California Institute on Global Conflict and Cooperation (IGCC), Policy Paper No. 27, June 1996.

[1] As a formal definition Lund (1997) offers a useful though somewhat lengthy definition: actions, policies, and institutions used to keep particular states or organized groups within them from threatening or using organized violence, armed force, or related forms of coercion as the way to settle either interstate or national political disputes, especially where and when the existing means cannot peacefully manage the destabilizing effects of economic, social, political, and international change.

- from regional multilateral organizations such as the Conference on (now Organization for) Security and Cooperation in Europe (CSCE/OSCE), which was committed in its 1990 Charter of Paris for a New Europe to "seek new forms of cooperation . . . [on] ways for preventing, through political means, conflicts which may emerge"; and the Organization of African Unity (OAU), which has established new mechanisms in the past few years which "have, as a primary objective, the anticipation and prevention of conflicts."
- from a broad range of nongovernmental organizations (NGOs), so many of which end up on the front lines of humanitarian relief efforts seeking to ameliorate the consequences of the failures of prevention;
- from elite associations, think tanks and scholars, which have been both issuing studies and pursuing action through "track-two" diplomacy, such as the Carnegie Commission for Preventing Deadly Conflict and the Council on Foreign Relations Center for Preventive Action.

Yet despite the unassailability of the basic logic and all the invocations and initial initiatives, the track record of these first years of the post-Cold War era is not particularly encouraging. Croatia, Bosnia, Somalia, Rwanda, Nagorno Karabakh, Chechnya, Tajikistan, "Kurdistan"—the list goes on to include over ninety armed conflicts since the fall of the Berlin Wall, the vast majority of which have been ethnic conflicts. Indeed, in the view of then-U.S. Defense Secretary William Perry, it is ethnic conflict that is driving "much of the need for military forces in the world today" (1994).

Some have questioned whether the whole concept of preventive diplomacy is yet another false and misleading "alchemy for a new world order" (Stedman 1995). That it has been oversold, its difficulties underestimated, and its risks undervalued is a fair criticism. But to simply write it off would be to commit the mirror-image mistake of those too eager and uncritical in their embrace. Instead, in my view we need to proceed from three basic postulates:

- preventive diplomacy is possible;
- preventive diplomacy is difficult;
- preventive diplomacy is necessary.

The purpose of this chapter is to develop and support these postulates as a step toward refining the concept of preventive diplomacy, de-reifying any remaining promises of panacea, and otherwise moving from appealing idea to usable foreign policy strategies (see also Jentleson, forthcoming 1998). After first developing a working definition for the term *preventive diplomacy* in the next section, I then address each of these postulates—possible, difficult, necessary—drawing both on theoretical-conceptual arguments and empirical evidence form recent major cases.

DEFINING PREVENTIVE DIPLOMACY

Two aspects of the definition need to be established:

- general conceptual parameters for a working definition of the term; and
- methodological considerations in measuring success and failure.

Conceptual Parameters for a Working Definition

Michael Lund (1996) attributes the coining of the term *preventive diplomacy* to UN Secretary General Dag Hammarksjold in 1960 when he referred, in the Cold War context, to UN efforts "to keep localized international disputes from provoking larger confrontations between the superpowers." More recently, it has been applied to an unmanageably broad range of activities, objectives, and policies, including people-to-people conflict-resolution dialogues, crisis-prevention mediation, war deescalation and termination, democracy building, economic development, and the eradication of poverty—even environmental preservation. No wonder that one former State Department official referred to it as "a buzz word among diplomats" (Stremlau 1995, 29).

Table 13.1 presents a framework drawing out the conceptual parameters of preventive diplomacy as differentiated from other major forms of diplomacy based on three criteria:

- the likelihood of mass violent conflict;
- the intended time frame in which the diplomatic activity seeks impact; and
- the principal objectives of the diplomatic action.

This is not intended as a comprehensive typology, but is suggested rather for definitional and heuristic utility. At one end is *normal diplomacy,* the day-to-day interactions of what Sir Harold Nicolson called "the management of relations between independent States by processes of negotiation" (Nicolson 1980: 41). Although such normal diplomacy regularly involves situations in which disputes and debates do exist (and thus it can be said to seek to be preventive), to the extent that there is no significant likelihood of mass violence, that there is a relatively nonpressing time frame, and that the objectives are regularized management through accepted channels, it is useful to acknowledge its normality and keep it distinct. At the other end is *war diplomacy,* involving situations in which violent conflict has already broken out, making the time frame an immediate one, with the objective of limiting or ending the conflict. One of the problems with the definition of preventive diplomacy laid out by UN Secretary General Boutros Boutros-Ghali in his *Agenda for Peace*—"action to prevent disputes from arising between parties, to prevent existing disputes from escalating into conflicts, and to limit the spread of the latter when they occur" (1992, 13)—is that the final clause blurs the distinction between preventing war or other mass violence from happening, and containing war and mass violence that have already begun. It is not that war and peace necessarily are dichotomous states of affairs, but in the same way that scholars who study war have needed to establish threshold criteria (Singer and Small 1972), it is useful to distinguish between diplomacy intended to prevent the occurrence of a war from diplomacy seeking to limit the intensification of a war.

We use the term *developmentalist diplomacy* to refer to efforts to address long-term societal and international problems which, if allowed to worsen, have the potential to lead to violent conflict. In this regard, John Stremlau cites a 1994 chapter of the Organization for Economic Cooperation and Development which

TABLE 13.1
Differentiating Preventive Diplomacy

	Normal diplomacy	Developmentalist diplomacy	Preventive diplomacy	War diplomacy
Likelihood of violent conflict	low	potential	imminent	existing
Time frame	ongoing	long-term	short, medium term	immediate
Principal objectives	management of relations	economic development, state-building	prevent crises and wars	war limitation and termination

stressed the importance of thinking about development in terms that extend beyond strictly economic calculations and recognize that "successfully managing competing interests and loyalties in societies is the vital prerequisite for both achieving successful development and for containing disputes and conflicts . . . (to) bring peace and development closer together" (Stremlau 1995, 35–36). Although this long-term perspective is valid, encompassing it in a working definition of preventive diplomacy would raise a problem of over-inclusiveness similar to that with the other two categories. There is a difference, as the Carnegie Commission for Preventing Deadly Conflict (1995, 4) points out, between prevention as "a long-term, structural approach" and situations that demand "immediate operational steps to build a firebreak against the outbreak and spread of mass violence."

The optimal conceptualization of *preventive diplomacy* is one that focuses on these firebreak-type objectives. It involves situations in which the likelihood of violent mass conflict is imminent—not yet existing, but also not low or just potential; the time frame is short to medium term—not immediate, but also not just a matter of ongoing relations or the long-term; and the objectives are to take the necessary diplomatic action within the limited time frame to prevent those crises or wars which seem imminent.

A further definitional point concerns the instruments and strategies included as part of the preventive diplomacy tool box. Although these are discussed further in a later section, the general point to be made here is that both coercive and noncoercive measures are included. The *Agenda for Peace* report explicitly identifies the preventive deployment of military forces as one of the strategies to which its definition of preventive diplomacy refers. Other efforts to define the term have sought to confine it to "nonviolent interactions that lead to constructive dialogue between adversaries," explicitly excluding "the use of armed forces" (Thompson and Gutlove 1994, 5). The problem with such a definition is that it ignores purposiveness and lapses into a posing of force and diplomacy as antithetical. They can be, of course, but they don't have to be. Preventive diplomacy, no less than other forms of diplomacy, often needs to be backed by the threat if not the actual use of force.

Methodological Considerations in Measuring Success and Failure

There are three complicating methodological problems in attempting to assess the record of preventive diplomacy.

The first is that in either assessment one must rely at least somewhat on *counterfactual* reasoning. To assess a case as a preventive diplomacy failure is to argue that violent conflict would have been avoided or at least limited if, irrespective of other factors, this particular factor had been different. Similarly, a case assessed as a success implies that were it not for the impact of preventive diplomacy it is at least likely that a major conflict would have occurred. This is a situation similar to that in other areas of international relations theory, such as deterrence and the debates over optimal explanations of deterrence failure and reliable identification of deterrence successes (see, for example, George and Smoke 1974; Lebow and Stein 1990). The key, as it has been for the deterrence literature and as it is for all efforts at counterfactual explanation, is both to establish the theoretical basis for the logic of the alternative hypothesized path and to support it empirically as strongly as possible (Tetlock and Belkin 1996; Fearon 1991).

The second problem is the need for a degree of *relativity* in the measurement scale sufficient to allow for shades of gray but not so much as to lose all evaluative reliability. On one end this means making some distinction between the success of avoiding the negative and the success of fully achieving the positive. With cases of failure, which often seem to have much less gray to them, it adds to the utility of analysis if any efficacious policies can be sifted out of the wreckage. There are very few cases of ethnic conflict that have ended up totally resolved, and it is doubtful there ever will be. But we do not serve our goal of gaining analytic insights into the sources of or the solutions for ethnic conflicts if our assessments are not sensitive to differences of degree.

The third problem is the frequent *transitoriness* of designations of success. A policy may initially appear to have achieved its objectives, but then at a later date may break down. What if the immediate goal of preventing a crisis is achieved, but a year later the ethnic groups are again warring? Or if a major conflict has been averted, but only because the peacekeeping mission continues to be deployed, with no end in sight? And when can societal conflict resolution initiatives be said to have taken hold? At what benchmark can we say that preventive-diplomacy institution building has reached robustness? Conceptually, if not as a matter of policy, we may need to develop a preventive-diplomacy equivalent to the criteria used in the economic domain, where countries "graduate" from such economic assistance programs as foreign aid and the Generalized System of Preferences.

THE POSSIBILITY OF PREVENTIVE DIPLOMACY

Working from this definition, the first key question is: How strong is the basis for postulating that preventive diplomacy is possible? This is not to go so far as to claim that some policy X definitely would have prevented ethnic cleansing in Bosnia, or some policy Y would surely have rebuilt the Somali state, or some policy Z prevented genocide in Rwanda. It is, however, also not to accept the assertion that nothing else could have been done, as if there was an inevitability in these conflicts degenerating to the levels of violence that they did.

There are three principal bases for asserting the possibility of preventive diplomacy: analysis of the purposive rather than primordialist sources of ethnic conflict; the case evidence of opportunities that did exist for effective preventive diplomacy, but which were missed; and the case evidence of conflicts that had the potential to escalate to war or other mass violence, but in which preventive action was taken with relative success (see also Jentleson, forthcoming 1998).

The Purposive Sources of Ethnic Conflict

A first point derives directly from the emphasis throughout this volume on the sources of ethnic conflict as being less "primordialist" than "purposive" in either or both of the instrumentalist and constructivist conceptualizations. If the primordialist view were valid and ethnicity was in fact a fixed and inherently deeply conflictual historical identity, such that the conflicts of the 1990s were primarily continuations of ones going back hundreds of years—such as "Balkan ghosts" going back to the fourteenth century, the tracing back of Somali clan rivalries to the precolonial pastoral period, the medieval *buhake* agricultural caste system of Tutsi dominance over Hutu—then it would be hard to hold out much prospect for preventive diplomacy. The problem with the primordialist view, though, as David Lake and Donald Rothchild state in their introductory essay, "is its assumption of fixed identities and its failure to account for variations in the level of conflict over time and place. In short, the approach founders on its inability to explain the emergence of new and transformed identities or account for the long periods in which either ethnicity is not a salient political characteristic or relations between different ethnic groups are comparatively peaceful."

Although Lake and Rothchild delineate differences in the instrumentalist and constructivist approaches, the complementarities between them as purposive explanations and their collective differentiation from primordialist theories bear more directly on my point here. Purposive explanations do acknowledge deep-seated intergroup dispositional antagonisms, but also bring out the ways in which ethnicity is a "socially constructed" identity linked to the distribution of political power and economic privilege within a society. They stress the calculated role played by what Timur Kuran calls "ethnic activists" in activating and fomenting these tensions in order to serve their own political objectives. Kuran (Chapter Two in this volume) cites Donald Horowitz on how "group identity tends to expand or contract to fill the political space available for expression." It follows that to the extent that international efforts can limit the available political space, group identity will be able to do less expanding. Similarly, in another chapter in this volume, Stephen Saideman stresses the impact of expectations of international opposition on the likelihood of secessions. And as we consider recent cases, this purposive view can better explain why, for example, the ethnic groups of the Balkans have not always been at each other's throats, only to be led into ethnic warfare by the "purposeful actions of political actors who actively create(d) violent conflict," serving their own domestic political agendas by "selectively drawing on history in order to portray it as historically inevitable." The Somali conflict also was not just an extension of historical tensions, but the consequence of the politicization of clan relations by the dictator Siad Barre and, ultimately, against him. In Rwanda the genocide was not "the spontaneous slaughter of one group by another" but rather was "actively promoted by political and military leaders" (Glenny 1993, 19; Gagnon 1994–1995; Hirsch and Oakley 1995; Adelman and Suhrke 1996, 2; Suhrke and Jones, forthcoming 1998). As with any purposeful action, calculations of costs and benefits were made in each of these cases, which means that, as Gagnon states for the ex-Yugoslavia case, "outside actors" could have prevented or moderated the conflict had they taken actions that would have made "the external costs of such conflict so high that the conflict itself would endanger the domestic power structure" (Gagnon 1994–1995, 164–65).

Case Evidence of Opportunities Missed

A second point is the strong evidence from a number of recent cases that the international community *did* have specific and identifiable opportunities to have some impact to limit if not prevent these conflicts, but its statecraft was flawed, inadequate, or even absent. Again, one must acknowledge the counterfactual limits to what could or would or might have happened. And one must self-consciously base any such arguments on what genuinely was knowable and doable at the time, and not just in retrospect, or be vulnerable to the "Monday morning quarterbacking" fallacy. Nevertheless, such caveats notwithstanding, the case literature from both analysts and policymakers strongly and credibly points to warnings that were available at the time, to options that were proposed, and to patterns in the behavior and responses of leaders and parties to the various conflicts that indicate that different policies were possible, and such policies had plausible chances of positive impact.

There is, of course, the question in identifying missed opportunities of how far to go back in the etiology of a conflict. In the Somalia case, for example, while U.S. support for dictator Siad Barre was deemed successful in terms of serving immediate 1970s–1980s geopolitical objectives against the Soviets and their client state Ethiopia, by paying little attention to the mounting corruption, economic mismanagement, and repression, it contributed to the eventual collapse of the Somali state. In a more proximate sense, Mohamed Sahnoun, a noted African diplomat who served in 1992 as head of the United Nations Operation in Somalia (UNOSOM), points specifically to the failure of the United States, the United Nations, and others in the international community to respond to the 1988 uprising in the north led by the Somali National Movement despite ample and available evidence ("early warning") of mass killings and wanton destruction by Siad

Barre's forces. The violence was documented both by human rights groups and by the U.S. State Department: "The world community was clearly witnessing a serious crisis in which a large population faced the dire consequences of what was to be a civil war. One would expect that in the absence of a democratic mechanism allowing for corrective measures, the international community would come to the rescue of the victimized population. It did not" (Sahnoun 1994, 6).

Sahnoun also cites three other missed opportunities: following the May 1990 Manifesto signed by 144 prominent political leaders, when "the world watched" while Siad Barre arrested many of the signatories; the fall of Siad Barre in January 1991 and the efforts by the Ethiopian and Eritrean governments to convene a reconciliation conference, which "came to nothing, however, because of lack of international and regional support"; and the ensuing attempt by the Djibouti government in July 1991 to organize a conference, only to have its request for support from the UN "refused with no explanation except that the matter was too complicated" (Sahnoun 1994, 8–10). Another study differs somewhat in the identification and analysis of the particular points of missed opportunity, but is no less adamant in arguing against inevitability (Menkhaus and Ortmayer, forthcoming 1998).

In the Yugoslavia case, again without going too far back but also keeping primary focus on the stages prior to the descent into mass violence, one finds a repeated emphasis on a number of particular points of inaction or flawed policies. Former U.S. Ambassador to Yugoslavia Warren Zimmerman is among those who point to the failure by Western governments, most blatantly Germany, to abide by the principle established by UN special envoys Cyrus Vance and Lord Carrington in the summer of 1991 not to grant diplomatic recognition to any Yugoslav republic until all had agreed on their mutual relationship. "If this simple principle had been maintained, less blood would have been shed in Bosnia," Zimmerman reasonably claims in measured terms. Zimmerman also points to the failure of NATO to respond to the shelling of Dubrovnik in October 1991: "Not only would damage to the city have been averted, but the Serbs would have been taught a lesson about Western resolve that might have deterred at least some of the aggression in Bosnia. As it was, the Serbs learned another lesson . . . that there was no Western resolve, and that they could push about as far as their power would take them" (Zimmerman 1995, 13–14).

In his analysis, Lawrence Freedman emphasizes the opportunity missed in the initial use of economic sanctions against Serbia; they were proclaimed with much fanfare but without any serious efforts at enforcement. Indeed, once the West became serious about enforcing the sanctions, they were a key factor pressuring Serbia to agree to peace terms; this reinforces the converse corollary of both the coercive opportunity missed and the credibility-damaging signal sent when the reality of the sanctions fell far short of the rhetoric. Freedman, Rieff, Malcolm, and others also point to a number of other aspects of U.S. and European policies in 1991–1992 that were much too little when it still may not have been too late (Freedman 1994–1995, 60; Rieff 1995; Malcolm 1994). The same logic fits the use of NATO air power which, when finally used brought substantial coercive leverage yet which earlier had been repeatedly threatened but not employed.

In the Rwanda case there is ample evidence of the availability of early warnings that were yet again met by flawed or otherwise inadequate preventive-diplomacy responses by the United Nations, the United States, France, and Belgium. Even going back to the late 1980s and early 1990s, information about violent conflicts, military buildups, human rights violations, and escalating political tensions came to policymakers from UN agencies such as the United Nations High Commission for Refugees (UNHCR), the OAU, Western ambassadors in the capital Kigali, human-rights and other NGOs, and others. This made for at least three "windows of opportunity" as identified in a detailed and revealing study by a Canadian–Norwegian research team (Adelman and Suhrke 1996; Suhrke and Jones, forthcoming 1998). First, in 1989 and early 1990, both the OAU and the UNHCR had gathered sufficient information on the increasing volatility of the long-standing refugee problem (mostly Tutsis in Uganda) to seek to take a series of initiatives, but they received little support from the United States or Western Europe. Less that a year later, on October 1, 1990, the Tutsi Rwandan Patriotic Front invaded from the refugee camps in Uganda and set off a civil war. Second, a key reason for the collapse of the 1992–1993 Arusha Accords which established Hutu–Tutsi power sharing was the failure of the international community to buttress them with tough and credible measures against violations and extremist violators. Proposals to make economic assistance conditional on respect for human rights were resisted by both the United States and the Europeans. The hatred-fomenting broadcasts of Radio Milles Collines were met with little more than yet another demarche to Hutu President Habyarimana. And although a UN peacekeeping force was authorized (UNAMIR, the United Nations Assistance Mission in Rwanda), it was slow to be deployed, it was staffed at less than one-third the level of recommended troops, and its mandate was limited despite repeated requests from its commander for greater authority. Consequently, when in April 1994 the genocide was launched, "UNAMIR lacked everything from sandbags to APCs [armored personnel carriers] to protect either its own troops or civilians" (Adelman and Suhrke 1996, 40). Again, although it was not conclusive or certain, there was substantial early warning available, including a leak in January 1994 from a Rwandan informant on a plan by Hutu extremists to launch an assassination campaign against Tutsi and moderate Hutu politicians.

Third, the first week of the crisis is pointed to as providing an opportunity to prevent the killing from reaching the extremes that it did. Adelman and Suhrke fault the UN for limiting the options to either building up UNAMIR sufficiently to be able to intervene between the two armies, or withdrawing. The UN did not recognize the possibility of a third option: increasing troop strength sufficiently to protect civilians. Adelman and Suhrke spread the fault between Secretary General Boutros-Ghali, who was off on a trip in the former Soviet Union and Eastern Europe during the critical days, and the unresponsiveness of the major powers, including the United States. However the blame is distributed, the point is that opportunities were missed (Adelman and Suhrke 1996, 12–16).

Case Evidence of Successful Preventive Diplomacy

The third basis for the assertion that preventive diplomacy can be successful comes from the comparative perspective of other cases that quite plausibly could have become deadly conflicts but in which preventive action was taken with relative success. In cases like Macedonia, another ex-Yugoslav republic with a volatile ethnic mix, and which shares a border with Serbia, or the Congo Republic, where internal ethnic violence was limited in 1992–1993 (although not in 1997), we are on solid analytical ground in contending that ethnic warfare was a distinct possibility. A brief discussion of each case shows the key role played by external actors and their preventive diplomacy in averting major conflict.

The earlier methodological point about transitoriness needs be borne in mind in attributing success to a case in progress like Macedonia (Leatherman 1996; Lund, forthcoming 1998). Any number of factors still may cause unforseen developments there. Nevertheless, the point will hold that although both Croatia and Bosnia exploded in mass violence, international diplomacy prevented its spread to Macedonia. Credit is widely shared. The Bush administration issued a firm and unequivocal warning to Milosevic against Serb repression and violence against the ethnic Albanians in Kosovo, a previously autonomous province within Serbia that borders Macedonia. Had violence broken out in Kosovo it could have drawn in Albania and also spread to Macedonia which has a large ethnic Albanian population. In addition, an international presence was established on the ground early in Macedonia. The CSCE sent an observer mission headed by a skilled American diplomat and with a broadly defined mandate. A number of NGOs also established themselves, and both provided an early-warning system and had some positive impact through conflict resolution and other multiethnic programs. Most significant was the actual deployment of a multinational military force before significant violence had been unleashed, originally as a division of the overall United Nations Protection Force (UNPROFOR) and then later with its own mandate and moniker as UNPREDEP (United Nations Preventive Deployment Force). U.S. troops were included first as about three hundred twenty-five of the original one thousand, and then up to over five hundred of a force that grew to about fifteen hundred. Even though its mandate was limited, its presence was felt. This was especially true for the U.S. troops, which, despite their small number and their being confined to low-risk duties, "carry weight," as Macedonian President Kiro Gligorov stressed. "It is a signal to all those who want to destabilize this region" (Roskin 1993–1994, 98).

In the Congo case, the transitoriness caveat is even more apt. A series of disputed elections in 1992–1993 set off conflict along ethnic and sectional lines. Violence broke out in April 1993 in Brazzaville and other cities, leaving over one thousand dead and about ten thousand displaced. The army restored some order, but there was little confidence that it would be more than temporary. The OAU interceded as mediators (with the same Mohamed Sahnoun who had been involved initially in Somalia as the special envoy), and succeeded in forging a viable compromise. Zartman and Vogeli (forthcoming 1998) cite a number of reasons for its success. The diplomatic effort was launched quickly, without the usual delays; Sahnoun was a skilled mediator in his own right and also made shrewd tactical decisions, such as drawing in the president of Gabon, who had family ties to both Congo presidential aspirants; the United States and European Community did not get directly involved but did provide valuable back-up support; and the Congolese leaders committed themselves to the importance of agreements that would avert escalation to ongoing and mass violence. These broke down in 1997, and mass violence ensued for reasons that at once violated the tenets and fit the logic of preventive diplomacy.

Summary

In sum, there are both analytic and empirical bases for affirming the possibility of preventive diplomacy. There is nothing inevitable about ethnic conflict resulting in mass violence. In those cases that have done so, there are identifiable points at which and policies by which international actors could have had preventive impact but did not. And in some key ethnic conflicts that did not result in mass violence, international preventive diplomacy played a key role.

POSSIBLE, BUT DIFFICULT

Affirming the possibility of preventive diplomacy, though, must not be done without also recognizing the difficulties that inhere in moving from the possible to the actual. Indeed, the very need for international actors to involve themselves in an ethnic conflict is evidence of the failure of the "ethnic contract" and other breakdowns of internal political order. And as any number of studies have shown, internal wars are in general more difficult to resolve through diplomacy than interstate wars (Licklider 1993; Stedman 1995; Pillar 1993; Walter 1997).

Although each case will naturally differ in some respects, as a basic framework we can identify five generic difficulties that must be overcome for mounting effective preventive diplomacy against ethnic conflicts: achieving early warning; mustering political will; devising a "fair-but-firm" strategy; breaking through the constraints of the sovereignty norm with respect to the internal dimension of ethnic conflict; and strengthening the capacities of international institutions.

Early Warning

As Alexander George has observed, although there may be disagreement "on how to define the scope of preventive diplomacy and . . . also on the utility of various tools and strategies that may be employed in specific situations . . . there is no disagreement on the central importance of obtaining timely warning of incipient or slowly developing crises if preventive diplomacy efforts are to make themselves felt" (George 1994, 1). As with other types of conflicts, achieving early warning of ethnic conflict requires overcoming two fundamental problems: the *informa-tional* problem of obtaining both the necessary quantity and quality of intelligence in a reliable and timely fashion, and the *analytic* problem of avoiding misperception or other faulty analysis of the likelihood of diffusion and/or escalation of the conflict, the impact on interests, and the potential risks and costs of both action and inaction (George and Holl 1995; Levite 1987).

In some respects the nature of what constitutes early warning of an ethnic conflict is even more difficult to ascertain in a manner that is both timely and reliable than is early warning of more classical problems such as an impending surprise attack or advances in an adversary's military capabilities. Although we should not underestimate the dangers and difficulties involved, the turning of a double agent or breaking an encrypted code or some other aspect of traditional espionage at least gives more concretely identifiable information as to what needs to be known than is the case when there is some form of early warning of an ethnic conflict. It is, as Joseph Nye (1994) put it when he was head of the National Intelligence Council, the difference between breaking "secrets" and solving "mysteries." The CIA thus has begun to put more emphasis on and expertise into its own ethnic conflict early-warning projects, and to draw on academic research and researchers, as have such bureaus within the State Department as Policy Planning and Intelligence and Research.

In the academic literature, although some advances have been made in providing the empirical basis as well as analytic methods and models with both explanatory and predictive power, the inherent analytic problem remains that, as David Carment (1994, 557) states on the basis of a review of relevant literature, "determining the necessary and sufficient conditions for ethnic conflict is a complex task. No two scholars seem to agree on the exact causes of ethnic strife." Indeed, even among the authors in this volume, the shared view of a purposive etiology notwithstanding, there are analytic differences as to the key variables affecting the likelihood both of ethnic conflict leading to mass violence and of its spread (diffusion or escalation).

Nevertheless, as we look at recent cases, early warning actually has been less of a problem than is often asserted and assumed. A great deal of information *was* available in the Yugoslav case, the Somali case, and the Rwandan case. Milosevic's 1987 Greater Serbia speech was right there in the Foreign Broadcast Information Service and other open sources. The Yugoslav Army's arms build-up and maneuvers were easily tracked by intelligence sources. Sahnoun (1994) cites missed opportunities in Somalia that go back to 1988, and, in addition to Amnesty International and Africa Watch reports, he cites a 1989 State Department report with the telling title *Why Somalis Flee: Synthesis of Accounts of Conflict Experience in Northern Somalia by Somali Refugees, Displaced Persons and Others*, as well as a follow-up study, also in 1989, by the U.S. Congress's General Accounting Office. And in the Rwanda case, although it should be acknowledged that no one could know "the swiftness, scale, thoroughness, and unique character of the genocide" that eventually transpired, "those with the capacity to prevent and mitigate the genocide [did] have the information upon which such a conclusion could be drawn" (Adelman and Suhrke 1996, 66). Many knew that organized extremist forces existed. Increasingly, the latter even gave public proof of their existence by words and deeds. A pattern of violence was discernible, and the state apparatus itself was implicated in arms distributions to paramilitary groups and extremist propaganda advocating the need to rid Rwanda of all Tutsis and their supporters. By early 1994, specific information about plans and conspiracies towards this end was picked up.

The analytic problem, however, has been more difficult to overcome. One reason is that the "signals" in all of these cases had to compete with quite a bit of "noise" from concomitant and louder international events: Somalis were being killed and were starving in large numbers in late 1990 and early 1991, but attention was riveted on Saddam Hussein's invasion of Kuwait; at the same time that Yugoslavia was breaking up in mid-1991, so too was the Soviet Union; the reverberation of the October 1993 failed operation in Mogadishu drowned out most everything else, especially another African ethnic conflict a few months later.

In addition, there are some basic cognitive and bureaucratic dispositions that impede early warning analysis. George and Holl (forthcoming 1998) cite basic psychological research which shows that the detection of a signal is not just a function of its strength relative to "background noise" but also the baseline receptivity, which is a function of "the expectations of observers called upon to evaluate such signals" and "the rewards and costs associated with recognizing and correctly appraising the signal." Given the strong tendency of policy makers to put off hard choices as long as possible, the cognitive dynamics are apt to be less receptive to information that if taken seriously would require "new decisions of a difficult or unpalatable character. . . . *Taking available warning seriously always carries the 'penalty' of deciding what to do about it*" (emphasis in original; for a different case but a similar problem, see Jentleson 1994).

The same disposition and disincentives detrimentally affect bureaucratic behavior. The intelligence analyst who pushes an early warning may endanger his or her career by being blamed for the bad news he or she brings—"shoot the messenger"—even if it is accurate. And if the news is inaccurate, the "cry wolf" label may follow, an appellation that damages one's professional reputation and also can bring its share of personal disdain among colleagues. For foreign service officers the bureaucratic disincentives are arguably even greater. One veteran ambassador offered the following assessment of the "habitual behavior" and "mind-sets" of the career Foreign Service: "The habits of planning ahead, of taking strategic diplomacy beyond the issues of the week, are not deeply ingrained. Preventive diplomacy requires the ability to sniff trouble in its early stages and then take steps to avoid it. This does not happen routinely or predictably." With this in mind, this same ambassador worked to add to the standard letter of instructions from the president to newly assigned chiefs of mission a statement that "achieving these goals . . . will require us to practice preventive diplomacy, to anticipate threats to our interests before they become crises and drain our human and material resources in wasteful ways." The intent was at least to create the expectation that ambassadors and their staffs should be providing early warning and "thinking and acting in terms of preventive diplomacy" (Grove 1994). A sentence in an instruction letter is not nearly enough, of course, to change habitual behavior and mind-sets. But in a sense that is the point.

Humanitarian relief and other nongovernmental organizations (NGOs) also can play important early warning roles. "The hallmark of NGOs," Larry Minear and Thomas Weiss write (1995, 49), "is their activity at the grass-roots level . . . working on the front lines to provide humanitarian assistance and protection." Thus, by both location and activity, NGOs often are the first external actors to become aware of conflicts in their early stages. Moreover, the reputation for non-partisanship and even apoliticalness that most have earned gives any information they provide and warnings they sound substantial credibility. However, this very reputation may be at risk as they seek on the one hand to fulfill their humanitarian mission, and on the other not to do so in ways that, however unintentionally, may end up supporting the principal propagators of violence (Rotberg 1997).

Political Will

Even if early warning is achievable, there remains the problem of mustering the political will necessary to act. Although the essence of the strategic logic of preventive diplomacy is to act early, before the problem becomes a crisis, it is often the same lack of a sense of crisis that makes it more difficult to build the political support necessary for taking early action. In a traditional realist calculus, such situations have had difficulty passing muster both because the immediate tends to take priority over the potential, and because many contemporary ethnic conflicts involve areas which, as the U.S. ambassador to Somalia candidly put it, are "not a critical piece of real estate for anybody in the post-Cold War world" (Richburg 1994). Or, as then-Soviet President Mikhail Gorbachev remarked only half-facetiously during his last official trip to Washington, "We are going to do a terrible thing to you . . . we're going to take away the enemy." Indeed the names of the various activist groups today—Civic Action Group, Refugees International, even Commission on Preventing Deadly Conflicts—just do not have the resonance of the old Committee on the Present Danger.

It is only partially parochial to say that this problem is particularly bad in post-Cold War American politics. But it is true in two senses. First, although the United States cannot and should not be expected to act unilaterally or always shoulder the major share of responsibility, U.S. leadership continues to be crucial to concerted multilateral action. In cases like Macedonia, although the CSCE and UNPROFOR were the vehicles, the United States played a key role both in the diplomatic intermediation and in the preventive military deployment, as the statement cited earlier by President Gligorov emphasized. In Bosnia, although there was plenty of responsibility to go around, the corollary to the impact that the United States had, once it finally became serious about playing a lead role, is the debilitating effect of its earlier halting policies. In Rwanda, despite the historically based lead roles of Belgium and France, Adelman and Suhrke (1996, 73) argue that "by acts of omission the United States ensured that neither an effective national response nor a collective UN effort to mitigate the genocide materialized."

Second, although other countries also have their own problems of pressing domestic agendas and limited resources, in the United States these have to be coped with in a political system that has the structural weaknesses of divided power (articulated by constitutional scholar Edward Corwin as a basic constitutional design with "an invitation to struggle" between the president and Congress), further exacerbated by partisan political divisions when one party controls one branch and the other party the other. Presidents always have had to prioritize among foreign policy concerns. Those that didn't, like Jimmy Carter, paid a political price. But even a foreign-policy president like Richard Nixon knew he also had to have a domestic agenda; and this was a lesson which George Bush learned the hard way. And within that part of the agenda which is dedicated to foreign policy, there are only so many times and on so many issues that a president can kick into gear the full effort to mobilize political support for any sort of substantial funding or significant action. As for Congress, it has been hard enough to get funding or commitments for immediate, let alone for prospective problems.

There also is a problem of political will for international institutions. Although the United Nations has institutional weaknesses that are its own fault and responsibility, it does also get unfairly blamed for inaction and indecisiveness when the lack of will really resides with its members. The UN authorities in charge of UNPROFOR deserve much of the criticism they received for how they managed the Croatia-Bosnia peacekeeping mission, but the exceedingly limited mandate UNPROFOR was given from the start was the doing largely of the key permanent members of the Security Council: the United States, Britain, France, and Russia. Similarly, in Rwanda one of UNAMIR's problems all along was the refusal by the major powers to provide sufficient financing or mandate. And when the early warning was sounded about another crisis brewing in Burundi in late 1994 and early 1995, including a charge by former President Jimmy Carter that the willingness to send troops to Bosnia but to keep doing very little in Burundi was racist, the most the Security Council mustered was a resolution for more contingency plans. Nor is this only true of the Security Council.

Thus the limits on political will have been a major constraint on preventive diplomacy. The question, though, is whether this has to be accepted as fixed, or could be malleable. Even taking this as an analytic question and not a normative judgment, there is reason to question whether the basic political calculus of how leaders can lower risks and avoid costs while still satisfying their interests is necessarily or even most often best served by inaction or deferred action. Conventional wisdom is that when interests are not compelling, one should not bother to run risks unless you absolutely have to; wait as long as you can to see if the conflict will be otherwise resolved or contained. Such thinking, however, is grounded in the assumption that there are no costs or risks to waiting whereas, as has happened repeatedly, the costs and risks may increase over time. Involvement thus may prove to be unavoidable, and if it does one risks ending up with fewer and less attractive options—to play on John Foster Dulles's famous dictum, having to get involved at a time and place not of one's own choosing. We return to this point later.

Fair but Firm Strategy

James Fearon poses the problem of ethnic conflict resolution and management as a "commitment problem that arises when two groups find themselves without a third party that can credibly guarantee agreements between them" (Chapter Five, 159). Both because of the questions just discussed about the extent to which their interests are at stake and because of the constraints of the norm of sovereignty, as is next discussed, it is unquestionably difficult for international actors to play that third-party role. But we again come back to the formulation of preventive diplomacy as being difficult yet possible. "It may be that the Western powers and relevant international organizations can do little to prevent this from happening," Fearon concludes with particular reference to ethnic conflicts in the former Soviet Union, "but it surely makes sense" to try (179).

How, then, can international actors make their intentions and actions sufficiently credible in the eyes of the ethnic parties to solve the problem of the lack of credibility of those parties' own agreements? It surely is not enough, as Stedman pointedly argues, to succumb to "the urge . . . to do something, anything" (1995, 17). Not only may such policies fail to achieve their objectives, but they run the "quagmire risk" of incurring costs and setbacks far more burdensome and damaging than if nothing had been done, as well as the "syndrome risk" of a paralysis carrying over to future situations, including some in which early action might actually have worked.

There cannot be a standard preventive diplomacy strategy, of course, any more than there could be a single strategy for deterrence or crisis management or any other area of foreign policy. But the guiding requisites should be along the lines of what I term a *fair but firm strategy*.

There is no doubt that the parties to the conflict must have confidence in the fairness of international third parties, with fairness defined as a fundamental commitment to peaceful and just resolution of the conflict rather than partisanship for or sponsorship of one or the other party to the conflict. This is key to overcoming the commitment problem Fearon writes about: both sides must have confidence that the international third parties will be even-handed in acting as guarantor of agreements they reach themselves and facilitator of agreements they are unable to reach on their own. Any promises made, rewards offered, or assurances given must be believable and stay that way. This requires a level of diplomatic skill in both the choosing and packaging of a particular diplomatic strategy and in the actual implementation of that strategy that too often is unappreciated. As to the particulars, some situations may be best served by straight-out third-party mediation; others might first require prenegotiations; others low-level conflict resolution techniques or track-two diplomacy. Lake and Rothchild summarize some of the confidence-building measures that may be helpful in this regard, and William Zartman in his chapter compares the relative merits of different internal power-sharing and political-constitutive formulas.

But my conception of fairness is not necessarily to be equated with impartiality, if the latter is defined as strict neutrality even if one side engages in gross and wanton acts of violence or other violations of efforts to prevent the intensification or spread of the conflict. This was one of the problems in both Bosnia and Somalia. Impartiality is relatively straightforward in genuinely humanitarian situations, as say the April 1991 military assistance mission sent to Bangladesh following the devastating cyclone that killed 139,000 people and wreaked $2 billion worth of damage. So too in genuine peacekeeping situations, meaning those in which the parties have reached agreement such that there is a peace to be kept and all parties need to feel assured that they will not be disadvantaged if they abide by the peace. But when the parties are still in conflict, what does it mean to be impartial? To apply the same strictures to both sides, even if these leave one side with major military advantages over the other? Not to coerce either side, irrespective of which one is doing more killing, seizing more territory, committing more war crimes (Jentleson 1996)? It is a "delusion" to think, as Richard Betts (1994) has put it, that in such situations impartiality should be the standard.

Fairness and firmness thus go together quite symmetrically. The parties to the conflict must know both that cooperation has its benefits and that those benefits will be fully equitable, and that noncooperation has its consequences and that the international parties are prepared to enforce those consequences differentially as warranted by who does and does not do what. Accordingly, although the preference may be to avoid having to use military force or economic sanctions or other coercive measures, the firmness of credible coercive threats needs to be projected more often and more quickly than has tended to be the case thus far. Going back to the analytic point made earlier of the purposive nature of ethnic conflicts, at least the credible threat of such coercive measures often needs to be posed so that the parties to the conflict have disincentives for pursuing their goals through their own military or other coercive means. At the most basic level, leaders such as an Aideed in Somalia or Milosevic and Karadzic in the former Yugoslavia "decided on civil war because they thought they could prevail militarily and that the international community was powerless to stop them," yet "if they had faced an early international willingness to use military force, then their calculations might have been different" (Stedman 1995, 18). To the extent that the parties to a conflict cannot achieve their objectives at acceptable costs, preventive diplomacy is strengthened.

Just how to convey or impose such costs will vary, and different situations must be analyzed to ensure that threats or preventive military deployments will be deterrents and not exacerbants. But in some form and to some degree a credible coercive component is no less an essential requisite than the political-diplomatic components of a preventive diplomacy strategy.

The Sovereignty Norm: Its Sanctity vs. Competing Interests and Principles

Because ethnic conflicts tend to be in whole or in part intrastate, preventive diplomacy in such cases has the added difficulty of the constraint of the norm of sovereignty, which limits intervention. Traditionally, for the more than three hundred years of the Westphalian system, the central organizing principle of international relations has been the supremacy of the nation state. "No agency exists above the individual states," write Robert Art and Robert Jervis (1992, 2), "with authority and power to make laws and settle disputes." John Ruggie (1988, 143) attributes the essence of sovereignty to "the institutionalization of public authority within mutually exclusive jurisdictional domains." If, then, there is no authority above the individual state and each state has its own jurisdictional exclusivity, there can be no legitimate basis for some other actor, whether another state or an international institution, to seek to insert itself in the domestic affairs of that state. Indeed, as Jack Donnelly observes, "the term 'intervention' usually implies illegality" (1992, 307).

Yet such strict notions of the sanctity of state sovereignty have been in tension with norms and values of humanitarianism and the place of the individual as the "right- and duty-bearing unit" in international society. This is the basis for and the purpose of the Genocide Convention, the Universal Declaration of Human Rights, and other affirmations of the inalienability of basic human rights, whether the offender is a foreign invader or one's own government. This tension of competing norms can be traced back to the earliest debates over just and unjust wars (Walzer 1977). It also is quite apparent in the United Nations Charter. On the one hand, for example, Article 2 (7) states that "nothing contained in the present Charter shall authorize the United Nations to intervene in matters which are essentially within the domestic jurisdiction of any state." On the other hand Article 3 affirms that "everyone has the right to life, liberty, and the security of person"; Article 55 commits the UN to "promote . . . universal respect for, and observance of, human rights and fundamental freedoms"; and Article 56 pledges all members "to take joint and separate action" toward this end.

Stephen Krasner (1993, 1995) rightly points out that the Westphalian system never has really been inviolate, and that there have been numerous breaches of sovereignty by great powers and other international actors in century after century. Surely, there were plenty of violations of sovereignty during the Cold War era. The difference, though, was that these were done more as manifestations of power politics than with a serious claim to principle. Khrushchev's January 1961 "wars of national liberation" speech was dressed up in claims of the justice and legitimacy of international socialist action to free downtrodden peoples from neo-colonialist domination, but in practice from the Warsaw Pact to Afghanistan the Soviets showed little genuine regard for the principle of sovereignty. As for the United States, whether in the cases when it did not intervene (Hungary 1956, Czechoslovakia 1968) or when it did (Vietnam, Iran 1953, Guatemala 1954, Lebanon 1958, Grenada 1983), the driving dynamic was realpolitik with claims of principle one way or the other more cover than cause. Indeed, the essence of the controversy surrounding the Reagan Doctrine in the 1980s was its claim that there could be no higher calling than to rid the world of Marxist-Leninist regimes, a claim that caused concern even among the Western allies because, as Robert Tucker (1985, 13) wrote, it risked subordinating "the traditional bases of international order to a particular vision of legitimacy." It is telling in this regard that on Afghanistan, where the Soviets were the violator of sovereignty, the United

States had strong support at the United Nations, winning General Assembly approval of a condemnatory resolution by wide margins year after year, but on Nicaragua, where the United States was seen as the violator, it was American policy that was the subject of repeated condemnatory resolutions.

Thus for the most part during the Cold War, the international community could maintain some claim to abiding by the principle of the sanctity of sovereignty even if the major powers acted differently. But in recent years this partial fiction has become much harder to sustain. The UN Security Council resolutions against the Iraqi invasion of Kuwait fell within the traditional rubric—against the sovereignty violator—but UNSC 688 passed in April 1991, authorizing the extended and sustained military intervention of Operation Provide Comfort to protect the Iraqi Kurds within the boundaries of Iraqi sovereignty, marked a substantial departure. Indeed, the creation of the UN Special Commission on Iraq and authorization of its unprecedented intrusive powers to ensure the disarming of Saddam's nonconventional weapons capability went even further in establishing that, at least in this case, there *was* an "agency above the individual state," that these were not always strictly "mutually exclusive jurisdictional domains."

It is telling that three members of the Security Council voted against UNSC 688 (Cuba, Yemen, Zimbabwe) and two abstained (China, India). The main reason was the concern about setting precedents that sovereignty might not be sacrosanct, which, for regimes as repressive as many of these, could have unpleasant repercussions. There have been other cases such as Haiti in which the Security Council also authorized interventions. On the other hand, when the Nigerian government murdered human rights leaders in the fall of 1995, the sovereignty-impinging, precedent-setting specter undermined effective UN action. And, even more to the point, one of the fundamental problems all along with UNPROFOR was that its mission was circumscribed by a strict definition of humanitarian relief that would not violate sovereignty, and indeed its very capacity to operate was predicated on the permission of the successor republic governments. John Steinbruner has been among those making the strongest case for the stake of the international community in "legal order" and the justification therefore to "impose these standards on all sovereign entities: states forfeit sovereignty if they do not or cannot execute these basic legal standards" (Wehling 1995, 8). Nicholas Onuf (1995) writes of "intervention for the common good," and Thomas Weiss and Jarat Chopra (1995) argue for "a qualitative shift from 'material interdependence' to 'moral interdependence.'" Gene Lyons and Michael Mastanduno (1995) conclude that the constraint of state sovereignty on humanitarian and other international involvements in internal affairs has been lessening but still remains a significant force, leading them to answer the question of whether we are moving "beyond Westphalia" with a question mark.

International Institutions: Stronger but Still Not Strong Enough

Unfortunately, much of the discussion in both academic and political circles on international institutions still rarely gets past intellectual and political straw men. We need to move beyond debating whether or not international institutions matter, and become more focused on middle-level theorizing about when, how, and why they do and do not. Similarly, the UN is far more competent than it is portrayed to be in the railings of conservative isolationists, but not nearly so capable as to play the preeminent role Boutros-Ghali sought to lay claim to in *Agenda for Peace*. A more balanced and more accurate view is that international institutions such as the UN and also the major regional multilateral organizations (RMOs) have become stronger and more capable but still are not as strong or as capable as needed to prevent the spread and reduce the occurrence of mass violent ethnic conflicts.

The UN brings two great strengths to preventive diplomacy. One is its unique legitimacy as authorizer of actions in the name of the international community. This always has been its raison d'être, and the problems notwithstanding, is crucial to efforts to strike a better balance between the rights and responsibilities of nation-state sovereignty. Second is its network of agencies, which do provide it with significant institutional capacity to help cope with refugee flows, help relieve starvation, and perform other humanitarian tasks. These UN agencies often work closely with NGOs, although there is extensive debate over how close this relationship should be in different situations. Minear and Weiss contend that when the goal is creating "humanitarian space," NGOs still benefit from UN funding but often can carry out the activities better on their own because their unofficial status allows them to be "more flexible and creative, and less constrained by the formalities of law" (1995, 38–45, 49).

The area in which the limits on UN capacity have perhaps become most evident in recent years, and in which little is likely to change, is in peace operations in situations other than traditional peacekeeping. The kinds of operations at which the UN is most effective—indeed, for which it won the 1988 Nobel Peace Prize—are those in which UN forces are brought in after the parties agree to the terms of a peace, with the mission of keeping that peace. Most of its recent failures have been in situations which in reality were more about peacemaking—even a Nobel laureate method will not succeed when applied to purposes as fundamentally different as is peacemaking from peacekeeping.

Shashi Tharoor (1996), the second-ranking UN official for peacekeeping, is realistic enough to identify a set of eight challenges that must be met, but is less realistic in his optimism that the UN can meet them. When one looks at some of these challenges, there is genuine question as to whether some are inherently insurmountable, given the nature of the United Nations. The "challenge of command," for example, takes us back to the issue of the Military Staff Committee and whether standing UN peace operations forces ever will be created. This surely is incompatible with prevailing political views in the United States. And, politics aside, there are real questions about command and control, logistics, training, and other aspects of building a force that would be sufficiently effective not only to be able to carry out preventive military deployments successfully, but more importantly that by its very existence could help deter ethnic parties from turning to violence. There are similar questions about "the challenge of choice." The issue Tharoor raises is how to choose among all the various conflicts around the globe for which a case for preventive diplomacy can be made. To this I would add that whatever choices are made need to be made decisively, yet there are concerns about the UN's capacity to act in such a concerted and expeditious manner, even at the Security Council level.

Similar balance is needed in assessing the potential of the RMOs. The leading example is the Organization for Security and Cooperation in Europe (OSCE). The name change from "Conference on" to "Organization for" reflects the efforts being made, as a former U.S. ambassador put it in an anonymous 1997 personal interview, to move from a "set of principles" as embodied in the 1975 Helsinki Final Act to "an operational organization." A key motivation has been the increased sense of a link between regional security and the peaceful resolution of ethnic and other internal conflicts. This interlinkage was a major theme of the November 1990 Charter of Paris for a New Europe. "We are convinced," one provision read, "that in order to strengthen peace and security among our states, the advancement of democracy, and respect for and effective exercise of human rights, are indispensable." And other parts of the charter make similar points:

> We affirm that the ethnic, cultural, linguistic, and religious identity of national minorities will be protected and that persons belonging to national minorities have the right freely to express, preserve, and develop that identity without any discrimination and in full equality before the law.
>
> We undertake to seek new forms of co-operation . . . in particular a range of methods for the peaceful settlement of disputes, including mandatory third-party involvement.
>
> We will cooperate to strengthen democratic institutions and to promote the application of the rule of law.

Building on the Paris Charter, the CSCE/OSCE has established some preventive diplomacy capabilities: for example, creation of a High Commissioner on National Minorities; establishment and deployment of its "missions of short and long duration" in a number of countries in East and Central Europe and the former Soviet Union to provide early warning and possibly a degree of deterrence through their monitoring; some limited successes in Estonia, Moldova, Macedonia, and Hungary-Romania, as well as elsewhere to some extent. But other efforts have been disappointing, as in Chechnya (Lapidus, forthcoming 1998) and Nagorno Karabakh (Maresca, forthcoming 1998). More generally, although courts of conciliation and arbitration were established by agreement at the December 1992 Stockholm summit, the one is authorized only to issue advisory opinions, and the other can issue binding judgments, but membership is optional, "and even those who join can place some limits on the court's jurisdiction," and then "only in exceptional cases will punitive actions be taken against recalcitrant states" (Walker 1993, 113–14). Also, operationally, the CSCE preventive diplomacy missions have been handicapped by lack of staff continuity (they are assigned, for instance, in two-month stints) and by overall limits on the sizes of missions host/target governments are willing to accept (Shorr 1993). And, most fundamentally, there remains the problem of "enforceable norms" (Chipman

1993b, 153). It is not quite like Stalin's apocryphal statement about the Pope, but it also is not totally different. There is value and importance to affirmation of norms of peaceful resolution of conflicts, democratic governance, and minority rights, but there also inevitably are situations in which affirmation is not enough and enforcement is necessary. Abram Chayes and Antonia Handler Chayes thus conclude that the OSCE can have the most success "in relatively low-level situations" (1996, 10).

Some developments with the OAU and the OAS do mark somewhat of a departure from their traditional sovereignty sanctity upholdings, but go even less far than the OSCE. Partly directed against the military coup in Haiti, but also consciously with more general applicability, the OAS approved the June 1991 "Santiago Resolution." It is replete with qualifiers about "due respect for the principle of nonintervention," but it does delineate as grounds for OAS interventionary action "the sudden or irregular interruption of the democratic political institutional process or of the legitimate exercise of power by the democratically elected government in any of the Organization's member states."

With reference to Haiti this was more corrective than preventive, but there was an intent to establish the threat of collective action as a preventive deterrent against future Haitis. What is particularly interesting is that whereas in the past most OAS members were reluctant to establish such principles and precedents for fear that the United States could use them as an interventionary blank check, now that most members are democracies there is a sense of a common interest vis-à-vis their own militaries or other potential domestic enemies in giving some legitimacy to regional multilateral intervention to protect democracy. This marked a significant shift in the self-interest assessment of governments which, although still qualified and cautious, did hold possibilities for further shifts legitimizing regional preventive diplomacy.

In the OAU case an important reference point is the June 1993 creation of a "Mechanism for Conflict Prevention, Management, and Resolution." The undeniability of regional security consequences of conflicts traditionally considered domestic has, as Edmond Keller points out in his chapter, encouraged African leaders seriously to reconsider the norms of external intervention for the purpose of settling domestic disputes (Chapter Twelve, 289–91). The OAU resolution still has significant qualifiers about "non-interference in the internal affairs of States," "the respect of sovereignty," and functioning "on the basis of consent and the cooperation of the parties to a conflict." Nevertheless, in relative terms there is some sense here as well of strengthening the regional multilateral organization in recognition of common regional interests in seeking to prevent conflicts which threaten regional security irrespective of their original venue.

In sum, international institutions have yet to fully measure up to the requisites for effective preventive diplomacy. Yet they have accomplished enough to dispel the low esteem and highly pessimistic prognosis of their potential held by some. Moreover, given that ethnic conflicts are so much more regionally rooted than globally transmitted, a role for the OSCE and other regional multilaterals in overall preventive diplomacy efforts is crucial.

CONCLUSION: POSSIBLE, DIFFICULT, . . . NECESSARY

It is always easiest if either a foreign policy strategy which is difficult is not really necessary, or if one which is necessary is not really difficult. Preventive diplomacy, however, is both difficult and necessary.

In using the term necessary, I do not mean anywhere and everywhere. But I do mean more places and more often than tends to be acknowledged in the prevailing preference for acting late, if at all.

There are three bases for this claim. The first goes back to the questions raised earlier about the validity of the common assumption by major outside powers like the United States that their interests are better served by waiting to see if the conflict will subside, not spread, or otherwise be self-contained. If it were the case that the fires of ethnic conflicts, however intense, would just burn upon themselves, and not have significant potential to spread regionally or destabilize more systematically, then in strict realist terms one could argue that major powers could afford to just let them be. The Bosnia and Rwanda experiences, though, particularly belie the realism of this assumption. Moreover, as Lake and Rothchild and other authors in this volume delineate, there is substantial analytic and theoretical basis for concluding that Bosnia and Rwanda are not exceptions, and that the risks of both diffusion and escalation of ethnic conflicts are quite substantial. There may be direct contagion through the actual physical movement of people and weapons, and/or demonstration effects (Kuran, Chapter Two in this volume), and/or other modes of diffusion. There also may be the horizontal escalation of drawing in outside powers even if not as direct combatants, which can have damaging effects on their overall relations and thus reverberate through the international system. This is why the UN and regional multilateral organizations have been increasing emphasis on regional security both in an absolute sense and also relative to the humanitarian rationale as the basis for sovereignty-abridging intermediations and interventions.

Second, the realistic question often is not "involvement, yes or no?" but "when and how?" And here policy makers need take more seriously the "Rubicon" problem: that as difficult as preventive diplomacy is, the onset of mass violence transforms the nature of the conflict in ways that make resolution and even limitation even more difficult. Much has been written on the question of "ripeness," the problem that the parties to a conflict simply may not have reached a point where they are willing to reach an agreement, even under substantial international pressures (Zartman 1989; Haass 1990). But on the other hand, there is the potentially countering process of "rotting," when situations may deteriorate with the passing of time, grow worse, and become too far gone (the crossing of that Rubicon) (Jentleson 1991). William Zartman, for example, his seminal work on ripeness notwithstanding, observes in this volume on the basis of a wide range of cases of ethnic and other internal conflicts, that autonomy and other compromise formulas for internal political order become less viable once "the conflict has built such a record of wrongs and hatreds that living together is no longer possible" (325). Stedman, too, along with his "alchemy" criticism, acknowledges that had there been an "early international willingness" to act with military force or in some other concerted manner, conflicts like those in the former Yugoslavia and Somalia might have followed less violent paths (1995a, 17).

The Bosnia conflict was never going to be easy, but—after all the killings, the rapes, the war crimes; with over a million people displaced internally and tens of thousands of other refugees outside the country; the economy shattered and in need of reconstruction in virtually every sector; and the interethnic bonds that had been built but shattered not only at the societal level but also with the "balka-nization" of intermarried families—the task is vastly harder. Or in Rwanda, as the question was posed rhetorically but tellingly in a UNHCR report, "what might have happened in Rwanda if the estimated $2 billion spent on refugee relief dur-ing the first two weeks of the emergency (and more since) had been devoted to keeping the peace, protecting human rights, and promoting development in the period which preceded the exodus?" (*Washington Post,* editorial, December 4, 1995).

Finally, there is fundamental humanitarian concern. The previous points estab-lish that preventive diplomacy has a pragmatic basis as well as a humanitarian one. But let us not go so far as to state or even imply that humanitarianism in itself does not impel a certain necessity.

One of the persistent frustrations of realists has been that American foreign policy never has been strictly a matter of "interests defined as power," in the clas-sic Morgenthau formulation. Indeed just a few years after writing *Politics among Nations* (1948) laying out this and other aspects of realism, Morgenthau felt com-pelled to write another book, *In Defense of the National Interest: A Critical Examination of American Foreign Policy* (1951), lambasting American statesmen for not acting in this manner and instead being "guided by moral abstractions with-out consideration of the national interest." Yet in the most fundamental sense "the distinction between interests and values," as Stanley Hoffmann argues (1996, 172; see also Hoffmann 1995–96), "is largely fallacious . . . a great power has an 'interest' in world order that goes beyond strict national security concerns, and its definition of world order is largely shaped by its values." To this should be added Joseph Nye's conception of "soft power" (1990), by which the values and ideals for which the United States stands are not just virtuous but also a source of inter-national influence, according to a pragmatic and indeed quite realist calculus.

Moreover, it is worth pondering whether in a globalist age we want to become a people that does not feel a moral imperative to seek to prevent genocide and other mass violence and destruction just because it may occur on a geopolitically unimportant piece of real estate. Again, this is both a moral question and a prag-matic one, as a "second image reversed" reverberation of how such hardening may affect domestic intersocietal relations. With ideas like these at stake, the search for effective strategies needs to continue.

CHAPTER FOURTEEN

Putting Humpty-Dumpty Together Again

I. WILLIAM ZARTMAN

ONCE ETHNIC CONFLICT has broken out and has then proceeded to a stage of violence, how can stable solutions be found? Although negotiations for a solution depend on the evolution of the conflict to a point of ripeness for settlement (Zartman 1989), the acceptability and durability of the solution depends on finding an appropriate formula made of identities and institutions for handling ethnic relations in the future (Zartman 1990). Temporary outcomes can be patched together and may well gain signatures from fatigued combatants, but more lasting arrangements need to incorporate both an identity principle to motivate, identify, and provide political community, and a working regime to manage ethnic relations. Most writing to date has focused on the causes and processes going into the conflict; more attention needs to be directed toward getting out of it.[1]

There is much discussion, more muddying than clarifying, about the notion of "solution." Conflicts as deep and complex as ethnic disputes have, of course, no solution. Solutions apply at best to legal divisions among consumables, or at least among possessables, that can be used, marked, carted away, or cut up. They do not adequately cover human feelings, memories, and relations, particularly when new generations can regenerate the conflict, using past histories to color current situations and current grievances to stain historic settlements. "Solutions" here will be used merely to indicate outcomes to which conflicting parties agree. Thus, "durable solutions" is not a redundancy but rather a quality to be enhanced, and outcomes need to be evaluated for durability, even if the sense of infinite permanence implied in the idea of solution is not to be found.

It is curious that some of the criticism leveled against the notion of solutions proposes its own criteria for permanence, decreeing that when basic human needs are satisfied by the intervenors, then the conflict will be so transformed as to disappear (Burton 1987, 1990a, 1990b). Yet human needs are always only temporarily satisfied: The sated today may be hungry tomorrow, the people who know who they are today may wonder tomorrow, those who have found dignity today may lose it tomorrow, and so on. Only time resolves, and time can also invent or revive conflict. If human agents can help time resolve by providing outcomes that at least address the question of durability, they will have made a respectable contribution to the well-being of the inheriting generation, which

---

[1] See, however, Horowitz (1985 and 1991) and Lijphart (1977).

thereafter is on its own. They do this by producing solutions that are processes and mechanisms, not judgments and awards.

IDENTITY PRINCIPLES AND CONFLICT SOLUTIONS

A state, the authoritative political institution that is sovereign over a recognized territory (Dawisha and Zartman 1988, 6–7), is an identity concept as well as a functional organism. These two natures are interdependent and they contain the requirements for a solution to ethnic conflict. A state needs an institutional arrangement or regime that enables it to manage conflict and handle the demands of its population (Zartman 1996a). It also needs an identity principle to hold its people together and to give cognitive content to the institutional aspects of legitimacy and sovereignty. Without such a regime, the state will fall apart in continuing and renewed conflict; without an identity principle, it becomes merely a bureaucratic administration with no standard terms for expressing allegiance.

The standard modern answer to the identity problem is the nation state, an historic and historiographic myth which claims that the political community and the political institution are coincident and that the first precedes the second. The historic falsity of the proposition need not be demonstrated here; generally, the two have moved forward in a parallel and uncoordinated way, ratcheting their relation into that of the modern state, as defined. When post colonial self-determination after World War II succeeded post imperial self-determination after World War I (Cobban 1994; Renan 1939), the relation between state and nation had to be reversed, and the state-nation was instituted (Zartman 1987, 50). Here the new successor state attempted to construct political community through a process of nation building (Deutsch and Foltz 1966). The process was necessary, since the legitimacy and capability of new states to hold onto their territory and people by military means alone was absent. That nation building often worked to cause ethnic conflict, either by being practiced well or by being practiced badly, does not diminish its necessity for the state. Nor does it hide the fact that states wracked by ethnic conflict will have to begin a process of nation building all over again.

Thus neither basis for the state as an identity principle has proven conflict-free. Ethnic nation states are faulted for being "backward-looking," weighed down by history and tradition, exclusionary in their effects, ascriptive rather than achievement-based in their criteria for membership. Furthermore, despite their apparent solidity, they tend to be inherently unstable, since the national self is not uncontestably predetermined and subgroups can break away on the same principle as that by which the original group sought to take control of its own destiny.

But just as ethnic solidarity can break down, so new national solidarity can break up. Although nation building allows for mobility, social promotion, tolerance, harmony, and the construction of a modern polity, these very values can also create conflict, exacerbate preexisting identity feelings, cause real or perceived discrimination, mobilize opposition, and break down modernizing institutions (Zartman 1995a). It should be no wonder that the nation-building emphasis of the 1960s and 1970s has been followed, in theory and in practice, by the ethnic conflicts of the 1980s and 1990s. Is stability to be found only in riding the wave, or are there elements of durability to be achieved?

Unfortunately and ultimately, the conflict between the two types of identity principle is decided only by force and violence, and these means in turn have an important impact on the durability of a solution. The two identity concepts (nation or ethnic state, and constructed state) cannot merely be debated, or the debate becomes truly academic (in the commonly perverted sense of the word). It would be hard to sustain a claim for the absolute superiority of one concept over another, since both have their drawbacks. Although both law and philosophy have sought to resolve the issue, they have not been able to decree or define away the use of violence as the final arbiter—the *ultima ratio regis*—as a sixteenth-century canon had stamped on its maul. International practice and law has devised the referendum as the final sanction of that right (Western Sahara case 1975; *UNGA/R* 1960) but the claim to hold a referendum has thus far required a serious use of force.[2] Independence is the highest political value of humankind, and it is worth the fight. The price is high and it should be, for the value is supreme, not to be taken lightly. Conflict, usually in its violent form, is generally required to assert the self that can claim its own determination.[3] It is also needed in order to mobilize and consolidate the self-identifying group and to claim possession of the right to self-rule. Consequently, in the midst of an effort to manage, resolve, and transform ethnic and other communitarian conflict, it must be remembered that conflict is about something and that for all the perverted forms it may take, it stems from grievances and causes that must be considered if solutions are to be durable.

Violent ethnic conflict arises from the breakdown of normal politics; grievances can no longer be brought to the government in a process of petition and redress. The grievances that trigger ethnic conflict are essentially those of perceived discrimination: A group feels that, because of its ascriptive (ethnic) identity, it is denied something to which it has a right. Hence, it is not merely an abstract choice between two identity principles that is being decided by violence, but an underlying grievance over perceived discrimination that makes one principle or the other inadequate for the situation. Thereafter, the rebellion may be in one of a number of stages in the life cycle of the conflict (Zartman 1995d, ch. 1).[4] Since these stages are functional phases, not periods of history marked by clear dates,

---

[2] The new Ethiopian constitution notwithstanding. The most recent legal discussion of the Saharan issue is found in Naldi (1989, ch. 2).

[3] Although I have pointed out in many other places that conflict is ubiquitous and inevitable but not always violent, the discussion here focuses on formulas for restoring normal politics and eliminating violent conflict. For earlier phases, see Deng et al (1996, 299 et passim) and Zartman (1990 and 1995c and 1997). For a good discussion about the possibilities and effects of managing ethnic conflict at the consolidation phase, see Rudolph and Thompson (1985). An apparent exception to the need for violence is Quebec, which was able to take advantage of its preexistence as a province to impose votes on self-determination without major violence.

[4] There are other interesting notions of phases, not totally irreconcilable with the above progression. On identity, legitimacy, distribution, and participation, see Rudolph and Thompson (1985); on equality, cultural rights, institutional political recognition, and secession, see Coakley (1993, 6–7); on reform group, nationalist movement, and revolutionary force, see Zartman (1980a).

they may well overlap or shade muddily into each other. Nonetheless, they do represent identifiable times in the evolution of the conflict.

The second stage is that of consolidation, when the attention of the rebels is turned inward in mobilizing their population, uniting their diverse organizations, challenging the legitimacy of the government, and building the means of combating it. This is usually not a time for solutions.[5] In fact, any attempt at finding a solution tends to be viewed as hostile and inimical to the consolidating purposes of the movement. The movement is consolidated by finding ways into the confrontation, not ways out of it. Only when the movement has completed its own consolidation can it turn to direct confrontation of the government, in an effort to raise its rebellion to a level of equality so that it can deal with the government on an even plane. This third, or confrontation, phase is also not a time of solutions, since the movement's aims now are to prepare for its own recognition, not to come to a premature agreement from a weaker position. Again, it is only when the confrontation phase has reached its goals that ethnic conflict is ready for a solution. By the nature of the conflict and the stage at which solutions can be sought, a return at this point to normal politics and redress of the original grievances will no longer suffice. A formula for a new political system needs to be created, one that will provide new governing structures and will handle the newly aroused population. Institutions and identity principles are the crucial ingredients of those formulas.

Force and violence, however, have their cost. They obviously take their toll of human lives in the course of the conflict, but more importantly for the present purposes, they mortgage future relations among the combatants. Once the war is over, relations are no longer the same among parties; it is hard to live together as before, both because of the effects of the violence and because of the identity mobilization that the conflict has required of the parties. Thus, conflict management does not merely need to address the course of the conflict to find an appropriate ending for it; it needs to take into account the effects of the conflict on potential solutions if they are to meet the test of durability.

Another ingredient of durability is viability. The one notion is inherent in the other, although, curiously, viability is often considered an inappropriate outsider to the debate. Notions of identity alone are generally considered to be trumps in the establishment of units for self-determination, and the criterion of viability is pushed aside with citations of the numerous examples of UN members that are patently unviable (Solarz 1980). But viability is more important to the matter of identity conflict than is usually recognized. To begin with, material fortunes are crucial elements in the cause of ethnic conflict. When the pie is large enough to go around, demands tend to be negotiable and satisfactory allocations can generally be found (Rothchild 1997c). It is when the pie shrinks and tough distributive

---

[5] Significantly, the cases in which conflict management at the consolidation phase has worked show that success involves not only government responsiveness but also an ability to coopt the leadership in a national process, pulling it away from its followers. It may also be significant that such cases tend to come from the developed world, where political processes are better established; see Rudolph and Thompson (1985).

choices need to be made that the specter of discrimination appears and groups emerge with the common cause of ascriptive deprivation relative to other groups (Zartman 1980a). The goal of the rebels is the end of discrimination against them.[6] When ethnic groups are mobilized and new political units are created on the basis of ethnic identities, there is an implicit promise to satisfy the group's needs that relies on available resources. Although Sekou Touré may well have proclaimed, "We prefer independence in poverty to servitude in riches" (*Agence France Presse-Guinée* 1958), that was a better mobilizing slogan than a sound political analysis; Guinea's problem was not that it enjoyed riches in its colonial status, but that the Korean War boom of the 1950s produced benefits unequally distributed between colonizing and colonized society. Colonized peoples have aspired to a better life, not just their own life. However, they feel that the better life is only possible when they have the levers of allocation in their own hands.

The problem with viability as a criterion is twofold: it is a future consideration with no guarantees, and it has no definitive measure. The collapse of once-rich states well-endowed with potentialities—like Guinea—makes the debate over the threshold of viability academic, just as the presence of ministate islands and enclaves among the well-to-do of the moment shows easy measures to be inaccurate (for the moment). But the difficulty of establishing the boundaries of a concept should not be taken as a test of its validity. Like the other absolutes already in the debate, viability is a necessary if imprecise ingredient whose absence will make itself felt on the matter of durability.

In sum, a number of criteria go into the formulation of a durable solution that both ends the violence and provides an outcome that replaces violence with politics. These include a usable identity principle—either ready-made or makeable—a promise of viability, support from the conflict process itself, and an institutional arrangement. The formula indicated will take different forms as a function of the context and the conflict, and cannot be found in one shape alone dictated by some external criterion. Therefore, the qualities of competing formulas for identity and territory and for regimes and institutions must next be examined.

Formulas for Identity and Territory

The initial element in determining the form of appropriate solutions is the geography of the conflict. If the rebel ethnic group is congregated in a contiguous area, it lends itself to more types of territorial solutions and different identity principles than if it is scattered around the country. Like many elements, this is not an immutable given. If the rebellious area is not homogeneous, it can be made so, by taking "foreign" populations and moving them out or doing them in—by forced migration or ethnic cleansing. Both leave deep wounds. In conflicts where

---

[6] Not necessarily to end all discrimination. One of the wisest and most encompassing things ever written in political science is Aristotle's Motor: "Inferiors become revolutionaries in order to be equals, and equals in order to be superiors," after which the cycle starts again (Aristotle as quoted from Barker 1948, 242).

territorial contiguity obtains and by providing a definable homeland contributes to the sense of identity of the rebellious group, it is only natural that territory will play a more important role in the solution.

If the ethnic rebellion has an identifiable territory, a number of territorial solutions are available, principally variations on two types: regional autonomy or federation, and secession (Lund 1996; Lapidoth 1996).[7] It is not necessary for present purposes to go into the differences and workings of these various forms. The purpose here is to evaluate the determinants for their appropriateness as a solution for ethnic conflicts. Although both autonomy and federation can contain varieties in the degree of self-rule, they differ from each other mainly in the relation between the sub-state units.[8] In the first, autonomous regions usually enjoy separate status from the rest of the country, whereas in the second, federated regions make up the entire country and have similar internal governance structures.

Opinion and practice at least since World War II has favored the maintenance of existing sovereign states, if only because they themselves are the units in charge of the international community. But beyond that conservative consideration, maintenance of established units works against balkanization, the creation of ever smaller and weaker states less and less capable of meeting the needs of their people and of combining the regional complementarities that create internal trade and markets for goods and labor.[9] Finally, it has been felt that accepting existing units reduces the danger of border disputes, irredenta, territorial wars, and so on; it favors a stable status quo. Even in the case of ethnic conflict, where violence has already broken out, an ethos supporting the status quo limits the damage caused by the conflict, working to keep it internal and containing its demands and effects.

Practice has confirmed this prescription. With a few exceptions to be discussed below, no contiguous state has broken apart in the postwar period. One of the most important norms that has worked to reinforce this condition is the uti possidetis juris doctrine operating in postcolonial Africa and inherited from postcolonial Latin America, which protects not only boundaries but the units they contain.[10] Thus, Latin America has settled down into constant units, after some initial rearranging, and its conflicts have been limited to boundary disputes over

---

[7] There is no such thing as confederation. If sovereignty does not remain with the over-arching unit, then the outcome is secession, whatever friendly relations may be established afterward. Divorce is divorce, even if we remain good friends.

[8] State will be used here to refer to the sovereign unit, and province or region to the autonomous or federated sub-state unit, even if in specific reality the latter are termed "states."

[9] It can well be argued that in the current era poor regions receive more attention and assistance as independent states than they would as parts of a larger state. Gambia does far better as a Gambia than it would as part of Senegal, and lives as a parasite on the Senegalese economic—and perhaps political—system; see Ka (1992). Independent Swaziland and Lesotho—and perhaps the bantustans—get more attention from South Africans than they would as part of South Africa. But the argument does more to explain why such microstates do not want to integrate into a larger unit than it does to prescribe a desirable and universal criterion for practice.

[10] For a fuller discussion of the African cases, see Zartman (1996a, 55–56).

where the *uti* properly is and to social unrest, but not to territorial secessionist movements. Similarly, Africa has seen no successful break-away units that do not fall under *uti possidetis;* even Eritrea and Somaliland were colonial units whose independence falls under the doctrine (Zartman 1996a). Salim Salim, secretary general of the Organization of African Unity (OAU), indicated in 1994 that the line stops at Eritrea and that secession attempts by southern Sudan or other regions would not be allowed by the OAU under the doctrine, although secessionism has risen since then among southern Sudanese.[11] In Cyprus, the ethnic cleansing of the northern part of the island and its secession as the Turkish Republic of Northern Cyprus has not received international recognition, beyond Turkey (Richarte 1995).

Three exceptions do occur under this norm. One involves noncontiguous states, and thus confirms the criterion of territorial contiguity. Pakistan is the best example. The second concerns two- or three-member federations. It is relatively well established in practice and solidly based in theory that federations composed of few units do not work. Two-unit federations are an institutionalized confrontation, leading either to the takeover of one by the other or to stalemate between two units seeking to defend themselves against the other's takeover attempts. Ethiopia, Mali, and Czechoslovakia are cases in point, and the strains in Tanzania and Cameroon (no longer a federation) are a further illustration.[12] Three-unit federations give rise to a similar situation of continual and unstable alliance politics of (any) two against one, leading either to takeover or breakup; even when the original units are themselves subdivided, the old shadows tend to remain. Libya is a case of the first and Nigeria of the second and third effects. Cases of federal breakup tend to come from the early histories of the states, as they experiment with new institutional forms, testing their durability.

The third set of exceptions comes from communist states that have broken up. This category has many sui generis cases, but collectively it is a situation in which ideology has proven insufficient as a functional equivalent of the identity principle; when one ideology breaks down (sub-)nationalisms rise again to provide more compelling and durable identity principles on which new states are constructed. It must be emphasized that the ideological glue broke down before the rise of nationalism and contributed to it, not the reverse. The examples are the breakup of the former Soviet Union, the former Yugoslav federation, and former Czechoslovakia (itself a case of the nondurability of two-unit federations, as noted Touval and Zartman 1996).

If the existing state provides a claim to being the acceptable framework for a solution, then the acceptable solution on the basis of the status quo comes in the form of autonomy or federation—separate legal control of one's own destiny within the boundaries of a sovereign larger unit. Federations and autonomies work when they are honestly applied, and contrary to many rulers' beliefs, they

---

[11] Interview with Salim Salim by the author, Washington, D.C. See the recent writings by Deng (1995).

[12] On Eritrea, see Sherman (1980) and Erlich (1983). On Mali, see Foltz (1965). On Czechoslovakia, see Kirschbaum (1993).

are not a prelude to secession. Secession comes when they are not honestly applied. The history of ten years of federation and thirty years of war in Eritrea is a case in point, and the wrenching evolution of attitudes in southern Sudan over forty years from autonomy to revolution to secession is another.[13] The cases show that the fragility of federation is not in the hands of the region but of the central governors. It is the despoiling of the federation that assures its unworkability. Once federation or autonomy has been granted and despoiled, the trustworthiness of the granting government has been weakened and the formula loses its value as a solution. There are no absolute guarantees to federation or autonomy except for the good faith of the government. The examples of Nigeria and Yugoslavia are more complex, but both vividly illustrate the same lesson—the need to handle distributive grievances within the framework of the federation, equalizing both allocation and the allocative mechanism itself, if the federation is to be maintained (Gboyega 1996; Woodward 1995a). Regional autonomy has gone far to relieve the particularist notions—even those of the Basques—that the unitarist regime of Franco fostered (Clark 1995), and autonomy of the five special regions of Italy—which deserves to be far better known than it is—has dampened some previously strong secessionist tendencies.

This rapid discussion shows that autonomy and federation are better solutions than usually considered, if they are honestly applied and carefully tended. It should also indicate that as a solution to ethnic conflict, autonomy and federation need to provide high degrees of self-rule to be acceptable and durable. It must be remembered that, as a negotiated solution, they come after the consolidation and confrontation phases of the conflict, when the rebellion has arrived at some sort of equality with the state and may be close to demanding formal equal—that is, sovereign—status as a result. That extreme outcome can only be precluded by its functional near equivalent, a high degree of autonomy that is the trade-off for the preservation of the larger unit. Later, that autonomy may soften, greater integration occur, and the identity principle of the constructed nation take greater prominence. But for the moment, the price of maintaining state sovereignty and its identity principle is the granting and respect of effective autonomy.

The ambiguity of the federal and autonomous solutions lies in the conflict of identity principles. Regional—frequently ethnic—identity is elevated to a level competing with the state principle, producing tension and perpetuating conflict. But that conflict is already present in the ethnic conflict to which autonomy is proposed as a solution; autonomy harnesses identity to regional tasks of self-government, and proves the broader identity by showing its breadth and tolerance. Seventy percent of the Spaniards in autonomous regions declare themselves to be both regionists and Spaniards (Moreno 1994). After 1972, southern Sudanese knew they were finally effectively Sudanese when they took control of their own affairs as an autonomous region (and learned their error by 1983 when they

---

[13] On Sudan, see note 14; on Eritrea, see note 12. Strictly, Eritrea should be considered an autonomous region rather than a federation because of its two-unit nature, but the same judgments apply.

found that control to be an illusion). It is sometimes suggested that ethnic regions in conflict need to be given their own independence, after which they will return to the larger unit when their symbolic needs have been satisfied. But giving independence is like introducing the shari'a; once established, it is hard to renounce. There is no example of voluntary return after secession. If return is the goal, it is much easier to accomplish from autonomy than from independence.

Yet in some cases, secession and independence are unavoidable. When solutions involving autonomy have been sullied and exhausted, when a government has proven its untrustworthiness, when the legitimacy of the central government to speak for and rule over the dissident region has been lost, when the conflict has built such a record of wrongs and hatreds that living together is no longer possible, when identity is conceived by the center in zero-sum terms in regard to the dissidents—in any of these cases, even autonomy is an unlikely solution. It may be striking that all these conditions but the last refer to dissidents' perceptions of the central state, not the reverse. That is because the central state is the unit that must integrate or from which the dissident region must secede, quite obviously, and because it is the state that is fighting for unity and the region for self-determination. Dissidents are fighting to show that their identity principle can only be protected in independence from the larger state. Nonetheless, it must be recognized that there are cases, such as Yugoslavia, in which the central government, or a major part of it, tries to be accommodating and is rebuffed precisely because sub-nationalist units' leaders arouse ethnic feelings of discrimination in order to build solidarity behind their rebellions (Woodward 1995a). Domestic and international reinforcement of the accommodating government is then needed, to show that separatism is not a viable option.

Other than in ideological terms, which decree a priori that ethnic identity may not furnish a state with an identity principle, it is hard to see why secession should not provide durable solutions when the conflict has gone too far, in terms defined above. Ethnic states are nation states, and their independence should release energies that can be profitably harnessed for the welfare of its people. But states newly created on an ethnic identity principle must face four questions related to their cause, and they had better face them before rather than after achieving independence.

One question is about viability. As has been noted already, small or poor states may provide momentary psychic satisfaction but they are dangerous responses to the challenge of self-determination. When the people's movement for national self-determination finds itself locked into a territory bereft of resources, it is likely to find itself under authoritarian control to keep its ruler in place and to prevent renewed rebellions of risen expectations against fallen satisfactions. If there are no examples to cite as yet, it is because the international community has held the line against secession, but not because of the inappropriateness of an ethnic identity principle.

The second question is about further secessions, addressing directly the implications of ethnic identity. No ethnic group is without its sub-groups, and many ethnic groups are held together principally by a common external enemy. When the enemy disappears as a threat, their national unity and cohesion go with it. Just as military rulers fear military coups, knowing from personal experience that coups topple governments, so ethnic secessionists should be wary of sub-group secessions. The cases of Somalia and Sudan are sadly eloquent on all these counts. When the Ethiopian danger receded in the late 1980s, the unity of the Somali nation dissolved. The clan-centered tactics of President Mohammed Siad Barre accelerated the process but only confirm the point, since they were facilitated by the Ethiopian collapse. The long-vaunted national unity of the country was broken by the secession of Somaliland in 1992. But Somaliland in turn was rent by clan warfare by 1995, as lesser clans rose against Isaak domination. When the northern Sudanese danger to the south was removed by the Addis Ababa agreement in 1972, smaller ethnic groups in the south began to fear domination by the largest ethnic group, the Dinka. It was easy for President Ja'far Nimeiry to play on these divisions and undermine the 1972 agreement. The national liberation war broke out again in 1983. Newly independent African states in the 1960s and states newly independent from the former Soviet Union in the 1990s were plagued by sub-national independence movements.

The third question, also on ethnic identity, is about ethnic minorities. Few territories are populated exclusively by one ethnic group. Sometimes there are mixed populations living together in harmony before the ethnic awakening. Most ethnically aroused countries, including Cyprus and Yugoslavia, had long periods in their recent past where populations mixed freely, lived in peace, and even intermarried. Sometimes there are pockets of minority populations living in enclaves within areas held by the majority. The Bosnian safe havens have their parallels in minority clan enclaves in Somalia, "southern" tribal groups in northern Sudan, and Igbo and Yoruba neighborhoods in northern Nigerian cities, among others. Other times populations are stratified by altitude or divided into urban and rural habitats. This is why ethnic maps are so hard to draw in Yugoslavia—as in Algeria, Liberia, and Nigeria—or why the borders in the Forgana valley among Tajikistan, Usbekistan, and Kyrgyzistan are so gerrymandered. Indeed, one practical barrier to sub-national secessions is the difficulty of drawing a line between "us" and "them." One of the reasons for the failure of the Somali offensive in the Ogaden War of 1977–1978 was the Somali inability to find a line where they could claim to have liberated all Somalis from Ethiopian rule and declare victory (Zartman 1989, 107–8).

The fourth question, also relating to ethnic identity, concerns exclusion. Newly built identity principles are by their nature inclusionary, since they are the property of no sub-group. But ethnic identity principles repell citizens who are in the state and its territory but out of the ethnic group. Making these principles inclusionary is a challenge. Traditionally, African ethnic groups did so by making strangers "honorary" members of the collectivity in identity as well as in habitation; in the longer run, some ethnic groups do so by marriage, although the foreigner may not always be fully accepted and may still have to live as a foreigner before meeting the future spouse. If the identity of the strangers is as aroused as the identity of the ethnic nation, inclusive identity on an ethnic basis will be hard to achieve and the conflict will be perpetuated within the new state. Minorities may move to more hospitable surroundings—to the former larger unit, to their "own" ethnic state, to a third land of opportunity. These are classic solutions, and are preferable to forced expulsion or genocide.

Viability, sub-secession, minorities, and exclusion are problems inherent in new states that are based on an ethnic identity principle. They are comparable to the problems in established states caused by continually repressed ethnic groups trying to live under a broader identity principle that denies their own identity and dignity. Before secession, the responsibility for resolving these challenges lies in the hands of those who activate ethnic identities through discrimination and who make life unlivable for ethnic minorities by refusing to accommodate ethnic identities under the constructed identity principle. After the fact, it lies in the hands of those who need to take into account the implications of constructing an ethnic state. There is no good answer to the search for a proper and durable identity principle. The real solution comes in proper implementation of whichever principle is adopted, so that old discriminations are eliminated and new discriminations do not appear to revive the old and cause new ethnic conflicts.

FORMULAS FOR REGIMES AND INSTITUTIONS

Ethnic conflicts are not ended by some belated attention to the original grievances or discriminations, as noted; they require a new political system (Zartman 1995a). The institutional arrangement or regime whereby the state manages its ongoing conflict and makes its policy decisions is the other fundamental component of a solution, besides its identity principle. Just as an identity principle comes in one of two forms—ethnic or constructed—so an institutional regime for ethnic relations comes in one of three forms—integration, separation, domination. This applies whether the rebellion is contained within a contiguous territory or not, and whether a new state is being established or not. Most ethnic conflicts—South Africa, Zimbabwe, Namibia, Liberia, Rwanda, Burundi, Sierra Leone, Somalia, Afghanistan, Peru, Guatemala, El Salvador, Nicaragua, Lebanon, among others—do (or did) not involve a contiguous territorial base or a new state, and so ethnic conflict is over the control and structure of an existing entity. For those with contiguous territory, one component of that regime is the provision of autonomy, federation, or independence, but even then, as we have seen, minorities in the autonomous, federated, or independent unit have to be handled in some way as well.

Indeed, it is the minorities, not the majority, who are the challenge to the institutional stability of the new regime. The majority—whether the former rebels or the state—has won; the challenge for durability is to keep the minority/ies from losing. Minorities institutionally condemned to a second-class position are merely the seeds for new ethnic conflict. But victorious ethnic nationalism is in a poor position to recognize the problem: It has prevailed on the identity principle of homogeneous solidarity and is not about to compromise on its integrity. In the short or the longer run, however, its minorities will cause it grief if not handled equitably in the new institutional order, as the Israeli ethnic democracy has learned and the Ethiopian guided democracy is learning. Two generic formulas— democracy and consociationalism—are usually posed as the solution, but both are inadequate (Sisk 1995).

Democracy is not the best mechanism for such solutions, for it will either reinforce a majority domination or have to be so contrived, engineered, and gerrymandered as to be a caricature of its spirit. Democracy can be turned on its head in times of ethnic conflict. The Bosnian referendum of February 1992, boycotted by the Bosnian Serbs, created an independent Bosnia without Serb representation, allowing the Serbs to refuse to live under Bosnian Muslim rule. The Serbian elections of December 1990 allowed Slobodan Milosevic to use ethnic appeals to delegitimize his rivals and win control of the state (Woodward 1995a, 121–22). Democracy is fine under a neutral state control, to assure fair use of the mechanisms and honest application of the rules, but no neutral state controls the democratic exercise in Burundi, Rwanda, Nigeria, Liberia, Somalia, Algeria, or even Tunisia. Foreign election observers provide some neutral control at the time of elections, but they have to go home thereafter, leaving the political system to its own devices.

Consociationalism (power sharing) is often presented as the answer (Lijphart 1985 and 1988),[14] but it is only one, and in reality (as opposed to theory) it is as hard both to define and to apply as it is to pronounce. Consociation has been used narrowly to mean a specific system with identifiable characteristics, corresponding essentially only to Belgium and Switzerland,[15] or loosely to refer to any system that includes component group representation at the top, with examples coming from many countries in the world. In the narrow sense, it works only where there are cohesive self-governing groups who can send trusted representatives to a collegial central authority with limited powers, and it does not handle the minority problem.

In the broad sense (which does not deserve the name of consociation), some mechanism for self-rule in the component communities and for representation at the top is a necessary characteristic of durable solutions. Ethnic conflicts can be settled only by the joint creation of a new political system and institutions, so that the handling of grievances and the management of conflicts are both autonomous and shared exercises in which the aggrieved community now has a hand. Autonomy is located at the local level, shared responsibility at the national level. As the motor of the state institutions, political parties built on the principles of interest aggregation and articulation, not of ascriptive representation, are required, although prohibitions against ethnic or regional parties are difficult to obtain when the parties are emerging from an ethnic conflict. Yugoslavia's—and, in microcosm, Bosnia's—problems with new institutions stemmed from the fact

---

[14] For critiques, see Horowitz (1991, esp. 137–45); Laitin (1987).

[15] And some people express doubt about Switzerland because of its use of direct democracy.

that the participant organizations were necessarily ethnic parties, the same bodies that were the cause of the conflict.

The best answer to the problem is not a pat formula but rather a process, a negotiation among the parties that not only translates their power in the conflict into positions in the new system, but that also provides both protection to the parties whatever their position, and trade-offs and incentives for all to preserve the regime. This sounds idealistic, to be sure, but so must any constitution-making process be, and it contains less of an assurance of failure than does consociation without the necessary preconditions or democracy in the hands of the demagogues. There are a few examples—the August 19, 1995, agreement on Liberia, the 1991 and 1993 constitutions in Colombia and South Africa, respectively (Eisenstadt and Garcia 1995; Zartman 1995a, 164, 285; and Sisk 1995) at two extremes—and many failures—the many *loya jirgas* in Afghanistan (Bokhari 1995; Rubin 1995a, 1995b; Weiner and Banuazizi 1994), the previous accords in Liberia (Lowenkopf 1995), the Arusha agreement of August 1993 in Rwanda, and on and on.

Because of the difficulty in negotiating ethnic conflicts (Zartman 1993b; Stedman 1995; and Rothchild 1997a), a mediator is usually necessary, a concerned party with long-range interests in a durable outcome to be put in charge of the process of finding a solution. This explains the importance of Dayton in 1995 for the Bosnian talks; Addis Ababa in 1972 for Sudan; Lancaster House in 1979 for Zimbabwe; Brazzaville and Governor's Island in 1988 for Namibia; Djibouti in 1991 and Addis Ababa in 1993 for Somalia; Yamasoukro in 1990–1991, Cotonou in 1993, and Abuja in 1995 for Liberia; Arusha in 1993 for Rwanda; Geneva in 1983, Lausanne in 1984, Damascus in 1988, and Taif in 1989 for Lebanon; Rome in 1992 for Mozambique; Bicesse in 1992 and Lusaka in 1994 for Angola; and other locations for other conflicts where a third party could keep negotiations on track and heading toward a durable solution. That some of these meetings were failures only shows that external mediation is a necessary but not sufficient condition for success. In some rare cases, such as Colombia and South Africa, the state is in sufficient control that it can watch over the fair implementation of the agreement, with an articulated civil society watching over its shoulder. In most others, there must be continuing international observation or even participation to keep the mechanism balanced until its component parts can be trusted by each other.

The mediator may come from many different levels—the United Nations through the secretary general's special representative, an external state's foreign secretary or ambassador, the relevant regional organization's conflict management mechanism, or a neighboring state's president or minister (see, among others, Bercovitch and Rubin 1992; Mitchell and Webb 1988; Zartman 1989; Touval and Zartman 1985; Myers 1991; and Rothchild 1997c). The mediator's role, ranging from communicator to formulator to manipulator (Touval and Zartman 1985; Zartman and Touval 1995), varies according to its power in the process and indicates whether the mediator is merely a passive catalyst or a major influence. It is more likely that mediation will need to play the latter, more intrusive roles in ethnic conflicts. The parties do not need merely a communicator; since they are from the same country, they generally know how to communicate with each other. What they do not know is how to provide the necessary balance in the parties' power or input, and in the eventual outcome or output, for them to construct a regime they can agree upon. Often, the mediator will need to play both roles, finding a formula and also maintaining the power balance. The dynamics of the negotiations usually involve parties' competing efforts to make a winning coalition with the mediator, and the mediator's efforts to play the parties' incremental agreement to parts of the package against each other. These dynamics came out particularly in Lord Carrington's role in Lancaster House in 1979 (Davidow 1984) and in the role of the United Nations Transitional Authority in Cambodia in 1993. However, it is unlikely in the future that solutions will be able to depend on the integral participation of the mediator's forces in the transitional government, as practiced in these two examples. This type of involvement is too costly for individual states or the world community to sustain; the colonial system is no longer present to provide candidates, and the world organization is not yet equipped to take up the task repeatedly. Instead, the mediator needs to use its position in the power relations to help devise and set in motion a mechanism that will run on its own.

Whatever the source of mediation, the regional constellation of states in which the conflict occurs needs to be brought along (Deng et al. 1996; Wriggins 1994; Midlarsky 1993; Brown 1996; Zartman 1989). Ethnic conflicts never stay within their internal limits; neighboring states are inevitably concerned, and even involved. Since they too are touched by the conflict, they need to be involved in its resolution, lest they be agents of its perpetuation. The lack of attention to regional stabilization has allowed the Rwandan and Burundian conflicts to perpetuate themselves, and the Sudanese conflict has become a constant element in the regional system of northeast Africa, as Cyprus is part of the Aegean conflict system, and so on. The role of neighboring states in stabilizing the ethnicized conflicts in Mozambique and Angola and the ethnic conflicts in Sri Lanka and Spain has been important, if not always determinant. That role is primarily one of facilitator and supporter; it must reinforce but it cannot replace the establishment of an internal regime.

Two elements determine the course of these negotiations over a regime to end ethnic conflicts: the input or results of the conflict—the current power relations between the parties; and the output or projection of the conflict—the prospective institutional relations between the parties. Although sometimes forgotten, both elements—where the parties are coming from and where the parties are going— are necessary ingredients in the durability of the solution. Simply dividing the spoils without providing for future mechanisms for handling the conflict, as happened at Geneva and Lausanne for Lebanon in 1983–1984, for example, is no solution, and attempts to set up a new regime without taking current power relations into account, as happened in Cotonou in 1993 for Liberia or Bicesse in 1992 for Angola, are doomed to failure.

The first matter to be decided in connection with power relations is, who is to be included in the negotiations, and how are their positions in the conflict to be translated into the new state institutions?[16] More specifically, are the aggressors, repressors, and rebels to be rewarded for their role in the conflict, and are new institutions to be handed over to the old villains, the new villains, or to new civic actors in an effort to bring in a reformed leadership? Parties to the problem should be parties to the settlement, a settlement which is made with them, not against them. This does not mean that no settlement should be concluded until every splinter faction is included, for that would be an invitation to factions to splinter and to splinters to turn to spoilers (Stedman 1997). It does mean that the net should be thrown as widely as possible, to include parties to the conflict, but that there should also be a demonstrated willingness to go on without them; they should be given a vote but not a veto. Afonso Dhlakama's ReNaMo in Mozambique, Jonas Savimbi's UNITA in Angola, and the Khmer Rouge in Cambodia were scarcely perfect partners to the agreements they signed, but those agreements gave a standard to use to bring them back to a peace process and would have been meaningless without them; the great weakness that destroyed the Yamoussoukro Accords on Liberia in 1991 was the absence of ULiMo, judged unworthy of inclusion in the negotiations.

It is hard to exclude the parties and leaders who have pursued the conflict, but it is important also to include political figures who tend to be more flexible, have a stake in the establishment of a workable system, and can make and implement a negotiated settlement. Durable settlements to end ethnic conflicts would not meet their purposes if they only hand over power to the next despot; they should be doing something more, and a new type of political system better equipped to handle its grievances should be provided by conflict management mechanisms as well as by the inclusion of new sectors and leaders who will keep those mechanisms in working order.

Power distribution at the time of negotiations takes the form of a mutually hurting stalemate reflecting several types of relations:[17] rebel predominance, with the government coming to terms (most frequently, as in Zimbabwe, South Africa, Liberia, Rwanda, Lebanon, and Namibia) (Stedman 1991; Davidow 1984; Zartman 1995d; Sisk 1995; Zartman 1989; Crocker 1992), government predominance with the rebellion coming to terms (as in Basque country or the Philippines) (Clark 1995; Druckman and Green 1995), or a real draw in which an ethnic group wins a place in the system without destroying the government (as in the Addis Ababa Agreement of 1972 on Sudan, the Lusaka Agreements on Angola, the Rome Agreement on Mozambique, and the 1989 agreement in Colombia). These differing relations determine the degree of newness in the new political system, either introducing a totally new regime, as in the first case, or providing a basic modification of the existing system, as in the latter two cases. Power relations should not be frozen in the new regime; indeed, they produce an artificial arrangement with pressures for change if they maintain a temporary

---

[16] On this and the other elements of pre-negotiation, see Zartman 1993a.

power relation longer than warranted. Such is the weakness of permanently entrenched seats, unlike those for a limited time in the Lancaster House Agreement in 1979 Zimbabwe, or exclusionary pacts, as in the National Front of 1960 in Colombia, or fixed apportionments, as in the Lebanese National Pact of 1943. Rather, they should be flexible, providing mechanisms for handling both shifting relations among the parties and the disappearance of the ethnic conflict entirely, by blending ethnicity into a new identity, either national or constructed.

Institutional arrangements for governing future relations and determining future payoffs—or outputs—vary among formulas based on: *integration*, which can range from a power-sharing arrangement that preserves the parties' integrity but makes them cooperate, to institutions such as national issue parties that cut up the sides and create new identities; *separation*, which can range from complete autonomy to the ingredients of consociation (where it overlaps with integration); and *dominance*, which can range from temporary mechanisms like elections to permanent arrangements like single-party status. In fact, these are rarely absolute systems but ingredients of a mix. Yet they do represent different outcomes and different bargaining positions. At Wright-Patterson Air Force Base in November 1995, the Bosnians and Croats came in with a position based on integration and the Serbians with separation (*Washington Post,* November 2, 1995, A23). Different positions can be bridged on the level of formula or of detail, but they require reconciliation rather than simply juxtaposition for an agreement to be durable.

There are many types of challenges to the task of institution building and constitution making, but the specific challenge in overcoming ethnic conflict is to prevent feelings of discrimination and provide mechanisms of conflict management on ethnic grounds, and this in the aftermath of wounding and mobilizing ethnic violence. Meeting this challenge involves incentives and constraints "built by constitutional engineers into the structure of the selfish calculations of politicians" (Horowitz 1991, 155). This challenge hangs on two dilemmas. One dilemma behind such provisions stems from the clash between the future and the past—outputs and inputs; durability comes from the gradual elimination of internal ethnic differences, yet ethnic discrimination and consciousness is the cause and result of the conflict. The other dilemma relates to the need for the parties to judge each mechanism from the point of view of the beneficiary and the victim, on the assumption that they could find themselves in either position. Although this is the underlying assumption of democracy—the right (indeed, likelihood) of the majority to become the minority, the assurance of the ins that they will not be punished for having been in when they become the outs—it is by no means the automatic consequence of either victory or accommodation in ethnic conflict.

Thus, one guideline for durability is that ethnic distinctions should be phased out, not reinforced, even though ethnic compensation—measures such as affirmative action—may well be needed initially. Ethnic distinctions and compensation can work against as well as for defined groups, as indicated by Aristotle's Motor, noted above. Even where an ethnic group has won a settlement based on separation—as in the creation of Israel—internal distinctions are likely to raise the same problem—as in the case of the Sephardim and, even more, the Falashas.

Or, looking toward the future, institutions of a new political system in Somalia should not reflect a clan confederation but should foster integration and cooperation of clans. Another guideline is the encouragement of multiethnic or transethnic coalitions, to overcome the effects of purely ethnic parties, ethnic majorities, and ethnic outbidding, even though coalition may actually reinforce component group discipline. The complex provisions of the Nigerian constitution to provide for cross-regional majorities, the provision for minority participation in the interim South African constitution, and the permanent provisions framing the Namibian constitution are examples, as were the unsuccessful arrangements of the Vance-Owen federal plan in Bosnia.

A third guideline is the provision of checks and balances, to prevent ethnicity from being reinforced by authoritarianism, even though such provisions may raise the possibility of interinstitutional paralysis. Structures that promote bargaining and accommodation are helpful to promoting openness and flexibility in the new system. The extraordinary structural complexity of the democratic regimes in Niger and Benin after 1992 were an antidote to the previous authoritarian regimes and their ethnic base, yet they contributed to the blockage that (coupled with ethnic rivalry and personal ambition) led to the military coup of January 1996 in Niger and the reemergence of Mathieu Kérékou in the presidential campaign of March 1996 in Benin. A fourth guideline calls for revisable and flexible rules, marked by periodic review and provisions for amendment, even though too much of the same good thing becomes instability and uncertainty. The regular revisions of the 1960 Cyprus regime in 1964, 1967, and 1973 were stages in the conflict, not in its resolution; but the 1943 National Pact in Lebanon would have been more durable—and perhaps would have prevented the fourteen-year civil war—if it had been subject to regular revisions. As both the guidelines and the examples show, every measure has its excess, and the challenge in each instance is to find self-enforcing mechanisms whose durability depends on the enlightened self-interest of the parties and not simply their goodwill.

Finally, mediated negotiations on outcomes to ethnic conflicts need to cover three projections of agreement: the constitution or long-term regime, the transitional arrangements, and the cease-fire or short-term regime. Constitutions involve procedures for government selection, minority protection, and indemnities, pardons, and judgments; transitions require a neutral administration and provisions for keeping the parties in the process; and cease-fires contain provisions for regroupment and monitors. The three steps are interrelated and build on each other, and again the most important requirements for durability are that all three be present and that they be consistent with each other. Cease-fires alone that do not provide for long-term institutionalization of relations are unlikely to last, and constitutions without the prior steps for getting there are unlikely to be attained. Similarly, an important tactical question concerns sequencing in negotiations. Much diplomatic experience suggests the appropriateness of a reverse order, putting the constitutional goal first and then providing for the more immediate steps. This was the pattern in the Zimbabwe negotiations in 1979 and, in modified form involving early constitutional principles and then negotiating principles, in the Namibian negotiations in 1983–1988; it is the pattern sought in the IGAD initiative on Sudan in 1994 and thereafter. At the same time, as this entire discussion emphasizes, there is no magic formula and no position among the three that is guaranteed to be superior.

ROLES FOR INSIDERS AND OUTSIDERS

How does this work out in Sudan, Yugoslavia, Bosnia, Sri Lanka, and Nigeria, among others? It means that external parties should help internal parties work for solutions of autonomy within existing states as long as possible, meeting ever-increasing pressure for ever greater separateness by ever more forthcoming measures of self-rule. Only when the central state becomes so untrustworthy that it cannot provide a legitimate framework for its component units should breakup and secession be considered legitimate. At that point, enforced marriage, even living in separate rooms, would be a more acrimonious solution than any kind of divorce, and divorce becomes the only solution. In terms of identity principles, generous conditions of cohabitation within a single state can actually restore and reinforce the perceived value of the overarching principle, up to a point. When that point is past and the overarching identity is emptied of its value, the only remaining principle for the dissidents is that of separate ethnic identity, with all its problems. Getting rid of the infected member can be used to help restore the cohesion of the remaining members under the overarching identity principle; it does not necessarily do so automatically. Through diverse policies and actions, the international community is contributing to the preservation of Sudanese, Sri Lankan, and Nigerian unity (Wriggins 1995; Nigerian Conference 1995); it failed miserably on Yugoslavia (Zimmerman 1995; Woodward 1995a) and is confused—understandably so—on Bosnia.

Tactical flexibility on identity principles also allows more creative trade-offs and solutions than does adherence to absolute criteria of either ethnic or nonethnic states. In Yugoslavia, for example, maintaining a multiethnic Bosnia within inherited borders allows for pluralist interactions among different ethnic or confessional groups and reduces the possibility of a Muslim—and hence potentially Islamicist—state. But it locks together people who have some very real and recent reasons to hate each other and who have very little promise of living in harmony. The alternative—to buy Serb agreement to a solution with an agreement for Bosnian Serbs to join Serbia (which may be more of a punishment than a payment to Serbia), even though this may provide a precedent for Bosnian Croats to join Croatia and Croatian Serbs to join Serbia, leaving a small Muslim Bosnia and a Croatian Croatia—is precluded more by geography than by principle. In Sudan, in a reverse example, a separate southern state would be landlocked with few resources to assure its viability and, more serious, would leave northern Sudan free to pursue its Islamicist policies at home and abroad; maintaining a multiethnic and multiconfessional state would work to curb such extremist tendencies, provided that the two communities have not already drifted too far apart into zero-sum forms of identity. Adherence to an absolute principle of either ethnic or multiethnic identity would not permit either tactical flexibility or choice of an identity principle that fits the evolution of the conflict.

External states have a powerful weapon that minimizes the intrusiveness of their interest, and that is the ability to recognize states and set standards. Such standards, of course, need to be clearly stated and followed; the European and American attempts to tell various Yugoslav entities about the criteria and preconditions for recognition were a parody of diplomacy. On the other hand, the international community's efforts to rule irredentism and secession illegitimate in the Horn of Africa (except for Eritrea) were clear and successful. Holding the line on criteria for lifting sanctions on Rhodesia and South Africa was important to their success. It is particularly important in a time of shifting rules and collapsing orders.

Beyond verbal policy, external states have a clear role before them in the need for third-party assistance in finding solutions for ethnic conflicts. If mediation is as necessary as described to the achievement of resolution in situations where conflict clouds the field and obstructs the vision of the parties, external actors must be willing to take up the role. There is no alternative, or rather the alternative is either a belated awakening of national consciences over inhuman bloodshed only after the fact, or a dulling of those consciences so that bloodshed is no longer troubling and national publics opt out of a common sense of humanity. There were identifiable points at which ethnic or confessional conflicts in Lebanon, Rwanda, Yugoslavia, Somalia, and Liberia could have been prevented by some direct and low-cost action by specific states—notably the United States—in the international community, and the opportunity was lost (Zartman n.d.).

That opportunity was lost in part because of a lack of responsibility and leadership, a failure of foreign policy. But some opportunities were also lost because of a lack of skill among those who did try to devise a solution. An absence of patience, a lack of preparedness, an ignorance of alternatives, and a shortfall in perseverance undermined demarches even when an initial effort was launched. Training and further research in formulating appropriate solutions are needed to increase the chances of success for positive intervention when it does occur.

CONCLUSION

This study has focused on the ingredients of durable solutions to ethnic conflicts, as conflicting parties grapple with the problems of finding a formula to end conflict and to provide the basis for workable relations within a new political community. It has sought to carry the requirements of negotiations to manage conflict beyond the contextual conditions of ripeness and conflict cycles into the substantive components of a durable solution. In so doing, it has tried to steer between notions of absolute requirements for stable outcomes and ad hoc processes determined only by power relations, by concentrating on the two fundamental components of such a formula. These are the identity principle, relating either to an ethnic nation or to a nation building, and the institutional regime. Although specifics need to be tailored to the situation, that regime should observe several important guidelines: protect those out of power (nonincumbents and minorities), phase out fixed (ethnic) distinctions, promote interethnic coalitions, install checks and balances, and be flexible and revisable.

PART FIVE

Conclusion

Ethnic Fears and Global Engagement

DAVID A. LAKE AND DONALD ROTHCHILD

TODAY, there are more than thirty-seven major internal conflicts underway around the world.[1] Almost all possess an important ethnic dimension. Nearly 38 million people have been displaced and 7 million killed in these devastating wars (Brown 1996, 4–7). At the close of the twentieth century, ethnic and other "social" conflicts are without a doubt the world's greatest cause of human suffering.[2]

Among the ethnic-related conflicts, almost half have begun since 1989, when the Cold War ended and the so-called "new world order" was inaugurated. To many observers, the ever-increasing number of identity-based conflicts suggests that we may be facing an epidemic of potentially catastrophic proportions—a new world disorder.

This volume began with two basic questions. How, why, and when do ethnic conflicts spread across state borders? And how can such transnational ethnic conflicts best be managed? In this final essay, we attempt to draw some general lessons for both theory and policy.

In a recent study of internal conflicts, Michael Brown notes that "a great deal of emphasis has been placed on 'contagion' and 'diffusion' effects, but their causal mechanisms are shrouded in mystery" (Brown 1996, 22). In this volume, we start to unravel this mystery, to probe the causes of transnational ethnic conflict. Our understanding remains tentative and preliminary; we are at the beginning, not the end, of what we believe is an important research effort. Nonetheless, we can draw five preliminary conclusions about the spread of ethnic conflict.

First, ethnic conflict within states and its spread across states is the product of strategic interactions between and within groups. In all conflicts, individuals and groups choose strategies based upon their expectations of the actions of others; outcomes, in turn, are the result of the strategies chosen. Within groups, ethnic activists (Kuran, Chapter Two) or political entrepreneurs (Saideman, Chapter Six) seek self-aggrandizement by polarizing society and outbidding moderate politicians within their community. By "playing the ethnic card," they seek to enhance

---

[1] A "major" internal conflict is defined as one with more than one thousand battle-related deaths. The number of "minor" conflicts is much larger.

[2] On social conflicts, see our discussion of ethnicity and ethnic conflict in Chapter One.

their position both within the group and in the larger social and political systems. Followers, in turn, support leaders when they anticipate personal or collective gains. Irrespective of whether ethnicity is an invented category, a leader's call for action to a people having some form of shared identity can awaken a consciousness of common grievances and a desire to rectify these perceived wrongs. The group can rapidly attract supporters not wanting to be left out, enabling its leaders to use their new influence and power to force centrist politicians to placate the membership on key issues. Provided that the aggressive nationalists continue to broaden their appeal and keep their movement unified, they can, in a multiethnic context, manipulate emotions, expand their demands, weaken the network of linkages across groups, and destroy the existing ethnic contract.

Between groups, violence arises from information failures, problems of credible commitment, or the security dilemma—and most commonly from a deadly syndrome of all three strategic dilemmas. Information failures occur as the state loses its ability to arbitrate between factions and as groups hold back information and suspect others of doing the same. Problems of credible commitment arise as ethnic contracts collapse and groups come to fear that others will not uphold their promises. Incentives to preempt drive groups to fight first and seek the basis for compromise later. In situations of increasing state weakness, the social fabric can be very weak and easily torn apart. One or more of these strategic dilemmas must exist for group leaders to choose conflict over compromise. Together, these within-group and between-group strategic interactions can combine to create a toxic brew of ethnic fear and, ultimately, violence.

Ethnic conflict spreads internationally in much the same way as it arises domestically. Ethnic conflict diffuses transnationally when it disrupts the ethnic balance of power in other states—through refugee flows, the retreat of armed insurgents, or other direct border penetrations—or when it leads individuals and groups to alter their demands or beliefs about the likely claims of others, to change their beliefs regarding the efficacy of political safeguards set forth in existing ethnic contracts, or to shift their assessments about the likely costs and benefits of protest, disturbance, or collective violence. Central to each of these causal pathways are elite actors within each ethnic group who make choices about how best to secure their positions and interests.

Ethnic conflict also escalates when third parties, often constrained by ethnic alliances, suffer from information failures, problems of credible commitment, and incentives to take preemptive action. Even though all parties to an escalating ethnic conflict are better off avoiding violence, and can normally be expected to do so, they may be prevented from reaching a stable compromise by any one of the strategic dilemmas we have identified. Just as these strategic dilemmas are a necessary condition for violence to arise between any two groups, they play a central role in determining whether or not conflicts will escalate.

If ethnic conflict is the product of strategic interactions between and within groups, we can equally conclude that it is not caused directly by the existence of "primordial" identities and ancient hatreds (contrary to Connor 1994), economic decline (contrary to Brown 1996, 587; Lipschutz and Crawford 1995; Woodward

1995a), democratization (contrary to Brown 1993, 9; Welsh 1993, 47), or the fall of communism (contrary to Kaplan 1993, 39–40; Snyder 1993; Welsh 1993, 46–47). Nor is the international spread of ethnic conflict merely the result of "bad leaders" and "bad neighbors" (contrary to Brown 1996, 25–26, 583). We recognize that these factors may all contribute to and even worsen the strategic dilemmas discussed above, but they cannot, by themselves, explain why groups choose to engage in violence rather than compromise their political differences.

Second, ethnic conflict does diffuse abroad, but largely to states that already contain the seeds of discord or to groups that can identify with the warring parties. The international diffusion of ethnic conflict is a compelling political problem that must be recognized and understood, but it is limited in nature.

As forcefully demonstrated by the penetration of eastern Zaire by Rwandan and local Tutsi military forces in fall 1996, direct diffusion stimulated by refugees, armed insurgents, and other cross-border "spillovers" is a real and practical concern. The popular fear is that a state plagued by ethnic conflict will "infect" its neighbors, who in turn will infect their neighbors until the entire region or even continent has been engulfed in an epidemic of violence. This image of ethnic conflict as a contagious disease, however, is overdrawn. Strong, robust states able to cope with potential information failures, problems of credible commitment, and security dilemmas are generally able to contain the cross-border spillovers produced by their weaker neighbors. On the other hand, states that are already at risk of ethnic violence—perhaps suffering from one or more of the strategic dilemmas in some limited form—are most likely to be affected detrimentally by such spillovers. Moreover, although the international community has been slow in responding to initial outbreaks of ethnic conflict, it has to date moved more effectively to head off direct forms of diffusion—with Macedonia being the great success story of the current Balkan conflict (but see our fourth point below). Although a legitimate source of worry, ethnic conflict is not highly contagious and is likely to diffuse directly only under fairly restrictive conditions. As Edmond Keller (Chapter Twelve) suggests, however, these conditions may now hold in much of Africa and, we might add, in the newly independent states of Eastern Europe and the former Soviet Union.

The indirect diffusion of ethnic conflict is far more subtle and hard to recognize. It may also prove, in the long run, more important and difficult to manage. Timur Kuran (Chapter Two) and Stuart Hill, Donald Rothchild, and Colin Cameron (Chapter Three) demonstrate theoretically and empirically that political bandwagons can occur, that conflict in one locale can diffuse indirectly to others. Moreover, they posit models in which diffusion is driven primarily by ideas and knowledge, both of which can traverse borders with ease and spread widely. Kuran and Hill, Rothchild, and Cameron also concur that large, prominent states typically "export" proportionately more discord than they "import" from others, suggesting that states in conflict are an important source of conflict elsewhere. Thus, as ethnic activists polarize society, mobilize ethnic associations for political purposes, and signal the potential for ethnic dissimilation abroad or as groups learn from the political tactics of others, conflict can diffuse rapidly and without geographic limits. Similarly, Sandra Halperin (Chapter Seven) finds that ethnic conflicts can spread widely when they become fused with socio-political struggles in states undergoing similar economic and political transformations. Indirect diffusion driven by ideas and knowledge is potentially universal in scope and domain.

At the same time, however, Hill, Rothchild, and Cameron posit explicitly that groups must be able to perceive and judge similarities between themselves, their conditions, and groups and situations elsewhere before they can learn from events abroad. Not all political tactics diffuse to all groups in all states. Groups must be able to identify at least some parallels in circumstances before they can infer that similar political tactics will work in their own struggles. This suggests that diffusion does have limits, but these limitations may be larger or smaller depending upon the political tactics and the characteristics of the groups in question. When political struggles are defined in universalistic terms and when political tactics are readily transportable to other settings, conflict is more likely to diffuse; the struggle for civil rights and the tactic of nonviolent protest that Hill, Rothchild, and Cameron examine resonated with oppressed groups elsewhere and did, in fact, spread widely. Conversely, when conflicts are defined in particularistic terms and employ political tactics specific to a time and place, diffusion is less likely to occur.

Equally important, both James Fearon (Chapter Five) and Stephen Saideman (Chapter Six) argue that even in the 1990s groups can draw mixed lessons from ethnic conflicts around the globe. For every instance of ethnic violence, there are several cases of successful ethnic compromise; for every Bosnia, there is a Czechoslovakia and a South Africa. As groups observe ethnic relations elsewhere, they may draw positive as well as negative lessons. Moreover, negative examples may lead groups to redouble their efforts to reach accommodation and avoid the slide into the vicious cycle of ethnic violence. Exactly what inferences groups draw from events elsewhere, and what lessons they draw from these inferences, remain important questions in need of further research.

Saideman reminds us, finally, that the wave of ethnic conflict now sweeping across the globe may not be the product of diffusion but, rather, a common reaction to simultaneous political changes, such as the weakening of state power following the collapse of communism in Eastern Europe and the former Soviet Union, and mounting economic and environmental crises in Africa and other developing regions. Coincidence in timing need not imply a causal linkage. The possible simultaneity of otherwise unrelated events stands as a caution to all analysts studying diffusion. It suggests that an enormous burden of proof is required before we can conclude that the recent conflicts are, in fact, causally linked.

Third, ethnic conflicts do escalate and draw in third parties. Will Moore and David Davis (Chapter Four) provide strong evidence that ethnic alliances that span borders are likely to generate higher levels of conflict between countries. At the aggregate level, ethnic conflicts are clearly prone to escalation. Paula Garb (Chapter Eight), in turn, emphasizes the socially constructed nature of ethnic identities and how alliances can be strengthened or, in the case of the North

Caucasus, weakened. She also demonstrates that ethnic alliances do not automatically result in cooperative efforts between related groups but depend, instead, upon the larger strategic context in which group leaders calculate their political strategies. Emphasizing the heavy-handed nature of the Russian response that deterred potential ethnic allies from rising to support the Chechens, she shows that the political strategies of the actors have important consequences for whether the conflict will escalate.

Fearon also argues that the escalation of ethnic conflicts is "self-limiting." Unlike ideological conflicts, which have universal appeal and can escalate to include virtually all states, ethnic conflicts eventually exhaust the number of countries with significant ethnic kin. However, Halperin finds that in the nineteenth century, at least, ethnic conflicts fused with other issues and thereby spread over nearly the whole of Europe, contributing to two world wars. Although she argues that these world wars eventually destroyed the pernicious socio-political structures that served to spread ethnic conflict throughout the continent, she finds that many of the same structures exist today in parts of the developing world, suggesting that we may continue to see a significant number of ethnic conflicts escalate beyond their initial belligerents.

Fourth, even if the international spread of ethnic conflict is limited, it is sensitive to the strategies of all relevant actors, including third parties. As a strategic process, ethnic conflict and its international spread are the products of strategies chosen by all groups, states, and international organizations. Any change in the strategies of these actors, therefore, can have widespread and often unanticipated effects.

Kuran (Chapter Two) suggests that the policy of multi-culturalism pursued by certain industrialized countries, and the legitimization and politicization of ethnicity that follows from the associated movement, may contribute to ethnic dissimilation abroad. Likewise, to the extent that the enforcement of ethnic contracts within multiethnic societies depends implicitly or explicitly upon noncoercive interventions—especially the benefits of inclusion or the pain of exclusion from the world community—or the possibility of coercive interventions, any decline in international vigilance may produce a new round of ethnic violence. Even if one concludes from the chapters above that ethnic conflict has not spread quickly or easily around the globe (that it is not the acute threat sometimes portrayed in popular debates), it would be a mistake to infer that the United States and other concerned countries can relax their efforts to stem the global tide of ethnic violence. Declaring victory against ethnic hatred and violence and retreating from the promotion of stable ethnic relations may, in fact, exacerbate latent ethnic fears. To inhibit the spread of ethnic conflict, the international community must continue to focus on ways of making existing ethnic contracts and relations more robust and less prone to information failures, problems of credible commitment, and security dilemmas.

Fifth, ethnic conflict is not unique. As the chapters above demonstrate, ethnic conflict can be usefully studied and understood through modern, rationalist approaches and theories. Many of the theories developed or used above have their roots in the study of interstate conflict. Nearly all are built upon general theories of human behavior that have been applied throughout the social sciences. Although it may be especially vicious and even perverse, ethnic conflict is closely related to other forms of conflict and can be studied with many of the same theoretical tools. Ultimately, we will want to examine the particulars of ethnic conflicts and how they differ from other types of disputes, but there is no reason to suspect that ethnic violence requires an entirely new conceptual foundation.

This conclusion carries both good and bad news for the study of ethnic conflict. By exploiting existing theories and tailoring them to the specifics of ethnic conflict, we can quickly gain some analytic leverage over the causes and patterns of such conflicts. However, our ability to explain and predict conflict in general remains limited. Realistic and helpful solutions to the problem of war, for instance, have yet to emerge despite decades of academic study. Existing theories can contribute to a richer understanding, but we, as analysts, still have a substantial distance to travel before we arrive at effective solutions.

The Management of Transnational Ethnic Conflict

Coping with the burgeoning ethnic conflicts of the post-Cold War world has been greatly complicated by the weakness of many states and by the lack of a third force to stand between internal adversaries and help reconcile their differences. Where states have lost the capacity to regulate internal political and ethnic competition, and external parties are unwilling to prevent the spread of violent conflicts, as in eastern Zaire in 1996, the conditions are ripe for the strategic dilemmas to take hold and for violence to emerge. Commenting on the paradox of the declining willingness of the great powers to intervene in African conflicts, for example, Francis Deng (1993, 34) remarks that "although the end of the Cold War has removed this aggravating external factor [of superpower ideological confrontation], it has also removed the moderating role of the superpowers, both as third parties and as mutually neutralizing allies." The result has been to create new and complex obstacles to dealing with information failures, problems of credible commitment, and security dilemmas and to confound analysts seeking to manage the spread of ethnic conflict across international borders. The chapters in this volume nonetheless offer some initial insights on the management of transnational ethnic conflict.

It is unwise to expect too much of conflict management initiatives. Most of the time, most ethnic groups live alongside with one another comfortably and amicably. Even in cases where ethnic minorities might otherwise be at risk, states have promoted stable ethnic relations and made concessions on minority group inclusion, participation, autonomy, and access to resources. However, an awareness that regimes can always change their preferences and retract these concessions leaves minorities fearful of the future. The three strategic dilemmas—information failures, problems of credible commitment, and the security dilemma—lurk in the background of all ethnically divided polities. Moreover, politicians can decide to outbid moderate competitors within their own ethnic group by making militant appeals to extreme elements. In situations of perceived group disadvantage, economic decline, hostile political memories, or widespread anomie, such appeals may awaken long dormant "malignant nationalisms" that set the stage for violence (Van Evera 1994, 8). Conflict always remains a possibility.

Confidence-building measures are essential to maintaining stable ethnic relations or restoring ethnic peace. Nonetheless, although confidence-building measures can restrain conflict in the short term, they cannot resolve the strategic dilemmas that continue to be firmly embedded in relations between ethnic groups. Because the prospect of future conflict cannot be dismissed, concessions made by state elites on inclusion, guarantees of proportionality, autonomy, and so forth are useful forms of reassurance, but they are inevitably fragile instruments for the protection of exposed peoples. In the final analysis, there are no reliable safety nets for vulnerable minorities.

Preventive efforts are more likely to keep ethnic conflicts manageable than measures taken after polarization and violence have undermined trust. As Bruce Jentleson observes (Chapter Thirteen), states can play an important role in keeping violent encounters and war from arising by structuring relations within society so as to reduce ethnic fears and promote cooperation. Confidence-building measures are important because they reassure minority peoples that their interests will be protected and that their representatives will be actively involved in making future decisions.

Preventing conflict by building democracy is more problematic. Democracy is important to stable intergroup relations because it establishes institutions that encourage the parties to commit themselves to regular political competition, albeit one which involves a degree of uncertainty for all actors. As Adam Przeworski (1991, 19) describes it: "Some institutions under certain conditions offer to the relevant political forces a prospect of eventually advancing their interests that is sufficient to incite them to comply with immediately unfavorable outcomes." Rather than fear the future, parties in a democratic regime can see opportunities to gain power, often through reconfigured coalitions that allow minorities an opportunity to compensate for their numerical weakness by forming political alliances with other interests.

But in multiethnic societies the opportunities of democracy are often contingent on other factors being securely in place. In the short term, ethnic demands must be reasonable, moderate politics must prevail, and, as I. William Zartman emphasizes (Chapter Fourteen), groups must not be shut out of the decision-making process. Where extremist politicians seek to outflank moderates within their own group and make militant appeals to their ethnic kinsmen for preferential treatment, the fragile ties between elites may snap and the democratic experiment may unravel. For democracy to prevent interethnic conflict from occurring, it must surmount the dangers of any transition period and emerge as a truly self-enforcing system for protecting minority rights.

International interventions can help prevent and manage conflict, but they depend for their success upon the credibility of the external actors. Fearful of the future, and recognizing the state's limited capacity to ensure their physical and cultural safety, political minorities often look outward to the international community for pro-tection. They hope that other states and international organizations will facilitate and, if necessary, restore an internal balance of power that has broken down or restrain a possibly threatening internal adversary.

State elites often place a high value on acquiring and maintaining legitimacy in the eyes of other world leaders and the international community in general. Other states, in turn, can manipulate this desire for legitimacy by rewarding efforts to build stable ethnic relations with continued inclusion or acceptance in the inter-national community or by punishing recalcitrant state elites with exclusion. The crumbling of the apartheid regime in South Africa was a victory not only for the black majority but for the political tool of international exclusion.

External actors can also play a more active role in preventing and containing ethnic conflicts. Seeking to clarify fears and objectives and to overcome informa-tion failures, private and public diplomats have undertaken the critically impor-tant task of facilitating communication between internal adversaries. This role proved crucial in the confrontation between north and south in the Sudan in the 1960s, where an unofficial mediator, the World Council of Churches/All Africa Conference of Churches, met regularly with both sides and organized their nego-tiations at Addis Ababa.

Third parties have also gone beyond facilitating communication between adversaries to forge settlements. They have made side payments and urged the adoption of confidence-building mechanisms to reassure minority populations about their future. At times, as in the Russian negotiations with Estonia on the troop withdrawal issue (discussed by Cynthia Kaplan in Chapter Eleven), third parties even pressed groups and their interstate allies to make important conces-sions—in this case the Russians, who were threatened with delays in forthcom-ing summit meetings and the postponement of economic assistance.

Finally, external parties have even engaged in multilateral peacekeeping and peacemaking initiatives. The impact of these efforts, as Edmond Keller indicates (Chapter Twelve), has been uneven. If the Organization of African Unity's inter-ventions in Chad in the early 1980s did little to bring about a resolution of the conflict, the initiative undertaken by the Economic Community of West African states in Liberia in the 1990s helped to contain the spreading violence. Likewise, although the French appeal to send international units to eastern Zaire in 1996 seemed promising to many, it ultimately failed because France had in the past been identified as a supporter of President Juvenal Habyarimana's Hutu-led gov-ernment in Rwanda and its political capital in the region remained questionable to the new, predominantly Tutsi government leaders. A prominent and, to date, reasonably successful intervention is the NATO-led initiative in Bosnia. It was the NATO bombings in September 1995 that led the parties to the bargaining table in Dayton, Ohio, and the subsequent peacekeeping forces in Bosnia have been essential to the restoration of the present political stability. Although the West can certainly be faulted for not acting earlier, and the undertaking may still fail in the long run because of a lack of external resources and commitment, events since the fall of 1995 demonstrate the power and potential of forceful external inter-ventions in deeply divided societies.

Yet, international intervention in intrastate disputes is not a cure-all. The international response has all too often been feeble and unconvincing. Under these circumstances, international intervention has typically failed to achieve its intended effects. The limits of international action are clearly shown by Daniel T. Froats and Stephen D. Krasner in Chapter Ten, where they analyze the efforts of the major European powers to secure guarantees for ethnic minorities in various treaties and agreements. In the nineteenth century, these interventions were decidedly limited. The external actors strongly protested human rights violations in the new Balkan states, but they did little to enforce their will. This changed under the Versailles settlement and the minority rights treaties that followed World War I. Here, the Western countries imposed very detailed arrangements and provided for monitoring and enforcement by the League of Nations and International Court of Justice. In the end, however, these carefully crafted treaties were no more able to ensure minority protections than the nineteenth-century Balkan treaties that preceded them, largely because of a lack of commitment by both the frail states and, especially, the great powers. No other lesson is more important than this. External interventions that lack credibility in the eyes of the local parties will fail.

The diffusion of ethnic conflict can be partially mitigated by managing information effectively. Confidence-building mechanisms and other forms of preventive action as well as external interventions are imperfect instruments for ensuring ethnic peace. Some measure of ethnic conflict may be inevitable. Confidence-building measures and external interventions are also targeted at particular ethnic conflicts—both actual and possible. They work primarily by influencing internal conditions and, thus, the probabilities of intrastate conflicts. As ethnic conflict requires fertile soil in which to grow, this emphasis on local conditions is necessary and appropriate—even in a volume such as ours that focuses on the international spread of ethnic conflict. By reducing the chances of violence in particular locations, various preventive measures and interventions affect indirectly the international processes of diffusion and escalation. Nonetheless, they do not address these processes directly.

With the exception of the first and most direct route, where conflict abroad alters the existing balance of ethnic power at home (Chapter One), diffusion occurs largely by changing the political strategies and, more fundamentally, the information and beliefs of ethnic groups. Ethnic conflict abroad may embolden groups to make more extreme demands, prompt groups to expect others to make extreme demands, and alter the evaluations groups make about the distribution of ethnic power within their societies, the efficacy of their existing safeguards, and the costs of using violence. Because of the selection bias in the international media and the self-aggrandizing strategies of egoistic politicians, conflict is more likely to diffuse through these channels than are peaceful interactions.

Recognizing the importance of information flows and the beliefs leaders and groups hold about the intentions and abilities of others, one of the most effective policy instruments available to the international community for limiting diffusion is to ensure that objective, unbiased and balanced information is widely available to all ethnic groups at risk of being engulfed by conflict. By providing impartial and unprejudiced information, states and the international community in general can seek to offset the selection bias in the media and the pronouncements of national political entrepreneurs and to correct the distortions in beliefs that follow from this bias. In this way, the international community can help to reduce the severity of both the between- and within-group strategic problems discussed in Chapter One. In turn, this directly limits the likelihood that ethnic conflicts will diffuse around the globe. Mediation in specific conflicts often serves this same purpose. But wider communication of accurate information can also create a general climate that inhibits the spread of conflict by mitigating the sources of ethnic fear and insecurity.

The need for readily available, objective information affirms the important international role played by relatively unbiased global broadcasters like the BBC. It also suggests a new mission for the information arms of the United States government, built up during the Cold War but now coming under the budgetary knife. Agencies like Radio Free Europe, which provided information on economic and political trends that was simply unavailable in the communist countries of Eastern Europe and the Soviet Union, could now serve equally well in disseminating even-handed reports on ethnic conflicts and, more important, successful cohabitations. Such impartial information might have made a difference in Bosnia and Rwanda, although, by itself, better information is unlikely to have prevented either conflict in its entirety.

External intervention should be carefully regulated and monitored by the international community. States must recognize and legitimate the need to protect minority rights within other countries. At the same time, the international community, acting through its regional and international bodies, should reserve to itself the sole right to sanction coercive interventions, lest the pursuit of this principle escalate rather than mitigate interstate conflicts.

Protecting minority rights is a double-edged sword. As Moore and Davis demonstrate in Chapter Four, transnational ethnic alliances are an important source of interstate conflict; through such alliances states are—willingly or unwillingly—drawn into neighboring conflicts. By legitimating the protection of minority rights in other countries, the international community risks stimulating or, at least, providing political cover for self-aggrandizing interventions by ethnic allies or other opportunistic states. To forestall this result, the international community should insist that efforts to protect minority rights be approved by some general regional or international body. By limiting the rights of co-ethnics in neighboring states to intervene unilaterally, the potential for transforming local conflicts into regional conflicts is greatly reduced. The pull of ethnic alliances can thereby be diminished.

At the same time, this insistence on international approval rather than unilateral initiatives obligates the international community to assume responsibility for protecting minorities—as it has done, with only limited success, with the Kurds in northern Iraq. If ethnic brethren are to be deterred from coming to the aid of their allies, the international community itself must assist besieged peoples. To prevent escalation, states without significant ethnic ties must be willing to assume responsibility for the protection of endangered minority peoples.

Toward Practical Initiatives

Recognizing the inherent limits on the ability of international interventions to solve the strategic dilemmas we have identified, as well as the limits of public support in outside states, we recommend four specific avenues of action.

Manage Information

Given the importance of private information and the beliefs that groups hold about the intentions of others, one of the most effective policy instruments in the hands of international actors today is to ensure that objective, unbiased and balanced information is made widely available in states threatened with intense conflict. This will require an ongoing but largely preventive effort. If conflict breaks out, in turn, outside states and international organizations can consider jamming radios that make inflammatory appeals, as did Radio Télévision Libre des Mille Collines in Rwanda. After the crisis has eased, external actors can use a variety of means—such as radio, fax, and the Internet—for sharing information with the warring parties to help verify compliance with new ethnic contracts.

Assist "Failing" States

Growing state weakness is a symptom of the strategic dilemmas discussed above. As information failures occur, problems of credible commitment arise, and security dilemmas begin to take hold, groups either turn away from the state or attempt to seize it to further their own quest for security. A state's increasing incapacity to arbitrate between groups and enforce ethnic contracts is a clear herald of violence. Preventing the breakdown of the state can, in turn, help mitigate the potential for violence. External actors should seek to ensure that confidence-building measures are in place and that elites live up to minimum standards of legal order and political and human rights. The support of the international community for the anti-apartheid struggle in South Africa is a prime example. Trade, financial aid, and other benefits from inclusion in the international community should be linked to the maintenance of minimum international standards of domestic order and justice.

Invest in Implementation

Negotiating a peace agreement between warring ethnic groups is only half the job. Implementing the agreement is just as important, and can be more difficult and complex than the negotiations. None of the strategies of external involvement discussed in this volume "solves" the problem of ethnic conflict. Even if external pressure brings the parties to the table and produces an agreement, the underlying strategic dilemmas remain in place. A stable peace can only arise as effective institutions of government are reestablished, the state once again begins to mediate effectively between distrustful ethnic groups, and the parties slowly gain confidence in the safeguards contained within their new ethnic contracts. This necessarily involves an element of state building and the possibility of forcible intervention to protect minorities. It is also a slow, incremental process that is likely to require years to bear fruit.

The United States and other countries, individually or collectively, should invest substantially in implementing peace agreements. That rival parties have consented to an agreement indicates they have jointly come to accept certain outcomes and understandings. At this stage, implementation becomes the decisive factor in the successful creation of internal political stability. Even when backed by a peacekeeping force, implementing a peace agreement involves a limited commitment on the part of an individual external state or a coalition of states; they are committed to this agreement, not others, and need not fall prey to the inevitable pressures for "mission creep." Successful implementation offers potentially large returns. The alternative is renewed or, in some cases, unending conflict.

Plan and Prevent

In the end, there can be no substitute for greater global commitment and concern. Planning and early action are essential in this endeavor. The international community has already been involved at nearly every stage of some confrontations around the globe, assembling data banks, setting up early warning systems, recognizing governments and insurgent movements, mediating before and after the formal negotiating process, dispatching peace keepers, engaging in peace-enforcement efforts, providing monitoring teams, assisting in the creation of new armies, and possibly holding war crimes trials. This is a hopeful sign. Yet, these international responses have been conducted separately, sporadically, and outside of any comprehensive strategy for achieving ethnic peace, thereby limiting their effectiveness. Planning for future ethnic crises means that states must act in advance of confrontations to develop norms, assemble information, establish early-warning mechanisms, and put mediators, military contingents, and monitoring teams on a stand-by basis. For former Secretary General Boutros Boutros-Ghali (1992, 47), a sense of confidence that the United Nations will react swiftly to uphold its charter "presupposes a strong, efficient and independent civil service . . . and an assured financial basis." Only such a decisive and effective global body can be counted upon to intercede in intense ethnic conflicts before they spread out of control and leave us all more fearful than ever about our own survival and well-being.

REFERENCES

Adam, Heribert. 1990. Exclusive nationalism versus inclusive patriotism: State ideologies for divided societies. *Innovation* 3, no. 4: 569–87.

Adam, Heribert, and Kogila Moodley. 1993. South Africa: The opening of the apartheid mind. In *The politics of ethnic conflict regulation*, edited by John McGarry and Brendan O'Leary. New York: Routledge.

Adam, Hussein. 1995. Somalia: Terrible beauty being born? In *Collapsed states: The disintegration and restoration of legitimate authority*, edited by I. W. Zartman. Boulder, CO: Lynne Rienner.

Adelman, Howard, and Astri Suhrke. 1996. *Early warning and conflict management* study 2 of the Joint Evaluation of Emergency Assistance to Rwanda. Copenhagen: DANIDA.

Agence France Presse. 1995a. OAU rapid deployment force. June 27.

———. 1995b. June 28.

———. *Agence France Presse-Guinée.* 1958. November 19.

Ake, Claude. 1985. Why is Africa not developing? *West Africa* 3538 (June 17).

Alba, Richard D. 1990. *Ethnic identity: The transformation of white America.* New Haven: Yale University Press.

Alcock, Antony. 1979. Three case studies. In *The future of cultural minorities,* edited by Antony Alcock, Brian Taylor, and John Welton. London: Macmillan; New York: St. Martin's Press.

Aldcroft, Derek H. 1978. *The European Economy, 1914-1970.* London: Croom Helm.

Allison, G. 1971. *The essence of decision.* Boston: Little, Brown.

Ames, Barry. 1987. *Political survival: Politicians and public policy in Latin America.* Berkeley and Los Angeles: University of California Press.

Amnesty International. 1995. *The tears of orphans: No future without human rights.* New York: Amnesty International.

ANC Daily News Briefing. 1996. SA will pay price for new constitution, FW. May 9, p. 9, as transmitted on gopher://gopher.anc.org.za.70/00/anc/newsbrief/ 1996/news0509.

Anchabadze, Yuri. 1995. The caucasian idea: The search for regional accord. In *Abstracts of conference "Interethnic conflicts in the Caucasus: Approaches to solutions"* 6. Moscow (January 19–20, 1994).

Anderson, Benedict. 1983. *Imagined communities: Reflections on the origins and spread of nationalism.* London: Verso.

Anderson, John R. 1990. *Cognitive psychology and its implications.* New York: W. H. Freeman.

Anderson, M. S. 1966. *The Eastern question, 1774–1923: A study in international relations.* London: Macmillan.

Anderson, Perry. 1974. *Lineages of the absolutist state.* London: Verso.

Arlen, Michael J. 1975. *Passage to Ararat.* New York: Farrar, Strauss, & Giroux.

Art, Robert J., and Robert Jervis. 1992. *International politics: Enduring concepts and contemporary issues.* 3rd ed. New York: HarperCollins.

Arutiunov, Sergei A. 1994. The languages of the Caucasus. In *Peoples of the Caucasus: Anthropology, linguistics, economy,* edited by M. G. Abdushelishvili, S. A. Arutiunov, and B. A. Kaloev. Moscow: Russian Academy of Sciences Institute of Ethnology and Anthropology.

Arutiunov, Sergei A. 1995. Ethnicity and conflict in the Caucasus. In *Ethnic conflict and Russian intervention in the Caucasus,* edited by Fred Wehling. Policy Paper 16. La Jolla: University of California Institute on Global Conflict and Cooperation (August).

Aspaturian, Vernon V. 1968. The non-Russian nationalities. In *Prospects for Soviet society*, edited by Allen Kassof. New York: Praeger.

Atwood, J. Brian. 1994. Suddenly, chaos. *Washington Post*, July 31, p. C9.

Aushev, Ruslan. 1995. If war goes on, it's to someone's advantage. *Komsomolskaya pravda*, January 18. p. 2

Avruch, Kevin, and Peter W. Black. 1991. The culture question and conflict resolution. *Peace-and-Change* 16, no. 1 (January): 22–45.

Axelrod, Robert. 1973. Schema theory: An information processing model of perception and cognition. *American Political Science Review* 67, no. 4 (December): 1,248–66.

Azar, Edward. 1980. The conflict and peace databank. *Journal of Conflict Resolution* 24, no. 1 (March): 143–52.

Azar, Edward E., and Thomas J. Sloan. 1975. *Dimensions of interaction*. Occasional Paper 8. Pittsburgh, PA: International Studies Association.

Azcárate, Pablo de. 1972. *League of Nations and national minorities: An experiment*. Translated from the Spanish. Washington, D.C.: Carnegie Endowment, 1945; New York: Klaus Reprint.

Baddeley, A. D. 1986. *Working memory*. Oxford: Oxford University Press.

Bahrick, H. P., and L. K. Hall. 1991. Lifetime maintenance of high school mathematics content. *Journal of Experimental Psychology: General* 120, no. 1 (March): 20–33.

Bainton, Roland H. 1951. *The travail of religious liberty: Nine biographical studies*. Philadelphia: The Westminster Press.

Banton, Michael. 1985. *Promoting racial harmony*. Cambridge: Cambridge University Press.

Banton, Michael, and Mohd Noor Mansor. 1992. The study of ethnic alignment: A new technique and an application in Malaysia. *Ethnic and Racial Studies* 15, no. 4 (October): 599–613.

Barker, Ernest, ed. 1948. *Politics* 2, sec. 2. New York: Oxford University Press.

Barkow, Jerome H., Leda Cosmides, and John Tooby, eds. 1992. *The adapted mind: Evolutionary psychology and the generation of culture*. New York: Oxford University Press.

Bartsch, Sebastian. 1995. *Minderheitenschutz in der internationalen Politik: Volkerbund und KSZE/OSZE in neuer Perspektive*. Oplanden, Germany: Westdeutscher Verlag.

Bates, Robert H. 1983. Modernization, ethnic competition, and the rationality of politics in contemporary Africa. In *State versus ethnic claims*, edited by Donald Rothchild and Victor A. Olorunsola. Boulder, CO: Westview.

Bates, Robert H., and Barry R. Weingast. 1995. Rationality and interpretation: The politics of transition. Paper presented to the annual meeting of the American Political Science Association, August 31–September 3 at Chicago.

Beller, E. A. 1970. The thirty years war. In *The new Cambridge modern history: The decline of Spain and the Thirty Years War 1609–48/59*. vol. 4. Cambridge: Cambridge University Press.

Bennigsen Broxup, Marie. 1992. Russia and the North Caucasus. In *The North Caucasus barrier: The Russian advance towards the Muslim world*, edited by Marie Bennigsen Broxup. London: Hurst.

Benns, Lee. 1930. *Europe since 1914*. New York: F. S. Crofts.

Bercovitch, Jacob, and Jeffrey Rubin, eds. 1992. *Mediation in international relations*. New York: St. Martin's Press.

Betts, Richard K. 1994. The delusion of impartial intervention. *Foreign Affairs* 73, no. 6 (November–December): 20–33.

Bilder, Richard. 1992. Can minorities treaties work? In *The protection of minorities and human rights*, edited by Yoram Dinstein and Mala Tabory. Dordrecht, Netherlands: Martinus Nijhoff.

Binder, David, with Barbara Crossette. 1993. As ethnic wars multiply, U.S. strives for a policy. *New York Times,* February 7, p. 1.

Blainey, Geoffrey. 1973. *The causes of war.* New York: Free Press.

Blaisdell, Donald C. 1929. *European financial control in the Ottoman Empire: A study of the establishment, activities, and significance of the administration of the Ottoman public debt.* New York: Columbia University Press.

Bloed, Arie. 1993. The CSCE and the protection of national minorities. In *The U.N. Minority Rights Declaration,* edited by Alex Phillips and Allen Rosas. London: Turku/Abo.

Bohlen, Celestine. 1993. Amid war for enclave, Amenia sees little hope. *New York Times,* February 12, A3.

Bokhari, Imtiaz. 1995. Internal negotiations among many actors: Afghanistan. In *Elusive peace: Negotiating an end of civil wars,* edited by I. William Zartman. Washington, D.C.: Brookings Institution.

Bookman, Milica Zarkovic. 1992. *The economics of secession.* New York: St. Martin's Press.

——. 1994. *Economic decline and nationalism in the Balkans.* New York: St. Martin's Press.

Boutros-Ghali, Boutros. 1992. *An agenda for peace.* New York: United Nations.

——. 1995. Supplement to *An agenda for peace:* Position paper of the secretary-general on the occasion of the fiftieth anniversary of the United Nations. United Nations, General Assembly, fiftieth sess., A/50/60 (January 3).

Brady, Henry E., and Cynthia S. Kaplan. 1994. Eastern Europe and the former Soviet Union. In *Referendums around the world: The growing use of direct democracy,* edited by David Butler and Austin Ranney. Washington, D.C.: AEI Press.

Brass, Paul, ed. 1985. *Ethnic groups and the state.* London: Croom-Helm.

Braudel, Fernand. 1979. *The wheels of commerce: Civilization and capitalism, fifteenth–eighteenth century.* New York: Harper and Row.

Brecher, Michael, and Jonathan Wilkenfeld. 1995. The ethnic dimension in twentieth-century crises. Paper presented at the annual meeting of the International Studies Association, February 22–25, at Chicago.

——. 1997. The ethnic dimension of international crises. In *Wars in the midst of peace: The international politics of ethnic conflict,* edited by D. W. Carment and P. James. Pittsburgh: University of Pittsburgh Press.

Bremer, Stuart A. 1993. Democracy and militarized interstate conflict, 1816–1965. *International Interactions* 18, no. 3: 231–49.

Bremmer, Ian, and Ray Taras, eds. 1993. *Nations and politics in the Soviet successor states.* Cambridge: Cambridge University Press.

Breuilly, John. 1994. *Nationalism and the state.* 2d ed. Chicago: University of Chicago Press.

Brown, Michael E., ed. 1993. *Ethnic conflict and international security.* Princeton: Princeton University Press.

——, ed. 1996. *The international dimensions of internal conflict.* Cambridge: MIT Press.

Brownlie, Ian, ed. 1992. *Basic Documents on Human Rights.* Oxford: Clareadon Press.

Broxup, Marie Bennigsen, ed. 1992. *The North Caucasus barrier: The Russian advance towards the Muslim world.* New York: St. Martin's Press.

Brubaker, Rogers. 1995. National minorities, nationalizing states, and external national homelands in the new Europe. *Daedalus* (Spring):107–32.

Bryce, Viscount James. 1972. *The treatment of the Armenians in the Ottoman Empire 1915–1916: Documents presented to the secretary of state for foreign affairs by Viscount Bryce.* Original edition, London, 1916; Beirut: G. Doniguiana and Sons.

Buerklin, W. P. 1987. Why study political cycles? An introduction. *European Journal of Political Research* 15, no. 1: 1–21.

Burt, Alfred LeRoy. 1956. *Evolution of the British empire and commonwealth*. Boston: Heath.

Burton, John. 1987. *Resolving deep-rooted conflict*. Lanham, MD: University Presses of America.

———, ed. 1990a. *Conflict: Resolution and prevention*. New York: St. Martin's Press.

———. 1990b. *Conflict: Human needs theory*. New York: St. Martin's Press.

Cairncross, Alec K. 1953. *Home and Foreign Investment, 1870–1914*. Cambridge: Cambridge University Press.

Cameron, A. Colin, and Frank A. G. Windmeijer. 1996. R-squared measures for count data regression models with applications to health care utilization. *Journal of Business and Economic Statistics* 14, no. 2: 209–20.

Cameron, Rondo. 1961. *France and the Economic Development of Europe, 1800–1914*. Princeton: Princeton University Press.

Carment, David W. 1993. The international dimensions of ethnic conflict: Concepts, indicators, and theory. *Journal of Peace Research* 30, no. 2 (May): 137–50.

———. 1994. The ethnic dimension in world politics: Theory, policy, and early warning. *Third World Quarterly* 15, no. 4: 551–82.

Carment, David, and Patrick James. 1995. Internal constraints and interstate ethnic conflict: Toward a crisis-based assessment of irredentism. *Journal of Conflict Resolution* 39, no. 1: 82–109.

———. 1997. Secession and irridenta in world politics: The neglected interstate dimension. In *Wars in the midst of peace: The international politics of ethnic conflict*, edited by D. W. Carment and P. James. Pittsburgh: University of Pittsburgh Press.

Carnegie Commission for Preventing Deadly Conflict. 1995. *Progress report*. Washington, D.C.: Carnegie Commission for Preventing Deadly Conflict (July).

Carr, Caleb. 1993. The consequences of Somalia. *World Policy Journal* 10, no. 3 (Fall): 1–4.

Castles, Stephen. 1984. *Here for good: Western Europe's new ethnic minorities*. London: Pluto Press.

Chan, Steve. 1984. Mirror, mirror on the wall . . . Are the freer countries more pacific? *Journal of Conflict Resolution* 28, no. 4 (December): 617–48.

Chayes, Abram, and Antonia Handler Chayes, eds. 1996. *Preventing conflict in the post-communist world: Mobilizing international and regional organizations*. Washington, D.C.: Brookings Institution.

Cederman, Lars-Erik. 1996. From primordialism to constructivism: The quest for flexible models of ethnic conflict. Paper presented at the Annual Meeting of the American Political Science Association, San Francisco.

Chernov, Igor. 1995. The Caucasus could explode if the hostilities in Chechnya are compounded by war in Abkhazia. *Trud*, January 10, p. 2.

Chesnov, Ian V. 1994. It's hard to be a Chechen: Teips, their past and contemporary role. *Nezavisimaya gazeta*, September 22, p. 5.

Chigas, Diana, et al. 1996. Preventive diplomacy and the organization for security and cooperation in Europe: Creating incentives for dialogue and cooperation. In *Preventing conflict in the post-communist world*, edited by Abram Chayes and Antonia Handler Chayes. Washington, D.C.: Brookings Institution.

Chipman, John. 1993a. Managing the politics of parochialism. In *Ethnic conflict and international security*, edited by Michael E. Brown. Princeton: Princeton University Press.

———. 1993b. Managing the politics of parochialism. *Survival* 35 (Spring): 143–69.

Chong, Dennis. 1991. *Collective action and the civil rights movement*. Chicago: University of Chicago Press.

Cigar, Norman. 1995. *Genocide in Bosnia: The policy of "ethnic cleansing."* College Station: Texas A & M University Press.

Clark, Robert. 1995. Negotiating with the Basque separatists. In *Elusive peace: Negotiating an end of civil wars,* edited by I. William Zartman. Washington, D.C.: Brookings Institution.

Claude, Inis L., Jr. 1955. *National minorities: An international problem.* Cambridge: Harvard University Press.

Coakley, John. 1993. Introduction to *The territorial management of ethnic conflict,* edited by John Coakley. London: Cass.

Cobban, Alfred. 1994. *National self-determination.* Chicago: University of Chicago Press.

Cohn, Bernard S. 1996. *Colonialism and its forms of knowledge: The British in India.* Princeton: Princeton University Press.

Connor, Walker. 1972. Nation-building or nation-destroying? *World Politics* 24 (April): 319–55.

———. 1979. Ethnonationalism in the first world: The present in historical perspective. In *Ethnic conflict in the Western world,* edited by Milton J. Esman. Ithaca: Cornell University Press.

———. 1987. Ethnonationalism. In *Understanding political development,* edited by Myron Weiner and Samuel Huntington. New York: HarperCollins.

———. 1993. Beyond reason: The nature of the ethnonational bond. *Ethnic and Racial Studies* 16, no. 3 (July): 373–89.

———. 1994. *Ethnonationalism: The quest for understanding.* Princeton: Princeton University Press.

Converse, Philip. 1964. The nature of belief systems in mass publics. In *Ideology and discontent,* edited by David Apter. New York: Free Press.

Cooper, Robert, and Mats Berdal. 1993. Outside intervention in ethnic conflicts. In *Ethnic conflict and international security,* edited by Michael E. Brown. Princeton: Princeton University Press.

Crocker, Chester A. 1992. *High noon in Southern Africa.* New York: W.W. Norton.

Cumhuriyet, October 22, 1993, 1, 15.

Current Digest of the Soviet Press. 1992a. 44, no. 37: 3.

———. 1992b. 44, no. 43: 15.

———. 1994a. 44, no. 28: 12.

———. 1994b. 46, no. 10: 23.

Cuthbertson, Ian M., and Jane Leibowitz, eds. 1993. *Minorities: The new Europe's old issue.* Boulder, CO: Westview.

Dakin, Douglas. 1973. *The Greek struggle for independence, 1821–1833.* Berkeley and Los Angeles: University of California Press.

Damrosch, Lori Fisler, ed. 1993. *Enforcing restraint: Collective intervention in internal conflicts.* New York: Council on Foreign Relations.

Davidson, Basil. 1992. *The black man's burden: Africa and the curse of the nation–state.* New York: Times Books.

Davidow, Jeffrey. 1984. *A peace in Southern Africa.* Boulder, CO: Westview.

Davis, David R., Keith Jaggers, and Will H. Moore. 1997. Ethnicity, minorities, and international conflict patterns. In *Wars in the midst of peace: The international politics of ethnic conflict,* edited by D. W. Carment and P. James. Pittsburgh: University of Pittsburgh Press.

Dawisha, Adeed, and I. William Zartman, eds. 1988. *Beyond coercion: The durability of the Arab state.* London: Croom-Helm.

Dawisha, Karen, and Bruce Parrott. 1994. *Russia and the new states of Eurasia: The politics of upheaval.* New York: Cambridge University Press.

de Waal, Alex. 1994. The genocidal state: Hutu extremism and the origins of the "final solution" in Rwanda. *Times Literary Supplement* (July), 3–4.

DeNardo, James. 1985. *Power in numbers*. Princeton: Princeton University Press.

———. 1995. *The amateur strategist*. Cambridge: Cambridge University Press.

Deng, Francis M. 1993. Africa and the new world disorder: Rethinking colonial borders. *Brookings Review* 11, no. 2: 32–35.

———. 1995. Negotiating a hidden agenda. In *Elusive peace, negotiating an end of civil wars*, edited by I. William Zartman. Washington, D.C.: Brookings Institution.

Deng, Francis M and I. William Zartman, eds. 1991. *Conflict resolution in Africa*. Washington, D.C.: Brookings Institution.

Deng, Francis M., Sadikel Kimaro, Terrence Lyons, Donald Rothchild, and I. William Zartman, eds. 1996. *Sovereignty as responsibility: Conflict management in Africa*. Washington, D.C.: Brookings Institution.

Derluguian, Georgii M. 1995. It's difficult to be a Chechen, unpublished manuscript.

Deutsch, Karl, and William Foltz. 1966. *Nation-building*. Boston: Little, Brown.

Dixon, William J. 1986. Reciprocity in United States-Soviet relations: Multiple symmetry or issue linkage? *American Journal of Political Science* 30, no. 2 (May): 421–45.

Djilas, Aleksa. 1995. Fear thy neighbor: The breakup of Yugoslavia. In *Nationalism and nationalities in the new Europe*, edited by Charles A. Kupchan. Ithaca: Cornell University Press.

Dobb, Maurice. 1960. *Economic Growth and Planning*. New York: Monthly Review Press.

Dominguez, Virginia R. 1989. *People as subject, people as object: Selfhood and peoplehood in contemporary Israel*. Madison: University of Wisconsin Press.

Donnelly, Jack. 1992. Humanitarian intervention and American foreign policy: Law, morality, and politics. In *Human rights in the world community: Issues and actions*, edited by Richard P. Claude and Burns H. Weston. Philadelphia: University of Pennsylvania Press.

Douglass, William A. 1988. A critique of recent trends in the analysis of ethnonationalism. *Ethnic and Racial Studies* 11, no. 1 (April), 192–206.

Doyle, Michael. 1986. Liberalism and world politics. *American Political Science Review* 80, no. 4 (December): 1, 151–61.

Drobizheva, L. M., et al. 1994. Problemy suvereniteta i mezhnatsional'nye otnosheniia v respublike Tatarstan v nachale 90-kh godov. In *Natsional'noe samosoznanie i nationalizm v Rossiiskoi Federatsii nachala 1990-kh godov*, edited by L. M. Drobizheva et al. Moscow: IEA RAN.

Druckman, Daniel, and Justin Green. 1995. Negotiating in the Philippines. In *Elusive peace: Negotiating an end of civil wars*, edited by I. William Zartman. Washington, D.C.: Brookings Institution.

Duby, Georges. 1980. *The three orders: Feudal society imagined*. Chicago: University of Chicago Press.

Dudwick, Nora. 1995. Armenia. The nation awakens. In *Nations and politics in Soviet successor states*, edited by Ian Bremmer and Raymond Taras. New York: Cambridge University Press.

Eisenstadt, Tod, and Daniel Garcia. 1995. Columbia. In *Elusive peace: Negotiating an end of civil wars*, edited by I. William Zartman. Washington, D.C.: Brookings Institution.

Erlich, Haggai. 1983. *The struggle over Eritrea*. Stanford: Hoover Institution Press.

Esman, Milton J. 1994. *Ethnic politics*. Ithaca: Cornell University Press.

Etzioni, Amitai. 1992–1993. The evils of self-determination. *Foreign Policy* 89 (Winter): 21–35.

Evans, Gareth. 1993. *Cooperating for peace: The global agenda for the 1990s and beyond.* London: Allen and Unwin.

Evans, Peter B. 1993. Building an integrative approach to international and domestic politics: Reflections and projections. In *Double-edged diplomacy: International bargaining and domestic politics,* edited by Peter B. Evans, Harold K. Jacobson, and Robert D. Putnam. Berkeley and Los Angeles: University of California Press.

Evans, Richard J. 1979. Red Wednesday in Hamburg: Social democrats, police, and Lumpenproletariat in the suffrage disturbances of 17 January 1906. *Social History* 4, no. 1 (January): 1–31.

Fahrmeier, L., and G. Tutz. 1994. *Multivariate statistical modelling based on generalized linear models.* New York: Springer-Verlag.

Fearon, James D. 1991. Counterfactuals and hypothesis testing in political science. *World Politics* 43 (January): 169–95.

———. 1993. Ethnic war as a commitment problem. University of Chicago. June. Unpublished manuscript.

———. 1994. Ethnic war as a commitment problem. Paper presented at the annual meetings of the American Political Science Association, September 2–5, 1994, at New York City.

———. 1995. Rationalist explanations for war. *International Organization* 49, no. 3 (Summer): 379–414.

Fearon, James D., and David D. Laitin. 1996. Explaining inter-ethnic cooperation. *American Political Science Review* 90, no. 4 (December): 715–35.

Felgengauer, Pavel. 1994. There will be no second Caucasus war: Shamil and his murids and holy wars are part of the past. *Segodnya* (December 17): 3.

Fiske, Susan. 1982. Schema-triggered affect: Applications to social perception. In *Affect and cognition,* edited by Margaret Clark and Susan Fiske. Hillsdale, NJ: Lawrence Erlbaum.

Fiske, Susan, and Patricia W. Linville. 1980. What does the schema concept buy us? *Personality and Social Psychology Bulletin* 6, no. 4 (December): 543–57.

Fiske, Susan, and Mark Pavelchak. 1986. Category-based versus piecemeal-based affective responses: Developments in schema-triggered affect. In *Handbook of motivation and cognition,* edited by Richard Sorrentino and E. Troy Higgins. New York: Guilford Press.

Fiske, Susan and Shelly Taylor. 1984. *Social cognition.* Reading: Addison-Wesley.

Fleischman, Janet. 1993. An uncivil war. *Africa Report* 38, no. 3 (May/June): 56-59.

Foltz, William. 1965. *From French West Africa to the Mali federation.* New Haven: Yale University Press.

Forsythe, David P. 1983. *Human rights and world politics.* Lincoln: University of Nebraska Press.

Fortna, Virginia P. 1995. Success and failure in Southern Africa: Peacekeeping in Namibia and Angola. In *Beyond traditional peacekeeping,* edited by Donald C. F. Daniel and Bradd C. Hayes. New York: St. Martin's.

Fouques-Duparc, Jacques. 1922. *La protection des minorites de race, de langue, et de religion: Étude de droit des gens.* Paris: Librairie Dalloz.

Freedman, Lawrence. 1994–1995. Why the West failed. *Foreign Policy* 97 (Winter): 58-69.

Frei, Daniel. 1976. Conditions affecting the effectiveness of international mediation. *Papers of the Peace Science Society* 26 (International): 67–84.

Frieden, Jeffry A., and Ronald Rogowski. 1996. The impact of the international economy on national policies: An analytic overview. In *Internationalization and domestic politics,* edited by Robert O. Keohane and Helen V. Milner. New York: Cambridge University Press.

Friedman, Thomas L. 1995. Boris, Bill, and Voltaire. *New York Times*, February 26, sec. 4, p. 15.

Friedman, Townsend. 1995. Statement . . . before the joint hearing of the Senate Foreign Relations Subcommittee on Africa and the House International Relations Subcommittee on Africa on Rwanda and Burundi. April 5. Washington, D.C.: 104th Session of Congress.

Furtado, Jr., Charles F., and Andrea Chandler, eds. 1992. *Perestroika in the Soviet republics: Documents on the national question.* Boulder, CO: Westview.

Furtado, Jr., Charles F., and Michael Hecter. 1992. The emergence of nationalist politics in the USSR: A comparison of Estonia and the Ukraine. In *Thinking theoretically about Soviet nationalities: History and comparison in the study of the USSR,* edited by Alexander J. Motyl. New York: Columbia University Press.

Gagliardo, John. 1991. *Germany under the old regime, 1600–1790.* London: Longman.

Gagnon, Jr., V. P. 1991. Yugoslavia: Prospects for stability. *Foreign Affairs* 70, no. 3: 17–35.

———. 1994–1995. Ethnic nationalism and international conflict: The case of Serbia. *International Security* 19, no. 3 (Winter): 130–66.

Galenson, Walter, and Harvey Leibenstein. 1955. Investment Criteria and Economic Development. *Quarterly Journal of Economics* 69 (August): 343–70.

Garb, Paula. 1994. Growing in age and wisdom: Abkhazian elders as mediators of conflict. In *Portraits of culture: Ethnographic originals,* edited by M. Ember and C. Ember. Englewood Cliffs, NJ: Prentice-Hall.

———. 1996. Mediation in the Caucasus. *Anthropological contributions to conflict resolution: Proceedings of the Southern Anthropological Association.* Atlanta: University of Georgia Press.

Gboyega, Alex. 1996. Nigeria: Unresolved conflicts. In *Elusive peace: Negotiating an end of civil wars,* edited by I. William Zartman. Washington, D.C.: Brookings Institution.

Geary, Dick. 1981. *European labour protest 1848–1939.* London: Croom-Helm.

Gellner, Ernest. 1992. Nationalism in the vacuum. In *Thinking theoretically about Soviet nationalities: History and comparison in the study of the USSR,* edited by Alexander J. Motyl. New York: Columbia University Press.

George, Alexander L. 1994. The warning-response problem in preventive diplomacy. Chapter presented to the Study Group on Preventive Diplomacy in the Post-Cold War World, United States Institute of Peace and the State Department Policy Planning Staff. January. Unpublished manuscript.

George, Alexander L., and Jane E. Holl. 1995. The warning-response problem in preventive diplomacy. Carnegie Commission for Preventing Deadly Conflict.

———. 1998. The warning-response problem and "missed opportunities" in preventive diplomacy. In *Opportunities missed, opportunities seized: Preventive diplomacy in the post-cold war world,* edited by Bruce W. Jentleson. Lanham, MD: Rowman and Littlefield, forthcoming.

George, Alexander L., and Richard Smoke. 1974. *Deterrence in American foreign policy: Theory and practice.* New York: Columbia University Press.

Gilpin, Robert. 1981. *War and change in world politics.* New York: Cambridge University Press.

Glazer, Nathan, and Daniel P. Moynihan. 1975. *Ethnicity: Theory and experience.* Cambridge: Harvard University Press.

Glenny, Misha. 1992a. *The fall of Yugoslavia.* New York: Penguin Books.

———. 1992b. The massacre of Yugoslavia. *New York Review of Books,* May 27.

———. 1993. *The fall of Yugoslavia: The third Balkan war.* Rev. ed. New York: Penguin Books.

Goldstein, Joshua S. 1991. Reciprocity in superpower relations: An empirical analysis. *International Studies Quarterly* 35, no. 2 (June): 195–209.

Goldstein, Joshua S., and John R. Freeman. 1990. *Three way street*. Chicago: University of Chicago Press.

———. 1991. U.S.-Soviet-Chinese relations: Routine, reciprocity, or rational expectations. *American Political Science Review* 85, no. 1 (March): 17–36.

Goldstein, Robert J. 1983. *Political repression in nineteenth-century Europe*. London: Croom-Helm.

Gourevitch, Peter. 1978. The second image reversed: The international sources of domestic politics. *International Organization* 32 (Autumn): 881–912.

Grove, Brandon. 1994. Chapter presented to the Study Group on Preventive Diplomacy in the Post-Cold War World, United States Institute of Peace and the State Department Policy Planning Staff. January. Unpublished manuscript.

Gurr, Ted Robert. 1992. The internationalization of protracted communal conflicts since 1945: Which groups, where, and how. In *The internationalization of communal strife*, edited by Manus Midlarsky. London: Routledge.

———. 1993. *Minorities at risk: A global view of ethnopolitical conflicts*. Washington, D.C.: United States Institute of Peace Press.

———. 1994. Peoples against states: Ethnopolitical conflict and the changing world system. *International Studies Quarterly* 38, no. 3 (September): 347–77.

Gurr, Ted Robert, Keith Jaggers, and Will H. Moore. 1989. *Polity II codebook*. Boulder, CO: Center for Comparative Politics.

Gutman, Yisrael, ed. 1989. *The Jews of Poland between two world wars*. Hanover, NH: Published for Brandeis University Press by University Press of New England.

Haas, Ernst. 1964. *Beyond the nation-state: Functionalism and international organization*. Stanford: Stanford University Press.

Haass, Richard N. 1990. *Unending conflicts: The United States and regional disputes*. New Haven: Yale University Press.

———. 1994. Military force: A user's guide. *Foreign Policy* 96 (Fall): 21–37.

Hailbronner, Kay. 1992. The legal status of population groups in a multinational state under public international law. In *The protection of minorities and human rights*, edited by Yoram Dinstein and Mala Tabory. Dordrecht, Netherlands: Martinus Nijhoff.

Halévy, Elie. 1930. *The world crisis of 1914–1918*. Oxford: Clarendon Press.

Halpern, Manfred. 1964. The morality and politics of intervention. In *International aspects of civil strife*, edited by J. N. Rosenau. Princeton: Princeton University Press.

Hardin, Russell. 1982. *Collective action*. Baltimore: Johns Hopkins University Press.

———. 1995. *One for all: The logic of group conflict*. Princeton: Princeton University Press.

Hayden, Robert M. 1992. Constitutional nationalism in the formerly Yugoslav republics. *Slavic Review* 51, no. 4 (Winter): 654–73.

Hazard, John N. 1993. Managing nationalism: State, law, and the national question in the USSR. In *Nations and politics in the Soviet successor states*, edited by Ian Bremmer and Raymond Taras. Cambridge: Cambridge University Press.

Hechter, Michael. 1987. *Principles of group solidarity*. Berkeley and Los Angeles: University of California Press.

Hechter, Michael, Debra Friedman, and Malka Appelbaum. 1982. A theory of ethnic collective action. *International Migration Review* 16, no. 2 (Summer): 412–34.

Henze, Paul B. 1992. Circassian resistance to Russia. In *The North Caucasus barrier: The Russian advance towards the Muslim world*, edited by Marie Bennigsen Broxup. London: Hurst.

Hill, Fiona. 1995. "Russia's tinderbox": Conflict in the North Caucasus and its implications for the future of the Russian federation. *Strengthening Democratic Institutions Project.* September. Cambridge: Harvard University John F. Kennedy School of Government.

Hill, Fiona, and Pamela Jewett. 1994. Back in the USSR: Russia's intervention in the internal affairs of the former Soviet republics and the implications for United States policy towards Russia. *Strengthening democratic institutions project.* Cambridge: John F. Kennedy School of Government.

Hill, Stuart. 1992. *Democratic values and technological choices.* Stanford: Stanford University Press.

Hill, Stuart, and Donald Rothchild. 1986. The contagion of political conflict in Africa and the world. *Journal of Conflict Resolution* 30, no. 4 (December): 716–35.

———. 1992. The impact of regime on the diffusion of political conflict. In *The internationalization of communal strife,* edited by Manus Midlarsky. London: Routledge.

Hirsch, John L., and Robert B. Oakley. 1995. *Somalia and Operation Restore Hope: Reflections on peacemaking and peacekeeping.* Washington, D.C.: United States Institute of Peace Press.

Hirschleifer, Jack. 1983. From weakest-link to best-shot: The voluntary provision of public goods. *Public Choice* 41, no. 3: 371–86.

———. 1987. The economic approach to conflict. In *Economic imperialism: The economic approach applied outside of the field of economics,* edited by Gerald Radnitzky and Peter Bernholz. New York: Paragon House.

Hirschman, Albert O. 1970. *Exit, voice, and loyalty: Responses to decline in firms, organizations, and states.* Cambridge: Harvard University Press.

Hitchens, Christopher. 1992. Appointment in Sarajevo. *The Nation* (September 14): 236–41.

Hoffmann, Stanley. 1995–1996. The politics and ethics of military intervention. *Survival* (Winter): 29–51.

———. 1996. In defense of Mother Theresa: Morality in foreign policy. *Foreign Affairs* 75 (March/April): 172–75.

Holborn, Hajo. 1959. *A history of modern Germany: The reformation.* New York: Alfred A. Knopf.

Horowitz, Donald L. 1975. Ethnic identity. In *Ethnicity: Theory and experience,* edited by Nathan Glazer and Daniel P. Moynihan. Cambridge: Harvard University Press.

———. 1985. *Ethnic groups in conflict.* Berkeley and Los Angeles: University of California Press.

———. 1990. Making moderation pay: The comparative politics of ethnic conflict management. In *Conflict and peacekeeping in multiethnic societies,* edited by Joseph Montville. Lexington, KY: Heath.

———. 1991. *A democratic South Africa? Constitutional engineering in a divided society.* Berkeley and Los Angeles: University of California Press.

Hughes, Michael. 1992. *Early modern Germany, 1477–1806.* London: Macmillan.

Human Rights Watch/Africa. 1994. *Civilian devastation: Abuses by all parties in the war in southern Sudan.* New York: Human Rights Watch.

Humanitarian Monitor. 1995. *Djibouti: Ending the war?* (February.)

Huntington, Samuel. 1993. The clash of civilizations? *Foreign Affairs* 72 (Summer): 22–49.

Huttenbach, Henry R. 1995. Letter to Paula Garb, December 6.

International Court of Justice. 1995. Western Sahara case. *International Court of Justice Reports 1995.* Hague: International Court of Justice.

International Monetary Fund. Various years. *International financial statistics.* New York: International Monetary Fund.

Iskhakov, D. M. 1992. Neformal'nye ob"edineniia v sovremennom Tatarskom obshchestve. In *Sovremennye national'nye protsessy v respublike Tatarstan*. Vol. 1, edited by R. N. Muchina, and D. M. Iskhakov. Kazan: Russian Academy of Sciences, 5–55.

Iskhakov, D. M. 1994. Politicheskoe razvitie Tatarstana v postkonstitutsionyi period. Unpublished manuscript.

Issacs, Harold. 1975. *Idols of the tribe: Group identity and political change*. New York: Harper and Row.

Iyengar, Shanto. 1991. *Is anyone responsible?* Chicago: University of Chicago Press.

Jackson, Henry F. 1982. *From the Congo to Soweto: U.S. foreign policy toward Africa since 1960*. New York: William Morrow.

Jackson, Robert H., and Carl G. Rosberg. 1982. Why Africa's weak states persist. *World Politics* 35, no. 1: 1–24.

Janics, K. 1975. Czechoslovakia's Magyar minority. *Canadian Review of Studies of Nationalism* 3, no. 1 (Autumn): 34–44.

Janowsky, Oscar Isaiah. 1945. *Nationalities and national minorities*. New York: Macmillan.

Jelavich, Charles, and Barbara Jelavich. 1977. *The establishment of the Balkan national states*. Seattle: University of Washington Press.

Jentleson, Bruce W. 1991. Review of *Unending conflicts*, by Richard N. Haass. *American Political Science Review* 85 (March): 337-38.

———. 1994. *With friends like these: Reagan, Bush, and Saddam, 1982–1990*. New York: W. W. Norton.

———. 1996. Who, why, what, and how: Debates over post-cold war military intervention. In *Eagle adrift: American foreign policy at the end of the century*, edited by Robert J. Lieber. New York: Longman.

———, ed. 1998. *Opportunities missed, opportunities seized: Preventive diplomacy in the post-cold war world*. Lanham, MD: Rowman & Littlefield, forthcoming.

Jervis, Robert. 1976. *Perception and misperception in international politics*. Princeton: Princeton University Press.

———. 1978. Cooperation under the security dilemma. *World Politics* 30, no. 2 (January): 167–214.

Joad, Cyril Edwin Mitchinson. 1951. What I still believe. *The New Statesman and Nation* (May 19): 557–58.

Jodice, D., and C. Taylor. 1981. *Codebook for political protest and government change, 1948–1977: The third world handbook of political and social indicators*. Berlin: Publication Series of the International Institute for Comparative Social Research.

Jones, Bryan D. 1994. *Reconceiving decision-making in democratic politics*. Chicago: University of Chicago Press.

Jones, Dorothy V. 1991. *Code of peace: Ethics and security in the world of the warlord states*. Chicago: University of Chicago Press.

Jones, Stephen F. 1993. Georgia: A failed democratic transition. In *Nations and politics in Soviet successor states*, edited by Ian Bremmer and Raymond Taras. Cambridge: Cambridge University Press.

Jordan, Wilbur K. 1932. *The development of religious toleration in England from the beginning of the English Reformation to the death of Queen Elizabeth*. London: Allen and Unwin.

Ka, Samba. 1992. Trade in the Senegambia. Ph.d. dissertation, Johns Hopkins University School of International Studies, Washington, D.C.

Kaempfer, William H., and Anton D. Lowenberg. 1992. Using threshold models to explain international relations. *Public Choice* 73 (June): 419–43.

Kalmykov, Yuri. 1993. Will Russia ever pursue a new nationalities policy? *Rossiskaya Gazeta* (January 6): 4.

Kampelman, Max M. 1993. Foreword to *Enforcing restraint: Collective intervention in internal conflicts,* edited by Lori Fisler Damrosch. New York: Council on Foreign Relations.

Kaplan, Cynthia S. 1992. Estonia: A plural society on the road to independence. In *Nations and politics in Soviet successor states,* edited by Ian Bremmer and Ray Taras. New York: Cambridge University Press.

———. 1995a. Political culture in Estonia: The impact of two traditions on political development. In *Political culture and civil society in Russia and the new states of Eurasia,* edited by Vladimir Tishmaneanu. Armonk, NY: M. E. Sharpe.

———. 1995b. Russian protest: Ethnic relations and state sovereignty. Paper presented at the International Spread and Management of Ethnic Conflict Conference. Davis: University of California Institute on Global Conflict and Cooperation (March 10).

Kaplan, Cynthia S., and Henry E. Brady. 1995. Igaunija: Divu Lopienu Raksturojums [Estonia: Portrait of two communities]. In *Nacionala politika baltijas valstis,* edited by Elmar Veber and Rasma Karklins. Riga, Latvia: Zinatne: 17–36.

Kaplan, Cynthia S., Henry E. Brady, William Smirnov, and Vladimir Andreenkov. 1992. Transition in Russia: Elite cleavages and political organizations. Paper presented at the annual meeting of the American Political Science Association at San Francisco (September 3).

Kaplan, Robert D. 1993. *Balkan ghosts: A journey through history.* New York: St. Martin's Press.

Karl, Terry L. 1986. Petroleum and political pacts: The transition to democracy in Venezuela. In *Transitions from authoritarian rule: Latin America,* edited by Guillermo O'Donnell, Philippe C. Schmitter, and Laurence Whitehead. Baltimore: Johns Hopkins University Press, 196–219.

Katzenstein, Peter J. 1976. International relations and domestic structures: Foreign economic policies of advanced industrial states. *International Organization* 30 (Winter): 1–45.

Kaufman, Stuart. 1996. Spiraling to ethnic war: Elites, masses, and Moscow in Moldova's civil war. *International Security* 21, no. 2 (Fall): 108–38.

Kaufmann, Chaim. 1996. Possible and impossible solutions to ethnic civil wars. *International Security* 20, no. 4 (Spring): 136–75.

Keller, Edmond J. 1997. Rethinking African regional security. In *Regional orders: Building security in a new world,* edited by David Lake and Patrick Morgan. State College: Pennsylvania State University Press, forthcoming.

Kempster, Norman, and Art Pine. 1995. Bosnia peace treaty approved: Use of U.S. troops is sought. *Los Angeles Times,* November 22, A1 and A16.

Kennedy, Paul. 1988. *The rise and fall of the great powers.* New York: Random House.

Kenny, George. 1993. From Bosnian crisis to all-out war. *New York Times,* June 20, sec. 4, p. 17.

Keohane, Robert. 1984. *After hegemony.* Princeton: Princeton University Press.

Keohane, Robert. 1989. *International institutions and state power. Essays in international relations theory.* Boulder: Westview Press.

Keohane, Robert, and Joseph S. Nye, Jr. 1977. *Power and interdependence.* Boston: Little Brown.

Khakimov, Rafel', ed. 1993. *Belaia kniga Tatarstana. Put' k suverenitetu 1990–1993.* Kazan: Belaia kniaga Tatarstana.

Khanakhu, Ruslan A., and O. M. Tsvetkov. 1995. Sociohistorical memory as a factor in public opinion promoting conflict. In *Abstracts of conference "Interethnic conflicts in the Caucasus: Approaches to solutions."* Moscow (January 19–20): 10–11.

Khasbulatov, Ruslan. 1995. The Chechen card—Yeltsin's trump card. *Zagreb vecernji list,* January 14, 15.

King, Gary. 1988. Statistical models for political science event counts: Bias in conventional procedures and evidence for the exponential poisson regression model. *American Journal of Political Science* 32, no. 3 (August): 838–63.

Kirschbaum, Stanislav. 1993. Czechoslovakia: The creation, federalization, and dissolution of a nation-state. In *Territorial management of ethnic conflict,* edited by John Coakley. London: Cass.

Klatt, Martin. 1994. Russians in the "near abroad." *RFE/RL Research Report* (August 19): 33–44.

Knopf, Jeffrey W. 1993. Beyond two-level games: Domestic-international interaction in the intermediate-range nuclear forces negotiations. *International Organization* 47 (Autumn): 599–628.

Krasner, Stephen. 1978. *Defending the national interest.* Princeton: Princeton University Press.

———. 1993. Westphalia and all that. In *Ideas and foreign policy: Beliefs, institutions, and political change,* edited by Judith Goldstein and Robert O. Keohane. Ithaca: Cornell University Press.

———. 1995. Sovereignty and intervention. In *Beyond Westphalia? State sovereignty and international intervention,* edited by Gene M. Lyons and Michael Mastanduno. Baltimore: Johns Hopkins University Press.

Krawchenko, Bohdan. 1993. Ukraine: The politics of independence. In *Nations and politics in Soviet successor states,* edited Ian Bremmer and Raymond Taras. New York: Cambridge University Press.

Krejci, Jaroslav, and Vitezslav Velimsky. 1981. *Ethnic and political nations in Europe.* London: Croom-Helm.

Krickus, Richard. 1993. Lithuania: Nationalism in the modern era. In *Nations and politics in the Soviet successor states,* edited by Ian Bremmer and Raymond Taras. New York: Cambridge University Press.

Kulischer, Eugene M. 1948. *Europe on the move: War and population changes, 1917–47.* New York: Columbia University Press.

Kuran, Timur. 1995. *Private truths, public lies: The social consequences of preference falsification.* Cambridge: Harvard University Press.

———. 1998. Ethnic norms and their transformation through reputational cascades. *Journal of Legal Studies* 27, no. 2 (June).

Kydd, Andrew. 1997. Game theory and the spiral model. *World Politics* 49, no. 3 (April): 371-400.

Laas, Jaan, ed. 1991. *Eesti kroonika 1990.* Tallinn, Estonia: A/S "Esintell."

Ladas, Stephen P. 1932. *The exchange of minorities: Bulgaria, Greece, and Turkey.* New York: Macmillan.

Laitin, David D. 1987. South Africa: Violence, myths, and democratic reform. *World Politics* 34, no. 2 (January): 258–79.

———. 1995a. Identity in formation: The Russian-speaking nationality in the post-Soviet diasporo. *Archives Européennes de Sociologie* 36, no. 2: 281–316.

———. 1995b. National revivals and violence. *Archives Européennes de Sociologie* 36, no. 1: 3–43.

Laitin, David, and Said Samatar. 1987. *Somalia: Nation in search of a state.* Boulder, CO: Westview.

Lake, David A. 1996. Anarchy, hierarchy, and the variety of international relations. *International Organization* 50, no. 1 (Winter): 1–33.

Lake, David A., and Donald Rothchild. 1996a. *Ethnic fears and global engagement: The international spread and management of ethnic conflict.* Policy Paper 20. La Jolla: University of California Institute on Global Conflict and Cooperation (January).

————. 1996b. Containing fear: The origins and management of ethnic conflict. *International Security* 21, no. 2 (Fall): 41–75.

Lake, David A., and Robert Powell, eds. n.d. *Strategic choice and international relations.* Princeton: Princeton University Press, forthcoming.

Landau, Jacob M. 1995. *Pan-Turkism: From irredentism to cooperation.* London: Hurst.

Landes, David S. 1969. *The unbound Prometheus. Technological change and industrial development in Western Europe from 1750 to the present.* Cambridge: Cambridge University Press.

Landy, Paul. 1961. Reforms in Yugoslavia. *Problems of communism* (November–December).

Langer, William L. 1964. *European alliances and alignments, 1871–1890.* 2d ed., with supplementary bibliographies. New York: Vintage Books.

Lapidoth, Ruth. 1996. *Autonomy: Flexible solutions to intra-state conflicts.* Washington, D.C.: United States Institute of Peace Press.

Lapidus, Gail W., and Renée de Nevers, eds. 1995. *Nationalism, ethnic identity, and conflict management in Russia today.* Stanford: Stanford University Center for International Security and Arms Control.

Lapidus, Gail W. 1998. The war in Chechnya: Opportunities missed and lessons to be learned. In *Opportunities missed, opportunities seized: Preventive diplomacy in the post-cold war world,* edited by Bruce W. Jentleson. Lanham, MD: Rowman and Littlefield, forthcoming.

Laponce, J. A. 1960. *The protection of minorities.* Berkeley and Los Angeles: University of California Press.

League of Nations. 1926. *Health organization handbook series no. 6: Official vital statistics of the Scandinavian countries and the Baltic Republics.* Geneva: League of Nations.

Leatherman, Janie. 1996. Untying Macedonia's Gordian knot: Preventive diplomacy in the southern Balkans. Paper presented at the annual meeting of the International Studies Association, at San Diego, April 1996.

Lebow, Richard Ned, and Janice Gross Stein. 1990. *When does deterrence succeed and how do we know?* Occasional Paper 8. Ottawa: Canadian Institute for International Peace and Security.

Legro, Jeffrey W. 1995. *Cooperation under fire: Anglo-German restraint during World War II.* Ithaca: Cornell University Press.

Legum, Colin. 1995. Sudan: Can they bring peace? *New African* (April), 32.

Lemarchand, René. 1994a. *Burundi: Ethnic conflict and genocide.* Cambridge: Cambridge University Press.

————. 1994b. Managing transitional anarchies: Rwanda, Burundi, and South Africa. *Journal of Modern African Studies* 32, no. 4 (December): 581–604.

Lemarchand, René, and David Martin. 1974. *Selective genocide in Burundi,* no. 20. London: Minority Rights Group.

Lemke, Douglas. 1995. Toward a general understanding of parity and war. *Conflict Management and Peace Science* 14, no. 2 (Fall): 143–62.

Lenin, V. I. 1948. *Imperialism: The highest stage of capitalism.* London: Lawrence and Wishart.

Lerner, N. 1993. The evolution of minority rights in international law. In *Peoples and minorities in international law,* edited by Catherine Brolmann, Rene Lefeber, and Marjoleine Zieck. Dordrecht, Netherlands: Martinus Nijhoff.

Levite, Ariel E. 1987. *Intelligence and strategic surprise*. New York: Columbia University Press.

Lévy, Maurice. 1951–52. *Histoire économique et sociale de la France depuis 1848*. Paris, Les Cours de Droit: Institute d'Etudes Politiques.

Lewis, Bernard. 1992. Muslims, Christians, and Jews: The dream of coexistence. *New York Review of Books* 39 (March 26): 48–52.

Lewis, W. Arthur. 1972. The historical record of international capital movements to 1913. In *International Investment: Selected Readings*, edited by J. H. Dunning. Harmondsworth: Penguin.

Lichbach, Mark I. 1995. *The rebel's dilemma*. Ann Arbor: University of Michigan Press.

Licklider, Roy, ed. 1993. *Stopping the killing: How civil wars end*. New York: New York University Press.

———. 1995. The consequences of negotiated settlements in civil wars, 1945–1993. *American Political Science Review* 89, no. 3 (September), 681–90.

Lieven, Anatol. 1993. *The Baltic revolution: Estonia, Latvia, Lithuania, and the path to independence*. New Haven: Yale University Press.

Lijphart, Arend. 1967. *The politics of accommodation: Pluralism and democracy in the Netherlands*. Berkeley and Los Angeles: University of California Press.

———. 1977. *Democracy in plural societies*. New Haven: Yale University Press.

———. 1985. Power-sharing in South Africa. Policy Paper in *International Affairs*, no. 24. Berkeley: University of California Institute of International Studies.

———. 1988. Ingredients for a viable power-sharing system in Angola. Paper presented to a Conference on Prospects for National Reconciliation in Angola. Department of State, April 20, at Washington, D.C.

———. 1990. The power sharing approach. In *Conflict and peacemaking in multiethnic societies*, edited by Joseph V. Montville. Lexington, MA: Lexington Books.

———. 1994. *Electoral systems and party systems*. Oxford: Oxford University Press.

Lipschutz, Ronnie, and Beverly Crawford. 1995. *Ethnic conflict isn't*. Policy Brief 2. La Jolla: University of California Institute on Global Conflict and Cooperation (March).

Lipski, Jan Josf. 1989–1990. In defense of socialism. *Across Frontiers* (Fall/Winter): 19–21.

Little, David. 1993. Religion catalyst or impediment to international law? The case of Hugo Grotius. Proceedings of the eighty-seventh annual meeting of the American Society of International Law, March 31–April 3, at Washington, D.C.

Lohmann, Susanne. 1994. The dynamics of informational cascades: The Monday demonstrations in Leipzig, East Germany, 1989–91. *World Politics* 47, no. 1 (October): 42–101.

Lorch, Donatella. 1994. Specter of hate stalks Burundi, too. *New York Times*, April 26, A9.

Lowenkopf, Martin. 1995. Liberia: Putting the state back together. In *Collapsed states: the disintegration and restoration of legitimate authority*. Boulder: Lynne Rienner Publishers.

Luard, Evan, ed. 1972. *The international regulation of civil wars*. London: Thames and Hudson.

Lund, Michael S. 1995. Underrating "preventive diplomacy." *Foreign Affairs* 74, no. 4 (July/August), 160–163.

———. 1996. *Preventing violent conflicts: A strategy for preventive diplomacy*. Washington, D.C.: United States Institute of Peace Press.

———. 1997. Preventive diplomacy. In *Encyclopedia of U.S. foreign relations*, edited by Bruce W. Jentleson and Thomas G. Patterson. New York: Oxford University Press.

———.1998. Preventive diplomacy for Macedonia: Containment becomes nation-building. In *Opportunities missed, opportunities seized: Preventive diplomacy in the post-cold war world*, edited by Bruce W. Jentleson. Lanham, MD: Rowman and Littlefield, forthcoming.

Lyman, Princeton N. 1991. Statement by bureau for refugee programs director. *U.S. Department of State Dispatch* 2, no. 29 (July 22). Washington, D.C.: U.S. House of Representatives Subcommittee on Africa.

Lyons, Gene M., and Michael Mastanduno, eds. 1995. *Beyond Westphalia? State sovereignty and international intervention.* Baltimore: Johns Hopkins University Press.

Macartney, Carlile Aylmer. 1934. *National states and national minorities.* London: Oxford University Press.

MacIver, Robert M. 1932. *The modern state.* London: Oxford University Press.

Madan, T. N. 1991. The double-edged sword: Fundamentalism and the Sikh religious tradition. In *Fundamentalisms observed,* edited by Martin E. Marty and R. Scott Appleby. Chicago: University of Chicago Press.

Malcolm, Noel. 1994. *Bosnia: A short history.* London: Macmillan; New York: New York University Press.

Mansfield, Peter. 1991. *A history of the Middle East.* New York: Viking.

Maoz, Zeev. 1997. Domestic political change and strategic response: The impact of domestic conflict on state behavior, 1816–1986. In *Wars in the midst of peace: The international politics of ethnic conflict,* edited by D. W. Carment and P. James. Pittsburgh: University of Pittsburgh Press.

Maoz, Zeev, and Bruce Russett. 1993. Normative and structural causes of the democratic peace. *American Political Science Review* 87, no. 3 (September): 624–38.

Maresca, John J. 1998. The international community and the conflict over Nagomo Karabakh. In *Opportunities missed, opportunities seized: Preventive diplomacy in the post-cold war world,* edited by Bruce W. Jentleson. Lanham, MD: Rowman and Littlefield, forthcoming.

Marshall, Monty G. 1993. Collective violence and war: Reconceptualizing the problem of political borders in security studies. Paper presented at the International Studies Association, Midwest annual meeting, at Chicago (March).

———. 1997. Systems at risk: Violence, diffusion, and disintegration in the Middle East. In *Wars in the midst of peace: The international politics of ethnic conflict,* edited by D. W. Carment and P. James. Pittsburgh: University of Pittsburgh Press.

Mason, David T. 1984. Individual participation in collective racial violence: A rational choice synthesis. *American Political Science Review* 78, no. 4 (December): 1,040–56.

Mattes, Robert B. 1993. Beyond "government and opposition": An independent South African legislature. *Politikon* 20, no. 2 (December): 64–91.

Mattingly, Garrett. 1955. *Renaissance diplomacy.* Baltimore: Penguin Books.

Maxwell, Constantia, ed. 1923. *Irish history from contemporary sources.* London: Allen and Unwin.

Mayer, Arno J. 1980. *The persistence of the ancien regime: Europe to the great war.* New York: Pantheon Books.

Mayhew, David R. 1974. *Congress: The electoral connection.* New Haven: Yale University Press.

Maynes, Charles William. 1993. Containing ethnic conflict. *Foreign Policy* 90 (Spring): 3–21.

———. 1995. Relearning intervention. *Foreign Policy* 98 (Spring): 96–113.

McAdam, Doug. 1982. *Political process and the development of black insurgency: 1930–1970.* Chicago: University of Chicago Press.

———. 1988. *Freedom summer.* Oxford: Oxford University Press.

McAdam, Doug, and Dieter Rucht. 1993. The cross-national diffusion of movement ideas. *Annals of the American Academy of Political and Social Science* 528 (July): 56–74.

McCarthy, John D., and Mayer N. Zald. 1973. *The trend of social movements in America: Professionalization and resource mobilization.* Morristown, NJ: General Learning Press.

————. 1977. Resource mobilization and social movements: A partial theory. *American Journal of Sociology* 82, no. 6 (May): 1,212–41.

McGarry, John, and Brendan O'Leary. 1993a. Introduction: The macro–political regulation of ethnic conflict. In *The politics of ethnic conflict regulation,* edited by John McGarry and Brendan O'Leary. London: Routledge.

————, eds. 1993b. *The politics of ethnic conflict regulation.* London: Routledge.

McWhirter, Cameron, and Gur Melamede. 1992. Ethiopia: The ethnicity factor. *Africa Report* 37, no. 5 (September/October): 30–33.

Meadwell, Hudson. 1989. Cultural and instrumental approaches to ethnic nationalism. *Ethnic and Racial Studies* 12 (July): 309–28.

Menkhaus, Ken, and Louis Ortmayer. 1998. Somalia: Misread crises and missed opportunities. In *Opportunity missed, opportunity seized: Preventive diplomacy in the post-cold war world,* edited by Bruce W. Jentleson. Lanham MD: Rowman & Littlefield, forthcoming.

Mercer, Jonathan. 1996. *Reputation and international politics.* Ithaca: Cornell University Press.

Midlarsky, Manus I. 1970. Mathematical models of instability and a theory of diffusion. *International Studies Quarterly* 14, no. 1 (March): 60–84.

————. 1988. *The onset of world war.* Boston: Unwin Hyman.

————. 1992. Communal strife and the origins of World War I. In *The internationalization of communal strife,* edited by Manus I. Midlarsky. New York: Routledge.

————, ed. 1993. *The internalization of civil strife.* New York: Macmillan.

Miller, G. A. 1956. The magical number seven, plus or minus two: Some limits on our capacity for processing information. *Psychological Review* 63, no. 1 (January): 81–97.

Milward, Alan S. 1984. *The Reconstruction of Western Europe, 1945–1951.* Berkeley and Los Angeles: University of California Press.

Minear, Larry, and Thomas G. Weiss. 1995. *Mercy under fire: War and the global humanitarian community.* Boulder, CO: Westview.

Misser, François. 1995. Rwanda: Searching for the killers. *New Africa* (April).

Mitchell, Chrostpher, and Keith Webb, eds. 1988. *New approaches to international mediation.* Westport, CT: Greenwood.

Modelski, George. 1964. International settlement of internal war. *International aspects of civil strife,* edited by J. N. Rosenau. Princeton: Princeton University Press.

Molodezh' Estonii. 1991. Sekretari TsK KPE o referendume (March 6).

Molodezh' Estonii. 1992. Referendum: Podvedeny itogi (March 5).

Monitor. 1996. Vol 2, no. 40 (February 27). Washington, D.C.: Jamestown Foundation.

Monroe, Kristen. 1996. *The heart of altruism: A perception of a common humanity.* Princeton: Princeton University Press.

Moravcsik, Andrew. 1993. Introduction: Integrating international and domestic theories of international bargaining. In *Double-edged diplomacy: International bargaining and domestic politics,* edited by Peter B. Evans, Harold K. Jacobson, and Robert D. Putnam. Berkeley and Los Angeles: University of California Press.

————. 1994. Lessons from the European human rights regime. In *Inter-American dialogue, advancing democracy and human rights in the Americas: What role of the OAS?* Washington, D.C.: Inter-American Dialogue.

Moreno, Luis. 1994. Ethnoterritorial accommodation and democratic development in Spain. Paper presented to the sixteenth world congress of the International Political Science Association, at Berlin.

Morgenthau, Hans. 1948. *Politics among nations*. New York: Alfred A. Knopf.

———. 1951. *In defense of the national interest: A critical examination of American foreign policy*. New York: Knopf.

Mortimer, Robert. 1996. ECOMOG, Liberia, and regional security in West Africa. In *Africa in the new international order: Rethinking state sovereignty and regional security,* edited by Edmond J. Keller and Donald Rothchild. Boulder, CO: Lynne Rienner.

Mowat, R. B. 1927. *A history of European diplomacy, 1914–1925*. New York: Longmans, Green.

Moynihan, Daniel Patrick. 1990. *On the law of nations*. Cambridge: Harvard University Press.

———. 1993. *Pandaemonium: Ethnicity in international politics*. New York: Oxford University Press.

Muiznieks, Nils. 1993. Latvia: Origins, evolution, and triumph. In *Nations and politics in Soviet successor states,* edited by Ian Bremmer and Raymond Taras. Cambridge: Cambridge University Press.

Mullen, Brian, Rupert Brown, and Colleen Smith. 1992. Ingroup bias as a function of salience, relevance, and status: An integration. *European Journal of Social Psychology* 22, no. 2 (Summer): 103–22.

Muller, Edward N., and Karl-Dieter Opp. 1986. Rational choice and rebellious collective action. *American Political Science Review* 80, no. 2 (June): 471–87.

Muller, Edward N., Henry A. Dietz, and Steven E. Finkel. 1991. Discontent and the expected utility of rebellion: The case of Peru. *American Political Science Review* 85, no. 4 (December): 1,261–82.

Munayev, Ismail (executive director, Association of the Commonwealth of Peoples). 1994. Conversation with Paula Garb. Moscow. December 23.

Myers, David, ed. 1991. *Regional hegemons*. Boulder, CO: Westview.

Naldi, Gino. 1989. *The organization of African unity: An analysis of its role*. London: Mansell.

Neuman, W. Russell. 1986. *The paradox of mass politics*. Cambridge: Harvard University Press.

Newbury, Catharine. 1988. *The cohesion of repression: Clientship and ethnicity in Rwanda, 1860–1960*. New York: Columbia University Press.

———. 1995. Background to genocide: Rwanda. *Issue* 23, no. 2: 12–17.

Newell, Allen, Paul S. Rosenbloom, and John E. Laird. 1989. Symbolic architectures for cognition. In *Foundations of cognitive science,* edited by Michael I. Posner. Cambridge: MIT Press.

Newland, Kathleen. 1993. Ethnic conflict and refugees. In *Ethnic conflict and international security*, edited by Michael E. Brown. Princeton: Princeton University Press.

New York Times. 1996. Serbia's apartheid victims. December 12, A12.

Nezavisimaya gazeta. 1993. (February 23).

Nicolson, Sir Harold. 1980. *Diplomacy*. 1939; reprint, New York: Oxford University Press.

Nigerian Conference. 1995. Conference report. Washington, D.C.: National Endowment for Democracy.

Nisbett, Richard, and Lee Ross. 1980. *Human inference: Strategies and shortcomings of social judgment*. Englewood Cliffs, NJ: Prentice-Hall.

Noam, Eli. 1991. *Television in Europe*. Oxford: Oxford University Press.

Nye, Joseph S., Jr. 1988. Neorealism and neoliberalism. *World Politics* 40, no. 2 (January): 235–51.

———. 1990. *Bound to lead: The changing nature of American power*. New York: Basic Books.

———. 1994. Speech as Director of the National Intelligence Council, U.S. Department of State Open Forum.

Obasanjo, Olusegun. 1996. The African region and the cold war: A balance sheet. In *Africa and the new international order: Studies of state sovereignty and regional security,* edited by Edmond J. Keller and Donald Rothchild. Boulder, CO: Lynne Rienner.

Oberoi, Harjot. 1993. Sikh fundamentalism: Translating history into theory. In *Fundamentalisms and the state: Remaking polities, economies, and militance,* edited by Martin E. Marty and R. Scott Appleby. Chicago: University of Chicago Press.

Ofosuhene, Kwabena, and Amma Osafo-Mensah. 1994. Lay down your arms. *Daily Graphic* (Accra), November 22.

Olson, Mancur. 1965. *The logic of collective action.* Cambridge: Harvard University Press.

———. 1982. *The rise and decline of nations: Economic growth, stagflation, and social rigidities.* New Haven: Yale University Press.

Onuf, Nicholas. 1995. Intervention for the common good. In *Beyond Westphalia? State sovereignty and international intervention,* edited by Gene M. Lyons and Michael Mastanduno. Baltimore: Johns Hopkins University Press.

Organization of African Unity. 1993. Declaration of the assembly of heads of state and government on the establishment within the OAU of a mechanism for conflict prevention, management and resolution. Twenty-ninth ordinary session, Assembly of Heads of State and Government, June 28–30, at Dakar, Senegal.

Organski, A.F.K. 1968. *World politics.* New York: Alfred A. Knopf

Organski, A.F.K., and Jacek Kugler. 1980. *The war ledger.* Chicago: University of Chicago Press.

Osgood, C. E. 1962. *An alternative to war or surrender.* Urbana: University of Illinois Press.

Otyrba, Gueorgui. 1994. War in Abkhazia: The regional significance of the Georgian-Abkhazian conflict. In *National identity and ethnicity in Russia and the new states of Eurasia,* edited by Karen Dawisha and Bruce Parrot. New York: M. E. Sharpe.

Pallis, A. A. 1925. Racial migrations in the Balkans during the years 1912–1924. *Geographical Journal* 66, no. 4 (October): 315–30.

Parkin, Frank. 1969. Class stratification in socialist societies. *British Journal of Sociology* 20, no. 4 (December): 255–74.

Pearson, Raymond. 1983. *National minorities in Eastern Europe, 1848–1945.* New York: St. Martin's Press; London: MacMillan.

Pehe, Jiri. 1993. Czechoslovakia: Toward dissolution. *RFE/RL Research Report* 2, no. 1: 84–88.

Percival, Valerie, and Thomas Homer-Dixon. 1995. *Environmental scarcity and violent conflict: The case of Rwanda.* Washington, D.C.: American Association for the Advancement of Science.

Perry, William. 1994. Ethnicity problems are driving military requirements. Washington, D.C.: Department of Defense report (May 5). News clip.

Pesic, Vesna. 1994. Bellicose virtues in elementary school readers. In *Warfare, patriotism, patriarchy: The analysis of elementary school textbooks,* edited by Ruzica Rosandic and Vesna Pesic. Belgrade: Centre for Anti-War Action.

Petersen, Roger. 1992. Rebellion and resistance. Ph.D. dissertation, University of Chicago.

Pfaff, William. 1993. *The wrath of nations: Civilization and the furies of nationalism.* New York: Simon & Schuster.

Pillar, Paul R. 1993. *Negotiating peace: War termination as a bargaining process.* Princeton: Princeton University Press.

Platias, Athananassior Georgios. 1986. High politics in small countries: An inquiry into the security policies of Greece, Israel, and Sweden. Ph.D. dissertation, Department of Government, Cornell University.

Poggi, Gianfranco. 1978. *The development of the modern state: A sociological introduction.* Stanford: Stanford University Press.

Posen, Barry R. 1993a. The security dilemma and ethnic conflict. In *Ethnic conflict and international security,* edited by Michael E. Brown. Princeton: Princeton University Press.

———. 1993b. The security dilemma and ethnic conflict. *Survival* 35, no. 1 (Spring): 27–47.

Postimees. 1995. Ratifitseeriti Eesti-Vene Juulilepped. December 21, p. 1.

Pretoria News. 1995. Miracles happen at OAU (June 24).

Przeworski, Adam. 1991. *Democracy and the market.* Cambridge: Cambridge University Press.

Purdie, Bob. 1990. *Politics in the streets.* Belfast: Blackstaff Press.

Putnam, Robert D. 1988. Diplomacy and domestic politics: The logic of two-level games. *International Organization* 42 (Summer): 427–60.

Radio Free Europe/Radio Liberty Daily Reports. 1992–1994.

Rajmaira, Sheen, and Michael D. Ward. 1990. Evolving foreign policy norms: Reciprocity in the superpower triad. *International Studies Quarterly* 34, no. 4 (December): 457–75.

Rasler, Karen A., and William R. Thompson. 1994. *The great powers and global struggle.* Lexington: University Press of Kentucky.

Raun, Tovio U. 1991. *Estonia and the Estonians.* 2d ed. Stanford, CA: Hoover Institution Press.

Raviot, Jean-Robert. 1994. Types of nationalism, society, and politics in Tatarstan. *Russian Politics and Law* 32 (March/April): 54–83.

Renan, Ernest. [1882] 1939. What is a nation? In *Modern political doctrines,* edited by Alfred Zimmern. London: Oxford University Press.

Restoration of the independence of the republic of Estonia: Selection of legal acts (1988–1991). 1991. Tallinn: Ministry of Foreign Affairs of the Republic of Estonia and Estonian Institute for Information.

Reynolds, Andrew. 1994. *South Africa: Elections 1994.* New York: St. Martin's Press.

Richarte, Marie-Pierre. 1995. La partition de Chypre. Ph.D. dissertation in Geography, University of the Sorbonne, Paris.

Richburg, Keith. 1994. Somalia slips back to bloodshed. *Washington Post,* September 4, p. A43.

Rieff, David. 1995. *Slaughterhouse: Bosnia and the failure of the West.* New York: Simon & Schuster.

Robinson, Jacob, et al. 1943. *Were the minorities treaties a failure?* New York: Institute of Jewish Affairs of the American Jewish Congress and the World Jewish Congress.

Roeder, Philip G. 1994. Politicians' incentives and the ethnic agenda in the Soviet successor states. Presented at the University of California Institute on Global Conflict and Cooperation Conference on the International Spread and Management of Ethnic Conflict, September 30, at La Jolla.

Romein, Jan. 1978. *The watershed of two eras: Europe in 1900.* Middletown, CT: Wesleyan University Press.

Roper Organization. 1991. *America's watching: Public attitudes toward television, 1991.* New York: Roper.

Rose, Richard. 1971. *Governing without consensus.* London: Faber and Faber.

Rosecrance, Richard. 1986. *The rise of the trading state.* New York: Basic Books.

Rosenau, James N. 1984. A pre-theory revisited: World politics in an era of cascading interdependence. *International Studies Quarterly* 28 (September): 245–305.

Roskin, Michael G. 1993–1994. Macedonia and Albania: The missing alliance. *Parameters* (Winter): 91–99.

Rotberg, Robert I., ed. 1997. *Vigilance and vengeance: NGOs preventing ethnic conflict in divided societies*. Washington, D.C.: Brookings Institution.

Rothchild, Donald. 1973. *Racial bargaining in independent Kenya: A study of minorities and decolonization*. London: Oxford University Press.

———. 1986a. Hegemonial exchange: An alternative model for managing conflict in Middle Africa. In *Ethnicity, politics, and development*, edited by Dennis L. Thompson and Dov Ronen. Boulder: Lynne Rienner.

———. 1986b. Interethnic conflict and policy analysis in Africa. *Ethnic and Racial Studies* 9, no. 1 (January), 66–86.

———. 1995. The United States and conflict management in Africa. In *Africa in world politics: Post–cold war challenges*, edited by John W. Harbeson and Donald Rothchild. Boulder, CO: Lynne Rienner.

———. 1997a. Management of conflict in West Africa. In *Governance as conflict management*, edited by I. William Zartman. Washington, D.C.: Brookings Institution.

———. 1997b. Ethnic bargaining and the management of intense conflict. *International Negotiation* 2: 1–20.

———. 1997c. *Managing ethnic conflict in Africa: Pressures and incentives for cooperation*. Washington, D.C.: Brookings Institution.

Rothchild, Donald, and Alexander J. Groth. 1995. Pathological dimensions of domestic and international ethnicity. *Political Science Quarterly* 110, no. 1 (Spring): 69–82.

Rothschild, Joseph. 1981. *Ethnopolitics: A conceptual framework*. New York: Columbia University Press.

Rubin, Barnett. 1995a. *The fragmentation of Afghanistan*. New Haven: Yale University Press.

———. 1995b. *The Search for peace in Afghanistan*. New Haven: Yale University Press.

Rudolph, Joseph, Jr., and Robert Thompson. 1985. Ethnoterritorial movements and the policy process: Accommodating nationalist demands in the developed world. *Comparative Politics* 17, no. 3 (April): 291–311.

Ruggie, John. 1988. Continuity and transformation in the world polity: Toward a neorealist synthesis. In *Neorealism and its critics*, edited by Robert O. Keohane. New York: Columbia University Press.

———. 1994. The UN: Between peacekeeping and enforcement. *Foreign affairs: Agenda 1994*. New York: Foreign Affairs.

Rule, James. 1988. *Theories of civil violence*. Berkeley and Los Angeles: University of California Press.

Rumelhart, David, and Andrew Ortony. 1977. The representatives of knowledge in memory. In *Schooling and the acquisition of knowledge*, edited by Richard Anderson, Rand Spiro, and William Montague. New York: Wiley.

Rummel, R. J. 1979. *Understanding conflict and war: Vol. 4: War, power and peace*. Beverly Hills: Sage.

Russett, Bruce. 1990. *Controlling the sword*. Cambridge: Harvard University Press.

Ryan, Stephen. 1990. *Ethnic conflict and international relations*. Aldershot, England: Dartmouth.

Saar, Andrus. 1990. Inter-ethnic relations in Estonia. *The Monthly Survey of Estonian and Soviet Politics* (November/December): 12–15.

Sahnoun, Mohamed. 1994. *Somalia: The missed opportunities*. Washington, D.C.: United States Institute of Peace Press.

Saideman, Stephen M. 1997. Explaining the international relations of secessionist conflicts: Vulnerability vs. ethnic ties. *International Organization* 51, no. 4 (Fall): 721–753.

Salih, Kamal Osman. 1991. The Sudan, 1985–89: The fading democracy. In *Sudan after Nimeiri*, edited by Peter Woodward. London: Routledge.

Schank, R., and R. Abelson. 1977. *Scripts, plans, goals, and understanding*. Hillsdale, NJ: Lawrence Erlbaum.

Schlessinger, Arthur M., Jr. 1991. *The disuniting of America: Reflections on a multicultural society*. Knoxville, TN: Whittle Books.

Schmidt, Fabian. 1993. Kosovo: The time bomb that has not gone off. *RFE/RL Report* 2, no. 39 (October 1): 21–29.

———. 1994. The former Yugoslavia: Refugees and war resisters. *RFE/RL Report* 3, no. 25 (June): 47–54.

Schmitt, Bernadotte. 1958. *The origins of the first world war*. London: Routledge and Kegan Paul.

Schmitz, Michael. 1992. Old and new nationalism in the former Yugoslavia. University of Chicago. Unpublished paper.

Schoppa, Leonard J. 1993. Two-level games and bargaining outcomes: Why *gaiatsu* succeeds in Japan in some cases but not others. *International Organization* 47 (Summer): 353–86.

Schumpeter, Joseph. A. 1947. *Capitalism, socialism, and democracy*. London: Harper and Brothers.

Schwartzberg, Stephen. 1988. The lion and the phoenix. *Journal of Middle Eastern Studies* 24, nos. 2 and 3: 139–177, 287–311.

Schweller, Randall L. 1994. Bandwagoning for profit: Bringing the revisionist state back in. *International Security* 19, no. 1 (Summer): 72–107.

Sciolino, Elaine. 1995. U.S. envoy advises caution on Bosnia peace agreement. *New York Times*, September 13, A6.

Scribner, R. W. 1990. Politics and the institutionalization of reform in Germany. In *The new Cambridge modern history*. Vol. 2: *The Reformation 1520–1559*, 2d ed., edited by G. R. Elton. Cambridge: Cambridge University Press.

Sée, Henri. 1942. *Histoire économique de la France II: Les temps modernes, 1789–1914*. Paris: Colin.

Sen, Amartya. 1960. *Choice of techniques: An aspect of the theory of planned economic development*. Oxford: Basil Blackwell.

Seton-Watson, Hugh. 1945. *Eastern Europe between the wars, 1918–1941*. Hamden, CT: Archon Books.

Sharp, Alan. 1979. Britain and the protection of minorities at the Paris Peace Conference, 1919. In *Minorities in history*, edited by A. C. Hepburn. New York: St. Martin's Press.

——— 1991. *The Versailles settlement: Peacemaking in Paris, 1919*. New York: St. Martin's Press.

Sheehy, Ann. 1992. Tatarstan asserts its sovereignty. *RFE/RL Research Report* 1 (April): 2.

Sherman, Richard. 1980. *Eritrea: The unfinished revolution*. New York: Praeger.

Shezi, Sipho. 1995. South Africa: State transition and the management of collapse. In *Collapsed States,* edited by I. W. Zartman. Boulder, CO: Lynne Rienner.

Shnirelman, Victor. 1996. *Who gets the past: Competing for ancestors among non-Russian intellectuals*. Baltimore: Johns Hopkins University Press.

Shorr, David. 1993. From treaties to crises. *Foreign Service Journal* (December), 35–37.

Shriver, Jr., Donald W. 1995. *An ethic for enemies: Forgiveness in politics*. New York: Oxford University Press.

Sigler, Jay A. 1983. *Minority rights: A comparative perspective*. Westport, CT: Greenwood Press.

Singer, J. David, and Melvin Small. 1972. *The wages of war, 1816–1965: A statistical handbook*. New York: Wiley.

Sisk, Timothy D. 1993. Choosing an electoral system: South Africa seeks new ground rules. *Journal of Democracy* 4, no. 1 (January): 79–91.

———. 1995. *Democratization in South Africa: The elusive social contract.* Princeton, NJ: Princeton University Press.

———. 1996. *Power sharing and international mediation in ethnic conflicts.* Washington, D.C.: United States Institute of Peace Press.

Siverson, Randolph M., and Harvey Starr. 1991. *The diffusion of war: A study of opportunity and willingness.* Ann Arbor: University of Michigan Press.

Skinner, Quentin. 1978. *The foundations of modern political thought.* Vol. 2: *The age of reformation.* Cambridge: Cambridge University Press.

Smith, Anthony D. 1986. *The ethnic origins of nations.* New York: Basil Blackwell.

———. 1991. *National identity.* London: Penguin Books.

———. 1993. The ethnic sources of nationalism. In *Ethnic conflict and international security,* edited by Michael E. Brown. Princeton: Princeton University Press.

Smith, Eric R.A.N. 1989. *The unchanging American voter.* Berkeley and Los Angeles: University of California Press.

Sniderman, Paul M., and Thomas Piazza. 1993. *The scar of race.* Cambridge: Harvard University Press.

Snyder, Jack. 1993. Nationalism and the crisis of the post-Soviet state. In *Ethnic conflict and international security,* edited by Michael E. Brown. Princeton: Princeton University Press.

Solarz, Stephen. 1980. *Arms for Morocco? U.S. policy toward the conflict in the Western Sahara.* Washington, D.C.: U.S. House of Representatives, Committee on Foreign Affairs (January): Appendix.

Sowell, Thomas. 1994. *Race and culture: A world view.* New York: Basic Books.

Starr J., and J. Collier, eds. 1989. *History and power in the study of law: New directions in legal anthropology.* Ithaca: Cornell University Press.

Starr, Harvey. 1991. Democratic dominoes: Diffusion approaches to the spread of democracy in the international system. *Journal of Conflict Resolution* 35, no. 2 (June): 356–81.

Stedman, Stephen John. 1991. *Peacemaking in civil wars: International mediation in Zimbabwe, 1974–1980.* Boulder: Lynne Rienner.

———. 1995. Alchemy for a new world order: Overselling "preventive diplomacy." *Foreign Affairs* 74, no. 3 (May/June): 14–20.

———. 1996. Negotiation and mediation in internal conflict. In *The international dimension of internal conflict,* edited by Michael Brown. Cambridge: MIT Press.

———.1997. Spoilers. *International security,* forthcoming.

Steele, Shelby. 1990. *The content of our character: A new vision of race in America.* New York: St. Martin's Press.

Stein, Arthur A. 1990. *Why nations cooperate: Circumstance and choice in international relations.* Ithaca: Cornell University Press.

Steinberg, Stephen. 1981. *The ethnic myth: Race, ethnicity, and class in America.* New York: Atheneum.

Steinberg, James B. 1993. International involvement in the Yugoslavia conflict. In *Enforcing restraint: Collective intervention in internal conflicts,* edited by Lori Fisler Damrosch. New York: Council on Foreign Relations.

Steinbruner, John. 1995. Remarks in *U.S. Intervention in Ethnic Conflict,* edited by Fred Wehling. Policy Paper 12. La Jolla: University of California Institute on Global Conflict and Cooperation, 7–11.

Stone, Julius. 1932. *International guarantees of minority rights.* London: Oxford University Press.

Strack, Harry R. 1978. *Sanctions: The case of Rhodesia*. Syracuse: Syracuse University Press.

Strayer, Joseph R. 1970. *On the medieval origins of the modern state*. Princeton: Princeton University Press.

Stremlau, John. 1991. The new global system and its implications for peace and security in Africa. U.S. Department of State Dispatch (September).

———. 1995. Antidote to anarchy. *The Washington Quarterly* 18 (Winter), 29–44.

Sudan Democratic Gazette. 1994. IGADD stays the course in spite of Khartoum's arrogance. No. 53 (October), 2–3 and 8–9.

———. 1995. El Mahdi publicly expresses self–determination for the South. No. 59 (April).

Suhrke, Astri, and Bruce Jones. 1998. Preventive diplomacies: Failure to act, or failure of actions taken? In *Opportunities missed, opportunities seized: Preventive diplomacy in the post-cold war world*, edited by Bruce W. Jentleson. Lanham, MD: Rowman and Littlefield, forthcoming.

Suhrke, Astri, and Lela Garner Noble, eds. 1977. *Ethnic conflict in international relations*. New York: Praeger.

Sullivan, Michael. 1990. *Power in contemporary international politics*. Columbia: University of South Carolina Press.

Taagepera, Rein. 1993. *Estonia: Return to independence*. Boulder, CO: Westview.

Taborsky, Edward, 1961. *Communism in Czechoslovakia*. Princeton: Princeton University Press.

Tambiah, Stanley. 1986. *Sri Lanka: Ethnic fratricide and the dismantling of democracy*. Chicago: University of Chicago Press.

Tarrow, Sidney. 1989. *Democracy and disorder: Protest and politics in Italy, 1965–1975*. Oxford: Oxford University Press.

———. 1995. *Power in movement: Social movements, collective action, and politics*. Cambridge: Cambridge University Press.

Taylor, A.J.P. 1961. *The origins of the Second World War*. New York: Atheneum.

Taylor, Shelly, and Jennifer Cracker. 1981. Schematic processing. In *Social cognition: The Ontario symposium*, edited by E. Tory Higgins, C. P. Herman, and M. P. Zanna. Hillsdale, NJ: Lawrence Erlbaum.

Teague, Elizabeth. 1994. Russia and Tatarstan sign power-sharing treaty. *Radio Free Europe/Radio Liberty Research Report* (April): 19–27.

Temperley, H. 1966. *The foreign policy of Canning, 1822–27*. Hamden, CT: Archon Books.

Tetlock, Philip E., and Aaron Belkin, eds. 1996. *Counterfactual thought experiments in world politics: Logical, methodological, and psychological perspectives*. Princeton: Princeton University Press.

Tharoor, Shashi. 1996. The role of the United Nations in European peacekeeping. In *Preventing conflict in the post-communist world*, edited by Abram Chayes and Antonia Handler Chayes. Washington, D.C.: Brookings Institution, 467–82.

The Economist. 1994. Minorities: That other Europe. December 25–January 7, p. 17.

Thompson, Gordon, and Paula Gutlove. 1994. Preventive diplomacy and national security: Incorporating conflict prevention and conflict resolution as elements of U.S. national security policy. Cambridge, MA: Institute for Resource and Security Studies. May. Unpublished manuscript.

Tilly, Charles. 1975. *The formation of national states in Western Europe*. Princeton: Princeton University Press.

———. 1978. *From mobilization to revolution*. Reading, MA: Addison-Wesley.

———. 1983. Speaking your mind without elections, surveys, or social movements. *Public Opinion Quarterly* 47, no. 4 (Winter): 461–78.

———. 1986. *The contentious French: Four centuries of popular struggle*. Cambridge. Harvard University Press.

Tipton, Frank B., and Robert Aldritch. 1987. *An economic and social history of Europe, from 1939 to the present*. Baltimore: Johns Hopkins University Press.

Tismaneanu, Vladimir. 1990. Democracy, what democracy? *East European Reporter* 4: 2 (Spring/Summer): 30–32.

Touval, Saadia. 1982. Managing the risks of accommodation. In *Termination of wars*, edited by Nissan Oren. Jerusalem: Magnes Press.

Touval, Saadia, and I. William Zartman. 1985. *International mediation and practice*. Boulder, CO: Westview.

———. 1989. Mediation in international conflicts. In *Mediation research*, edited by K. Kressel and D. G. Pruitt. San Francisco: Jossey-Bass.

———. eds. 1996. Negotiations in the former Soviet Union and the former Yugoslavia. Special issue of *International Negotiation*, vol. 1: 3.

Trachtenberg, Marc. 1993. Intervention in historical perspective. In *Emerging norms of justified intervention: A collection of essays from a project of the American Academy of Arts and Sciences*, edited by Laura W. Reed and Carl Kaysen. Cambridge, MA: American Academy of Arts and Sciences.

Treaty of Berlin, July 13, 1878. In *Major peace treaties of modern history, 1648–1967*, edited by Fred L. Israel. Vol. 2. 1967. New York: McGraw-Hill.

Treaty of Münster, October 24, 1648. In *Major peace treaties of modern history, 1648–1967*, edited by Fred L. Israel. Vol. 1. 1967. New York: McGraw-Hill.

Treaty of Osnabruck, 1648. In *The consolidated treaty series: 1648–1649*, edited by Clive Parry. Vol. 1. 1969. Dobbs Ferry, NY: Oceana.

Trebilcock, Clive. 1981. *Industrialization of the continental powers: 1780–1914*. London: Longmans.

Tucker, Robert W. 1985. *Intervention and the Reagan doctrine*. New York: Council on Religion and International Affairs.

Tullock, Gordon. 1971. The paradox of revolution. *Public Choice* 11 (Fall): 89–99.

Turner, John C. 1982. Towards a cognitive redefinition of the social group. In *Social identity and intergroup relations*, edited by Henri Tajfel. Cambridge: Cambridge University Press.

UNGA/R 1960. 1,215, no. 15. Geneva: United Nations.

Urusov, Sergei Dmitrievich. 1908. *Memoirs of a Russian governor*. Translated by Herman Rosenthal. London: Harper and Brothers.

United States Arms Control and Disarmament Agency (USACDA). Various years. *World military expenditures and arms transfers*. Washington, D.C.: U.S. Government Printing Office.

van den Berghe, Pierre L. 1981. *The ethnic phenomenon*. New York: Elsevier.

Van Evera, Stephen. 1994. Hypotheses on nationalism and war. *International Security* 18, no. 4: 5–39.

Van Houten, Pieter. 1995. The role of the homeland in ethnic relations. Master's thesis, University of Chicago.

Vares, Peeter. 1993. Dimensions and orientations in the foreign and security policies of the Baltic states. In *New actors on the international arena: The foreign policies of the Baltic countries*, edited by Pertii Joenniemi and Peeter Vares. Tampere, Finland: Tampere Peace Research Institute.

Vayrynen, Raimo. 1994. Towards a theory of ethnic conflicts and their resolution. Lecture delivered to the Joan B. Kroc Institute for International Peace Studies, University of Notre Dame Hesburgh Center for International Studies, March 15, at Notre Dame, IN.

Veatch, Richard. 1983. Minorities and the League of Nations. In *The League of Nations in retrospect: Proceedings of the symposium*. Series E. Serial Publications, United Nations Library Geneva, Series E. Berlin and New York: Gruyter.

Viorst, Milton. 1995. Sudan's Islamic experiment. *Foreign Affairs* 74, no. 3: 45–58.

Vogt, Margaret A. 1996. The involvement of ECOWAS in peacekeeping in Liberia. In *Africa in the new international order: Rethinking state sovereignty and regional security,* edited by Edmond J. Keller and Donald Rothchild. Boulder, CO: Lynne Rienner.

von Lazar, J. 1966. Class struggle and socialist construction: The Hungarian paradox. *Slavic Review* 25 (June): 303–13.

Wagner, R. Harrison. 1993. The causes of peace. In *Stopping the killing: How civil wars end*, edited by Roy Licklider. New York: New York University Press.

Walker, Jennone. 1993. International mediation of ethnic conflicts. *Survival* 35 (Spring): 102–17.

Walter, Barbara F. 1997. The critical barrier to civil war settlement. *International Organization* 51 (Spring): 335–64.

Waltz, Kenneth W. 1959. *Man, the state, and war*. New York: Columbia University Press.

———. 1979. *Theory of international politics*. New York: Columbia University Press.

Walzer, Michael. 1977. *Just and unjust wars*. New York: Basic Books.

Ward, Michael D. 1982. Cooperation and conflict in foreign policy behavior: Reaction and memory. *International Studies Quarterly* 28, no. 1 (March): 87–126.

Ward, Michael D., and Sheen Rajmaira. 1992. Reciprocity and norms in U.S.-Soviet foreign policy. *Journal of Conflict Resolution* 36, no. 2 (June): 342–68.

Washington Office on Africa. 1995. *Support for peacekeeping at risk in new congress*. Washington, D.C.: Washington Office on Africa (February).

Watts, Larry L. 1995. Ethnic tensions: How the West can help. *World Policy Journal* 12, no. 1 (Spring): 89–96.

Wehling, Fred. ed. 1995. *U.S. intervention in ethnic conflict*. Policy Paper 12. La Jolla: University of California Institute on Global Conflict and Cooperation.

Weiner, Myron, and Ali Banuazizi, eds. 1994. *The politics of social transformation in Afghanistan, Iran, and Pakistan*. Syracuse: Syracuse University Press.

Weingast, Barry R. 1997. Constructing trust: The political and economic roots of ethnic and regional conflict. In *Where is the new institutionalism now?* edited by Virginia Haufler, Karol Soltan, and Eric Uslaner. Ann Arbor: University of Michigan Press.

Weinstein, Warren. 1972. Conflict and confrontation in Central Africa: The revolt in Burundi, 1972. *Africa Today* 19, no. 4 (Fall), 17–37.

Weisbrot, Robert. 1990. *Freedom bound*. New York: W. W. Norton.

Weiss, Thomas G., and Jarat Chopra. 1995. Sovereignty under siege: From intervention to humanitarian space. In *Beyond Westphalia? State sovereignty and international intervention,* edited by Gene M. Lyons and Michael Mastanduno. Baltimore: Johns Hopkins University Press.

Welsh, David. 1993. Domestic politics and ethnic conflict. In *Ethnic conflict and international security*, edited by Michael E. Brown. Princeton: Princeton University Press: 43–60.

Williams, Robin. 1994. The sociology of ethnic conflicts: Comparative international perspectives. *Annual Review of Sociology* vol. 20 (annual 1994): 49–80.

Williamson, Oliver. 1985. *The economic institutions of capitalism: Firms, markets, and relational contracting*. New York: Free Press.

Wilson, James Q. 1993. *The moral sense*. New York: The Free Press.

Wippman, David. 1993. Enforcing the peace: ECOWAS and the Liberian civil war. In *Enforcing restraint: Collective intervention in internal conflicts,* edited by Lori Fisler Damrosch. New York: Council on Foreign Relations.

Wiskemann, E. 1956. *Germany's eastern neighbors: Problems relating to the Oder-Neisse Line and the Czech frontier regions.* London: Oxford University Press.

Wittman, Donald. 1979. How a war ends: A rational model approach. *Journal of Conflict Resolution* 23 (December): 743–63.

Wolf, Eric. 1990. Facing power—Old insights, new questions. *American Anthropologist* 92, no. 3: 586–96.

Woodward, Peter. 1990. *Sudan, 1898–1989: The unstable state.* Boulder, CO: Lynne Rienner.

Woodward, Susan. 1995a. *Balkan tragedy: Chaos and dissolution after the cold war.* Washington, D.C.: Brookings Institution.

———. 1995b. *Socialist unemployment: The political economy of Yugoslavia, 1945–1990.* Princeton: Princeton University Press.

Wriggins, Howard, ed. 1994. *Dynamics of regional politics.* New York: Columbia University Press.

———, ed. 1995. Negotiating with the Tamil rebellion. In *Elusive peace, negotiating an end of civil wars,* edited by I. William Zartman. Washington, D.C.: Brookings Institution.

Yankelovich Partners Inc. 1994. New York. (Acquired through the Roper Center for Public Opinion Research, University of Connecticut.)

Yinger, J. Milton. 1981. Toward a theory of assimilation and dissimilation. *Ethnic and Racial Studies* 4, no. 3 (July): 250–64.

Young, M. Crawford. 1992. The national and colonial question and Marxism: A view from the South. In *Thinking theoretically about Soviet nationalities: History and comparison in the study of the USSR,* edited by Alexander J. Motyl. New York: Columbia University Press.

———. 1993. *The rising tide of cultural pluralism: The nation-state at bay?* Madison: University of Wisconsin Press.

Zaller, John R. 1992. *The nature and origins of mass opinion.* Cambridge: Cambridge University Press.

Zanga, Louis. 1992. Albania afraid of war over Kosovo. *RFE/RL Report* 1, no. 46 (November 20): 20–23.

Zartman, I. William. 1980a. Toward a theory of elite circulation. In *Elites in the Middle East,* edited by I. William Zartman. New York: Praeger.

———, ed. 1980b. *Elites in the Middle East.* New York: Praeger.

———. 1985. *Ripe for resolution: Conflict and intervention in Africa.* New York: Oxford University Press.

———. 1987. *International relations in the new Africa.* Lanham, MD: University Presses of America.

———. 1989. *Ripe for resolution: Conflict and intervention in Africa.* 2d ed. New York: Oxford University Press.

———. 1990. Negotiations and prenegotiations in ethnic conflict: The beginning, the middle, and the ends. In *Conflict and peacemaking in multiethnic societies,* edited by Joseph Montville. Lexington, KY: Heath.

———. 1993a. Prenegotiation phases and functions. In *Getting to the table,* edited by Janice Stein. Baltimore: Johns Hopkins University Press.

———. 1993b. The unfinished agenda: Negotiating internal conflicts. In *Stopping the killing,* edited by Roy Licklider. New York: New York University Press.

———. 1995a. Conclusion: The last mile. In *Elusive peace,* edited by I. William Zartman. Washington, D.C.: Brookings Institution.

————. 1995b. Negotiating the South African conflict. In *Elusive peace,* edited by I. William Zartman. Washington, D.C.: Brookings Institution.

————, ed. 1995c. *Collapsed states: The disintegration and restoration of legitimate authority.* Boulder, CO: Lynne Rienner.

————, ed. 1995d. *Elusive peace, negotiating an end of civil wars.* Washington, D.C.: Brookings Institution.

————. 1996a. African regional security and changing patterns of relations. In *Africa in the new international order,* edited by Edmond Keller and Donald Rothchild. Boulder, CO: Lynne Rienner.

————, ed. 1997. *Governance as conflict management: Politics and violence in West Africa.* Washington, D.C.: Brookings Institution.

————. N.d. *Preventing collapse.* New York: Carnegie Commission on Preventing Deadly Conflicts, forthcoming.

Zartman, I. William, and Saadia Touval. 1995. Mediation after the Cold War. In *Peacemaking in the new era,* edited by Chester Crocker and Fen Osler Hampson. Washington, D.C.: United States Institute of Peace Press.

Zartman, I. William, and Katharina Vogeli. 1998. Preventing coup and collapse: Delivering competition out of monopoly in Congo. In *Opportunities missed, opportunities seized: Preventive diplomacy in the post-cold war world,* edited by Bruce W. Jentleson. Lanham, MD: Rowman and Littlefield, forthcoming.

Zeger, S. L., and B. Qaqish. 1988. A regression model for time series of counts. *Biometrics:* 44 (December): 1,019–31.

Zhuryari-Ossipova, Olga. 1993. Russian factor in Estonian foreign policy: Reaction to the limitation of sovereignty. In *New actors on the international arena: The foreign policies of the Baltic countries,* edited by Pertii Joenniemi and Peeter Vares. Tampere, Finland: Tampere Peace Research Institute.

Zimmerman, Warren. 1995. The last ambassador: A memoir of the collapse of Yugoslavia. *Foreign Affairs* 74 (March/April): 2–20.